75 Thematic Readings

An Anthology

75 Thematic Readings

An Anthology

Boston Burr Ridge, IL Dubuque, IA Madison, WI New York
San Francisco St. Louis Bangkok Bogotá Caracas Kuala Lumpur
Lisbon London Madrid Mexico City Milan Montreal New Delhi
Santiago Seoul Singapore Sydney Taipei Toronto

McGraw-Hill Higher Education ⚛

*A Division of The **McGraw-Hill** Companies*

75 THEMATIC READINGS: AN ANTHOLOGY
Published by McGraw-Hill, a business unit of The McGraw-Hill Companies, Inc., 1221
Avenue of the Americas, New York, NY, 10020. Copyright © 2003 by The McGraw-Hill
Companies, Inc. All rights reserved. No part of this publication may be reproduced or
distributed in any form or by any means, or stored in a database or retrieval system,
without the prior written consent of The McGraw-Hill Companies, Inc., including, but
not limited to, in any network or other electronic storage or transmission, or broadcast for
distance learning.
Some ancillaries, including electronic and print components, may not be available to
customers outside the United States.

This book is printed on acid-free paper.

8 9 0 DOC/DOC 0 9

ISBN-13: 978-0-07-246931-8
ISBN-10: 0-07-246931-5

President of McGraw-Hill Humanities/Social Sciences: *Steve Debow*
Executive editor: *Lisa Moore*
Editorial coordinator: *Victoria Fullard*
Senior marketing manager: *David S. Patterson*
Senior media producer: *Todd Vaccaro*
Project manager: *Jean R. Starr*
Production supervisor: *Susanne Riedell*
Cover design: *Gino Cieslik*
Cover image: *©PhotoDisc*
Typeface: *10/12 Palatino*
Compositor: *GAC Indianapolis*
Printer: *R.R. Donnelley and Sons Co.*

Library of Congress Cataloging-in-Publication Data

75 thematic readings : an anthology / McGraw-Hill.
   p. cm.
   Includes index.
   ISBN 0-07-246931-5 (softcover : acid-free paper)
   1. College readers. 2. English language--Rhetoric--Problems, exercises, etc. 3.
Report writing--Problems, exercises, etc. I Title: Seventy-five thematic readings. II.
McGraw-Hill Companies.
PE1417.A13 2003
808'.0427--dc21

2002071753

http://www.mhhe.com/commcentral

Contents

"My mother! My father! After English became my primary language I no longer knew what words to use in addressing my parents."

"During the first silent year, I spoke to no one at school, did not ask before going to the lavatory, and flunked kindergarten."

"For a people who are neither Spanish nor live in a country in which Spanish is the first language; for a people who live in a country in which English is the reigning tongue but who are not Anglo; for people who cannot entirely identify with either standard (formal, Castillian) Spanish nor standard English, what recourse is left to them but to create their own language?"

"Words themselves are innocuous; it is the consensus that gives them true power."

Chapter 2
EDUCATION AND LEARNING   67

*"Beginning in the late 1950s, Americans began to change their
ideas about the individual's obligations to family and society.
Broadly described, this change was away from an ethic of
obligation to others and toward an obligation to self."*

*"I want a wife who will take care of my physical needs. I want a
wife who will keep my house clean. A wife who will pick up
after me."*

*"Women told me that men were guilty of having kept all the
joys and privileges of the earth for themselves. . . . What
privileges? . . . Warriors and toilers: those seemed, in my
boyhood vision, to be the chief destinies for men."*

*"One of the most difficult tasks to accomplish in American
society is to be a solid, caring, and loving black father."*

*"Gay marriage is a radical notion for straight people and a
conservative notion for gay ones."*

*"No other fairy tale renders so well as the 'Cinderella' stories
the inner experiences of the young child in the throes of sibling
rivalry, when he feels hopelessly outclassed by his brothers and
sisters."*

". . . always squeeze bread to make sure it's fresh; but what if
the baker won't let me feel the bread; *you mean to say that
after all you are really going to be the kind of woman the baker
won't let near the bread?"*

Contents

Chapter 5
GOVERNMENT, POWER, AND JUSTICE 263

Niccolò Machiavelli: *"The Qualities of the Prince"* 265

". . . a prince must be little concerned with conspiracies when the people are well disposed toward him; but when the populace is hostile and regards him with hatred, he must fear everything and everyone."

Thomas Jefferson: *"The Declaration of Independence"* 276

"We hold these truths to be self-evident, that all men are created equal, that they are endowed by their Creator with certain unalienable Rights, that among these are Life, Liberty, and the pursuit of Happiness."

Elizabeth Cady Stanton: *"Declaration of Sentiments"* 280

"The history of mankind is a history of repeated injuries and usurpations on the part of man toward woman, having in direct object the establishment of an absolute tyranny over her."

Sojourner Truth: *"Ain't I a Woman?"* 283

"I have borne thirteen children, and seen them almost all sold off into slavery, and when I cried out with my mother's grief, none but Jesus heard me!"

Henry David Thoreau: *"Civil Disobedience"* 284

"'That government is best which governs not at all'; and when men are prepared for it, that will be the kind of government which they will have.

Martin Luther King, Jr.: *"Letter from Birmingham City Jail"* 305

"We know through painful experience that freedom is never voluntarily given by the oppressor, it must be demanded by the oppressed."

Chapter 6
ECONOMICS, WORK, AND
CONSUMER CULTURE   365

Chapter 8
NATURE, SCIENCE, AND
TECHNOLOGY   539

Index of Rhetorical Modes

NARRATION

DESCRIPTION

EXEMPLIFICATION

PROCESS

CAUSE AND EFFECT

COMPARISON/CONTRAST

DIVISION / CLASSIFICATION

DEFINITION

ARGUMENT

Preface

PROVEN SELECTIONS

Although *75 Thematic Readings* is new, McGraw-Hill has been publishing textbooks since 1901. In that time we've done a tremendous amount of research on what books professors want to use for their courses—through trial and error and through field-based surveys—and particularly on what selections instructors have found are the best springboards for writing and critical thought. For *75 Thematic Readings* in particular, we've also analyzed thematic readers popular among college instructors today, and we've consulted countless instructors about the readings they have found engaged their students. This collection of 75 readings, organized thematically, is the result of our research into the most popular readings for college composition organized around a basic core of liberal arts and culturally oriented themes.

CORE THEMES

These themes, which were also selected based on research, reflect an interest in promoting substantive discussion on topics related to fields of study in college. Themes in particular on Communication, Education, Economics, Government, Philosophy, and Science directly examine issues related to those disciplines. In addition, historical and cultural (particularly ethnic and sexual) contexts have become an integral part of academic study, and themes related specifically to culture, sexual politics, the environment, and consumer culture are included as well. It is our hope that the introduction of such topics as areas of inquiry will introduce the kinds of critical thinking and analysis that college represents.

DIVERSE AUTHORS AND SUBJECTS

It has been a goal of this collection to include works by a spectrum of diverse writers and to represent a complex collage of experience. Diversity in 75 *Thematic Readings* means including the voices of those with disabilities, such as Nancy Mairs's "On Being a Cripple," and the perspectives of those with different sexual orientations (see Anna Quindlen's "Evan's Two Moms"), as well as an examination of both male and female gender roles (see Scott Russell Sanders, "The Men We Carry in Our Minds" as well as Margaret Atwood's "The Female Body"). In addition, 75 *Thematic Readings* includes works by Gloria Anzaldúa, Leslie Marmon Silko, Judith Cofer, Maxine Hong Kingston, N. Scott Momaday, Langston Hughes, Gloria Naylor, Maya Angelou, Brent Staples, Alice Walker, and others.

PROVOCATIVE AND ISSUE-ORIENTED SELECTIONS

75 *Thematic Readings* also includes a wide range of provocative works by contemporary writers who are influencing discussion of issues important today—writers such as Cornel West, "On Black Fathering," Ronald Takaki on "The Harmful Myth of Asian Superiority," Noel Ignatiev, who discusses "How the Irish Became White," and Camille Paglia on the war between the sexes. Serious issues are addressed in 75 *Thematic Readings* by seminal writers, such as Studs Terkel, Barbara Ehrenreich, Mike Rose, Shelby Steele, and Henry Louis Gates, Jr. An assortment of perspectives are included as well from William Bennett to Jesse Jackson.

HISTORICAL AND DISCIPLINARY WORKS

Careful attention has also been given to the inclusion of a historical range of works, as well as works from a variety of disciplinary
perspectives. Popular science writers such as Stephen Jay Gould
and Lewis Thomas are included, along with the sociological
analysis of James Q. Wilson, and literary voices such as Langston
Hughes and Virginia Woolf. Plato's "Allegory of the Cave" is included in the Philosophy section. Frederick Douglass's "Learning
to Read and Write" grounds the section on Education. The section
on Government, Power, and Justice pairs Thomas Jefferson's "The
Declaration of Independence" with Elizabeth Cady Stanton's "Declaration of Sentiments."

PROSE MODELS

75 Thematic Readings also includes works that are models of writing at its finest, from arguments such as Thomas Jefferson's "The
Declaration of Independence" and Thoreau's "Civil Disobedience" to the introspective and powerful elegance of Joan Didion's
"On Keeping a Notebook" and James Baldwin's "Notes of a Native Son." Classic works by stylists noted for clarity and grace,
such as George Orwell and E. B. White, are also included.

FLEXIBLE

Containing 75 complete essays, *75 Thematic Readings* can be used
to support a variety of approaches to composition. Its themes introduce areas of study from across the curriculum and seminal
thinkers within those themes (for example, Plato in Philosophy
and Machiavelli in Government). Many works can be examined
as arguments, such as Susan Brownmiller's essay on the first
amendment, "Let's Put Pornography Back in the Closet"; or
works can be read in tandem to see a range of perspectives on a
particular issue (for example, "Silence" by Maxine Hong Kingston
and "Aria" by Richard Rodriguez, which both address bilingual

education). These selections were particularly designed to promote critical thinking through a broad range of themes. Those
who focus on cultural issues will find a range of essays of cultural
analysis, such as Deborah Tannen's "I'm Sorry, I'm Not Apologizing" or "Sex, Lies, and Advertising" by Gloria Steinem. The text
can also be used in a rhetorically focused course, by using the
alternative table of contents arranged by rhetorical modes.

A VALUE PRICE

Time and time again we at McGraw-Hill have heard from professors that you want your students to have a range of quality selections at a price that is less than other readers available for your
composition courses. This new reader, *75 Thematic Readings*, is our
answer—especially for those instructors who teach with a thematic reader. At less than half the price of thematic readers currently popular among college instructors, it is part of a franchise
of value-priced titles put together by McGraw-Hill to address the
very real concerns about textbook costs for students. Other value-
priced books available through McGraw-Hill include *75 Readings*
(a rhetorically organized reader), *75 Readings Plus* (that same
rhetorically organized reader with editorial apparatus), and *Rules
of Thumb* (a handbook for writers).

To keep the cost low, *75 Thematic Readings* has been compiled
by the editors at McGraw-Hill and designed as a reader first: that
is, only readings—no headnotes, no questions before or after the
selections, no writing assignments, no introductions to the writing
process—which we hope appeals particularly to professors who
value flexibility and prefer to develop their own sequence of discussion questions to support the points of emphasis and particular goals of their courses. (Editorial apparatus for each selection is
available, however, on a website that accompanies the text,
www.mhhe.com/75thematic.) It is our hope as well that without
this editorial apparatus in the book, this reader will feel more like
a real book. Equally important, we hope that you will find the selections useful for your students, and that the price of this text will
make it one you feel good about assigning in your classes.

ACKNOWLEDGMENTS

No book is put together in a vacuum, and this book in particular has depended on a number of editors and editorial consultants for McGraw-Hill. Marcia Muth's in-depth analysis of readers across the board was the foundation stone for the project. Alexis Walker brought her keen instincts, her teaching experience, and her research for Primis's custom readers to the final shape of this manuscript. Laura Barthule coordinated the extensive market research that told the editors when they veered too much to the right and then again too much to the left, striking in the end what we hope is a balanced presentation. Victoria Fullard and Todd Vaccaro made sure the website was well-oiled and ready when this book hit the presses.

However, most of our thanks are due to those who reviewed this text at various stages. Some of these became our friends and indeed our collaborators in creating a book at a value price that would help them fulfill their goals as composition instructors. Without them, no book would have been possible: Laurie Buchholz, *Porterville College;* Lisa Buranen, *California State University, Los Angeles;* David Calonne, *Eastern Michigan University;* Patricia A. Conti, *Sacred Heart University;* Lawrence Coates, *Southern Utah University;* Frank Day, *Clemson University;* Lynda Del Valle, *El Paso Community College;* Elizabeth Elchlepp, *Santiago Canyon College;* Eric Fallen, *Brooklyn College/CUNY;* Janet Fetzer, *University of Texas at San Antonio;* Cara A. Finnegan, *University of Illinois at Urbana-Champaign;* Richard Frohock, *Oklahoma State University;* Kate Gray, *Clackamas Community College;* Bob Harrison, *Southwestern Community College;* Betty Hart, *University of Southern Indiana;* Michael Hennessey, *Southwest Texas State University;* Roderick Hughes, *St. Bonaventure University;* Heather Bryant Jordan, *Extension School of Harvard University;* Michael Kilduff, *University of Colorado;* Loel Kim, *University of Memphis;* Mary Ann Klein, *Quincy University;* Erika Koss-Smith, *San Diego State University;* Kristina E. L. Ladnier, *Kennesaw State University;* Jen Jie Li, *Brooklyn College, CUNY;* Gorge Lober, *Monterey Peninsula College;* Gerald T. McCarthy, *San Antonio College;* Tim Morris, *University of Texas at Arlington;* John W. Munns, *University of South Florida;* Mary L.

Navarro, *Sinclair Community College;* Katherine Powell, *Berry College;* Robert E. Preissle, *DeVry Institute of Technology;* Mike Rose, *University of California, Los Angeles;* Margarite Roumas, *Fitchburg State College;* Abby Shapiro, *Boston University;* Angela M. Thompson, *University of Oregon;* Daniel Traber, *Texas A&M University;* Paula Vehlow, *University of Akron;* William G. Wall, *Santa Fe Community College;* Margaret Walsh, *U-Mass, Boston;* Kathleen Wax, *Northern Virginia Community College;* Kimberley A. Wells, *Texas A&M University;* Arnold Wood Jr., *Florida Community College at Jacksonville, South.*

Lisa Moore

Executive Editor

McGraw-Hill

Chapter

Language and Communication

"Language is the most significant and colossal work that the human spirit has evolved," notes linguist Edward Sapir. "It is the most inclusive art we know, a mountainous and anonymous work of unconscious generations." Language has been credited with human civilization, and it is a supreme expression of our social selves, so it is little wonder that politics and language would inevitably be intertwined. George Orwell indicates in "Politics and the English Language" that language shapes us, and conversely, we it. He argues, for example, that without clear language there can be no clear thought, and though he wrote during the rise of Fascism and World War II, his words provoke us today when he argues that political deception relies on the use of grand political clichés and that "all issues are political issues." While we are accustomed to thinking of political debate as a realm where politics and language meet, such as when Susan Brownmiller argues that the First Amendment right to free speech should not encompass pornography's degradation of women, politics and language can have a more subtle connection when it is an expression of one's own marginalized identity. In "How to Tame a Wild Tongue," Gloria Anzaldúa explores her "mestizo" language of Spanish dialects and English and considers her language to express a political and potentially revolutionary borderland of personal identity. The distinctions between public and private languages are explored by Richard Rodriguez and Maxine Hong Kingston as they recount their struggles with the power and the loss they felt in gaining fluency in the public language of English over their native tongues. Leslie Marmon Silko, on the other hand, comes from a Pueblo culture that embraced many different tribes and their

1

tribal languages. It wasn't the particular language itself that defined the individual in the Pueblo imagination, she indicates, but rather the individual's story and how it connected that person to others. Such stories absorbed the stories around them, which were thus kept alive in this oral culture. In the Pueblo culture, the written word itself was considered suspicious for its potential to purposely deceive. Gloria Naylor, the novelist, also imagines the written word to be a poor substitute for the spoken, and much of the frustration novelists feel with their work, she postulates, is that "even the most transcendent passage falls far short of the richness of life." She goes further to say that "words themselves are innocuous; it is the consensus that gives them true power," and she examines the power of the shifting meaning of one word in particular, when it comes from the mouth of a white person or when it is said within the black family. While words can define us publicly—and Deborah Tannen's "I'm Sorry, I'm Not Apologizing" examines the ways gender differences in speech can have deleterious effects on a woman's public image—words are finally also so intimate. Joan Didion eloquently reveals this intimacy in her reminiscence "On Keeping a Notebook." In it, she shows that while language is certainly public and can define us publicly, its privacy is powerful as well. Privately, she reveals, language is used to "remember what it is was like to be me."

Aria

Richard Rodriguez

1   Supporters of bilingual education today imply that students like me miss a great deal by not being taught in their family's language. What they seem not to recognize is that, as a socially disadvantaged child, I considered Spanish to be a private language. What I needed to learn in school was that I had the right—and the obligation—to speak the public language of *los gringos*. The odd truth is that my first-grade classmates could have become bilingual, in the conventional sense of that word, more easily than I. Had they been taught (as upper-middle-class children are often taught early) a second language like Spanish or French, they could have regarded it simply as that: another public language. In my case such bilingualism could not have been so quickly achieved. What I did not believe was that I could speak a single public language.

2   Without question, it would have pleased me to hear my teachers address me in Spanish when I entered the classroom. I would have felt much less afraid. I would have trusted them and responded with ease. But I would have delayed—for how long postponed?—having to learn the language of public society. I would have evaded—and for how long could I have afforded to delay?—learning the great lesson of school, that I had a public identity.

3   Fortunately, my teachers were unsentimental about their responsibility. What they understood was that I needed to speak a public language. So their voices would search me out, asking me questions. Each time I'd hear them, I'd look up in surprise to see a nun's face frowning at me. I'd mumble, not really meaning to answer. The nun would persist, "Richard, stand up. Don't look at the floor. Speak up. Speak to the entire class, not just to me!" But I couldn't believe that the English language was mine to use. (In part, I did not want to believe it.) I continued to mumble. I resisted the teacher's demands. (Did I somehow suspect that once I learned public language my pleasing family life would be

changed?) Silent, waiting for the bell to sound, I remained dazed, diffident, afraid.

Because I wrongly imagined that English was intrinsically a public language and Spanish an intrinsically private one, I easily noted the difference between classroom language and the language of home. At school, words were directed to a general audience of listeners. ("Boys and girls.") Words were meaningfully ordered. And the point was not self-expression alone but to make oneself understood by many others. The teacher quizzed: "Boys and girls, why do we use that word in this sentence? Could we think of a better word to use there? Would the sentence change its meaning if the words were differently arranged? And wasn't there a better way of saying much the same thing?" (I couldn't say. I wouldn't try to say.)

Three months. Five. Half a year passed. Unsmiling, ever watchful, my teachers noted my silence. They began to connect my behavior with the difficult progress my older sister and brother were making. Until one Saturday morning three nuns arrived at the house to talk to our parents. Stiffly, they sat on the blue living room sofa. From the doorway of another room, spying the visitors, I noted the incongruity—the clash of two worlds, the faces and voices of school intruding upon the familiar setting of home. I overheard one voice gently wondering, "Do your children speak only Spanish at home, Mrs. Rodriguez?" While another voice added, "That Richard especially seems so timid and shy."

That Rich-heard!

With great tact the visitors continued, "Is it possible for you and your husband to encourage your children to practice their English when they are home?" Of course, my parents complied. What would they not do for their children's well-being? And how could they have questioned the Church's authority which those women represented? In an instant, they agreed to give up the language (the sounds) that had revealed and accentuated our family's closeness. The moment after the visitors left, the change was observed. *"Ahora,* speak to us *en inglés,* my father and mother united to tell us.

At first, it seemed a kind of game. After dinner each night, the family gathered to practice "our" English. (It was still then *inglès,* a language foreign to us, so we felt drawn as strangers to it.) Laughing, we would try to define words we could not pronounce. We played with strange English sounds, often overanglicizing our pronunciations. And we filled the smiling gaps of our sentences with familiar Spanish sounds. But that was cheating, somebody shouted. Everyone laughed. In school, meanwhile, like my brother and sister, I was required to attend a daily tutoring session. I needed a full year of special attention. I also needed my teachers to keep my attention from straying in class by calling out, *Rich-heard*—their English voices slowing prying loose my ties to my other name, its three notes, *Ri-car-do*. Most of all I needed to hear my mother and father speak to me in a moment of seriousness in broken—suddenly heartbreaking—English. The scene was inevitable: One Saturday morning I entered the kitchen where my parents were talking in Spanish. I did not realize that they were talking in Spanish however until, at the moment they saw me, I heard their voices change to speak English. Those *gringo* sounds they uttered startled me. Pushed me away. In that moment of trivial misunderstanding and profound insight, I felt my throat twisted by unsounded grief. I turned quickly and left the room. But I had no place to escape to with Spanish. (The spell was broken.) My brothers and sisters were speaking English in another part of the house.

9   Again and again in the days following, increasingly angry, I was obliged to hear my mother and father: "Speak to us *en inglés*" (*Speak.*) Only then did I determine to learn classroom English. Weeks after, it happened: One day in school I raised my hand to volunteer an answer. I spoke out in a loud voice. And I did not think it remarkable when the entire class understood. That day, I moved very far from the disadvantaged child I had been only days earlier. The belief, that calming assurance that I belonged in public, had at last taken hold.

10   Shortly after, I stopped hearing the high and loud sounds of *los gringos*. A more and more confident speaker of English, I didn't trouble to listen to *how* strangers sounded, speaking to me. And there simply were too many English-speaking people in my day for me to hear American accents anymore. Conversations quickened. Listening to persons who sounded eccentrically

pitched voices, I usually noted their sounds for an initial few seconds before I concentrated on *what* they were saying. Conversations became content-full. Transparent. Hearing someone's *tone* of voice—angry or questioning or sarcastic or happy or sad—I didn't distinguish it from the words it expressed. Sound and word were thus tightly wedded. At the end of a day, I was often bemused, always relieved, to realize how "silent," though crowded with words, my day in public had been. (This public silence measured and quickened the change in my life.)

At last, seven years old, I came to believe what had been technically true since my birth: I was an American citizen. 11

But the special feeling of closeness at home was diminished 12
by then. Gone was the desperate, urgent, intense feeling of being at home, rare was the experience of feeling myself individualized by family intimates. We remained a loving family, but one greatly changed. No longer so close; no longer bound tight by the pleasing and troubling knowledge of our public separateness. Neither my older brother nor sister rushed home after school anymore. Nor did I. When I arrived home there would often be neighborhood kids in the house. Or the house would be empty of sounds.

Following the dramatic Americanization of their children, 13
even my parents grew more publicly confident. Especially my mother. She learned the names of all the people on our block. And she decided we needed to have a telephone installed in the house. My father continued to use the word *gringo*. But it was no longer charged with the old bitterness or distrust. (Stripped of any emotional content, the word simply became a name for those Americans not of Hispanic descent.) Hearing him, sometimes, I wasn't sure if he was pronouncing the Spanish word *gringo* or saying gringo in English.

Matching the silence I started hearing in public was a new 14
quiet at home. The family's quiet was partly due to the fact that, as we children learned more and more English, we shared fewer and fewer words with our parents. Sentences needed to be spoken slowly when a child addressed his mother or father. (Often the parent wouldn't understand.) The child would need to repeat himself. (Still the parent misunderstood.) The young voice, frustrated, would end up saying, "Never mind"—the subject was

closed. Dinners would be noisy with the clinking of knives and forks against dishes. My mother would smile softly between her remarks; my father at the other end of the table would chew and chew at his food, while he stared over the heads of his children.

15   My *mother!* My *father!* After English became my primary language, I no longer knew what words to use in addressing my parents. The old Spanish words (those tender accents of sound) I had used earlier—*mamá* and *papá*—I couldn't use anymore. They would have been too painful reminders of how much had changed in my life. On the other hand, the words I heard neighborhood kids call their parents seemed equally unsatisfactory. *Mother* and *Father; Ma, Papa, Pa, Dad, Pop* (how I hated the all American sound of that last word especially)—all these terms I felt were unsuitable, not really terms of address for my parents. As a result, I never used them at home. Whenever I'd speak to my parents, I would try to get their attention with eye contact alone. In public conversations, I'd refer to "my parents" or "my mother and father."

16   My mother and father, for their part, responded differently, as their children spoke to them less. She grew restless, seemed troubled and anxious at the scarcity of words exchanged in the house. It was she who would question me about my day when I came home from school. She smiled at small talk. She pried at the edges of my sentences to get me to say something more. (What?) She'd join conversations she overheard, but her intrusions often stopped her children's talking. By contrast, my father seemed reconciled to the new quiet. Though his English improved somewhat, he retired into silence. At dinner he spoke very little. One night his children and even his wife helplessly giggled at his garbled English pronunciation of the Catholic Grace before Meals. Thereafter he made his wife recite the prayer at the start of each meal, even on formal occasions, when there were guests in the house. Hers became the public voice of the family. On official business, it was she, not my father, one would usually hear on the phone or in stores, talking to strangers. His children grew so accustomed to his silence that, years later, they would speak routinely of his shyness. (My mother would often try to explain: Both his parents died when he was eight. He was raised by an uncle who treated him like little more

than a menial servant. He was never encouraged to speak. He
grew up alone. A man of few words.) But my father was not shy, I
realized, when I'd watch him speaking Spanish with relatives. Using Spanish, he was quickly effusive. Especially when talking with
other men, his voice would spark, flicker, flare alive with sounds.
In Spanish, he expressed ideas and feelings he rarely revealed in
English. With firm Spanish sounds, he conveyed confidence and
authority English would never allow him.

The silence at home, however, was finally more than a literal 17
silence. Fewer words passed between parent and child, but more
profound was the silence that resulted from my inattention to
sounds. At about the time I no longer bothered to listen with care
to the sounds of English in public, I grew careless about listening
to the sounds family members made when they spoke. Most of
the time I heard someone speaking at home and didn't distinguish his sounds from the words people uttered in public. I didn't
even pay much attention to my parents' accented and ungrammatical speech. At least not at home. Only when I was with them
in public would I grow alert to their accents. Though, even then,
their sounds caused me less and less concern. For I was increasingly confident of my own public identity.

I would have been happier about my public success had I not 18
sometimes recalled what it had been like earlier, when my family
had conveyed its intimacy through a set of conveniently private
sounds. Sometimes in public, hearing a stranger, I'd hark back to
my past. A Mexican farmworker approached me downtown to
ask directions to somewhere, "*¿Hijito. . .?*" he said. And his voice
summoned deep longing. Another time, standing beside my
mother in the visiting room of a Carmelite convent, before the
dense screen which rendered the nuns shadowy figures, I heard
several Spanish-speaking nuns—their busy, singsong overlapping
voices—assure us that yes, yes, we were remembered, all our family was remembered in their prayers. (Their voices echoed far-
away family sounds.) Another day, a dark-faced old woman—her
hand light on my shoulder—steadied herself against me as she
boarded a bus. She murmured something I couldn't quite comprehend. Her Spanish voice came near, like the face of a never-
before-seen relative in the instant before I was kissed. Her voice,

like so many of the Spanish voices I'd hear in public, recalled the golden age of my youth. Hearing Spanish then, I continued to be a careful, if sad, listener to sounds. Hearing a Spanish-speaking family walking behind me, I turned to look. I smiled for an instance, before my glance found the Hispanic-looking faces of strangers in the crowd going by.

19   Today I hear bilingual educators say that children lose a degree of "individuality" by becoming assimilated into public society. Bilingual schooling was popularized in the seventies, that decade when middle-class ethics began to resist the process of assimilation—the American melting pot). But the bilingualists simplistically scorn the value and necessity of assimilation. They do not seem to realize that there are *two* ways a person is individualized. So they do not realize that while one suffers a diminished sense of *private* individuality by becoming assimilated into public society, such assimilation makes possible the achievement of *public* individuality.

20   The bilingualists insist that a student should be reminded of his difference from others in mass society, his heritage. But they equate mere separateness with individuality. The fact is that only in private—with intimates—is separateness from the crowd a prerequisite for individuality (An intimate draws me apart, tells me that I am unique, unlike all others.) In public, by contrast, full individuality is achieved, paradoxically, by those who are able to consider themselves members of the crowd. Thus it happened for me: Only when I was able to think of myself as an American, no longer an alien in *gringo* society, could I seek the rights and opportunities necessary for full public individuality. The social and political advantages I enjoy as a man result from the day that I came to believe that my name, indeed, is *Rich-heard Road-ree-guess*. It is true that my public society today is often impersonal. (My public society is usually mass society.) Yet despite the anonymity of the crowd and despite the fact that the individuality I achieve in public is often tenuous—because it depends on my being one in a crowd—I celebrate the day I acquired my new name. Those middle-class ethics who scorn assimilation seem to me filled with decadent self-pity, obsessed by the burden of

public life. Dangerously, they romanticize public separateness and they trivialize the dilemma of the socially disadvantaged.

My awkward childhood does not prove the necessity of bilin-   21
gual education. My story discloses instead an essential myth of childhood—inevitable pain. If I rehearse here the changes in my private life after my Americanization, it is finally to emphasize the public gain. The loss implies the gain: The house I returned to each afternoon was quiet. Intimate sounds no longer rushed to the door to greet me. There were other noises inside. The telephone rang. Neighborhood kids ran past the door of the bedroom where I was reading my school-books—covered with shopping-bag paper. Once I learned public language, it would never again be easy for me to hear intimate family voices. More and more of my day was spent hearing words. But that may only be a way of saying that the day I raised my hand in class and spoke loudly to an entire roomful of faces, my childhood started to end.

1981

Tongue Tied

Maxine Hong Kingston

When I went to kindergarten and had to speak English for the   1
first time, I became silent. A dumbness—a shame—still cracks my voice in two, even when I want to say "hello" casually, or ask an easy question in front of the check-out counter, or ask directions of a bus driver. I stand frozen, or I hold up the line with the complete, grammatical sentence that comes squeaking out at impossible length. "What did you say?" says the cab driver, or "Speak up," so I have to perform again, only weaker the second time. A telephone call makes my throat bleed and takes up that day's courage. It spoils my day with self-disgust when I hear my broken voice come skittering out into the open. It makes people wince to hear it. I'm getting better, though. Recently I asked the postman for special-issue stamps; I've waited since childhood for postmen

to give me some of their own accord. I am making progress, a little every day.

2   My silence was thickest—total—during the three years that I covered my school paintings with black paint. I painted layers of black over houses and flowers and suns, and when I drew on the blackboard, I put a layer of chalk on top. I was making a stage curtain, and it was the moment before the curtain parted or rose. The teachers called my parents to school, and I saw they had been saving my pictures, curling and cracking, all alike and black. The teachers pointed to the pictures and looked serious, talked seriously too, but my parents did not understand English. ("The parents and teachers of criminals were executed," said my father.) My parents took the pictures home. I spread them out (so black and full of possibilities) and pretended the curtains were swinging open, flying up, one after another, sunlight underneath, mighty operas.

3   During the first silent year I spoke to no one at school, did not ask before going to the lavatory, and flunked kindergarten. My sister also said nothing for three years, silent in the playground and silent at lunch. There were other quiet Chinese girls not of our family, but most of them got over it sooner than we did. I enjoyed the silence. At first it did not occur to me I was supposed to talk or to pass kindergarten. I talked at home and to one or two of the Chinese kids in class. I made motions and even made some jokes. I drank out of a toy saucer when the water spilled out of the cup, and everybody laughed, pointing at me, so I did it some more. I didn't know that Americans don't drink out of saucers.

4   I liked the Negro students (Black Ghosts) best because they laughed the loudest and talked to me as if I were a daring talker too. One of the Negro girls had her mother coil braids over her ears Shanghai-style like mine; we were Shanghai twins except that she was covered with black like my paintings. Two Negro kids enrolled in Chinese school, and the teachers gave them Chinese names. Some Negro kids walked me to school and home, protecting me from the Japanese kids, who hit me and chased me and stuck gum in my ears. The Japanese kids were noisy and tough. They appeared one day in kindergarten, released from concentration camp, which was a tic-tac-toe mark, like barbed wire, on the map.

It was when I found out I had to talk that school become a ₅
misery, that the silence became a misery. I did not speak and felt
bad each time that I did not speak. I read aloud in first grade,
though, and heard the barest whisper with little squeaks come out
of my throat. "Louder," said the teacher, who scared the voice
away again. The other Chinese girls did not talk either, so I knew
the silence had to do with being a Chinese girl.

Reading out loud was easier than speaking because we did not ₆
have to make up what to say, but I stopped often, and the teacher
would think I'd gone quiet again. I could not understand "I." The
Chinese "I" has seven strokes, intricacies. How could the American "I," assuredly wearing a hat like the Chinese, have only three
strokes, the middle so straight? Was it out of politeness that this
writer left off the strokes the way a Chinese has to write her own
name small and crooked? No, it was not politeness; "I" is a capital
and "you" is lower-case. I stared at that middle line and waited so
long for its black center to resolve into tight strokes and dots that I
forgot to pronounce it. The other troublesome word was "here," no
strong consonant to hang on to, and so flat, where "here" is two
mountainous ideographs. The teacher, who had already told me
every day how to read "I" and "here," put me in the low corner
under the stairs again, where the noisy boys usually sat.

When my second grade class did a play, the whole class went ₇
to the auditorium except the Chinese girls. The teacher, lovely and
Hawaiian, should have understood about us, but instead left us
behind in the classroom. Our voices were too soft or nonexistent,
and our parents never signed the permission slips anyway. They
never signed anything unnecessary. We opened the door a crack
and peeked out, but closed it again quickly. One of us (not me)
won every spelling bee, though.

I remember telling the Hawaiian teacher, "We Chinese can't ₈
sing 'land where our fathers died.'" She argued with me about
politics, while I meant because of curses. But how can I have that
memory when I couldn't talk? My mother says that we, like the
ghosts, have no memories.

After American school, we picked up our cigar boxes, in ₉
which we had arranged books, brushes, and an inkbox neatly, and
went to Chinese school, from 5:00 to 7:30 P.M. There we chanted to-

gether, voices rising and falling, loud and soft, some boys shouting, everybody reading together, reciting together and not alone with one voice. When we had a memorization test, the teacher let each of us come to his desk and say the lesson to him privately, while the rest of the class practiced copying or tracing. Most of the teachers were men. The boys who were so well behaved in the American school played tricks on them and talked back to them. The girls were not mute. They screamed and yelled during recess, when there were no rules; they had fistfights. Nobody was afraid of children hurting themselves or of children hurting school property. The glass doors to the red and green balconies with the gold joy symbols were left wide open so that we could run out and climb the fire escapes. We played capture-the-flag in the auditorium, where Sun Yat-sen and Chiang Kai-shek's pictures hung at the back of the stage, the Chinese flag on their left and the American flag on their right. We climbed the teak ceremonial chairs and made flying leaps off the stage. One flag headquarters was behind the glass door and the other on stage right. Our feet drummed on the hollow stage. During recess the teachers locked themselves up in their office with the shelves of books, copybooks, inks from China. They drank tea and warmed their hands at a stove. There was no play supervision. At recess we had the school to ourselves, and also we could roam as far as we could go—downtown, Chinatown stores, home—as long as we returned before the bell rang.

10   At exactly 7.30 the teacher again picked up the brass bell that sat on his desk and swung it over our heads, while we charged down the stairs, our cheering magnified in the stairwell. Nobody had to line up.

11   Not all of the children who were silent at American school found voice at Chinese school. One new teacher said each of us had to get up and recite in front of the class, who was to listen. My sister and I had memorized the lesson perfectly. We said it to each other at home, one chanting, one listening. The teacher called on my sister to recite first. It was the first time a teacher had called on the secondborn to go first. My sister was scared. She glanced at me and looked away; I looked down at my desk. I hoped that she could do it because if she could, then I would have to. She opened her mouth and a voice came out that wasn't

a whisper, but it wasn't a proper voice either. I hoped that she would not cry, fear breaking up her voice like twigs underfoot. She sounded as if she were trying to sing through weeping and strangling. She did not pause or stop to end the embarrassment. She kept going until she said the last word, and then she sat down. When it was my turn, the same voice came out, a crippled animal running on broken legs. You could hear splinters in my voice, bones rubbing jagged against one another. I was loud, though. I was glad I didn't whisper.

How strange that the emigrant villagers are shouters, holler- 12 ing face to face. My father asks, "Why is it I can hear Chinese from blocks away? Is it that I understand the language? Or is it they talk loud?" They turn the radio up full blast to hear the operas, which do not seem to hurt their ears. And they yell over the singers that wail over the drums, everybody talking at once, big arm gestures, spit flying. You can see the disgust on American faces looking at women like that. It isn't just the loudness. It is the way Chinese sounds, ching-chong ugly, to American ears, not beautiful like Japanese sayonara words with the consonants and vowels as regular as Italian. We make gutteral peasant noise and have Ton Duc Thang names you can't remember. And the Chinese can't hear Americans at all; the language is too soft and western music unhearable. I've watched a Chinese audience laugh, visit, talk-story, and holler during a piano recital, as if the musician could not hear them. A Chinese-American, somebody's son, was playing Chopin, which has no punctuation, no cymbals, no gongs. Chinese piano music is five black keys. Normal Chinese women's voices are strong and bossy. We American-Chinese girls had to whisper to make ourselves American-feminine. Apparently we whispered even more softly than the Americans. Once a year the teachers referred my sister and me to speech therapy, but our voices would straighten out, unpredictably normal, for the thera-pists. Some of us gave up, shook our heads, and said nothing, not one word. Some of us could not even shake our heads. At times shaking my head no is more self-assertion than I can manage. Most of us eventually found some voice, however faltering. We invented an American-feminine speaking personality.

1976

How to Tame a Wild Tongue

Gloria Anzaldúa

1   "We're going to have to control your tongue," the dentist says, pulling out all the metal from my mouth. Silver bits plop and tinkle into the basin. My mouth is a motherlode.

2   The dentist is cleaning out my roots. I get a whiff of the stench when I gasp. "I can't cap that tooth yet, you're still draining," he says.

3   "We're going to have to do something about your tongue," I hear the anger rising in his voice. My tongue keeps pushing out the wads of cotton, pushing back the drills, the long thin needles. "I've never seen anything as strong or as stubborn," he says. And I think, how do you tame a wild tongue, train it to be quiet, how do you bridle and saddle it? How do you make it lie down?

4   "Who is to say that robbing a people of
         its language is less violent than war?"
         —Ray Gwyn Smith[1]

5   I remember being caught speaking Spanish at recess—that was good for three licks on the knuckles with a sharp ruler. I remember being sent to the corner of the classroom for "talking back" to the Anglo teacher when all I was trying to do was tell her how to pronounce my name. "If you want to be American, speak 'American.' If you don't like it, go back to Mexico where you belong."

6   "I want you to speak English. *Pa' hallar buen trabajo tienes que saber hablar el inglés bien. Qué vale toda tu educación si todavía hablas inglé con un* 'accent,'" my mother would say, mortified that I spoke English like a Mexican. At Pan American University, I and all Chicano students were required to take two speech classes. Their purpose: to get rid of our accents.

7   Attacks on one's form of expression with the intent to censor are a violation of the First Amendment. *El Anglo con cara de inocente nos arrancó la lengua.* Wild tongues can't be tamed, they can only be cut out.

[1]Ray Gwyn Smith, *Moorland Is Cold Country,* unpublished book.

OVERCOMING THE TRADITION OF SILENCE

> *Abogadas, escupimos el oscuro.*   8
> *Peleando con nuestra propia sombra*
> *el silencio nos sepulta.*

En boca cerrada no entran moscas. "Flies don't enter a closed   9
mouth" is a saying I kept hearing when I was a child. *Ser habladora*
was to be a gossip and a liar, to talk too much. *Muchachitas bien cri-*
adas, well-bred girls don't answer back. *Es una falta de respeto* to
talk back to one's mother or father. I remember one of the sins I'd
recite to the priest in the confession box the few times I went to
confession: talking back to my mother, *hablar pa' 'trás, repelar, Ho-*
cicona, repelona, chismosa, having a big mouth, questioning, carrying tales are all signs of being *mal criada.* In my culture they are all
words that are derogatory if applied to women—I've never heard
them applied to men.

The first time I heard two women, a Puerto Rican and a   10
Cuban, say the word *"nosotras,"* I was shocked. I had not known
the word existed. Chicanas use *nosotros* whether we're male or female. We are robbed of our female being by the masculine plural.
Language is a male discourse.

> And our tongues have become   11
> dry   the wilderness has
> dried out our tongues   and
> we have forgotten speech.
>   —Irena Klepfisz[2]

Even our own people, other Spanish speakers *nos quieren*   12
poner candados en la boca. They would hold us back with their bag
of *reglas de academia.*

---

[2]Irena Klepfisz, *"Di rayze aheym/*The Journey Home," in *The Tribe of Dina: A Jewish*
Women's Anthology, Melanie Kaye/Kontrowitz and Irena Klepfisz, eds. (Mont-
pelier, VT: Sinister Wisdom Books, 1986), 49.

OYÉ COMO LADRA: EL LENGUAJE DE LA FRONTERA

13
> *Quien tiene boca se equivoca.*
> —Mexican saying

14 "*Pocho,* cultural traitor, you're speaking the oppressor's language by speaking English, you're ruining the Spanish language," I have been accused by various Latinos and Latinas. Chicano Spanish is considered by the purist and by most Latinos deficient, a mutilation of Spanish.

15 But Chicano Spanish is a border tongue which developed naturally. Change, *evolución, enriquecimiento de palabras nuevas por invención o adopción* have created variants of Chicano Spanish, *un nuevo lenguaje. Un lenguaje que corrésponde a un moda de vivir.* Chicano Spanish is not incorrect, it is a living language.

16 For a people who are neither Spanish nor live in a country in which Spanish is the first language; for a people who live in a country in which English is the reigning tongue but who are not Anglo; for a people who cannot entirely identify with either standard (formal, Castillian) Spanish or standard English, what recourse is left to them but to create their own language? A language which they can connect their identity to, one capable of communicating the realities and values true to themselves—a language with terms that are neither *español ni inglés,* but both. We speak a patois, a forked tongue, a variation of two languages.

17 Chicano Spanish sprang out of the Chicanos' need to identify ourselves as a distinct people. We needed a language with which we could communicate with ourselves, a secret language. For some of us, language is a homeland closer than the Southwest— for many Chicanos today live in the Midwest and the East. And because we are a complex, heterogeneous people, we speak many languages. Some of the languages we speak are:

1. Standard English

2. Working class and slang English

3. Standard Spanish

4. Standard Mexican Spanish

5. North Mexican Spanish dialect

6. Chicano Spanish (Texas, New Mexico, Arizona and California have regional variations)

7. Tex-Mex

8. *Pachuco* (called *caló*)

My "home" tongues are the languages I speak with my sister 18 and brothers, with my friends. They are the last five listed, with 6 and 7 being closest to my heart. From school, the media and job situations, I've picked up standard and working class English. From Mamagrande Locha and from reading Spanish and Mexican literature, I've picked up Standard Spanish and Standard Mexican Spanish. From *los recién llegados*, Mexican immigrants, and *braceros*, I learned the North Mexican dialect. With Mexicans I'll try to speak either Standard Mexican Spanish or the North Mexican dialect. From my parents and Chicanos living in the Valley, I picked up Chicano Texas Spanish, and I speak it with my mom, younger brother (who married a Mexican and who rarely mixes Spanish with English), aunts and older relatives.

With Chicanas from *Nuevo México* or *Arizona* I will speak Chi- 19 cano Spanish a little, but often they don't understand what I'm saying. With most California Chicanas I speak entirely in English (unless I forget). When I first moved to San Francisco, I'd rattle off something in Spanish, unintentionally embarrassing them. Often it is only with another Chicana *tejana* that I can talk freely.

Words distorted by English are known as anglicisms or 20 *pochismos*. The *pocho* is an anglicized Mexican or American of Mexican origin who speaks Spanish with an accent characteristic of North Americans and who distorts and reconstructs the language according to the influence of English.[3] Tex-Mex, or Spanglish, comes most naturally to me. I may switch back and forth

[3]R. C. Ortega, *Dialectología Del Barrio*. trans. Hortencia S. Alwan (Los Angeles, CA: R. C. Ortega Publisher and Bookseller, 1977), 132.

from English to Spanish in the same sentence or in the same word. With my sister and my brother Nune and with Chicano *tejano* contemporaries I speak in Tex-Mex.

21   From kids and people my own age I picked up *Pachuco*. *Pachuco* (the language of the zoot suiters) is a language of rebellion, both against Standard Spanish and Standard English. It is a secret language. Adults of the culture and outsiders cannot understand it. It is made up of slang words from both English and Spanish. *Ruca* means girl or woman, *vato* means guy or dude, *chale* means no, *simón* means yes, *churo* is sure, talk is *periquiar, pigionear* means petting, *que gacho* means how nerdy, *ponte águila* means watch out, death is called *la pelona*. Through lack of practice and not having others who can speak it, I've lost most of the *Pachuco* tongue.

CHICANO SPANISH

22 Chicanos, after 250 years of Spanish/Anglo colonization have developed significant differences in the Spanish we speak. We collapse two adjacent vowels into a single syllable and sometimes shift the stress in certain words such as *maíz/maiz, cohete/cuete*. We leave out certain consonants when they appear between vowels: *lado/lao, mojado/mojao*. Chicanos from South Texas pronounced *f* as *j* as in *jue* (*fue*). Chicanos use "archaisms," words that are no longer in the Spanish language, words that have been evolved out. We say *semos, truje, hiaga, ansina*, and *naiden*. We retain the "archaic" *j*, as in *jalar*, that derives from an earlier *h* (the French *halar* or the Germanic *halon* which was lost to standard Spanish in the 16th century), but which is still found in several regional dialects such as the one spoken in South Texas. (Due to geography, Chicanos from the Valley of South Texas were cut off linguistically from other Spanish speakers. We tend to use words that the Spaniards brought over from Medieval Spain. The majority of the Spanish colonizers in Mexico and the Southwest came from Extremadura—Hernán Cortés was one of them—and Andalucía. Andalucians pronounce *ll* like a *y*, and their *d*'s tend to be absorbed by adjacent vowels:

tirado becomes *tirao*. They brought *el lenguaje popular, dialectos y regionalismos.*[4]).

Chicanos and other Spanish speakers also shift *ll* to *y* and *z* to   23 *s.*[5] We leave out initial syllables, saying *tar* for *estar, toy* for *estoy, hora* for *ahora* (*cubanos* and *puertorriqueños* also leave out initial letters of some words). We also leave out the final syllable such as *pa* for *para*. The intervocalic *y*, the *ll* as in *tortilla, ella, botella,* gets replaced by *tortia* or *tortiya, ea, botea*. We add an additional syllable at the beginning of certain words: *atocar* for *tocar, agastar* for *gastar*. Sometimes we'll say *lavaste las vacijas,* other time *lavates* (substituting the *ates* verb endings for the *aste*).

We use anglicisms, words borrowed from English: *bola* from   24 ball, *carpeta* from carpet, *máchina de lavar* (instead of *lavadora*) from washing machine. Tex-Mex argot, created by adding a Spanish sound at the beginning or end of an English word such as *cookiar* for cook, *watchar* for watch, *parkiar* for park, and *rapiar* for rape, is the result of the pressures on Spanish speakers to adapt to English.

We don't use the word *vosotros/as* or its accompanying verb   25 form. We don't say *claro* (to mean yes), *imagínate,* or *me emociona,* unless we picked up Spanish from Latinas, out of a book, or in a classroom. Other Spanish-speaking groups are going through the same, or similar, development in their Spanish.

LINGUISTIC TERRORISM

> *Deslenguadas. Somos los del español deficiente.* We are your linguis-   26 tic nightmare, your linguistic aberration, your linguistic *mesti- zaje,* the subject of your *burla.* Because we speak with tongues of fire we are culturally crucified. Racially, culturally and linguistically *somos huérfanos*—we speak an orphan tongue.

Chicanas who grew up speaking Chicano Spanish have internal-   27 ized the belief that we speak poor Spanish. It is illegitimate, a bas-

---

[4]Eduardo Hernandéz-Chávez, Andrew D. Cohen, and Anthony F. Beltramo, *El Lenguaje de los Chicanos: Regional and Social Characteristics of Language Used by Mexican Americans* (Arlington, VA: Center for Applied Linguistics, 1975), 39.
[5]Hernandéz-Chávez, xvii.

tard language. And because we internalize how our language has been used against us by the dominant culture, we use our language differences against each other.

28   Chicana feminists often skirt around each other with suspicion and hesitation. For the longest time I couldn't figure it out. Then it dawned on me. To be close to another Chicana is like looking into the mirror. We are afraid of what we'll see there. *Pena.* Shame. Low estimation of self. In childhood we are told that our language is wrong. Repeated attacks on our native tongue diminish our sense of self. The attacks continue throughout our lives.

29   Chicanas feel uncomfortable talking in Spanish to Latinas, afraid of their censure. Their language was not outlawed in their countries. They had a whole lifetime of being immersed in their native tongue; generations, centuries in which Spanish was a first language, taught in school, heard on radio and TV, and read in the newspaper.

30   If a person, Chicana or Latina, has a low estimation of my native tongue, she also has a low estimation of me. Often with *mexicanas y latinas* we'll speak English as a neutral language. Even among Chicanas we tend to speak English at parties or conferences. Yet, at the same time, we're afraid the other will think we're *agringadas* because we don't speak Chicano Spanish. We oppress each other trying to out-Chicano each other, vying to be the "real" Chicanas, to speak like Chicanos. There is no one Chicano language Just as there is no one Chicano experience. A monolingual Chicana whose first language is English or Spanish is just as much a Chicana as one who speaks several variants of Spanish. A Chicana from Michigan or Chicago or Detroit is just as much as Chicana as one from the Southwest. Chicano Spanish is as diverse linguistically as it is regionally.

31   By the end of this century, Spanish speakers will comprise the biggest minority group in the U.S., a country where students in high schools and colleges are encouraged to take French classes because French is considered more "cultured." But for a language to remain alive it must be used.[6] By the end of this century

[6]Irena Klepfisz, "Secular Jewish Identity: Yidishkayt in America," in *The Tribe of Dina*, Kaye/Kantrowitz and Klepfisz, eds., 43

English, and not Spanish, will be the mother tongue of most Chicanos and Latinos.

So, if you want to really hurt me, talk badly about my language. Ethnic identity is twin skin to linguistic identity—I am my language. Until I can take pride in my language, I cannot take pride in myself. Until I can accept as legitimate Chicano Texas Spanish, Tex-Mex and all the other languages I speak, I cannot accept the legitimacy of myself. Until I am free to write bilingually and to switch codes without having always to translate, while I still have to speak English or Spanish when I would rather speak Spanglish, and as long as I have to accommodate the English speakers rather than having them accommodate me, my tongue will be illegitimate. [32]

I will no longer be made to feel ashamed of existing. I will have my voice: Indian, Spanish, white. I will have my serpent's tongue—my woman's voice, my sexual voice, my poet's voice. I will overcome the tradition of silence. [33]

> My fingers [34]
> move sly against your palm
> Like women everywhere, we speak in code . . . .
> —Melanie Kaye/Kantrowitz[7]

1987

A Question of Language

Gloria Naylor

Language is the subject. It is the written form with which I've managed to keep the wolf away from the door and, in diaries, to keep my sanity. In spite of this, I consider the written word infe- [1]

---

[7]Melanie Kaye/Kantrowitz, "Sign," in *We Speak in Code: Poems and Other Writings* (Pittsburgh, PA: Motheroot Publications, Inc., 1980), 85.

rior to the spoken, and much of the frustration experienced by
novelists is the awareness that whatever we manage to capture in
even the most transcendent passages falls far short of the richness
of life. Dialogue achieves its power in the dynamics of a fleeting
moment of sight, sound, smell, and touch.

2   I'm not going to enter the debate here about whether it is language that shapes reality or vice versa. That battle is doomed to be
waged whenever we seek intermittent reprieve from the chicken
and egg dispute. I will simply take the position that the spoken
word, like the written word, amounts to a nonsensical arrangement of sounds or letters without a consensus that assigns "meaning." And building from the meanings of what we hear, we order
reality. Words themselves are innocuous; it is the consensus that
gives them true power.

3   I remember the first time I heard the word *nigger*. In my third-
grade class, our math tests were being passed down the rows, and
as I handed the papers to a little boy in back of me, I remarked that
once again he had received a much lower mark than I did. He
snatched his test from me and spit out that word. Had he called me
a nymphomaniac or a necrophiliac, I couldn't have been more puzzled. I didn't know what a nigger was, but I knew that whatever it
meant, it was something he shouldn't have called me. This was
verified when I raised my hand, and in a loud voice repeated what
he had said and watched the teacher scold him for using a "bad"
word. I was later to go home and ask the inevitable question that
every black parent must face—"Mommy, what does *nigger* mean?"

4   And what exactly did it mean? Thinking back, I realize that
this could not have been the first time the word was used in my
presence. I was part of a large extended family that had migrated
from the rural South after World War II and formed a close-knit
network that gravitated around my maternal grandparents. Their
ground-floor apartment in one of the buildings they owned in
Harlem was a weekend mecca for my immediate family, along
with countless aunts, uncles, and cousins who brought along assorted friends. It was a bustling and open house with assorted
neighbors and tenants popping in and out to exchange bits of gossip, pick up an old quarrel, or referee the ongoing checkers game
in which my grandmother cheated shamelessly. They were all

there to let down their hair and put up their feet after a week of labor in the factories, laundries, and shipyards of New York.

Amid the clamor, which could reach deafening proportions— two or three conversations going on simultaneously, punctuated by the sound of a baby's crying somewhere in the back rooms or out on the street—there was still a rigid set of rules about what was said and how. Older children were sent out of the living room when it was time to get into the juicy details about "you-know-who" up on the third floor who had gone and gotten herself "p-r-e-g-n-a-n-t!" But my parents, knowing that I could spell well beyond my years, always demanded that I follow the others out to play. Beyond sexual misconduct and death, everything else was considered harmless for our young ears. And so among the anecdotes of the triumphs and disappointments in the various workings of their lives, the word *nigger* was used in my presence, but it was set within contexts and inflections that caused it to register in my mind as something else.

In the singular, the word was always applied to a man who had distinguished himself in some situation that brought their approval for his strength, intelligence, or drive:

"Did Johnny *really* do that?"

"I'm telling you, that nigger pulled in $6,000 of overtime last year. Said he got enough for a down payment on a house."

When used with a possessive adjective by a woman—"my nigger"—it became a term of endearment for her husband or boyfriend. But it could be more than just a term applied to a man. In their mouths it became the pure essence of manhood—a disembodied force that channeled their past history of struggle and present survival against the odds into a victorious statement of being: "Yeah, that old foreman found out quick enough—you don't mess with a nigger."

In the plural, it became a description of some group within the community that had overstepped the bounds of decency as my family defined it. Parents who neglected their children, a drunken couple who fought in public, people who simply refused to look for work, those with excessively dirty mouths or unkempt households were all "trifling niggers." This particular circle could forgive hard times, unemployment, the occasional bout of depression—they had gone through all of that themselves—but the unforgivable sin was a lack of self-respect.

11   A woman could never be a "nigger" in the singular, with its connotation of confirming worth. The noun *girl* was its closest equivalent in that sense, but only when used in direct address and regardless of the gender doing the addressing. *Girl* was a token of respect for a woman. The one-syllable word was drawn out to sound like three in recognition of the extra ounce of wit, nerve, or daring that the woman had shown in the situation under discussion.

12   "G-i-r-l, stop. You mean you said that to his face?"

13   But if the word was used in a third-person reference or shortened so that it almost snapped out of the mouth, it always involved some element of communal disapproval. And age became an important factor in these exchanges. It was only between individuals of the same generation, or from any older person to a younger (but never the other way around), that *girl* would be considered a compliment.

14   I don't agree with the argument that use of the word *nigger* at this social stratum of the black community was an internalization of racism. The dynamics were the exact opposite: the people in my grandmother's living room took a word that whites used to signify worthlessness or degradation and rendered it impotent. Gathering there together, they transformed *nigger* to signify the varied and complex human beings they knew themselves to be. If the word was to disappear totally from the mouths of even the most liberal of white society, no one in that room was naive enough to believe it would disappear from white minds. Meeting the word head-on, they proved it had absolutely nothing to do with the way they were determined to live their lives.

15   So there must have been dozens of times that *nigger* was spoken in front of me before I reached the third grade. But I didn't "hear" it until it was said by a small pair of lips that had already learned it could be a way to humiliate me. That was the word I went home and asked my mother about. And since she knew that I had to grow up in America, she took me in her lap and explained.

1986

Language and Literature from a Pueblo Indian Perspective

Leslie Marmon Silko

Where I come from, the words that are most highly valued are [1] those which are spoken from the heart, unpremeditated and unrehearsed. Among the Pueblo people, a written speech or statement is highly suspect because the true feelings of the speaker remain hidden as he reads words that are detached from the occasion and the audience. I have intentionally not written a formal paper to read to this session because of this and because I want you to hear and to experience English in a nontraditional structure, a structure that follows patterns from the oral tradition. For those of you accustomed to a structure that moves from point A to point B to point C, this presentation may be somewhat difficult to follow because the structure of Pueblo expression resembles something like a spider's web—with many little threads radiating from a center, criss-crossing each other. As with the web, the structure will emerge as it is made and you must simply listen and trust, as the Pueblo people do, that meaning will be made.

I suppose the task that I have today is a formidable one be- [2] cause basically I come here to ask you, at least for a while, to set aside a number of basic approaches that you have been using and probably will continue to use in approaching the study of English or the study of language; first of all, I come to ask you to see language from the Pueblo perspective, which is a perspective that is very much concerned with including the whole of creation and the whole of history and time. And so we very seldom talk about breaking language down into words. As I will continue to relate to you, even the use of a specific language is less important than the one thing—which is the "telling," or the storytelling. And so, as Simon Ortiz has written, if you approach a Pueblo person and want to talk words or, worse than that, to break down an individ-

---

This "essay" is an edited transcript of an oral presentation. The "author" deliberately did not read from a prepared paper so that the audience could experience firsthand one dimension of the oral tradition—non-linear structure. Her remarks were intended to be heard, not read.

ual word into its components, ofttimes you will just get a blank stare, because we don't think of words as being isolated from the speaker, which, of course, is one element of the oral tradition. Moreover, we don't think of words as being alone: words are always with other words, and the other words are almost always in a story of some sort.

3   Today I have brought a number of examples of stories in English because I would like to get around to the question that has been raised, or the topic that has come along here, which is what changes we Pueblo writers might make with English as a language for literature. But at the same time I would like to explain the importance of storytelling and how it relates to a Pueblo theory of language.

4   So first I would like to go back to the Pueblo Creation story. The reason I go back to that story is because it is an all-inclusive story of creation and how life began. Tséitsínako, Thought Woman, by thinking of her sisters, and together with her sisters, thought of everything which is, and this world was created. And the belief was that everything in this world was a part of the original creation, and that the people at home realized that far away there were others—other human beings. There is even a section of the story which is a prophesy—which describes the origin of the European race, the African, and also remembers the Asian origins.

5   Starting out with this story, with this attitude which includes all things, I would like to point out that the reason the people are more concerned with story and communication and less with a particular language is in part an outgrowth of the area [pointing to a map] where we find ourselves. Among the twenty Pueblos there are at least six distinct languages, and possibly seven. Some of the linguists argue—and I don't set myself up to be a linguist at all—about the number of distinct languages. But certainly Zuni is all alone, and Hopi is all alone, and from mesa to mesa there are subtle differences in languages—very great differences. I think that this might be the reason that what particular language was being used wasn't as important as what a speaker was trying to say. And this, I think, is reflected and stems or grows out of a particular view of the story—that is, that language *is* story. At Laguna many words have stories which make them. So when one is telling a story, and one is using words to tell the story, each word

that one is speaking has a story of its own too. Often the speakers or tellers go into the stories of the words they are using to tell one story so that you get stories within stories, so to speak. This structure becomes very apparent in the storytelling, and what I would like to show you later on by reading some pieces that I brought is that this structure also informs the writing and the stories which are currently coming from Pueblo people. I think what is essential is this sense of story, and story within story, and the idea that one story is only the beginning of many stories, and the sense that stories never truly end. I would like to propose that these views of structure and the dynamics of storytelling are some of the contributions which Native American cultures bring to the English language or at least to literature in the English language.

First of all, a lot of people think of storytelling as something 6 that is done at bedtime—that is something that is done for small children. When I use the term storytelling, I include a far wider range of telling activity. I also do not limit storytelling to simply old stories, but to again go back to the original view of creation, which sees that it is all part of a whole; we do not differentiate or fragment stories and experiences. In the beginning, Tséitsínako, Thought Woman, thought of all these things, and all of these things are held together as one holds many things together in a single thought.

So in the telling (and today you will hear a few of the dimen- 7 sions of this telling) first of all, as was pointed out earlier, the storytelling always includes the audience and the listeners, and, in fact, a great deal of the story is believed to be inside the listener, and the storyteller's role is to draw the story out of the listeners. This kind of shared experience grows out of a strong community base. The storytelling goes on and continues from generation to generation.

The Origin story functions basically as a maker of our iden- 8 tity—with the story we know who we are. We are the Lagunas. This is where we came from. We came this way. We came by this place. And so from the time you are very young, you hear these stories, so that when you go out into the wider world, when one asks who you are, or where are you from, you immediately know: we are the people who came down from the north. We are the people of these stories. It continues down into clans so that you are not just talking about Laguna Pueblo people, you are talking about your own clan. Within the clans there are stories which identify the clan.

9   In the Creation story, Antelope says that he will help knock a hole in the earth so that the people can come up, out into the next world. Antelope tries and tries, and he uses his hooves and is unable to break through; and it is then that Badger says, "Let me help you." And Badger very patiently uses his claws and digs a way through, bringing the people into the world. When the Badger clan people think of themselves, or when the Antelope people think of themselves, it is as people who are of *this* story, and this is *our* place, and we fit into the very beginning when the people first came, before we began our journey south.

10   So you can move, then, from the idea of one's identity as a tribal person into clan identity. Then we begin to get to the extended family, and this is where we begin to get a kind of story coming into play which some people might see as a different kind of story, though Pueblo people do not. Anthropologists and ethnologists have, for a long time, differentiated the types of oral language they find in the Pueblos. They tended to rule out all but the old and sacred and traditional stories and were not interested in family stories and the family's account of itself. But these family stories are just as important as the other stories—the older stories. These family stories are given equal recognition. There is no definite, pre-set pattern for the way one will hear the stories of one's own family, but it is a very critical part of one's childhood, and it continues on throughout one's life. You will hear stories of importance to the family—sometimes wonderful stories—stories about the time a maternal uncle got the biggest deer that was ever seen and brought back from the mountains. And so one's sense of who the family is, and who you are, will then extend from that—"I am from the family of my uncle who brought in this wonderful deer, and it was a wonderful hunt"—so you have this sort of building or sense of identity.

11   There are also other stories, stories about the time when another uncle, perhaps, did something that wasn't really acceptable. In other words, this process of keeping track, of telling, is

an all-inclusive process which begins to create a total picture. So it is very important that you know all of the stories—both positive and not so positive—about one's own family. The reason that it is very important to keep track of all the stories in one's own family is because you are liable to hear a story from somebody else who is perhaps an enemy of the family, and you are liable to hear a version which has been changed, a version which makes your family sound disreputable—something that will taint the honor of the family. But if you have already heard the story, you know your family's version of what *really* happened that night, so when somebody else is mentioning it, you will have a version of the story to counterbalance it. Even when there is no way around it—old Uncle Pete did a terrible thing—by knowing the stories that come out of other families, by keeping very close watch, listening constantly to learn the stories about other families, one is in a sense able to deal with terrible sorts of things that might happen within one's own family. When a member of one's own family does something that cannot be excused, one always knows stories about similar things which happened in other families. And it is not done maliciously. I think it is very important to realize this. Keeping track of all the stories within the community gives a certain distance, a useful perspective which brings incidents down to a level we can deal with. If others have done it before, it cannot be so terrible. If others have endured, so can we.

The stories are always bringing us together, keeping this 12 whole together, keeping this family together, keeping this clan together. "Don't go away, don't isolate yourself, but come here, because we have all had these kinds of experiences"—this is what the people are saying to you when they tell you these other stories. And so there is this constant pulling together to resist what seems to me to be a basic part of human nature: when some violent emotional experience takes place, people get the urge to run off and hide or separate themselves from others. And of course, if we do that, we are not only talking about endangering the group, we are also talking about the individual or the individual family never being able to recover or to survive. Inherent in this belief is the feel-

ing that one does not recover or get well by one's self, but it is together that we look after each other and take care of each other.

13   In the storytelling, then, we see this process of bringing people together, and it works not only on the family level, but also on
the level of the individual. Of course, the whole Pueblo concept of
the individual is a little bit different from the usual Western concept of the individual. But one of the beauties of the storytelling is
that when something happens to an individual, many people will
come to you and take you aside, or maybe a couple of people will
come and talk to you. These are occasions of storytelling. These
occasions of storytelling are continuous; they are a way of life.

14   Storytelling lies at the heart of the Pueblo people, and so
when someone comes in and says, "When did they tell the stories,
or what time of day does the storytelling take place?" that is a
ridiculous question. The storytelling goes on constantly—as some
old grandmother puts on the shoes of a little child and tells the
child the story of a little girl who didn't wear her shoes. At the
same time somebody comes into the house for coffee to talk with
an adolescent boy who has just been into a lot of trouble, to reassure him that *he* got into that kind of trouble, or somebody else's
son got into that kind of trouble too. You have this constant ongoing process, working on many different levels.

15   One of the stories I like to bring up about helping the individual in crisis is a recent story, and I want to remind you that we
make no distinctions between the stories—whether they are history, whether they are fact, whether they are gossip—these distinctions are not useful when we are talking about this particular
experience with language. Anyway, there was a young man who,
when he came back from the war in Vietnam, had saved up his
Army pay and bought a beautiful red Volkswagen Beetle. He was
very proud of it, and one night drove up to a place right across the
reservation line. It is a very notorious place for many reasons, but
one of the more notorious things about the place is a deep arroyo
behind the place. This is the King's Bar. So he ran in to pick up a
cold six-pack to take home, but he didn't put on his emergency
brake. And his little red Volkswagen rolled back into the arroyo
and was all smashed up. He felt very bad about it, but within a

few days everybody had come to him and told him stories about other people who had lost cars to that arroyo. And probably the story that made him feel the best was about the time that George Day's station wagon, with his mother-in-law and kids in the back, rolled into that arroyo. So everybody was saying, "Well, at least your mother-in-law and kids weren't in the car when it rolled in," and you can't argue with that kind of story. He felt better then because he wasn't alone anymore. He and his smashed-up Volkswagen were now joined with all the other stories of cars that fell into that arroyo. . . .

There are a great many parallels between Pueblo experiences 16 and the remarks that have been made about South Africa and the Caribbean countries—similarities in experiences so far as language is concerned. More specifically, with the experience of English being imposed upon the people. The Pueblo people, of course, have seen intruders come and intruders go. The first they watched come were the Spaniards; while the Spaniards were there, things had to be conducted in Spanish. But as the old stories say, if you wait long enough, they'll go. And sure enough, they went. Then another bunch came in. And old stories say, well, if you wait around long enough, not so much that they'll go, but at least their ways will go. One wonders now, when you see what's happening to technocratic-industrial culture, now that we've used up most of the sources of energy, you think perhaps the old people are right.   17

But anyhow, our experience with English has been different because the Bureau of Indian Affairs schools were so terrible that we never heard of Shakespeare. There was Dick and Jane, and I can remember reading that the robins were heading south for winter, but I knew that all winter the robins were around Laguna. It took me a long time to figure out what was going on. I worried for quite a while about the robins because they didn't leave in the winter, not realizing that the textbooks were written in Boston. The big textbook companies are up here in Boston and *their* robins do go south in the winter. But this freed us and encouraged us to stay with our narratives. Whatever literature we received at school (which was damn little), at home the storytelling, the special regard for telling and bringing together through the telling, was going on constantly. It has continued, and so we have a great body of classical oral literature, both in the narratives and in the chants and songs.

18   As the old people say, "If you can remember the stories, you will be all right. Just remember the stories." And, or course, usually when they say that to you, when you are young, you wonder what in the world they mean. But when I returned—I had been away from Laguna Pueblo for a couple of years, well more than a couple of years after college and so forth—I returned to Laguna and I went to Laguna-Acoma high school to visit an English class, and I was wondering how the telling was continuing, because Laguna Pueblo, as the anthropologists have said, is one of the more acculturated pueblos. So I walked into this high school English class and there they were sitting, these very beautiful Laguna and Acoma kids. But I knew that out in their lockers they had cassette tape recorders, and I knew that at home they had stereos, and they were listening to "Kiss" and Led Zeppelin and all those other things. I was almost afraid, but I had to ask—I had with me a book of short fiction (it's called *The Man to Send Rain Clouds* [New York: Viking Press, 1974]), and among the stories of other Native American writers, it has stories that I have written and Simon Ortiz has written. And there is one particular story in the book about the killing of a state policeman in New Mexico by three Acoma Pueblo men. It was an act that was committed in the early fifties. I was afraid to ask, but I had to. I looked at the class and I said, "How many of you heard this story before you read it in the book?" And I was prepared to hear this crushing truth that indeed the anthropologists were right about the old traditions dying out. But it was amazing, you know, almost all but one or two students raised their hands. They had heard that story, just as Simon and I heard it, when we were young. That was my first indication that storytelling continues on. About half of them had heard it in English, about half of them had heard it in Laguna. I think again, getting back to one of the original statements, that if you begin to look at the core of the importance of the language and how it fits in with the culture, it is the *story* and the feeling of the story which matters more than what language it's told in. . . .

1979

On Keeping a Notebook

Joan Didion

"'That woman Estelle,'" the note reads, "'is partly the reason why 1
George Sharp and I are separated today.' *Dirty crepe-de-Chine
wrapper, hotel bar, Wilmington RR, 9:45 a.m. August Monday morning.*"

Since the note is in my notebook, it presumably has some 2
meaning to me. I study it for a long while. At first I have only the
most general notion of what I was doing on an August Monday
morning in the bar of the hotel across from the Pennsylvania Railroad station in Wilmington, Delaware (waiting for a train? missing one? 1960? 1961? why Wilmington?), but I do remember being
there. The woman in the dirty crepe-de-Chine wrapper had come
down from her room for a beer, and the bartender had heard before the reason why George Sharp and she were separated today.
"Sure," he said, and went on mopping the floor. "You told me." At
the other end of the bar is a girl. She is talking, pointedly, not to
the man beside her but to a cat lying in the triangle of sunlight
cast through the open door. She is wearing a plaid silk dress from
Peck & Peck, and the hem is coming down.

Here is what it is: the girl has been on the Eastern Shore, and 3
now she is going back to the city, leaving the man beside her, and
all she can see ahead are the viscous summer sidewalks and the
3 a.m. long-distance calls that will make her lie awake and then
sleep drugged through all the steaming mornings left in August
(1960? 1961?). Because she must go directly from the train to
lunch in New York, she wishes that she had a safety pin for the
hem of the plaid silk dress, and she also wishes that she could
forget about the hem and the lunch and stay in the cool bar that
smells of disinfectant and malt and make friends with the
woman in the crepe-de-Chine wrapper. She is afflicted by a little
self-pity, and she wants to compare Estelles. That is what that
was all about.

Why did I write it down? In order to remember, of course, but 4
exactly what was it I wanted to remember? How much of it actually happened? Did any of it? Why do I keep a notebook at all? It

is easy to deceive oneself on all those scores. The impulse to write things down is a peculiarly compulsive one, inexplicable to those who do not share it, useful only accidentally, only secondarily, in the way that any compulsion tries to justify itself. I suppose that it begins or does not begin in the cradle. Although I have felt compelled to write things down since I was five years old, I doubt that my daughter ever will, for she is a singularly blessed and accepting child, delighted with life exactly as life presents itself to her, unafraid to go to sleep and unafraid to wake up. Keepers of private notebooks are a different breed altogether, lonely and resistant rearrangers of things, anxious malcontents, children afflicted apparently at birth with some presentiment of loss.

5   My first notebook was a Big Five tablet, given to me by my mother with the sensible suggestion that I stop whining and learn to amuse myself by writing down my thoughts. She returned the tablet to me a few years ago; the first entry is an account of a woman who believed herself to be freezing to death in the Arctic night, only to find, when day broke, that she had stumbled onto the Sahara Desert, where she would die of the heat before lunch. I have no idea what turn of a five-year-old's mind could have prompted so insistently "ironic" and exotic a story, but it does reveal a certain predilection for the extreme which has dogged me into adult life; perhaps if I were analytically inclined I would find it a truer story than any I might have told about Donald Johnson's birthday party or the day my cousin Brenda put Kitty Litter in the aquarium.

6   So the point of my keeping a notebook has never been, nor is it now, to have an accurate factual record of what I have been doing or thinking. That would be a different impulse entirely, an instinct for reality which I sometimes envy but do not possess. At no point have I ever been able successfully to keep a diary; my approach to daily life ranges from the grossly negligent to the merely absent, and on those few occasions when I have tried dutifully to record a day's events, boredom has so overcome me that the results are mysterious at best. What is this business about "shopping, typing piece, dinner with E, depressed"? Shopping for what? Typing what piece? Who is E? Was this "E" depressed, or was I depressed? Who cares?

In fact I have abandoned altogether that kind of pointless en-   7
try; instead I tell what some would call lies. "That's simply not
true," the members of my family frequently tell me when they
come up against my memory of a shared event. "The party was
not for you, the spider was *not* a black widow, *it wasn't that way at
all.*" Very likely they are right, for not only have I always had trouble distinguishing between what happened and what merely
might have happened, but I remain unconvinced that the distinction, for my purposes, matters. The cracked crab that I recall having for lunch the day my father came home from Detroit in 1945
must certainly be embroidery, worked into the day's pattern to
lend verisimilitude; I was ten years old and would not now remember the cracked crab. The day's events did not turn on
cracked crab. And yet it is precisely that fictitious crab that makes
me see the afternoon all over again, a home movie run all too often, the father bearing gifts, the child weeping, an exercise in family love and guilt. Or that is what it was to me. Similarly, perhaps
it never did snow that August in Vermont; perhaps there never
were flurries in the night wind, and maybe no one else felt the
ground hardening and summer already dead even as we pretended to bask in it, but that was how it felt to me, and it might as
well have snowed, could have snowed, did snow.

  How it felt to me: that is getting closer to the truth about a note-   8
book. I sometimes delude myself about why I keep a notebook,
imagine that some thrifty virtue derives from preserving everything observed. See enough and write it down, I tell myself, and
then some morning when the world seems drained of wonder,
some day when I am only going through the motions of doing
what I am supposed to do, which is write—on that bankrupt
morning I will simply open my notebook and there it will all be, a
forgotten account with accumulated interest, paid passage back to
the world out there: dialogue overheard in hotels and elevators
and at the hatcheck counter in Pavillon (one middle-aged man
shows his hatcheck to another and says, "That's my old football
number"); impressions of Bettina Aptheker and Benjamin Son-
nenberg and Teddy ("Mr. Acapulco") Stauffer; careful *apercus*
about tennis bums and failed fashion models and Greek shipping
heiresses, one of whom taught me a significant lesson (a lesson I
could have learned from F. Scott Fitzgerald, but perhaps we all

must meet the very rich for ourselves) by asking, when I arrived
to interview her in her orchid-filled sitting room on the second
day of a paralyzing New York blizzard, whether it was snowing
outside.

9   I imagine, in other words, that the notebook is about other
people. But of course it is not. I have no real business with what
one stranger said to another at the hatcheck counter in Pavillon; in
fact I suspect that the line "That's my old football number"
touched not my own imagination at all, but merely some memory
of something once read, probably "The Eighty-Yard Run." Nor is
my concern with a woman in a dirty crepe-de-Chine wrapper in a
Wilmington bar. My stake is always, of course, in the unmen-
tioned girl in the plaid silk dress. *Remember what it was to be me:*
that is always the point.

10   It is a difficult point to admit. We are brought up in the ethic
that others, any others, all others, are by definition more interesting than ourselves; taught to be diffident, just this side of self-
effacing. ("You're the least important person in the room and
don't you forget it," Jessica Mitford's governess would hiss in her
ear on the advent of any social occasion; I copied that into my
notebook because it is only recently that I have been able to enter
a room without hearing some such phrase in my inner ear.) Only
the very young and the very old may recount their dreams at breakfast, dwell upon self, interrupt with memories of beach picnics and
favorite Liberty lawn dresses and the rainbow trout in a creek near
Colorado Springs. The rest of us are expected, rightly, to affect ab-
sorption in other people's favorite dresses, other people's trout.

11   And so we do. But our notebooks give us away, for however
dutifully we record what we see around us, the common denominator of all we see is always, transparently, shamelessly, the implacable "I." We are not talking here about the kind of notebook
that is patently for public consumption, a structural conceit for
binding together a series of graceful *pensées;* we are talking about
something private, about bits of the mind's string too short to use,
an indiscriminate and erratic assemblage with meaning only for
its maker.

12   And sometimes even the maker has difficulty with the meaning. There does not seem to be, for example, any point in my knowing for the rest of my life that, during 1964, 720 tons of soot fell on

every square mile of New York City, yet there it is in my notebook, labeled "FACT." Nor do I really need to remember that Ambrose Bierce liked to spell Leland Stanford's name "£eland $tanford" or that "smart women almost always wear black in Cuba," a fashion hint without much potential for practical application. And does not the relevance of these notes seem marginal at best?

> In the basement museum of the Inyo County Courthouse in Independence, California, sign pinned to a mandarin coat: This MANDARIN COAT was often worn by Mrs. Minnie S. Brooks when giving lectures on her TEAPOT COLLECTION." Redhead getting out of car in front of Beverly Wilshire Hotel, chinchilla stole, Vuitton bags with tags reading: 13
>
>
>
> MRS. LOU FOX
> HOTEL SAHARA
> VEGAS
>
>

Well, perhaps not entirely marginal. As a matter of fact, Mrs. Minnie S. Brooks and her MANDARIN COAT pull me back into my own childhood, for although I never knew Mrs. Brooks and did not visit Inyo County until I was thirty, I grew up in just such a world, in houses cluttered with Indian relics and bits of gold ore and ambergris and the souvenirs my Aunt Mercy Farnsworth brought back from the Orient. It is a long way from that world to Mrs. Lou Fox's world, where we all live now, and is it not just as well to remember that? Might not Mrs. Minnie S. Brooks help me to remember what I am? Might not Mrs. Lou Fox help me to remember what I am not?   14

But sometimes the point is harder to discern. What exactly did I have in mind when I noted down that it cost the father of someone I know $650 a month to light the place on the Hudson in which he lived before the Crash? What use was I planning to make of this line by Jimmy Hoffa: "I may have my faults, but being wrong ain't one of them"? And although I think it interesting to know where the girls who travel with the Syndicate have their hair done when they find themselves on the West Coast, will I ever make suitable use of it? Might I not be better off just passing it on to John O'Hara? What is a recipe for sauerkraut doing in my notebook? What kind of magpie keeps this notebook? *"He was born the night the Titanic went down."* That seems a nice enough   15 line, and I even recall who said it, but is it not really a better line in life than it could ever be in fiction?

16   But of course that is exactly it: not that I should ever use the line, but that I should remember the woman who said it and the afternoon I heard it. We were on her terrace by the sea, and we were finishing the wine left from lunch, trying to get what sun there was, a California winter sun. The woman whose husband was born the night the *Titanic* went down wanted to rent her house, wanted to go back to her children in Paris. I remember wishing that I could afford the house, which cost $1,000 a month. "Someday you will," she said lazily. "Someday it all comes." There in the sun on her terrace it seemed easy to believe in someday, but later I had a low-grade afternoon hangover and ran over a black snake on the way to the supermarket and was flooded with inexplicable fear when I heard the checkout clerk explaining to the man ahead of me why she was finally divorcing her husband. "He left me no choice," she said over and over as she punched the register. "He has a little seven-month-old baby by her, he left me no choice." I would like to believe that my dread then was for the human condition, but of course it was for me, because I wanted a baby and did not then have one and because I wanted to own the house that cost $1,000 a month to rent and because I had a hangover.

17   It all comes back. Perhaps it is difficult to see the value in having one's self back in that kind of mood, but I do see it; I think we are well advised to keep on nodding terms with the people we used to be whether we find them attractive company or not. Otherwise they turn up unannounced and surprise us, come hammering on the mind's door at 4 a.m. of a bad night and demand to know who deserted them, who betrayed them, who is going to make amends. We forget all too soon the things we thought we could never forget. We forget the loves and the betrayals alike, forget what we whispered and what we screamed, forget who we were. I have already lost touch with a couple of people I used to be; one of them, a seventeen-year-old, presents little threat, although it would be of some interest to me to know again what it feels like to sit on a river levee drinking vodka-and-orange-juice and listening to Les Paul and Mary Ford and their echoes sing

"How High the Moon" on the car radio. (You see I still have the scenes, but I no longer perceive myself among those present, no longer could even improvise the dialogue.) The other one, a twenty-three-year-old, bothers me more. She was always a good deal of trouble, and I suspect she will reappear when I least want to see her, skirts too long, shy to the point of aggravation, always the injured party, full of recriminations and little hurts and stories I do not want to hear again, at once saddening me and angering me with her vulnerability and ignorance, an apparition all the more insistent for being so long banished.

It is a good idea, then, to keep in touch, and I suppose that keeping in touch is what notebooks are all about. And we are all on our own when it comes to keeping those lines open to ourselves: your notebook will never help me, nor mine you. *"So what's new in the whiskey business?"* What could that possibly mean to you? To me it means a blonde in a Pucci bathing suit sitting with a couple of fat men by the pool at the Beverly Hills Hotel. Another man approaches, and they all regard one another in silence for a while. "So what's new in the whiskey business?" one of the fat men finally says by way of welcome, and the blonde stands up, arches one foot and dips it in the pool, looking all the while at the cabana where Baby Pignatari is talking on the telephone. That is all there is to that, except that several years later I saw the blonde coming out of Saks Fifth Avenue in New York with her California complexion and a voluminous mink coat. In the harsh wind that day she looked old and irrevocably tired to me, and even the skins in the mink coat were not worked the way they were doing them that year, not the way she would have wanted them done, and there is the point of the story. For a while after that I did not like to look in the mirror, and my eyes would skim the newspapers and pick out only the deaths, the cancer victims, the premature coronaries, the suicides, and I stopped riding the Lexington Avenue IRT because I noticed for the first time that all the strangers I had seen for years—the man with the seeing-eye dog, the spinster who read the classified pages every day, the fat girl who always got off with me at Grand Central—looked older than they once had.

It all comes back. Even that recipe for sauerkraut: even that brings it back. I was on Fire Island when I first made that sauerkraut, and it was raining, and we drank a lot of bourbon and ate the sauerkraut and went to bed at ten, and I listened to the rain and the Atlantic and felt safe. I made the sauerkraut again last night and it did not make me feel any safer, but that is, as they say, another story.

1966

"I'm Sorry, I'm Not Apologizing": Conversational Rituals

Deborah Tannen

1   Conversation is a ritual. We say things that seem the thing to say, without thinking of the literal meaning of our words any more than we expect the question "How are you?" to call forth a detailed account of aches and pains. On the job, the meat of the work that has to be done is held together, made pleasant and possible, by the ketchup, relish, and bun of conversational rituals. But people have different habits for using these rituals, and when a ritual is not recognized, the words spoken are taken literally. I have heard visitors to the United States complain that Americans are hypocritical because they ask how you are but aren't interested in the answer. And American in Burma are puzzled when Burmese ask, "Have you eaten yet?"—and show no sign of inviting them to lunch.[1] In the Philippines, people ask each other, "Where are you going?"—which may seem rather intrusive to Americans, who don't realize that the only reply expected is, "Over there."[2]

2   It is easy, and entertaining, to notice different rituals in foreign countries, as did the Briton who spent a year working in France

---

[1] "*And Americans in Burma are puzzled when Burmese ask, 'Have you eaten yet?'—and show no sign of inviting them to lunch.*" My source for the Burmese greeting ritual is personal conversation with A. L. Becker.

[2] "*. . . Americans, who don't realize that the only reply expected is, 'Over there.'*" Mary Catherine Bateson mentions this Philippine greeting ritual in *Peripheral Visions*.

and was amused that everyone ceremoniously shook hands and said "*Bonjour*" to everyone else when they arrived at work in the morning—and again when they left for lunch, returned from lunch, and left at the end of the day. He even observed elementary-school children shaking each other's hands in greeting when they met on their way to school. We expect rituals at points of transition like greetings, and we expect them to be different—and those differences to cause confusion—when we go to foreign countries. But we don't expect differences, and are far less likely to recognize the ritual nature of our conversations, among other Americans at work. Our differing rituals are even more problematic when we think we're all speaking the same language.

SAYING "I'M SORRY" WHEN YOU'RE NOT

One conversational ritual that can differ from one person to the next and cause trouble at work is apologizing.   3

I had been interviewed by a well-known columnist who ended our friendly conversation by giving me the number of her direct telephone line in case I ever wanted to call her. Some time later, I did want to call her but had misplaced her direct number and had to go through the newspaper receptionist to get through to her. When our conversation was ending, and we had both uttered ending-type remarks, I remembered that I wanted to get her direct number for the future and said, "Oh, I almost forgot—last time you gave me your direct number, but I lost it: I wondered if I could get it again." "Oh, I'm sorry," she came back instantly. "It's . . ." And she gave me the number. I laughed because she had just done something I had mentioned in our interview: said "I'm sorry" when an apology was not called for. She had done nothing wrong; I was the one who lost the number. But in fact she was not apologizing; she was just uttering an automatic conversational smoother to assure me she had no intention of rushing me off the phone or denying me her number. . . .   4

Sometimes a tone of self-deprecation is heard as an apology even without the word "sorry" being spoken. In another tape of a conversation recorded for me, a manager named Kristin was ex-   5 plaining to a computer-support manager named Herb why she invited him to a meeting, even though she wasn't sure he was the right person:

> Kristin: Just 'cause, you know, I'd worked with him and then you came and I—I didn't know. . .what his schedule was. And I wasn't sure who [laughing] the head of that group was! [Herb also laughs.] To tell you the truth! So. . .
> Herb: No, don't—don't apologize.

Many women are frequently told, "Don't apologize" or "You're always apologizing." The reason "apologizing" is seen as something they should stop doing is that it seems synonymous with putting oneself down. But for many women, and a fair number of men, saying "I'm sorry" isn't literally an apology; it is a ritual way of restoring balance to a conversation. "I'm sorry," spoken in this spirit, if it has any literal meaning at all, does not mean "I apologize," which would be tantamount to accepting blame, but rather "I'm sorry that happened." To understand the ritual nature of apologies, think of a funeral at which you might say, "I'm so sorry about Reginald's death." When you say that, you are not pleading guilty to a murder charge. You're expressing regret that something happened without taking or assigning blame. In other words, "I'm sorry" can be an expression of understanding—and caring—about the other person's feelings rather than an apology.[3]

6   That an apology can be a routinized way of taking the other person's feelings into account becomes clear in the following example. When professional pool player Ewa Mataya, who is regarded as one of the top female pool players in the world, was being bested in a tournament by amateur Julie Nogiac, Mataya said of Nogiac, "She's very sweet. She kept apologizing." I doubt

---

[3]*"I'm sorry' can be an expression of understanding—and caring—about the other person's feelings rather than an apology."* Linguist Amy Sheldon uses the term "double-voice discourse" to describe how the little girls in a day care center talked in ways that took account of both their own and others' interests and goals. She contrasts this with the "single-voice discourse" that typified the boys' talk: Each pursued his own goal, leaving it to others to pursue theirs. (Sheldon, "Preschool Girls' Discourse Competence")

Nogiac actually regretted that she was beating the champion; she was simply expressing her awareness that her doing so must have been making Mataya feel bad.[4]

This is not to say that "I'm sorry" is never an apology. But when   7 it is, in the sense of accepting responsibility for something that went wrong, it is often assumed to be the first step in a two-step ritual: I say "I'm sorry" and take half the blame; then you take the other half. A secretary told me she liked working for her boss because, if he said, "When you typed this letter, you missed this phrase that I inserted," and she said, "Oh, I'm sorry. I'll fix it," he would usually follow up, "Well, I wrote it so small it was easy to miss."

Admitting fault can be experienced as taking a one-down po-   8 sition. When both parties share the blame, they end up on an equal footing. That is the logic behind the ritual sharing of blame in response to an apology. It's a mutual face-saving device. Someone who feels that an apology requires a ritualized sharing of blame might even make up a fault to admit, in order to seal off the interchange in an appropriate way. And those who share an understanding of the ritual will not take that admission of fault literally, but will simply appreciate it as an attempt to save face for them. Put another way, it is a courteous way of not leaving the apologizer in the one-down position.

Someone, on the other hand, who does not use apologies rit-   9 ually may well take them all literally. And this can lead to resentment on the part of the ritual apologizer. If I say "I'm sorry" and you say "I accept your apology," then my attempt to achieve balance has misfired, and I think you have put me in a one-down position, though you probably think I put myself there. (Sensing this, people sometimes make a joke of preserving the imbalance following an apology: "Okay, just make sure it doesn't happen again." It's funny because it is obvious that is not the way the exchange is supposed to go.)

Ritual apologies—like other conversational rituals—work   10 fine when both parties share assumptions about their use. But

[4]My information about and quotation from pool champion Ewa Mataya are taken from "Pool's Reigning Hot Shot," by Marcia Froelke Coburn, *Know-How* magazine, Fall 1993, pp. 58–60. The quotation is from p. 60.

people who utter frequent ritual apologies when others don't may end up seeming to be taking blame for mishaps that are not their fault. When they are partly at fault, they come out looking entirely so. There are cultural as well as gender influences on how likely people are to use apologies in this way, but research on Americans by Nessa Wolfson and on New Zealanders by Janet Holmes shows that women are more likely to do it than men. Holmes found that women uttered the most apologies to other women and far fewer to men, while men uttered very few to other men and slightly more to women. . . .

GIVING PRAISE

11   Giving praise is also a conversational ritual, and here too there are cultural as well as gender patterns, as the next two examples show.

12   Lester had been on his new job only six months when he heard that some of the women reporting to him were deeply dissatisfied. When he talked to them, they erupted; two were on the verge of quitting, they said, because they weren't happy working for someone who didn't appreciate their work. They were convinced that Lester didn't think they were doing a good job, and they preferred to quit rather than wait to be fired. Lester was dumbfounded. He believed they were doing a fine job and had never thought otherwise. Surely, he had said nothing to give them the impression he didn't like their work. And indeed he hadn't. That was the problem. He had said nothing. The women expected him to praise their work if he liked it, and to show interest in what they were doing by asking about it from time to time. When he said nothing about the job they were doing, they assumed he was following the adage, "If you can't say something nice, don't say anything." He thought he was showing confidence in them by leaving them alone. To him, everything was fine unless he corrected them. To them, unless he told them everything was fine, there must be a problem.

13   Vince had a similar experience by which he learned there is no right amount of praise and attention to give. He supervised a group of eight people who reported directly to him. He believed

in keeping in touch with his group, so he made a point of checking in with each one, even if briefly, at least once a day. Certain he was being a responsible and caring boss, he was shocked when a new system of soliciting evaluations from subordinates was instituted. Though there were some who were pleased with his style of management, the complaints of others ranged from, "He's always looking over my shoulder; he doesn't seem to trust me to do the work" to "He rarely shows any interest in what I'm doing; he doesn't seem to care about it, so why should I care?" It turned out that checking once a day was too much attention for some in his group and too little for others. Those who saw his visits as too brief were interpreting them in terms of power: He's my superior, he's checking on me. Those who saw them as too brief were interpreting them in terms of rapport: He's not interested enough to spend more time. In Vince's case, it turned out that those who took the first tack were men, and those who took the second were women.

Praise is a very special form of feedback. Although I heard [14] many men and women mention that they got more thanks and praise from women than from men, I never heard anyone say they resented receiving praise.[5] I frequently heard from men that they did not mind not getting feedback; if they didn't hear anything, they felt they were doing okay. But when they had a boss who praised them often, they always said they liked it. "It's a problem," one man joked, "because it's habit-forming. The more praise you get, the more you want!"

"I don't know where I stand with you," a woman complained [15] to her boss. "You're not giving me any signals." This is a complaint I heard frequently from women who worked for men. But I also heard it from many men who work for women. I suspect it is not a matter of women or men not sending out signals, but of their sending different signals, which are more likely to be missed by those of the other gender. Another possibility is that many men

---

[5]*"I never heard anyone say they resented receiving praise."* Actually, there was one exception: One woman said she cried when, on her first job, all she got from her boss was praise. Since she couldn't believe she was doing everything right, she took the unalloyed praise as lack of caring.

feel women don't tell them directly enough if they are doing something wrong, and many women feel that men don't tell them directly enough if they are doing well. . . .

"WHICH WAY IS RIGHT?"

16   Someone who is told, "Stop apologizing" rarely thinks of replying, "It's just a ritual; you should say, 'I'm sorry' more. It would make you more likable." She is more likely to say, or think, "What's wrong with me? Why do I apologize all the time?" Our understanding of language inclines us to look for literal rather than ritual meanings in words. And many of us are also inclined to look for individual psychological problems to explain the way we talk. It is easy to make someone who has spoken indirectly feel guilty: "Why do I do that? What's wrong with me?" But few people wonder why they speak as they do when they are talking to others who share their conversational rituals. It's only when our rituals fail that we question them.

17   I have described in this chapter a number of conversational rituals (by no means all) that can differ from one person to the next. Many readers will wonder, "Which way is best?" There is no one best way. Any style of speaking will work just fine in some situations with those who share the style. The most common culprit is style differences. (This is not to imply that misunderstandings or other tensions will never arise when styles are shared. Discord can result from ill intentions or conflicts of interest, and all styles have built-in liabilities that can cause problems in some situations.) But all styles will at times fail with others who don't share or understand them, just as your language won't do you much good if you try to speak it to someone who doesn't know that language. It's not that you are no longer speaking a good language; it will still work fine to express your ideas. But if what you're after is not just self-expression but communication—getting others to understand what you say—then it's not enough for language to be right; it has to be shared—or at least understood.

1990

Let's Put Pornography Back in the Closet

Susan Brownmiller

Free speech is one of the great foundations on which our democ-   1
racy rests. I am old enough to remember the Hollywood Ten, the
screenwriters who went to jail in the late 1940s because they refused to testify before a congressional committee about their political affiliations. They tried to use the First Amendment as a
defense, but they went to jail because in those days there were few
civil liberties lawyers around who cared to champion the First
Amendment right to free speech, when the speech concerned the
Communist Party.

The Hollywood Ten were correct in claiming the First Amend-   2
ment. Its high purpose is the protection of unpopular ideas and
political dissent. In the dark, cold days of the 1950s, few civil libertarians were willing to declare themselves First Amendment ab-
solutists. But in the brighter, though frantic, days of the 1960s, the
principle of protecting unpopular political speech was gradually
strengthened.

It is fair to say now that the battle has largely been won. Even   3
the American Nazi Party has found itself the beneficiary of the
dedicated, tireless work of the American Civil Liberties Union.
But—and please notice the quotation marks coming up—"To
equate the free and robust exchange of ideas and political debate
with commercial exploitation of obscene material demeans the
grand conception of the First Amendment and its high purposes
in the historic struggle for freedom. It is a misuse of the great
guarantees of free speech and free press."

I didn't say that, although I wish I had, for I think the words   4
are thrilling. Chief Justice Warren Burger said it in 1973, in the
United States Supreme Court's majority opinion in *Miller v. California*. During the same decades that the right to political free
speech was being strengthened in the courts, the nation's obscenity laws also were undergoing extensive revision.

5   It's amazing to recall that in 1934 the question of whether James Joyce's *Ulysses* should be banned as pornographic actually went before the Court. The battle to protect *Ulysses* as a work of literature with redeeming social value was won. In later decades, Henry Miller's *Tropic* books, *Lady Chatterley's Lover* and the *Memoirs of Fanny Hill* also were adjudged not obscene. These decisions have been important to me. As the author of *Against Our Will*, a study of the history of rape that does contain explicit sexual material, I shudder to think how my book would have fared if James Joyce, D. H. Lawrence, and Henry Miller hadn't gone before me.

6   I am not a fan of *Chatterley* or the *Tropic* books, I should quickly mention. They are not to my literary taste, nor do I think they represent female sexuality with any degree of accuracy. But I would hardly suggest that we ban them. Such a suggestion wouldn't get very far anyway. The battle to protect these books is ancient history. Time does march on, quite methodically. What, then, is unlawfully obscene, and what does the First Amendment have to do with it?

7   In the Miller case of 1973 (not Henry Miller, by the way, but a porn distributor who sent unsolicited stuff through the mails), the Court came up with new guidelines that it hoped would strengthen obscenity laws by giving more power to the states. What it did in actuality was throw everything into confusion. It set up a three part test by which materials can be adjudged obscene. The materials are obscene if they depict patently offensive, hard-core sexual conduct; lack serious scientific, literary, artistic or political value; and appeal to the prurient interest of an average person—as measured by contemporary community standards.

8   "Patently offensive," "prurient interest," and "hard-core" are indeed words to conjure with. "Contemporary community standards" are what we're trying to redefine. The feminist objection to pornography is not based on prurience, which the dictionary defines as lustful, itching desire. We are not opposed to sex and desire, with or without the itch, and we certainly believe that explicit sexual material has its place in literature, art, science and education. Here we part company rather swiftly with old-line conservatives who don't want sex education in the high schools, for example.

No, the feminist objection to pornography is based on our be- 9
lief that pornography represents hatred of women, that pornography's intent is to humiliate, degrade and dehumanize the female
body for the purpose of erotic stimulation and pleasure. We are
unalterably opposed to the presentation of the female body being
stripped, bound, raped, tortured, mutilated and murdered in the
name of commercial entertainment and free speech.

These images, which are standard pornographic fare, have 10
nothing to do with the hallowed right of political dissent. They
have everything to do with the creation of a cultural climate in
which a rapist feels he is merely giving in to a normal urge and
a woman is encouraged to believe that sexual masochism is
healthy, liberated fun. Justice Potter Stewart once said about
hard-core pornography "You know it when you see it," and that
certainly used to be true. In the good old days, pornography
looked awful. It was cheap and sleazy, and there was no mistaking
it for art.

Nowadays, since the porn industry has become a multimil- 11
lion dollar business, visual technology has been employed in its
service. Pornographic movies are skillfully filmed and edited,
pornographic still shots using the newest tenets of good design
artfully grace the covers of *Hustler, Penthouse,* and *Playboy,* and the
public—and the courts—are sadly confused.

The Supreme Court neglected to define "hard-core" in the 12
Miller decision. This was a mistake. If "hard-core" refers only to
explicit sexual intercourse, then that isn't good enough. When
women or children or men—no matter how artfully—are shown
tortured or terrorized in the service of sex, that's obscene. And
"patently offensive," I would hope, to our "contemporary community standards."

Justice William O. Douglas wrote in his dissent to the Miller 13
case that no one is "compelled to look." This is hardly true. To buy
a paper at the corner newsstand is to subject oneself to a forcible
immersion in pornography, to be demeaned by an array of dehu-
manized, chopped-up parts of the female anatomy, packaged like
cuts of meat at the supermarket. I happen to like my body and I
work hard at the gym to keep it in good shape, but I am embarrassed for my body and for the bodies of all women when I see

the fragmented parts of us, so frivolously, and so flagrantly, displayed.

14   Some constitutional theorists (Justice Douglas was one) have maintained that any obscenity law is a serious abridgement of free speech. Others (and Justice Earl Warren was one) have maintained that the First Amendment was never intended to protect obscenity. We live quite compatibly with a host of free-speech abridgements. There are restraints against false and misleading advertising or statements—shouting "fire" without cause in a crowded movie theater, etc.—that do not threaten, but strengthen, our societal values. Restrictions on the public display of pornography belong in this category.

15   The distinction between permission to publish and permission to display publicly is an essential one and one which I think consonant with First Amendment principles. Justice Burger's words which I quoted above support this without question. We are not saying "Smash the presses" or "Ban the bad ones," but simply "Get the stuff out of our sight." Let the legislatures decide—using realistic and humane contemporary community standards—what can be displayed and what cannot. The courts, after all, will be the final arbiters.

1979

Politics and the English Language
George Orwell

1   Most people who bother with the matter at all would admit that the English language is in a bad way, but it is generally assumed that we cannot by conscious action do anything about it. Our civilization is decadent and our language—so the argument runs—

must inevitably share in the general collapse. It follows that any struggle against the abuse of language is a sentimental archaism, like preferring candles to electric light or hansom cabs to aeroplanes. Underneath this lies the half-conscious belief that language is a natural growth and not an instrument which we shape for our own purposes.   2

Now, it is clear that the decline of a language must ultimately have political and economic causes: it is not due simply to the bad influence of this or that individual writer. But an effect can become a cause, reinforcing the original cause and producing the same effect in an intensified form, and so on indefinitely. A man may take to drink because he feels himself to be a failure, and then fail all the more completely because he drinks. It is rather the same thing that is happening to the English language. It becomes ugly and inaccurate because our thoughts are foolish, but the slovenliness of our language makes it easier for us to have foolish thoughts. The point is that the process is reversible. Modern English, especially written English, is full of bad habits which spread by imitation and which can be avoided if one is willing to take the necessary trouble. If one gets rid of these habits one can think more clearly, and to think clearly is a necessary first step towards political regeneration: so that the fight against bad English is not frivolous and is not the exclusive concern of professional writers. I will come back to this presently, and I hope by that time the meaning of what I have said here will have become clearer. Meanwhile, here are five specimens of the English language as it is now habitually written.   3

These five passages have not been picked out because they are especially bad—I could have quoted far worse if I had chosen—but because they illustrate various of the mental vices from which we now suffer. They are a little below the average, but are fairly representative samples. I number them so that I can refer back to them when necessary:

> "(1) I am not, indeed, sure whether it is not true to say that the Milton who once seemed not unlike a seventeenth-century Shelly had not become, out of an experience ever more bitter in each year, more alien [sic] to the founder of that Jesuit sect which nothing could induce him to tolerate."
>
>   Professor Harold Laski (Essay in *Freedom of Expression*)

"(2) Above all, we cannot play ducks and drakes with a native battery of idioms which prescribes such egregious collocations of vocables as the Basic *put up with* for *tolerate* or *put at a loss* for *bewilder*."

Professor Lancelot Hogben (Interglossa)

"(3) On the one side we have the free personality: by definition it is not neurotic, for it has neither conflict nor dream. Its desires, such as they are, are transparent, for they are just what institutional approval keeps in the forefront of consciousness; another institutional pattern would alter their number and intensity; there is little in them that is natural, irreducible, or culturally dangerous. But *on the other* side, the social bond itself is nothing but the mutual reflection of these self-secure integrities. Recall the definition of love. Is not this the very picture of a small academic? Where is there a place in this hall of mirrors for either personality or fraternity?"

Essay on psychology in Politics (New York)

"(4) All the 'best people' from the gentlemen's clubs, and all the frantic fascist captains, united in common hatred of Socialism and bestial horror of the rising tide of the mass revolutionary movement, have turned to acts of provocation, to foul incendiarism, to medieval legends of poisoned wells, to legalize their own destruction of proletarian organizations, and rouse the agitated petty-bourgeoisie to chauvinistic fervour on behalf of the fight against the revolutionary way out of the crisis."

Communist pamphlet

"(5) If a new spirit *is* to be infused into this old country, there is one thorny and contentious reform which must be tackled, and that is the humanization and galvanization of the B.B.C. Timidity here will bespeak cancer and atrophy of the soul. The heart of Britain may be sound and of strong beat, for instance, but the British lion's roar at present is like that of Bottom in Shakespeare's *Midsummer Night's Dream*—as gentle as any sucking dove. A virile new Britain cannot continue indefinitely to be traduced in the eyes or rather ears, of the world by the effete languors of Langham Place, brazenly masquerading as 'standard English.' When the Voice of Britain is heard at nine o'clock, better far and infinitely less ludicrous to hear aitches honestly dropped than the present priggish, inflated, inhibited, schoolma'amish arch braying of blameless bashful mewing maidens!"

Letter in Tribune

Each of these passages has faults of its own, but, quite apart   4
from avoidable ugliness, two qualities are common to all of them.
The first is staleness of imagery: the other is lack of precision. The
writer either has a meaning and cannot express it, or he inadvertently says something else, or he is almost indifferent as to
whether his words mean anything or not. This mixture of vagueness and sheer incompetence is the most marked characteristic of
modern English prose, and especially of any kind of political writing. As soon as certain topics are raised, the concrete melts into
the abstract and no one seems able to think of turns of speech that
are not hackneyed: prose consists less and less of *words* chosen for
the sake of their meaning, and more and more of *phrases* tacked
together like the sections of a prefabricated hen-house. I list below, with notes and examples, various of the tricks by means of
which the work or prose-construction is habitually dodged.

DYING METAPHORS

A newly invented metaphor assists thought by evoking a visual   5
image, while on the other hand a metaphor which is technically
"dead" (e.g. *iron resolution*) has in effect reverted to being an ordinary word and can generally be used without loss of vividness.
But in between these two classes there is a huge dump of worn-
out metaphors which have lost all evocative power and are
merely used because they save people the trouble of inventing
phrases for themselves. Examples are: *Ring the changes on, take up
the cudgels for, toe the line, ride roughshod over, stand shoulder to shoulder with, play into the hands of, no axe to grind, grist to the mill, fishing
in troubled waters, on the order of the day, Achilles' heel, swan song,
hotbed.* Many of these are used without knowledge of their meaning (what is a "rift," for instance?), and incompatible metaphors
are frequently mixed, a sure sign that the writer is not interested
in what he is saying. Some metaphors now current have been
twisted out of their original meaning without those who use them
even being aware of the fact. For example, *toe the line* is sometimes
written *tow the line*. Another example is *the hammer and the anvil,*
now really used with the implication that the anvil gets the worst
of it. In real life it is always the anvil that breaks the hammer,

never the other way about: a writer who stopped to think what he was saying would be aware of this, and would avoid perverting the original phrase.

OPERATORS OR VERBAL FALSE LIMBS

6 These save the trouble of picking out appropriate verbs and nouns, and at the same time pad each sentence with extra sylla-bles which give it an appearance of symmetry. Characteristic phrases are: *render inoperative, militate against, make contact with, be subjected to, give rise to, give grounds for, have the effect of, play a lead-ing part (role) in, make itself felt, take effect, exhibit a tendency to, serve the purpose of, etc., etc.* The keynote is the elimination of simple verbs. Instead of being a single word, such as *break, stop, spoil, mend, kill*, a verb becomes a *phrase*, made up of a noun or adjec-tive tacked on to some general-purposes verb such as *prove, serve, form, play, render*. In addition, the passive voice is wherever possi-ble used in preference to the active, and noun constructions are used instead of gerunds (*by examination of* instead of *by examin-ing*). The range of verbs is further cut down by means of the *-ize* and *de-* formation, and the banal statements are given an appear-ance of profundity by means of the *not un-* formation. Simple conjunctions and prepositions are replaced by such phrases as *with respect to, having regard to, the fact that, by dint of, in view of, in the interests of, on the hypotheses that;* and the ends of sentences are saved from anticlimax by such resounding commonplaces as *greatly to be desired, cannot be left out of account, a development to be expected in the near future, deserving of serious consideration, brought to a satisfactory conclusion*, and so on and so forth.

PRETENTIOUS DICTION

7 Words like *phenomenon, element, individual* (as noun), *objective, cat-egorical, effective, virtual, basic, primary, promote, constitute, exhibit, exploit, utilize, eliminate, liquidate*, are used to dress up simple state-ments and give an air of scientific impartiality to biased judg-ments. Adjectives like *epoch-making, epic, historic, unforgettable*,

triumphant, age-old, inevitable, inexorable, veritable, are used to dignify the sordid processes of international politics, while writing that aims at glorifying war usually takes on an archaic color, its characteristic words being: *realm, throne, chariot, mailed fist, trident, sword, shield, buckler, banner, jackboot, clarion.* Foreign words and expressions such as *cul de sac, ancien régime, deus ex machina, mutatis mutandis, status quo, gleichschaltung, weltanschauung,* are used to give an air of culture and elegance. Except for the useful abbreviations *i.e., e.g.,* and *etc.,* there is no real need for any of the hundreds of foreign phrases now current in English. Bad writers, and especially scientific, political and sociological writers, are nearly always haunted by the notion that Latin or Greek words are grander than Saxon ones, and unnecessary words like *expedite, ameliorate, predict, extraneous, deracinated, clandestine, subaqueous,* and hundreds of others constantly gain ground from their Anglo-Saxon opposite numbers.[1] The jargon peculiar to Marist writing (*hyena, hangman, cannibal, petty bourgeois, these gentry, lackey, flunky, mad dog, White Guard,* etc.) consists largely of words and phrases translated from Russian, German or French; but the normal way of coining a new word is to use a Latin or Greek root with the appropriate affix and, where necessary, the *-ize* formation. It is often easier to make up words of this kind (*deregionalize, impermissible, extramarital, nonfragmentatory,* and so forth) than to think up the English words that will cover one's meaning. The result, in general, is an increase in slovenliness and vagueness.

MEANINGLESS WORDS

In certain kinds of writing, particularly in art criticism and literary criticism, it is normal to come across long passages which are al-

---

[1]An interesting illustration of this is the way in which the English flower names which were in use till very recently are being ousted by Greek ones, *snapdragon* becoming *antirrhinum, forget-me-not* becoming *myosotis,* etc. It is hard to see any practical reason for this change of fashion: it is probably due to an instinctive turning-away from the more homely word and vague feeling that the Greek word is scientific.

most completely lacking in meaning.[2] Words like *romantic, plastic, values, human, dead, sentimental, natural, vitality,* as used in art criticism, are strictly meaningless in the sense that they not only do not point to any discoverable object, but are hardly ever expected to do so by the reader. When one critic writes, "The outstanding feature of Mr. X's work is its living quality," while another writes, "The immediately striking thing about Mr. X's work is its peculiar deadness," the reader accepts this as a simple difference of opinion. If words like *black* and *white* were involved, instead of the jargon words *dead* and *living,* he would see at once that language was being used in an improper way. Many political words are similarly abused. The word *Fascism* has now no meaning except in so far as it signifies "something not desirable." The words *democracy, socialism, freedom, patriotic, realistic, justice,* have each of them several different meanings which cannot be reconciled with one another. In the case of a word like *democracy,* not only is there no agreed definition, but the attempt to make one is resisted from all sides. It is almost universally felt that when we call a country democratic we are praising it: consequently the defenders of every kind of régime claim that it is a democracy, and fear that they might have to stop using the word if it were tied down to any one meaning. Words of this kind are often used in a consciously dishonest way. That is, the person who uses them has his own private definition, but allows his hearer to think he means something quite different. Statements like *Marshal Pétain was a true patriot, The Soviet Press is the freest in the world, The Catholic Church is opposed to persecution,* are almost always made with intent to deceive. Other words used in variable meanings, in most cases more or less dishonestly, are: *class, totalitarian, science, progressive, reactionary, bourgeois, equality.*

9   Now that I have made this catalog of swindles and perversions, let me give another example of the kind of writing that they

[2]Example: "Comfort's catholicity of perception and image, strangely Whitmanesque in range, almost the exact opposite in aesthetic compulsion, continues to evoke that trembling atmospheric accumulative hinting at a cruel, an inexorably serene timelessness. . .Wrey Gardiner scores by aiming at simple bull's-eyes with precision. Only they are not so simple, and through this contented sadness runs more than the surface bittersweet of resignation" (*Poetry Quarterly*).

lead to. This time it must of its nature be an imaginary one. I am going to translate a passage of good English into modern English of the worst sort. Here is a well-known verse from *Ecclésiastes:*

> "I returned and saw under the sun, that the race is not to the swift, nor the battle to the strong, neither yet bread to the wise, nor yet riches to men of understanding, nor yet favor to men of skill; but time and chance happeneth to them all."

Here it is in modern English:

> "Objective consideration of contemporary phenomena compels the conclusion that success or failure in competitive activities exhibits no tendency to be commensurate with innate capacity, but that a considerable element of the unpredictable must invariably be taken into account."

This is a parody, but not a very gross one. Exhibit (3), above, 10 for instance, contains several patches of the same kind of English. It will be seen that I have not made a full translation. The beginning and ending of the sentence follow the original meaning fairly closely, but in the middle the concrete illustrations—race, battle, bread—dissolve into the vague phrase "success or failure in competitive activities." This had to be so, because no modern writer of the kind I am discussing—no one capable of using phrases like "objective consideration of contemporary phenomena"—would ever tabulate his thoughts in that precise and detailed way. The whole tendency of modern prose is away from concreteness. Now analyse these two sentences a little more closely. The first contains forty-nine words but only sixty syllables, and all its words are those of everyday life. The second contains thirty-eight words of ninety syllables: eighteen of its words are from Latin roots, and one from Greek. The first sentence contains six vivid images, and only one phrase ("time and chance") that could be called vague. The second contains not a single fresh, arresting phrase, and in spite of its ninety syllables it gives only a shortened version of the meaning contained in the first. Yet without a doubt it is the second kind of sentence that is gaining ground in modern English. I do not want to exaggerate. This kind of writing is not yet universal, and outcrops of simplicity will occur here and there in the worst-written page. Still, if you or I were told to write a few lines on the uncertainty of human fortunes, we should probably come much nearer to my imaginary sentence than to the one from *Ecclésiastes*.

11   As I have tried to show, modern writing at its worst does not consist in picking out words for the sake of their meaning and inventing images in order to make the meaning clearer. It consists in gumming together long strips of words which have already been set in order by someone else, and making the results presentable by sheer humbug. The attraction of this way of writing is that it is easier. It is easier—even quicker, once you have the habit—to say *In my opinion it is a not unjustifiable assumption that* than to say *I think*. If you use ready-made phrases, you not only don't have to hunt about for words; you also don't have to bother with the rhythms of your sentences, since these phrases are generally so arranged as to be more or less euphonious. When you are composing in a hurry—when you are dictating to a stenographer, for instance, or making a public speech—it is natural to fall into a pretentious, Latinized style. Tags like *a consideration which we should do well to bear in mind* or *a conclusion to which all of us would readily assent* will save many a sentence from coming down with a bump. By using stale metaphors, similes and idioms, you save much mental effort, at the cost of leaving your meaning vague, not only for your reader but for yourself. This is the significance of mixed metaphors. The sole aim of a metaphor is to call up a visual image. When these images clash—as in *The Fascist octopus has sung its swan song, the jackboot is thrown into the melting pot*—it can be taken as certain that the writer is not seeing a mental image of the objects he is naming; in other words he is not really thinking. Look again at the examples I gave at the beginning of this essay. Professor Laski (1) uses five negatives in fifty-three words. One of these is superfluous, making nonsense of the whole passage, and in addition there is the slip *alien* for akin, making further nonsense, and several avoidable pieces of clumsiness which increase the general vagueness. Professor Hogben (2) plays ducks and drakes with a battery which is able to write prescriptions, and, while disapproving of the everyday phrase *put up with*, is willing to look *egregious* up in the dictionary and see what it means. (3), if one takes an uncharitable attitude towards it, is simply meaningless: probably one could work out its intended meaning by reading the

whole of the article in which it occurs. In (4), the writer knows more or less what he wants to say, but an accumulation of stale phrases chokes him like tea leaves blocking a sink. In (5), words and meaning have almost parted company. People who write in this manner usually have a general emotional meaning—they dislike one thing and want to express solidarity with another—but they are not interested in the detail of what they are saying. A scrupulous writer, in every sentence that he writes, will ask himself at least four questions, thus: What am I trying to say? What words will express it? What image or idiom will make it clearer? Is this image fresh enough to have an effect? And he will probably ask himself two more: Could I put it more shortly? Have I said anything that is avoidably ugly? But you are not obliged to go to all this trouble. You can shirk it by simply throwing your mind open and letting the ready-made phrases come crowding in. They will construct your sentences for you—even think your thoughts for you, to a certain extent—and at need they will perform the important service of partially concealing your meaning even from yourself. It is at this point that the special connection between politics and the debasement of language becomes clear.

In our time it is broadly true that political writing is bad writing. Where it is not true, it will generally be found that the writer is some kind of rebel, expressing his private opinions and not a "party line." Orthodoxy, or whatever color, seems to demand a lifeless, imitative style. The political dialects to be found in pamphlets, leading articles, manifestos, White Papers and the speeches of under-secretaries do, our course, vary from party to party, but they are all alike in that one almost never finds in them a fresh, vivid, home-made turn of speech. When one watches some tired phrases—*bestial atrocities, iron heel, bloodstained tyranny, free peoples of the world, stand shoulder to shoulder*—one often has a curious feeling that one is not watching a live human being but some kind of dummy: a feeling which suddenly becomes stronger at moments when the light catches the speaker's spectacles and turns them into blank discs which seem to have no eyes behind them. And this is not altogether fanciful. A speaker who uses that kind of phraseology has gone some distance towards turning himself into a machine. The appropriate noises are coming out of his larynx, but his brain is not involved as it would be if he were choosing his words for himself. If the speech he is making is one that he is accustomed to make over and over again, he may be almost unconscious of what he is saying, as one is when one utters the responses in church. And this reduced state of consciousness, if not indispensable, is at any rate favorable to political conformity.

13   In our time, political speech and writing are largely the defense of the indefensible. Things like the continuance of British rule in India, the Russian purges and deportations, the dropping of the atom bombs on Japan, can indeed be defended, but only by arguments which are too brutal for most people to face, and which do not square with the professed aims of political parties. Thus political language has to consist largely of euphemism, question-begging and sheer cloudy vagueness. Defenseless villages are bombarded from the air, the inhabitants driven out into the countryside, the cattle machine-gunned, the huts set on fire with incendiary bullets: this is called *pacification*. Millions of peasants are robbed of their farms and sent trudging along the roads with no more than they can carry: this is called *transfer of population* or *rectification of frontiers*. People are imprisoned for years without trial, or shot in the back of the neck or sent to die of scurvy in Arctic lumber camps: this is called *elimination of unreliable elements*. Such phraseology is needed if one wants to name things without calling up mental pictures of them. Consider for instance some comfortable English professor defending Russian totalitarianism. He cannot say outright, "I believe in killing off your opponents when you can get good results by doing so." Probably, therefore, he will say something like this:

14   "While freely conceding that the Soviet régime exhibits certain features which the humanitarian may be inclined to deplore, we must, I think, agree that a certain curtailment of the right to political opposition is an unavoidable concomitant of transitional periods, and that the rigors which the Russian people have been called upon to undergo have been amply justified in the sphere of concrete achievement."

15   The inflated style is itself a kind of euphemism. A mass of Latin words falls upon the facts like soft snow, blurring the outlines and covering up all the details. The great enemy of clear

language is insincerity. When there is a gap between one's real and one's declared aims, one turns as it were instinctively to long words and exhausted idioms, like a cuttlefish squirting out ink. In our age there is no such thing as "keeping out of politics." All issues are political issues, and politics itself is a mass of lies, evasions, folly, hatred and schizophrenia. When the general atmosphere is bad, language must suffer. I should expect to find—this is a guess which I have not sufficient knowledge to verify—that the German, Russian and Italian languages have all deteriorated in the last ten or fifteen years, as a result of dictatorship.

But if thought corrupts language, language can also corrupt 16 thought. A bad usage can spread by tradition and imitation, even among people who should and do know better. The debased language that I have been discussing is in some ways very convenient. Phrases like *a not unjustifiable assumption, leaves much to be desired, would serve no good purpose, a consideration which we should do well to bear in mind,* are a continuous temptation, a packet of aspirins always at one's elbow. Look back through this essay, and for certain you will find that I have again and again committed the very faults I am protesting against. By this morning's post I have received a pamphlet dealing with conditions in Germany. The author tells me that he "felt impelled" to write it. I open it at random, and here is almost the first sentence that I see: "(The Allies) have an opportunity not only of achieving a radical transformation of Germany's social and political structure in such a way as to avoid a nationalistic reaction in Germany itself, but at the same time of laying the foundations of a cooperative and unified Europe." You see, he "feels impelled" to write—feels, presumable, that he has something new to say—and yet his words, like cavalry horses answering the bugle, group themselves automatically into the familiar dreary pattern. This invasion of one's mind by ready-made phrases (*lay the foundations, achieve a radical transformation*) can only be prevented if one is constantly on guard against them, and every such phrase anaesthetizes a portion of one's brain.

I said earlier that the decadence of our language is probably 17 curable. Those who deny this would argue, if they produced an argument at all, that language merely reflects existing social conditions, and that we cannot influence its development by any direct tinkering with words and constructions. So far as the general tone or spirit of a language goes, this may be true, but it is not true in detail. Silly words and expressions have often disappeared, not through any evolutionary process but owing to the conscious action of a minority. Two recent examples were *explore every avenue* and *leave no stone unturned*, which were killed by the jeers of a few journalists. There is a long list of flyblown metaphors which could similarly be got rid of if enough people would interest themselves in the job; and it should also be possible to laugh the *not un-* formation out of existence,[3] to reduce the amount of Latin and Greek in the average sentence, to drive out foreign phrases and strayed scientific words, and, in general, to make pretentiousness unfashionable. But all these are minor points. The defense of the English language implies more than this, and perhaps it is best to start by saying what it does *not* imply.

18   To begin with it has nothing to do with archaism, with the salvaging of obsolete words and turns of speech, or with the setting up of a "standard English" which must never be departed from. On the contrary, it is especially concerned with the scrapping of every word or idiom which has outworn its usefulness. It has nothing to do with correct grammar and syntax, which are of no importance so long as one makes one's meaning clear, or with the avoidance of Americanisms, or with having what is called a "good prose style." On the other hand it is not concerned with fake simplicity and the attempt to make written English colloquial. Nor does it even imply in every case preferring the Saxon word to the Latin one, though it does imply using the fewest and shortest words that will cover one's meaning. What is above all needed is to let the meaning choose the word, and not the other way about. In prose, the worst thing one can do with words is to surrender to them. When you think of a concrete object, you think wordlessly, and then, if you want to describe the thing you have been visualizing you probably hunt about till you find the exact words that seem to fit. When you think of something abstract you are more inclined to use words from the start, and unless you

---

[3]One can cure oneself of the *not un-* formation by memorizing this sentence. *A not unblack dog was chasing a not unsmall rabbit across a not ungreen field.*

make a conscious effort to prevent it, the existing dialect will come rushing in and do the job for you, at the expense of blurring or even changing your meaning. Probably it is better to put off using words as long as possible and get one's meaning as clear as one can through pictures or sensations. Afterwards one can choose— not simply *accept*—the phrases that will best cover the meaning, and then switch round and decide what impression one's words are likely to make on another person. This last effort of the mind cuts out all stale or mixed images, all prefabricated phrases, need- less repetitions, and humbug and vagueness generally. But one can often be in doubt about the effect of a word or a phrase, and one needs rules that one can rely on when instinct fails. I think the following rules will cover most cases:

(i)   Never use a metaphor, simile or other figure of speech which you are used to seeing in print.

(ii) Never use a long word where a short one will do.

(iii) If it is possible to cut a word out, always cut it out.

(iv) Never use the passive where you can use the active.

(v)   Never use a foreign phrase, a scientific word or a jargon word if you can think of an everyday English equivalent.

(vi) Break any of these rules sooner than say anything out- right barbarous.

These rules sound elementary, and so they are, but they demand a 19 deep change of attitude in anyone who has grown used to writing in the style now fashionable. One could keep all of them and still write bad English, but one could not write the kind of stuff that I quoted in those five specimens at the beginning of this article.

I have not here been considering the literary use of language, 20 but merely language as an instrument for expressing and not for concealing or preventing thought. Stuart Chase and others have come near to claiming that all abstract words are meaningless, and have used this as a pretext for advocating a kind of political quietism. Since you don't know what Fascism is, how can you struggle against Fascism? One need not swallow such absurdities as this, but one ought to recognize that the present political chaos is connected with the decay of language, and that one can probably bring about some improvement by starting at the verbal end. If you simplify your English, you are freed from the worst follies of orthodoxy. You cannot speak any of the necessary dialects, and when you make a stupid remark its stupidity will be obvious, even to yourself. Political language—and with variations this is true of all political parties, from Conservatives to Anarchists—is designed to make lies sound truthful and murder respectable, and to give an appearance of solidity to pure wind. One cannot change this all in a moment, but one can at least change one's own habits, and from time to time one can even, if one jeers loudly enough, send some worn-out and useless phrase—some *jackboot, Achilles' heel, hotbed, melting pot, acid test, veritable inferno* or other lump of verbal refuse—into the dustbin where it belongs.

1946

2

Education and Learning

The struggle for literacy has been marked by politics and revolution. It is not just the ability to read that literacy offers, but also access to a wider range of ideas that can change the course of a life or a country. There has always been a privileged class that had greater access to literacy, because literacy is a defining feature of self-determination. The printing press, however, gave wider (though still limited) access to literacy, and also sparked painful religious reform, which was often coupled with nationalist revolutions. This in turn led to a philosophy of enlightenment and a belief in the reason of the individual that was a founding principle for this country. Nevertheless, tension between who holds the word and who holds power is ever present. Laws governing who could be taught to read reflected hostility toward social mobility, especially among people of color and women. Frederick Douglass, son of a white man and a slave, had to bribe local white boys with bread to teach him to write, but eventually he escaped slavery and founded his own abolitionist newspaper—proof of the power those who held him in slavery were afraid literacy would afford him. But for every one story of this kind of victory, there are a thousand stories of voices and minds silenced. To this day, the debate about education has ended up in the political arena; *Brown* v. *Board of Education* is just one example of the disenfranchised and their fight for equal access. "Graduation" by Maya Angelou is a moving story of double standards in education, but it is also a story of triumph as those who are disenfranchised begin to tell their own tale. Still, it can be prejudice that translates into indifference that denies access to education, as Mike Rose reveals in "I Just Wanna Be Average." Class and how it plays into ambivalence toward an education that is "owned" by the privileged is analyzed by bell hooks. Both bell hooks and Adrienne Rich, however, see the possibilities of empowerment that literacy affords if each of us takes responsibility for our own minds and stories. Henry Louis Gates, Jr., discusses the stories and authors that are taught in the academy as part of how we make a place for ourselves within a privileged institution. Finally, Shelby Steele reveals the tensions between white guilt and black anxieties that are brought to the college environment—and our opportunity to make up for lost time in our fight for equality. The promise of technology to widen the net of literacy is examined by Neil Postman, who believes that for all its advantages, technology will not erase the divisions human nature brings to our struggle for an education that elevates and affirms.

Learning to Read and Write

Frederick Douglass

1   I lived in Master Hugh's family about seven years. During this time, I succeeded in learning to read and write. In accomplishing this, I was compelled to resort to various stratagems. I had no regular teacher. My mistress, who had kindly commenced to instruct me, had, in compliance with the advice and direction of her husband, not only ceased to instruct, but had set her face against my being instructed by any one else. It is due, however, to my mistress to say of her, that she did not adopt this course of treatment immediately. She at first lacked the depravity indispensable to shutting me up in mental darkness. It was at least necessary for her to have some training in the exercise of irresponsible power, to make her equal to the task of treating me as though I were a brute.

2   My mistress was, as I have said, a kind and tender-hearted woman; and in the simplicity of her soul she commenced, when I first went to live with her, to treat me as she supposed one human being ought to treat another. In entering upon the duties of a slaveholder, she did not seem to perceive that I sustained to her the relation of a mere chattel, and that for her to treat me as a human being was not only wrong, but dangerously so. Slavery proved as injurious to her as it did to me. When I went there, she was a pious, warm, and tender-hearted woman. There was no sorrow or suffering for which she had not a tear. She had bread for the hungry, clothes for the naked, and comfort for every mourner that came within her reach. Slavery soon proved its ability to divest her of these heavenly qualities. Under its influence, the tender heart became stone, and the lamb-like disposition gave way to one of tiger-like fierceness. The first step in her downward course was in her ceasing to instruct me. She now commenced to practise her husband's precepts. She finally became even more violent in her opposition than her husband himself. She was not satisfied with simply doing as well as he had commanded; she seemed anxious to do better. Nothing seemed to make her more angry than to see me with a newspaper. She seemed to think that here

lay the danger. I have had her rush at me with a face made all up of fury, and snatch from me a newspaper, in a manner that fully revealed her apprehension. She was an apt woman; and a little experience soon demonstrated, to her satisfaction, that education and slavery were incompatible with each other.

From this time I was most narrowly watched. If I was in a sep- 3 arate room any considerable length of time, I was sure to be suspected of having a book, and was at once called to give an account of myself. All this, however, was too late. The first step had been taken. Mistress, in teaching me the alphabet, had given me the *inch*, and no precaution could prevent me from taking the *ell*.

The plan which I adopted, and the one by which I was most 4 successful, was that of making friends of all the little white boys whom I met in the street. As many of these as I could, I converted into teachers. With their kindly aid, obtained at different times and in different places, I finally succeeded in learning to read. When I was sent on errands, I always took my book with me, and by doing one part of my errand quickly, I found time to get a lesson before my return. I used also to carry bread with me, enough of which was always in the house, and to which I was always welcome; for I was much better off in this regard than many of the poor white children in our neighborhood. This bread I used to bestow upon the hungry little urchins, who, in return, would give me that more valuable bread of knowledge. I am strongly tempted to give the names of two or three of those little boys, as a testimonial of the gratitude and affection I bear them; but prudence forbids:—not that it would injure me, but it might embarrass them; for it is almost an unpardonable offence to teach slaves to read in this Christian country. It is enough to say of the dear little fellows, that they lived on Philpot Street, very near Durgin and Bailey's shipyard. I used to talk this matter of slavery over with them. I would sometimes say to them, I wished I could be as free as they would be when they got to be men. "You will be free as soon as you are twenty-one, *but I am a slave for life!* Have not I as good a right to be free as you have?" These words used to trouble them; they would express for me the liveliest sympathy, and console me with the hope that something would occur by which I might be free.

5   I was now about twelve years old, and the thought of being *a slave for life* began to bear heavily upon my heart. Just about this time, I got hold of a book entitled "The Columbian Orator." Every opportunity I got, I used to read this book. Among much of other interesting matter, I found in it a dialogue between a master and his slave. The slave was represented as having run away from his master three times. The dialogue represented the conversation which took place between them, when the slave was retaken the third time. In this dialogue, the whole argument in behalf of slavery was brought forward by the master, all of which was disposed of by the slave. The slave was made to say some very smart as well as impressive things in reply to his master—things which had the desired though unexpected effect; for the conversation resulted in the voluntary emancipation of the slave on the part of the master.

6   In the same book, I met with one of Sheridan's mighty speeches on and in behalf of Catholic emancipation. These were choice documents to me. I read them over and over again with unabated interest. They gave tongue to interesting thoughts of my own soul, which had frequently flashed through my mind, and died away for want of utterance. The moral which I gained from the dialogue was the power of truth over the conscience of even a slaveholder. What I got from Sheridan was a bold denunciation of slavery, and a powerful vindication of human rights. The reading of these documents enabled me to utter my thoughts, and to meet the arguments brought forward to sustain slavery; but while they relieved me of one difficulty, they brought on another even more painful than the one of which I was relieved. The more I read, the more I was led to abhor and detest my enslavers. I could regard them in no other light than a band of successful robbers, who had left their homes, and gone to Africa, and stolen us from our homes, and in a strange land reduced us to slavery. I loathed them as being the meanest as well as the most wicked of men. As I read and contemplated the subject, behold! that very discontentment which Master Hugh had predicted would follow my learning to read had already come, to torment and sting my soul to unutterable anguish. As I writhed under it, I would at times feel that learning to read had been a curse rather than a blessing. It had given me a

view of my wretched condition, without the remedy. It opened my eyes to the horrible pit, but to no ladder upon which to get out. In moments of agony, I envied my fellow-slaves for their stupidity. I have often wished myself a beast. I preferred the condition of the meanest reptile to my own. Any thing, no matter what, to get rid of thinking! It was this everlasting thinking of my condition that tormented me. There was no getting rid of it. It was pressed upon me by every object within sight or hearing, animate or inanimate. The silver trump of freedom had roused my soul to eternal wakefulness. Freedom now appeared, to disappear no more forever. It was heard in every sound, and seen in every thing. It was ever present to torment me with a sense of my wretched condition. I saw nothing without seeing it, I heard nothing without hearing it, and felt nothing without feeling it. It looked from every star, it smiled in every calm, breathed in every wind, and moved in every storm.

I often found myself regretting my own existence, and wish- 7
ing myself dead; and but for the hope of being free, I have no doubt but that I should have killed myself, or done something for which I should have been killed. While in this state of mind, I was eager to hear anyone speak of slavery. I was a ready listener. Every little while, I could hear something about the abolitionists. It was some time before I found what the word meant. It was always used in such connections as to make it an interesting word to me. If a slave ran away and succeeded in getting clear, or if a slave killed his master, set fire to a barn, or did any thing very wrong in the mind of a slaveholder, it was spoken of as the fruit of *abolition.* Hearing the word in this connection very often, I set about learning what it meant. The dictionary afforded me little or no help. I found it was "the act of abolishing;" but then I did not know what was to be abolished. Here I was perplexed. I did not dare to ask any one about its meaning, for I was satisfied that it was something they wanted me to know very little about. After a patient waiting, I got one of our city papers, containing an account of the number of petitions from the north, praying for the abolition of slavery in the District of Columbia, and of the slave trade between the States. From this time I understood the words *abolition* and *abolitionist,* and always drew near when that word

was spoken, expecting to hear something of importance to myself and fellow-slaves. The light broke in upon me by degrees. I went one day down on the wharf of Mr. Waters; and seeing two Irishmen unloading a scow of stone, I went, unasked, and helped them. When we had finished, one of them came to me and asked me if I were a slave. I told him I was. He asked, "Are ye a slave for life?" I told him that I was. The good Irishman seemed to be deeply affected by the statement. He said to the other that it was a pity so fine a little fellow as myself should be a slave for life. He said it was a shame to hold me. They both advised me to run away to the north; that I should find friends there, and that I should be free. I pretended not to be interested in what they said, and treated them as if I did not understand them; for I feared they might be treacherous. White men have been known to encourage slaves to escape, and then, to get the reward, catch them and return them to their masters. I was afraid that these seemingly good men might use me so; but I nevertheless remembered their advice, and from that time I resolved to run away. I looked forward to a time at which it would be safe for me to escape. I was too young to think of doing so immediately; besides, I wished to learn how to write, as I might have occasion to write my own pass. I consoled myself with the hope that I should one day find a good chance. Meanwhile, I would learn to write.

The idea as to how I might learn to write was suggested to me by being in Durgin and Bailey's ship-yard, and frequently seeing the ship carpenters, after hewing, and getting a piece of timber ready for use, write on the timber the name of that part of the ship for which it was intended. When a piece of timber was intended for the larboard side, it would be marked thus—"L." When a piece was for the starboard side, it would be marked thus—"S." A piece for the larboard side forward, would be marked thus—"L. F." When a piece was for starboard side forward, it would be marked thus—"S. F." For larboard aft, it would be marked thus—"L. A." For starboard aft, it would be marked thus—"S. A." I soon learned the names of these letters, and for what they were intended when placed upon a piece of timber in the ship-yard. I immediately commenced copying them, and in a short time was able to make the four letters named. After that, when I met with any boy who I knew could write, I would tell him I could write as well as he. The next word would be, "I don't believe you. Let me see you try it." I would then make the letters which I had been so fortunate as to learn, and ask him to beat that. In this way I got a good many lessons in writing, which it is quite possible I should never have gotten in any other way. During this time, my copy-book was the board fence, brick wall, and pavement; my pen and ink was a lump of chalk. With these, I learned mainly how to write. I then commenced and continued copying the Italics in Webster's Spelling Book, until I could make them all without looking on the book. By this time, my little Master Thomas had gone to school, and learned how to write, and had written over a number of copy-books. These had been brought home, and shown to some of our near neighbors, and then laid aside. My mistress used to go to class meeting at the Wilk Street meetinghouse every Monday afternoon, and leave me to take care of the house. When left thus, I used to spend the time in writing in the spaces left in Master Thomas's copy-book, copying what he had written. I continued to do this until I could write a hand very similar to that of Master Thomas. Thus, after a long, tedious effort for years, I finally succeeded in learning how to write.

1845

Graduation
Maya Angelou

The children in Stamps[1] trembled visibly with anticipation. Some   1
adults were excited too, but to be certain the whole young population had come down with graduation epidemic. Large classes were graduating from both the grammar school and the high school. Even those who were years removed from their own day of glorious release were anxious to help with preparations as a

[1] A rural, segregated town in Arkansas.

kind of dry run. The junior students who were moving into the vacating classes' chairs were tradition-bound to show their talents for leadership and management. They strutted through the school and around the campus exerting pressure on the lower grades. Their authority was so new that occasionally if they pressed a little too hard it had to be overlooked. After all, next term was coming, and it never hurt a sixth grader to have a play sister in the eighth grade, or a tenth-year student to be able to call a twelfth grader Bubba. So all was endured in a spirit of shared understanding. But the graduating classes themselves were the nobility. Like travelers with exotic destinations on their minds, the graduates were remarkably forgetful. They came to school without their books, or tablets or even pencils. Volunteers fell over themselves to secure replacements for the missing equipment. When accepted, the willing workers might or might not be thanked, and it was of no importance to the pregraduation rites. Even teachers were respectful of the now quiet and aging seniors, and tended to speak to them, if not as equals, as being only slightly lower than themselves. After tests were returned and grades given, the student body, which acted like an extended family, knew who did well, who excelled, and what piteous ones had failed.

2   Unlike the white high school, Lafayette County Training School distinguished itself by having neither lawn, nor hedges, nor tennis court, nor climbing ivy. Its two buildings (main classrooms, the grade school and home economics) were set on a dirt hill with no fence to limit either its boundaries or those of bordering farms. There was a large expanse to the left of the school which was used alternately as a baseball diamond or basketball court. Rusty hoops on swaying poles represented the permanent recreational equipment, although bats and balls could be borrowed from the P.E. teacher if the borrower was qualified and if the diamond wasn't occupied.

3   Over this rocky area relieved by a few shady tall persimmon trees the graduating class walked. The girls often held hands and no longer bothered to speak to the lower students. There was a sadness about them, as if this old world was not their home and they were bound for higher ground. The boys, on the other hand, had become more friendly, more outgoing. A decided change

from the closed attitude they projected while studying for finals. Now they seemed not ready to give up the old school, the familiar paths and classrooms. Only a small percentage would be continuing on to college—one of the South's A & M (agricultural and mechanical) schools, which trained Negro youths to be carpenters, farmers, handymen, masons, maids, cooks and baby nurses. Their future rode heavily on their shoulders, and blinded them to the collective joy that had pervaded the lives of the boys and girls in the grammar school graduating class.

Parents who could afford it had ordered new shoes and ready-made clothes for themselves from Sears and Roebuck or Montgomery Ward. They also engaged the best seamstresses to make the floating graduating dresses and to cut down secondhand pants which would be pressed to a military slickness for the important event. 4

Oh, it was important, all right. Whitefolks would attend the ceremony, and two or three would speak of God and home, and the Southern way of life, and Mrs. Parsons, the principal's wife, would play the graduation march while the lower-grade graduates paraded down the aisles and took their seats below the platform. The high school seniors would wait in empty classrooms to make their dramatic entrance. 5

In the Store I was the person of the moment. The birthday girl. The center. Bailey had graduated the year before, although to do so he had had to forfeit all pleasures to make up for his time lost in Baton Rouge. 6

My class was wearing butter-yellow piqué dresses, and Momma launched out on mine. She smocked the yoke into tiny crisscrossing puckers, then shirred the rest of the bodice. Her dark fingers ducked in and out of the lemony cloth as she embroidered raised daisies around the hem. Before she considered herself finished she had added a crocheted cuff on the puff sleeves, and a point crocheted collar. 7

I was going to be lovely. A walking model of all the various styles of fine hand sewing and it didn't worry me that I was only twelve years old and merely graduating from the eighth grade. Besides, many teachers in Arkansas Negro schools had only that diploma and were licensed to impart wisdom. 8

9   The days had become longer and more noticeable. The faded beige of former times had been replaced with strong and sure colors. I began to see my classmates' clothes, their skin tones, and the dust that waved off pussy willows. Clouds that lazed across the sky were objects of great concern to me. Their shiftier shapes might have held a message that in my new happiness and with a little bit of time I'd soon decipher. During that period I looked at the arch of heaven so religiously my neck kept a steady ache. I had taken to smiling more often, and my jaws hurt from the unaccustomed activity. Between the two physical sore spots, I suppose I could have been uncomfortable, but that was not the case. As a member of the winning team (the graduating class of 1940) I had outdistanced unpleasant sensations by miles. I was headed for the freedom of open fields.

10   Youth and social approval allied themselves with me and we trammeled memories of slights and insults. The wind of our swift passage remodeled my features. Lost tears were pounded to mud and then to dust. Years of withdrawal were brushed aside and left behind, as hanging ropes of parasitic moss.

11   My work alone had awarded me a top place and I was going to be one of the first called in the graduating ceremonies. On the classroom blackboard, as well as on the bulletin board in the auditorium, there were blue stars and white stars and red stars. No absences, no tardinesses, and my academic work was among the best of the year. I could say the preamble to the Constitution even faster than Bailey. We timed ourselves often: "Wethepeople-oftheUnitedStatesinordertoformamoreperfectunion. . . ." I had memorized the Presidents of the United States from Washington to Roosevelt in chronological as well as alphabetical order.

12   My hair pleased me too. Gradually the black mass had lengthened and thickened, so that it kept at last to its braided pattern, and I didn't have to yank my scalp off when I tried to comb it.

13   Louise and I had rehearsed the exercises until we tired out ourselves. Henry Reed was class valedictorian. He was a small, very black boy with hooded eyes, a long, broad nose and an oddly shaped head. I had admired him for years because each term he and I vied for the best grades in our class. Most often he bested me, but instead of being disappointed I was pleased that we

shared top places between us. Like many Southern Black children, he lived with his grandmother, who was as strict as Momma and as kind as she knew how to be. He was courteous, respectful and soft-spoken to elders, but on the playground he chose to play the roughest games. I admired him. Anyone, I reckoned, sufficiently afraid or sufficiently dull could be polite. But to be able to operate at a top level with both adults and children was admirable.

His valedictory speech was entitled "To Be or Not to Be." The 14 rigid tenth-grade teacher had helped him write it. He'd been working on the dramatic stresses for months.

The weeks until graduation were filled with heady activities. 15 A group of small children were to be presented in a play about buttercups and daisies and bunny rabbits. They could be heard throughout the building practicing their hops and their little songs that sounded like silver bells. The older girls (non-graduates, of course) were assigned the task of making refreshments for the night's festivities. A tangy scent of ginger, cinnamon, nutmeg and chocolate wafted around the home economics building as the budding cooks made samples for themselves and their teachers.

In every corner of the workshop, axes and saws split fresh 16 timber as the woodshop boys made sets and stage scenery. Only the graduates were left out of the general bustle. We were free to sit in the library at the back of the building or look in quite de-tachedly, naturally, on the measures being taken for our event.

Even the minister preached on graduation the Sunday before. 17 His subject was, "Let your light so shine that men will see your good works and praise your Father, Who is in Heaven." Although the sermon was purported to be addressed to us, he used the occa-sion to speak to backsliders, gamblers and general ne'er-do-wells. But since he had called our names at the beginning of the service we were mollified.

Among Negroes the tradition was to give presents to children 18 going only from one grade to another. How much more important this was when the person was graduating at the top of the class. Uncle Willie and Momma had sent away for a Mickey Mouse watch like Bailey's. Louise gave me four embroidered handkerchiefs. (I gave her crocheted doilies.) Mrs. Sneed, the minister's wife, made me an undershirt to wear for graduation, and nearly every customer gave me a nickel or maybe even a dime with the instruction, "Keep on moving to higher ground," or some such encouragement.

19   Amazingly the great day finally dawned and I was out of bed before I knew it. I threw open the back door to see it more clearly, but Momma said, "Sister, come away from that door and put your robe on."

20   I hoped the memory of that morning would never leave me. Sunlight was itself young, and the day had none of the insistence maturity would bring it in a few hours. In my robe and barefoot in the backyard, under cover of going to see about my new beans, I gave myself up to the gentle warmth and thanked God that no matter what evil I had done in my life He had allowed me to live to see this day. Somewhere in my fatalism I had expected to die, accidentally, and never have the chance to walk up the stairs in the auditorium and gracefully receive my hard-earned diploma. Out of God's merciful bosom I had won reprieve.

21   Bailey came out in his robe and gave me a box wrapped in Christmas paper. He said he had saved his money for months to pay for it. It felt like a box of chocolates, but I knew Bailey wouldn't save money to buy candy when we had all we could want under our noses.

22   He was as proud of the gift as I. It was a soft-leather-bound copy of a collection of poems by Edgar Allan Poe, or, as Bailey and I called him, "Eap." I turned to "Annabel Lee" and we walked up and down the garden rows, the cool dirt between our toes, reciting the beautifully sad lines.

23   Momma made a Sunday breakfast although it was only Friday. After we finished the blessing, I opened my eyes to find the watch on my plate. It was a dream of a day. Everything went smoothly and to my credit. I didn't have to be reminded or scolded for anything. Near evening I was too jittery to attend to chores, so Bailey volunteered to do all before his bath.

24   Days before, we had made a sign for the Store, and as we turned out the lights Momma hung the cardboard over the doorknob. It read clearly: CLOSED. GRADUATION.

My dress fitted perfectly and everyone said that I looked like a   25
sunbeam in it. On the hill, going toward the school, Bailey walked
behind with Uncle Willie, who muttered, "Go on, Ju." He wanted
him to walk ahead with us because it embarrassed him to have to
walk so slowly. Bailey said he'd let the ladies walk together, and
the men would bring up the rear. We all laughed, nicely.

Little children dashed by out of the dark like fireflies. Their   26
crepe-paper dresses and butterfly wings were not made for running and we heard more than one rip, dryly, and the regretful "uh
uh" that followed.

The school blazed without gaiety. The windows seemed cold   27
and unfriendly from the lower hill. A sense of ill-fated timing crept
over me, and if Momma hadn't reached for my hand I would have
drifted back to Bailey and Uncle Willie, and possibly beyond. She
made a few slow jokes about my feet getting cold, and tugged me
along to the now-strange building.

Around the front steps, assurance came back. There were my   28
fellow "greats," the graduating class. Hair brushed back, legs oiled,
new dresses and pressed pleats, fresh pocket handkerchiefs and
little handbags, all homesewn. Oh, we were up to snuff, all right.
I joined my comrades and didn't even see my family go in to find
seats in the crowded auditorium.

The school band struck up a march and all classes filed in as   29
had been rehearsed. We stood in front of our seats, as assigned,
and on a signal from the choir director, we sat. No sooner had this
been accomplished than the band started to play the national anthem. We rose again and sang the song, after which we recited the
pledge of allegiance. We remained standing for a brief minute before the choir director and the principal signaled to us, rather desperately I thought, to take our seats. The command was so
unusual that our carefully rehearsed and smooth-running machine was thrown off. For a full minute we fumbled for our chairs
and bumped into each other awkwardly. Habits change or solid-
ify under pressure, so in our state of nervous tension we had been
ready to follow our usual assembly pattern: the American national anthem, then the pledge of allegiance, then the song every
Black person I knew called the Negro National Anthem. All done

in the same key, with the same passion and most often standing on the same foot.

30   Finding my seat at last, I was overcome with a presentiment of worse things to come. Something unrehearsed, unplanned, was going to happen, and we were going to be made to look bad. I distinctly remember being explicit in the choice of pronoun. It was "we," the graduating class, the unit, that concerned me then.

31   The principal welcomed "parents and friends" and asked the Baptist minister to lead us in prayer. His invocation was brief and punchy, and for a second I thought we were getting on the high road to right action. When the principal came back to the dais, however, his voice had changed. Sounds always affected me profoundly and the principal's voice was one of my favorites. During assembly it melted and lowed weakly into the audience. It had not been in my plan to listen to him, but my curiosity was piqued and I straightened up to give him my attention.

32   He was talking about Booker T. Washington, our "late great leader," who said we can be as close as the fingers on the hand, etc. . . . Then he said a few vague things about friendship and the friendship of kindly people to those less fortunate than themselves. With that his voice nearly faded, thin, away. Like a river diminishing to a stream and then to a trickle. But he cleared his throat and said, "Our speaker tonight, who is also our friend, came from Texarkana to deliver the commencement address but due to the irregularity of the train schedule, he's going to, as they say, 'speak and run.'" He said that we understood and wanted the man to know that we were most grateful for the time he was able to give us and then something about how we were willing always to adjust to another's program, and without more ado—"I give you Mr. Edward Donleavy."

33   Not one but two white men came through the door off-stage. The shorter one walked to the speaker's platform, and the tall one moved to the center seat and sat down. But that was our principal's seat, and already occupied. The dislodged gentleman bounced around for a long breath or two before the Baptist minister gave him his chair, then with more dignity than the situation deserved, the minister walked off the stage.

Donleavy looked at the audience once (on reflection, I'm sure 34
that he wanted only to reassure himself that we were really there),
adjusted his glasses and began to read from a sheaf of papers.

He was glad "to be here and to see the work going on just as 35
it was in the other schools."

At the first "Amen" from the audience I willed the offender to 36
immediate death by choking on the word. But Amens and Yes, sir's
began to fall around the room like rain through a ragged umbrella.

He told us of the wonderful changes we children in Stamps 37
had in store. The Central School (naturally, the white school was
Central) had already been granted improvements that would be
in use in the fall. A well-known artist was coming from Little Rock
to teach art to them. They were going to have the newest micro-
scopes and chemistry equipment for the laboratory. Mr. Donleavy
didn't leave us long in the dark over who made these improvements available to Central High. Nor were we to be ignored in the
general betterment scheme he had in mind.

He said that he had pointed out to people at a very high level 38
that one of the first-line football tacklers at Arkansas Agricultural
and Mechanical College had graduated from good old Lafayette
County Training School. Here fewer Amen's were heard. Those
few that did break through lay dully in the air with the heaviness
of habit.

He went on to praise us. He went on to say how he had bragged 39
that "one of the best basketball players at Fisk sank his first ball
right here at Lafayette County Training School."

The white kids were going to have a chance to become 40
Galileos and Madame Curies and Edisons and Gauguins, and our
boys (the girls weren't even in on it) would try to be Jesse Owenses
and Joe Louises.

Owens and the Brown Bomber were great heroes in our world, 41
but what school official in the white-goddom of Little Rock had
the right to decide that those two men must be our only heroes?
Who decided that for Henry Reed to become a scientist he had to
work like George Washington Carver, as a bootblack, to buy a
lousy microscope? Bailey was obviously always going to be too
small to be an athlete, so which concrete angel glued to what
county seat had decided that if my brother wanted to become a

lawyer he had to first pay penance for his skin by picking cotton and hoeing corn and studying correspondence books at night for twenty years?

42   The man's dead words fell like bricks around the auditorium and too many settled in my belly. Constrained by hard-learned manners I couldn't look behind me, but to my left and right the proud graduating class of 1940 had dropped their heads. Every girl in my row had found something new to do with her handkerchief. Some folded the tiny squares into love knots, some into triangles, but most were wadding them, then pressing them flat on their yellow laps.

43   On the dais, the ancient tragedy was being replayed. Professor Parsons sat, a sculptor's reject, rigid. His large, heavy body seemed devoid of will or willingness, and his eyes said he was no longer with us. The other teachers examined the flag (which was draped stage right) or their notes, or the windows which opened on our now-famous playing diamond.

44   Graduation, the hush-hush magic time of frills and gifts and congratulations and diplomas, was finished for me before my name was called. The accomplishment was nothing. The meticulous maps, drawn in three colors of ink, learning and spelling decasyllabic words, memorizing the whole of *The Rape of Lucrece*—it was for nothing. Donleavy had exposed us.

45   We were maids and farmers, handymen and washerwomen, and anything higher that we aspired to was farcical and presumptuous.

46   Then I wished that Gabriel Prosser and Nat Turner had killed all whitefolks in their beds and that Abraham Lincoln had been assassinated before the signing of the Emancipation Proclamation, and that Harriet Tubman had been killed by that blow on her head and Christopher Columbus had drowned in the *Santa Maria*.

47   It was awful to be a Negro and have no control over my life. It was brutal to be young and already trained to sit quietly and listen to charges brought against my color with no chance of defense. We should all be dead. I thought I should like to see us all dead, one on top of the other. A pyramid of flesh with the whitefolks on the bottom, as the broad base, then the Indians with their silly tomahawks and teepees and wigwams and treaties, the

Negroes with their mops and recipes and cotton sacks and spirituals sticking out of their mouths. The Dutch children should all
stumble in their wooden shoes and break their necks. The French
should choke to death on the Louisiana Purchase (1803) while silk-
worms ate all the Chinese with their stupid pigtails. As a species,
we were an abomination. All of us.

Donleavy was running for election, and assured our parents 48
that if he won we could count on having the only colored paved
playing field in that part of Arkansas. Also—he never looked up
to acknowledge the grunts of acceptance—also, we were bound to
get some new equipment for the home economics building and
the workshop.

He finished, and since there was no need to give any more 49
than the most perfunctory thank-you's, he nodded to the men on
the stage, and the tall white man who was never introduced
joined him at the door. They left with the attitude that now they
were off to something really important. (The graduation ceremonies at Lafayette County Training School had been a mere
preliminary.)

The ugliness they left was palpable. An uninvited guest who 50
wouldn't leave. The choir was summoned and sang a modern
arrangement of "Onward, Christian Soldiers," with new words
pertaining to graduates seeking their place in the world. But it
didn't work. Elouise, the daughter of the Baptist minister, recited
"Invictus," and I could have cried at the impertinence of "I am the
master of my fate, I am the captain of my soul."

My name had lost its ring of familiarity and I had to be 51
nudged to go and receive my diploma. All my preparations had
fled. I neither marched up to the stage like a conquering Amazon,
nor did I look in the audience for Bailey's nod of approval. Marguerite Johnson,[2] I heard the name again, my honors were read,
there were noises in the audience of appreciation, and I took my
place on the stage as rehearsed.

I thought about colors I hated: ecru, puce, lavender, beige and 52
black.

[2]Maya Angelou was born Marguerite Johnson in 1928; married Tosh Angelou
(divorced 1952); took the name of Maya Angelou in her early twenties.

53   There was shuffling and rustling around me, then Henry Reed was giving his valedictory address, "To Be or Not to Be." Hadn't he heard the whitefolks? We couldn't *be*, so the question was a waste of time. Henry's voice came out clear and strong. I feared to look at him. Hadn't he got the message? There was no "nobler in the mind" for Negroes because the world didn't think we had minds, and they let us know it. "Outrageous fortune"? Now, that was a joke. When the ceremony was over I had to tell Henry Reed some things. That is, if I still cared. Not "rub," Henry, "erase." "Ah, there's the erase." Us.

54   Henry had been a good student in elocution. His voice rose on tides of promise and fell on waves of warnings. The English teacher had helped him to create a sermon winging through Hamlet's soliloquy. To be a man, a doer, a builder, a leader, or to be a tool, an unfunny joke, a crusher of funky toadstools. I marveled that Henry could go through with the speech as if we had a choice.

        I had been listening and silently rebutting each sentence with
55 my eyes closed; then there was a hush, which in an audience warns that something unplanned is happening. I looked up and saw Henry Reed, the conservative, the proper, the A student, turn his back to the audience and turn to us (the proud graduating class of 1940) and sing, nearly speaking,

> "Lift ev'ry voice and sing
> Till earth and heaven ring
> Ring with the harmonies of Liberty . . ."

It was the poem written by James Weldon Johnson. It was the music composed by J. Rosamond Johnson. It was the Negro National Anthem. Out of habit we were singing it.

        Our mothers and fathers stood in the dark hall and joined the
56 hymn of encouragement. A kindergarten teacher led the small children onto the stage and the buttercups and daisies and bunny rabbits marked time and tried to follow:

> "Stony the road we trod
> Bitter the chastening rod
> Felt in the days when hope, unborn, had died.
> Yet with a steady beat

Have not our weary feet
Come to the place for which our fathers sighed?"

Each child I knew had learned that song with his ABC's and 57
along with "Jesus Loves Me This I Know." But I personally had
never heard it before. Never heard the words, despite the thousands of times I had sung them. Never thought they had anything
to do with me.

On the other hand, the words of Patrick Henry had made such 58
an impression on me that I had been able to stretch myself tall and
trembling and say, "I know not what course others may take, but
as for me, give me liberty or give me death."

And now I heard, really for the first time: 59

"We have come over a way that with tears
has been watered,
We have come, treading our path through
the blood of the slaughtered."

While echoes of the song shivered in the air, Henry Reed 60
bowed his head, said "Thank you," and returned to his place in
the line. The tears that slipped down many faces were not wiped
away in shame.

We were on top again. As always, again. We survived. The 61
depths had been icy and dark, but now a bright sun spoke to our
souls. I was no longer simply a member of the proud graduating
class of 1940; I was a proud member of the wonderful, beautiful
Negro race.

Oh, Black known and unknown poets, how often have your 62
auctioned pains sustained us? Who will compute the only nights
made less lonely by your songs, or the empty pots made less
tragic by your tales?

If we were a people much given to revealing secrets, we might 63
raise monuments and sacrifice to the memories of our poets, but
slavery cured us of that weakness. It may be enough, however, to
have it said that we survive in exact relationship to the dedication
of our poets (include preachers, musicians and blues singers).

1970

"I Just Wanna Be Average"

Mike Rose

1   Some people who manage to write their way out of the working class describe the classroom as an oasis of possibility. It became their intellectual playground, their competitive arena. Given the richness of my memories of this time, it's funny how scant are my recollections of school. I remember the red brick building of St. Regina's itself, and the topography of the playground: the swings and basketball courts and peeling benches. There are images of a few students: Erwin Petschaur, a muscular German boy with a strong accent; Dave Sanchez, who was good in math; and Sheila Wilkes, everyone's curly-haired heartthrob. And there are two nuns: Sister Monica, the third-grade teacher with beautiful hands for whom I carried a candle and who, to my dismay, had wedded herself to Christ; and Sister Beatrice, a woman truly crazed, who would sweep into class, eyes wide, to tell us about the Apocalypse.

2   All the hours in class tend to blend into one long, vague stretch of time. What I remember best, strangely enough, are the two things I couldn't understand and over the years grew to hate: grammar lessons and mathematics. I would sit there watching a teacher draw her long horizontal line and her short, oblique lines and break up sentences and put adjectives here and adverbs there and just not get it, couldn't see the reason for it, turned off to it. I would hide by slumping down in my seat and page through my reader, carried along by the flow of sentences in a story. She would test us, and I would dread that, for I always got Cs and Ds. Mathematics was a bit different. For whatever reasons, I didn't learn early math very well, so when it came time for more complicated operations, I couldn't keep up and started daydreaming to avoid my inadequacy. This was a strategy I would rely on as I grew older. I fell further and further behind. A memory: The teacher is faceless and seems very far away. The voice is faint and is discussing an equation written on the board. It is raining, and I am watching the streams of water form patterns on the windows.

I realize now how consistently I defended myself against the ₃
lessons I couldn't understand and the people and events of South
L.A. that were too strange to view head-on. I got very good at
watching a blackboard with minimum awareness. And I drifted
more and more into a variety of protective fantasies. I was lucky
in that although my parents didn't read or write very much and
had no more than a few books around the house, they never de-
bunked my pursuits. And when they could, they bought me what
I needed to spin my web.

One early Christmas they got me a small chemistry set. My fa- ₄
ther brought home an old card table from the secondhand store,
and on that table I spread out my test tubes, my beaker, my Erlen-
meyer flask, and my gas-generating apparatus. The set came
equipped with chemicals, minerals, and various treated papers—
all in little square bottles. You could send away to someplace in
Maryland for more, and I did, saving pennies and nickels to get
the substances that were too exotic for my set, the Junior Chem-
craft: Congo red paper, azurite, glycerine, chrome alum,
cochineal—this from female insects!—tartaric acid, chameleon paper, logwood. I would sit before my laboratory and play for
hours. My father rested on the purple couch in front of me watching wrestling or *Gunsmoke* while I measured powders or heated
crystals or blew into solutions that my breath would turn red or
pink. I was taken by the blends of names and by the colors that
swirled through the beaker. My equations were visual and pho-
netic. I would hold a flask up to the hall light, imagining the veils
of a million atoms dancing. Sulfur and alcohol hung in the air. I
wanted to shake down the house.

One day my mother came home from Coffee Dan's with an ₅
awful story. The teenage brother of one of her waitress friends
was in the hospital. He had been fooling around with explosives
in his garage "where his mother couldn't see him," and something happened, and "he blew away part of his throat. For God's
sake, be careful," my mother said. "Remember poor Ada's brother."
Wow! I thought. How neat! Why couldn't my experiments be that
dangerous? I really lost heart when I realized that you could probably eat the chemicals spread across my table.

6   I knew what I had to do. I saved my money for a week and then walked with firm resolve past Walt's Malts, past the brake shop, across Ninetieth Street, and into Palazolla's market. I bought a little bottle of Alka-Seltzer and ran home. I chopped up the wafers and mixed them into a jar of white crystals. When my mother came home, dog tired, and sat down on the edge of my couch to tell me and Dad about her day, I gravely poured my concoction into a beaker of water, cried something about the unexpected, and ran out from behind my table. The beaker foamed ominously. My father swore in Italian. The second time I tried it, I got something milder—in English. And by my third near-miss with death, my parents were calling my behavior cute. Cute! Who wanted cute? I wanted to toy with the disaster that befell Ada Pendleton's brother. I wanted all those wonderful colors to collide in ways that could blow your voice box right off.

7   But I was limited by the real. The best I could do was create a toxic antacid. I loved my chemistry set—its glassware and its intriguing labels—but it wouldn't allow me to do the things I wanted to do. St. Regina's had an all-purpose room, one wall of which was lined with old books—and one of those shelves held a row of plastic-covered space novels. The sheen of their covers was gone, and their futuristic portraits were dotted with erasures and grease spots like a meteor shower of the everyday. I remember the rockets best. Long cylinders outfitted at the base with three slick fins, tapering at the other end to a perfect conical point, ready to pierce out of the stratosphere and into my imagination: X-fifteens and Mach 1, the dark side of the moon, the Red Planet, Jupiter's Great Red Spot, Saturn's rings—and beyond the solar system to swirling wisps of galaxies, to stardust.

8   I would check out my books two at a time and take them home to curl up with a blanket on my chaise lounge, reading, sometimes, through the weekend, my back aching, my thoughts lost between galaxies. I became the hero of a thousand adventures, all with intricate plots and the triumph of good over evil, all many dimensions removed from the dim walls of the living room. We were given time to draw in school, so, before long, all this worked itself onto paper. The stories I was reading were reshaping themselves

into pictures. My father got me some butcher paper from Palazolla's, and I continued to draw at home. My collected works rendered the Horsehead Nebula, goofy space cruisers, robots, and
Saturn. Each had its crayon, a particular waxy pencil with mood
and meaning: rust and burnt sienna for Mars, yellow for the Sun,
lime and rose for Saturn's rings, and bright red for the Jovian spot.
I had a little sharpener to keep the points just right. I didn't write
any stories; I just read and drew. I wouldn't care much about writing until late in high school.

The summer before the sixth grade, I got a couple of jobs. The ⁹
first was at a pet store a block or so away from my house. Since I
was still small, I could maneuver around in breeder cages, scraping the heaps of parakeet crap from the tin floor, cleaning the water troughs and seed trays. It was pretty awful. I would go home
after work and fill the tub and soak until all the fleas and bird
mites came floating to the surface, little Xs in their multiple eyes.
When I heard about a job selling strawberries door-to-door, I
jumped at it. I went to work for a white-haired Chicano named
Frank. He would carry four or five kids and dozens of crates of
strawberries in his ramshackle truck up and down the avenues of
the better neighborhoods: houses with mowed lawns and petunia
beds. We'd work all day for seventy-five cents, Frank dropping
pairs of us off with two crates each, then picking us up at preas-
signed corners. We spent lots of time together, bouncing around
on the truck bed redolent with strawberries or sitting on a corner,
cold, listening for the sputter of Frank's muffler. I started telling
the other kids about my books, and soon it was my job to fill up
that time with stories.

Reading opened up the world. There I was, a skinny book- ¹⁰
worm drawing the attention of street kids who, in any other circumstances, would have had me for breakfast. Like an epic
tale-teller, I developed the stories as I went along, relying on a flexible plot line and a repository of heroic events. I had a great time. I
sketched out trajectories with my finger on Frank's dusty truck
bed. And I stretched out each story's climax, creating cliffhangers
like the ones I saw in the Saturday serials. These stories created
for me a temporary community.

11   It was around this time that fiction started leading me circuitously to a child's version of science. In addition to the space novels, St. Regina's library also had half a dozen books on astronomy—*The Golden Book of Planets* and stuff like that—so I checked out a few of them. I liked what I read and wheedled enough change out of my father to enable me to take the bus to the public library. I discovered star maps, maps of lunar seas, charts upon charts of the solar system and the planetary moons: Rhea, Europa, Callisto, Miranda, Io. I didn't know that most of these moons were named for women—I didn't know classical mythology—but I would say their names to myself as though they had a woman's power to protect: Europa, Miranda, Io . . . . The distances between stars fascinated me, as did the sizes of the big telescopes. I sent away for catalogs. Then prices fascinated me too. I wanted to drape my arm over a thousand-dollar scope and hear its motor drive whirr. I conjured a twelve-year-old's life of the astronomer: sitting up all night with potato chips and the stars, tracking the sky for supernovas, humming "Earth Angel" with the Penguins. What was my mother to do but save her tips and buy me a telescope?!

12   It was a little reflecting job, and I solemnly used to carry it out to the front of the house on warm summer nights, to find Venus or Alpha Centauri or trace the stars in Orion or lock onto the moon. I would lay out my star maps on the concrete, more for their magic than anything else, for I had trouble figuring them out. I was no geometer of the constellations; I was their balladeer. Those nights were very peaceful. I was far enough away from the front door and up enough from the sidewalk to make it seem as if I rested on a mound of dark silence, a mountain in Arizona, perhaps, watching the sky alive with points of light. Poor Freddie, toothless Lester whispering promises about making me feel good, the flat days, the gang fights—all this receded, for it was now me, the star child, lost in an eyepiece focused on a reflecting mirror that cradled, in its center, a shimmering moon.

---

13   The loneliness in Los Angeles fosters strange arrangements. Lou Minton was a wiry man with gaunt, chiseled features and

prematurely gray hair, combed straight back. He had gone to college in the South for a year of two and kicked around the country for many more before settling in L.A. He lived in a small downtown apartment with a single window and met my mother at the counter of Coffee Dan's. He had been alone too long and eventually came to our house and became part of the family. Lou repaired washing machines, and he had a car, and he would take me to the vast, echoing library just west of Pershing Square and to the Museum of Science and Industry in Exposition Park. He bought me astronomy books, taught me how to use tools, and helped me build model airplanes from balsa wood and rice paper. As my father's health got worse, Lou took care of him.

My rhapsodic and prescientific astronomy carried me into my   14
teens, consumed me right up till high school, losing out finally, and only, to the siren call of pubescence—that endocrine hoodoo that transmogrifies nice boys into gawky flesh fiends. My mother used to bring home *Confidential* magazine, a peep-show rag specializing in the sins of the stars, and it beckoned me mercilessly: Jayne Mansfield's cleavage, Gina Lollobrigida's eyes, innuendos about deviant sexuality, ads for Frederick's of Hollywood—spiked heels, lacy brassieres, the epiphany of silk panties on a mannequin's hips. Along with Phil Everly, I was through with counting the stars above.

Budding manhood. Only adults talk about adolescence bud-   15
ding. Kids have no choice but to talk in extremes; they're being wrenched and buffeted, rabbit-punched from inside by systemic thugs. Nothing sweet and pastoral here. Kids become ridiculous and touching at one and the same time: passionate about the trivial, fixed before the mirror, yet traversing one of the most important rites of passage in their lives—liminal people, silly and profoundly human. Given my own expertise, I fantasized about concocting the fail-safe aphrodisiac that would bring Marianne Bilpusch, the cloakroom monitor, rushing into my arms or about commanding a squadron of bosomy, linguistically mysterious astronauts like Zsa Zsa Gabor. My parents used to say that their son would have the best education they could afford. Maybe I would be a doctor. There was a public school in our neighborhood and

several Catholic schools to the west. They had heard that quality schooling meant private, Catholic schooling, so they somehow got the money together to send me to Our Lady of Mercy, fifteen or so miles southwest of Ninety-first and Vermont. So much for my fantasies. Most Catholic secondary schools then were separated by
16 gender.

It took two buses to get to Our Lady of Mercy. The first started deep in South Los Angeles and caught me at midpoint. The second drifted through neighborhoods with trees, parks, big lawns, and lots of flowers. The rides were long but were livened up by a group of South L.A. veterans whose parents also thought that Hope had set up shop in the west end of the county. There was Christy Biggars, who, at sixteen, was dealing and was, according to rumor, a pimp as well. There were Bill Cobb and Johnny Gonzales, grease-pencil artists extraordinaire, who left Nembutal-enhanced swirls of "Cobb" and "Johnny" on the corrugated walls of the bus. And then there was Tyrrell Wilson. Tyrrell was the coolest kid I knew. He ran the dozens like a metric halfback, laid down a rap that outrhymed and outpointed Cobb, whose rap was good but not great—the curse of a moderately soulful kid trapped in white skin. But it was Cobb who would sneak a radio onto the bus, and thus underwrote his patter with Little Richard, Fats Domino, Chuck Berry, the Coasters, and Ernie K. Doe's mother-in-law, an awful woman who was "sent from down below." And so it was that Christy and Cobb and Johnny G. and Tyrrell and I and assorted others picked up along the way passed our days in the back of the bus, a funny mix brought together by geography and
17 parental desire.

Entrance to school brings with it forms and releases and assessments. Mercy relied on a series of tests, mostly the Stanford-Binet, for placement, and somehow the results of my tests got confused with those of another student named Rose. The other Rose apparently didn't do very well, for I was placed in the vocational track, a euphemism for the bottom level. Neither I nor my parents realized what this meant. We had no sense that Business Math, Typing, and English–Level D were dead ends. The current spate of reports on the schools criticizes parents for not involving themselves in the education of their children. But how would someone like Tommy Rose, with his two years of Italian schooling, know what to ask? And what sort of pressure could an exhausted waitress apply? The error went undetected, and I remained in the vocational track for two years. What a place.

My homeroom was supervised by Brother Dill, a troubled [18] and unstable man who also taught freshman English. When his class drifted away from him, which was often, his voice would rise in paranoid accusations, and occasionally he would lose control and shake or smack us. I hadn't been there two months when one of his brisk, face-turning slaps had my glasses sliding down the aisle. Physical education was also pretty harsh. Our teacher was a stubby ex-lineman who had played old-time pro ball in the Midwest. He routinely had us grabbing our ankles to receive his stinging paddle across our butts. He did that, he said, to make men of us. "Rose," he bellowed on our first encounter; me standing geeky in line in my baggy shorts. "'Rose'? What the hell kind of name is that?"

"Italian, sir," I squeaked.   [19]

"Italian! Ho. Rose, do you know the sound a bag of shit makes [20] when it hits the wall?"

"No, sir."   [21]

"Wop!"   [22]

Sophomore English was taught by Mr. Mitropetros. He was a [23] large, bejeweled man who managed the parking lot at the Shrine Auditorium. He would crow and preen and list for us the stars he'd brushed against. We'd ask questions and glance knowingly and snicker, and all that fueled the poor guy to brag some more. Parking cars was his night job. He had little training in English, so his lesson plan for his day work had us reading the district's required text, *Julius Caesar*, aloud for the semester. We'd finish the play way before the twenty weeks was up, so he'd have us switch parts again and again and start again: Dave Snyder, the fastest guy at Mercy, muscling through Caesar to the breathless squeals of Calpurnia, as interpreted by Steve Fusco, a surfer who owned the school's most envied paneled wagon. Week ten and Dave and Steve would take on new roles, as would we all, and render a waterlogged Cassius and a Brutus that are beyond my powers of description.

24   Spanish I—taken in the second year—fell into the hands of a new recruit. Mr. Montez was a tiny man, slight, five foot six at the most, soft-spoken and delicate. Spanish was a particularly rowdy class, and Mr. Montez was as prepared for it as a doily maker at a hammer throw. He would tap his pencil to a room in which Steve Fusco was propelling spitballs from his heavy lips, in which Mike Dweetz was taunting Billy Hawk, a half-Indian, half-Spanish, reed-thin, quietly explosive boy. The vocational track at Our Lady of Mercy mixed kids traveling in from South L.A. with South Bay surfers and a few Slavs and Chicanos from the harbors of San Pedro. This was a dangerous miscellany: surfers and hodads and South-Central blacks all ablaze to the metronomic tapping of Hector Montez's pencil.

25   One day Billy lost it. Out of the corner of my eye I saw him strike out with his right arm and catch Dweetz across the neck. Quick as a spasm, Dweetz was out of his seat, scattering desks, cracking Billy on the side of the head, right behind the eye. Snyder and Fusco and others broke it up, but the room felt hot and close and naked. Mr. Montez's tenuous authority was finally ripped to shreds, and I think everyone felt a little strange about that. That charade was over, and when it came down to it, I don't think any of the kids really wanted it to end this way. They has pushed and pushed and bullied their way into a freedom that both scared and embarrassed them.

26   Students will float to the mark you set. I and the others in the vocational classes were bobbing in pretty shallow water. Vocational education has aimed at increasing the economic opportunities of students who do not do well in our schools. Some serious programs succeed in doing that, and through exceptional teachers—like Mr. Gross in *Horace's Compromise*—students learn to develop hypotheses and troubleshoot, reason through a problem, and communicate effectively—the true job skills. The vocational track, however, is most often a place for those who are just not making it, a dumping group for the disaffected. There were a few teachers who worked hard at education; young Brother Slattery, for example, combined a stern voice with weekly quizzes to try to pass along to us a skeletal outline of world history. But mostly the

teachers had no idea of how to engage the imaginations of us kids who were scuttling along at the bottom of the pond.

And the teachers would have needed some inventiveness, 27 for none of us was groomed for the classroom. It wasn't just that I didn't know things—didn't know how to simplify algebraic fractions, couldn't identify different kinds of clauses, bungled Spanish translations—but that I had developed various faulty and inadequate ways of doing algebra and making sense of Spanish. Worse yet, the years of defensive tuning out in elementary school had given me a way to escape quickly while seeming at least half alert. During my time in Voc. Ed., I developed further into a mediocre student and a somnambulant problem solver, and that affected the subjects I did have the wherewithal to handle: I detested Shakespeare; I got bored with history. My attention flitted here and there. I fooled around in class and read my books indifferently—the intellectual equivalent of playing with your food. I did what I had to do to get by, and I did it with half a mind.

But I did learn things about people and eventually came into 28 my own socially. I liked the guys in Voc. Ed. Growing up where I did, I understood and admired physical prowess, and there was an abundance of muscle here. There was Dave Snyder, a sprinter and halfback of true quality. Dave's ability and his quick wit gave him a natural appeal, and he was welcome in any clique, though he always kept a little independent. He enjoyed acting the fool and could care less about studies, but he possessed a certain maturity and never caused the faculty much trouble. It was a testament to his independence that he included me among his friends—I eventually went out for track, but I was no jock. Owing to the Latin alphabet and a dearth of *R*s and *S*s, Snyder sat behind Rose and we started exchanging one-liners and became friends.

There was Ted Richard, a much-touted Little League pitcher. 29 He was chunky and had a baby face and came to our Lady of Mercy as a seasoned street fighter. Ted was quick to laugh and he had a loud, jolly laugh, but when he got angry he'd smile a little smile, the kind that simply raises the corner of the mouth a quarter of an inch. For those who knew, it was an eerie signal. Those who didn't found themselves in big trouble, for Ted was very quick. He loved to carry on what we would come to call philosophical discussions: What is courage? Does God exist? He also loved words, enjoyed picking up big ones like *salubrious* and *equivocal* and using them in our conversations—laughing at himself as the word hit a chuckhole rolling off his tongue. Ted didn't do all that well in school—baseball and parties and testing the courage he'd speculated about took up his time. His textbooks were *Argosy* and *Field and Stream*, whatever newspapers he'd find on the bus stop—from the *Daily Worker* to pornography—conversations with uncles or hobos or businessmen he'd meet in a coffee shop, *The Old Man and the Sea*. With hindsight, I can see that Ted was developing into one of those rough-hewn intellectuals whose sources are a mix of the learned and the apocryphal, whose discussions are both assured and sad.

30   And then there was Ken Harvey. Ken was good-looking in a puffy way and had a full and oily ducktail and was a car enthusiast . . . a hodad. One day in religion class, he said the sentence that turned out to be one of the most memorable of the hundreds of thousands I heard in those Voc. Ed. years. We were talking about the parable of the talents, about achievement, working hard, doing the best you can do, blah-blah-blah, when the teacher called on the restive Ken Harvey for an opinion. Ken thought about it, but just for a second, and said (with studied, minimal affect), "I just wanna be average." That woke me up. Average?! Who wants to be average? Then the athletes chimed in with the clichés that make you want to laryngectomize them, and the exchange became a platitudinous melee. At the time, I though Ken's assertion was stupid, and I wrote him off. But his sentence has stayed with me all these years, and I think I am finally coming to understand it.

31   Ken Harvey was gasping for air. School can be a tremendously disorienting place. No matter how bad the school, you're going to encounter notions that don't fit with the assumptions and beliefs that you grew up with—maybe you'll hear these dissonant notions from teachers, maybe from the other students, and maybe you'll read them. You'll also be thrown in with all kinds of kids from all kinds of backgrounds, and that can be unsettling— this is especially true in places of rich ethnic and linguistic mix, like the L.A. basin. You'll see a handful of students far excel you in courses that sound exotic and that are only in the curriculum of the elite: French, physics, trigonometry. And all this is happening while you're trying to shape an identity; your body is changing,

and your emotions are running wild. If you're a working-class kid in the vocational track, the options you'll have to deal with this will be constrained in certain ways: You're defined by your school as "slow"; you're placed in a curriculum that isn't designed to liberate you but to occupy you, or, if you're lucky, train you, though the training is for work the society does not esteem; other students are picking up the cues from your school and your curriculum and interacting with you in particular ways. If you're a kid like Ted Richard, you turn your back on all this and let your mind roam where it may. But youngsters like Ted are rare. What Ken and so many others do is protect themselves from such suffocating madness by taking on with a vengeance the identity implied in the vocational track. Reject the confusion and frustration by openly defining yourself as the Common Joe. Champion the average. Rely on your own good sense. F— this bull——. Bull——, of course, is everything you—and the others—fear is beyond you: books, essays, tests, academic scrambling, complexity, scientific reasoning, philosophical inquiry.

The tragedy is that you have to twist the knife in your own 32 gray matter to make this defense work. You'll have to shut down, have to reject intellectual stimuli or diffuse them with sarcasm, have to cultivate stupidity, have to convert boredom from a malady into a way of confronting the world. Keep your vocabulary simple, act stoned when you're not or act more stoned than you are, flaunt ignorance, materialize your dreams. It is a powerful and effective defense—it neutralizes the insult and the frustration of being a vocational kid and, when perfected, it drives teachers up the wall, a delightful secondary effect. But like all strong magic, it exacts a price.

————————

My own deliverance from the Voc. Ed. world began with 33 sophomore biology. Every student, college prep to vocational, had to take biology, and unlike the other courses, the same person taught all sections. When teaching the vocational group, Brother Clint probably slowed down a bit or omitted a little of the fundamental biochemistry, but he used the same book and more or less the same syllabus across the board. If one class got tough, he could get tougher. He was young and powerful and very handsome, and looks and physical strength were high currency. No one gave him any trouble.

34   I was pretty bad at the dissecting table, but the lectures and the textbook were interesting: plastic overlays that, with each turned page, peeled away skin, then veins and muscle, then organs, down to the very bones that Brother Clint, pointer in hand, would tap out on our hanging skeleton. Dave Snyder was in big trouble, for the study of life—versus the living of it—was sticking in his craw. We worked out a code for our multiple-choice exams. He'd poke me in the back: once for the answer under *A*, twice for *B*, and so on: and when he'd hit the right one, I'd look up to the ceiling as though I were lost in thought. Poke: cytoplasm. Poke, poke: methane. Poke, poke, poke: William Harvey. Poke, poke, poke, poke: islets of Langerhans. This didn't work out perfectly, but Dave passed the course, and I mastered the dreamy look of a guy on a record jacket. And something else happened. Brother Clint puzzled over this Voc. Ed. kid who was racking up 98s and 99s on his tests. He checked the school's records and discovered the error. He recommended that I begin my junior year in the College Prep program. According to all I've read since, such a shift, as one report put it, is virtually impossible. Kids at that level rarely cross tracks. The telling thing is how chancy both my placement into and exit from Voc. Ed. was; neither I nor my parents had anything to do with it. I lived in one world during spring semester, and when I came back to school in the fall, I was living in another.

1989

keeping close to home: class and education

bell hooks

1   We are both awake in the almost dark of 5 a.m. Everyone else is sound asleep. Mama asks the usual questions. Telling me to look

around, make sure I have everything, scolding me because I am
uncertain about the actual time the bus arrives. By 5:30 we are
waiting outside the closed station. Alone together, we have a chance
to really talk. Mama begins. Angry with her children, especially
the ones who whisper behind her back, she says bitterly, "Your
childhood could not have been that bad. You were fed and
clothed. You did not have to do without—that's more than a lot of
folks have and I just can't stand the way y'all go on." The hurt in
her voice saddens me. I have always wanted to protect mama
from hurt, to ease her burdens. Now I am part of what troubles.
Confronting me, she says accusingly, "It's not just the other children. You talk too much about the past. You don't just listen." And
I do talk. Worse, I write about it.

Mama has always come to each of her children seeking differ-   2
ent responses. With me she expresses the disappointment, hurt,
and anger of betrayal: anger that her children are so critical, that
we can't even have the sense to like the presents she sends. She
says, "From now on there will be no presents. I'll just stick some
money in a little envelope the way the rest of you do. Nobody
wants criticism. Everybody can criticize me but I am supposed to
say nothing." When I try to talk, my voice sounds like a twelve
year old. When I try to talk, she speaks louder, interrupting me,
even though she has said repeatedly, "Explain it to me, this talk
about the past." I struggle to return to my thirty-five year old self
so that she will know by the sound of my voice that we are two
women talking together. It is only when I state firmly in my very
adult voice, "Mama, you are not listening," that she becomes
quiet. She waits. Now that I have her attention, I fear that my explanations will be lame, inadequate. "Mama," I begin, "people
usually go to therapy because they feel hurt inside, because they
have pain that will not stop, like a wound that continually breaks
open, that does not heal. And often these hurts, that pain has to do
with things that have happened in the past, sometimes in childhood, often in childhood, or things that we believe happened."
She wants to know, "What hurts, what hurts are you talking about?"
"Mom, I can't answer that. I can't speak for all of us, the hurts are
different for everybody. But the point is you try to make the hurt
better, to heal it, by understanding how it came to be. And I know

you feel mad when we say something happened or hurt that you don't remember being that way, but the past isn't like that, we don't have the same memory of it. We remember things differently. You know that. And sometimes folk feel hurt about stuff and you just don't know or didn't realize it, and they need to talk about it. Surely you understand the need to talk about it."

3   Our conversation is interrupted by the sight of my uncle walking across the park toward us. We stop to watch him. He is on his way to work dressed in a familiar blue suit. They look alike, these two who rarely discuss the past. This interruption makes me think about life in a small town. You always see someone you know. Interruptions, intrusions are part of daily life. Privacy is difficult to maintain. We leave our private space in the car to greet him. After the hug and kiss he has given me every year since I was born, they talk about the day's funerals. In the distance the bus approaches. He walks away knowing that they will see each other later. Just before I board the bus I turn, staring into my mother's face. I am momentarily back in time, seeing myself eighteen years ago, at this same bus stop, staring into my mother's face, continually turning back, waving farewell as I returned to college—that experience which first took me away from our town, from family. Departing was as painful then as it is now. Each movement away makes return harder. Each separation intensifies distance, both physical and emotional.

4   To a southern black girl from a working-class background who had never been on a city bus, who had never stepped on an escalator, who had never travelled by plane, leaving the comfortable confines of a small town Kentucky life to attend Stanford University was not just frightening; it was utterly painful. My parents had not been delighted that I had been accepted and adamantly opposed my going so far from home. At the time, I did not see their opposition as an expression of their fear that they would lose me forever. Like many working-class folks, they feared what college education might do to their children's minds even as they unenthusiastically acknowledged its importance. They did not understand why I could not attend a college nearby, an all-black college. To them, any college would do. I would graduate, become a school teacher, make a decent living and a good

marriage. And even though they reluctantly and skeptically supported my educational endeavors, they also subjected them to
constant harsh and bitter critique. It is difficult for me to talk
about my parents and their impact on me because they have always felt wary, ambivalent, mistrusting of my intellectual aspirations even as they have been caring and supportive. I want to
speak about these contradictions because sorting through them,
seeking resolution and reconciliation has been important to me
both as it affects my development as a writer, my effort to be fully
self-realized, and my longing to remain close to the family and
community that provided the groundwork for much of my thinking, writing, and being.

Studying at Stanford, I began to think seriously about class 5
differences. To be materially underprivileged at a university where
most folks (with the exception of workers) are materially privileged provokes such thought. Class differences were boundaries
no one wanted to face or talk about. It was easier to downplay
them, to act as though we were all from privileged backgrounds,
to work around them, to confront them privately in the solitude of
one's room, or to pretend that just being chosen to study at such
an institution meant that those of us who did not come from privilege were already in transition toward privilege. To not long for
such transition marked one as rebellious, as unlikely to succeed. It
was a kind of treason not to believe that it was better to be identified with the world of material privilege than with the world of
the working class, the poor. No wonder our working-class parents
from poor backgrounds feared our entry into such a world, intuit-
ing perhaps that we might learn to be ashamed of where we had
come from, that we might never return home, or come back only
to lord it over them.

Though I hung with students who were supposedly radical 6
and chic, we did not discuss class. I talked to no one about the
sources of my shame, how it hurt me to witness the contempt
shown the brown-skinned Filipina maids who cleaned our rooms,
or later my concern about the $100 a month I paid for a room off-
campus which was more than half of what my parents paid for
rent. I talked to no one about my efforts to save money, to send a
little something home. Yet these class realities separated me from

fellow students. We were moving in different directions. I did not intend to forget my class background or alter my class allegiance. And even though I received an education designed to provide me with a bourgeois sensibility, passive acquiescence was not my only option. I knew that I could resist. I could rebel. I could shape the direction and focus of the various forms of knowledge available to me. Even though I sometimes envied and longed for greater material advantages (particularly at vacation times when I would be one of few if any students remaining in the dormitory because there was no money for travel), I did not share the sensibility and values of my peers. That was important—class was not just about money; it was about values which showed and determined behavior. While I often needed more money, I never needed a new set of beliefs and values. For example, I was profoundly shocked and disturbed when peers would talk about their parents without respect, or would even say that they hated their parents. This was especially troubling to me when it seemed that these parents were caring and concerned. It was often explained to me that such hatred was "healthy and normal." To my white, middle-class California roommate, I explained the way we were taught to value our parents and their care, to understand that they were not obligated to give us care. She would always shake her head, laughing all the while, and say, "Missy, you will learn that it's different here, that we think differently." She was right. Soon, I lived alone, like the one Mormon student who kept to himself as he made a concentrated effort to remain true to his religious beliefs and values. Later in graduate school I found that classmates believed "lower class" people had no beliefs and values. I was silent in such discussions, disgusted by their ignorance.

7   Carol Stack's anthropological study, *All Our Kin*, was one of the first books I read which confirmed my experiential understanding that within black culture (especially among the working class and poor, particularly in southern states), a value system emerged that was counter-hegemonic, that challenged notions of individualism and private property so important to the maintenance of white-supremacist, capitalist patriarchy. Black folk created in marginal spaces a world of community and collectivity where resources were shared. In the preface to *Feminist Theory:*

from margin to center, I talked about how the point of difference, this marginality can be the space for the formation of an oppositional world view. That world view must be articulated, named if it is to provide a sustained blueprint for change. Unfortunately, there has existed no consistent framework for such naming. Consequently both the experience of this difference and documentation of it (when it occurs) gradually loses presence and meaning.

Much of what Stack documented about the "culture of 8 poverty," for example, would not describe interactions among most black poor today irrespective of geographical setting. Since the black people she described did not acknowledge (if they recognized it in theoretical terms) the oppositional value of their world view, apparently seeing it more as a survival strategy determined less by conscious efforts to oppose oppressive race and class biases than by circumstance, they did not attempt to establish a framework to transmit their beliefs and values from generation to generation. When circumstances changed, values altered. Efforts to assimilate the values and beliefs of privileged white people, presented through media like television, undermine and destroy potential structures of opposition.

Increasingly, young black people are encouraged by the dom- 9 inant culture (and by those black people who internalize the values of this hegemony) to believe that assimilation is the only possible way to survive, to succeed. Without the framework of an organized civil rights or black resistance struggle, individual and collective efforts at black liberation that focus on the primacy of self-definition and self-determination often go unrecognized. It is crucial that those among us who resist and rebel, who survive and succeed, speak openly and honestly about our lives and the nature of our personal struggles, the means by which we resolve and reconcile contradictions. This is no easy task. Within the educational institutions where we learn to develop and strengthen our writing and analytical skills, we also learn to think, write, and talk in a manner that shifts attention away from personal experience. Yet if we are to reach our people and all people, if we are to remain connected (especially those of us whose familial backgrounds are poor and working-class), we must understand that ti.. telling of ..e's personal story provides a meaningful example, a way for folks to identify and connect.

10   Combining personal with critical analysis and theoretical perspectives can engage listeners who might otherwise feel estranged, alienated. To speak simply with language that is accessible to as many folks as possible is also important. Speaking about one's personal experience or speaking with simple language is often considered by academics and/or intellectuals (irrespective of their political inclinations) to be a sign of intellectual weakness or even anti-intellectualism. Lately, when I speak, I do not stand in place—reading my paper, making little or no eye contact with audiences—but instead make eye contact, talk extemporaneously, digress, and address the audience directly. I have been told that people assume I am not prepared, that I am anti-intellectual, unprofessional (a concept that has everything to do with class as it determines actions and behavior), or that I am reinforcing the stereotype of black people as non-theoretical and gutsy.

11   Such criticism was raised recently by fellow feminist scholars after a talk I gave at Northwestern University at a conference on "Gender, Culture, Politics" to an audience that was mainly students and academics. I deliberately chose to speak in a very basic way, thinking especially about the few community folks who had come to hear me. Weeks later, Kum-Kum Sangari, a fellow participant who shared with me what was said when I was no longer present, and I engaged in quite rigorous critical dialogue about the way my presentation had been perceived primarily by privileged white female academics. She was concerned that I not mask my knowledge of theory, that I not appear anti-intellectual. Her critique compelled me to articulate concerns that I am often silent about with colleagues. I spoke about class allegiance and revolutionary commitments, explaining that it was disturbing to me that intellectual radicals who speak about transforming society, ending the domination of race, sex, class, cannot break with behavior patterns that reinforce and perpetuate domination, or continue to use as their sole reference point how we might be or are perceived by those who dominate, whether or not we gain their acceptance and approval.

This is a primary contradiction which raises the issue of ₁₂ whether or not the academic setting is a place where one can be truly radical or subversive. Concurrently, the use of a language and style of presentation that alienate most folks who are not also academically trained reinforces the notion that the academic world is separate from real life, that everyday world where we constantly adjust our language and behavior to meet diverse needs. The academic setting is separate only when we work to make it so. It is a false dichotomy which suggests that academics and/or intellectuals can only speak to one another, that we cannot hope to speak with the masses. What is true is that we make choices, that we choose our audiences, that we choose voices to hear and voices to silence. If I do not speak in a language that can be understood, then there is little chance for dialogue. This issue of language and behavior is a central contradiction all radical intellectuals, particularly those who are members of oppressed groups, must continually confront and work to resolve. One of the clear and present dangers that exists when we move outside our class of origin, our collective ethnic experience, and enter hierarchical institutions which daily reinforce domination by race, sex, and class, is that we gradually assume a mindset similar to those who dominate and oppress, that we lose critical consciousness because it is not reinforced or affirmed by the environment. We must be ever vigilant. It is important that we know who we are speaking to, who we most want to hear us, who we most long to move, motivate, and touch with our words.

When I first came to New Haven to teach at Yale, I was truly ₁₃ surprised by the marked class divisions between black folks—students and professors—who identify with Yale and those black folks who work at Yale or in surrounding communities. Style of dress and self-presentation are most often the central markers of one's position. I soon learned that the black folks who spoke on the street were likely to be part of the black community and those who carefully shifted their glance were likely to be associated with Yale. Walking with a black female colleague one day, I spoke to practically every black person in sight (a gesture which reflects my upbringing), an action which disturbed my companion. Since I addressed black folk who were clearly not associated with Yale, she wanted to know whether or not I knew them. That was funny to me. "Of course not," I answered. Yet when I thought about it seriously, I realized that in a deep way, I knew them for they, and not my companion or most of my colleagues at Yale, resemble my family. Later that year, in a black women's support group I started for undergraduates, students from poor backgrounds spoke about the shame they sometimes feel when faced with the reality of their connection to working-class and poor black people. One student confessed that her father is a street person, addicted to drugs, someone who begs from passersby. She, like other Yale students, turns away from street people often, sometimes showing anger or contempt; she hasn't wanted anyone to know that she was related to this kind of person. She struggles with this, wanting to find a way to acknowledge and affirm this reality, to claim this connection. The group asked me and one another what we do to remain connected, to honor the bonds we have with working-class and poor people even as our class experience alters.

14   Maintaining connections with family and community across class boundaries demands more than just summary recall of where one's roots are, where one comes from. It requires knowing, naming, and being ever-mindful of those aspects of one's past that have enabled and do enable one's self-development in the present, that sustain and support, that enrich. One must also honestly confront barriers that do exist, aspects of that past that do diminish. My parent's ambivalence about my love for reading led to intense conflict. They (especially my mother) would work to ensure that I had access to books, but would threaten to burn the books or throw them away if I did not conform to other expectations. Or they would insist that reading too much would drive me insane. Their ambivalence nurtured in me a like uncertainty about the value and significance of intellectual endeavor which took years for me to unlearn. While this aspect of our class reality was one that wounded and diminished, their vigilant insistence that being smart did not make me a "better" or "superior" person (which often got on my nerves because I think I wanted to have that sense that it did indeed set me apart, make me better) made a profound impression. From them I learned to value and respect various skills and talents folk might have, not just to value people who

read books and talk about ideas. They and my grandparents might say about somebody, "Now he don't read nor write a lick, but he can tell a story," or as my grandmother would say, "call out the hell in words."

Empty romanticization of poor or working-class backgrounds   15 undermines the possibility of true connection. Such connection is based on understanding difference in experience and perspective and working to mediate and negotiate these terrains. Language is a crucial issue for folk whose movement outside the boundaries of poor and working-class backgrounds changes the nature and direction of their speech. Coming to Stanford with my own version of a Kentucky accent, which I think of always as a strong sound quite different from Tennessee or Georgia speech, I learned to speak differently while maintaining the speech of my region, the sound of my family and community. This was of course much easier to keep up when I returned home to stay often. In recent years, I have endeavored to use various speaking styles in the classroom as a teacher and find it disconcerts those who feel that the use of a particular patois excludes them as listeners, even if there is translation into the usual, acceptable mode of speech. Learning to listen to different voices, hearing different speech challenges the notion that we must all assimilate—share a single, similar talk— in educational institutions. Language reflects the culture from which we emerge. To deny ourselves daily use of speech patterns that are common and familiar, that embody the unique and distinctive aspect of our self is one of the ways we become estranged and alienated from our past. It is important for us to have as many languages on hand as we can know or learn. It is important for those of us who are black, who speak in particular patois as well as standard English to express ourselves in both ways.

Often I tell students from poor and working-class backgrounds   16 that if you believe what you have learned and are learning in schools and universities separates you from your past, this is precisely what will happen. It is important to stand firm in the conviction that nothing can truly separate us from our pasts when we nurture and cherish that connection. An important strategy for maintaining contact is ongoing acknowledgement of the primacy of one's past, of one's background, affirming the reality that such bonds are not severed automatically solely because one enters a new environment or moves toward a different class experience.

17   Again, I do not wish to romanticize this effort, to dismiss the reality of conflict and contradiction. During my time at Stanford, I did go through a period of more than a year when I did not return home. That period was one where I felt that it was simply too difficult to mesh my profoundly disparate realities. Critical reflection about the choice I was making, particularly about why I felt a choice had to be made, pulled me through this difficult time. Luckily I recognized that the insistence on choosing between the world of family and community and the new world of privileged white people and privileged ways of knowing was imposed upon me by the outside. It is as though a mythical contract had been signed somewhere which demanded of us black folks that once we entered these spheres we would immediately give up all vestiges of our underprivileged past. It was my responsibility to formulate a way of being that would allow me to participate fully in my new environment while integrating and maintaining aspects of the old.

18   One of the most tragic manifestations of the pressure black people feel to assimilate is expressed in the internalization of racist perspectives. I was shocked and saddened when I first heard black professors at Stanford downgrade and express contempt for black students, expecting us to do poorly, refusing to establish nurturing bonds. At every university I have attended as a student or worked at as a teacher, I have heard similar attitudes expressed with little or no understanding of factors that might prevent brilliant black students from performing to their full capability. Within universities, there are few educational and social spaces where students who wish to affirm positive ties to ethnicity—to blackness, to working-class backgrounds—can receive affirmation and support. Ideologically, the message is clear—assimilation is the way to gain acceptance and approval from those in power.

19   Many white people enthusiastically supported Richard Rodriguez's vehement contention in his autobiography, *Hunger of Memory*, that attempts to maintain ties with his Chicano background impeded his progress, that he had to sever ties with community and kin to succeed at Stanford and in the larger world, that family language, in his case Spanish, had to be made secondary or

discarded. If the terms of success as defined by the standards of ruling groups within white-supremacist, capitalist patriarchy are the only standards that exist, then assimilation is indeed necessary. But they are not. Even in the face of powerful structures of domination, it remains possible for each of us, especially those of us who are members of oppressed and/or exploited groups as well as those radical visionaries who may have race, class, and sex privilege, to define and determine alternative standards, to decide on the nature and extent of compromise. Standards by which one's success is measured, whether student or professor, are quite different for those of us who wish to resist reinforcing the domination of race, sex, and class, who work to maintain and strengthen our ties with the oppressed, with those who lack material privilege, with our families who are poor and working-class.

When I wrote my first book, *Ain't I A Woman: black women and* 20 *feminism,* the issue of class and its relationship to who one's reading audience might be came up for me around my decision not to use footnotes, for which I have been sharply criticized. I told people that my concern was that footnotes set class boundaries for readers, determining who a book is for. I was shocked that many academic folks scoffed at this idea. I shared that I went into working-class black communities as well as talked with family and friends to survey whether or not they ever read books with footnotes and found that they did not. A few did not know what they were, but most folks saw them as indicating that a book was for college-educated people. These responses influenced my decision. When some of my more radical, college-educated friends freaked out about the absence of footnotes, I seriously questioned how we could ever imagine revolutionary transformation of society if such a small shift in direction could be viewed as threatening. Of course, many folks warned that the absence of footnotes would make the work less credible in academic circles. This information also highlighted the way in which class informs our choices. Certainly I did feel that choosing to use simple language, absence of footnotes, etc. would mean I was jeopardizing the possibility of being taken seriously in academic circles but then this was a political matter and a political decision. It utterly delights me that this has proven not to be the case and that the book is read by many academics as well as by people who are not college-educated.

21   Always our first response when we are motivated to conform or compromise within structures that reinforce domination must be to engage in critical reflection. Only by challenging ourselves to push against oppressive boundaries do we make the radical alternative possible, expanding the realm and scope of critical inquiry. Unless we share radical strategies, ways of rethinking and revisioning with students, with kin and community, with a larger audience, we risk perpetuating the stereotype that we succeed because we are the exception, different from the rest of our people. Since I left home and entered college, I am often asked, usually by white people, if my sisters and brothers are also high achievers. At the root of this question is the longing for reinforcement of the belief in "the exception" which enables race, sex, and class biases to remain intact. I am careful to separate what it means to be exceptional from a notion of "the exception."

22   Frequently I hear smart black folks, from poor and working-class backgrounds, stressing their frustration that at times family and community do not recognize that they are exceptional. Absence of positive affirmation clearly diminishes the longing to excel in academic endeavors. Yet it is important to distinguish between the absence of basic positive affirmation and the longing for continued reinforcement that we are special. Usually liberal white folks will willingly offer continual reinforcement of us as exceptions—as special. This can be both patronizing and very seductive. Since we often work in situations where we are isolated from other black folks, we can easily begin to feel that encouragement from white people is the primary or only source of support and recognition. Given the internalization of racism, it is easy to view this support as more validating and legitimizing than similar support from black people. Still, nothing takes the place of being valued and appreciated by one's own, by one's family and community. We share a mutual and reciprocal responsibility for affirming one another's successes. Sometimes we have to talk to our folks about the fact that we need their ongoing support and affirmation, that it is unique and special to us. In some cases we may never receive desired recognition and acknowledgement of specific achievements from kin. Rather than seeing this as a basis for estrangement, for severing connection, it is useful to explore other sources of nourishment and support.

I do not know that my mother's mother ever acknowledged 23 my college education except to ask me once, "How can you live so far away from your people?" Yet she gave me sources of affirmation and nourishment, sharing the legacy of her quilt-making, of family history, of her incredible way with words. Recently, when our father retired after more than thirty years of work as a janitor, I wanted to pay tribute to this experience, to identify links between his work and my own as writer and teacher. Reflecting on our family past, I recalled ways he had been an impressive example of diligence and hard work, approaching tasks with a seriousness of concentration I work to mirror and develop, with a discipline I struggle to maintain. Sharing these thoughts with him keeps us connected, nurtures our respect for each other, maintaining a space, however large or small, where we can talk.

Open, honest communication is the most important way we 24 maintain relationships with kin and community as our class experience and backgrounds change. It is as vital as the sharing of resources. Often financial assistance is given in circumstances where there is no meaningful contact. However helpful, this can also be an expression of estrangement and alienation. Communication between black folks from various experiences of material privilege was much easier when we were all in segregated communities sharing common experiences in relation to social institutions. Without this grounding, we must work to maintain ties, connection. We must assume greater responsibility for making and maintaining contact, connections that can shape our intellectual visions and inform our radical commitments.

The most powerful resource any of us can have as we study 25 and teach in university settings is full understanding and appreciation of the richness, beauty, and primacy of our familial and community backgrounds. Maintaining awareness of class differences, nurturing ties with the poor and working-class people who are our most intimate kin, our comrades in struggle, transforms and enriches our intellectual experience. Education as the practice of freedom becomes not a force which fragments or separates, but one that brings us closer, expanding our definitions of home and community.

1988

Claiming an Education

Adrienne Rich

1   For this convocation, I planned to separate my remarks into two parts: some thoughts about you, the women students here, and some thoughts about us who teach in a women's college. But ultimately, those two parts are indivisible. If university education means anything beyond the processing of human beings into expected roles, through credit hours, tests, and grades (and I believe that in a women's college especially it *might* mean much more), it implies an ethical and intellectual contract between teacher and student. This contract must remain intuitive, dynamic, unwritten; but we must turn to it again and again if learning is to be reclaimed from the depersonalizing and cheapening pressures of the present-day academic scene.

2   The first thing I want to say to you who are students, is that you cannot afford to think of being here to *receive* an education; you will do much better to think of yourselves as being here to *claim* one. One of the dictionary definitions of the verb "to claim" is: *to take as the rightful owner; to assert in the face of possible contradiction.* "To receive" is *to come into possession of; to act as receptacle or container for; to accept as authoritative or true.* The difference is that between acting and being acted-upon, and for women it can literally mean the difference between life and death.

3   One of the devastating weaknesses of university learning, of the store of knowledge and opinion that has been handed down through academic training, has been its almost total erasure of women's experience and thought from the curriculum, and its exclusion of women as members of the academic community. Today, with increasing numbers of women students in nearly every branch of higher learning, we still see very few women in the upper levels of faculty and administration in most institutions. Douglass College itself is a women's college in a university administered overwhelmingly by men, who in turn are answerable to the state legislature, again composed predominantly of men. But

This address was given at the Douglass College Convocation, September 6, 1977.

the most significant fact for you is that what you learn here, the very texts you read, the lectures you hear, the way your studies are divided into categories and fragmented one from the other—all this reflects, to a very large degree, neither objective reality, nor an accurate picture of the past, nor a group of rigorously tested observations about human behavior. What you can learn here (and I mean not only at Douglass but any college in any university) is how *men* have perceived and organized their experience, their history, their ideas of social relationships, good and evil, sickness and health, etc. When you read or hear about "great issues," "major texts," "the mainstream of Western thought," you are hearing about what men, above all white men, in their male subjectivity, have decided is important.

Black and other minority peoples have for some time recog- 4 nized that their racial and ethnic experience was not accounted for in the studies broadly labeled human; and that even the sciences can be racist. For many reasons, it has been more difficult for women to comprehend our exclusion, and to realize that even the sciences can be sexist. For one thing, it is only within the last hundred years that higher education has grudgingly been opened up to women at all, even to white, middle-class women. And many of us have found ourselves poring eagerly over books with titles like: *The Descent of Man; Man and His Symbols; Irrational Man; The Phenomenon of Man: The Future of Man; Man and the Machine; From Man to Man; May Man Prevail?; Man, Science, and Society,* or *One-Dimensional Man*—books pretending to describe a "human" reality that does not include over one-half the human species.

Less than a decade ago, with the rebirth of a feminist move- 5 ment in this country, women students and teachers in a number of universities began to demand and set up women's studies courses—to *claim* a woman-directed education. And, despite the inevitable accusations of "unscholarly," "group therapy," "faddism," etc., despite backlash and budget cuts, women's studies are still growing, offering to more and more women a new intellectual grasp on their lives, new understanding of our history, a fresh vision of the human experience, and also a critical basis for evaluating what they hear and read in other courses, and in the society at large.

6   But my talk is not really about women's studies, much as I believe in their scholarly, scientific, and human necessity. While I think that any Douglass student has everything to gain by investigating and enrolling in women's studies courses, I want to suggest that there is a more essential experience that you owe yourselves, one which courses in women's studies can greatly enrich, but which finally depends on you, in all your interactions with yourself and your world. This is the experience of *taking responsibility toward yourselves.* Our upbringing as women has so often told us that this should come second to our relationships and responsibilities to other people. We have been offered ethical models of the self-denying wife and mother; intellectual models of the brilliant but slapdash dilettante who never commits herself to anything the whole way, or the intelligent woman who denies her intelligence in order to seem more "feminine," or who sits in passive silence even when she disagrees inwardly with everything that is being said around her.

7   Responsibility to yourself means refusing to let others do your thinking, talking, and naming for you; it means learning to respect and use your own brains and instincts; hence, grappling with hard work. It means that you do not treat your body as a commodity with which to purchase superficial intimacy or economic security; for our bodies and minds are inseparable in this life, and when we allow our bodies to be treated as objects, our minds are in mortal danger. It means insisting that those to whom you give your friendship and love are able to respect your mind. It means being able to say, with Charlotte Brontë's *Jane Eyre:* "I have an inward treasure born with me, which can keep me alive if all the extraneous delights should be withheld or offered only at a price I cannot afford to give."

8   Responsibility to yourself means that you don't fall for shallow and easy solutions—predigested books and ideas, weekend encounters guaranteed to change your life, taking "gut" courses instead of ones you know will challenge you, bluffing at school and life instead of doing solid work, marrying early as an escape from real decisions, getting pregnant as an evasion of already existing problems. It means that you refuse to sell your talents and aspirations short, simply to avoid conflict and confrontation. And

this, in turn, means resisting the forces in society which say that women should be nice, play safe, have low professional expectations, drown in love and forget about work, live through others, and stay in the places assigned to us. It means that we insist on a life of meaningful work, insist that work be as meaningful as love and friendship in our lives. It means, therefore, the courage to be "different"; not to be continuously available to others when we need time for ourselves and our work; to be able to demand of others—parents, friends, roommates, teachers, lovers, husbands, children—that they respect our sense of purpose and our integrity as persons. Women everywhere are finding the courage to do this, more and more, and we are finding that courage both in our study of women in the past who possessed it, and in each other as we look to other women for comradeship, community, and challenge. The difference between a life lived actively, and a life of passive drifting and dispersal of energies, is an immense difference. Once we begin to feel committed to our lives, responsible to ourselves, we can never again be satisfied with the old, passive way.

Now comes the second part of the contract. I believe that in a women's college you have the right to expect your faculty to take you seriously. The education of women has been a matter of debate for centuries, and old, negative attitudes about women's role, women's ability to think and take leadership, are still rife both in and outside the university. Many male professors (and I don't mean only at Douglass) still feel that teaching in a women's college is a second-rate career. Many tend to eroticize their women students—to treat them as sexual objects—instead of demanding the best of their minds. (At Yale, a legal suit [*Alexander* v. *Yale*] has been brought against the university by a group of women students demanding a stated policy against sexual advances toward female students by male professors.) Many teachers, both men and women, trained in the male-centered tradition, are still handing the ideas and texts of that tradition on to students without teaching them to criticize its antiwoman attitudes, its omission of women as part of the species. Too often, all of us fail to teach the most important thing, which is that clear thinking, active discussion, and excellent writing are all necessary for intellectual freedom, and that these require *hard work.* Sometimes, perhaps in discouragement with a culture which is both antiintellectual and antiwoman, we may resign ourselves to low expectations for our students before we have given them half a chance to become more thoughtful, expressive human beings. We need to take to heart the words of Elizabeth Barrett Browning, a poet, a thinking woman, and a feminist, who wrote in 1845 of her impatience with studies which cultivate a "passive recipiency" in the mind, and asserted that "women want to be made to *think actively:* their apprehension is quicker than that of men, but their defect lies for the most part in the logical faculty and in the higher mental activities." Note that she implies a defect which can be remedied by intellectual training; *not* an inborn lack of ability.

10   I have said that the contract on the student's part involves that you demand to be taken seriously so that you can also go on taking yourself seriously. This means seeking out criticism, recognizing that the most affirming thing anyone can do for you is demand that you push yourself further, show you the range of what you *can* do. It means rejecting attitudes of "take-it-easy," "why-be-so-serious," "why-worry-you'll-probably-get-married-anyway." It means assuming your share of responsibility for what happens in the classroom, because that affects the quality of your daily life here. It means that the student sees herself engaged *with* her teachers in an active, ongoing struggle for a real education. But for her to do this, her teachers must be committed to the belief that women's minds and experience are intrinsically valuable and indispensable to any civilization worthy the name; that there is no more exhilarating and intellectually fertile place in the academic world today than a women's college—*if* both students and teachers in large enough numbers are trying to fulfill this contract. The contract is really a pledge of mutual seriousness about women, about language, ideas, methods, and values. It is our shared commitment toward a world in which the inborn potentialities of so many women's minds will no longer be wasted, raveled-away, paralyzed, or denied.

1977

Whose Canon Is It, Anyway?

Henry Louis Gates Jr.

William Bennett and Allan Bloom, the dynamic duo of the new   1
cultural right, have become the easy targets of the cultural left,
which I am defining here loosely and generously as that uneasy,
shifting set of alliances formed by feminist critics, critics of so-
called minority culture and Marxist and post-structuralist critics
generally—in short, the rainbow coalition of contemporary critical theory. These two men (one a former United States Secretary of
Education and now President Bush's "drug czar,"[1] the other a
professor at the University of Chicago and author of "The Closing
of the American Mind") symbolize the nostalgic return to what I
think of as the "antebellum esthetic position," when men were
men and men were white, when scholar-critics were white men
and when women and people of color were voiceless, faceless servants and laborers, pouring tea and filling brandy snifters in the
boardrooms of old boys' clubs. Inevitably, these two men have
come to play the roles that George Wallace and Orville Faubus
played for the civil rights movement, or that Richard Nixon and
Henry Kissinger played during Vietnam—the "feel good" targets
who, despite internal differences and contradictions, the cultural
left loves to hate.

And how tempting it is to juxtapose their "civilizing mission"   2
to the racial violence that has swept through our campuses since
1986—at traditionally liberal Northern institutions such as the
University of Massachusetts at Amherst, Mount Holyoke College,
Smith College, the University of Chicago, Columbia, the University of Pennsylvania, and at Southern institutions such as the University of Alabama, the University of Texas and the Citadel. Add
to this the fact that affirmative action programs on campus have
become window dressing operations, necessary "evils" maintained
to preserve the fiction of racial fairness and openness but deprived of the power to enforce their stated principles. When un-

[1]President George Bush (b. 1924), term 1989–1993, father of President George W.
Bush.

employment among black youth is 40 percent, when 44 percent of black Americans can't read the front page of a newspaper, when less than 2 percent of the faculty on campuses is black and when only 40 percent of black students in higher education are men, well, you look for targets close at hand.

3   And yet there's a real danger of localizing our grievances; of the easy personification, assigning celebrated faces to the forces of reaction and so giving too much credit to a few men who are really symptomatic of a larger political current. (In a similar vein, our rhetoric sometimes depicts the high canonical as the reading matter of the power elite. You have to imagine James Baker curling up with the "Pisan Cantos," Dan Quayle leafing through "The Princess Casamassima.") Maybe our eagerness to do so reflects a certain vanity that academic cultural critics are prone to. We make dire predictions, and when they come true, we think we've changed the world.

4   It's a tendency that puts me in mind of my father's favorite story about Father Divine, that historic con man of the cloth. In the 1930's, he was put on trial and convicted for using the mails to defraud. At sentencing, Father Divine stood up and told the judge: I'm warning you, you send me to jail, something terrible is going to happen to you. Father Divine, of course, was sent to prison, and a week later, by sheer coincidence, the Judge had a heart attack and died. When the warden and the guards found out about it in the middle of the night, they raced to Father Divine's cell and woke him up. Father Divine, they said, your judge just dropped dead of a heart attack. Without missing a beat, Father Divine lifted his head and told them: "I *hated* to do it."

5   As writers, teachers or intellectuals, most of us would like to claim greater efficacy for our labors than we're entitled to. These days, literary criticism likes to think of itself as "war by other means." But it should start to wonder: have its victories come too easily? The recent turn toward politics and history in literary studies has turned the analysis of texts into a marionette theater of the political, to which we bring all the passions of our real-world commitments. And that's why it is sometimes necessary to remind ourselves of the distance from the classroom to the streets. Academic critics write essays, "readings" of literature, where the

bad guys (you know, racism or patriarchy) lose, where the forces of oppression are subverted by the boundless powers of irony and allegory that no prison can contain, and we glow with hard-won triumph. We pay homage to the marginalized and demonized, and it feels almost as if we've righted an actual injustice. (Academic battles are so fierce—the received wisdom has it—because so little is truly at stake.) I always think of the folk tale about the fellow who killed seven with one blow: flies, not giants.

Ours was the generation that took over buildings in the late 6 1960's and demanded the creation of black and women's studies programs and now, like the return of the repressed, has come back to challenge the traditional curriculum. And some of us are even attempting to redefine the canon by editing anthologies. Yet it sometimes seems that blacks are doing better in the college curriculum than they are in the streets or even on the campuses.

This is not a defeatist moan, just an acknowledgment that the 7 relation between our critical postures and the social struggles they reflect is far from transparent. That doesn't mean there's no relation, of course, only that it's a highly mediated one. In all events, I do think we should be clear about when we've swatted a fly and when we've toppled a giant. Still, you can't expect people who spend their lives teaching literature to be dispassionate about the texts they teach; no one went into literature out of an interest in literature-in-general.

I suppose the literary canon is, in no very grand sense, the 8 commonplace book of our shared culture, the archive of those texts and titles we wish to remember. And how else did those of us who teach literature fall in love with our subject than through our very own commonplace books, in which we inscribed secretly, as we might in a private diary, those passages of books that named for us what we had deeply felt, but could not say?

I kept mine from the age of 12, turning to it to repeat those 9 marvelous words that named me in some private way. From H. H. Munro to Dickens and Austen, to Hugo and de Maupassant, each resonant sentence would find its way into my book. (There's no point in avoiding the narcissism here: we are always transfixed by those passages that seem to read *us*.) Finding James Baldwin and writing him down at an Episcopal church camp in 1965—I was 15, and the Watts riots were raging—probably determined the direction of my intellectual life more than anything else I could name. I wrote and rewrote verbatim his elegantly framed paragraphs, full of sentences that were somehow both Henry Jamesian and King Jamesian, garbed as they were in the figures and cadences of the spirituals. Of course, we forget the private pleasures that brought us to the subject in the first place once we adopt the alienating strategies of formal analysis; our professional vanity is to insist that the study of literature be both beauty and truth, style and politics and everything in between.

10   In the swaddling clothes of our academic complacencies, then, few of us are prepared when we bump against something hard, and sooner or later, we do. One of the first talks I ever gave was to a packed audience at a college honors seminar, and it was one of those mistakes you don't make twice. Fresh out of graduate school, immersed in the arcane technicalities of contemporary literary theory, I was going to deliver a crunchy structuralist analysis of a slave narrative by Frederick Douglass, tracing the intricate play of its "binary oppositions." Everything was neatly schematized, formalized, analyzed; this was my Sunday-best structuralism: crisp white shirt and shiny black shoes. And it wasn't playing. If you've seen an audience glaze over, this was double glazing. Bravely, I finished my talk and, of course, asked for questions. "Yeah, brother," said a young man in the very back of the room, breaking the silence that ensued, "all we want to know is, was Booker T. Washington an Uncle Tom or not?"

11   The funny thing is, this happens to be an interesting question, a lot more interesting than my talk was. It raised all the big issues about the politics of style: about what it means to speak for another, about how you were to distinguish between canny subversion and simple co-optation—who was manipulating whom? And while I didn't exactly appreciate it at the time, the exchange did draw my attention, a little rudely perhaps, to the yawning chasm between our critical discourse and the traditions they discourse upon.

12   Obviously, some of what I'm saying is by way of *mea culpa*, because I'm speaking here as a participant in a moment of canon

formation in a so-called marginal tradition. As it happens, W. W. Norton, the "canonical" anthology publisher, will be publishing "The Norton Anthology of Afro-American Literature." The editing of this anthology has been a great dream of mine for a long time, and it represents, in the most concrete way, the project of black canon formation. But my pursuit of this project has required me to negotiate a position between those on the cultural right who claim that black literature can have no canon, no masterpieces, and those on the cultural left who wonder why anyone wants to establish the existence of a canon, any canon, in the first place.

We face the outraged reactions of those custodians of Western 13 culture who protest that the canon, that transparent decanter of Western values, may become—breathe the word—*politicized.* That people can maintain a straight face while they protest the irruption of politics into something that has always been political—well, it says something about how remarkably successful official literary histories have been in presenting themselves as natural objects, untainted by worldly interests.

I agree with those conservatives who have raised the alarm 14 about our students' ignorance of history. But part of the history we need to teach has to be the history of the very idea of the "canon," which involves the history both of literary pedagogy and of the very institution of the school. One function of literary history is then to conceal all connections between institutionalized interests and the literature we remember. Pay no attention to the men behind the curtain, booms the Great Oz of literary history.

Cynthia Ozick once chastised feminists by warning that strate- 15 gies become institutions. But isn't that really another way of warning that their strategies, Heaven forfend, may *succeed?*

Here we approach the scruples of those on the cultural left 16 who worry about, well, the price of success. "Who's co-opting whom?" might be their slogan. To them, the very idea of the canon is hierarchical, patriarchal and otherwise politically suspect. They'd like us to disavow it altogether.

But history and its institutions are not just something we 17 study, they're also something we live, and live through. And how effective and how durable our interventions in contemporary cultural politics will be depends upon the ability to mobilize the institutions that buttress and reproduce that culture. We could seclude ourselves from the real world and keep our hands clean, free from the taint of history. But that is to pay obeisance to the status quo, to the entrenched arsenal of sexual and racial authority, to say that things shouldn't change, become something other and, let's hope, better.

18   Indeed, this is one case where we've got to borrow a leaf from the right, which is exemplarily aware of the role of education in the reproduction of values. We must engage in this sort of canon reformation precisely because Mr. Bennett is correct: the teaching of literature *is* the teaching of values, not inherently, no, but contingently, yes; it is—it has become—the teaching of an esthetic and political order, in which no person of color, no woman, was ever able to discover the reflection or representation of his or her cultural image or voice. The return of "the" canon, the high canon of Western masterpieces, represents the return of an order in which my people were the subjugated, the voiceless, the invisible, the unpresented and the unrepresentable.

19   Let me be specific. Those of us working in my own tradition confront the hegemony of the Western tradition, generally, and of the larger American tradition, more locally, as we theorize about our tradition and engage in canon formation. Long after white American literature has been anthologized and canonized, and recanonized, our efforts to define a black American canon are often decried as racist, separatist, nationalist, or "essentialist." Attempts to derive theories about our literary tradition from the black tradition—a tradition, I might add, that must include black vernacular forms as well as written literary forms—are often greeted by our colleagues in traditional literature departments as a misguided desire to secede from a union that only recently, and with considerable kicking and screaming, has been forged. What is *wrong* with you people? our friends ask us in genuine passion and concern; after all, aren't we all just citizens of literature here?

20   Well, yes and no. Every black American text must confess to a complex ancestry, one high and low (that is, literary and vernacular)

but also one white and black. There can be no doubt that white
texts inform and influence black texts (and vice versa), so that a
thoroughly integrated canon of American literature is not only politically sound, it is intellectually sound as well. But the attempts
of black scholars to define a black American canon, and to derive
indigenous theories of interpretation from within this canon, are
not meant to refute the soundness of these gestures of integration.
Rather, it is a question of perspective, a question of emphasis. Just
as we can and must cite a black text within the larger American
tradition, we can and must cite it within its own tradition, a tradition not defined by a pseudoscience of racial biology, or a mysti-
cally shared essence called blackness, but by the repetition and
revision of shared themes, topoi and tropes, the call and response
of voices, their music and cacophony.

And this is our special legacy: what in 1849 Frederick Douglass   21
called the "live, calm, grave, clear, pointed, warm, sweet, melodi-
ous and powerful human voice." The presence of the past in the
African-American tradition comes to us most powerfully as *voice*,
a voice that is never quite our own—or *only* our own—however
much we want it to be. One of my earliest childhood memories
tells this story clearly.

I remember my first public performance, which I gave at the   22
age of 4 in the all-black Methodist church that my mother attended, and that her mother had attended for 50 years. It was a religious program, at which each of the children of the Sunday
school was to deliver a "piece"—as the people in our church referred to a religious recitation. Mine was the couplet "Jesus was a
boy like me, / And like Him I want to be." Not much of a recitation, but then I *was* only 4. So, after weeks of practice in elocution,
hair pressed and greased down, shirt starched and pants pressed,
I was ready to give my piece. I remember skipping along to the
church with all of the other kids, driving everyone crazy, repeating that couplet over and over, "Jesus was a boy like me, / And
like Him I want to be."

Finally we made it to the church, and it was packed—bulging   23
and glistening with black people, eager to hear pieces, despite the
fact that they had heard all of the pieces already, year after year,

like bits and fragments of a repeated master text. Because I was the youngest child on the program, I was the first to go. Miss Sarah Russell (whom we called Sister Holy Ghost—behind her back, of course) started the program with a prayer, then asked if little Skippy Gates would step forward. I did so.

24   And then the worst happened: I completely forgot the words of my piece. Standing there, pressed and starched, just as clean as I could be, in front of just about everybody in our part of town, I could not for the life of me remember one word of that piece.

25   After standing there I don't know how long, struck dumb and captivated by all of those staring eyes, I heard a voice from near the back of the church proclaim, "Jesus was a boy like me, / And like Him I want to be."

26   And my mother, having arisen to find my voice, smoothed her dress and sat down again. The congregation's applause lasted as long as its laughter as I crawled back to my seat.

27   What this moment crystallizes for me is how much of my scholarly and critical work has been an attempt to learn how to speak in the strong, compelling cadences of my mother's voice. As the black feminist scholar Hortense Spillers has recently insisted, in moving words that first occasioned this very recollection, it is "the heritage of the *mother* that the African-American male must regain as an aspect of his own personhood—the power of 'yes' to the 'female' within."

28   To reform core curriculums, to account for the comparable eloquence of the African, the Asian and the Middle Eastern traditions, is to begin to prepare our students for their roles as citizens of a world culture, educated through a truly human notion of "the humanities," rather than—as Mr. Bennett and Mr. Bloom would have it—as guardians at the last frontier outpost of white male Western culture, the keepers of the master's pieces. And for us as scholar-critics, learning to speak in the voice of the black mother is perhaps the ultimate challenge of producing a discourse of the Other.

1989

The Recoloring of Campus Life

Shelby Steele

In the past few years, we have witnessed what the National Insti-   1
tute Against Prejudice and Violence calls a "proliferation" of racial
incidents on college campuses around the country. Incidents of
on-campus "intergroup conflict" have occurred at more than 160
colleges in the last two years, according to the institute. The nature of these incidents has ranged from open racial violence—
most notoriously, the October 1986 beating of a black student at
the University of Massachusetts at Amherst after an argument
about the World Series turned into a racial bashing, with a crowd
of up to three thousand whites chasing twenty blacks—to the harassment of minority students and acts of racial or ethnic insensi-
tivity, with by far the greatest number of episodes falling in the
last two categories. At Yale last year, a swastika and the words
"white power" were painted on the university's Afro-American
cultural center. Racist jokes were aired not long ago on a campus
radio station at the University of Michigan. And at the University
of Wisconsin at Madison, members of the Zeta Beta Tau fraternity
held a mock slave auction in which pledges painted their faces
black and wore Afro wigs. Two weeks after the president of Stanford University informed the incoming freshmen class last fall
that "bigotry is out, and I mean it," two freshmen defaced a poster
of Beethoven—gave the image thick lips—and hung it on a black
student's door.

   In response, black students around the country have redis-   2
covered the militant protest strategies of the sixties. At the University of Massachusetts at Amherst, Williams College, Penn State
University, University of California–Berkeley, UCLA, Stanford University, and countless other campuses, black students have sat in,
marched, and rallied. But much of what they were marching and
rallying about seemed less a response to specific racial incidents
than a call for broader action on the part of the colleges and uni-

versities they were attending. Black students have demanded everything from more black faculty members and new courses on racism to the addition of "ethnic" foods in the cafeteria. There is the sense in these demands that racism runs deep. Is the campus becoming the battleground for a renewed war between the races? I don't think so, not really. But if it is not a war, the problem of campus racism does represent a new and surprising hardening of racial lines within the most traditionally liberal and tolerant of America's institutions—its universities.

3   As a black who has spent his entire adult life on predominantly white campuses, I found it hard to believe that the problem of campus racism was as dramatic as some of the incidents seemed to make it. The incidents I read or heard about often seemed prankish and adolescent, though not necessarily harmless. There is a meanness in them but not much menace; no one is proposing to reinstitute Jim Crow on campus. On the California campus where I now teach, there have been few signs of racial tension.

4   And, or course, universities are not where racial problems tend to arise. When I went to college in the mid-sixties, colleges were oases of calm and understanding in a racially tense society; campus life—with its traditions of tolerance and fairness, its very distance from the "real" world—imposed a degree of broadmindedness on even the most provincial students. If I met whites who were not anxious to be friends with blacks, most were at least vaguely friendly to the cause of our freedom. In any case, there was no guerrilla activity against our presence, no "mine field of racism" (as one black student at Berkeley recently put it to me) to negotiate. I wouldn't say that the phrase "campus racism" is a contradiction in terms, but until recently it certainly seemed an incongruence.

5   But a greater incongruence is the generational timing of this new problem on the campuses. Today's undergraduates were born after the passage of the 1964 Civil Rights Act. They grew up in an age when racial equality was for the first time enforceable by law.

This too was a time when blacks suddenly appeared on television, as mayors of big cities, as icons of popular culture, as teachers, and in some cases even as neighbors. Today's black and white college students, veterans of "Sesame Street" and often of integrated grammar and high schools, have had more opportunities to know each other than any previous generation in American history. Not enough opportunities, perhaps, but enough to make the notion of racial tension on campus something of a mystery, at least to me.

To look at this mystery, I left my own campus with its burden 6 of familiarity and talked with black and white students at California schools where racial incidents had occurred: Stanford, UCLA, and Berkeley. I spoke with black and white students—not with Asians and Hispanics—because, as always, blacks and white represent the deepest lines of division, and because I hesitate to wander onto the complex territory of other minority groups. A phrase by William H. Gass—"the hidden internality of things"—describes, with maybe a little too much grandeur, what I hoped to find. But it is what I wanted to find, for this is the kind of problem that makes a black person nervous, which is not to say that it doesn't unnerve whites as well. Once every six months or so someone yells "nigger" at me from a passing car. I don't like to think that these solo artists might soon make up a chorus, or worse, that this chorus might one day soon sing to me from the paths of my own campus.

I have long believed that the trouble between the races is sel- 7 dom what it appears to be. It was not hard to see after my first talks with students that racial tension on campus is a problem that misrepresents itself. It has the same look, the archetypal pattern, of America's timeless racial conflict—white racism and black protest. And I think part of our concern over it comes from the fact that it has the feel of a relapse, illness gone and come again. But if we are seeing the same symptoms, I don't believe we are dealing with the same illness. For one thing, I think racial tension on campus is more the result of racial equality than inequality.

How to live with racial difference has been America's pro- 8 found social problem. For the first hundred years or so following emancipation it was controlled by a legally sanctioned inequality that kept the races from each other. No longer is this the case. On campuses today, as throughout society, blacks enjoy equality under the law—a profound social advancement. No student may be kept out of a class or a dormitory or an extracurricular activity because of his or her race. But there is a paradox here: on a campus where members of all races are gathered, mixed together in the classroom as well as socially, differences are more exposed than ever. And this is where the trouble starts. For members of each race—young adults coming into their own, often away from home for the first time—bring to this site of freedom, exploration, and (now, today) equality, very deep fears, anxieties, inchoate feelings of racial shame, anger, and guilt. These feelings could lie dormant in the home, in familiar neighborhoods, in simpler days of childhood. But the college campus, with its structures of interaction and adult-level competition—the big exam, the dorm, the mixer—is another matter. I think campus racism is born of the rub between racial difference and a setting, the campus itself, devoted to interaction and equality. On our campuses, such concentrated microsocieties, all that remains unresolved between blacks and whites, all the old wounds and shames that have never been addressed, present themselves for attention—and present our youth with pressures they cannot always handle.

I have mentioned one paradox: racial fears and anxieties among blacks and whites, bubbling up in an era of racial equality under the law, in settings that are among the freest and fairest in society. But there is another, related paradox, stemming from the notion of—and practice of—affirmative action. Under the provisions of the Equal Employment Opportunity Act of 1972, all state governments and institutions (including universities) were forced to initiate plans to increase the proportion of minority and women employees and, in the case of universities, of students too. Affirmative action plans that establish racial quotas were ruled unconstitutional more than ten years ago in *University of California* v. *Bakke,* but such plans are still thought by some to secretly exist, and lawsuits having to do with alleged quotas are still very much with us. But quotas are only the most controversial aspect of affirmative action; the principal of affirmative action is reflected in various university programs aimed at redressing and overcoming past patterns of discrimination. Of course, to be conscious of past patterns of discriminations—the fact, say, that public schools in the black inner cities are more crowded and employ fewer top-notch teachers than a white suburban public school, and that this is a factor in student performance—is only reasonable. But in doing this we also call attention quite obviously to difference: in the case of blacks and whites, racial difference. What has emerged on campus in recent years—as a result of the new equality and of affirmative action and, in a sense, as a result of progress—is a *politics of difference,* a troubling, volatile politics in which each group justifies itself, its sense of worth and its pursuit of power, through difference alone.

In this context, racial, ethnic, and gender differences become 10 forms of sovereignty, campuses become balkanized, and each group fights with whatever means are available. No doubt there are many factors that have contributed to the rise of racial tension on campus: What has been the role of fraternities, which have returned to campus with their inclusions and exclusions? What role has the heightened notion of college as some first step to personal, financial success played in increasing competition, and thus tension? But mostly, what I sense is that in interactive settings, fighting the fights of "difference," old ghosts are stirred and haunt again. Black and white Americans simply have the power to make each other feel shame and guilt. In most situations, we may be able to deny these feelings, keep them at bay. But these feelings are likely to surface on college campuses, where young people are groping for identity and power, and where difference is made to matter so greatly. In a way, racial tension on campus in the eighties might have been inevitable.

I would like, first, to discuss black students, their anxieties 11 and vulnerabilities. The accusation black Americans have always lived with is that they are inferior—inferior simply because they are black. And this accusation has been too uniform, too ingrained in cultural imagery, too enforced by law, custom, and every form of power not to have left a mark. Black inferiority was a precept accepted by the founders of this nation; it was a principle of social organization that relegated blacks to the sidelines of American life. So when young black students find themselves on white campuses surrounded by those who have historically claimed superiority, they are also surrounded by the myth of their inferiority.

12   Of course, it is true that many young people come to college with some anxiety about not being good enough. But only blacks come wearing a color that is still, in the minds of some, a sign of inferiority. Poles, Jews, Hispanics, and other groups also endure degrading stereotypes. But two things make the myth of black inferiority a far heavier burden—the broadness of its scope and its incarnation in color. There are not only more stereotypes of blacks than of other groups, but these stereotypes are also more dehumanizing, more focused on the most despised human traits: stupidity, laziness, sexual immorality, dirtiness, and so on. In America's racial and ethnic hierarchy, blacks have clearly been relegated to the lowest level—have been burdened with an ambiguous, animalistic humanity. Moreover, this is made unavoidable for blacks by sheer visibility of black skin, a skin that evokes the myth of inferiority on sight. Today this myth is sadly reinforced for many black students by affirmative action programs, under which blacks may often enter college with lower test scores and high school grade point averages than whites. "They see me as an affirmative action case," one black student told me at UCLA. This reinforces the myth of inferiority by implying that blacks are not good enough to make it into college on their own.

13   So when a black student enters college, the myth of inferiority compounds the normal anxiousness over whether he or she will be good enough. This anxiety is not only personal but also racial. The families of these students will have pounded into them the fact that blacks are not inferior. And probably more than anything it is this pounding that finally leaves the mark. If I am not inferior, why the need to say so?

14   This myth of inferiority constitutes a very sharp and ongoing anxiety for young blacks, the nature of which is very precise: it is the terror that somehow, through one's actions or by virtue of some "proof" (a poor grade, a flubbed response in class), one's fear of inferiority—inculcated in ways large and small by society—will be confirmed as real. On a university campus where intelligence itself is the ultimate measure, this anxiety is bound to be triggered.

A black student I met at UCLA was disturbed a little when I 15
asked him if he ever felt vulnerable—anxious about "black inferiority"—as a black student. But after a long pause, he finally said,
"I think I do." The example he gave was of a large lecture class
he'd taken with over three hundred students. Fifty or so black students sat in the back of the lecture hall and "acted out every
stereotype in the book." They were loud, ate food, came in late—
and generally got lower grades than whites in the class. "I knew I
would be seen like them, and I didn't like it. I never sat by them."
Seen like what, I asked, though we both knew the answer. "As
lazy, ignorant, and stupid," he said sadly.

Had the group at the back been white fraternity brothers, they 16
would not have been seen as dumb whites, of course. And a frat
brother who worried about his grades would not worry that he
been seen "like them." The terror in this situation for the black
student I spoke with was that his own deeply buried anxiety
would be given credence, that the myth would be verified, and
that he would feel shame and humiliation not because of who he
was but simply because he was black. In this lecture hall his race,
quite apart from his performance, might subject him to four
unendurable feelings—diminishment, accountability to the pre-
conceptions of whites, a powerlessness to change those precon-
ceptions, and finally, shame. These are the feelings that make up
his racial anxiety, and that of all blacks on any campus. On a white
campus a black is never far from these feelings, and even his unconscious knowledge that he is subject to them can undermine his
self-esteem. There are blacks on any campus who are not up to
doing good college-level work. Certain black students may not be
happy or motivated or in the appropriate field of study—*just like
whites*. (Let us not forget that many white students get poor
grades, fail, drop out.) Moreover, many more blacks than whites
are not quite prepared for college, may have to catch up, owing to
factors beyond their control: poor previous schooling, for example. But the white who has to catch up will not be anxious that his
being behind is a matter of his whiteness, of his being racially inferior. The black student may well have such a fear.

This, I believe, is one reason why black colleges in America 17
turn out 37 percent of all black college graduates though they

enroll only 16 percent of black college students. Without whites around on campus, the myth of inferiority is in abeyance and, along with it, a great reservoir of culturally imposed self-doubt. On black campuses, feelings of inferiority are personal; on campuses with a white majority, a black's problems have a way of becoming a "black" problem.

18   But this feeling of vulnerability a black may feel, in itself, is not as serious a problem as what he or she does with it. To admit that one is made anxious in integrated situations about the myth of racial inferiority is difficult for young blacks. It seems like admitting that one is racially inferior. And so, most often, the student will deny harboring the feelings. This is where some of the pangs of racial tension begin, because denial always involves distortion.

19   In order to deny a problem we must tell ourselves that the problem is something different from what it really is. A black student at Berkeley told me that he felt defensive every time he walked into a classroom of white faces. When I asked why, he said, "Because I know they're all racists. They think blacks are stupid." Of course, it may be true that some whites feel this way, but the singular focus on white racism allows this student to obscure his own underlying racial anxiety. He can now say that his problem—facing a classroom of white faces, *fearing* that they think he is dumb—is entirely the result of certifiable white racism and has nothing to do with his own anxieties, or even that this particular academic subject may not be his best. Now all the terror of his anxiety, its powerful energy, is devoted to simply *seeing* racism. Whatever evidence of racism he finds—and looking this hard, he will no doubt find some—can be brought in to buttress his distorted view of the problem while his actual deep-seated anxiety goes unseen.

20   Denial, and the distortion that results, places the problem *outside* the self and in the world. It is not that I have any inferiority anxiety because of my race; it is that I am going to school with people who don't like blacks. This is the shift in thinking that allows black students to reenact the protest pattern of the sixties. *Denied racial anxiety–distortion–reenactment* is the process by which feelings of inferiority are transformed into an exaggerated white menace—which is then protested against with the techniques of

the past. Under the sway of this process, black students believe that history is repeating itself, that it's just like the sixties, or fifties. In fact, it is not-yet-healed wounds from the past, rather than the inequality that created the wounds, that is the real problem.

This process generates an unconscious need to exaggerate the level of racism on campus—to make it a matter of the system, not just a handful of students. Racism is the avenue away from the true inner anxiety. How many students demonstrating for black theme dorms—demonstrating in the style of the sixties, when the battle was to win for blacks a place on campus—might be better off spending their time reading and studying? Black students have the highest dropout rate and the lowest grade point average of any group in American universities. This need not be so. And it is not the result of not having black theme dorms. 21

It was my very good fortune to go to college in 1964, when the question of black "inferiority" was openly talked about among blacks. The summer before I left for college, I heard Martin Luther King speak in Chicago, and he laid it on the line for black students everywhere: "When you are behind in a footrace, the only way to get ahead is to run faster than the man in front of you. So when your white roommate says he's tired and goes to sleep, you stay up and burn the midnight oil." His statement that we were "behind in a footrace" acknowledged that, because of history, of few opportunities, of racism, we were, in a sense, "inferior." But this had to do with what had been done to our parents and their parents, not with inherent inferiority. And because it was acknowledged, it was presented to us as a challenge rather than a mark of shame. 22

Of the eighteen black students (in a student body of one thousand) who were on campus in my freshman year, all graduated, though a number of us were not from the middle class. At the university where I currently teach, the dropout rate for black students in 72 percent, despite the presence of several academic support programs, a counseling center with black counselors, an Afro-American studies department, black faculty, administrators, and staff, a general education curriculum that emphasizes 23 "cultural pluralism," an Educational Opportunities Program, a mentor program, a black faculty and staff association, and an administration and faculty that often announce the need to do more for black students.

24   It may be unfair to compare my generation with the current one. Parents do this compulsively and to little end but self-congratulation. But I don't congratulate my generation. I think we were advantaged. We came along at a time when racial integration was held in high esteem. And integration was a very challenging social concept for both blacks and whites. We were remaking ourselves—that's what one did at college—and making history. We had something to prove. This was a profound advantage; it gave us clarity and a challenge. Achievement in the American mainstream was the goal of integration, and the best thing about this challenge was its secondary message—that we *could* achieve.

25   There is much irony in the fact that black power would come along in the late sixties and change all this. Black power was a movement of uplift and pride, and yet it also delivered the weight of pride—a weight that would burden black students from then on. Black power "nationalized" the black identity, made blackness itself an object of celebration, an allegiance. But if it transformed a mark of shame into a mark of pride, it also, in the name of pride, required the denial of racial anxiety. Without a frank account of one's anxieties, there is no clear direction, no concrete challenge. Black students today do not get as clear a message from their racial identity as my generation got. They are not filled with the same urgency to prove themselves because black pride has said, *You're already proven, already equal, as good as anybody.*

26   The "black identity" shaped by black power most forcefully contributes to racial tensions on campuses by basing entitlement more on race than on constitutional rights and standards of merit. With integration, black entitlement derived from constitutional principles of fairness. Black power changed this by skewing the formula from rights to color—if you were black, you were entitled. Thus the United Coalition Against Racism (UCAR) at the University of Michigan could "demand" two years ago that all

black professors be given immediate tenure, that there is a special pay incentive for black professors, and that money be provided for an all-black student union. In this formula, black becomes the very color of entitlement, an extra right in itself, and a very dangerous grandiosity is promoted in which blackness amounts to specialness.

Race is, by any standard, an unprincipled source of power. 27 And on campuses the use of racial power by one group makes racial, ethnic, or gender difference a currency of power for all groups. When I make my *difference* into power, other groups must seize upon their difference to contain my power and maintain their position relative to me. Very quickly a kind of politics of difference emerges in which racial, ethnic, and gender groups are forced to assert their entitlement and vie for power based on the single quality that makes them different from one another.

On many campuses today academic departments and pro- 28 grams are established on the basis of difference—black studies, women's studies, Asian studies, and so on—despite the fact that there is nothing in these "difference" departments that cannot be studied within traditional academic disciplines. If their rationale is truly past exclusion from the mainstream curriculum, shouldn't the goal now be complete inclusion rather than separateness? I think this logic is overlooked because those groups are too interested in the power their difference can bring, and they insist on separate departments and programs as tribute to that power.

This politics of difference makes everyone on campus a mem- 29 ber of a minority group. It also makes racial tension inevitable. To highlight one's difference as a source of advantage is also, indirectly, to inspire the enemies of that difference. When blackness (and femaleness) become power, then white maleness is also sanctioned as power. A white male student I spoke with at Stanford said, "One of my friends said the other day that we should get together and start up a white student union and come up with a list of demands."

It is certainly true that white maleness has long been an unfair 30 source of power. But the sin of white male power is precisely its use of race and gender as a source of entitlement. When minorities and women use their race, ethnicity, and gender in the same way, they not only commit the same sin but also, indirectly, sanction the very form of power that oppressed them in the first place. The politics of difference is based on a tit-for-tat sort of logic in which every victory only calls one's enemies to arms.

31   This elevation of difference undermines the communal impulse by making each group foreign and inaccessible to others. When difference is celebrated rather than remarked, people must think in terms of difference, they must find meaning in difference, and this meaning comes from an endless process of contrasting one's group with other groups. Blacks use whites to define themselves as different, women use men, Hispanics use whites and blacks, and on it goes. And in the process each group mythologizes and mystifies its difference, puts it beyond the full comprehension of outsiders. Difference becomes inaccessible preciousness toward which outsiders are expected to be simply and uncomprehendingly reverential. But beware: in this world, even the insulated world of the college campus, preciousness is a balloon asking for a needle. At Smith College graffiti appears: "Niggers, spics, and chinks. Quit complaining or get out."

32   I think that those who run our colleges and universities are every bit as responsible for the politics of difference as are minority students. To correct the exclusions once caused by race and gender, universities—under the banner of affirmative action—have relied too heavily on race and gender as criteria. So rather than break the link between difference and power, they have reinforced it. On most campuses today, a well-to-do black student with two professional parents is qualified by his race for scholarship monies that are not available to a lower-middle-class white student. A white female with a private school education and every form of cultural advantage comes under the affirmative action umbrella. This kind of inequity is an invitation to backlash.

33   What universities are quite rightly trying to do is compensate people for past discrimination and the deprivations that followed from it. But race and gender alone offer only the grossest measure of this. And the failure of universities has been their backing away from the challenge of identifying principles of fairness and merit that make finer and more equitable distinctions. The real challenge is not simply to include a certain number of blacks, but to

end discrimination against all blacks and to offer special help to those with talent who have also been economically deprived.

With regard to black students, affirmative action has led uni- 34 versities to correlate color with poverty and disadvantage in so absolute a way as to encourage the politics of difference. But why have they gone along with this? My belief is that it is due to the specific form of racial anxiety to which whites are most subject.

Most of the white students I talked with spoke as if from un- 35 der a faint cloud of accusation. There was always a ring of defensiveness in their complaints about blacks. A white student I spoke to at UCLA told me: "Most white students on this campus think the black student leadership here is made up of oversensitive crybabies who spend all their time looking for things to kick up a ruckus about." A white student at Stanford said, "Blacks do nothing but complain and ask for sympathy when everyone really knows that they don't do well because they don't try. If they worked harder, they could do as well as everyone else."

That these students felt accused was most obvious in their 36 compulsion to assure me that they were not racist. Oblique versions of some-of-my-best-friends-are stories came ritualistically before or after critiques of black students. Some said flatly, "I am not a racist, but . . ." Of course, we all deny being racist, but we only do this compulsively, I think, when we are working against an accusation of bias. I think it was the color of my skin itself that accused them.

This was the meta-message that surrounded these conversa- 37 tions like an aura, and it is, I believe, the core of white American racial anxiety. My skin not only accused them; it judged them. And this judgment was a sad gift of history that brought them to account whether they deserved such accountability or not. It said that wherever and whenever blacks were concerned, they had reason to feel guilt. And whether it was earned or unearned, I think it was guilt that set off the compulsion in these students to disclaim. I believe it is true that, in America, black people make white people feel guilty.

Guilt is the essence of white anxiety just as inferiority is the 38 essence of black anxiety. And the terror that it carries for whites is the terror of discovering that one has reason to feel guilt where blacks are concerned—not so much because of what blacks might think but because of what guilt can say about oneself. If the darkest fear of blacks is inferiority, the darkest fear of whites is that their better lot in life is at least partially the result of their capacity for evil—their capacity to dehumanize an entire people for their own benefit and then to be indifferent to the devastation their dehumanization has wrought on successive generations of their victims. This is the terror that whites are vulnerable to regarding blacks. And the mere fact of being white is sufficient to feel it, since even whites with hearts clean of racism benefit from being white—benefit at the expense of blacks. This is a conditional guilt having nothing to do with individual intentions or actions. And it makes for a very powerful anxiety because it threatens whites with a view of themselves as inhuman, just as inferiority threatens blacks with a similar view of themselves. At the dark core of both anxieties is a suspicion of incomplete humanity.

39   So, the white students I met were not just meeting me; they were also meeting the possibility of their own inhumanity. And this, I think, is what explains how some young white college students in the late eighties could so frankly take part in racially insensitive and outright racist acts. They were expected to be cleaner of racism than any previous generation—they were born into the Great Society. But this expectation overlooks the fact that, for them, color is still an accusation and judgment. In black faces there is a discomforting reflection of white collective shame. Blacks remind them that their racial innocence is questionable, that they are the beneficiaries of past and present racism, and the sins of the father may well have been visited on the children.

40   And yet young whites tell themselves that they had nothing to do with the oppression of black people. They have a stronger belief in their racial innocence than any previous generation of whites and a natural hostility toward anyone who would challenge that innocence. So (with a great deal of individual variation) they can end up in the paradoxical position of being hostile to blacks as a way of defending their own racial innocence.

41   I think this is what the young white editors of the *Dartmouth Review* were doing when they harassed black music professor William Cole. Weren't they saying, in effect, I am so free of racial

guilt that I can afford to attack blacks ruthlessly and still be racially innocent? The ruthlessness of these attacks was a form of denial, a badge of innocence. The more they were charged with racism, the more ugly and confrontational their harassment became (an escalation unexplained even by the serious charges against Professor Cole). Racism became a means of rejecting racial guilt, a way of showing that they were not, ultimately, racists.

The politics of difference sets up a struggle for innocence 42 among all groups. When difference is the currency of power, each group must fight for the innocence that entitles it to power. To gain this innocence, blacks sting whites with guilt, remind them of their racial past, accuse them of new and more subtle forms of racism. One way whites retrieve their innocence is to discredit blacks and deny their difficulties, for in this denial is the denial of their own guilt. To blacks this denial looks like racism, a racism that feeds black innocence and encourages them to throw more guilt at whites. And so the cycle continues. The politics of difference leads each group to pick at the vulnerabilities of the other.

Men and women who run universities—whites, mostly—par- 43 ticipate in the politics of difference because they handle their guilt differently than do many of their students. They don't deny it, but still they don't want to *feel* it. And to avoid this feeling of guilt they have tended to go along with whatever blacks put on the table rather than work with them to assess their real needs. University administrators have too often been afraid of guilt and have relied on negotiation and capitulation more to appease their own guilt than to help blacks and other minorities. Administrators would never give white students a racial theme dorm where they could be "more comfortable with people of their own kind," yet more and more universities are doing this for black students, thus fostering a kind of voluntary segregation. To avoid the anxieties of integrated situations blacks ask for theme dorms; to avoid guilt, white administrators give theme dorms.

When everyone is on the run from their anxieties about race, 44 race relations on campus can be reduced to the negotiation of avoidances. A pattern of demand and concession develops in which both sides use the other to escape themselves. Black studies departments, black deans of student affairs, black counseling programs, Afro houses, black theme dorms, black homecoming dances and graduation ceremonies—black students and white administrators have slowly engineered a machinery of separatism that, in the name of sacred difference, redraws the ugly lines of segregation.

45   Black students have not sufficiently helped themselves, and universities, despite all their concessions, have not really done much for blacks. If both faced their anxieties, I think they would see the same thing: academic parity with all other groups should be the overriding mission of black students, and it should also be the first goal that universities have for their black students. Blacks can only *know* they are as good as others when they are, in fact, as good—when their grades are higher and their dropout rate lower. Nothing under the sun will substitute for this, and no amount of concessions will bring it about.

46   Universities can never be free of guilt until they truly help black students, which means leading and challenging them rather than negotiating and capitulating. It means inspiring them to achieve academic parity, nothing less, and helping them to see their own weaknesses as their greatest challenge. It also means dismantling the machinery of separatism, breaking the link between difference and power, and skewing the formula for entitlement away from race and gender and toward the fundamental rights.

47   As for the young white students who have rediscovered swastikas and the word "nigger," I think that they suffer from an exaggerated sense of their own innocence, as if they were incapable of evil and beyond the reach of guilt. But it is also true that the politics of difference creates an environment that threatens their innocence and makes them defensive. White students are not invited to the negotiating table from which they see blacks and others walk away with concessions. The presumption is that they do not deserve to be there because they are white. So they can only be defensive, and the less mature among them will be aggressive. Guerrilla activity will ensue. Of course this is wrong, but it is also a reflection of an environment where difference carries power and where whites have the wrong "difference."

I think universities should emphasize commonality as a higher 48
value than "diversity" and "pluralism"—buzzwords for the politics of difference. Difference that does not rest on a clearly delin-
eated foundation of commonality is not only inaccessible to those
who are not part of the ethnic or racial group, but also antagonistic
to them. Difference can enrich only the common ground.

Integration has become an abstract term today, having to do 49
with little more than numbers and racial balances. But it once
stood for a high and admirable set of values. It made difference
second to commonality, and it asked members of all races to face
whatever fears they inspired in each other. I doubt the word will
have a new vogue, but the values, under whatever name, are
worth working for.

1989

Virtual Students, Digital Classroom

Neil Postman

1

If one has a trusting relationship with one's students (let us say,
graduate students), it is not altogether gauche to ask them if they
believe in God (with a capital G). I have done this three or four
times and most students say they do. Their answer is preliminary
to the next question: If someone you love were desperately ill, and
you had to choose between praying to God for his or her recovery
or administering an antibiotic (as prescribed by a competent
physician), which would you choose?   2

Most say the question is silly since the alternatives are not
mutually exclusive. Of course. But suppose they were—which
would you choose? God helps those who help themselves, some
say in choosing the antibiotic, therefore getting the best of two

possible belief systems. But if pushed to the wall (e.g., God does not always help those who help themselves; God helps those who pray and who believe), most choose the antibiotic, after noting that the question is asinine and proves nothing. Of course, the question was not asked, in the first place, to prove anything but to begin a discussion of the nature of belief. And I do not fail to inform the students, by the way, that there has recently emerged evidence of a "scientific" nature that when sick people are prayed for they do better than those who aren't.

3   As the discussion proceeds, important distinctions are made among the different meanings of "belief," but at some point it becomes far from asinine to speak of the god of Technology—in the sense that people believe technology works, that they rely on it, that it makes promises, that they are bereft when denied access to it, that they are delighted when they are in its presence, that for most people it works in mysterious ways, that they condemn people who speak against it, that they stand in awe of it and that, in the "born again" mode, they will alter their life-styles, their schedules, their habits, and their relationships to accommodate it. If this be not a form of religious belief, what is?

4   In all strands of American cultural life, you can find so many examples of technological adoration that it is possible to write a book about it. And I would if it had not already been done so well. But nowhere do you find more enthusiasm for the god of Technology than among educators. In fact, there are those, like Lewis Perelman, who argue (for example, in his book, *School's Out*) that modern information technologies have rendered schools entirely irrelevant since there is now much more information available outside the classroom than inside it. This is by no means considered an outlandish idea. Dr. Diane Ravitch, former Assistant Secretary of Education, envisions, with considerable relish, the challenge that technology presents to the tradition that "children (and adults) should be educated in a specific place, for a certain number of hours, and a certain number of days during the week and year." In other words, that children should be educated in school. Imagining the possibilities of an information superhighway offering perhaps a thousand channels, Dr. Ravitch assures us that:

In this new world of pedagogical plenty, children and adults will be able to dial up a program on their home television to learn whatever they want to know, at their own convenience. If Little Eva cannot sleep, she can learn algebra instead. At her home-learning station, she will tune in to a series of interesting problems that are presented in an interactive medium, much like video games. . . .

Young John may decide that he wants to learn the history of modern Japan, which he can do by dialing up the greatest authorities and teachers on the subject, who will not only use dazzling graphs and illustrations, but will narrate a historical video that excites his curiosity and imagination.

In this vision there is, it seems to me, a confident and typical 5 sense of unreality. Little Eva can't sleep, so she decides to learn a little algebra? Where does Little Eva come from? Mars? If not, it is more likely she will tune in to a good movie. Young John decides that he wants to learn the history of modern Japan? How did young John come to this point? How is it that he never visited a library up to now? Or is that he, too, couldn't sleep and decided that a little modern Japanese history was just what he needed?

What Ravitch is talking about here is not a new technology 6 but a new species of child, one who, in any case, no one has seen up to now. Of course, new technologies do make new kinds of people, which leads to a second objection to Ravitch's conception of the future. There is a kind of forthright determinism about the imagined world described in it. The technology is here or will be; we must use it because it is there; we will become the kind of people the technology requires us to be, and whether we like it or not, we will remake our institutions to accommodate technology. All of this must happen because it is good for us, but in any case, we have no choice. This point of view is present in very nearly every statement about the future relationship of learning to technology. And, as in Ravitch's scenario, there is always a cheery, gee-whiz tone to the prophecies. Here is one produced by the National Academy of Sciences, written by Hugh McIntosh.

School for children of the Information Age will be vastly different than it was for Mom and Dad.

Interested in biology? Design your own life forms with computer simulation.

Having trouble with a science project? Teleconference about it with a research scientist.

Bored with the real world? Go into a virtual physics lab and rewrite the laws of gravity.

These are the kinds of hands-on learning experiences schools could be providing right now. The technologies that make them possible are already here, and today's youngsters, regardless of economic status, know how to use them. They spend hours with them every week—not in the classroom, but in their own homes and in video game centers at every shopping mall.

7   It is always interesting to attend to the examples of learning, and the motivations that ignite them, in the songs of love that technophiles perform for us. It is, for example, not easy to imagine research scientists all over the world teleconferencing with thousands of students who are having difficulty with their science projects. I can't help thinking that most research scientists would put a stop to this rather quickly. But I find it especially revealing that in the scenario above we have an example of a technological solution to a psychological problem that would seem to be exceedingly serious. We are presented with a student who is "bored with the real world." What does it mean to say someone is bored with the real world, especially one so young? Can a journey into virtual reality cure such a problem? And if it can, will our troubled youngster want to return to the real world? Confronted with a student who is bored with the real world, I don't think we can solve the problem so easily by making available a virtual reality physics lab.

8   The role that new technology should play in schools or anywhere else is something that needs to be discussed without the hyperactive fantasies of cheerleaders. In particular, the computer and its associated technologies are awesome additions to a culture, and are quite capable of altering the psychic, not to mention the sleeping, habits of our young. But like all important technologies of the past, they are Faustian bargains,[1] giving and taking away, sometimes in equal measure, sometimes more in one way

---

[1] The legendary Doctor Faustus exchanged his soul for infinite knowledge in a pact with the Devil.

than the other. It is strange—indeed, shocking—that with the twenty-first century so close, we can still talk of new technologies as if they were unmixed blessings—gifts, as it were, from the gods. Don't we all know what the combustion engine has done for us and against us? What television is doing for us and against us? At the very least, what we need to discuss about Little Eva, Young John, and McIntosh's trio is what they will lose, and what we will lose, if they enter a world in which computer technology is their chief source of motivation, authority, and, apparently, psychological sustenance. Will they become, as Joseph Weizenbaum warns,[2] more impressed by calculation than human judgment? Will speed of response become, more than ever, a defining quality of intelligence? If, indeed, the idea of a school will be dramatically altered, what kinds of learning will be neglected, perhaps made impossible? Is virtual reality a new form of therapy? If it is, what are its dangers?

These are serious matters, and they need to be discussed by 9 those who know something about children from the planet Earth, and whose vision of children's needs, and the needs of society, go beyond thinking of school mainly as a place for the convenient distribution of information. Schools are not now and have never been largely about getting information to children. That has been on the schools' agenda, of course, but has always been way down on the list. For technological utopians, the computer vaults information access to the top. This reshuffling of priorities comes at a most inopportune time. The goal of giving people greater access to more information faster, more conveniently, and in more diverse forms was the main technological thrust of the nineteenth century. Some folks haven't noticed it but that problem was largely solved, so that for almost a hundred years there has been more information available to the young outside the school than inside. That fact did not make the schools obsolete, nor does it now make them obsolete. Yes, it is true that Little Eva, the insomniac from Mars, could turn on an algebra lesson, thanks to the

[2]Weizenbaum's 1976 book, *Computer Power and Human Reason: From Judgment to Calculation*, raises these questions.

computer, in the wee hours of the morning. She could also, if she wished, read a book or magazine, watch television, turn on the radio or listen to music. All of this she could have done before the computer. The computer does not solve any problem she has but does exacerbate one. For Little Eva's problem is not how to get access to a well-structured algebra lesson but what to do with all the information available to her during the day, as well as during sleepless nights. Perhaps this is why she couldn't sleep in the first place. Little Eva, like the rest of us, is overwhelmed by information. She lives in a culture that has 260,000 billboards, 17,000 newspapers, 12,000 periodicals, 27,000 video outlets for renting tapes, 400 million television sets, and well over 500 million radios, not including those in automobiles. There are 40,000 new book titles published every year, and each day 41 million photographs are taken. And thanks to the computer, more than 60 billion pieces of advertising junk come into our mailboxes every year. Everything from telegraphy and photography in the nineteenth century to the silicon chip in the twentieth has amplified the din of information intruding on Little Eva's consciousness. From millions of sources all over the globe, through every possible channel and medium—light waves, air waves, ticker tape, computer banks, telephone wires, television cables, satellites, and printing presses—information pours in. Behind it in every imaginable form of storage—on paper, on video, on audiotape, on disks, film, and silicon chips—is an even greater volume of information waiting to be retrieved. In the face of this we might ask: What can schools do for Little Eva besides making still more information available? If there is nothing, then new technologies will indeed make schools obsolete. But in fact, there is plenty.

10   One thing that comes to mind is that schools can provide her with a serious form of technology education. Something quite different from instruction in using computers to process information, which, it strikes me, is a trivial thing to do, for two reasons. In the first place, approximately 35 million people have already learned how to use computers without the benefit of school instruction. If the schools do nothing, most of the population will know how to use computers in the next ten years, just as most of the population learns how to drive a car without school instruction. In the second

place, what we needed to know about cars—as we need to know about computers, television, and other important technologies—is not how to use them but how they use *us*. In the case of cars, what we needed to think about in the early twentieth century was not how to drive them but what they would do to our air, our landscape, our social relations, our family life, and our cities. Suppose in 1946 we had started to address similar questions about television: What will be its effects on our political institutions, our psychic habits, our children, our religious conceptions, our economy? Would we be better positioned today to control TV's massive assault on American culture? I am talking here about making technology itself an object of inquiry so that Little Eva and Young John are more interested in asking questions about the computer than getting answers from it.

I am not arguing against using computers in school. I am 11 arguing against our sleepwalking attitudes toward it, against allowing it to distract us from important things, against making a god of it. This is what Theodore Roszak warned against in *The Cult of Information:* "Like all cults," he wrote, "this one also has the intention of enlisting mindless allegiance and acquiescence. People who have no clear idea of what they mean by information or why they should want so much of it are nonetheless prepared to believe that we live in an Information Age, which makes every computer around us what the relics of the True Cross were in the Age of Faith: emblems of salvation." To this, I would add the sage observation of Alan Kay of Apple Computer. Kay is widely associated with the invention of the personal computer, and certainly has an interest in schools using them. Nonetheless, he has repeatedly said that any problems the schools cannot solve without computers, they cannot solve with them. What are some of those problems? There is, for example, the traditional task of teaching children how to behave in groups. One might even say that schools have never been essentially about individualized learning. It is true, of course, that groups do not learn, individuals do. But the idea of a school is that individuals must learn in a setting in which individual needs are subordinated to group interests. Unlike other media of mass communication, which celebrate individual response and are experienced in private, the classroom is intended to tame the ego, to connect the individual with others, to demonstrate the value and necessity of group cohesion. At present, most scenarios describing the uses of computers have children solving problems alone; Little Eva, Young John, and the others are doing just that. The presence of other children may, indeed, be an annoyance.

12   Like the printing press before it, the computer has a powerful bias toward amplifying personal autonomy and individual problem-solving. That is why educators must guard against computer technology's undermining some of the important reasons for having the young assemble (to quote Ravitch) "in a specific place, for a certain number of hours, and a certain number of days during the week and year."

13   Although Ravitch is not exactly against what she calls "state schools," she imagines them as something of a relic of a pretechnological age. She believes that the new technologies will offer all children equal access to information. Conjuring up a hypothetical Little Mary who is presumably from a poorer home than Little Eva, Ravitch imagines that Mary will have the same opportunities as Eva "to learn any subject, and to learn it from the same master teachers as children in the richest neighborhood." For all of its liberalizing spirit, this scenario makes some important omissions. One is that though new technologies may be a solution to the learning of "subjects," they work against the learning of what are called "social values," including an understanding of democratic processes. If one reads the first chapter of Robert Fulghum's *All I Really Need to Know I Learned in Kindergarten*, one will find an elegant summary of a few things Ravitch's scenario has left out. They include learning the following lessons: Share everything, play fair, don't hit people, put things back where you found them, clean up your own mess, wash your hands before you eat, and, of course, flush. The only thing wrong with Fulghum's book is that no one has learned all these things at kindergarten's end. We have ample evidence that it takes many years of teaching these values in school before they have been accepted and internalized. That is why it won't do for children to learn in "settings of their own choosing." That is also why schools require children to be in a certain place at a

certain time and to follow certain rules, like raising their hands when they wish to speak, not talking when others are talking, not chewing gum, not leaving until the bell rings, exhibiting patience toward slower learners, etc. This process is called making civilized people. The god of Technology does not appear interested in this function of schools. At least, it does not come up much when technology's virtues are enumerated.

The god of Technology may also have a trick or two up its 14 sleeve about something else. It is often asserted that new technologies will equalize learning opportunities for the rich and poor. It is devoutly to be wished for, but I doubt it will happen. In the first place, it is generally understood by those who have studied the history of technology that technological change always produces winners and losers. There are many reasons for this, among them economic differences. Even in the case of the automobile, which is a commodity most people can buy (although not all), there are wide differences between the rich and poor in the quality of what is available to them. It would be quite astonishing if computer technology equalized all learning opportunities, irrespective of economic differences. One may be delighted that Little Eva's parents could afford the technology and software to make it possible for her to learn algebra at midnight. But Little Mary's parents may not be able to, may not even know such things are available. And if we say that the school could make the technology available to Little Mary (at least during the day), there may [be] something else Little Mary is lacking.

It turns out, for example, that Little Mary may be having 15 sleepless nights as frequently as Little Eva but not because she wants to get a leg up on her algebra. Maybe because she doesn't know who her father is, or, if she does, where he is. Maybe we can understand why McIntosh's kid is bored with the real world. Or is the child confused about it? Or terrified? Are there educators who seriously believe that these problems can be addressed by new technologies?

I do not say, of course, that schools can solve the problems of 16 poverty, alienation, and family disintegration, but schools can *respond* to them. And they can do this because there are people in them, because these people are concerned with more than algebra lessons or modern Japanese history, and because these people can identify not only one's level of competence in math but one's level of rage and confusion and depression. I am talking here about children as they really come to us, not children who are invented to show us how computers may enrich their lives. Of course, I suppose it is possible that there are children who, waking at night, want to study algebra or who are so interested in their world that they yearn to know about Japan. If there be such children, and one hopes there are, they do not require expensive computers to satisfy their hunger for learning. They are on their way, with or without computers. Unless, of course, they do not care about others or have no friends, or little respect for democracy or are filled with suspicion about those who are not like them. When we have machines that know how to do something about these problems, that is the time to rid ourselves of the expensive burden of schools or to reduce the function of teachers to "coaches" in the uses of machines (as Ravitch envisions). Until then, we must be more modest about this god of Technology and certainly not pin our hopes on it.

17   We must also, I suppose, be empathetic toward those who search with good intentions for technological panaceas. I am a teacher myself and know how hard it is to contribute to the making of a civilized person. Can we blame those who want to find an easy way, through the agency of technology? Perhaps not. After all, it is an old quest. As early as 1918, H. L. Mencken[3] (although completely devoid of empathy) wrote, "There is no sure-cure so idiotic that some superintendent of schools will not swallow it. The aim seems to be reduce the whole teaching process to a sort of automatic reaction, to discover some master formula that will not only take the place of competence and resourcefulness in the teacher but that will also create an artificial receptivity in the child."

18   Mencken was not necessarily speaking of technological panaceas but he may well have been. In the early 1920s a teacher wrote the following poem:

[3]American journalist (1880–1956).

Mr. Edison says
That the radio will supplant the teacher.
Already one may learn languages by means of
    Victrola records.
The moving picture will visualize
What the radio fails to get across.
Teachers will be relegated to the backwoods,
With fire-horses,
And long-haired women;
Or, perhaps shown in museums.
Education will become a matter
Of pressing the button.
Perhaps I can get a position at the switchboard.

I do not go as far back as the radio and Victrola, but I am old 19
enough to remember when 16-millimeter film was to be the sure-
cure. Then closed-circuit television. Then 8-millimeter film. Then
teacher-proof textbooks. Now computers.

I know a false god when I see one.   20

1995

3

Culture, Race, and Ethnicity

Identity is the core issue behind inquiries about culture, race, and ethnicity here. Are we shaped by our race? Brent Staples, Zora Neale Hurston, and James Baldwin talk about not being aware of their race as children. Zora Neale Hurston indicates that sometimes she doesn't "feel her race, she just feels *me*." Not until adulthood did race begin to define them, and often through prejudice. Some say that you can never escape the centrally defining characteristic of race, for even if you do not define yourself through it, the world defines you by it, as both Brent Staples and James Baldwin examine in their essays here. James Baldwin, in particular, reflects on the rage prejudice creates, and his own struggle with his hatred of those who degraded him. Like Staples, Ronald Takaki explores racial and ethnic stereotypes, and how even positive stereotypes are harmful when they get in the way of truth. However, culture is not always about marginalization or discrimination. Langston Hughes looks at his own culture as an insider, and how religion was central to it. His own alienation at not being able to embrace this positive feature of his childhood is depicted with humor and its own kind of grace. N. Scott Momaday, on the other hand, reflects on his native Kiowa religion—which was practiced by his grandmother who later became Christian—and finds it affirming to remember the heritage of his ancestors. This recognition of self is a critical aspect of good psychological health and is like going home, which is where Momaday, Baldwin, and Cofer's essays are located. Nevertheless, cultural definitions of a member of a particular group—as Takaki and Staples point out—can often be meaningless metaphors. Further, nothing innate might be involved in the definition that seems as basic as the color of a

153

person's skin. Judith Ortiz Cofer's article is a case in point about how culture is transmitted generation to generation—and the terms of what makes one a "Puerto Rican woman" can change over time, even when—like the tree in today's Christmas celebrations—precepts seem self-evident. Noel Ignatiev examines the changing definition of who one is in his biting essay on "How the Irish Became White." Ultimately, identity is a malleable concept, but injustice is not. The economic consequences of prejudice are clear. James Baldwin says in his essay that we must make peace with the fallibility of man but never accept it.

The Harmful Myth of Asian Superiority

Ronald Takaki

1   Asian Americans have increasingly come to be viewed as a "model minority." But are they as successful as claimed? And for whom are they supposed to be a model?

2   Asian Americans have been described in the media as "excessively, even provocatively" successful in gaining admission to universities. Asian American shopkeepers have been congratulated, as well as criticized, for their ubiquity and entrepreneurial effectiveness.

3   If Asian Americans can make it, many politicians and pundits ask, why can't African Americans? Such comparisons pit minorities against each other and generate African American resentment toward Asian Americans. The victims are blamed for their plight, rather than racism and an economy that has made many young African American workers superfluous.

4   The celebration of Asian Americans has obscured reality. For example, figures on the high earnings of Asian Americans relative to Caucasians are misleading. Most Asian Americans live in California, Hawaii, and New York—states with higher incomes and higher costs of living than the national average.

5   Even Japanese Americans, often touted for their upward mobility, have not reached equality. While Japanese American men in California earned an average income comparable to Caucasian men in 1980, they did so only by acquiring more education and working more hours.

6   Comparing family incomes is even more deceptive. Some Asian American groups do have higher family incomes than Caucasians. But they have more workers per family.

7   The "model minority" image homogenizes Asian Americans and hides their differences. For example, while thousands of Vietnamese American young people attend universities, others are on the streets. They live in motels and hang out in pool halls in places like East Los Angeles; some join gangs.

8   Twenty-five percent of the people in New York City's Chinatown lived below the poverty level in 1980, compared with 17 percent

of the city's population. Some 60 percent of the workers in the Chinatowns of Los Angeles and San Francisco are crowded into low-paying jobs in garment factories and restaurants.

"Most immigrants coming into Chinatown with a language 9 barrier cannot go outside this confined area into the mainstream of American industry," a Chinese immigrant said. "Before, I was a painter in Hong Kong, but I can't do it here. I got no license, no education. I want a living; so it's dishwasher, janitor, or cook."

Hmong and Mien refugees from Laos have unemployment 10 rates that reach as high as 80 percent. A 1987 California study showed that three out of ten Southeast Asian refugee families had been on welfare for four to ten years.

Although college-educated Asian Americans are entering the 11 professions and earning good salaries, many hit the "glass ceiling"— the barrier through which high management positions can be seen but not reached. In 1988, only 8 percent of Asian Americans were "officials" and "managers," compared with 12 percent for all groups.

Finally, the triumph of Korean immigrants has been exagger- 12 ated. In 1988, Koreans in the New York metropolitan area earned only 68 percent of the median income of non-Asians. More than three-quarters of Korean greengrocers, those so-called paragons of bootstrap entrepreneurialism, came to America with a college education. Engineers, teachers, or administrators while in Korea, they became shopkeepers after their arrival. For many of them, the greengrocery represents dashed dreams, a step downward in status.

For all their hard work and long hours, most Korean shop- 13 keepers do not actually earn very much: $17,000 to $35,000 a year, usually representing the income from the labor of an entire family.

But most Korean immigrants do not become shopkeepers. In- 14 stead, many find themselves trapped as clerks in grocery stores, service workers in restaurants, seamstresses in garment factories, and janitors in hotels.

Most Asian Americans know their "success" is largely a myth. 15 They also see how the celebration of Asian Americans as a "model minority" perpetuates their inequality and exacerbates relations between them and African Americans.

1990

How It Feels to Be Colored Me

Zora Neale Hurston

1   I am colored but I offer nothing in the way of extenuating circumstances except the fact that I am the only Negro in the United States
whose grandfather on the mother's side was *not* an Indian chief.

2   I remember the very day that I became colored. Up to my thirteenth year I lived in the little Negro town of Eatonville, Florida.
It is exclusively a colored town. The only white people I knew
passed through the town going to or coming from Orlando. The
native whites rode dusty horses, the Northern tourists chugged
down the sandy village road in automobiles. The town knew the
Southerners and never stopped cane chewing when they passed.
But the Northerners were something else again. They were peered
at cautiously from behind curtains by the timid. The more ven-
turesome would come out on the porch to watch them go past
and got just as much pleasure out of the tourists as the tourists got
out of the village.

3   The front porch might seem a daring place for the rest of the
town, but it was a gallery seat for me. My favorite place was atop
the gate-post. Proscenium box for a born first-nighter. Not only
did I enjoy the show, but I didn't mind the actors knowing that I
liked it. I usually spoke to them in passing. I'd wave at them and
when they returned my salute, I would say something like this:
"Howdy-do-well-I-thank-you-where-you-goin'?" Usually automobile or the horse paused at this, and after a queer exchange of
compliments, I would probably "go a piece of the way" with
them, as we say in farthest Florida. If one of my family happened
to come to the front in time to see me, of course negotiations
would be rudely broken off. But even so, it is clear that I was the
first "welcome-to-our-state" Floridian, and I hope the Miami
Chamber of Commerce will please take notice.

4   During this period, white people differed from colored to me
only in that they rode through town and never lived there. They
liked to hear me "speak pieces" and sing and wanted to see me
dance the parse-me-la, and gave me generously of their small silver

for doing these things, which seemed strange to me for I wanted to do them so much that I needed bribing to stop. Only they didn't know it. The colored people gave no dimes. They deplored any joyful tendencies in me, but I was their Zora nevertheless. I belonged to them, to the nearby hotels, to the county—everybody's Zora.

But changes came in the family when I was thirteen, and I was sent to school in Jacksonville. I left Eatonville, the town of the oleanders, as Zora. When I disembarked from the river-boat at Jacksonville, she was no more. It seemed that I had suffered a sea change. I was not Zora of Orange County any more, I was now a little colored girl. I found it out in certain ways. In my heart as well as in the mirror, I became a fast brown—warranted not to rub nor run.

But I am not tragically colored. There is no great sorrow dammed up in my soul, nor lurking behind my eyes. I do not mind at all. I do not belong to the sobbing school of Negrohood who hold that nature somehow has given them a low-down dirty deal and whose feelings are all hurt about it. Even in the helter-skelter skirmish that is my life, I have seen that the world is to the strong regardless of a little pigmentation more or less. No, I do not weep at the world—I am too busy sharpening my oyster knife.

Someone is always at my elbow reminding me that I am the granddaughter of slaves. It fails to register depression with me. Slavery is sixty years in the past. The operation was successful and the patient is doing well, thank you. The terrible struggle that made me an American out of a potential slave said "On the line!" The Reconstruction said "Get set!"; and the generation before said "Go!" I am off to a flying start and I must not halt in the stretch to look behind and weep. Slavery is the price I paid for civilization, and the choice was not with me. It is a bully adventure and worth all that I have paid through my ancestors for it. No one on earth ever had a greater chance for glory. The world to be won and nothing to be lost. It is thrilling to think—to know that for any act of mine, I shall get twice as much praise or twice as much blame. It is quite exciting to hold the center of the national stage, with the spectators not knowing whether to laugh or to weep.

8   The position of my white neighbor is much more difficult. No brown specter pulls up a chair beside me when I sit down to eat. No dark ghost thrusts its leg against mine in bed. The game of keeping what one has is never so exciting as the game of getting.

9   I do not always feel colored. Even now I often achieve the unconscious Zora of Eatonville before the Hegira. I feel most colored when I am thrown against a sharp white background.

10   For instance at Barnard. "Beside the waters of the Hudson" I feel my race. Among the thousand white persons, I am a dark rock surged upon, and overswept, but through it all, I remain myself. When covered by the waters, I am; and the ebb but reveals me again.

11   Sometimes it is the other way around. A white person is set down in our midst, but the contrast is just as sharp for me. For instance, when I sit in the drafty basement that is The New World Cabaret with a white person, my color comes. We enter chatting about any little nothing that we have in common and are seated by the jazz waiters. In the abrupt way that jazz orchestras have, this one plunges into a number. It loses no time in circumlocutions, but gets right down to business. It constricts the thorax and splits the heart with its tempo and narcotic harmonies. This orchestra grows rambunctious, rears on its hind legs and attacks the tonal veil with primitive fury, rending it, clawing it until it breaks through to the jungle beyond. I follow those heathen—follow them exultingly. I dance wildly inside myself; I yell within, I whoop; I shake my assegai above my head, I hurl it true to the mark *yeeeeooww!* I am in the jungle and living in the jungle way. My face is painted red and yellow and my body is painted blue. My pulse is throbbing like a war drum. I want to slaughter something—give pain, give death to what, I do not know. But the piece ends. The men of the orchestra wipe their lips and rest their fingers. I creep back slowly to the veneer we call civilization with the last tone and find the white friend sitting motionless in his seat, smoking calmly.

12   "Good music they have here," he remarks, drumming the table with his fingertips.

Music. The great blobs of purple and red emotion have not   13
touched him. He has only heard what I felt. He is far away and I
see him but dimly across the ocean and the continent that have
fallen between us. He is so pale with his whiteness then and I am
so colored.

At certain times I have no race. I am *me*. When I set my hat at   14
a certain angle and saunter down Seventh Avenue, Harlem City,
feeling as snooty as the lions in front of the Forty-Second Street Library, for instance. So far as my feelings are concerned, Peggy
Hopkins Joyce on the Boule Mich with her gorgeous rainment,
stately carriage, knees knocking together in a most aristocratic
manner, has nothing on me. The cosmic Zora emerges. I belong to
no race nor time. I am the eternal feminine with its string of beads.

I have no separate feeling about being an American citizen   15
and colored. I am merely a fragment of the Great Soul that surges
within the boundaries. My country, right or wrong.

Sometimes, I feel discriminated against, but it does not make   16
me angry. It merely astonishes me. How *can* any deny themselves
the pleasure of my company? It's beyond me.

But in the main, I feel like a brown bag of miscellany propped   17
against a wall. Against a wall in company with other bags, white,
red and yellow. Pour out the contents, and there is discovered a
jumble of small things priceless and worthless. A first-water diamond, an empty spool, bits of broken glass, lengths of string, a
key to a door long since crumbled away, a rusty knife-blade, old
shoes saved for a road that never was and never will be, a nail
bent under the weight of things too heavy for any nail, a dried
flower or two still a little fragrant. In your hand is the brown bag.
On the ground before you is the jumble it held—so much like the
jumble in the bags, could they be emptied, that all might be
dumped in a single heap and the bags refilled without altering the
content of any greatly. A bit of colored glass more or less would
not matter. Perhaps that is how the Great Stuffer of Bags filled
them in the first place—who knows?

1928

Notes of a Native Son*

James Baldwin

1   On the 29th of July, in 1943, my father died. On the same day, a few hours later, his last child was born. Over a month before this, while all our energies were concentrated in waiting for these events, there had been, in Detroit, one of the bloodiest race riots of the century. A few hours after my father's funeral, while he lay in state in the undertaker's chapel, a race riot broke out in Harlem. On the morning of the 3rd of August, we drove my father to the graveyard through a wilderness of smashed plate glass.

2   The day of my father's funeral had also been my nineteenth birthday. As we drove him to the graveyard, the spoils of injustice, anarchy, discontent, and hatred were all around us. It seemed to me that God himself had devised, to mark my father's end, the most sustained and brutally dissonant of codas. And it seemed to me, too, that the violence which rose all about us as my father left the world had been devised as a corrective for the pride of his eldest son. I had declined to believe in that apocalypse which had been central to my father's vision; very well, life seemed to be saying, here is something that will certainly pass for an apocalypse until the real thing comes along. I had inclined to be contemptuous of my father for the conditions of his life, for the conditions of our lives. When his life had ended I began to wonder about that life and also, in a new way, to be apprehensive about my own.

3   I had not known my father very well. We had got on badly, partly because we shared, in our different fashions, the voice of stubborn pride. When he was dead I realized that I had hardly ever spoken to him. When he had been dead a long time I began to wish I had. It seems to be typical of life in America, where opportunities, real and fancied, are thicker than anywhere else on the globe, that the second generation has no time to talk to the first. No one, including my father, seems to have known exactly

---

*"Notes of a Native Son" takes its title from Richard Wright's classic novel about black rage, *Native Son* (1940).

how old he was, but his mother had been born during slavery. He was of the first generation of free men. He, along with thousands of other Negroes, came North after 1919 and I was part of that generation which had never seen the landscape of what Negroes sometimes call the Old Country.

He had been born in New Orleans and had been a quiet 4 young man there during the time that Louis Armstrong, a boy, was running errands for the dives and honky-tonks of what was always presented to me as one of the most wicked of cities—to this day, whenever I think of New Orleans, I also helplessly think of Sodom and Gomorrah. My father never mentioned Louis Armstrong, except to forbid us to play his records; but there was a picture of him on our wall for a long time. One of my father's strong-willed female relatives had placed it there and forbade my father to take it down. He never did, but he eventually maneuvered her out of the house and when, some years later, she was in trouble and near death, he refused to do anything to help her.

He was, I think, very handsome. I gather this from photo- 5 graphs and from my own memories of him, dressed in his Sunday best and on his way to preach a sermon somewhere, when I was little. Handsome, proud, and ingrown, "like a toe-nail," somebody said. But he looked to me, as I grew older, like pictures I had seen of African tribal chieftains: he really should have been naked, with war-paint on and barbaric mementos, standing among spears. He could be chilling in the pulpit and indescribably cruel in his personal life and he was certainly the most bitter man I have ever met; yet it must be said that there was something else in him, buried in him, which lent him his tremendous power and, even, a rather crushing charm. It had something to do with his blackness, I think—he was very black—with his blackness and his beauty, and with the fact that he knew that he was black but did not know that he was beautiful. He claimed to be proud of his blackness but it had also been the cause of much humiliation and it had fixed bleak boundaries to his life. He was not a young man when we were growing up and he had already suffered many kinds of ruin; in his outrageously demanding and protective way he loved his children, who were black like him and menaced, like him; and all these things sometimes showed in his face when he tried, never to my knowledge with any success, to establish contact with any of us. When he took one of his children on his knee to play, the child always became fretful and began to cry; when he tried to help one of us with our homework the absolutely unabating tension which emanated from him caused our minds and our tongues to become paralyzed, so that he, scarcely knowing why, flew into a rage and the child, not knowing why, was punished. If it ever entered his head to bring a surprise home for his children, it was, almost unfailingly, the wrong surprise and even the big watermelons he often brought home on his back in the summertime led to the most appalling scenes. I do not remember, in all those years, that one of his children was ever glad to see him come home. From what I was able to gather of his early life, it seemed that this inability to establish contact with other people had always marked him and had been one of the things which had driven him out of New Orleans. There was something in him, therefore, groping and tentative, which was never expressed and which was buried with him. One saw it most clearly when he was facing new people and hoping to impress them. But he never did, not for long. We went from church to smaller and more improbable church, he found himself in less and less demand as a minister, and by the time he died none of his friends had come to see him for a long time. He had lived and died in an intolerable bitterness of spirit and it frightened me, as we drove him to the graveyard through those unquiet, ruined streets, to see how powerful and overflowing this bitterness could be and to realize that this bitterness now was mine.

6   When he died I had been away from home for a little over a year. In that year I had had time to become aware of the meaning of all my father's bitter warnings, had discovered the secret of his proudly pursed lips and rigid carriage: I had discovered the weight of white people in the world. I saw that this had been for my ancestors and now would be for me an awful thing to live with and that the bitterness which had helped to kill my father could also kill me.

7   He had been ill a long time—in the mind, as we now realized, reliving instances of his fantastic intransigence in the new light of his affliction and endeavoring to feel a sorrow for him which never, quite, came true. We had not known that he was being eaten up by

paranoia, and the discovery that his cruelty, to our bodies and our minds, had been one of the symptoms of his illness was not, then, enough to enable us to forgive him. The younger children felt, quite simply, relief that he would not be coming home anymore. My mother's observation that it was he, after all, who had kept them alive all these years meant nothing because the problems of keeping children alive are not real for children. The older children felt, with my father gone, that they could invite their friends to the house without fear that their friends would be insulted or, as had sometimes happened with me, being told that their friends were in league with the devil and intended to rob our family of everything we owned. (I didn't fail to wonder, and it made me hate him, what on earth we owned that anybody would want.)

His illness was beyond all hope of healing before anyone re- 8 alized that he was ill. He had always been so strange and had lived, like a prophet, in such unimaginably close communication with the Lord that his long silences which were punctuated by moans and hallelujahs and snatches of old songs while he sat at the living-room window never seemed odd to us. It was not until he refused to eat because, he said, his family was trying to poison him that my mother was forced to accept as a fact what had, until then, been only an unwilling suspicion. When he was committed, it was discovered that he had tuberculosis and, as it turned out, the disease of his mind allowed the disease of his body to destroy him. For the doctors could not force him to eat, either, and, though he was fed intravenously, it was clear from the beginning that there was no hope for him.

In my mind's eye I could see him, sitting at the window, 9 locked up in his terrors; hating and fearing every living soul including his children who had betrayed him, too, by reaching towards the world which had despised him. There were nine of us. I began to wonder what it could have felt like for such a man to have had nine children whom he could barely feed. He used to make little jokes about our poverty, which never, of course, seemed very funny to us; they could not have seemed very funny to him, either, or else our all too feeble response to them would never have caused such rages. He spent great energy and achieved, to our chagrin, no small amount of success in keeping

us away from the people who surrounded us, people who had all-
night rent parties to which we listened when we should have been
sleeping, people who cursed and drank and flashed razor blades
on Lenox Avenue. He could not understand why, if they had so
much energy to spare, they could not use it to make their lives
better. He treated almost everybody on our block with a most uncharitable asperity and neither they, nor, of course, their children
were slow to reciprocate.

10   The only white people who came to our house were welfare
workers and bill collectors. It was almost always my mother who
dealt with them, for my father's temper, which was at the mercy
of his pride, was never to be trusted. It was clear that he felt their
very presence in his home to be a violation: this was conveyed by
his carriage, almost ludicrously stiff, and by his voice, harsh and
vindictively polite. When I was around nine or ten I wrote a play
which was directed by a young, white schoolteacher, a woman,
who then took an interest in me, and gave me books to read and, in
order to corroborate my theatrical bent, decided to take me to see
what she somewhat tactlessly referred to as "real" plays. Theater-
going was forbidden in our house, but, with the really cruel intu-
itiveness of a child, I suspected that the color of this woman's skin
would carry the day for me. When, at school, she suggested taking me to the theater, I did not, as I might have done if she had
been a Negro, find a way of discouraging her, but agreed that she
should pick me up at my house one evening. I then, very cleverly,
left all the rest to my mother, who suggested to my father, as I
knew she would, that it would not be very nice to let such a kind
woman make the trip for nothing. Also, since it was a schoolteacher, I imagine that my mother countered the idea of sin with
the idea of "education," which word, even with my father, carried
a kind of bitter weight.

11   Before the teacher came my father took me aside to ask *why*
she was coming, what *interest* she could possibly have in our
house, in a boy like me. I said I didn't know but I, too, suggested
that it had something to do with education. And I understood that
my father was waiting for me to say something—I didn't quite
know what; perhaps that I wanted his protection against this
teacher and her "education." I said none of these things and the

teacher came and we went out. It was clear, during the brief interview in our living room, that my father was agreeing very much
against his will and that he would have refused permission if he
had dared. The fact that he did not dare caused me to despise him:
I had no way of knowing that he was facing in that living room a
wholly unprecedented and frightening situation.

   Later, when my father had been laid off from his job, this   12
woman became very important to us. She was really a very sweet
and generous woman and went to a great deal of trouble to be of
help to us, particularly during one awful winter. My mother
called her by the highest name she knew: she said she was a
"christian." My father could scarcely disagree but during the four
or five years of our relatively close association he never trusted
her and was always trying to surprise in her open, Midwestern
face the genuine, cunningly hidden, and hideous motivation. In
later years, particularly when it began to be clear that this "education" of mine was going to lead me to perdition, he became
more explicit and warned me that my white friends in high school
were not really my friends and that I would see, when I was older,
how white people would do anything to keep a Negro down.
Some of them could be nice, he admitted, but none of them were
to be trusted and most of them were not even nice. The best thing
was to have as little to do with them as possible. I did not feel this
way and I was certain, in my innocence, that I never would.

   But the year which preceded my father's death had made a   13
great change in my life. I had been living in New Jersey, working
in defense plants, working and living among southerners, white
and black. I knew about the south, of course, and about how
southerners treated Negroes and how they expected them to behave, but it had never entered my mind that anyone would look
at me and expect *me* to behave that way. I learned in New Jersey
that to be a Negro meant, precisely, that one was never looked at
but was simply at the mercy of the reflexes the color of one's skin
caused in other people. I acted in New Jersey as I had always acted,
that is as though I thought a great deal of myself—I had to *act* that
way—with results that were, simply, unbelievable. I had scarcely
arrived before I had earned the enmity, which was extraordinarily
ingenious, of all my superiors and nearly all my co-workers. In

the beginning, to make matters worse, I simply did not know what was happening. I did not know what I had done, and I shortly began to wonder what *anyone* could possibly do, to bring about such unanimous, active, and unbearably vocal hostility. I knew about jim-crow but I had never experienced it. I went to the same self-service restaurant three times and stood with all the Princeton boys before the counter, waiting for a hamburger and coffee; it was always an extraordinarily long time before anything was set before me; but it was not until the fourth visit that I learned that, in fact, nothing had ever been set before me: I had simply picked something up. Negroes were not served there, I was told, and they had been waiting for me to realize that I was always the only Negro present. Once I was told this, I determined to go there all the time. But now they were ready for me and, though some dreadful scenes were subsequently enacted in that restaurant, I never ate there again.

14   It was the same story all over New Jersey, in bars, bowling alleys, diners, places to live. I was always being forced to leave, silently, or with mutual imprecations. I very shortly became notorious and children giggled behind me when I passed and their elders whispered or shouted—they really believed that I was mad. And it did begin to work on my mind, of course; I began to be afraid to go anywhere and to compensate for this I went to places to which I really should not have gone and where, God knows, I had no desire to be. My reputation in town naturally enhanced my reputation at work and my working day became one long series of acrobatics designed to keep me out of trouble. I cannot say that these acrobatics succeeded. It began to seem that the machinery of the organization I worked for was turning over, day and night, with but one aim: to eject me. I was fired once, and contrived, with the aid of a friend from New York, to get back on the payroll; was fired again, and bounced back again. It took a while to fire me for the third time, but the third time took. There were no loopholes anywhere. There was not even any way of getting back inside the gates.

15   That year in New Jersey lives in my mind as though it were the year during which, having an unsuspected predilection for it, I first contracted some dread, chronic disease, the unfailing symptom of

which is a kind of blind fever, a pounding in the skull and fire in the bowels. Once this disease is contracted, one can never be really carefree again, for the fever, without an instant's warning, can recur at any moment. It can wreck more important things than race relations. There is not a Negro alive who does not have this rage in his blood—one has the choice, merely, of living with it consciously or surrendering to it. As for me, this fever has recurred in me, and does, and will until the day I die.

My last night in New Jersey, a white friend from New York 16 took me to the nearest bit town, Trenton, to go to the movies and have a few drinks. As it turned out, he also saved me from, at the very least, a violent whipping. Almost every detail of that night stands out very clearly in my memory. I even remember the name of the movie we saw because its title impressed me as being so patly ironical. It was a movie about the German occupation of France, starring Maureen O'Hara and Charles Laughton and called *This Land Is Mine.* I remember the name of the diner we walked into when the movie ended: it was the "American Diner." When we walked in the counterman asked what we wanted and I remember answering with the casual sharpness which had become my habit: "We want a hamburger and a cup of coffee, what do you think we want?" I do not know why, after a year of such rebuffs, I so completely failed to anticipate his answer, which was, of course, "We don't serve Negroes here." This reply failed to discompose me, at least for the moment. I made some sardonic comment about the name of the diner and we walked out into the streets.

This was the time of what was called the "brown-out," when 17 the lights in all American cities were very dim. When we reentered the streets something happened to me which had the force of an optical illusion, or a nightmare. The streets were very crowded and I was facing north. People were moving in every direction but it seemed to me, in that instant, that all of the people I could see, and many more than that, were moving toward me, against me, and that everyone was white. I remember how their faces gleamed. And I felt, like a physical sensation, a *click* at the nape of my neck as though some interior string connecting my head to my body had been cut. I began to walk. I heard my friend call after me, but I ignored him. Heaven only knows what was going on in his mind, but he had the good sense not to touch me—I don't know what would have happened if he had—and to keep me in sight. I don't know what was going on in my mind, either; I certainly had no conscious plan. I wanted to do something to crush these white faces, which were crushing me. I walked for perhaps a block or two until I came to an enormous, glittering, and fashionable restaurant in which I knew not even the intercession of the Virgin would cause me to be served. I pushed through the doors and took the first vacant seat I saw, at a table for two, and waited.

18   I do not know how long I waited and I rather wonder, until today, what I could possibly have looked like. Whatever I looked like, I frightened the waitress who shortly appeared, and the moment she appeared all of my fury flowed towards her. I hated her for her white face, and for her great, astounded, frightened eyes. I felt that if she found a black man so frightening I would make her fright worth-while.

19   She did not ask me what I wanted, but repeated, as though she had learned it somewhere, "We don't serve Negroes here." She did not say it with the blunt, derisive hostility to which I had grown so accustomed, but, rather, with a note of apology in her voice, and fear. This made me colder and more murderous than ever. I felt I had to do something with my hands. I wanted her to come close enough for me to get her neck between my hands.

20   So I pretended not to have understood her, hoping to draw her closer. And she did step a very short step closer, with her pencil poised incongruously over her pad, and repeated the formula: ". . . don't serve Negroes here."

21   Somehow, with the repetition of that phrase, which was already ringing in my head like a thousand bells of a nightmare, I realized that she would never come any closer and that I would have to strike from a distance. There was nothing on the table but an ordinary watermug half full of water, and I picked this up and hurled it with all my strength at her. She ducked and it missed her and shattered against the mirror behind the bar. And, with that sound, my frozen blood abruptly thawed, I returned from wherever I had been, I *saw*, for the first time, the restaurant, the people with their mouths open, already, as it seemed to me, rising as one

man, and I realized what I had done, and where I was, and I was frightened. I rose and began running for the door. A round, pot-bellied man grabbed me by the nape of the neck just as I reached the doors and began to beat me about the face. I kicked him and got loose and ran into the streets. My friend whispered, *"Run!"* and I ran.

My friend stayed outside the restaurant long enough to mis- 22 direct my pursuers and the police, who arrived, he told me, at once. I do not know what I said to him when he came to my room that night. I could not have said much. I felt, in the oddest, most awful way, that I had somehow betrayed him. I lived it over and over and over again, the way one relives an automobile accident after it has happened and one finds oneself alone and safe. I could not get over two facts, both equally difficult for the imagination to grasp, and one was that I could have been murdered. But the other was that I had been ready to commit murder. I saw nothing very clearly but I did see this: that my life, my *real* life, was in dan-ger, and not from anything other people might do but from the hatred I carried in my own heart.

2

I had returned home around the second week in June—in great 23 haste because it seemed that my father's death and my mother's confinement were both but a matter of hours. In the case of my mother, it soon became clear that she had simply made a miscal-culation. This had always been her tendency and I don't believe that a single one of us arrived in the world, or has since arrived anywhere else, on time. But none of us dawdled so intolerably about the business of being born as did my baby sister. We some-times amused ourselves, during those endless, stifling weeks, by picturing the baby sitting within in the safe, warm dark, bitterly regretting the necessity of becoming a part of our chaos and stub-bornly putting it off as long as possible. I understood her perfectly and congratulated her on showing such good sense so soon. Death, however, sat as purposefully at my father's bedside as life stirred within my mother's womb and it was harder to under-

stand why he so lingered in that long shadow. It seemed that he had bent, and for a long time, too, all of his energies towards dy-
24 ing. Now death was ready for him but my father held back.

All of Harlem, indeed, seemed to be infected by waiting. I had never before known it to be so violently still. Racial tensions throughout this country were exacerbated during the early years of the war, partly because the labor market brought together hundreds of thousands of ill-prepared people and partly because Negro soldiers, regardless of where they were born, received their military training in the south. What happened in defense plants and army camps had repercussions, naturally, in every Negro ghetto. The situation in Harlem had grown bad enough for clergymen, policemen, educators, politicians, and social workers to assert in one breath that there was no "crime wave" and to offer, in the very next breath, suggestions as how to combat it. These suggestions always seemed to involve playgrounds, despite the fact that racial skirmishes were occurring in the playgrounds, too. Playground or not, crime wave or not, the Harlem police force had been augmented in March, and the unrest grew—perhaps, in fact, partly as a result of the ghetto's instinctive hatred of policemen. Perhaps the most revealing news item, out of the steady parade of reports of muggings, stabbings, shootings, assaults, gang wars, and accusations of police brutality, is the item concerning six Negro girls who set upon a white girl in the subway because, as they all too accurately put it, she was stepping on their toes. In-
25 deed she was, all over the nation.

I had never before been so aware of policemen, on foot, on horseback, on corners, everywhere, always two by two. Nor had I ever been so aware of small knots of people. They were on stoops and on corners and in doorways, and what was striking about them, I think, was that they did not seem to be talking. Never, when I passed these groups, did the usual sound of a curse or a laugh ring out and neither did there seem to be any hum of gossip. There was certainly, on the other hand, occurring between them communication extraordinarily intense. Another thing that was striking was the unexpected diversity of the people who made up these groups. Usually, for example, one would see a group of sharpies standing on the street corner, jiving the passing chicks; or a group of older men, usually, for some reason, in the vicinity of a barber shop, discussing baseball scores, or the numbers,[1] or making rather chilling observations about women they had known. Women, in a general way, tended to be seen less often together—unless they were church women, or very young girls, or prostitutes met together for an unprofessional instant. But that summer I saw the strangest combinations: large, respectable, churchly matrons standing on the stoops or the corners with their hair tied up, together with a girl in sleazy satin whose face bore the marks of gin and the razor, or heavy-set, abrupt, no-nonsense older men, in company with the most disreputable and fanatical "race" men, or these same "race" men with the sharpies, or these sharpies with the churchly women. Seventh Day Adventists and Methodists and Spiritualists seemed to be hobnobbing with Holy-rollers and they were all, alike, entangled with the most flagrant disbelievers; something heavy in their stance seemed to indicate that they had all, incredibly, seen a common vision, and on each face there seemed to be the same strange, bitter shadow.

The churchly women and the matter-of-fact, no-nonsense 26 men had children in the Army. The sleazy girls they talked to had lovers there, the sharpies and the "race" men had friends and brothers there. It would have demanded an unquestioning patriotism, happily as uncommon in this country as it is undesirable, for these people not to have been disturbed by the bitter letters they received, by the newspaper stories they read, not to have been enraged by the posters, then to be found all over New York, which described the Japanese as "yellow-bellied Japs." It was only the "race" men, to be sure, who spoke ceaselessly of being revenged—how this vengeance was to be exacted was not clear—for the indignities and dangers suffered by Negro boys in uniform; but everybody felt a directionless, hopeless bitterness, as well as that panic which can scarcely be suppressed when one knows that a human being one loves is beyond one's reach, and in danger. This helplessness and this gnawing uneasiness does something, at length, to even the toughest mind. Perhaps the best

---

[1] **the numbers** Popular street gambling game based on winning numbers at a given race track.

way to sum all this up is to say that the people I knew felt, mainly, a peculiar kind of relief when they knew that their boys were being shipped out of the south, to do battle overseas. It was, perhaps, like feeling that the most dangerous part of a dangerous journey had been passed and that now, even if death should come, it would come with honor and without the complicity of their countrymen. Such a death would be, in short, a fact with which one could hope to live.

27   It was on the 28th of July, which I believe was a Wednesday, that I visited my father for the first time during his illness and for the last time in his life. The moment I saw him I knew why I had put off this visit so long. I had told my mother that I did not want to see him because I hated him. But this was not true. It was only that I *had* hated him and I wanted to hold on to this hatred. I did not want to look at him as a ruin: it was not a ruin I had hated. I imagine that one of the reasons people cling to their hates so stubbornly is because they sense, once hate is gone, that they will be forced to deal with pain.

28   We traveled out to him, his older sister and myself, to what seemed to be the very end of a very Long Island. It was hot and dusty and we wrangled, my aunt and I, all the way out, over the fact that I had recently begun to smoke and, as she said, to give myself airs. But I knew that she wrangled with me because she could not bear to face the fact of her brother's dying. Neither could I endure the reality of her despair, her unstated bafflement as to what had happened to her brother's life, and her own. So we wrangled and I smoked and from time to time she fell into a heavy reverie. Covertly, I watched her face, which was the face of an old woman; it had fallen in, the eyes were sunken and lightless; soon she would be dying too.

29   In my childhood—it had not been so long ago—I had thought her beautiful. She had been quick-witted and quick-moving and very generous with all the children and each of her visits had been an event. At one time one of my brothers and myself had thought of running away to live with her. Now she could no longer produce out of her handbag some unexpected and yet familiar delight. She made me feel pity and revulsion and fear. It was awful to realize that she no longer caused me to feel affection. The closer

we came to the hospital the more querulous she became and at the same time, naturally, grew more dependent on me. Between pity and guilt and fear I began to feel that there was another me trapped in my skull like a jack-in-the-box who might escape my control at any moment and fill the air with screaming.

She began to cry the moment we entered the room and she   30
saw him lying there, all shriveled and still, like a little black monkey. The great, gleaming apparatus which fed him and would have compelled him to be still even if he had been able to move brought to mind, not beneficence, but torture; the tubes entering his arm made me think of pictures I had seen when a child, of Gulliver, tied down by the pygmies on that island. My aunt wept and wept, there was a whistling sound in my father's throat; nothing was said; he could not speak. I wanted to take his hand, to say something. But I do not know what I could have said, even if he could have heard me. He was not really in that room with us, he had at last really embarked on his journey; and though my aunt told me that he said he was going to meet Jesus, I did not hear anything except that whistling in his throat. The doctor came back and we left, into that unbearable train again, and home. In the morning came the telegram saying that he was dead. Then the house was suddenly full of relatives, friends, hysteria, and confusion and I quickly left my mother and the children to the care of those impressive women, who, in Negro communities at least, automatically appear at times of bereavement armed with lotions, proverbs, and patience, and an ability to cook. I went downtown. By the time I returned, later the same day, my mother had been carried to the hospital and the baby had been born.

3

For my father's funeral I had nothing black to wear and this posed   31
a nagging problem all day long. It was one of those problems, simple, or impossible of solution, to which the mind insanely clings in order to avoid the mind's real trouble. I spent most of the day at the downtown apartment of a girl I knew, celebrating my birthday with whiskey and wondering what to wear that night. When planning a birthday celebration one naturally does not expect that

it will be up against competition from a funeral and this girl had anticipated taking me out that night, for a big dinner and a night club afterwards. Sometime during the course of that long day we decided that we would go out anyway, when my father's funeral service was over. I imagine *I* decided it, since, as the funeral hour approached, it became clearer and clearer to me that I would not know what to do with myself when it was over. The girl, stifling her very lively concern as to the possible effects of the whiskey on one of my father's chief mourners, concentrated on being conciliatory and practically helpful. She found a black shirt for me somewhere and ironed it and, dressed in the darkest pants and jacket I owned, ₃₂ and slightly drunk, I made my way to my father's funeral.

The chapel was full, but not packed, and very quiet. There were, mainly, my father's relatives, and his children, and here and there I saw faces I had not seen since childhood, the faces of my father's one-time friends. They were very dark and solemn now, seeming somehow to suggest that they had known all along that something like this would happen. Chief among the mourners was my aunt, who had quarreled with my father all his life; by which I do not mean to suggest that her mourning was insincere or that she had not loved him. I suppose that she was one of the few people in the world who had, and their incessant quarreling proved precisely the strength of the tie that bound them. The only other person in the world, as far as I knew, whose relationship to my father rivaled my aunt's in depth was my mother, who was ₃₃ not there.

It seemed to me, of course, that it was a very long funeral. But it was, if anything, a rather shorter funeral than most, nor, since there were no overwhelming, uncontrollable expressions of grief, could it be called—if I dare to use the word—successful. The minister who preached my father's funeral sermon was one of the few my father had still been seeing as he neared his end. He presented to us in his sermon a man whom none of us had ever seen—a man thoughtful, patient, and forbearing, a Christian inspiration to all who knew him, and a model for his children. And no doubt the children, in their disturbed and guilty state, were almost ready to believe this; he had been remote enough to be anything and, anyway, the shock of the incontrovertible, that it was really our father lying up there in that casket, prepared the mind for anything. His sister moaned and this grief-stricken moaning was taken for corroboration. The other faces held a dark, noncommittal thoughtfulness. This was not the man they had known, but they had scarcely expected to be confronted with *him;* this was, in a sense deeper than question of fact, the man they had not known, and the man they had not known may have been the real one. The real man, whoever he had been, had suffered and now he was dead: this was all that was sure and all that mattered now. Every man in the chapel hoped that when his hour came he, too, would be eulogized, which is to say forgiven, and that all of his lapses, greeds, errors, and strayings from the truth would be invested with coherence and looked upon with charity. This was perhaps the last thing human beings could give each other and it was what they demanded, after all, of the Lord. Only the Lord saw the midnight tears, only He was present when one of His children, moaning and wringing hands, paced up and down the room. When one slapped one's child in anger the recoil in the heart reverberated through heaven and became part of the pain of the universe. And when the children were hungry and sullen and distrustful and one watched them, daily, growing wilder, and further away, and running headlong into danger, it was the Lord who knew what the charged heart endured as the strap was laid to the backside; the Lord alone knew what one *would* have said if one had had, like the Lord, the gift of the living word. It was the Lord who knew of the impossibility every parent in the room faced: how to prepare the child for the day when the child would be despised and how to *create* in the child—by what means?—a stronger antidote to this poison that one had found for oneself. The avenues, side streets, bars, billiard halls, hospitals, police stations, and even the playgrounds of Harlem—not to mention the houses of correction, the jails, and the morgue—testified to the potency of the poison while remaining silent as to the efficacy of whatever antidote, irresistibly raising the question of whether or not such an antidote existed; raising, which was worse, the question of whether or not an antidote was desirable; perhaps poison should be fought with poison. With these several schisms in the mind and with more terrors in the heart than could be named, it was better not to judge the man who had gone down under an impossible burden. It was better to remember: *Thou knowest this man's fall; but thou knowest not his wrassling.*

34   While the preacher talked and I watched the children—years of changing their diapers, scrubbing them, slapping them, taking them to school, and scolding them had had the perhaps inevitable result of making me love them, though I am not sure I knew this then—my mind was busily breaking out with a rash of disconnected impressions. Snatches of popular songs, indecent jokes, bits of books I had read, movie sequences, faces, voices, political issues—I thought I was going mad; all these impressions suspended, as it were, in the solution of the faint nausea produced in me by the heat and liquor. For a moment I had the impression that my alcoholic breath, inefficiently disguised with chewing gum, filled the entire chapel. Then someone began singing one of my father's favorite songs and, abruptly, I was with him, sitting on his knee, in the hot, enormous, crowded church which was the first church we attended. It was the Abysinia Baptist Church on 138th Street. We had not gone there long. With this image, a host of others came. I had forgotten, in the rage of my growing up, how proud my father had been of me when I was little. Apparently, I had had a voice and my father had liked to show me off before the members of the church. I had forgotten what he had looked like when he was pleased but now I remembered that he had always been grinning with pleasure when my solos ended. I even remembered certain expressions on his face when he teased my mother—had he loved her? I would never know. And when had it all begun to change? For now it seemed that he had not always been cruel. I remembered being taken for a haircut and scraping my knee on the footrest of the barber's chair and I remembered my father's face as he soothed my crying and applied the stinging iodine. Then I remembered our fights, fights which had been of the worse possible kind because my technique had been silence.

35   I remembered the one time in all our life together when we had really spoken to each other.

36   It was on a Sunday and it must have been shortly before I left home. We were walking, just the two of us, in our usual silence, to or from church. I was in high school and had been doing a lot of writing and I was, at about this time, the editor of the high school

magazine. But I had also been a Young Minister and had been preaching from the pulpit. Lately, I had been taking fewer engagements and preached as rarely as possible. It was said in the church, quite truthfully, that I was "cooling off."

My father asked me abruptly, "You'd rather write than preach, wouldn't you?" 37

I was astonished at his question—because it was a real question. I answered, "Yes." 38

That was all we said. It was awful to remember that that was all we had *ever* said. 39

The casket now was opened and the mourners were being led up the aisle to look for the last time on the deceased. The assumption was that the family was too overcome with grief to be allowed to make this journey alone and I watched while my aunt was led to the casket and, muffled in black, and shaking, led back to her seat. I disapproved of forcing the children to look on their dead father, considering that the shock of his death, or more truthfully, the shock of death as a reality, was already a little more than a child could bear, but my judgment in this matter had been overruled and there they were, bewildered and frightened and very small, being led, one by one, to the casket. But there is also something very gallant about children at such moments. It has something to do with their silence and gravity and with the fact that one cannot help them. Their legs, somehow, seemed *exposed*, so that it is at once incredible and terribly clear that their legs are all they have to hold them up. 40

I had not wanted to go to the casket myself and I certainly had not wished to be led there, but there was no way of avoiding either of these forms. One of the deacons led me up and I looked on my father's face. I cannot say that it looked like him at all. His blackness had been equivocated by powder and there was no suggestion in that casket of what his power had or could have been. He was simply an old man dead, and it was hard to believe that he had ever given anyone either joy or pain. Yet, his life filled that room. Further up the avenue his wife was holding his newborn child. Life and death so close together, and love and hatred, and right and wrong, said something to me which I did not want to hear concerning man, concerning the life of man. 41

42   After the funeral, while I was downtown desperately celebrating my birthday, a Negro soldier, in the lobby of the Hotel Braddock, got into a fight with a white policeman over a Negro girl. Negro girls, white policemen, in or out of uniform, and Negro males—in or out of uniform—were part of the furniture of the lobby of the Hotel Braddock and this was certainly not the first time such an incident had occurred. It was destined, however, to receive an unprecedented publicity, for the fight between the policeman and the soldier ended with the shooting of the soldier. Rumor, flowing immediately to the streets outside, stated the soldier had been shot in the back, an instantaneous and revealing invention, and that the soldier had died protecting a Negro woman. The facts were somewhat different—for example, the soldier had not been shot in the back, and was not dead, and the girl seems to have been as dubious a symbol of womanhood as her white counterpart in Georgia usually is, but no one was interested in the facts. They preferred the invention because this invention expressed and corroborated their hates and fears so perfectly. It is just as well to remember that people are always doing this. Perhaps many of those legends, including Christianity, to which the world clings began their conquest of the world with just some such concerted surrender to distortion. The effect, in Harlem, of this particular legend was like the effect of a lit match in a tin of gasoline. The mob gathered before the doors of the Hotel Braddock simply began to swell and to spread in every direction, and Harlem exploded.

43   The mob did not cross the ghetto lines. It would have been easy, for example, to have gone over Morningside Park on the west side or to have crossed the Grand Central railroad tracks at 125th Street on the east side, to wreak havoc in the white neighborhoods. The mob seems to have been mainly interested in something more potent and real than the white face, that is, in white power, and the principal damage done during the riot of the summer of 1943 was to white business establishments in Harlem. It might have been a far bloodier story, of course, if, at the hour the riot began, these establishments had still been open. From the Hotel Braddock the mob fanned out, east and west along 125th Street, and for the entire length of Lenox, Seventh, and Eighth avenues. Along each of these avenues, and along each

major side street—116th, 125th, 135th, and so on—bars, stores, pawnshops, restaurants, even little luncheonettes had been smashed open and entered and looted—looted, it might be added, with more haste than efficiency. The shelves really looked as though a bomb had struck them. Cans of beans and soup and dog food, along with toilet paper, corn flakes, sardines and milk tumbled every which way, and abandoned cash registers and cases of beer leaned crazily out of the splintered windows and were strewn along the avenues. Sheets, blankets, and clothing of every description formed a kind of path, as though people had dropped them while running. I truly had not realized that Harlem *had* so many stores until I saw them all smashed open; the first time the word *wealth* ever entered my mind in relation to Harlem was when I saw it scattered in the streets. But one's first, incongruous impression of plenty was countered immediately by an impression of waste. None of this was doing anybody any good. It would have been better to have left the plate glass as it had been and the goods lying in the stores.

It would have been better, but it would also have been intol- 44 erable, for Harlem had needed something to smash. To smash something is the ghetto's chronic need. Most of the time it is the members of the ghetto who smash each other, and themselves. But as long as the ghetto walls are standing there will always come a moment when these outlets do not work. That summer, for example, it was not enough to get into a fight on Lenox Avenue, or curse out one's cronies in the barber shops. If ever, indeed, the violence which fills Harlem's churches, pool halls, and bars erupts outward in a more direct fashion, Harlem and its citizens are likely to vanish in an apocalyptic flood. That this is not likely to happen is due to a great many reasons, most hidden and powerful among them the Negro's real relation to the white American. This relation prohibits, simply, anything as uncomplicated and satisfactory as pure hatred. In order really to hate white people, one has to blot so much out of the mind—and the heart— that this hatred itself becomes an exhausting and self-destructive pose. But this does not mean, on the other hand, that love comes easily: the white world is too powerful, too complacent, too ready with gratuitous humiliation, and, above all, too ignorant and too innocent for that. One is absolutely forced to make perpetual qualifications and one's own reactions are always canceling each other out. It is this, really, which has driven so many people mad, both white and black. One is always in the position of having to decide between amputation and gangrene. Amputation is swift but time may prove that the amputation was not necessary—or one may delay the amputation too long. Gangrene is slow, but it is impossible to be sure that one is reading one's symptoms right. The idea of going through life as a cripple is more than one can bear, and equally unbearable is the risk of swelling up slowly, in agony, with poison. And the trouble, finally, is that the risks are real even if the choices do not exist.

45   "But as for me and my house," my father had said, "we will serve the Lord." I wondered, as we drove him to his resting place, what this line had meant for him. I had heard him preach it many times. I had preached it once myself, proudly giving it an inter-pretation different from my father's. Now the whole thing came back to me, as though my father and I were on our way to Sunday school and I were memorizing the golden text: *And if it seem evil unto you to serve the Lord, choose you this day whom you will serve; whether the gods which your fathers served that were on the other side of the flood, or the gods of the Amorites, in whose land ye dwell: but as for me and my house, we will serve the Lord.* I suspected in these familiar lines a meaning which had never been there for me before. All of my father's texts and songs, which I hade decided were meaning-less, were arranged before me at his death like empty bottles, waiting to hold the meaning which life would give them for me. This was his legacy: nothing is ever escaped. That bleakly memo-rable morning I hated the unbelievable streets and the Negroes and whites who had, equally, made them that way. But I knew that it was folly, as my father would have said, this bitterness was folly. It was necessary to hold on to the things that mattered. The dead man mattered, the new life mattered; blackness and whiteness did not matter; to believe that they did was to acquiesce in one's own destruction. Hatred, which could destroy so much, never failed to destroy the man who hated and this was an immutable law.

It began to seem that one would have to hold in the mind for- 46
ever two ideas which seemed to be in opposition. The first idea
was acceptance, the acceptance, totally without rancor, of life as it
is, and men as they are: in the light of this idea, it goes without
saying that injustice is a commonplace. But this did not mean that
one could be complacent, for the second idea was of equal power:
that one must never, in one's own life, accept these injustices as
commonplace but must fight them with all one's strength. This
fight begins, however, in the heart and it now had been laid to my
charge to keep my own heart free of hatred and despair. This inti-
mation made my heart heavy and, now that my father was ir-
recoverable, I wished that he had been beside me so that I could
have searched his face for the answers which only the future
would give me now.

1955

Black Men and Public Spaces

Brent Staples

My first victim was a woman—white, well dressed, probably in 1
her early twenties. I came upon her late one evening on a deserted
street in Hyde Park, a relatively affluent neighborhood in an otherwise mean, impoverished section of Chicago. As I swung onto
the avenue behind her, there seemed to be a discreet, uninflamma-
tory distance between us. Not so. She cast back a worried glance.
To her, the youngish black man—a broad six feet two inches with
a beard and billowing hair, both hands shoved into the pockets of
a bulky military jacket—seemed menacingly close. After a few
more quick glimpses, she picked up her pace and was soon running in earnest. Within seconds she disappeared into a cross street.

That was more than a decade ago. I was twenty-two years old, 2
a graduate student newly arrived at the University of Chicago. It

was in the echo of that terrified woman's footfalls that I first began to know the unwieldy inheritance I'd come into—the ability to alter public space in ugly ways. It was clear that she thought herself the quarry of a mugger, a rapist, or worse. Suffering a bout of insomnia, however, I was stalking sleep, not defenseless wayfarers. As a softy who is scarcely able to take a knife to a raw chicken—let alone hold it to a person's throat—I was surprised, embarrassed, and dismayed all at once. Her flight made me feel like an accomplice in tyranny. It also made it clear that I was indistinguishable from the muggers who occasionally seeped into the area from the surrounding ghetto. That first encounter, and those that followed, signified that a vast, unnerving gulf lay between nighttime pedestrians—particularly women—and me. And I soon gathered that being perceived as dangerous is a hazard in itself. I only needed to turn a corner into a dicey situation, or crowd some frightened, armed person in a foyer somewhere, or make an errant move after being pulled over by a policeman. Where fear and weapons meet—and they often do in urban America—there is always the possibility of death.

3   In that first year, my first away from my hometown, I was to become thoroughly familiar with the language of fear. At dark, shadowy intersections in Chicago, I could cross in front of a car stopped at a traffic light and elicit the *thunk, thunk, thunk* of the driver—black, white, male, or female—hammering down the door locks. On less traveled streets after dark, I grew accustomed to but never comfortable with people who crossed to the other side of the street rather than pass me. Then there were the standard unpleasantries with police, doormen, bouncers, cabdrivers, and others whose business is to screen out troublesome individuals *before* there is any nastiness.

4   I moved to New York nearly two years ago and I have remained an avid night walker. In central Manhattan, the near-constant crowd cover minimizes tense one-on-one street encounters. Elsewhere—visiting friends in SoHo, where sidewalks are narrow and tightly spaced buildings shut out the sky—things can get very taut indeed.

Black men have a firm place in New York mugging literature. 5
Norman Podhoretz in his famed (or infamous) 1963 essay, "My
Negro Problem—And Ours," recalls growing up in terror of black
males; they "were tougher than we were, more ruthless," he
writes—and as an adult on the Upper West Side of Manhattan, he
continues, he cannot constrain his nervousness when he meets
black men on certain streets. Similarly, a decade later, the essayist
and novelist Edward Hoagland extols a New York where once
"Negro bitterness bore down mainly on other Negroes." Where
some see mere panhandlers, Hoagland sees "a mugger who is
clearly screwing up his nerve to do more than just *ask* for money."
But Hoagland has "the New Yorker's quick-hunch posture for
broken-field maneuvering," and the bad guy swerves away.

I often witness that "hunch posture," from women after dark 6
on the warrenlike streets of Brooklyn where I live. They seem to
set their faces on neutral and, with their purse straps strung across
their chests bandolier style, they forge ahead as though bracing
themselves against being tackled. I understand, of course, that the
danger they perceive is not a hallucination. Women are particularly vulnerable to street violence, and young black males are dras-
tically overrepresented among the perpetrators of that violence.
Yet these truths are no solace against the kind of alienation that
comes of being ever the suspect, against being set apart, a fear-
some entity with whom pedestrians avoid making eye contact.

It is not altogether clear to me how I reached the ripe old age 7
of twenty-two without being conscious of the lethality nighttime
pedestrians attributed to me. Perhaps it was because in Chester,
Pennsylvania, the small, angry industrial town where I came of
age in the 1960s, I was scarcely noticeable against a backdrop of
gang warfare, street knifings, and murders. I grew up one of the
good boys, had perhaps a half-dozen fistfights. In retrospect, my
shyness of combat has clear sources.

Many things go into the making of a young thug. One of those 8
things is the consummation of the male romance with the power to
intimidate. An infant discovers that random flailings send the baby
bottle flying out of the crib and crashing to the floor. Delighted, the
joyful babe repeats those motions again and again, seeking to
duplicate the feat. Just so, I recall the points at which some of
my boyhood friends were finally seduced by the perception of

themselves as tough guys. When a mark cowered and surrendered his money without resistance, myth and reality merged—and paid off. It is, after all, only manly to embrace the power to frighten and intimidate. We, as men, are not supposed to give an inch of our lane on the highway; we are to seize the fighter's edge in work and in play and even in love; we are to be valiant in the face of hostile forces.

9   Unfortunately, poor and powerless young men seem to take all this nonsense literally. As a boy, I saw countless tough guys locked away; I have since buried several, too. They were babies, really—a teenage cousin, a brother of twenty-two, a childhood friend in his midtwenties—all gone down in episodes of bravado played out in the streets. I came to doubt the virtues of intimidation early on. I chose, perhaps even unconsciously, to remain a shadow—timid, but a survivor.

10   The fearsomeness mistakenly attributed to me in public places often has a perilous flavor. The most frightening of these confusions occurred in the late 1970s and early 1980s when I worked as a journalist in Chicago. One day, rushing into the office of a magazine I was writing for with a deadline story in hand, I was mistaken for a burglar. The office manager called security and, with an ad hoc posse, pursued me through the labyrinthine halls, nearly to my editor's door. I had no way of proving who I was. I could only move briskly toward the company of someone who knew me.

11   Another time I was on assignment for a local paper and killing time before an interview. I entered a jewelry store on the city's affluent Near North Side. The proprietor excused herself and returned with an enormous red Doberman pinscher straining at the end of a leash. She stood, the dog extended toward me, silent to my questions, her eyes bulging nearly out of her head. I took a cursory look around, nodded, and bade her good night. Relatively speaking, however, I never fared as badly as another black male journalist. He went to nearby Waukegan, Illinois, a couple of summers ago to work on a story about a murderer who was born there. Mistaking the reporter for the killer, police hauled him from his car at gunpoint and but for his press credentials would probably have tried to book him. Such episodes are not uncommon. Black men trade tales like this all the time.

In "My Negro Problem—And Ours," Podhoretz writes that 12
the hatred he feels for blacks makes itself known to him through a
variety of avenues—one being his discomfort with that "special
brand of paranoid touchiness" to which he says blacks are prone.
No doubt he is speaking here of black men. In time, I learned to
smother the rage I felt at so often being taken for a criminal. Not
to do so would surely have led to madness—via that special
"paranoid touchiness" that so annoyed Podhoretz at the time he
wrote the essay.

I began to take precautions to make myself less threatening. I 13
move about with care, particularly late in the evening. I give a
wide berth to nervous people on subway platforms during the wee
hours, particularly when I have exchanged business clothes for
jeans. If I happen to be entering a building behind some people
who appear skittish, I may walk by, letting them clear the lobby
before I return, so as not to seem to be following them. I have been
calm and extremely congenial on those rare occasions when I've
been pulled over by the police.

And on late-evening constitutionals along streets less traveled 14
by, I employ what has proved to be an excellent tension-reducing
measure: I whistle melodies from Beethoven and Vivaldi and the
more popular classical composers. Even steely New Yorkers
hunching toward nighttime destinations seem to relax, and occasionally they even join in the tune. Virtually everybody seems to
sense that a mugger wouldn't be warbling bright, sunny selections from Vivaldi's *Four Seasons*. It is my equivalent of the cow-
bell that hikers wear when they know they are in bear country.

1986

How the Irish Became White

Noel Ignatiev

Throughout most of the eighteenth century, Ireland was governed 1
under a series of codes which have become known collectively as

the Penal Laws. Under the terms of these Laws, Catholics were not permitted to vote or serve in Parliament or hold public office in any of the municipal corporations, or live within the limits of incorporated towns; they were forbidden to practice law or hold a post in the military or the civil service. Catholics were forbidden to open or teach in a school, serve as private tutors, attend university, or educate their sons abroad. They were forbidden to take part in the manufacture or sale of arms, newspapers, or books, or possess or carry arms. No Catholic might own a horse worth more than five pounds. Except in the linen trade, they might take on no more than two apprentices, and Protestants might not take on Catholic apprentices. Catholics might not buy, inherit, or receive gifts of land from Protestants, nor rent land worth more than thirty shillings a year, nor lease land for longer than thirty-one years, nor make a profit from land of more than one-third of the rent paid; no Catholic estate could be entailed but instead had to be divided at death among all the children. By converting to Protestantism, a Catholic son could dispossess his father and disinherit all his brothers. A Protestant landowner lost his civil rights if he married a Catholic, a Protestant heiress her inheritance. All bishops of the Catholic Church were ordered to leave the country under penalty of death if they remained or returned; no priest might enter the country from anywhere, and only one priest was permitted per parish, forbidden to set foot outside it without special permission. Like all Irish, Catholics paid taxes to support the Protestant Church of Ireland. Catholic orphans were to be brought up as Protestants. As can be seen, the Penal Laws regulated every aspect of Irish life, civil, domestic, and spiritual. In effect they established Ireland as a country in which Irish Catholics formed an oppressed race.

. . .

2   Eighteenth-century Ireland presents a classic case of racial oppression. Catholics there were known as native Irish, Celts, or Gaels (as well as "Papists" and other equally derogatory names), and were regarded, and frequently spoke of themselves, as a "race," rather than a nation. The Penal Laws imposed upon them a caste status out of which no Catholic, no matter how wealthy, could escape.

. . .

On their arrival in America, the Irish were thrown together 3
with black people on jobs and in neighborhoods, with predictable
results. The Census of 1850 was the first to include a class it called
"mulatto"; it enumerated 406,000 nationwide, including 15,000 in
Pennsylvania, the largest number for any free state. There is no
closer breakdown, but they made up a little over a quarter of the
state's "colored" population. Applying that ratio to the 3,000 Negroes living in the heavily Irish Moyamensing district (whose total population was 24,000) gives a figure of over eight hundred
persons of mixed ancestry, or one out of every thirty. Even if most
of these were the children of slaveholders who had been manu-
mitted and migrated north, an Irish resident of that district must
have seen on the street constant reminders of the fact and possibility of sexual union between European-Americans and Negroes . . .
In 1853 a Philadelphia grand jury issued a report on living conditions in the Moyamensing district; attached to its report was an article entitled "The Mysteries and Miseries of Philadelphia," which
originally appeared in the *Evening Bulletin:*

> We will essay a description of a hovel we visited which was kept
> by a hideous looking Irishman, known as Jemmy Quinn. The
> house is a tavern and lodging-house, and is located in Small
> Street, above Fifth. It is a two-story frame of quite a small size,
> but is nevertheless divided into a numbers of rooms which are
> about ten feet square. The bar room is in front on the ground
> floor. With the exception of this apartment, no other part of the
> house contained a single article of furniture, except some dam-
> aged furnaces and miserable stoves. The walls were discolored
> by smoke and filth, the glass was broken from the windows,
> chinks in the frame work let in the cold air, and every thing was
> as wretchedly uncomfortable as it is possible to conceive. Yet in
> every one of these squalid apartments, including the cellar and
> the loft, men and women—blacks and whites by dozens—were
> huddled together promiscuously, squatting or lying upon the
> bare floors, and keeping themselves from freezing by covering
> their bodies with such filthy rags as chance threw in their way.[1]

[1]Anne Warren Weston to Elizabeth Pease, January 30, 1842, William Lloyd Garrison Papers, cited by Gilbert Osofsky in "Abolitionists, Irish Immigrants, and Romantic Nationalism," *American Historical Review* 80:4 (October 1975): 889–912.

268954383. . ...

4   In New York, the majority of cases of "mixed" matings involved Irish women. The same was true of Boston. A list of employed of the Narragansett and National Brick Company in 1950 includes a number described as of Irish nationality who are also listed as "mulatto."

5   The interaction between Irish- and Afro-American was not limited to sexual affairs: In New Orleans Irish moved into the black district, and frequented "Black Rookeries." Irish grocers regularly received stolen sugar and flour brought to them by slaves, and sold them liquor, etc. In one case that came before a Philadelphia court, a white man charged two Negroes with stealing his money. His testimony revealed that the three were friends and had been drinking together at Fourth Street oyster cellar. Nor did the crossing over always take place under hellish circumstances; heaven had its turn as well: The Twelfth Presbyterian Church in Philadelphia was presided over after 1837 by an Afro-American minister; baptismal records for the next twenty years suggest that one-third of the members were Irish.

6   The first Congress of the United States voted in 1790 that only "white" persons could be naturalized as citizens. Coming as immigrants rather than as captives or hostages undoubtedly affected the potential racial status of the Irish in America, but it did not settle the issue, since it was by no means obvious who was "white."

. . .

7   [T]he Irish in America . . . opted . . . for the privileges and burdens of whiteness. The outcome was not a foregone conclusion. . . . While the white skin made the Irish eligible for membership in the white race, it did not guarantee their admission; they had to earn it.

. . .

8   Strong tendencies existed in antebellum America to consign the Irish if not to the black race, then to an intermediate race located socially between black and white. Nativism [a party and movement espousing the privilege of those born in America over immigrants] expressed this tendency, and Nativism appealed to many artisans who were resentful of immigrants coming into the country. Many craftsmen of the time, and some historians subsequently, have spoken of "low-paid" immigrant (like "cheap" black) labor, as if cheapness were some quality in the labor itself. . . . If, therefore, the Democratic Party decided, after some vacillation,

to reject Nativism, the decision had far-reaching consequences. . . .
Everywhere, the movement that expanded the franchise for
whites curtailed it for persons of color.

. . .

The United States of North America, after the electoral re- 9
forms of the Jacksonian period [1828–1860, led by Andrew Jackson's Democratic party], was perhaps the most truly democratic
republic the world had ever seen up to that time, and arguably
more democratic than any it has seen since. That assertion is
based first, on the lack of significant property restrictions on the
franchise[2] among the free population, and, second, on the weakness of the state, that is, the relative absence of administrative organs and bodies of armed men, differentiated from the general
population and therefore insulated from politics, charged with
maintaining order. Karl Marx was probably thinking of this situation when he referred to the U.S. workingmen as "the true political power of the North.". . . The entire passage reads:

> While the workingmen, the true political power of the North, al-
> lowed slavery to defile their own republic; while before the Ne-
> gro, mastered and sold without his concurrence, they boasted it
> the highest prerogative of the white-skinned laborer to sell him-
> self and choose his own master; they were unable to attain the
> true freedom of labor or to support their European brethren in
> the struggle for emancipation, but this barrier to progress has
> been swept off by the red sea of civil war.[3]

In a certain sense, this study may be understood as a meditation
on how the Irish, an important contingent of "the true political
power of the North," came to boast the white skin as their highest
prerogative.

Slaveholder ideologists understood full well the importance 10
of gaining the support of Northern laborers, and made special appeals to them. . . . In the combination of the Southern planters and
the "plain Republicans" of the North, the Irish were to become a

---

[2]The vote.
[3]*National Anti-Slavery Standard*, March 24, 1842, cited by Gilbert Osofsky in "Abolitionists, Irish Immigrants, and Romantic Nationalism," *American Historical Review* 80:4 (October 1975): 889–912.

key element. . . . The need to gain the loyalty of the Irish explains why the Democratic Party, on the whole, rejected Nativism. It also explains why not merely slavery but the color line became so important to it. To trace, therefore, the movement from the Republican Party that carried out the "civil revolution of 1801" to the Democratic Party that served as the center of parliamentary opposition to the civil revolution of 1845–1877 (counting from the first shots fired in Kansas to the withdrawal of the last federal troops from the South) is to explain the link between the Jacobin, agitator, conspirator, gunrunner, and jailbird who left Ireland in 1801 and the alderman who swore his allegiance to the Constitution and slavery in 1838. It is also to answer the question, how did the Irish become white in America?

1995

Casa

Judith Ortiz Cofer

1   At three or four o'clock in the afternoon, the hour of *café con leche,* the women of my family gathered in Mamá's living room to speak of important things and retell familiar stories meant to be overheard by us young girls, their daughters. In Mamá's house (everyone called my grandmother Mamá) was a large parlor built by my grandfather to his wife's exact specifications so that it was always cool, facing away from the sun. The doorway was on the side of the house so no one could walk directly into her living room. First they had to take a little stroll through and around her beautiful garden where prize-winning orchids grew in the trunk of an ancient tree she had hollowed out for that purpose. This room was furnished with several mahogany rocking chairs, acquired at the births of her children, and one intricately carved rocker that had passed down to Mamá at the death of her own mother.

2   It was on these rockers that my mother, her sisters, and my grandmother sat on these afternoons of my childhood to tell their

stories, teaching each other, and my cousin and me, what it was like to be a woman, more specifically, a Puerto Rican woman. They talked about life on the island, and life in *Los Nueva Yores,* their way of referring to the United States from New York City to California: the other place, not home, all the same. They told real-life stories though, as I later learned, always embellishing them with a little or a lot of dramatic detail. And they told *cuentos,* the morality and cautionary tales told by the women in our family for generations: stories that became a part of my subconscious as I grew up in two worlds, the tropical island and the cold city, and that would later surface in my dreams and in my poetry.

One of these tales was about the woman who was left at the altar. Mamá liked to tell that one with histrionic intensity. I remember the rise and fall of her voice, the sighs, and her constantly gesturing hands, like two birds swooping through her words. This particular story usually would come up in a conversation as a result of someone mentioning a forthcoming engagement or wedding. The first time I remember hearing it, I was sitting on the floor at Mamá's feet, pretending to read a comic book. I may have been eleven or twelve years old, at that difficult age when a girl was no longer a child who could be ordered to leave the room if the women wanted freedom to take their talk into forbidden zones, nor really old enough to be considered a part of their conclave. I could only sit quietly, pretending to be in another world, while absorbing it all in a sort of unspoken agreement of my status as silent auditor. On this day, Mamá had taken my long, tangled mane of hair into her ever-busy hands. Without looking down at me and with no interruption of her flow of words, she began braiding my hair, working at it with the quickness and determination that characterized all her actions. My mother was watching us impassively from her rocker across the room. On her lips played a little ironic smile. I would never sit still for *her* ministrations, but even then, I instinctively knew that she did not possess Mamá's matriarchal power to command and keep everyone's attention. This was never more evident than in the spell she cast when telling a story.

"It is not like it used to be when I was a girl," Mamá announced. "Then, a man could leave a girl standing at the church altar with a bouquet of fresh flowers in her hands and disappear off the face of the earth. No way to track him down if he was from another town. He could be a married man, with maybe even two or three families all over the island. There was no way to know. And there were men who did this. Hombres with the devil in their flesh who would come to a pueblo, like this one, take a job at one of the haciendas, never meaning to stay, only to have a good time and to seduce the women."

5   The whole time she was speaking, Mamá would be weaving my hair into a flat plait that required pulling apart the two sections of hair with little jerks that made my eyes water; but knowing how grandmother detested whining and *boba* (sissy) tears, as she called them, I just sat up as straight and stiff as I did at La Escuela San Jose, where the nuns enforced good posture with a flexible plastic ruler they bounced off of slumped shoulders and heads. As Mamá's story progressed, I noticed how my young Aunt Laura lowered her eyes, refusing to meet Mamá's meaningful gaze. Laura was seventeen, in her last year of high school, and already engaged to a boy from another town who had staked his claim with a tiny diamond ring, then left for Los Nueva Yores to make his fortune. They were planning to get married in a year. Mamá had expressed serious doubts that the wedding would ever take place. In Mamá's eyes, a man set free without a legal contract was a man lost. She believed that marriage was not something men desired, but simply the price they had to pay for the privilege of children and, of course, for what no decent (synonymous with "smart") woman would give away for free.

6   "María La Loca was only seventeen when *it* happened to her." I listened closely at the mention of this name. María was a town character, a fat middle-aged woman who lived with her old mother on the outskirts of town. She was to be seen around the pueblo delivering the meat pies the two women made for a living. The most peculiar thing about María, in my eyes, was that she walked and moved like a little girl though she had the thick body and wrinkled face of an old woman. She would swing her hips in an exaggerated, clownish way, and sometimes even hop and skip up to someone's house. She spoke to no one. Even if you asked her a question, she would just look at you and smile, showing her

yellow teeth. But I had heard that if you got close enough, you could hear her humming a tune without words. The kids yelled out nasty things at her, calling her *La Loca,* and the men who hung out at the bodega playing dominoes sometimes whistled mockingly as she passed by with her funny, outlandish walk. But María seemed impervious to it all, carrying her basket of *pasteles* like a grotesque Little Red Riding Hood through the forest.

María La Loca interested me, as did all the eccentrics and ⁷ crazies of our pueblo. Their weirdness was a measuring stick I used in my serious quest for a definition of normal. As a Navy brat shuttling between New Jersey and the pueblo, I was constantly made to feel like an oddball by my peers, who made fun of my two-way accent: a Spanish accent when I spoke English, and when I spoke Spanish I was told that I sounded like a *Gringa.* Being the outsider had already turned my brother and me into cultural chameleons. We developed early on the ability to blend into a crowd, to sit and read quietly in a fifth story apartment building for days and days when it was too bitterly cold to play outside, or, set free, to run wild in Mamá's realm, where she took charge of our lives, releasing Mother for a while from the intense fear for our safety that our father's absences instilled in her. In order to keep us from harm when Father was away, Mother kept us under strict surveillance. She even walked us to and from Public School No. 11, which we attended during the months we lived in Paterson, New Jersey, our home base in the States. Mamá freed all three of us like pigeons from a cage. I saw her as my liberator and my model. Her stories were parables from which to glean the *Truth.*

"María La Loca was once a beautiful girl. Everyone thought ⁸ she would marry the Méndez boy." As everyone knew, Rogelio Méndez was the richest man in town. "But," Mamá continued, knitting my hair with the same intensity she was putting into her story, "this *macho* made a fool out of her and ruined her life." She paused for the effect of her use of the word "macho," which at that time had not yet become a popular epithet for an unliberated man. This word had for us the crude and comical connotation of "male of the species," stud; a *macho* was what you put in a pen to increase your stock.

9   I peeked over my comic book at my mother. She too was under Mamá's spell, smiling conspiratorially at this little swipe at men. She was safe from Mamá's contempt in this area. Married at an early age, an unspotted lamb, she had been accepted by a good family of strict Spaniards whose name was old and respected, though their fortune had been lost long before my birth. In a rocker Papa had painted sky blue sat Mamá's oldest child, Aunt Nena. Mother of three children, stepmother of two more, she was a quiet woman who liked books but had married an ignorant and abusive widower whose main interest in life was accumulating wealth. He too was in the mainland working on his dream of returning home rich and triumphant to buy the *finca* of his dreams. She was waiting for him to send for her. She would leave her children with Mamá for several years while the two of them slaved away in factories. He would one day be a rich man, and she a sadder woman. Even now her life-light was dimming. She spoke little, an aberration in Mamá's house, and she read avidly, as if storing up spiritual food for the long winters that awaited her in Los Nueva Yores without her family. But even Aunt Nena came alive to Mamá's words, rocking gently, her hands over a thick book in her lap.

10   Her daughter, my cousin Sara, played jacks by herself on the tile porch outside the room where we sat. She was a year older than I. We shared a bed and all our family's secrets. Collaborators in search of answers, Sara and I discussed everything we heard the women say, trying to fit it all together like a puzzle that, once assembled, would reveal life's mysteries to us. Though she and I still enjoyed taking part in boys' games—chase, volleyball, and even *vaqueros,* the island version of cowboys and Indians involving cap-gun battles and violent shoot-outs under the mango tree in Mamá's backyard—we loved best the quiet hours in the afternoon when the men were still at work, and the boys had gone to play serious baseball at the park. Then Mamá's house belonged only to us women. The aroma of coffee perking in the kitchen, the mesmerizing creaks and groans of the rockers, and the women telling their lives in *cuentos* are forever woven into the fabric of my imagination, braided like my hair that day I felt my grandmother's hands teaching me about strength, her voice convincing me of the power of storytelling.

That day Mamá told how the beautiful María had fallen prey 11
to a man whose name was never the same in subsequent versions
of the story; it was Juan one time, José, Rafael, Diego, another. We
understood that neither the name or any of the *facts* were important, only that a woman had allowed love to defeat her. Mamá put
each of us in María's place by describing her wedding dress in
loving detail: how she looked like a princess in her lace as she
waited at the altar. Then, as Mamá approached the tragic denoue-
ment of her story, I was distracted by the sound of my Aunt
Laura's violent rocking. She seemed on the verge of tears. She
knew the fable was intended for her. That week she was going to
have her wedding gown fitted, though no firm date had been set
for the marriage. Mamá ignored Laura's obvious discomfort, dig-
ging out a ribbon from the sewing basket she kept by her rocker
while describing María's long illness, "a fever that would not
break for days." She spoke of a mother's despair: "that woman
climbed the church steps on her knees every morning, wore only
black as a *promesa* to the Holy Virgin in exchange for her daughter's health." By the time María returned from her honeymoon
with death, she was ravished, no longer young or sane. "As you
can see, she is almost as old as her mother already," Mamá
lamented while tying the ribbon to the ends of my hair, pulling it
back with such force that I just knew I would never be able to
close my eyes completely again.

"That María's getting crazier every day." Mamá's voice 12
would take a lighter tone now, expressing satisfaction, either for
the perfection of my braid, or for a story well told—it was hard to
tell. "You know that tune María is always humming?" Carried
away by her enthusiasm, I tried to nod, but Mamá still had me
pinned between her knees.

"Well, that's the wedding march." Surprising us all, Mamá 13
sang out, "Da, da, dara . . . da, da, dara." Then lifting me off the
floor by my skinny shoulders, she would lead me around the room
in an impromptu waltz—another session ending with the laughter
of women, all of us caught up in the infectious joke of our lives.

1990

Salvation

Langston Hughes

1   I was saved from sin when I was going on thirteen. But not really
saved. It happened like this. There was a big revival at my Auntie
Reed's church. Every night for weeks there had been much preaching, singing, praying, and shouting, and some very hardened
sinners had been brought to Christ, and the membership of the
church had grown by leaps and bounds. Then just before the revival ended, they held a special meeting for children, "to bring the
young lambs to the fold." My aunt spoke of it for days ahead.
That night I was escorted to the front row and placed on the
mourners' bench with all the other young sinners, who had not
yet been brought to Jesus.

2   My aunt told me that when you were saved you saw a light,
and something happened to you inside! And Jesus came into your
life! And God was with you from then on! She said you could see
and hear and feel Jesus in your soul. I believed her. I had heard a
great many old people say the same thing and it seemed to me
they ought to know. So I sat there calmly in the hot, crowded
church, waiting for Jesus to come to me.

3   The preacher preached a wonderful rhythmical sermon, all
moans and shouts and lonely cries and dire pictures of hell, and then
he sang a song about the ninety and nine safe in the fold, but one little lamb was left out in the cold. Then he said: "Won't you come?
Won't you come to Jesus? Young lambs, won't you come?" And he
held out his arms to all us young sinners there on the mourners'
bench. And the little girls cried. And some of them jumped up and
went to Jesus right away. But most of us just sat there.

4   A great many older people came and knelt around us and
prayed, old women with jet-black faces and braided hair, old men
with work-gnarled hands. And the church sang a song about the
lower lights are burning, some poor sinners to be saved. And the
whole building rocked with prayer and song.

5   Still I kept waiting to *see* Jesus.

Finally all the young people had gone to the altar and were 6
saved, but one boy and me. He was a rounder's son named Westley. Westley and I were surrounded by sisters and deacons praying. It was very hot in the church, and getting late now. Finally
Westley said to me in a whisper: "God damn! I'm tired o' sitting
here. Let's get up and be saved." So he got up and was saved.

Then I was left all alone on the mourners' bench. My aunt 7
came and knelt at my knees and cried, while prayers and songs
swirled all around me in the little church. The whole congregation
prayed for me alone, in a mighty wail of moans and voices. And I
kept waiting serenely for Jesus, waiting, waiting—but he didn't
come. I wanted to see him, but nothing happened to me. Nothing!
I wanted something to happen to me, but nothing happened.

I heard the songs and the minister saying: "Why don't you 8
come? My dear child, why don't you come to Jesus? Jesus is waiting for you. He wants you. Why don't you come? Sister Reed,
what is this child's name?"

"Langston," my aunt sobbed.   9

"Langston, why don't you come? Why don't you come and be 10
saved? Oh, Lamb of God! Why don't you come?"

Now it was really getting late. I began to be ashamed of my- 11
self, holding everything up so long. I began to wonder what God
thought about Westley, who certainly hadn't seen Jesus either, but
who was now sitting proudly on the platform, swinging his
knickerbockered legs and grinning down at me, surrounded by
deacons and old women on their knees praying. God had not
struck Westley dead for taking his name in vain or for lying in the
temple. So I decided that maybe to save further trouble, I'd better
lie, too, and say that Jesus had come, and get up and be saved.

So I got up.   12

Suddenly the whole room broke into a sea of shouting, as 13
they saw me rise. Waves of rejoicing swept the place. Women
leaped in the air. My aunt threw her arms around me. The minister took me by the hand and let me to the platform.

When things quieted down, in a hushed silence, punctuated 14
by a few ecstatic "Amens," all the new young lambs were blessed
in the name of God. Then joyous singing filled the room.

That night, for the last time in my life but one—for I was a big 15
boy twelve years old—I cried. I cried, in bed alone, and couldn't

stop. I buried my head under the quilts, but my aunt heard me. She woke up and told my uncle I was crying because the Holy Ghost had come into my life, and because I had seen Jesus. But I was really crying because I couldn't bear to tell her that I had lied, that I had deceived everybody in the church, and I hadn't seen Jesus, and that now I didn't believe there was a Jesus any more, since he didn't come to help me.

1940

The Way to Rainy Mountain

N. Scott Momaday

1   A single knoll rises out of the plain in Oklahoma, north and west of the Wichita range. For my people, the Kiowas, it is an old landmark, and they gave it the name Rainy Mountain. The hardest weather in the world is there. Winter brings blizzards, hot tornadic winds arise in the spring, and in summer the prairie is an anvil's edge. The grass turns brittle and brown, and it cracks beneath your feet. There are green belts along the rivers and creeks, linear groves of hickory and pecan, willow and witch hazel. At a distance in July or August the steaming foliage seems almost to writhe in fire. Great green and yellow grasshoppers are everywhere in the tall grass, popping up like corn to sting the flesh, and tortoises crawl about on the red earth, going nowhere in the plenty of time. Loneliness is an aspect of the land. All things in the plain are isolate; there is no confusion of objects in the eye, but *one* hill or *one* tree or *one* man. To look upon that landscape in the early morning, with the sun at your back, is to lose the sense of proportion. Your imagination comes to life, and this, you think, is where Creation was begun.

2   I returned to Rainy Mountain in July. My grandmother had died in the spring, and I wanted to be at her grave. She had lived to be very old and at last infirm. Her only living daughter was with her when she died, and I was told that in death her face was that of a child.

I like to think of her as a child. When she was born, the Kiowas ₃
were living the last great moment of their history. For more than a
hundred years they had controlled the open range from the Smoky
Hill River to the Red, from the headwaters of the Canadian to the
fork of the Arkansas and Cimarron. In alliance with the Co-
manches, they had ruled the whole of the Southern Plains. War
was their sacred business, and they were the finest horsemen the
world has ever known. But warfare for the Kiowas was pre-emi-
nently a matter of disposition rather than of survival, and they
never understood the grim, unrelenting advance of the U.S. Cavalry. When at last, divided and ill provisioned, they were driven
onto the Staked Plains in the cold of autumn, they fell into panic.
In Palo Duro Canyon they abandoned their crucial stores to pillage
and had nothing then but their lives. In order to save themselves,
they surrendered to the soldiers at Fort Sill and were imprisoned
in the old stone corral that now stands as a military museum. My
grandmother was spared the humiliation of those high gray walls
by eight or ten years, but she must have known from birth the affliction of defeat, the dark brooding of old warriors.

Her name was Aho, and she belonged to the last culture to ₄
evolve in North America. Her forebears came down from the high
country in western Montana nearly three centuries ago. They
were a mountain people, a mysterious tribe of hunters whose language has never been classified in any major group. In the late
seventeenth century they began a long migration to the south and
east. It was a journey toward the dawn, and it led to a golden age.
Along the way the Kiowas were befriended by the Crows, who
gave them the culture and religion of the Plains. They acquired
horses, and their ancient nomadic spirit was suddenly free of the
ground. They acquired Tai-me, the sacred sun-dance doll, from
that moment the object and symbol of their worship, and so
shared in the divinity of the sun. Not least, they acquired the
sense of destiny, therefore courage and pride. When they entered
upon the Southern Plains they had been transformed. No longer
were they slaves to the simple necessity of survival; they were a
lordly and dangerous society of fighters and thieves, hunters and
priests of the sun. According to their origin myth, they entered the
world through a hollow log. From one point of view, their migra-

tion was the fruit of an old prophecy, for indeed they emerged from a sunless world.

5   Though my grandmother lived out her long life in the shadow of Rainy Mountain, the immense landscape of the continental interior lay like memory in her blood. She could tell of the Crows, whom she had never seen, and of the Black Hills, where she had never been. I wanted to see in reality what she had seen more perfectly in the mind's eye, and drove fifteen hundred miles to begin my pilgrimage.

6   A dark mist lay over the Black Hills, and the land was like iron. At the top of a ridge I caught sight of Devil's Tower upthrust against the gray sky as if in the birth of time the core of the earth had broken through its crust and the motion of the world was begun. There are things in nature that engender an awful quiet in the heart of man; Devil's Tower is one of them. Two centuries ago, because of their need to explain it, the Kiowas made a legend at the base of the rock. My grandmother said:

7   "Eight children were there at play, seven sisters and their brother. Suddenly the boy was struck dumb; he trembled and began to run upon his hands and feet. His fingers became claws, and his body was covered with fur. There was a bear where the boy had been. The sisters were terrified; they ran, and the bear after them. They came to the stump of a great tree, and the tree spoke to them. It bade them climb upon it, and as they did so, it began to rise into the air. The bear came to kill them, but they were just beyond its reach. It reared against the tree and scored the bark all around with its claws. The seven sisters were borne into the sky, and they became the stars of the Big Dipper." From that moment, and so long as the legend lives, the Kiowas have kinsmen in the night sky. Whatever they were in the mountains, they could be no more. However tenuous their well-being, however much they had suffered and would suffer again, they had found a way out of the wilderness.

8   My grandmother had a reverence for the sun, a holy regard that now is all but gone out of mankind. There was a wariness in her, and an ancient awe. She was a Christian in her later years, but she had come a long way about, and she never forgot her birthright. As a child she had been to the sun dances; she had taken part

in that annual rite, and by it she had learned the restoration of her people in the presence of Tai-me. She was about seven when the last Kiowa sun dance was held in 1887 on the Washita River above Rainy Mountain Creek. The buffalo were gone. In order to consummate the ancient sacrifice—to impale the head of a buffalo bull upon the Tai-me tree—a delegation of old men journeyed into Texas, there to beg and barter for an animal from the Goodnight herd. She was ten when the Kiowas came together for the last time as a living sun-dance culture. They could find no buffalo; they had to hang an old hide from the sacred tree. Before the dance could begin, a company of soldiers rode out from Fort Sill under orders to disperse the tribe. Forbidden without cause the essential act of their faith, having seen the wild herds slaughtered and left to rot upon the ground, the Kiowas backed away forever from the tree. That was July 20, 1890, at the great bend of the Washita. My grandmother was there. Without bitterness, and for as long as she lived, she bore a vision of deicide.

Now that I can have her only in memory, I see my grand- 9
mother in the several postures that were peculiar to her: standing at the wood stove on a winter morning and turning meat in a great iron skillet; sitting at the south window, bent above her beadwork, and afterwards, when her vision failed, looking down for a long time into the fold of her hands; going out upon a cane, very slowly as she did when the weight of age came upon her; praying. I remember her most often at prayer. She made long, rambling prayers out of suffering and hope, having seen many things. I was never sure that I had the right to hear, so exclusive were they of all mere custom and company. The last time I saw her she prayed standing by the side of the bed at night, naked to the waist, the light of a kerosene lamp moving upon her dark skin. Her long black hair, always drawn and braided in the day, lay upon her shoulders and against her breasts like a shawl. I do not speak Kiowa, and I never understood her prayers, but there was something inherently sad in the sound, some merest hesitation upon the syllables of sorrow. She began in a high and descending pitch, exhausting her breath to silence; then again and again—and always the same intensity of effort, of something that

is, and is not, like urgency in the human voice. Transported so in the dancing light among the shadows of her room, she seemed beyond the reach of time. But that was illusion; I think I knew then that I should not see her again.

10   Houses are like sentinels in the plain, old keepers of the weather watch. There, in a very little while, wood takes on the appearance of great age. All colors wear soon away in the wind and rain, and then the wood is burned gray and the grain appears and the nails turn red with rust. The window panes are black and opaque; you imagine there is nothing within, and indeed there are many ghosts, bones given up to the land. They stand here and there against the sky, and you approach them for a longer time than you expect. They belong in the distance; it is their domain.

11   Once there was a lot of sound in my grandmother's house, a lot of coming and going, feasting and talk. The summers there were full of excitement and reunion. The Kiowas are a summer people; they abide the cold and keep to themselves, but when the season turns and the land becomes warm and vital they cannot hold still; an old love of going returns upon them. The aged visitors who came to my grandmother's house when I was a child were made of lean and leather, and they bore themselves upright. They wore great black hats and bright ample shirts that shook in the wind. They rubbed fat upon their hair and wound their braids with strips of colored cloth. Some of them painted their faces and carried the scars of old and cherished enmities. They were an old council of warlords, come to remind and be reminded of who they were. Their wives and daughters served them well. The women might indulge themselves; gossip was at once the mark and compensation of their servitude. They made loud and elaborate talk among themselves, full of jest and gesture, fright and false alarm. They went abroad in fringed and flowered shawls, bright beadwork and German silver. They were at home in the kitchen, and they prepared meals that were banquets.

12   There were frequent prayer meetings, and nocturnal feasts. When I was a child I played with my cousins outside, where the lamplight fell upon the ground and the singing of the old people rose up around us and carried away into the darkness. There were a lot of good things to eat, a lot of laughter and surprise. And

afterwards, when the quiet returned, I lay down with my grandmother and could hear the frogs away by the river and feel the
motion of the air.

Now there is a funereal silence in the rooms, the endless wake   13
of some final word. The walls have closed in upon my grandmother's house. When I returned to it in mourning, I saw for the
first time in my life how small it was. It was late at night, and
there was a white moon, nearly full. I sat for a long time on the
stone steps by the kitchen door. From there I could see out across
the land; I could see the long row of trees by the creek, the low
light upon the rolling plains, and the stars of the Big Dipper. Once
I looked at the moon and caught sight of a strange thing. A cricket
had perched upon the handrail, only a few inches away. My line
of vision was such that the creature filled the moon like a fossil. It
had gone there, I thought, to live and die, for there, of all places,
was its small definition made whole and eternal. A warm wind
rose up and purled like the longing within me.

The next morning, I awoke at dawn and went out on the dirt   14
road to Rainy Mountain. It was already hot, and the grasshoppers
began to fill the air. Still, it was early in the morning, and birds
sang out of the shadows. The long yellow grass on the mountain
shone in the bright light, and a scissortail hied above the land.
There, where it ought to be, at the end of a long and legendary
way, was my grandmother's grave. She had at last succeeded to
that holy ground. Here and there on the dark stones were ancestral
names. Looking back once, I saw the mountain and came away.

1967

Relationships and Sexual Politics

In this post-feminist generation, gender is more analyzed, scruti-
nized, and debated than ever. Despite a new openness, some of
this freedom is confusing rather than liberating. Media exploitation, for example, continues to alienate women from their own
bodies, as Margaret Atwood describes in her essay on "The Female Body." Whatever progress has been made, Camille Paglia
controversially argues that recognizing inequality in the arena of
sexual politics is still necessary common sense if women are to be
kept out of harm's way. Ellen Goodman talks about inequality as
well, but in the workplace, and how issues of sexual harassment
need to be resolved by standards reasonable people share. Scott
Russell Sanders explains on the other hand that the idea of men as
having all the power doesn't reflect his own working class roots
where a life of hardship was the rule. Judy Brady counters that the
life of a traditional wife is one of constant sacrifice. However, it is
just this sacrifice by both men and women that Barbara Dafoe
Whitehead feels has been lost in the current culture of divorce,
along with the idea that children are important stakeholders in
a marriage. While divorce has left many children fatherless, a
father's significance in a child's psychological well-being is reflected on by Cornel West. Marriage, parenthood, and relationships between the sexes are being redefined—and Anna Quindlen
asks about same-sex marriage to legally protect those who love
each other. Family and its powerful effect on our sense of who we
are in the world are explored by Alice Walker in "Beauty: When
the Other Dancer Is the Self" as she comes to terms with a disfig-
uring childhood accident. Bruno Bettelheim situates sexual politics in psychodynamic struggles that define childhood and are

reflected in the most popular children's literature. In "Cinderella," Bruno Bettelheim aptly reveals that childhood is not free of social pressures, and Jamaica Kincaid's "Girl" depicts the ironies of the relationship between the sexes as it explores the sexual socialization of a spirited West Indies girl.

Beauty: When the Other Dancer Is the Self

Alice Walker

1   It is a bright summer day in 1947. My father, a fat, funny man with beautiful eyes and a subversive wit, is trying to decide which of his eight children he will take with him to the county fair. My mother, of course, will not go. She is knocked out from getting most of us ready: I hold my neck stiff against the pressure of her knuckles as she hastily completes the braiding and the beribboning of my hair.

2   My father is the driver for the rich old white lady up the road. Her name is Miss Mey. She owns all the land for miles around, as well as the house in which we live. All I remember about her is that she once offered to pay my mother thirty-five cents for cleaning her house, raking up piles of her magnolia leaves, and washing her family's clothes, and that my mother—she of no money, eight children, and a chronic earache—refused it. But I do not think of this in 1947. I am two-and-a-half years old. I want to go everywhere my daddy goes. I am excited at the prospect of riding in a car. Someone has told me fairs are fun. That there is room in the car for only three of us doesn't faze me at all. Whirling happily in my starchy frock, showing off my biscuit-polished patent-leather shoes and lavender socks, tossing my head in a way that makes my ribbons bounce, I stand, hands on hips, before my father. "Take me, Daddy," I say with assurance; "I'm the prettiest!"

3   Later, it does not surprise me to find myself in Miss Mey's shiny black car, sharing the back seat with the other lucky ones. Does not surprise me that I thoroughly enjoy the fair. At home that night I tell the unlucky ones all I can remember about the merry-go-round, the man who eats live chickens, and the teddy bears, until they say: that's enough, baby Alice. Shut up now, and go to sleep.

4   It is Easter Sunday, 1950. I am dressed in a green, flocked, scalloped-hem dress (handmade by my adoring sister, Ruth) that

has its own smooth satin petticoat and tiny hot-pink roses tucked into each scallop. My shoes, new T-strap patent leather, again highly biscuit-polished. I am six years old and have learned one of the longest Easter speeches to be heard that day, totally unlike the speech I said when I was two: "Easter lilies/pure and white/blossom in/the morning light." When I rise to give my speech I do so on a great wave of love and pride and expectation. People in the church stop rustling their new crinolines. They seem to hold their breath. I can tell they admire my dress, but it is my spirit, bordering on sassiness (womanishness), they secretly applaud.

"That girl's a little *mess*," they whisper to each other, pleased. 5

Naturally I say my speech without stammer or pause, unlike 6 those who stutter, stammer, or, worst of all, forget. This is before the word "beautiful" exists in people's vocabulary, but "Oh, isn't she the *cutest* thing!" frequently floats my way. "And got so much sense!" they gratefully add . . . for which thoughtful addition I thank them to this day.

It was great fun being cute. But then, one day, it ended. 7

I am eight years old and a tomboy. I have a cowboy hat, cow- 8 boy boots, checkered shirt and pants, all red. My playmates are my brothers, two and four years older than I. Their colors are black and green, the only difference in the way we are dressed. On Saturday nights we all go to the picture show, even my mother; Westerns are her favorite kind of movie. Back home, "on the ranch," we pretend we are Tom Mix, Hopalong Cassidy, Lash LaRue (we've even named one of our dogs Lash LaRue); we chase each other for hours rustling cattle, being outlaws, delivering damsels from distress. Then my parents decide to buy my brothers guns. These are not "real" guns. They shoot BBs, copper pellets my brothers say will kill birds. Because I am a girl, I do not get a gun. Instantly I am relegated to the position of Indian. Now there appears a great distance between us. They shoot and shoot at everything with their new guns. I try to keep up with my bow and arrows.

One day while I am standing on top of our makeshift 9 "garage"—pieces of tin nailed across some poles—holding my bow and arrow and looking out toward the fields, I feel an incredible blow in my right eye. I look down just in time to see my brother lower his gun.

10   Both brothers rush to my side. My eye stings, and I cover it with my hand. "If you tell," they say, "we will get a whipping. You don't want that to happen, do you?" I do not. "Here is a piece of wire," says the older brother, picking it up from the roof; "say you stepped on one end of it and the other flew up and hit you." The pain is beginning to start. "Yes," I say. "Yes, I will say that is what happened." If I do not say this is what happened, I know my brothers will find ways to make me wish I had. But now I will say anything that gets me to my mother.

11   Confronted by our parents we stick to the lie agreed upon. They place me on a bench on the porch and I close my left eye while they examine the right. There is a tree growing from underneath the porch that climbs past the railing to the roof. It is the last thing my right eye sees. I watch as its trunk, its branches, and then its leaves are blotted out by the rising blood.

12   I am in shock. First there is intense fever, which my father tries to break using lily leaves bound around my head. Then there are chills: my mother tries to get me to eat soup. Eventually, I do not know how, my parents learn what has happened. A week after the "accident" they take me to see a doctor. "Why did you wait so long to come?" he asks, looking into my eye and shaking his head. "Eyes are sympathetic," he says. "If one is blind, the other will likely become blind too."

13   This comment of the doctor's terrifies me. But it is really how I look that bothers me most. Where the BB pellet struck there is a glob of whitish scar tissue, a hideous cataract, on my eye. Now when I stare at people—a favorite pastime, up to now—they will stare back. Not at the "cute" little girl, but at her scar. For six years I do not stare at anyone, because I do not raise my head.

14   Years later, in the throes of a mid-life crisis, I ask my mother and sister whether I changed after the "accident." "No," they say, puzzled. "What do you mean?"

15   *What do I mean?*

16   I am eight, and, for the first time, doing poorly in school, where I have been something of a whiz since I was four. We have

just moved to the place where the "accident" occurred. We do not know any of the people around us because this is a different county. The only time I see the friends I knew is when we go back to our old church. The new school is the former state penitentiary. It is a large stone building, cold and drafty, crammed to overflowing with boisterous, ill-disciplined children. On the third floor there is a huge circular imprint of some partition that has been torn out.

"What used to be here?" I ask a sullen girl next to me on our 17 way past it to lunch.

"The electric chair," says she. 18

At night I have nightmares about the electric chair, and about 19 all the people reputedly "fried" in it. I am afraid of the school, where all the students seem to be budding criminals.

"What's the matter with your eye?" they ask, critically. 20

When I don't answer (I cannot decide whether it was an "ac- 21 cident" or not), they shove me, insist on a fight.

My brother, the one who created the story about the wire, 22 comes to my rescue. But then brags so much about "protecting" me, I become sick.

After months of torture at the school, my parents decide to 23 send me back to our old community, to my old school. I live with my grandparents and the teacher they board. But there is no room for Phoebe, my cat. By the time my grandparents decide there is room, and I ask for my cat, she cannot be found. Miss Yarborough, the boarding teacher, takes me under her wing, and begins to teach me to play the piano. But soon she marries an African—a "prince," she says—and is whisked away to his continent.

At my old school there is at least one teacher who loves me. 24 She is the teacher who "knew me before I was born" and bought my first baby clothes. It is she who makes life bearable. It is her presence that finally helps me turn on the one child at the school who continually calls me "one-eyed bitch." One day I simply grab him by his coat and beat him until I am satisfied. It is my teacher who tells me my mother is ill.

My mother is lying in bed in the middle of the day, something 25 I have never seen. She is in too much pain to speak. She has an ab- scess in her ear. I stand looking down on her, knowing that if she dies, I cannot live. She is being treated with warm oils and hot bricks held against her cheek. Finally a doctor comes. But I must go back to my grandparents' house. The weeks pass but I am hardly aware of it. All I know is that my mother might die, my father is not so jolly, my brothers still have their guns, and I am the one sent away from home.

26   "You did not change," they say.

27   *Did I imagine the anguish of never looking up?*

28   I am twelve. When relatives come to visit I hide in my room. My cousin Brenda, just my age, whose father works in the post office and whose mother is a nurse, comes to find me. "Hello," she says. And then she asks, looking at my recent school picture, which I did not want taken, and on which the "glob," as I think of it, is clearly visible, "You still can't see out of that eye?"

29   "No," I say, and flop back on the bed over my book.

30   That night, as I do almost every night, I abuse my eye. I rant and rave at it, in front of the mirror. I plead with it to clear up before morning. I tell it I hate and despise it. I do not pray for sight. I pray for beauty.

31   "You did not change," they say.

32   I am fourteen and baby-sitting for my brother Bill, who lives in Boston. He is my favorite brother and there is a strong bond between us. Understanding my feelings of shame and ugliness he and his wife take me to a local hospital, where the "glob" is removed by a doctor named O. Henry. There is still a small bluish crater where the scar tissue was, but the ugly white stuff is gone. Almost immediately I become a different person from the girl who does not raise her head. Or so I think. Now that I've raised my head I win the boyfriend of my dreams. Now that I've raised my head I have plenty of friends. Now that I've raised my head classwork comes from my lips as faultlessly as Easter speeches did, and I leave high school as valedictorian, most popular student, and *queen,* hardly believing my luck. Ironically, the girl who was voted most beautiful in our class (and was) was later shot twice through the chest by a male companion, using a "real" gun, while she was pregnant. But that's another story in itself. Or is it?

"You did not change," they say.　　33

It is now thirty years since the "accident." A beautiful jour- 34
nalist comes to visit and to interview me. She is going to write a
cover story for her magazine that focuses on my latest book. "Decide how you want to look on the cover," she says. "Glamorous,
or whatever."

Never mind "glamorous," it is the "whatever" that I hear. 35
Suddenly all I can think of is whether I will get enough sleep the
night before the photography session: If I don't, my eye will be
tired and wander, as blind eyes will.

At night in bed with my lover I think up reasons why I should 36
not appear on the cover of a magazine. "My meanest critics will
say I've sold out," I say. "My family will now realize I write scan-
dalous books."

"But what's the real reason you don't want to do this?" he asks. 37

"Because in all probability," I say in a rush, "my eye won't be 38
straight."

"It will be straight enough," he says. Then, "Besides, I 39
thought you'd made your peace with that."

And I suddenly remember that I have. 40

I remember: 41

I am talking to my brother Jimmy, asking if he remembers 42
anything unusual about the day I was shot. He does not know I
consider that day the last time my father, with his sweet home
remedy of cool lily leaves, chose me, and that I suffered and raged
inside because of this. "Well," he says, "all I remember is standing
by the side of the highway with Daddy, trying to flag down a car.
A white man stopped, but when Daddy said he needed somebody
to take his little girl to the doctor, he drove off."

I remember: 43

I am in the desert for the first time. I fall totally in love with it. 44
I am so overwhelmed by its beauty, I confront for the first time,
consciously, the meaning of the doctor's words years ago: "Eyes
are sympathetic. If one is blind, the other will likely become blind
too." I realize I have dashed about the world madly, looking at
this, looking at that, storing up images against the fading of the

light. *But I might have missed seeing the desert!* The shock of that possibility—and gratitude for over twenty-five years of sight—sends me literally to my knees. Poem after poem comes—which is perhaps how poets pray.

45   *On Sight*

I am so thankful I have seen
The Desert
And the creatures in the desert
And the desert Itself.

The desert has its own moon
Which I have seen
With my own eye.
There is no flag on it.

Trees of the desert have arms
All of which are always up
That is because the moon is up
The sun is up
Also the sky
The Stars
Clouds
None with flags.

If there were flags, I doubt
the trees would point.
Would you?

46   *But mostly, I remember this:*

47   I am twenty-seven, and my baby daughter is almost three. Since her birth I have worried about her discovery that her mother's eyes are different from other people's. Will she be embarrassed? I think. What will she say? Every day she watches a television program called *Big Blue Marble*. It begins with a picture of the earth as it appears from the moon. It is bluish, a little battered-looking, but full of light, with whitish clouds swirling around it. Every time I see it I weep with love, as if it is a picture of Grandma's house. One day when I am putting Rebecca down for

her nap, she suddenly focuses on my eye. Something inside me cringes, gets ready to try to protect myself. All children are cruel about physical differences, I know from experience, and that they don't always mean to be is another matter. I assume Rebecca will be the same.

But no-o-o-o. She studies my face intently as we stand, her inside and me outside her crib. She even holds my face maternally between her dimpled little hands. Then, looking every bit as serious and lawyerlike as her father, she says, as if it may just possibly have slipped my attention: "Mommy, there's a *world* in your eye." (As in, "Don't be alarmed, or do anything crazy.") And then, gently, but with great interest: "Mommy, where did you *get* that world in your eye?"

For the most part, the pain left then. (So what, if my brothers grew up to buy even more powerful pellet guns for their sons and to carry real guns themselves. So what, if a young "Morehouse man" once nearly fell off the steps of Trevor Arnett Library because he thought my eyes were blue.) Crying and laughing I ran to the bathroom, while Rebecca mumbled and sang herself to sleep. Yes indeed, I realized, looking into the mirror. There *was* a world in my eye. And I saw that it was possible to love it: that in fact, for all it had taught me of shame and anger and inner vision, I *did* love it. Even to see it drifting out of orbit in boredom, or rolling up out of fatigue, not to mention floating back at attention in excitement (bearing witness, a friend has called it), deeply suitable to my personality, and even characteristic of me.

That night I dream I am dancing to Stevie Wonder's song "Always" (the name of the song is really "As," but I hear it as "Always"). As I dance, whirling and joyous, happier than I've ever been in my life, another bright-faced dancer joins me. We dance and kiss each other and hold each other through the night. The other dancer has obviously come through all right, as I have done. She is beautiful, whole, and free. And she is also me.

1983

The Female Body

Margaret Atwood

1

1 I agree, it's a hot topic. But only one? Look around, there's a wide range. Take my own, for instance.

2   I get up in the morning. My topic feels like hell. I sprinkle it with water, brush parts of it, rub it with towels, powder it, add lubricant. I dump in the fuel and away goes my topic, my topical topic, my controversial topic, my capacious topic, my limping topic, my nearsighted topic, my topic with back problems, my badly behaved topic, my vulgar topic, my outrageous topic, my aging topic, my topic that is out of the question and anyway still can't spell, in its oversized coat and worn winter boots, scuttling along the sidewalk as if it were flesh and blood, hunting for what's out there, an avocado, an alderman, an adjective, hungry as ever.

2

3 The basic Female Body comes with the following accessories: garter belt, panti-girdle, crinoline, camisole, bustle, brassiere, stomacher, chemise, virgin zone, spike heels, nose ring, veil, kid gloves, fishnet stockings, fichu, bandeau, Merry Widow, weepers, chokers, barrettes, bangles, beads, lorgnette, feather boa, basic black, compact, Lycra stretch one-piece with modesty panel, designer peignoir, flannel nightie, lace teddy, bed, head.

3

4 The Female Body is made of transparent plastic and lights up when you plug it in. You press a button to illuminate the different

systems. The circulatory system is red, for the heart and arteries, purple for the veins; the respiratory system is blue; the lymphatic system is yellow; the digestive system is green, with liver and kidneys in aqua. The nerves are done in orange and the brain is pink. The skeleton, as you might expect, is white.

The reproductive system is optional, and can be removed. It comes with or without a miniature embryo. Parental judgment can thereby be exercised. We do not wish to frighten or offend. 5

4

He said, I won't have one of those things in the house. It gives a young girl a false notion of beauty, not to mention anatomy. If a real woman was built like that she'd fall on her face. 6

She said, If we don't let her have one like all the other girls she'll feel singled out. It'll become an issue. She'll long for one and she'll long to turn into one. Repression breeds sublimation. You know that. 7

He said, It's not just the pointy plastic tits, it's the wardrobes. The wardrobes and that stupid male doll, what's his name, the one with the underwear glued on. 8

She said, Better to get it over with when she's young. He said, All right, but don't let me see it. 9

She came whizzing down the stairs, thrown like a dart. She was stark naked. Her hair had been chopped off, her head was turned back to front, she was missing some toes and she'd been tattooed all over her body with purple ink in a scrollwork design. She hit the potted azalea, trembled there for a moment like a botched angel, and fell. 10

He said, I guess we're safe. 11

5

The Female Body has many uses. It's been used as a door knocker, a bottle opener, as a clock with a ticking belly, as something to hold up lampshades, as a nutcracker, just squeeze the brass legs together and out comes your nut. It bears torches, lifts victorious 12 wreaths, grows copper wings and raises aloft a ring of neon stars; whole buildings rest on its marble heads.

13   It sells cars, beer, shaving lotion, cigarettes, hard liquor; it sells diet plans and diamonds, and desire in tiny crystal bottles. Is this the face that launched a thousand products? You bet it is, but don't get any funny big ideas, honey, that smile is a dime a dozen.

14   It does not merely sell, it is sold. Money flows into this country or that country, flies in, practically crawls in, suitful after suitful, lured by all those hairless pre-teen legs. Listen, you want to reduce the national debt, don't you? Aren't you patriotic? That's the spirit. That's my girl.

15   She's a natural resource, a renewable one luckily, because those things wear out so quickly. They don't make 'em like they used to. Shoddy goods.

6

16 One and one equals another one. Pleasure in the female is not a re-quirement. Pair-bonding is stronger in geese. We're not talking about love, we're talking about biology. That's how we all got here, daughter.

17   Snails do it differently. They're hermaphrodites, and work in threes.

7

18 Each Female Body contains a female brain. Handy. Makes things work. Stick pins in it and you get amazing results. Old popular songs. Short circuits. Bad dreams.

19   Anyway: each of these brains has two halves. They're joined together by a thick cord; neural pathways flow from one to the other, sparkles of electric information washing to and fro. Like light on waves. Like a conversation. How does a woman know? She listens. She listens in.

20   The male brain, now, that's a different matter. Only a thin con-nection. Space over here, time over there, music and arithmetic in their own sealed compartments. The right brain doesn't know

what the left brain is doing. Good for aiming through, for hitting the target when you pull the trigger. What's the target? Who's the target? Who cares? What matters is hitting it. That's the male brain for you. Objective.

This is why men are so sad, why they feel so cut off, why they 21 think of themselves as orphans cast adrift, footloose and stringless in the deep void. What void? she asks. What are you talking about? The void of the universe, he says, and she says Oh and looks out the window and tries to get a handle on it, but it's no use, there's too much going on, too many rustlings in the leaves, too many voices, so she says, Would you like a cheese sandwich, a piece of cake, a cup of tea? And he grinds his teeth because she doesn't understand, and wanders off, not just alone but Alone, lost in the dark, lost in the skull, searching for the other half, the twin who could complete him.

Then it comes to him: he's lost the Female Body! Look, it 22 shines in the gloom, far ahead, a vision of wholeness, ripeness, like a giant melon, like an apple, like a metaphor for "breast" in a bad sex novel; it shines like a balloon, like a foggy noon, a watery moon, shimmering in its egg of light.

Catch it. Put it in a pumpkin, in a high tower, in a compound, 23 in a chamber, in a house, in a room. Quick, stick a leash on it, a lock, a chain, some pain, settle it down, so it can never get away from you again.

1994

A Reasonable Standard

Ellen Goodman

Since the volatile mix of sex *and* harassment exploded under the 1 Capitol dome, it hasn't been just senators scurrying for cover. The case of the Professor *and* the Judge has left a gender gap that looks more like a crater.

2   We have discovered that men *and* women see this issue differently. Stop the presses. Sweetheart, get me rewrite. On the "Today" show, Bryant Gumbel asks something about a man's right to have a pinup on the wall, *and* Katie Couric says what she thinks of that.

3   On the normally sober "MacNeil/Lehrer" hour, the usual panel of legal experts doesn't break down between left and right but between male and female.

4   On a hundred radio talk shows, women are sharing experiences *and* men are asking for proof. In 10,000 offices, the order of the day is the nervous joke. One boss asks his secretary if he can still say, "Good morning," or is that sexual harassment. Heh, heh. The women aren't laughing. OK boys *and* girls, back to your corners. Can we talk? Can we hear? The good news is that women have stopped rolling their eyes at each other *and* started speaking out. The bad news is that we may each assume the other gender not only doesn't understand but can't understand. "They don't get it" becomes "They can't get it."

5   Let's start with the fact that sexual harassment is a concept as new as date rape. Date rape, that should-be oxymoron, assumes a different perspective on the part of the man *and* the woman. His date, her rape.

6   Sexual harassment comes with some of the same assumptions. What he labels sexual she labels harassment. This produces what many men tend to darkly call a "murky" area of the law. Murky, however, is a step in the right direction. When everything was clear, it was clearly biased. The old single standard was male standard.

7   The only options a working woman had were to grin, bear it or quit. Sexual-harassment rules are based on the point of view of the victim, nearly always a woman. The rules ask, not just whether she has been physically assaulted, but whether the environment in which she works is intimidating or coercive. Whether she feels harassed. It says that her feelings matter.

This, of course, raises all sorts of hackles about women's feel- 8
ings, women's sensitivity. How can you judge the sensitivity level
of every single woman you work with? What's a poor man to do?

But the law isn't psychiatry. It doesn't adapt to individual sen- 9
sitivity levels. There is a standard emerging by which the courts can
judge these cases *and* by which people can judge them as well. It's
called "the *reasonable* woman standard." How would a *reasonable*
woman interpret this? How would a *reasonable* woman behave?

This is not an entirely new idea, although perhaps the law's 10
belief in the reasonableness of women is. There has long been a
"reasonable man" in the law not to mention a *"reasonable* pilot," a
reasonable innkeeper," a *"reasonable* train operator."

Now the law is admitting that a *reasonable* woman may see 11
these situations differently than a man. That truth—available in
your senator's mailbag—is also apparent in research. We tend to
see sexualized situations from our own gender's perspective. Kim
Lane Scheppele, a political science *and* law professor at the University of Michigan, summarizes the miscues this way: "Men see
the sex first *and* miss the coercion. Women see the coercion *and*
miss the sex." Does that mean that we are genetically doomed to
our double vision? Scheppele is quick to say no. Our justice system rests on the belief that one person can get in another's head,
walk in her shoes, see things from another perspective. *And* so
does our hope for change.

If a jury of car drivers can understand how a *"reasonable* pilot" 12
would see one situation, a jury of men can see how a *reasonable*
woman would see another event. The crucial ingredient is empathy.

Check it out in the office tomorrow. He's coming on, she's 13
backing off, he keeps coming. Read the body language. There's a
Playboy calendar on the wall *and* a PMS joke in the board room,
and the boss is just being friendly.

How would a *reasonable* woman feel? At this moment, when 14
the air is crackling with hostility *and* consciousness-raising has the

hair sticking up on the back of many necks, guess what? Men can "get it." *Reasonable* men.

1991

Rape: A Bigger Danger Than Feminists Know

Camille Paglia

1   Rape is an outrage that cannot be tolerated in civilized society. Yet feminism, which has waged a crusade for rape to be taken more seriously, has put young women in danger by hiding the truth about sex from them.

2   In dramatizing the pervasiveness of rape, feminists have told young women that before they have sex with a man, they must give consent as explicit as a legal contract's. In this way, young women have been convinced that they have been the victims of rape. On elite campuses in the Northeast and on the West Coast, they have held consciousness-raising sessions, petitioned administrations, demanded inquests. At Brown University, outraged, panicky "victims" have scrawled the names of alleged attackers on the walls of women's rest rooms. What marital rape was to the '70s, "date rape" is to the '90s.

3   The incidence and seriousness of rape do not require this kind of exaggeration. Real acquaintance rape is nothing new. It has been a horrible problem for women for all of recorded history. Once, father and brothers protected women from rape. Once, the penalty for rape was death. I come from a fierce Italian tradition where, not so long ago in the motherland, a rapist would end up knifed, castrated, and hung out to dry.

4   But the old clans and small rural communities have broken down. In our cities, on our campuses far from home, young women are vulnerable and defenseless. Feminism has not prepared them for this. Feminism keeps saying the sexes are the same. It keeps telling women they can do anything, go anywhere,

say anything, wear anything. No, they can't. Women will always be in sexual danger.

One of my male students recently slept overnight with a friend 5 in a passageway of the Great Pyramid in Egypt. He described the moon and sand, the ancient silence and eerie echoes. I am a woman. I will never experience that. I am not stupid enough to believe I could ever be safe there. There is a world of solitary adventure I will never have. Women have always known these somber truths. But feminism, with its pie-in-the-sky fantasies about the perfect world, keeps young women from seeing life as it is.

We must remedy social injustice whenever we can. But there 6 are some things we cannot change. There are sexual differences that are based in biology. Academic feminism is lost in a fog of social constructionism. It believes we are totally the product of our environment. This idea was invented by Rousseau. He was wrong. Emboldened by dumb French language theory, academic feminists repeat the same hollow slogans over and over to each other. Their view of sex is naive and prudish. Leaving sex to the feminists is like letting your dog vacation at the taxidermist's.

The sexes are at war. Men must struggle for identity against 7 the overwhelming power of their mothers. Women have menstruation to tell them they are women. Men must do or risk something to be men. Men become masculine only when other men say they are. Having sex with a woman is one way a boy becomes a man.

College men are at their hormonal peak. They have just left 8 their mothers and are questing for their male identity. In groups, they are dangerous. A woman going to a fraternity party is walking into Testosterone Flats, full of prickly cacti and blazing guns. If she goes, she should be armed with resolute alertness. She should arrive with girlfriends and leave with them. A girl who lets herself get dead drunk at a fraternity party is a fool. A girl who goes upstairs alone with a brother at a fraternity party is an idiot. Feminists call this "blaming the victim." I call it common sense.

For a decade, feminists have drilled their disciples to say, 9 "Rape is a crime of violence but not of sex." This sugar-coated Shirley Temple nonsense has exposed young women to disaster. Misled by feminism, they do not expect rape from the nice boys from good homes who sit next to them in class.

10   Aggression and eroticism, in fact, are deeply intertwined. Hunt, pursuit and capture are biologically programmed into male sexuality. Generation after generation, men must be educated, refined, and ethically persuaded away from their tendency toward anarchy and brutishness. Society is not the enemy, as feminism ignorantly claims. Society is woman's protection against rape. Feminism, with its solemn Carry Nation repressiveness, does not see what is for men the eroticism or fun element in rape, especially the wild, infectious delirium of gang rape. Women who do not understand rape cannot defend themselves against it.

11   The date-rape controversy shows feminism hitting the wall of its own broken promises. The women of my '60s generation were the first respectable girls in history to swear like sailors, get drunk, stay out all night—in short, to act like men. We sought total sexual freedom and equality. But as time passed, we woke up to cold reality. The old double standard protected women. When anything goes, it's women who lose.

12   Today's young women don't know what they want. They see that feminism has not brought sexual happiness. The theatrics of public rage over date rape are their way of restoring the old sexual rules that were shattered by my generation. Yet nothing about the sexes has really changed. The comic film *Where the Boys Are* (1960), the ultimate expression of '50s man-chasing, still speaks directly to our time. It shows smart, lively women skillfully anticipating and fending off the dozens of strategies with which horny men try to get them into bed. The agonizing date-rape subplot and climax are brilliantly done. The victim, Yvette Mimieux, makes mistake after mistake, obvious to the other girls. She allows herself to be lured away from her girlfriends and into isolation with boys whose character and intentions she misreads. *Where the Boys Are* tells the truth. It shows courtship as a dangerous game in which the signals are not verbal but subliminal.

13   Neither militant feminism, which is obsessed with politically correct language, nor academic feminism, which believes that knowledge and experience are "constituted by" language, can understand preverbal or nonverbal communication. Feminism, focusing on sexual politics, cannot see that sex exists in and through the body. Sexual desire and arousal cannot be fully translated into

verbal terms. This is why men and women misunderstand each other.

Trying to remake the future, feminism cut itself off from sex- 14
ual history. It discarded and suppressed the sexual myths of literature, art and religion. Those myths show us the turbulence, the mysteries and passions of sex. In mythology we see men's sexual anxiety, their fear of woman's dominance. Much sexual violence is rooted in men's sense of psychological weakness toward women. It takes many men to deal with one woman. Woman's voracity is a persistent motif. Clara Bow, it was rumored, took on the USC football team on weekends. Marilyn Monroe, singing "Diamonds Are a Girl's Best Friend," rules a conga line of men in tuxes. Half-clad Cher, in the video for "If I Could Turn Back Time," deranges a battleship of screaming sailors and straddles a pink-lit cannon. Feminism, coveting social power, is blind to woman's cosmic sexual power.

To understand rape, you must study the past. There never 15
was and never will be sexual harmony. Every woman must be prudent and cautious about where she goes and with whom. When she makes a mistake, she must accept the consequences and, through self-criticism, resolve never to make that mistake again. Running to mommy and daddy on the campus grievance committee is unworthy of strong women. Posting lists of guilty men in the toilet is cowardly, infantile stuff.

The Italian philosophy of life espouses high-energy con- 16
frontation. A male student makes a vulgar remark about your breasts? Don't slink off to whimper with the campus shrinking violets. Deal with it. On the spot. Say, "Shut up, you jerk! And crawl back to the barnyard where you belong!" In general, women who project this take-charge attitude toward life get harassed less often. I see too many dopey, immature, self-pitying women walking around like melting sticks of butter. It's the Yvette Mimieux syndrome: make me happy. And listen to me weep when I'm not.

The date-rape debate is already smothering in propaganda 17
churned out by the expensive Northeastern colleges and universities, with their overconcentration of boring, uptight academic feminists and spoiled, affluent students. Beware of the deep ma-

nipulativeness of rich students who were neglected by their parents. They love to turn the campus into hysterical psychodramas of sexual transgression, followed by assertions of parental authority and concern. And don't look for sexual enlightenment from academe, which spews out mountains of books but never looks at life directly.

18   As a fan of football and rock music, I see in the simple, swaggering masculinity of the jock and in the noisy posturing of the heavy-metal guitarist certain fundamental, unchanging truths about sex. Masculinity is aggressive, unstable, combustible. It is also the most creative cultural force in history. Women must reorient themselves toward the elemental powers of sex, which can strengthen or destroy.

19   The only solution to date rape is female self-awareness and self-control. A woman's number-one line of defense against rape is herself. When a real rape occurs, she should report it to the police. Complaining to college committees because the courts "take too long" is ridiculous. College administrations are not a branch of the judiciary. They are not equipped or trained for legal inquiry. Colleges must alert incoming students to the problems and dangers of adulthood. Then colleges must stand back and get out of the sex game.

1988

The Making of a Divorce Culture
Barbara Dafoe Whitehead

1   Divorce is now part of everyday American life. It is embedded in our laws and institutions, our manners and mores, our movies and television shows, our novels and children's storybooks, and our closest and most important relationships. Indeed, divorce has become so pervasive that many people naturally assume it has seeped into the social and cultural mainstream over a long period

of time. Yet this is not the case. Divorce has become an American way of life only as the result of recent and revolutionary change.

The entire history of American divorce can be divided into 2 two periods, one evolutionary and the other revolutionary. For most of the nation's history, divorce was a rare occurrence and an insignificant feature of family and social relationships. In the first sixty years of the twentieth century, divorce became more common, but it was hardly commonplace. In 1960, the divorce rate stood at a still relatively modest level of nine per one thousand married couples. After 1960, however, the rate accelerated at a dazzling pace. It doubled in roughly a decade and continued its upward climb until the early 1980s, when it stabilized at the highest level among advanced Western societies. As a consequence of this sharp and sustained rise, divorce moved from the margins to the mainstream of American life in the space of three decades.

Ideas are important in revolutions, yet surprisingly little at- 3 tention has been devoted to the ideas that gave impetus to the divorce revolution. Of the scores of books on divorce published in recent decades, most focus on its legal, demographic, economic, or (especially) psychological dimensions. Few, if any, deal fully with its intellectual origins. Yet trying to comprehend the divorce revolution and its consequences without some sense of its ideological origins, is like trying to understand the American Revolution without taking into account the thinking of John Locke, Thomas Jefferson, or Thomas Paine. This more recent revolution, like the revolution of our nation's founding, has its roots in a distinctive set of ideas and claims.

This book is about the ideas behind the divorce revolution 4 and how these ideas have shaped a culture of divorce. The making of a divorce culture has involved three overlapping changes: first, the emergence and widespread diffusion of a historically new and distinctive set of ideas about divorce in the last third of the twentieth century; second, the migration of divorce from a minor place within a system governed by marriage to a freestanding place as a major institution governing family relationships; and third, a widespread shift in thinking about the obligations of marriage and parenthood.

5   Beginning in the late 1950s, Americans began to change their ideas about the individual's obligations to family and society. Broadly described, this change was away from an ethic of obligation to others and toward an obligation to self. I do not mean that people suddenly abandoned all responsibilities to others, but rather that they became more acutely conscious of their responsibility to attend to their own individual needs and interests. At least as important as the moral obligation to look after others, the new thinking suggested, was the moral obligation to look after oneself.

6   This ethical shift had a profound impact on ideas about the nature and purpose of the family. In the American tradition, the marketplace and the public square have represented the realms of life devoted to the pursuit of individual interest, choice, and freedom, while the family has been the realm defined by voluntary commitment, duty, and self-sacrifice. With the greater emphasis on individual satisfaction in family relationships, however, family well-being became subject to a new metric. More than in the past, satisfaction in this sphere came to be based on subjective judgments about the content and quality of individual happiness rather than on such objective measures as level of income, material nurture and support, or boosting children onto a higher rung on the socioeconomic ladder. People began to judge the strength and "health" of family bonds according to their capacity to promote individual fulfillment and personal growth. As a result, the conception of the family's role and place in the society began to change. The family began to lose its separate place and distinctive identity as the realm of duty, service, and sacrifice. Once the domain of the obligated self, the family was increasingly viewed as yet another domain for the expression of the unfettered self.

7   These broad changes figured centrally in creating a new conception of divorce which gained influential adherents and spread broadly and swiftly throughout the society—a conception that represented a radical departure from earlier notions. Once regarded mainly as a social, legal, and family event in which there were other stakeholders, divorce now became an event closely linked to the pursuit of individual satisfactions, opportunities, and growth.

The new conception of divorce drew upon some of the oldest, and most resonant, themes in the American political tradition. The nation, after all, was founded as the result of a political divorce, and revolutionary thinkers explicitly adduced a parallel between the dissolution of marital bonds and the dissolution of political bonds. In political as well as marital relationships, they argued, bonds of obligation were established voluntarily on the basis of mutual affection and regard. Once such bonds turned cold and oppressive, peoples, like individuals, had the right to dissolve them and to form more perfect unions.

In the new conception of divorce, this strain of eighteenth- 9 century political thought mingled with a strain of twentieth-century psychotherapeutic thought. Divorce was not only an individual right but also a psychological resource. The dissolution of marriage offered the chance to make oneself over from the inside out, to refurbish and express the inner self, and to acquire certain valuable psychological assets and competencies, such as initiative, assertiveness, and a stronger and better self-image.

The conception of divorce as both an individual right and an 10 inner experience merged with and reinforced the new ethic of obligation to the self. In family relationships, one had an obligation to be attentive to one's own feelings and to work toward improving the quality of one's inner life. This ethical imperative completed the rationale for a sense of individual entitlement to divorce. Increasingly, mainstream America saw the legal dissolution of marriage as a matter of individual choice, in which there were no other stakeholders or larger social interests. This conception of divorce strongly argued for removing the social, legal, and moral impediments to the free exercise of the individual right to divorce.

Traditionally, one major impediment to divorce was the pres- 11 ence of children in the family. According to well-established popular belief, dependent children had a stake in their parents' marriage and suffered hardship as a result of the dissolution of the marriage. Because children were vulnerable and dependent, parents had a moral obligation to place their children's interests in the marital partnership above their own individual satisfactions. This notion was swiftly abandoned after the 1960s. Influential voices in the society, including child-welfare professionals, claimed that the happiness of individual parents, rather than an intact marriage, was the key determinant of children's family well-being. If divorce could make one or both parents happier, then it was likely to improve the well-being of children as well.

12   In the following decades, the new conception of divorce spread through the law, therapy, etiquette, the social sciences, popular advice literature, and religion. Concerns that had dominated earlier thinking on divorce were now dismissed as old-fashioned and excessively moralistic. Divorce would not harm children but would lead to greater happiness for children and their single parents. It would not damage the institution of marriage but would make possible better marriages and happier individuals. Divorce would not damage the social fabric by diminishing children's life chances but would strengthen the social fabric by improving the quality of affective bonds between parents and children, whatever form the structural arrangements of their families might happen to take.

13   As the sense of divorce as an individual freedom and entitlement grew, the sense of concern about divorce as a social problem diminished. Earlier in the century, each time the divorce rate increased sharply, it had inspired widespread public concern and debate about the harmful impact of divorce on families and the society. But in the last third of the century, as the divorce rate rose to once unthinkable levels, public anxiety about it all but vanished. At the very moment when divorce had its most profound impact on the society, weakening the institution of marriage, revolutionizing the structure of families and reorganizing parent-child relationships, it ceased to be a source of concern or debate.

14   The lack of attention to divorce became particularly striking after the 1980s, as a politically polarized debate over the state of the American family took shape. On one side, conservatives pointed to abortion, illegitimacy, and homosexuality as forces destroying the family. On the other, liberals cited domestic violence, economic insecurity, and inadequate public supports as the key problems afflicting the family. But politicians on both sides had almost nothing to say about divorce. Republicans did not want to alienate their upscale constituents or their libertarian wing, both of whom tended to favor easy divorce, nor did they want to call attention to the divorces among their own leadership. Democrats did not want to anger their large constituency among women

who saw easy divorce as a hard-won freedom and prerogative, nor did they wish to seem unsympathetic to single mothers. Thus, except for bipartisan calls to get tougher with deadbeat dads, both Republicans and Democrats avoided the issue of divorce and its consequences as far too politically risky.

But the failure to address divorce carried a price. It allowed the middle class to view family breakdown as a "them" problem rather than an "us" problem. Divorce was not like illegitimacy or welfare dependency, many claimed. It was a matter of individual choice, imposing few, if any, costs or consequences on others. Thus, mainstream America could cling to the comfortable illusion that the nation's family problems had to do with the behavior of unwed teenage mothers or poor women on welfare rather than with the instability of marriage and family life within its own ranks. [15]

Nonetheless, after thirty years of persistently high levels of divorce, this illusion, though still politically attractive, is increasingly difficult to sustain in the face of a growing body of experience and evidence. To begin with, divorce has indeed hurt children. It has created economic insecurity and disadvantage for many children who would not otherwise be economically vulnerable. It has led to more fragile and unstable family households. It has caused a mass exodus of fathers from children's households and, all too often, from their lives. It has reduced the levels of parental time and money invested in children. In sum, it has changed the very nature of American childhood. Just as no patient would have designed today's system of health care, so no child would have chosen today's culture of divorce. [16]

Divorce figures prominently in the altered economic fortunes of middle-class families. Although the economic crisis of the middle class is usually described as a problem caused by global economic changes, changing patterns in education and earnings, and ruthless corporate downsizing, it owes more to divorce than is commonly acknowledged. Indeed, recent data suggest that marriage may be a more important economic resource than a college degree. According to an analysis of 1994 income patterns, the median income of married-parent households whose heads have only a high school diploma is ten percent higher than the median [17] income of college-educated single-parent households.[1] Parents who are college graduates *and* married form the new economic elite among families with children. Consequently, those who are concerned about what the downsizing of corporations is doing to workers should also be concerned about what the downsizing of families through divorce is doing to parents and children.

18   Widespread divorce depletes social capital as well. Scholars tell us that strong and durable family and social bonds generate certain "goods" and services, including money, mutual assistance, information, caregiving, protection, and sponsorship. Because such bonds endure over time, they accumulate and form a pool of social capital which can be drawn down upon, when needed, over the entire course of a life. An elderly couple, married for fifty years, is likely to enjoy a substantial body of social and emotional capital, generated through their long-lasting marriage, which they can draw upon in caring for each other and for themselves as they age. Similarly, children who grow up in stable, two-parent married households are the beneficiaries of the social and emotional capital accumulated over time as a result of an enduring marriage bond. As many parents know, children continue to depend on these resources well into young adulthood. But as family bonds become increasingly fragile and vulnerable to disruption, they become less permanent and thus less capable of generating such forms of help, financial resources, and mutual support. In short, divorce consumes social capital and weakens the social fabric. At the very time that sweeping socioeconomic changes are mandating

---

[1]An analysis of income data provided by The Northeastern University Center for Labor Market Studies shows the following distribution by education and marital status:

MEDIAN INCOMES FOR U.S. FAMILIES WITH CHILDREN, 1994

Education of household head	Married Couple Familes	Single Parent Families
College Graduate	$71,263	$36,006
High School Graduate	$40,098	$14,698

Based on 1994 Current Population Statistics. Families with one or more children under 18. Age of household head: 22–62.

greater investment of social capital in children, widespread divorce is reducing the pool of social capital. As the new economic and social conditions raise the hurdles of child-rearing higher, divorce digs potholes in the tracks.

It should be stressed that this book is not intended as a brief 19 against divorce as such. We must assume that divorce is necessary as a remedy for irretrievably broken marriages, especially those that are marred by severe abuse such as chronic infidelity, drug addiction, or physical violence. Nor is its argument directed against those who are divorced. It assumes that divorce is difficult, painful, and often unwanted by at least one spouse, and that divorcing couples require compassion and support from family, friends, and their religious communities. Nor should this book be taken as an appeal for a return to an earlier era of American family life. The media routinely portray the debate over the family as one between nostalgists and realists, between those who want to turn back the clock to the fifties and those who want to march bravely and resolutely forward into the new century. But this is a lazy and misguided approach, driven more by the easy availability of archival photos and footage from 1950s television sitcoms than by careful consideration of the substance of competing arguments.

More fundamentally, this approach overlooks the key issue. 20 And that issue is not how today's families might stack up against those of an earlier era; indeed, no reliable empirical data for such a comparison exist. In an age of diverse family structures, the heart of the matter is what kinds of contemporary family arrangements have the greatest capacity to promote children's well-being, and how we can ensure that more children have the advantages of growing up in such families.

In the past year or so, there has been growing recognition of 21 the personal and social costs of three decades of widespread divorce. A public debate has finally emerged. Within this debate, there are two separate and overlapping discussions.

The first centers on a set of specific proposals that are in- 22 tended to lessen the harmful impact of divorce on children: a federal system of child-support collection, tougher child-support enforcement, mandatory counseling for divorcing parents, and refu.. n of no-fa .lt divorce laws in the states. What is striking about this discussion is its narrow focus on public policy, particularly on changes in the system of no-fault divorce. In this, as in so many other crucial discussions involving social and moral questions, the most vocal and visible participants come from the world of government policy, electoral politics, and issue advocacy. The media, which are tongue-tied unless they can speak in the language of left-right politics, reinforce this situation. And the public is offered needlessly polarized arguments that hang on a flat yes-or-no response to this or that individual policy measure. All too often, this discussion of divorce poses what *Washington Post* columnist E. J. Dionne aptly describes as false choices.

23   Notably missing is a serious consideration of the broader moral assumptions and empirical claims that define our divorce culture. Divorce touches on classic questions in American public philosophy—on the nature of our most important human and social bonds, the duties and obligations imposed by bonds we voluntarily elect, the "just causes" for the dissolution of those bonds, and the differences between obligations volunteered and those that must be coerced. Without consideration of such questions, the effort to change behavior by changing a few public policies is likely to founder.

24   The second and complementary discussion does try to place divorce within a larger philosophical framework. Its proponents have looked at the decline in the well-being of the nation's children as the occasion to call for a collective sense of commitment by all Americans to all of America's children. They pose the challenging question: "What are Americans willing to do 'for the sake of *all* children'?" But while this is surely an important question, it addresses only half of the problem of declining commitment. The other half has to do with how we answer the question: "What are individual parents obliged to do 'for the sake of their own children'?"

25   Renewing a *social* ethic of commitment to children is an urgent goal, but it cannot be detached from the goal of strengthening the *individual* ethic of commitment to children. The state of one affects the standing of the other. A society that protects the rights of parents to easy, unilateral divorce, and flatly rejects the idea that parents should strive to preserve a marriage "for the sake of the

children," faces a problem when it comes to the question of public sacrifice "for the sake of the children." To put it plainly, many of the ideas we have come to believe and vigorously defend about adult prerogatives and freedoms in family life are undermining the foundations of altruism and support for children.

With each passing year, the culture of divorce becomes more   26 deeply entrenched. American children are routinely schooled in divorce. Mr. Rogers teaches toddlers about divorce. An entire children's literature is devoted to divorce. Family movies and videos for children feature divorced families. *Mrs. Doubtfire*, originally a children's book about divorce and then a hit movie, is aggressively marketed as a holiday video for kids. Of course, these books and movies are designed to help children deal with the social reality and psychological trauma of divorce. But they also carry an unmistakable message about the impermanence and unreliability of family bonds. Like romantic love, the children's storybooks say, family love comes and goes. Daddies disappear. Mommies find new boyfriends. Mommies' boyfriends leave. Grandparents go away. Even pets must be left behind.

More significantly, in a society where nearly half of all chil-   27 dren are likely to experience parental divorce, family breakup becomes a defining event of American childhood itself. Many children today know nothing but divorce in their family lives. And although children from divorced families often say they want to avoid divorce if they marry, young adults whose parents divorced are more likely to get divorced themselves and to bear children outside of marriage than young adults from stable married-parent familes.

Precisely because the culture of divorce has generational mo-   28 mentum, this book offers no easy optimism about the prospects for change. But neither does it counsel passive resignation or acceptance of the culture's relentless advance. What it does offer is a critique of the ideas behind current divorce trends. Its argument is directed against the ideas about divorce that have gained ascendancy, won our support, and lodged in our consciousness as "proven" and incontrovertible. It challenges the popular idea of divorce as an individual right and freedom to be exercised in the pursuit of individual goods and satisfactions, without due regard for other stakeholders in the marital partnership, especially children. This may be a fragile and inadequate response to a profoundly consequential set of changes, but it seeks the abandonment of ideas that have misled us and failed our children.

29   In a larger sense, this book is both an appreciation and a criticism of what is peculiarly American about divorce. Divorce has spread throughout advanced Western societies at roughly the same pace and over roughly the same period of time. Yet nowhere else has divorce been so deeply imbued with the larger themes of a nation's political traditions. Nowhere has divorce so fully reflected the spirit and susceptibilities of a people who share an extravagant faith in the power of the individual and in the power of positive thinking. Divorce in America is not unique, but what we have made of divorce is uniquely American. In exploring the cultural roots of divorce, therefore, we look at ourselves, at what is best and worst in our traditions, what is visionary and what is blind, and how the two are sometimes tragically commingled and confused.

1997

Why I [Still] Want a Wife
Judy Brady

1   I belong to that classification of people known as wives. I am A Wife. And, not altogether incidentally, I am a mother. Not too long ago a male friend of mine appeared on the scene fresh from a recent divorce. He had one child; who is, of course, with his ex-wife. He is obviously looking for another wife. As I thought about him while I was ironing one evening, it suddenly occurred to me that I, too, would like to have a wife. Why do I want a wife?

2   I would like to go back to school so that I can become economically independent, support myself, and, if need be, support those dependent upon me. I want a wife who will work and send me to school. And while I am going to school I want a wife to take

care of my children. I want a wife to keep track of the children's doctor and dentist appointments. And to keep track of mine, too. I want a wife to make sure my children eat properly and are kept clean. I want a wife who will wash the children's clothes and keep them mended. I want a wife who is a good nurturant attendant to my children, who arranges for their schooling, makes sure that they have an adequate social life with their peers, takes them to the park, the zoo, etc. I want a wife who takes care of the children when they are sick, a wife who arranges to be around when the children need special care, because, of course, I cannot miss classes at school. My wife must arrange to lose time at work and not lose the job. It may mean a small cut in my wife's income from time to time, but I guess I can tolerate that. Needless to say, my wife will arrange and pay for the care of the children while my wife is working.

I want a wife who will take care of *my* physical needs. I want 3 a wife who will keep my house clean. A wife who will pick up after me. I want a wife who will keep my clothes clean, ironed, mended, replaced when need be, and who will see to it that my personal things are kept in their proper place so that I can find what I need the minute I need it. I want a wife who cooks the meals, a wife who is a *good* cook. I want a wife who will plan the menus, do the necessary grocery shopping, prepare the meals, serve them pleasantly, and then do the cleaning up while I do my studying. I want a wife who will care for me when I am sick and sympathize with my pain and loss of time from school. I want a wife to go along when our family takes a vacation so that some-one can continue to care for me and my children when I need a rest and change of scene.

I want a wife who will not bother me with rambling com- 4 plaints about a wife's duties. But I want a wife who will listen to me when I feel the need to explain a rather difficult point I have come across in my course of studies. And I want a wife who will type my papers for me when I have written them.

I want a wife who will take care of the details of my social life. 5 When my wife and I are invited out by my friends, I want a wife who will take care of the babysitting arrangements. When I meet people at school that I like and want to entertain, I want a wife who will have the house clean, will prepare a special meal, serve it to me and my friends, and not interrupt when I talk about the things that interest me and my friends. I want a wife who will have arranged that the children are fed and ready for bed before my guests arrive so that the children do not bother us.

6   And I want a wife who knows that sometimes I need a night out by myself.

7   I want a wife who is sensitive to my sexual needs, a wife who makes love passionately and eagerly when I feel like it, a wife who makes sure I am satisfied. And, of course, I want a wife who will not demand sexual attention when I am not in the mood for it. I want a wife who assumes the complete responsibility for birth control, because I do not want more children. I want a wife who will remain sexually faithful to me so that I do not have to clutter up my intellectual life with jealousies. And I want a wife who understands that *my* sexual needs may entail more than strict adherence to monogamy. I must, after all, be able to relate to people as fully as possible.

8   If, by chance, I find another person more suitable as a wife than the wife I already have, I want the liberty to replace my present wife with another one. Naturally, I will expect a fresh, new life; my wife will take the children and be solely responsible for them so that I am left free.

9   When I am through with school and have a job, I want my wife to quit working and remain at home so that my wife can more fully and completely take care of a wife's duties.

10   My God, who *wouldn't* want a wife?

1970/Revised 1991

The Men We Carry in Our Minds

Scott Russell Sanders

1 The first men, besides my father, I remember seeing were black convicts and white guards, in the cottonfield across the road from

our farm on the outskirts of Memphis. I must have been three or four. The prisoners wore dingy gray-and-black zebra suits, heavy as canvas, sodden with sweat. Hatless, stooped, they chopped weeds in the fierce heat, row after row, breathing the acrid dust of boll-weevil poison. The overseers wore dazzling white shirts and broad shadowy hats. The oiled barrels of their shotguns flashed in the sunlight. Their faces in memory are utterly blank. Of course those men, white and black, have become for me an emblem of racial hatred. But they have also come to stand for the twin poles of my early vision of manhood—the brute toiling animal and the boss.

When I was a boy, the men I knew labored with their bodies. 2 They were marginal farmers, just scraping by, or welders, steel workers, carpenters; they swept floors, dug ditches, mined coal, or drove trucks, their forearms ropy with muscle; they trained horses, stoked furnaces, built tires, stood on assembly lines wrestling parts onto cars and refrigerators. They got up before light, worked all day long whatever the weather, and when they came home at night they looked as though somebody had been whipping them. In the evenings and on weekends they worked on their own places, tilling gardens that were lumpy with clay, fixing broken-down cars, hammering on houses that were always too drafty, too leaky, too small.

The bodies of the men I knew were twisted and maimed in 3 ways visible and invisible. The nails of their hands were black and split, the hands tattooed with scars. Some had lost fingers. Heavy lifting had given many of them finicky backs and guts weak from hernias. Racing against conveyor belts had given them ulcers. Their ankles and knees ached from years of standing on concrete. Anyone who had worked for long around machines was hard of hearing. They squinted, and the skin of their faces was creased like the leather of old work gloves. There were times, studying them, when I dreaded growing up. Most of them coughed, from dust or cigarettes, and most of them drank cheap wine or whiskey, so their eyes looked bloodshot and bruised. The fathers of my friends always seemed older than the mothers. Men wore out sooner. Only women lived into old age.

As a boy I also knew another sort of men, who did not sweat 4 and break down like mules. They were soldiers, and so far as I could tell they scarcely worked at all. During my early school years we lived on a military base, an arsenal in Ohio, and every day I saw GIs in the guardshacks, on the stoops of barracks, at the wheels of olive drab Chevrolets. The chief fact of their lives was boredom. Long after I left the Arsenal I came to recognize the sour smell the soldiers gave off as that of souls in limbo. They were all waiting—for wars, for transfers, for leaves, for promotions, for the end of their hitch—like so many braves waiting for the hunt to begin. Unlike the warriors of older tribes, however, they would have no say about when the battle would start or how it would be waged. Their waiting was broken only when they practiced for war. They fired guns at targets, drove tanks across the churned-up fields of the military reservation, set off bombs in the wrecks of old fighter planes. I knew this was all play. But I also felt certain that when the hour for killing arrived, they would kill. When the real shooting started, many of them would die. This was what soldiers were *for*, just as a hammer was for driving nails.

5   Warriors and toilers: those seemed, in my boyhood vision, to be the chief destinies for men. They weren't the only destinies, as I learned from having a few male teachers, from reading books, and from watching television. But the men on television—the politicians, the astronauts, the generals, the savvy lawyers, the philosophical doctors, the bosses who gave orders to both soldiers and laborers—seemed as remote and unreal to me as the figures in tapestries. I could no more imagine growing up to become one of these cool, potent creatures than I could imagine becoming a prince.

6   A nearer and more hopeful example was that of my father, who had escaped from a red-dirt farm to a tire factory, and from the assembly line to the front office. Eventually he dressed in a white shirt and tie. He carried himself as if he had been born to work with his mind. But his body, remembering the earlier years of slogging work, began to give out on him in his fifties, and it quit on him entirely before he turned sixty-five. Even such partial escape from man's fate as he had accomplished did not seem possible for most of the boys I knew. They joined the Army, stood in line for jobs in the smoky plants, helped build highways. They were bound to work as their fathers had worked, killing themselves or preparing to kill others.

A scholarship enabled me not only to attend college, a rare ₈ enough feat in my circle, but even to study in a university meant for the children of the rich. Here I met for the first time young men who had assumed from birth that they would lead lives of comfort and power. And for the first time I met women who told me that men were guilty of having kept all the joys and privileges of the earth for themselves. I was baffled. What privileges? What joys? I thought about the maimed, dismal lives of most of the men back home. What had they stolen from their wives and daughters? The right to go five days a week, twelve months a year, for thirty or forty years to a steel mill or a coal mine? The right to drop bombs and die in war? The right to feel every leak in the roof, every gap in the fence, every cough in the engine, as a wound they must mend? The right to feel, when the layoff comes or the plant shuts down, not only afraid but ashamed?

I was slow to understand the deep grievances of women. This ₇ was because, as a boy, I had envied them. Before college, the only people I had ever known who were interested in art or music or literature, the only ones who read books, the only ones who ever seemed to enjoy a sense of ease and grace were the mothers and daughters. Like the menfolk, they fretted about money, they scrimped and made-do. But, when the pay stopped coming in, they were not the ones who had failed. Nor did they have to go to war, and that seemed to me a blessed fact. By comparison with the narrow, ironclad days of fathers, there was an expansiveness, I thought, in the days of mothers. They went to see neighbors, to shop in town, to run errands at school, at the library, at church. No doubt, had I looked harder at their lives, I would have envied them less. It was not my fate to become a woman, so it was easier for me to see the graces. Few of them held jobs outside the home, and those who did filled thankless roles as clerks and waitresses. I didn't see, then, what a prison a house could be, since houses seemed to me brighter, handsomer places than any factory. I did not realize—because such things were never spoken of—how often women suffered from men's bullying. I did learn about the wretchedness of abandoned wives, single mothers, widows; but I also learned about the wretchedness of lone men. Even then I could see how exhausting it was for a mother to cater all day to the needs of young children. But if I had been asked, as a boy, to choose between tending a baby and tending a machine, I think I would have chosen the baby. (Having now tended both, I know I would choose the baby.)

9   So I was baffled when the women at college accused me and my sex of having cornered the world's pleasures. I think something like my bafflement has been felt by other boys (and by girls as well) who grew up in dirt-poor farm country, in mining country, in black ghettos, in Hispanic barrios, in the shadows of factories, in Third World nations—any place where the fate of men is as grim and bleak as the fate of women. Toilers and warriors. I realize now how ancient these identities are, how deep the tug they exert on men, the undertow of a thousand generations. The miseries I saw, as a boy, in the lives of nearly all men I continue to see in the lives of many—the body-breaking toil, the tedium, the call to be tough, the humiliating powerlessness, the battle for a living and for territory.

10   When the women I met at college thought about the joys and privileges of men, they did not carry in their minds the sort of men I had known in my childhood. They thought of their fathers, who were bankers, physicians, architects, stockbrokers, the big wheels of the big cities. These fathers rode the train to work or drove cars that cost more than any of my childhood houses. They were attended from morning to night by female helpers, wives and nurses and secretaries. They were never laid off, never short of cash at month's end, never lined up for welfare. These fathers made decisions that mattered. They ran the world.

11   The daughters of such men wanted to share in this power, this glory. So did I. They yearned for a say over their future, for jobs worthy of their abilities, for the right to live at peace, unmolested, whole. Yes, I thought, yes yes. The difference between me and these daughters was that they saw me, because of my sex, as destined from birth to become like their fathers, and therefore as an enemy to their desires. But I knew better. I wasn't an enemy, in fact or in feeling. I was an ally. If I had known, then, how to tell them so, would they have believed me? Would they now?

1984

On Black Fathering

Cornel West

One of the most difficult tasks to accomplish in American society 1
is to be a solid, caring, and loving black father. To be a good black
father, first you have to negotiate all of the absurd attacks and
assaults on your humanity and on your capacity and status as a
human being. Second, you have to provide materially and economically, as well as nurture psychologically, personally, and ex-
istentially. All of this requires a deep level of maturity. By
maturity I mean a solid understanding of who one is as a person,
and a sense of sacrifice and courage. For black men to reach that
level of maturity and understanding is almost miraculous given
the dehumanizing context for black men, and yet millions and
millions have done it. It is a tribute to fulfill the highest standards
of fatherhood. When I think of my own particular case, I think of
my father, my grandfather, and his father, because what they were
able to do was to sustain some sense of dignity and sacrifice even
as they dealt with all the arrows that were coming at them on
every level in American society.

Let's consider the economic level. In America, generally 2
speaking, patriarchal definitions of men in relation to the economic front mean you have a job and provide for your family.
Many black men did not (and do not) make enough money to
provide for their families adequately because of their exclusion
from jobs with a living wage. They then oftentimes tended, and
tend, to accent certain patriarchal identities (e.g., predatory or
abusive behavior) in lieu of the fact that they could not perform
the traditional patriarchal roles in American society.

Then on the home front, where black men had and have, of- 3
tentimes, wives who were and are subject to such white suprema-
cist abuse, either at the white home where these sisters work(ed)
or as a service worker in other parts of white society, most black
men had to deal with the kinds of scars and bruises that come
from knowing that you were supposed to protect your woman, as
it were, which is also part of the patriarchal identity in America—
a man ought to be able to protect his woman but could not protect

her from the vicious abuse. Many black men also recognized that there was a relation between their not being able to get a job given the discrimination and segregation on the one hand and the tremendous power wielded by those white men who were often condoning the abuse of their own wives.

4   How children perceive their father is another interesting component of the dynamic that black fathers have to negotiate. How are black fathers able to convey to their children some affirmative sense of self, some sense of reality—given what is happening to these men on the economic front, given what many of them know is happening to their wives outside of the house, and given the perception by their own children that they are unable to fulfill the expected patriarchal role? In the tradition of the black father, the best ones—I think my grandfather and dad are good examples—came up with ways of negotiating a balance so that they would recognize that exclusion from the economic sphere was real, and recognize that possible abuse of their wives was real, and also recognize that they had to sustain a connection with their kids in which their kids could see the best in them despite the limited and dehumanizing circumstances under which they functioned.

5   My mother happened to be a woman who was not abused in the fashion described above. I remember one incident when a white policeman disrespected my mother. Dad went at him verbally and, in the eyes of the police, ended up violating the law. At that point he just drew a line in the sand that said, "You're going too far." I thank God that a number of incidents like that didn't happen, or he would have ended up in jail forever—like so many other brothers who just do not allow certain levels of disrespect of their mother, wife, sister, or daughter. As a man, what I was able to see in Dad was his ability to transform his own pain with a sense of laughter, and a sense of empathy, and a sense of compassion for others. This was a real act of moral genius Dad accomplished, and I think that it is part of the best of a tradition of moral genius. Unfortunately, large numbers of black men do not reach that level because the rage and the anger are just too deep; they just burn them out and consume their soul. Fortunately, on the other hand, you do have many black men that achieve this level and some that go beyond it.

In my own case as a father, I certainly tried to emulate and im- 6
itate Dad's very ingenious ways of negotiating the balances between what was happening on these different fronts, but because
of the sacrifices he and Mom made, I had access to opportunities
that he did not. When my son Cliff was born, I was convinced that
I wanted to try to do for him what Dad had done for me. But it
was not to be—there was no way that I could be the father to my
son that my dad was to me. Part of it was that my circumstances
were very different. Another part was simply that I was not the
man that my father was. My brother is actually the shining example
of building on the rich legacy of my dad as a father much more
than I am, because he gives everything—right across the board.
He is there—whatever the circumstance—has spent time with the
kids; he is always there in the same way that Dad was there for us.
I'll always try to be a rich footnote to my brother, yet as a father I
have certainly not been the person that he was. The effort has
been there, the endeavor too, but the circumstances (as well as
my not being as deep a person as he or my father) have not enabled me to measure up. On the other hand, my son Cliff turned
out to be a decent and fascinating person—and he is still in
process, of course.

The bottom line for my dad was always love, and he was a 7
deeply Christian man—his favorite song was "I Will Trust in the
Lord." He had a profound trust. His trust was much more profound than mine in some ways, even though I work at it. He had
a deep love, and that's the thing I've tried to build on with Cliff.
My hope and my inclination are that Cliff feels this love, but certainly it takes more than love to nurture and father a son or a
daughter.

The most important things for black fathers to try to do are to 8
give of themselves, to try to exemplify in their own behavior what
they want to see in their sons and daughters, and, most important,
to spend time with and give attention to their children. This is a
big challenge, yet it is critical as we move into the twenty-first
century.

The most difficult task of my life was to give the eulogy for 9
my father. Everything else pales in the face of this challenge.
Hence what Dad means to me—like my family, Cliff and Elleni—
constitutes who and what I am and will be.

EULOGY

10   Clifton Lincoln West, Jr. What a man. What an individual. What a person. What a servant. We gather here this afternoon in this sacred place and this consecrated space to say good-bye. To bid farewell to a good man, a great Christian who lived a grand and loving life. When I think of my father, I cannot but think of what he said to that reporter from the *Sacramento Bee* when they asked him, "What is it about you and what is it about your family—do you have a secret?" Dad said, "No, we live by Grace—in addition to that, me and his mother, we try to *be there*." I shall never forget that my father was not simply a man of quiet dignity, steadfast integrity, and high intelligence, but fundamentally and quintessentially he was a man of love, and love means being there for others. That's why when I think of Dad I recall that precious moment in the fifteenth chapter of John in the eleventh and twelfth verse: "These things have I given unto you that my joy might remain in you, and that your joy might be full. This is my commandment that ye love one another as I have loved you."

11   In the midst of Dad's sophistication and refinement he was always for real. He was someone who was down-to-earth because he took this commandment seriously, and it meant he had to cut against the grain in a world in which he was going to endure lovingly and with compassion. Isn't that what the very core of the gospel is about? The thirteenth chapter of I Corinthians—that great litany of love that Dr. King talked about—deals with it. Dad used to read it all the time. I will never forget when he took me to college in Cambridge, the first time I ever flew on an airplane (it cost about ninety-five dollars then). Dad told me, "Corn, we're praying for you, and always remember: 'Though I speak with the tongues of men and of angels and have not love, I become as a sounding brass or a tinkling cymbal. And though I have the gift of prophecy, and understand all mysteries, and all knowledge; and though I have all faith, so that I could remove mountains, and have not love, I am nothing.'"

12   As we stand here on these stormy banks of Jordan and watch Dad's ship go by, may I remind each and every one of you that we come from a loving family, a courageous people of African descent, and a rich Christian tradition. We have seen situations in

which history has pushed our backs against the wall, and life has knocked us to our knees. In the face of despair and degradation sometimes we know that all we can do is sing a song, or crack a smile, or say a prayer. Yet we refuse to allow grief and misery to have the last word.

Dad was a man of love, and if I was to adopt his perspective 13 at this very moment, he would say, "Corn, don't push me in the limelight, keep your mother in mind, don't focus on me, keep the family in mind—I'm just a servant passing through." That's the kind of father I had.

But he didn't come to it by himself, you see. He was part of a 14 family, he was part of a people, he was part of a tradition that went all the way back to gut-bucket Jim Crow Louisiana, September 7, 1928. He was not supposed to make it, you see. Nobody would have believed that Clifton Lincoln West, Jr., the third child of C. L. West and Lovey West, would have been able to aspire to the heights that he did. No one would have predicted or projected that he would make it through the first three months in Louisiana—Cliff was not supposed to make that trip, you know. He was born the year before the stock market crashed. His family stayed three months in Louisiana, and Grandfather and Grandmother, with three young children in a snowstorm, journeyed on a train to Tulsa, Oklahoma. You all know what Tulsa, Oklahoma, was like. It was seven years after the major riot in this country in which over three hundred folks—black folks—were killed and Greenwood, Archer and Pine—that GAP corner—the Wall Street of black America was all burned out. But Grandmama had something else in mind, and the Lord did too.

Dad went on to Paul Laurence Dunbar Elementary School—to 15 give you an idea of what side of town they were living on—and George Washington Carver Junior High School, and Booker T. Washington High School. It was there that he got to choose the idea of pulling from the best of the world but remaining not of the world. I like that about Dad. He wasn't so excessively pious or so excessively rigid that he became naive and got caught up in narrow doctrines and creeds and thought he was better than anybody else. That's not the kind of man he was. No. His faith was grounded in a love because he knew that he had fallen short of the glory of God.

He knew he had inadequacies and shortcomings, but he was going to struggle anyhow; he was going to keep keeping on anyway.

16   After high school he went on to the military for three years. He could have easily given his life for this country. When he returned to Tulsa, Oklahoma, he was refused admission at the University of Tulsa, and then went on to that grand institution, Fisk University, where he met that indescribably wonderful, beautiful, lovable honor student from Orange, Texas—Irene Bias. I'll never forget when we were at Fisk together, he described the place right outside Jubilee Hall where they met. I said, "Dad, that's a special place," and he said, "Yes, that meeting was the beginning of the peak of my life." As their love began to grow and multiply, the army grabbed him back again for eighteen months, but in the years to come they had young Clifton, my brother, to whom I'm just a footnote; myself, of course; and Cynthia and Cheryl. We moved from Oklahoma through Topeka, Kansas, on our way to 8008 48th Avenue, Glen Elder. Yes, how proud we were driving up in that bright orange Mercury. We were at the cutting edge of residential breakdown in Sacramento, but along the way, for almost a decade, Dad, and the men of Glen Elder—Mr. Peters, Mr. Pool, Mr. Powell, Mr. Reed—these were black men who cared and who worked together. These overworked yet noble men built the little league diamond by themselves, and then they organized the league into ten teams—minor and major leagues for the neighborhood. They provided a means by which character and integrity could be shaped among the young brothers. Then every Sunday, onto Shiloh—"can't wait for the next sermon of Reverend Willie P. Cooke, just hope that he didn't go too long"—but we knew that the Lord was working in him. Dad would always tell us, "You know how blessed I am, how blessed we are. Never think that we've come as far as we have on our own."

17   When we were in trouble, there was Mr. Fields, Mrs. Ray, and Mrs. Harris—there were hundreds of folks who made a difference. You all remember when Dad went to the hospital when he was thirty-one years old and the doctors had given up on him. There was a great sadness on Forty-eighth Avenue because he had left Mom with four little children. Granddad—the Reverend C. L. West, left his church for months to come and be with Mom—

Grandmom came as well—and Dad was in the hospital in Oakland. They had given up on him; the medical profession had reached its conclusion and said they could do nothing. And we said, "We know the power. Let Him step in." We knew that Reverend Cook hadn't been preaching that "Jesus is a rock in a weary land, and water in dry places, and food when you are hungry, and a mind regulator and a heart fixer" for nothing. And we came to Calvary in prayer.

Can you imagine how different our lives would have been if 18 we had lost Dad then, in 1961, rather than 1994? Even in the midst of our fear we rejoice. It would have been a different world for each and every one of us, especially the children. Dad kept going after his recovery. He worked at McClellan Air Force Base— steadily missed some of those promotions he should have got, but he stayed convinced that he was going to teach people right no matter what, even given his own situation.

That's another thing I loved about him. People always ask 19 me, "West, why do you still talk about love? It's played out. Why when you talk about blackness is it always linked to white brothers and sisters and yellow brothers and sisters and red brothers and sisters and brown brothers and sisters?" And I tell them about John 15:11–12. I tell them that I dedicated my life a long time ago to the same Jesus that Dad dedicated his life to, to the same Jesus that Reverend C. L. West dedicated his life, to the same Jesus that my grandfather on my mother's side and my grandmother on my mother's side dedicated their lives to, but, more important, I saw in the concrete, with Dad and Mom, a love that transcends skin pigmentation. I saw it on the ground. Dad taught us that even as you keep track of the injustice, you don't lose track of the humanity. That's what love and being there are all about. Dad made it a priority and preference to be there for us. He made a choice. It meant that he would live a life of interruptions because those who are fundamentally committed to being there are going to be continually interrupted—your own agenda, your own project, are going to be interfered with. Dad was always open to that kind of interruption. He was able to translate a kind of unpredictable interruption into a supportive intervention in somebody else's life. More important, Dad realized that a being-there kind of love meant that you had to have follow up and follow through. One could not just show up—one has to follow up and follow through. This is the most difficult aspect of it. Love is inseparable from pain and hurt and sadness and sorrow and disappointment, but Dad knew that you had to have follow up and follow through. He knew that you had to struggle in the midst of that pain and that hurt—you had to have just not simply the high moments of love, but the funk of love, the stink and the stench of love. In all of his relationships Dad embodied precisely that struggle with the high moments of love and the low moments of love. He knew that the cross was not just about smiles and that it was not just about celebration—it was about sadness, stench, and funk. That is what the blood was about, not Kool-aid but blood. That's how inseparable scars, bruises, and wounds are from joy, affirmation, and wholeness. If you were serious about love, if you were serious about being there for people you were going to be there in in the midst of any situation, any circumstances, any condition. Dad realized that God being there for us in any situation and circumstance meant that if he was going to be Godlike, he had to be there in any situation for us. I've been alive now for forty years, and on Thursday I'll be forty-one years old, and *not once has my mother or father disappointed me.* They have always been there. That is a blessing, and I do not deserve it. It's a blessing, and I am thankful for it.

20   So as we bid farewell to Dad, I want you all to know that I am looking forward to a family reunion. I am looking forward to union together on the other side of the Jordan. I am looking forward to seeing Dad in a place where the wicked will cease their troubling and the weary shall be at rest. I tell you when I get there, I'm going down Revelation Boulevard to the corner of John Street, right around the corner from Mark's place. But I want to go to Nahum's place. I don't want to be in Jeremiah's house, it would be too crowded. I don't even want to be down on Peter Street, too many people there—I want some quiet time. I want to sit down with C. L. West, I want to sit down with Nick Bias, and I want to sit down with Aunt Juanita, and I want to sit down with Aunt Tiny. And I want to sit down with Dad! I want to let them know that we did the best that we could to keep alive the best of the

legacy of love that they left to us. And when we come together, we will come together in a way in which there will be no more tears, no more heartache, no more heartbreak, no more sadness and sorrow, no more agony and anguish. We shall sit at the feet of the Lord and be blessed, and our souls will look back and wonder how we got over, how we got over.

1988

Evan's Two Moms

Anna Quindlen

Evan has two moms. This is no big thing. Evan has always had   1
two moms—in his school file, on his emergency forms, with his friends. "Ooooh, Evan, you're lucky," they sometimes say. "You have two moms." It sounds like a sitcom, but until last week it was emotional truth without legal bulwark. That was when a judge in New York approved the adoption of a six-year-old boy by his biological mother's lesbian partner. Evan. Evan's mom. Evan's other mom. A kid, a psychologist, a pediatrician. A family.

The matter of Evan's two moms is one in a series of events   2
over the last year that lead to certain conclusions. A Minnesota appeals court granted guardianship of a woman left a quadriplegic in a car accident to her lesbian lover, the culmination of a seven-year battle in which the injured woman's parents did everything possible to negate the partnership between the two. A lawyer in Georgia had her job offer withdrawn after the state attorney general found out that she and her lesbian lover were planning a marriage ceremony; she's brought suit. The computer company Lotus announced that the gay partners of employees would be eligible for the same benefits as spouses.

Add to these public events the private struggles, the couples   3
who go from lawyer to lawyer to approximate legal protections their straight counterparts take for granted, the AIDS survivors who find themselves shut out of their partners' dying days by bio-

logical family members and shut out of their apartments by leases with a single name on the dotted line, and one solution is obvious.

4   Gay marriage is a radical notion for straight people and a conservative notion for gay ones. After years of being sledgehammered by society, some gay men and lesbian women are deeply suspicious of participating in an institution that seems to have "straight world" written all over it.

5   But the rads of twenty years ago, straight and gay alike, have other things on their minds today. Family is one, and the linchpin of family has commonly been a loving commitment between two adults. When same-sex couples set out to make that commitment, they discover that they are at a disadvantage: No joint tax returns. No health insurance coverage for an uninsured partner. No survivor's benefits from Social Security. None of the automatic rights, privileges, and responsibilities society attaches to a marriage contract. In Madison, Wisconsin, a couple who applied at the Y with their kids for a family membership were turned down because both were women. It's one of those small things that can make you feel small.

6   Some took marriage statutes that refer to "two persons" at their word and applied for a license. The results were court decisions that quoted the Bible and embraced circular argument: marriage is by definition the union of a man and a woman because that is how we've defined it.

7   No religion should be forced to marry anyone in violation of its tenets, although ironically it is now only in religious ceremonies that gay people can marry, performed by clergy who find the blessing of two who love each other no sin. But there is no secular reason that we should take a patchwork approach of corporate, governmental, and legal steps to guarantee what can be done simply, economically, conclusively, and inclusively with the words "I do."

8   "Fran and I chose to get married for the same reasons that any two people do," said the lawyer who was fired in Georgia. "We fell in love; we wanted to spend our lives together." Pretty simple.

9   Consider the case of *Loving* v. *Virginia,* aptly named. At the time, sixteen states had laws that barred interracial marriage, relying on natural law, that amorphous grab bag for justifying prejudice. Sounding a little like God throwing Adam and Eve out of paradise, the trial judge suspended the one-year sentence of

Richard Loving, who was white, and his wife, Mildred, who was black, provided they got out of the State of Virginia.

In 1967 the Supreme Court found such laws to be unconstitu-   10
tional. Only twenty-five years ago and it was a crime for a black woman to marry a white man. Perhaps twenty-five years from now we will find it just as incredible that two people of the same sex were not entitled to legally commit themselves to each other. Love and commitment are rare enough; it seems absurd to thwart them in any guise.

1992

Cinderella: A Story of Sibling Rivalry and Oedipal Conflicts

Bruno Bettelheim

By all accounts, "Cinderella" is the best-known fairy tale, and   1
probably also the best-liked. It is quite an old story; when first written down in China during the ninth century A.D., it already had a history. The unrivaled tiny foot size as a mark of extraordinary virtue, distinction, and beauty, and the slipper made of precious material are facets which point to an Eastern, if not necessarily Chinese, origin. The modern hearer does not connect sexual attractiveness and beauty in general with extreme smallness of the foot, as the ancient Chinese did, in accordance with their practice of binding women's feet.

"Cinderella," as we know it, is experienced as a story about   2
the agonies and hopes which form the essential content of sibling rivalry; and about the degraded heroine winning out over her siblings who abused her. Long before Perrault gave "Cinderella" the form in which it is now widely known, "having to live among the ashes" was a symbol of being debased in comparison to one's siblings, irrespective of sex. In Germany, for example, there were stories in which such an ash-boy later becomes king, which parallels Cinderella's fate. "Aschenputtel" is the title of the Brothers

Grimm's version of the tale. The term originally designated a lowly, dirty kitchenmaid who must tend to the fireplace ashes.

3   There are many examples in the German language of how being forced to dwell among the ashes was a symbol not just of degradation, but also of sibling rivalry, and of the sibling who finally surpasses the brother or brothers who have debased him. Martin Luther in his *Table Talks* speaks about Cain as the God-forsaken evildoer who is powerful, while pious Abel is forced to be his ash-brother *(Aschebrüdel)*, a mere nothing, subject to Cain; in one of Luther's sermons he says that Esau was forced into the role of Jacob's ash-brother. Cain and Abel, Jacob and Esau are Biblical examples of one brother being suppressed or destroyed by the other.

4   The fairy tale replaces sibling relations with relations between stepsiblings—perhaps a device to explain and make acceptable an animosity which one wishes would not exist among true siblings. Although sibling rivalry is universal and "natural" in the sense that it is the negative consequence of being a sibling, this same re-lation also generates equally as much positive feeling between siblings, highlighted in fairy tales such as "Brother and Sister."

5   No other fairy tale renders so well as the "Cinderella" stories the inner experiences of the young child in the throes of sibling ri-valry, when he feels hopelessly outclassed by his brothers and sis-ters. Cinderella is pushed down and degraded by her stepsisters; her interests are sacrificed to theirs by her (step)mother; she is ex-pected to do the dirtiest work and although she performs it well, she receives no credit for it; only more is demanded of her. This is how the child feels when devastated by the miseries of sibling ri-valry. Exaggerated though Cinderella's tribulations and degrada-tions may seem to the adult, the child carried away by sibling rivalry feels, "That's me; that's how they mistreat me, or would want to; that's how little they think of me." And there are mo-ments—often long time periods—when for inner reasons a child feels this way even when his position among his siblings may seem to give him no cause for it.

6   When a story corresponds to how the child feels deep down—as no realistic narrative is likely to do—it attains an emotional quality of "truth" for the child. The events of "Cinderella" offer him vivid images that give body to his overwhelming but

nevertheless often vague and nondescript emotions; so these episodes seem more convincing to him than his life experiences.

The term "sibling rivalry" refers to a most complex constella- 7 tion of feelings and their causes. With extremely rare exceptions, the emotions aroused in the person subject to sibling rivalry are far out of proportion to what his real situation with his sisters and brothers would justify, seen objectively. While all children at times suffer greatly from sibling rivalry, parents seldom sacrifice one of their children to the others, nor do they condone the other children's persecuting one of them. Difficult as objective judgments are for the young child—nearly impossible when his emotions are aroused—even he in his more rational moments "knows" that he is not treated as badly as Cinderella. But the child often feels mistreated, despite all his "knowledge" to the contrary. That is why he believes in the inherent truth of "Cinderella," and then he also comes to believe in her eventual deliverance and victory. From her triumph he gains the exaggerated hopes for his future which he needs to counteract the extreme misery he experiences when ravaged by sibling rivalry.

Despite the name "sibling rivalry," this miserable passion has 8 only incidentally to do with a child's actual brothers and sisters. The real source of it is the child's feelings about his parents. When a child's older brother or sister is more competent than he, this arouses only temporary feelings of jealousy. Another child being given special attention becomes an insult only if the child fears that, in contrast, he is thought little of by his parents, or feels rejected by them. It is because of such an anxiety that one or all of a child's sisters or brothers may become a thorn in his flesh. Fearing that in comparison to them he cannot win his parents' love and esteem is what inflames sibling rivalry. This is indicated in stories by the fact that it matters little whether the siblings actually possess greater competence. The Biblical story of Joseph tells that it is jealousy of parental affection lavished on him which accounts for the destructive behavior of his brothers. Unlike Cinderella's, Joseph's parent does not participate in degrading him, and, on the contrary, prefers him to his other children. But Joseph, like Cinderella, is turned into a slave, and, like her, he miraculously escapes and ends by surpassing his siblings.

9   Telling a child who is devastated by sibling rivalry that he will grow up to do as well as his brothers and sisters offers little relief from his present feelings of dejection. Much as he would like to trust our assurances, most of the time he cannot. A child can see things only with subjective eyes, and comparing himself on this basis to his siblings, he has no confidence that he, on his own, will someday be able to fare as well as they. If he could believe more in himself, he would not feel destroyed by his siblings no matter what they might do to him, since then he could trust that time would bring about a desired reversal of fortune. But since the child cannot, on his own, look forward with confidence to some future day when things will turn out all right for him, he can gain relief only through fantasies of glory—a domination over his siblings— which he hopes will become reality through some fortunate event.

10   Whatever our position within the family, at certain times in our lives we are beset by sibling rivalry in some form or other. Even an only child feels that other children have some great advantages over him, and this makes him intensely jealous. Further, he may suffer from the anxious thought that if he did have a sibling, his parents would prefer this other child to him. "Cinderella" is a fairy tale which makes nearly as strong an appeal to boys as to girls, since children of both sexes suffer equally from sibling rivalry, and have the same desire to be rescued from their lowly position and surpass those who seem superior to them.

11   On the surface, "Cinderella" is as deceptively simple as the story of Little Red Riding Hood, with which it shares greatest popularity. "Cinderella" tells about the agonies of sibling rivalry, of wishes coming true, of the humble being elevated, of true merit being recognized even when hidden under rags, of virtue rewarded and evil punished—a straightforward story. But under this overt content is concealed a welter of complex and largely unconscious material, which details of the story allude to just enough to set our unconscious associations going. This makes a contrast between surface simplicity and underlying complexity which arouses deep interest in the story and explains its appeal to the millions over centuries. To begin gaining an understanding of these hidden meanings, we have to penetrate behind the obvious sources of sibling rivalry discussed so far.

As mentioned before, if the child could only believe that it is 12
the infirmities of his age which account for his lowly position, he
would not have to suffer so wretchedly from sibling rivalry, because he could trust the future to right matters. When he thinks
that his degradation is deserved, he feels his plight is utterly
hopeless. Djuna Barnes's perceptive statement about fairy
tales—that the child knows something about them which he cannot tell (such as that he likes the idea of Little Red Riding Hood
and the wolf being in bed together)—could be extended by di-
viding fairy tales into two groups: one group where the child responds only unconsciously to the inherent truth of the story and
thus cannot tell about it; and another large number of tales
where the child preconsciously or even consciously knows what
the "truth" of the story consists of and thus could tell about it,
but does not want to let on that he knows. Some aspects of "Cinderella" fall into the latter category. Many children believe that
Cinderella probably deserves her fate at the beginning of the
story, as they feel they would, too; but they don't want anyone
to know it. Despite this, she is worthy at the end to be exalted,
as the child hopes he will be too, irrespective of his earlier
shortcomings.

Every child believes at some period of his life—and this is not 13
only at rare moments—that because of his secret wishes, if not
also his clandestine actions, he deserves to be degraded, banned
from the presence of others, relegated to a netherworld of smut.
He fears this may be so, irrespective of how fortunate his situation
may be in reality. He hates and fears those others—such as his siblings—whom he believes to be entirely free of similar evilness,
and he fears that they or his parents will discover what he is really
like, and then demean him as Cinderella was by her family. Because he wants others—most of all, his parents—to believe in his
innocence, he is delighted that "everybody" believes in Cinderella's. This is one of the great attractions of this fairy tale. Since
people give credence to Cinderella's goodness, they will also believe in his, so the child hopes. And "Cinderella" nourishes this
hope, which is one reason it is such a delightful story.

Another aspect which holds large appeal for the child is the 14
vileness of the stepmother and stepsisters. Whatever the short-

comings of a child may be in his own eyes, these pale into insignificance when compared to the stepsisters' and stepmother's falsehood and nastiness. Further, what these stepsisters do to Cinderella justifies whatever nasty thoughts one may have about one's siblings: they are so vile that anything one may wish would happen to them is more than justified. Compared to their behavior, Cinderella is indeed innocent. So the child, on hearing her story, feels he need not feel guilty about his angry thoughts.

15   On a very different level—and reality considerations coexist easily with fantastic exaggerations in the child's mind—as badly as one's parents or siblings seem to treat one, and much as one thinks one suffers because of it, all this is nothing compared to Cinderella's fate. Her story reminds the child at the same time how lucky he is, and how much worse things could be. (Any anxiety about the latter possibility is relieved, as always in fairy tales, by the happy ending.)

16   The behavior of a five-and-a-half-year-old girl, as reported by her father, may illustrate how easily a child may feel that she is a "Cinderella." This little girl had a younger sister of whom she was very jealous. The girl was very fond of "Cinderella," since the story offered her material with which to act out her feelings, and because without the story's imagery she would have been hard pressed to comprehend and express them. This little girl had used to dress very neatly and liked pretty clothes, but she became unkempt and dirty. One day when she was asked to fetch some salt, she said as she was doing so, "Why do you treat me like Cinderella?"

17   Almost speechless, her mother asked her, "Why do you think I treat you like Cinderella?"

18   "Because you make me do all the hardest work in the house!" was the little girl's answer. Having thus drawn her parents into her fantasies, she acted them out more openly, pretending to sweep up all the dirt, etc. She went even further, playing that she prepared her little sister for the ball. But she went the "Cinderella" story one better, based on her unconscious understanding of the contradictory emotions fused into the "Cinderella" role, because at another moment she told her mother and sister, "You shouldn't be jealous of me just because I am the most beautiful in the family."

This shows that behind the surface humility of Cinderella lies 19 the conviction of her superiority to mother and sisters, as if she would think: "You can make me do all the dirty work, and I pretend that I am dirty, but within me I know that you treat me this way because you are jealous of me because I am so much better than you." This conviction is supported by the story's ending, which assures every "Cinderella" that eventually she will be discovered by her prince.

Why does the child believe deep within himself that Cin- 20 derella deserves her dejected state? This question takes us back to the child's state of mind at the end of the oedipal period. Before he is caught in oedipal entanglements, the child is convinced that he is lovable, and loved, if all is well within his family relationships. Psychoanalysis describes this stage of complete satisfaction with oneself as "primary narcissism." During this period the child feels certain that he is the center of the universe, so there is no reason to be jealous of anybody.

The oedipal disappointments which come at the end of this 21 developmental stage cast deep shadows of doubt on the child's sense of his worthiness. He feels that if he were really as deserving of love as he had thought, then his parents would never be critical of him or disappoint him. The only explanation for parental criticism the child can think of is that there must be some serious flaw in him which accounts for what he experiences as rejection. If his desires remain unsatisfied and his parents disappoint him, there must be something wrong with him or his desires, or both. He cannot yet accept that reasons other than those residing within him could have an impact on his fate. In his oedipal jealousy, wanting to get rid of the parent of the same sex had seemed the most natural thing in the world, but now the child realizes that he cannot have his own way, and that maybe this is so because the desire was wrong. He is no longer so sure that he is preferred to his siblings, and he begins to suspect that this may be due to the fact that *they* are free of any bad thoughts or wrongdoing such as his.

All this happens as the child is gradually subjected to ever 22 more critical attitudes as he is being socialized. He is asked to behave in ways which run counter to his natural desires, and he resents this. Still he must obey, which makes him very angry. This anger is directed against those who make demands, most likely his parents; and this is another reason to wish to get rid of them, and still another reason to feel guilty about such wishes. This is why the child also feels that he deserves to be chastised for his feelings, a punishment he believes he can escape only if nobody learns what he is thinking when he is angry. The feeling of being unworthy to be loved by his parents at a time when his desire for their love is very strong leads to the fear of rejection, even when in reality there is none. This rejection fear compounds the anxiety that others are preferred and also maybe preferable—the root of sibling rivalry.

23   Some of the child's pervasive feelings of worthlessness have their origin in his experiences during and around toilet training and all other aspects of his education to become clean, neat, and orderly. Much has been said about how children are made to feel dirty and bad because they are not as clean as their parents want or require them to be. As clean as a child may learn to be, he knows that he would much prefer to give free rein to his tendency to be messy, disorderly, and dirty.

24   At the end of the oedipal period, guilt about desires to be dirty and disorderly becomes compounded by oedipal guilt, because of the child's desire to replace the parent of the same sex in the love of the other parent. The wish to be the love, if not also the sexual partner, of the parent of the other sex, which at the beginning of the oedipal development seemed natural and "innocent," at the end of the period is repressed as bad. But while this wish as such is repressed, guilt about it and about sexual feelings in general is not, and this makes the child feel dirty and worthless.

25   Here again, lack of objective knowledge leads the child to think that he is the only bad one in all these respects—the only child who has such desires. It makes every child identify with Cinderella, who is relegated to sit among the cinders. Since the child has such "dirty" wishes, that is where he also belongs, and where he would end up if his parents knew of his desires. This is why every child needs to believe that even if he were thus degraded, eventually he would be rescued from such degradation and experience the most wonderful exaltation—as Cinderella does.

For the child to deal with his feelings of dejection and worth- 26
lessness aroused during this time, he desperately needs to gain
some grasp on what these feelings of guilt and anxiety are all
about. Further, he needs assurance on a conscious and an unconscious level that he will be able to extricate himself from these
predicaments. One of the greatest merits of "Cinderella" is that, irrespective of the magic help Cinderella receives, the child understands that essentially it is through her own efforts, and because
of the person she is, that Cinderella is able to transcend magnifi-
cently her degraded state, despite what appear as insurmountable
obstacles. It gives the child confidence that the same will be true
for him, because the story relates so well to what has caused both
his conscious and his unconscious guilt.

Overtly "Cinderella" tells about sibling rivalry in its most ex- 27
treme form: the jealousy and enmity of the stepsisters, and Cinderella's sufferings because of it. The many other psychological
issues touched upon in the story are so covertly alluded to that the
child does not become consciously aware of them. In his unconscious, however, the child responds to these significant details
which refer to matters and experiences from which he consciously
has separated himself, but which nevertheless continue to create
vast problems for him.

1975

Girl

Jamaica Kincaid

Wash the white clothes on Monday and put them on the stone 1
heap; wash the color clothes on Tuesday and put them on the
clothesline to dry; don't walk barehead in the hot sun; cook
pumpkin fritters in very hot sweet oil; soak your little clothes
right after you take them off; when buying cotton to make yourself a nice blouse, be sure that it doesn't have gum on it, because

that way it won't hold up well after a wash; soak salt fish overnight before you cook it; is it true that you sing benna in Sunday school?; always eat your food in such a way that it won't turn someone else's stomach; on Sundays try to walk like a lady and not like the slut you are so bent on becoming; don't sing benna in Sunday school; you mustn't speak to wharf-rat boys, not even to give directions; don't eat fruits on the street—flies will follow you; *but I don't sing benna on Sundays at all and never in Sunday school;* this is how to sew on a button; this is how to make a buttonhole for the button you have just sewed on; this is how to hem a dress when you see the hem coming down and so to prevent yourself from looking like the slut I know you are so bent on becoming; this is how you iron your father's khaki shirt so that it doesn't have a crease; this is how you iron your father's khaki pants so that they don't have a crease; this is how you grow okra—far from the house, because okra tree harbors red ants; when you are growing dasheen, make sure it gets plenty of water or else it makes your throat itch when you are eating it; this is how you sweep a corner; this is how you sweep a whole house; this is how you sweep a yard; this is how you smile to someone you don't like too much; this is how you smile to someone you don't like at all; this is how you smile to someone you like completely; this is how you set a table for tea; this is how you set a table for dinner; this is how you set a table for dinner with an important guest; this is how you set a table for lunch; this is how you set a table for breakfast; this is how to behave in the presence of men who don't know you very well, and this way they won't recognize immediately the slut I have warned you against becoming; be sure to wash every day, even if it is with your own spit; don't squat down to play marbles—you are not a boy, you know; don't pick people's flowers—you might catch something; don't throw stones at blackbirds, because it might not be a blackbird at all; this is how to make a bread pudding; this is how to make doukona; this is how to make pepper pot; this is how to make a good medicine for a cold; this is how to make a good medicine to throw away a child before it even becomes a child; this is how to catch a fish; this is how to throw back a fish you don't like, and that way something bad won't fall on you; this is how to bully a man; this is how a man bullies you; this is how to love a man, and if this doesn't work there are other ways, and if they don't work don't feel too bad about giving up; this is how to spit up in the air if you feel like it, and this is how to move quick so that it doesn't fall on you; this is how to make ends meet; always squeeze bread to make sure it's fresh; *but what if the baker won't let me feel the bread?;* you mean to say that after all you are really going to be the kind of woman who the baker won't let near the bread?

1983

5

Government, Power, and Justice

How does a government gain power, and keep it? Is it a matter of who has the most might? The most cunning? Though *Machiavellian* is most often used to characterize a ruthless philosophy where "the ends justify the means," Machiavelli's vision of princely power as dependent on a prince's relationship with the people (rather than divine right) presages the beginnings of the modern nation state. Machiavelli wrote with an eye toward the model of republican Rome, but in his own sixteenth-century Italy, the acquisition of power was chaotic and unstable where the prince of one city was in competition with the prince of another. Out of this environment and his own study of history came Machiavelli's ad vice—which he defended as a pragmatic rather than idealistic view of power —to those who would rule in "The Qualities of the Prince." Over 250 years later, Thomas Jefferson eloquently argues in "The Declaration of Independence" that it is the people who grant a government its power, though, unlike Machiavelli, Jefferson sees the people as a dynamic force in the expression of a nation's conduct toward its citizens. But who *are* the people? In her "Declaration of Sentiments," suffragist Elizabeth Cady Stanton argues in an imitation of the grand elocution of Jefferson's declaration that both "men and women are created equal" and that women should not be submitted to laws that they had no voice in creating. It has often been argued that women are too delicate for the responsibilities that men endure, but the abolitionist and escaped slave Sojourner Truth joined voices with those in the suffrage movement when she delivered her speech, "Ain't I a Woman?" In this speech, Sojourner Truth reveals the hypocrisy of the delicacy argument through her examples of the treatment of black women, and slave women in particular. Henry David Thoreau, himself an abolitionist, muses on his night in jail for "disobey[ing] unjust laws" in what would become a manifesto for justice, "Civil Disobedience." In another meditation from a jail on justice and what makes a just state, Martin Luther King, Jr., refutes those who would have stability over justice. It is just this appeal for stability and the status quo that are often the tools used by those who rule to maintain their power, as Hannah Arendt movingly describes in her examination of the systematic slaughter of European Jews. In "Deportations from Western Europe," Arendt notes that much of the deportation rested on such appeals, which Germany made to manipulate its conquered neighbors into delivering non–native-born Jews for deportation, as the first step toward a breakdown in resistance to deportations. Jews native to a country were soon to follow. One nation, Denmark, employed civil disobedience effectively against this us–them tyranny. The distinction between native and non-native has deep roots—the British took from "them" the Irish, observes Jonathan Swift in his famous satire, "A Modest Proposal," where he bitterly proposes that the Irish eat their children, since they had been left with nothing else to eat. Born in India, George Orwell knew firsthand the tyranny of empire and has written extensively against colonialism. In his classic work "Shooting an Elephant," he describes the dissolution of the rulers' character that such an us–them mind-set creates. Tyranny is no stranger to any epoch, nor is justice. E.B. White provides a lasting statement on the compact between the people and its government in "The Meaning of Democracy."

The Qualities of the Prince

Niccolò Machiavelli

ON THOSE THINGS FOR WHICH MEN, AND PARTICULARLY PRINCES, ARE PRAISED OR BLAMED

1 Now there remains to be examined what should be the methods and procedures of a prince in dealing with his subjects and friends. And because I know that many have written about this, I am afraid that by writing about it again I shall be thought of as presumptuous, since in discussing this material I depart radically from the procedures of others. But since my intention is to write something useful for anyone who understands it, it seemed more suitable to me to search after the effectual truth of the matter rather than its imagined one. And many writers have imagined for themselves republics and principalities that have never been seen nor known to exist in reality; for there is such a gap between how one lives and how one ought to live that anyone who abandons what is done for what ought to be done learns his ruin rather than his preservation: for a man who wishes to make a vocation of being good at all times will come to ruin among so many who are not good. Hence it is necessary for a prince who wishes to maintain his position to learn how not to be good, and to use this knowledge or not to use it according to necessity.

2   Leaving aside, therefore, the imagined things concerning a prince, and taking into account those that are true, I say that all men, when they are spoken of, and particularly princes, since they are placed on a higher level, are judged by some of these qualities which bring them either blame or praise. And this is why one is considered generous, another miserly (to use a Tuscan word, since "avaricious" in our language is still used to mean one who wishes to acquire by means of theft; we call "miserly" one who excessively avoids using what he has); one is considered a giver, the

other rapacious; one cruel, another merciful; one treacherous, another faithful; one effeminate and cowardly, another bold and courageous; one humane, another haughty; one lascivious, another chaste; one trustworthy, another cunning; one harsh, another lenient; one serious, another frivolous; one religious, another unbelieving; and the like. And I know that everyone will admit that it would be a very praiseworthy thing to find in a prince, of the qualities mentioned above, those that are held to be good, but since it is neither possible to have them nor to observe them all completely, because human nature does not permit it, a prince must be prudent enough to know how to escape the bad reputation of those vices that would lose the state for him, and must protect himself from those that will not lose it for him, if this is possible; but if he cannot, he need not concern himself unduly if he ignores these less serious vices. And, moreover, he need not worry about incurring the bad reputation of those vices without which it would be difficult to hold his state; since, carefully taking everything into account, one will discover that something which appears to be a virtue, if pursued, will end in his destruction; while some other thing which seems to be a vice, if pursued, will result in his safety and his well-being.

ON GENEROSITY AND MISERLINESS

Beginning, therefore, with the first of the above-mentioned qualities, I say that it would be good to be considered generous; nevertheless, generosity used in such a manner as to give you a reputation for it will harm you; because if it is employed virtuously and as one should employ it, it will not be recognized and you will not avoid the reproach of its opposite. And so, if a prince wants to maintain his reputation for generosity among men, it is necessary for him not to neglect any possible means of lavish display; in so doing such a prince will always use up all his resources and he will be obliged, eventually, if he wishes to maintain his reputation for generosity, to burden the people with excessive taxes and to do everything possible to raise funds. This will begin to make him hateful to his subjects, and, becoming impoverished, he will not be much esteemed by anyone; so that, as a consequence of his generosity, having offended many and rewarded few, he will feel the effects of any slight unrest and will be ruined at the first sign of danger; recognizing this and wishing to alter his policies, he immediately runs the risk of being reproached as a miser.

4   A prince, therefore, unable to use this virtue of generosity in a manner which will not harm himself if he is known for it, should, if he is wise, not worry about being called a miser; for with time he will come to be considered more generous once it is evident that, as a result of his parsimony, his income is sufficient, he can defend himself from anyone who makes war against him, and he can undertake enterprises without overburdening his people, so that he comes to be generous with all those from whom he takes nothing, who are countless, and miserly with all those to whom he gives nothing, who are few. In our times we have not seen great deeds accomplished except by those who were considered miserly; all others were done away with. Pope Julius II, although he made use of his reputation for generosity in order to gain the papacy, then decided not to maintain it in order to be able to wage war; the present King of France has waged many wars without imposing extra taxes on his subjects, only because his habitual parsimony has provided for the additional expenditures; the present King of Spain, if he had been considered generous, would not have engaged in nor won so many campaigns.

5   Therefore, in order not to have to rob his subjects, to be able to defend himself, not to become poor and contemptible, and not to be forced to become rapacious, a prince must consider it of little importance if he incurs the name of miser, for this is one of those vices that permits him to rule. And if someone were to say: Caesar with his generosity came to rule the empire, and many others, because they were generous and known to be so, achieved very high positions; I reply: you are either already a prince or you are on the way to becoming one; in the first instance such generosity is damaging; in the second it is very necessary to be thought generous. And Caesar was one of those who wanted to gain the principality of Rome; but if, after obtaining this, he had lived and had not moderated his expenditures, he would have destroyed that empire. And if someone were to reply: there have existed many

princes who have accomplished great deeds with their armies who have been reputed to be generous; I answer you: a prince either spends his own money and that of his subjects or that of others; in the first case he must be economical; in the second he must not restrain any part of his generosity. And for that prince who goes out with his soldiers and lives by looting, sacking, and ransoms, who controls the property of others, such generosity is necessary; otherwise he would not be followed by his troops. And with what does not belong to you or to your subjects you can be a more liberal giver, as were Cyrus, Caesar, and Alexander; for spending the wealth of others does not lessen your reputation but adds to it; only the spending of your own is what harms you. And there is nothing that uses itself up faster than generosity, for as you employ it you lose the means of employing it, and you become either poor or despised or, in order to escape poverty, rapacious and hated. And above all other things a prince must guard himself against being despised and hated; and generosity leads you to both one and the other. So it is wiser to live with the reputation of a miser, which produces reproach without hatred, than to be forced to incur the reputation of rapacity, which produces reproach along with hatred, because you want to be considered as generous.

ON CRUELTY AND MERCY AND WHETHER IT IS BETTER TO BE LOVED THAN TO BE FEARED OR THE CONTRARY

Proceeding to the other qualities mentioned above, I say that every 6 prince must desire to be considered merciful and not cruel; nevertheless, he must take care not to misuse this mercy. Cesare Borgia was considered cruel; nonetheless, his cruelty had brought order to Romagna, united it, restored it to peace and obedience. If we examine this carefully, we shall see that he was more merciful than the Florentine people, who, in order to avoid being considered cruel, allowed the destruction of Pistoia. Therefore, a prince must not worry about the reproach of cruelty when it is a matter of keeping his subjects united and loyal; for with a very few examples of cruelty he will be more compassionate than those who, out of excessive mercy, permit disorders to continue, from which arise murders and plundering; for these usually harm the community at large, while the executions that come from the prince harm one individual in particular. And the new prince, above all other princes, cannot escape the reputation of being called cruel, since new states are full of dangers. And Virgil, through Dido, states: "My difficult condition and the newness of my rule make me act in such a manner, and to set guards over my land on all sides."

7   Nevertheless, a prince must be cautious in believing and in acting, nor should he be afraid of his own shadow; and he should proceed in such a manner, tempered by prudence and humanity, so that too much trust may not render him imprudent nor too much distrust render him intolerable.

8   From this arises an argument: whether it is better to be loved than to be feared, or the contrary. I reply that one should like to be both one and the other; but since it is difficult to join them together, it is much safer to be feared than to be loved when one of the two must be lacking. For one can generally say this about men: that they are ungrateful, fickle, simulators and deceivers, avoiders of danger, greedy for gain; and while you work for their good they are completely yours, offering you their blood, their property, their lives, and their sons, as I said earlier, when danger is far away; but when it comes nearer to you they turn away. And that prince who bases his power entirely on their words, finding himself stripped of other preparations, comes to ruin; for friendships that are acquired by a price and not by greatness and nobility of character are purchased but are not owned, and at the proper moment they cannot be spent. And men are less hesitant about harming someone who makes himself loved than one who makes himself feared because love is held together by a chain of obligation which, since men are a sorry lot, is broken on every occasion in which their own self-interest is concerned; but fear is held together by a dread of punishment which will never abandon you.

9   A prince must nevertheless make himself feared in such a manner that he will avoid hatred, even if he does not acquire love; since to be feared and not to be hated can very well be combined; and this will always be so when he keeps his hands off the property and the women of his citizens and his subjects. And if he must take

someone's life, he should do so when there is proper justification and manifest cause; but, above all, he should avoid the property of others; for men forget more quickly the death of their father than the loss of their patrimony. Moreover, the reasons for seizing their property are never lacking; and he who begins to live by stealing always finds a reason for taking what belongs to others; on the contrary, reasons for taking a life are rarer and disappear sooner.

But when the prince is with his armies and has under his 10 command a multitude of troops, then it is absolutely necessary that he not worry about being considered cruel; for without that reputation he will never keep an army united or prepared for any combat. Among the praiseworthy deeds of Hannibal is counted this: that, having a very large army, made up of all kinds of men, which he commanded in foreign lands, there never arose the slightest dissension, neither among themselves nor against their prince, both during his good and his bad fortune. This could not have arisen from anything other than his inhuman cruelty, which, along with his many other abilities, made him always respected and terrifying in the eyes of his soldiers; and without that, to attain the same effect, his other abilities would not have sufficed. And the writers of history, having considered this matter very little, on the one hand admire these deeds of his and on the other condemn the main cause of them.

And that it be true that his other abilities would not have been 11 sufficient can be seen from the example of Scipio, a most extraordinary man not only in his time but in all recorded history, whose armies in Spain rebelled against him; this came about from nothing other than his excessive compassion, which gave to his soldiers more liberty than military discipline allowed. For this he was censured in the senate by Fabius Maximus, who called him the corruptor of the Roman militia. The Locrians, having been ruined by one of Scipio's officers, were not avenged by him, nor was the arrogance of that officer corrected, all because of his tolerant nature; so that someone in the senate who tried to apologize for him said that there were many men who knew how not to err better than they knew how to correct errors. Such a nature would have, in time, damaged Scipio's fame and glory if he had maintained it during the empire; but, living under the control of the senate, this harmful characteristic of his not only concealed itself but brought him fame.

12   I conclude, therefore, returning to the problem of being feared and loved, that since men love at their own pleasure and fear at the pleasure of the prince, a wise prince should build his foundation upon that which belongs to him, not upon that which belongs to others: he must strive only to avoid hatred, as has been said.

HOW A PRINCE SHOULD KEEP HIS WORD

13 How praiseworthy it is for a prince to keep his word and to live by integrity and not by deceit everyone knows; nevertheless, one sees from the experience of our times that the princes who have accomplished great deeds are those who have cared little for keeping their promises and who have known how to manipulate the minds of men by shrewdness; and in the end they have surpassed those who laid their foundations upon honesty.

14   You must, therefore, know that there are two means of fighting: one according to the laws, the other with force; the first way is proper to man, the second to beasts; but because the first, in many cases, is not sufficient, it becomes necessary to have recourse to the second. Therefore, a prince must know how to use wisely the natures of the beast and the man. This policy was taught to princes allegorically by the ancient writers, who described how Achilles and many other ancient princes were given to Chiron the Centaur to be raised and taught under his discipline. This can only mean that, having a half-beast and half-man as a teacher, a prince must know how to employ the nature of the one and the other; and the one without the other cannot endure.

15   Since, then, a prince must know how to make good use of the nature of the beast, he should choose from among the beasts the fox and the lion; for the lion cannot defend itself from traps and the fox cannot protect itself from wolves. It is therefore necessary to be a fox in order to recognize the traps and a lion in order to frighten the wolves. Those who play only the part of the lion do

not understand matters. A wise ruler, therefore, cannot and should not keep his word when such an observance of faith would be to his disadvantage and when the reasons which made him promise are removed. And if men were all good, this rule would not be good; but since men are a sorry lot and will not keep their promises to you, you likewise need not keep yours to them. A prince never lacks legitimate reasons to break his promises. Of this one could cite an endless number of modern examples to show how many pacts, how many promises have been made null and void because of the infidelity of princes; and he who has known best how to use the fox has come to a better end. But it is necessary to know how to disguise this nature well and to be a great hypocrite and a liar: and men are so simpleminded and so controlled by their present necessities that one who deceives will always find another who will allow himself to be deceived.

I do not wish to remain silent about one of these recent in-   16
stances. Alexander VI did nothing else, he thought about nothing else, except to deceive men, and he always found the occasion to do this. And there never was a man who had more forcefulness in his oaths, who affirmed a thing with more promises, and who honored his word less; nevertheless, his tricks always succeeded perfectly since he was well acquainted with this aspect of the world.

Therefore, it is not necessary for a prince to have all of the   17
above-mentioned qualities, but it is very necessary for him to appear to have them. Furthermore, I shall be so bold as to assert this: that having them and practicing them at all times is harmful; and appearing to have them is useful; for instance, to seem merciful, faithful, humane, forthright, religious, and to be so; but his mind should be disposed in such a way that should it become necessary not to be so, he will be able and know how to change to the contrary. And it is essential to understand this: that a prince, and especially a new prince, cannot observe all those things by which men are considered good, for in order to maintain the state he is often obliged to act against his promise, against charity, against humanity, and against religion. And therefore, it is necessary that he have a mind ready to turn itself according to the way the winds of Fortune and the changeability of affairs require him; and, as I

said above, as long as it is possible, he should not stray from the good, but he should know how to enter into evil when necessity commands.

18   A prince, therefore, must be very careful never to let anything slip from his lips which is not full of the five qualities mentioned above: he should appear, upon seeing and hearing him, to be all mercy, all faithfulness, all integrity, all kindness, all religion. And there is nothing more necessary than to seem to possess this last quality. And men in general judge more by their eyes than their hands; for everyone can see but few can feel. Everyone sees what you seem to be, few perceive what you are, and those few do not dare to contradict the opinion of the many who have the majesty of the state to defend them; and in the actions of all men, and especially of princes, where there is no impartial arbiter, one must consider the final result.[1] Let a prince therefore act to seize and to maintain the state; his methods will always be judged honorable and will be praised by all; for ordinary people are always deceived by appearances and by the outcome of a thing; and in the world there is nothing but ordinary people; and there is no room for the few, while the many have a place to lean on. A certain prince of the present day, whom I shall refrain from naming, preaches nothing but peace and faith, and to both one and the other he is entirely opposed; and both, if he had put them into practice, would have cost him many times over either his reputation or his state.

ON AVOIDING BEING DESPISED AND HATED

19 But since, concerning the qualities mentioned above, I have spoken about the most important, I should like to discuss the others briefly in this general manner: that the prince, as was noted above, should think about avoiding those things which make him hated and despised; and when he has avoided this, he will have

[1]The Italian original, *si guarda al fine,* has often been mistranslated as "the ends justify the means," something Machiavelli never wrote. [Translators' note]

carried out his duties and will find no danger whatsoever in other vices. As I have said, what makes him hated above all else is being rapacious and a usurper of the property and the women of his subjects; he must refrain from this; and in most cases, so long as you do not deprive them of either their property or their honor, the majority of men live happily; and you have only to deal with the ambition of a few, who can be restrained without difficulty and by many means. What makes him despised is being considered changeable, frivolous, effeminate, cowardly, irresolute; from these qualities a prince must guard himself as if from a reef, and he must strive to make everyone recognize in his actions greatness, spirit, dignity, and strength; and concerning the private affairs of his subjects, he must insist that his decision be irrevocable; and he should maintain himself in such a way that no man could imagine that he can deceive or cheat him.

That prince who projects such an opinion of himself is greatly esteemed; and it is difficult to conspire against a man with such a reputation and difficult to attack him, provided that he is understood to be of great merit and revered by his subjects. For a prince must have two fears: one, internal, concerning his subjects; the other, external, concerning foreign powers. From the latter he can defend himself by his good troops and friends; and he will always have good friends if he has good troops; and internal affairs will always be stable when external affairs are stable, provided that they are not already disturbed by a conspiracy; and even if external conditions change, if he is properly organized and lives as I have said and does not lose control of himself, he will always be able to withstand every attack, just as I said that Nabis the Spartan did. But concerning his subjects, when external affairs do not change, he has to fear that they may conspire secretly: the prince secures himself from this by avoiding being hated or despised and by keeping the people satisfied with him; this is a necessary matter, as was treated above at length. And one of the most powerful remedies a prince has against conspiracies is not to be hated by the masses; for a man who plans a conspiracy always believes that he will satisfy the people by killing the prince; but when he thinks he might anger them, he cannot work up the courage to undertake such a deed; for the problems on the side of the conspirators are countless. And experience demonstrates that conspiracies have been many but few have been concluded successfully; for anyone who conspires cannot be alone, nor can he find companions except from amongst those whom he believes to be dissatisfied; and as soon as you have uncovered your intent to one dissatisfied man, you give him the means to make himself happy, since he can have everything he desires by uncovering the plot; so much is this so that, seeing a sure gain on the one hand and one doubtful and full of danger on the other, if he is to maintain faith with you he has to be either an unusually good friend or a completely determined enemy of the prince. And to treat the matter briefly, I say that on the part of the conspirator there is nothing but fear, jealousy, and the thought of punishment that terrifies him; but on the part of the prince there is the majesty of the principality, the laws, the defenses of friends and the state to protect him; so that, with the good will of the people added to all these things, it is impossible for anyone to be so rash as to plot against him. For, where usually a conspirator has to be afraid before he executes his evil deed, in this case he must be afraid, having the people as an enemy, even after the crime is performed, nor can he hope to find any refuge because of this.

21   One could cite countless examples on this subject; but I want to satisfy myself with only one which occurred during the time of our fathers. Messer Annibale Bentivoglio, prince of Bologna and grandfather of the present Messer Annibale, was murdered by the Canneschi family, who conspired against him; he left behind no heir except Messer Giovanni, then only a baby. As soon as this murder occurred, the people rose up and killed all the Canneschi. This came about because of the good will that the house of the Bentivoglio enjoyed in those days; this good will was so great that with Annibale dead, and there being no one of that family left in the city who could rule Bologna, the Bolognese people, having heard that in Florence there was one of the Bentivoglio blood who was believed until that time to be the son of a blacksmith, went to Florence to find him, and they gave him the control of that city; it was ruled by him until Messer Giovanni became of age to rule.

I conclude, therefore, that a prince must be little concerned 22
with conspiracies when the people are well disposed toward him;
but when the populace is hostile and regards him with hatred, he
must fear everything and everyone. And well-organized states and
wise princes have, with great diligence, taken care not to anger the
nobles and to satisfy the common people and keep them contented;
for this is one of the most important concerns that a prince has.

1513

The Declaration of Independence

Thomas Jefferson

In Congress, July 4, 1776
The unanimous Declaration of the
thirteen united States of America

When in the Course of human events it becomes necessary for one 1
people to dissolve the political bands which have connected them
with another, and to assume among the powers of the earth, the
separate and equal station to which the Laws of Nature and of
Nature's God entitle them, a decent respect to the opinions of
mankind requires that they should declare the causes which impel
them to the separation.

     We hold these truths to be self-evident, that all men are cre- 2
ated equal, that they are endowed by their Creator with certain
unalienable Rights, that among these are Life, Liberty and the
pursuit of Happiness. That to secure these rights, Governments
are instituted among Men, deriving their just powers from the
consent of the governed. That whenever any Form of Government
becomes destructive of these ends, it is the Right of the People to
alter or to abolish it, and to institute new Government, laying its
foundation on such principles and organizing its powers in such
form, as to them shall seem most likely to affect their Safety and

Happiness. Prudence, indeed, will dictate that Governments long established should not be changed for light and transient causes; and accordingly all experience hath shewn that mankind are more disposed to suffer, while evils are sufferable, than to right themselves by abolishing the forms to which they are accustomed. But when a long train of abuses and usurpations, pursuing invariably the same Object evinces a design to reduce them under absolute Despotism, it is their right, it is their duty, to throw off such Government, and to provide new Guards for their future security. Such has been the patient sufferance of these Colonies; and such is now the necessity which constrains them to alter their former Systems of Government. The history of the present King of Great Britain is a history of repeated injuries and usurpations, all having in direct object the establishment of an absolute Tyranny over these States. To prove this, let Facts be submitted to a candid world.

3   He has refused his Assent to Laws, the most wholesome and necessary for the public good.

4   He has forbidden his Governors to pass laws of immediate and pressing importance, unless suspended in their operation till his Assent should be obtained; and when so suspended, he has utterly neglected to attend to them.

5   He has refused to pass other Laws for the accommodation of large districts of people, unless those people would relinquish the right of Representation in the Legislature, a right inestimable to them and formidable to tyrants only.

6   He has called together legislative bodies at places unusual, uncomfortable, and distant from the depository of their Public Records, for the sole purpose of fatiguing them into compliance with his measures.

7   He has dissolved Representative Houses repeatedly, for opposing with manly firmness his invasions on the rights of the people.

8   He has refused for a long time, after such dissolutions, to cause others to be elected; whereby the Legislative Powers, incapable of Annihilation, have returned to the People at large for their exercise; the State remaining in the mean time exposed to all the dangers of invasion from without, and convulsions within.

9   He has endeavored to prevent the population of these States; for that purpose obstructing the Laws for Naturalization of

Foreigners; refusing to pass others to encourage their migration hither, and raising the conditions of new Appropriations of Lands.

He has obstructed the Administration of Justice, by refusing his Assent to Laws for Establishing Judiciary Powers. 10

He has made judges dependent on his Will alone, for the tenure of their offices, and the amount and payment of their salaries. 11

He has erected a multitude of New Offices, and sent hither swarms of Officers to harass our people, and eat out their substance. 12

He has kept among us, in times of peace, Standing Armies without the Consent of our legislatures. 13

He has affected to render the Military independent of and superior to the Civil Power. 14

He has combined with others to subject us to a jurisdiction foreign to our constitution, and unacknowledged by our laws; giving his Assent to the Acts of pretended Legislation: For quartering large bodies of armed troops among us: For protecting them, by a mock Trial, from punishment for any Murders which they should commit on the Inhabitants of these States: For cutting off our Trade with all parts of the world: For imposing Taxes on us without our Consent: For depriving us in many cases, of the benefits of Trial by Jury: For Transporting us beyond Seas to be tried for pretended offenses: For abolishing the free System of English Laws in a neighboring Province, establishing therein an Arbitrary government, and enlarging its Boundaries so as to render it at once an example and fit instrument for introducing the same absolute rule into these Colonies: For taking away our Charters, abolishing our most valuable Laws and altering fundamentally the Forms of our Governments: For suspending our own Legislatures, and declaring themselves invested with power to legislate for us in all cases whatsoever. 15

He has abdicated Government here, by declaring us out of his Protection and waging War against us. 16

He has plundered our seas, ravaged our Coasts, burnt our towns, and destroyed the lives of our people. 17

He is at this time transporting large Armies of foreign Mercenaries to complete the works of death, desolation and tyranny, already begun with circumstances of Cruelty & Perfidy scarcely 18 paralleled in the most barbarous ages, and totally unworthy the Head of a civilized nation.

19   He has constrained our fellow Citizens taken Captive on the high Seas to bear Arms against their Country, to become the executioners of their friends and Brethren, or to fall themselves by their Hands.

20   He has excited domestic insurrections amongst us, and has endeavored to bring on the inhabitants of our frontiers, the merciless Indian Savages, whose known rule of warfare is an undistinguished destruction of all ages, sexes, and conditions.

21   In every stage of these Oppressions We have Petitioned for Redress in the most humble terms: Our repeated petitions have been answered only by repeated injury. A Prince, whose character is thus marked by every act which may define a Tyrant, is unfit to be the ruler of a free people.

22   Nor have we been wanting in attention to our British brethren. We have warned them from time to time of attempts by their legislature to extend an unwarrantable jurisdiction over us. We have reminded them of the circumstances of our emigration and settlement here. We have appealed to their native justice and magnanimity, and we have conjured them by the ties of our common kindred to disavow these usurpations, which would inevitably interrupt our connections and correspondence. They too have been deaf to the voice of justice and of consanguinity. We must, therefore, acquiesce in the necessity, which denounces our Separation, and hold them, as we hold the rest of mankind, Enemies in War, in Peace Friends.

23   We, THEREFORE, the Representatives of the UNITED STATES OF AMERICA, in General Congress, Assembled, appealing to the Supreme Judge of the world for the rectitude of our intentions, do, in the Name, and by Authority of the good People of these Colonies, solemnly publish and declare, That these United Colonies are, and of Right ought to be FREE AND INDEPENDENT STATES: that they are Absolved from all Allegiance to the British Crown, and that all political connection between them and the State of Great Britain, is and ought to be totally dissolved; and that as Free and Independent States; they have full Power to levy

War, conclude Peace, contract Alliances, establish Commerce, and to do all the Acts and Things which Independent States may of right do. And for the support of this Declaration, with a firm reliance on the protection of Divine Providence, we mutually pledge to each other our Lives, our Fortunes, and our sacred Honor.

1776

Declaration of Sentiments
Elizabeth Cady Stanton

When, in the course of human events, it becomes necessary for one portion of the family of man to assume among the people of the earth a position different from that which they have hitherto occupied, but one to which the laws of nature and of nature's God entitle them, a decent respect to the opinions of mankind requires that they should declare the causes that impel them to such a course.   1

We hold these truths to be self-evident: that all men and women are created equal; that they are endowed by their Creator with certain inalienable rights; that among these are life, liberty, and the pursuit of happiness; that to secure these rights governments are instituted, deriving their just powers from the consent of the governed. Whenever any form of government becomes destructive of these ends, it is the right of those who suffer from it to refuse allegiance to it, and to insist upon the institution of a new government, laying its foundation on such principles, and organizing its powers in such form, as to them shall seem most likely to effect their safety and happiness. Prudence, indeed, will dictate that governments long established should not be changed for light and transient causes; and accordingly all experience hath shown that mankind are more disposed to suffer, while evils are sufferable, than to right themselves by abolishing the forms to which they were accustomed. But when a long train of abuses and usurpations, pursuing invariably the same object evinces a   2 design to reduce them under absolute despotism, it is their duty to throw off such government, and to provide new guards for their future security. Such has been the patient sufferance of the women under this government, and such is now the necessity which constrains them to demand the equal station to which they are entitled.

3   The history of mankind is a history of repeated injuries and usurpations on the part of man toward woman, having in direct object the establishment of an absolute tyranny over her. To prove this, let facts be submitted to a candid world.

4   He has never permitted her to exercise her inalienable right to the elective franchise.

5   He has compelled her to submit to laws, in the formation of which she had no voice.

6   He has withheld from her rights which are given to the most ignorant and degraded men—both natives and foreigners.

7   Having deprived her of this first right of a citizen, the elective franchise, thereby leaving her without representation in the halls of legislation, he has oppressed her on all sides.

8   He has made her, if married, in the eye of the law, civilly dead.

9   He has taken from her all right in property, even to the wages she earns.

10   He has made her, morally, an irresponsible being, as she can commit many crimes with impunity, provided they be done in the presence of her husband. In the covenant of marriage, she is compelled to promise obedience to her husband, he becoming, to all intents and purposes, her master—the law giving him power to deprive her of her liberty, and to administer chastisement.

11   He has so framed the laws of divorce, as to what shall be the proper causes, and in case of separation, to whom the guardianship of the children shall be given, as to be wholly regardless of the happiness of women—the law, in all cases, going upon a false supposition of the supremacy of man, and giving all power into his hands.

12   After depriving her of all rights as a married woman, if single, and the owner of property, he has taxed her to support a government which recognizes her only when her property can be made profitable to it.

He has monopolized nearly all the profitable employments, 13
and from those she is permitted to follow, she receives but a
scanty remuneration. He closes against her all the avenues to
wealth and distinction which he considers most honorable to himself. As a teacher of theology, medicine, or law, she is not known.

He has denied her the facilities for obtaining a thorough edu- 14
cation, all colleges being closed against her.

He allows her in Church, as well as State, but a subordinate 15
position, claiming Apostolic authority for her exclusion from the
ministry, and, with some exceptions, from any public participa-
tion in the affairs of the Church.

He has created a false public sentiment by giving to the world 16
a different code of morals for men and women, by which moral
delinquencies which exclude women from society, are not only
tolerated, but deemed of little account in man.

He has usurped the prerogative of Jehovah himself, claiming 17
it as his right to assign for her a sphere of action, when that belongs to her conscience and to her God.

He has endeavored, in every way that he could, to destroy her 18
confidence in her own powers, to lessen her self-respect, and to
make her willing to lead a dependent and abject life.

Now in view of this entire disfranchisement of one-half the 19
people of this country, their social and religious degradation—in
view of the unjust laws above mentioned, and because women do
feel themselves aggrieved, oppressed, and fraudulently deprived
of their most sacred rights, we insist that they have immediate admission to all the rights and privileges which belong to them as
citizens of the United States.

In entering upon the great work before us, we anticipate no 20
small amount of misconception, misrepresentation, and ridicule;
but we shall use every instrumentality within our power to effect
our object. We shall employ agents, circulate tracts, petition the State
and National legislatures, and endeavor to enlist the pulpit and the
press in our behalf. We hope this Convention will be followed by a
series of Conventions embracing every part of the country.

1848

Ain't I a Woman?

Sojourner Truth

1   Well, children, where there is so much racket there must be something out of kilter. I think that 'twixt the negroes of the South and the women of the North, all talking about rights, the white men will be in a fix pretty soon. But what's all this here talking about?

2   That man over there says that women need to be helped into carriages, and lifted over ditches, and to have the best place everywhere. Nobody ever helps me into carriages, or over mud-puddles, or gives me any best place! And ain't I a woman? Look at me! Look at my arm! I have ploughed and planted, and gathered into barns, and no man could head me! And ain't I a woman? I could work as much and eat as much as a man—when I could get it—and bear the lash as well! And ain't I a woman? I have borne thirteen children, and seen them most all sold off to slavery, and when I cried out with my mother's grief, none but Jesus heard me! And ain't I a woman?

3   Then they talk about this thing in the head; what's this they call it? [Intellect, someone whispers.] That's it, honey. What's that got to do with women's rights or negro's rights? If my cup won't hold but a pint, and yours holds a quart, wouldn't you be mean not to let me have my little half-measure full?

4   Then that little man in black there, he says women can't have as much rights as men, 'cause Christ wasn't a woman! Where did your Christ come from? Where did your Christ come from? From God and a woman! Man had nothing to do with Him.

5   If the first woman God ever made was strong enough to turn the world upside down all alone, these women together ought to be able to turn it back, and get it right side up again! And now they is asking to do it, the men better let them.

6   Obliged to you for hearing me, and now old Sojourner ain't got nothing more to say.

1851

Civil Disobedience

Henry David Thoreau

I heartily accept the motto—"That government is best which gov-   1
erns least;" and I should like to see it acted up to more rapidly
and systematically. Carried out, it finally amounts to this, which
also I believe,—"That government is best which governs not at
all;" and when men are prepared for it, that will be the kind of
government which they will have. Government is at best but an
expedient; but most governments are usually, and all governments are sometimes, inexpedient. The objections which have
been brought against a standing army, and they are many and
weighty, and deserve to prevail, may also at last be brought
against a standing government. The standing army is only an arm
of the standing government. The government itself, which is only
the mode which the people have chosen to execute their will, is
equally liable to be abused and perverted before the people can
act through it. Witness the present Mexican war, the work of comparatively a few individuals using the standing government as
their tool; for, in the outset, the people would not have consented
to this measure.

     This American government,—what is it but a tradition,   2
though a recent one, endeavoring to transmit itself unimpaired to
posterity, but each instant losing some of its integrity? It has not
the vitality and force of a single living man; for a single man can
bend it to his will. It is a sort of wooden gun to the people themselves; and, if ever they should use it in earnest as a real one
against each other, it will surely split. But it is not the less necessary for this; for the people must have some complicated machinery or other, and hear its din, to satisfy that idea of government
which they have. Governments show thus how successfully men
can be imposed on, even impose on themselves, for their own advantage. It is excellent, we must all allow; yet this government
never of itself furthered any enterprise, but by the alacrity with
which it got out of its way. *It* does not keep the country free. *It*
does not settle the West. *It* does not educate. The character inher-

ent in the American people has done all that has been accomplished; and it would have done somewhat more, if the government had not sometimes got in its way. For government is an expedient by which men would fain succeed in letting one another alone; and, as has been said, when it is most expedient, the governed are most let alone by it. Trade and commerce, if they were not made of India rubber, would never manage to bounce over the obstacles which legislators are continually putting in their way; and, if one were to judge these men wholly by the effects of their actions, and not partly by their intentions, they would deserve to be classed and punished with those mischievous persons who put obstructions on the railroads.

3   But, to speak practically and as a citizen, unlike those who call themselves no-government men, I ask for, not at once no government, but *at once* a better government. Let every man make known what kind of government would command his respect, and that will be one step toward obtaining it.

4   After all, the practical reason why, when the power is once in the hands of the people, a majority are permitted, and for a long period continue, to rule, is not because they are most likely to be in the right, nor because this seems fairest to the minority, but because they are physically the strongest. But a government in which the majority rule in all cases cannot be based on justice, even as far as men understand it. Can there not be a government in which majorities do not virtually decide right and wrong, but conscience?—in which majorities decide only those questions to which the rule of expediency is applicable? Must the citizen ever for a moment, or in the least degree, resign his conscience to the legislator? Why has every man a conscience, then? I think that we should be men first, and subjects afterward. It is not desirable to cultivate a respect for the law, so much as for the right. The only obligation which I have a right to assume, is to do at any time what I think right. It is truly enough said, that a corporation has no conscience; but a corporation of conscientious men is a corporation *with* a conscience. Law never made men a whit more just; and, by means of their respect for it, even the well-disposed are daily made the agents of injustice. A common and natural result of an undue respect for law is, that you may see a file of soldiers,

colonel, captain, corporal, privates, powder-monkeys and all, marching in admirable order over hill and dale to the wars, against their wills, aye, against their common sense and consciences, which makes it very steep marching indeed, and produces a palpitation of the heart. They have no doubt that it is a damnable business in which they are concerned; they are all peaceably inclined. Now, what are they? Men at all? or small moveable forts and magazines, at the service of some unscrupulous man in power? Visit the Navy Yard, and behold a marine, such a man as an American government can make, or such as it can make a man with its black arts, a mere shadow and reminiscence of humanity, a man laid out alive and standing, and already, as one may say, buried under arms with funeral accompaniments, though it may be

> "Not a drum was heard, nor a funeral note,
> As his corse to the ramparts we hurried;
> Not a soldier discharged his farewell shot
> O'er the grave where our hero we buried."

The mass of men serve the State thus, not as men mainly, but as machines, with their bodies. They are the standing army, and the militia, jailers, constables, *posse comitatus,* &c. In most cases there is no free exercise whatever of the judgment or of the moral sense; but they put themselves on a level with wood and earth and stones; and wooden men can perhaps be manufactured that will serve the purpose as well. Such command no more respect than men of straw, or a lump of dirt. They have the same sort of worth only as horses and dogs. Yet such as these even are commonly esteemed good citizens. Others, as most legislators, politicians, lawyers, ministers, and office-holders, serve the State chiefly with their heads; and, as they rarely make any moral distinctions, they are as likely to serve the devil, without intending it, as God. A very few, as heroes, patriots, martyrs, reformers in the great sense, and *men,* serve the State with their consciences also, and so necessarily resist it for the most part; and they are commonly treated by it as enemies. A wise man will only be useful as

a man, and will not submit to be "clay," and "stop a hole to keep
the wind away," but leave that office to his dust at least:—

> "I am too high-born to be propertied,
> To be a secondary at control,
> Or useful serving-man and instrument
> To any sovereign state throughout the world."

6   He who gives himself entirely to his fellow-men appears to
them useless and selfish; but he who gives himself partially to
them is pronounced a benefactor and philanthropist.

7   How does it become a man to behave toward this American
government to-day? I answer that he cannot without disgrace be
associated with it. I cannot for an instant recognize that political organization as *my* government which is the *slave's* government also.

8   All men recognize the right of revolution; that is, the right to
refuse allegiance to and to resist the government, when its
tyranny or its inefficiency are great and unendurable. But almost
all say that such is not the case now. But such was the case, they
think, in the Revolution of '75. If one were to tell me that this was
a bad government because it taxed certain foreign commodities
brought to its ports, it is most probable that I should not make an
ado about it, for I can do without them: all machines have their
friction; and possibly this does enough good to counterbalance
the evil. At any rate, it is a great evil to make a stir about it. But
when the friction comes to have its machine, and oppression and
robbery are organized, I say, let us not have such a machine any
longer. In other words, when a sixth of the population of a nation
which has undertaken to be the refuge of liberty are slaves, and a
whole country is unjustly overrun and conquered by a foreign
army, and subjected to military law, I think that it is not too soon
for honest men to rebel and revolutionize. What makes this duty
the more urgent is the fact, that the country so overrun is not our
own, but ours is the invading army.

9   Paley, a common authority with many on moral questions,
in his chapter on the "Duty of Submission to Civil Government,"
resolves all civil obligation into expediency; and he proceeds to
say, "that so long as the interest of the whole society requires it,

that is, so long as the established government cannot be resisted or changed without public inconveniency, it is the will of God that the established government be obeyed, and no longer."—"This principle being admitted, the justice of every particular case of resistance is reduced to a computation of the quantity of the danger and grievance on the one side, and of the probability and expense of redressing it on the other." Of this, he says, every man shall judge for himself. But Paley appears never to have contemplated those cases to which the rule of expediency does not apply, in which a people, as well as an individual, must do justice, cost what it may. If I have unjustly wrested a plank from a drowning man, I must restore it to him though I drown myself. This, according to Paley, would be inconvenient. But he that would save his life, in such a case, shall lose it. This people must cease to hold slaves, and to make war on Mexico, though it cost them their existence as a people.

In their practice, nations agree with Paley; but does any one think that Massachusetts does exactly what is right at the present crisis? 10

> "A drab of state, a cloth-o'-silver slut,
> To have her train borne up, and her soul trail
>   in the dirt."

Practically speaking, the opponents to a reform in Massachusetts are not a hundred thousand politicians at the South, but a hundred thousand merchants and farmers here, who are more interested in commerce and agriculture than they are in humanity, and are not prepared to do justice to the slave and to Mexico, *cost what it may*. I quarrel not with far-off foes, but with those who, near at home, co-operate with, and do the bidding of those far away, and without whom the latter would be harmless. We are accustomed to say, that the mass of men are unprepared; but improvement is slow, because the few are not materially wiser or better than the many. It is not so important that many should be as good as you, as that there be some absolute goodness somewhere; for that will leaven the whole lump. There are thousands who are *in opinion* opposed to slavery and to the war, who yet in effect do nothing to put an end to them; who, esteeming themselves children of Washington and Franklin, sit down with their hands in their pockets, and say that they know not what to do, and do nothing; who even postpone the question of freedom to the question of free-trade, and quietly read the prices-current along with the latest advices from Mexico, after dinner, and, it may be, fall asleep over them both. What is the price-current of an honest man and patriot to-day? They hesitate, and they regret, and sometimes they petition; but they do nothing in earnest and with effect. They will wait, well disposed, for others to remedy the evil, that they may no longer have it to regret. At most, they give only a cheap vote, and a feeble countenance and God-speed, to the right, as it goes by them. There are nine hundred and ninety-nine patrons of virtue to one virtuous man; but it is easier to deal with the real possessor of a thing than with the temporary guardian of it.

11   All voting is a sort of gaming, like chequers or backgammon, with a slight moral tinge to it, a playing with right and wrong, with moral questions; and betting naturally accompanies it. The character of the voters is not staked. I cast my vote, perchance, as I think right; but I am not vitally concerned that that right should prevail. I am willing to leave it to the majority. Its obligation, therefore, never exceeds that of expediency. Even voting *for the right* is *doing* nothing for it. It is only expressing to men feebly your desire that it should prevail. A wise man will not leave the right to the mercy of chance, nor wish it to prevail through the power of the majority. There is but little virtue in the action of masses of men. When the majority shall at length vote for the abolition of slavery, it will be because they are indifferent to slavery, or because there is but little slavery left to be abolished by their vote. *They* will then be the only slaves. Only *his* vote can hasten the abolition of slavery who asserts his own freedom by his vote.

12   I hear of a convention to be held at Baltimore, or elsewhere, for the selection of a candidate for the Presidency, made up chiefly of editors, and men who are politicians by profession; but I think, what is it to any independent, intelligent, and respectable man what decision they may come to, shall we not have the advantage of his wisdom and honesty, nevertheless? Can we not count upon

some independent votes? Are there not many individuals in the
country who do not attend conventions? But no: I find that the respectable man, so called, has immediately drifted from his position, and despairs of his country, when his country has more
reason to despair of him. He forthwith adopts one of the candi-
dates thus selected as the only *available* one, thus proving that he
is himself *available* for any purposes of the demagogue. His vote is
of no more worth than that of any unprincipled foreigner or
hireling native, who may have been bought. Oh for a man who is
a *man*, and, as my neighbor says, has a bone in his back which you
cannot pass your hand through! Our statistics are at fault: the
population has been returned too large. How many *men* are there
to a square thousand miles in this country? Hardly one. Does not
America offer any inducement for men to settle here? The American has dwindled into an Odd Fellow,—one who may be known
by the development of his organ of gregariousness, and a manifest lack of intellect and cheerful self-reliance; whose first and
chief concern, on coming into the world, is to see that the alms-
houses are in good repair; and, before yet he has lawfully donned
the virile garb, to collect a fund for the support of the widows and
orphans that may be; who, in short, ventures to live only by the
aid of the mutual insurance company, which has promised to
bury him decently.

It is not a man's duty, as a matter of course, to devote himself ¹³
to the eradication of any, even the most enormous wrong; he may
still properly have other concerns to engage him; but it is his duty,
at least, to wash his hands of it, and, if he gives it no thought
longer, not to give it practically his support. If I devote myself to
other pursuits and contemplations, I must first see, at least, that I
do not pursue them sitting upon another man's shoulders. I must
get off him first, that he may pursue his contemplations too. See
what gross inconsistency is tolerated. I have heard some of my
townsmen say, "I should like to have them order me out to help
put down an insurrection of the slaves, or to march to Mexico,—
see if I would go;" and yet these very men have each, directly by
their allegiance, and so indirectly, at least, by their money, furnished
a substitute. The soldier is applauded who refuses to serve in an

unjust war by those who do not refuse to sustain the unjust government which makes the war; is applauded by those whose own act and authority he disregards and sets at nought; as if the State were penitent to that degree that it hired one to scourge it while it sinned, but not to that degree that it left off sinning for a moment. Thus, under the name of order and civil government, we are all made at last to pay homage to and support our own meanness. After the first blush of sin, comes its indifference; and from immoral it becomes, as it were, *un*moral, and not quite unnecessary to that life which we have made.

14   The broadest and most prevalent error requires the most disinterested virtue to sustain it. The slight reproach to which the virtue of patriotism is commonly liable, the noble are most likely to incur. Those who, while they disapprove of the character and measures of a government, yield to it their allegiance and support, are undoubtedly its most conscientious supporters, and so frequently the most serious obstacles to reform. Some are petitioning the State to dissolve the Union, to disregard the requisitions of the President. Why do they not dissolve it themselves—the union between themselves and the State,—and refuse to pay their quota into its treasury? Do not they stand in the same relation to the State, that the State does to the Union? And have not the same reasons prevented the State from resisting the Union, which have prevented them from resisting the State?

15   How can a man be satisfied to entertain an opinion merely, and enjoy *it?* Is there any enjoyment in it, if his opinion is that he is aggrieved? If you are cheated out of a single dollar by your neighbor, you do not rest satisfied with knowing that you are cheated, or with saying that you are cheated, or even with petitioning him to pay you your due; but you take effectual steps at once to obtain the full amount, and see that you are never cheated again. Action from principle,—the perception and the performance of right,—changes things and relations; it is essentially revolutionary, and does not consist wholly with any thing which was. It not only divides states and churches, it divides families; aye, it divides the *individual,* separating the diabolical in him from the divine.

Unjust laws exist: shall we be content to obey them, or shall ₁₆
we endeavor to amend them, and obey them until we have succeeded, or shall we transgress them at once? Men generally, under
such a government as this, think that they ought to wait until they
have persuaded the majority to alter them. They think that, if they
should resist, the remedy would be worse than the evil. But it is
the fault of the government itself that the remedy is worse than
the evil. *It* makes it worse. Why is it not more apt to anticipate and
provide for reform? Why does it not cherish its wise minority?
Why does it cry and resist before it is hurt? Why does it not encourage its citizens to be on the alert to point out its faults, and *do*
better than it would have them? Why does it always crucify Christ,
and excommunicate Copernicus and Luther, and pronounce
Washington and Franklin rebels?

One would think, that a deliberate and practical denial of its ₁₇
authority was the only offence never contemplated by government; else, why has it not assigned its definite, its suitable and
proportionate penalty? If a man who has no property refuses but
once to earn nine shillings for the State, he is put in prison for a
period unlimited by any law that I know, and determined only by
the discretion of those who placed him there; but if he should steal
ninety times nine shillings from the State, he is soon permitted to
go at large again.

If the injustice is part of the necessary friction of the machine ₁₈
of government, let it go, let it go: perchance it will wear smooth,—
certainly the machine will wear out. If the injustice has a spring,
or a pulley, or a rope, or a crank, exclusively for itself, then perhaps you may consider whether the remedy will not be worse
than the evil; but if it is of such a nature that it requires you to be
the agent of injustice to another, then, I say, break the law. Let your
life be a counter friction to stop the machine. What I have to do is
to see, at any rate, that I do not lend myself to the wrong which I
condemn.

As for adopting the ways which the State has provided for ₁₉
remedying the evil, I know not of such ways. They take too much
time, and a man's life will be gone. I have other affairs to attend
to. I came into this world, not chiefly to make this a good place to
live in, but to live in it, be it good or bad. A man has not every

thing to do, but something; and because he cannot do *every thing*, it is not necessary that he should do *something* wrong. It is not my business to be petitioning the governor or the legislature any more than it is theirs to petition me; and, if they should not hear my petition, what should I do then? But in this case the State has provided no way: its very Constitution is the evil. This may seem to be harsh and stubborn and unconciliatory; but it is to treat with the utmost kindness and consideration the only spirit that can appreciate or deserves it. So is all change for the better, like birth and death which convulse the body.

20   I do not hesitate to say, that those who call themselves abolitionists should at once effectually withdraw their support, both in person and property, from the government of Massachusetts, and not wait till they constitute a majority of one, before they suffer the right to prevail through them. I think that it is enough if they have God on their side, without waiting for that other one. Moreover, any man more right than his neighbors, constitutes a majority of one already.

21   I meet this American government, or its representative the State government, directly, and face to face, once a year, no more, in the person of its tax-gatherer; this is the only mode in which a man situated as I am necessarily meets it; and it then says distinctly, Recognize me; and the simplest, the most effectual, and, in the present posture of affairs, the indispensablest mode of treating with it on this head, of expressing your little satisfaction with and love for it, is to deny it then. My civil neighbor, the tax-gatherer, is the very man I have to deal with,—for it is, after all, with men and not with parchment that I quarrel,—and he has voluntarily chosen to be an agent of the government. How shall he ever know well what he is and does as an officer of the government, or as a man, until he is obliged to consider whether he shall treat me, his neighbor, for whom he has respect, as a neighbor and well-disposed man, or as a maniac and disturber of the peace, and see if he can get over this obstruction to his neighborliness without a ruder and more impetuous thought or speech corresponding with his action? I know this well, that if one thousand, if one hundred, if ten men whom I could name,—if ten *honest* men only, —aye, if *one* HONEST man, in this State of Massachusetts, *ceasing to hold slaves,*

were actually to withdraw from this copartnership, and be locked up in the county jail therefor, it would be the abolition of slavery in America. For it matters not how small the beginning may seem to be: what is once well done is done for ever. But we love better to talk about it: that we say is our mission. Reform keeps many scores of newspapers in its service, but not one man. If my esteemed neighbor, the State's ambassador, who will devote his days to the settlement of the question of human rights in the Council Chamber, instead of being threatened with the prisons of Carolina, were to sit down the prisoner of Massachusetts, that State which is so anxious to foist the sin of slavery upon her sister,—though at present she can discover only an act of inhospitality to be the ground of a quarrel with her,—the Legislature would not wholly waive the subject the following winter.

Under a government which imprisons any unjustly, the true place for a just man is also a prison. The proper place to-day, the only place which Massachusetts has provided for her freer and less desponding spirits, is in her prisons, to be put out and locked out of the State by her own act, as they have already put themselves out by their principles. It is there that the fugitive slave, and the Mexican prisoner on parole, and the Indian come to plead the wrongs of his race, should find them; on that separate, but more free and honorable ground, where the State places those who are not *with* her but *against* her,—the only house in a slave-state in which a free man can abide with honor. If any think that their influence would be lost there, and their voices no longer afflict the ear of the State, that they would not be as an enemy within its walls, they do not know by how much truth is stronger than error, nor how much more eloquently and effectively he can combat injustice who has experienced a little in his own person. Cast your whole vote, not a strip of paper merely, but your whole influence. A minority is powerless while it conforms to the majority; it is not even a minority then; but it is irresistible when it clogs by its whole weight. If the alternative is to keep all just men in prison, or give up war and slavery, the State will not hesitate which to choose. If a thousand men were not to pay their tax-bills this year, that would not be a violent and bloody measure, as it would be to pay them, and enable the State to commit violence and shed innocent blood. This is, in fact, the definition of a peaceable revolution, if any such is possible. If the tax-gatherer, or any other public officer, asks me, as one has done, "But what shall I do?" my answer is, "If you really wish to do any thing, resign your office." When the subject has refused allegiance, and the officer has resigned his office, then the revolution is accomplished. But even suppose blood should flow. Is there not a sort of blood shed when the conscience is wounded? Through this wound a man's real manhood and immortality flow out, and he bleeds to an everlasting death. I see this blood flowing now.

23   I have contemplated the imprisonment of the offender, rather than the seizure of his goods,—though both will serve the same purpose,—because they who assert the purest right, and consequently are most dangerous to a corrupt State, commonly have not spent much time in accumulating property. To such the State renders comparatively small service, and a slight tax is wont to appear exorbitant, particularly if they are obliged to earn it by special labor with their hands. If there were one who lived wholly without the use of money, the State itself would hesitate to demand it of him. But the rich man—not to make any invidious comparison—is always sold to the institution which makes him rich. Absolutely speaking, the more money, the less virtue; for money comes between a man and his objects, and obtains them for him; and it was certainly no great virtue to obtain it. It puts to rest many questions which he would otherwise be taxed to answer; while the only new question which it puts is the hard but superfluous one, how to spend it. Thus his moral ground is taken from under his feet. The opportunities of living are diminished in proportion as what are called the "means" are increased. The best thing a man can do for his culture when he is rich is to endeavour to carry out those schemes which he entertained when he was poor. Christ answered the Herodians according to their condition. "Show me the tribute-money," said he;—and one took a penny out of his pocket;—If you use money which has the image of Caesar on it, and which he has made current and valuable, that is, *if you are men of the State,* and gladly enjoy the advantages of Caesar's government, then pay him back some of his own when he demands it; "Render therefore to Caesar that which is Caesar's,

and to God those things which are God's,"—leaving them no
wiser than before as to which was which; for they did not wish
to know.

When I converse with the freest of my neighbors, I perceive 24
that, whatever they may say about the magnitude and seriousness
of the question, and their regard for the public tranquility, the
long and the short of the matter is, that they cannot spare the protection of the existing government, and they dread the consequences of disobedience to it to their property and families. For
my own part, I should not like to think that I ever rely on the protection of the State. But, if I deny the authority of the State when it
presents its tax-bill, it will soon take and waste all my property,
and so harass me and my children without end. This is hard. This
makes it impossible for a man to live honestly and at the same
time comfortably in outward respects. It will not be worth the
while to accumulate property; that would be sure to go again. You
must hire or squat somewhere, and raise but a small crop, and eat
that soon. You must live within yourself, and depend upon yourself, always tucked up and ready for a start, and not have many
affairs. A man may grow rich in Turkey even, if he will be in all respects a good subject of the Turkish government. Confucius
said,—"If a State is governed by the principles of reason, poverty
and misery are subjects of shame; if a State is not governed by the
principles of reason, riches and honors are the subjects of shame."
No: until I want the protection of Massachusetts to be extended to
me in some distant southern port, where my liberty is endan-
gered, or until I am bent solely on building up an estate at home
by peaceful enterprise, I can afford to refuse allegiance to Massachusetts, and her right to my property and life. It costs me less in
every sense to incur the penalty of disobedience to the State, than
it would to obey. I should feel as if I were worth less in that case.

Some years ago, the State met me in behalf of the church, and 25
commanded me to pay a certain sum toward the support of a clergyman whose preaching my father attended, but never I myself.
"Pay it," it said, "or be locked up in the jail." I declined to pay.
But, unfortunately, another man saw fit to pay it. I did not see
why the schoolmaster should be taxed to support the priest, and
not the priest the schoolmaster; for I was not the State's school-

master, but I supported myself by voluntary subscription. I did not see why the lyceum should not present its tax-bill, and have the State to back its demand, as well as the church. However, at the request of the selectmen, I condescended to make some such statement as this in writing:—"Know all men by these presents, that I, Henry Thoreau, do not wish to be regarded as a member of any incorporated society which I have not joined." This I gave to the town-clerk; and he has it. The State, having thus learned that I did not wish to be regarded as a member of that church, has never made a like demand on me since; though it said that it must adhere to its original presumption that time. If I had known how to name them, I should then have signed off in detail from all the societies which I never signed on to; but I did not know where to find a complete list.

26   I have paid no poll-tax for six years. I was put into a jail once on this account, for one night; and, as I stood considering the walls of solid stone, two or three feet thick, the door of wood and iron, a foot thick, and the iron grating which strained the light, I could not help being struck with the foolishness of that institution which treated me as if I were mere flesh and blood and bones, to be locked up. I wondered that it should have concluded at length that this was the best use it could put me to, and had never thought to avail itself of my services in some way. I saw that, if there was a wall of stone between me and my towns-men, there was a still more difficult one to climb or break through, before they could get to be as free as I was. I did not for a moment feel confined, and the walls seemed a great waste of stone and mortar. I felt as if I alone of all my townsmen had paid my tax. They plainly did not know how to treat me, but behaved like persons who are underbred. In every threat and in every compliment there was a blunder; for they thought that my chief desire was to stand the other side of that stone wall. I could not but smile to see how industriously they locked the door on my meditations, which followed them out again without let or hinderance, and *they* were really all that was dangerous. As they could not reach me, they had resolved to punish my body; just as boys, if they cannot come at some person against whom they have a spite, will abuse his dog. I saw that the State was half-witted, that it was

timid as a lone woman with her silver spoons, and that it did not know its friends from its foes, and I lost all my remaining respect for it, and pitied it.

Thus the State never intentionally confronts a man's sense, in-   27
tellectual or moral, but only his body, his senses. It is not armed with superior wit or honesty, but with superior physical strength. I was not born to be forced. I will breathe after my own fashion. Let us see who is the strongest. What force has a multitude? They only can force me who obey a higher law than I. They force me to become like themselves. I do not hear of *men* being *forced* to live this way or that by masses of men. What sort of life were that to live? When I meet a government which says to me, "Your money or your life," why should I be in haste to give it my money? It may be in a great strait, and not know what to do: I cannot help that. It must help itself; do as I do. It is not worth the while to snivel about it. I am not responsible for the successful working of the machinery of society. I am not the son of the engineer. I perceive that, when an acorn and a chestnut fall side by side, the one does not remain inert to make way for the other, but both obey their own laws, and spring and grow and flourish as best they can, till one, perchance, overshadows and destroys the other. If a plant cannot live according to its nature, it dies; and so a man.

The night in prison was novel and interesting enough. The   28
prisoners in their shirtsleeves were enjoying a chat and the evening air in the door-way, when I entered. But the jailer said, "Come, boys, it is time to lock up;" and so they dispersed, and I heard the sound of their steps returning into the hollow apart-ments. My room-mate was introduced to me by the jailer, as "a first-rate fellow and a clever man." When the door was locked, he showed me where to hang my hat, and how he managed matters there. The rooms were whitewashed once a month; and this one, at least, was the whitest, most simply furnished, and probably the neatest apartment in the town. He naturally wanted to know where I came from, and what brought me there; and, when I had told him, I asked him in my turn how he came there, presuming him to be an honest man, of course; and, as the world goes, I be-lieve he was. "Why," said he, "they accuse me of burning a barn; but I never did it." As near as I could discover, he had probably

gone to bed in a barn when drunk, and smoked his pipe there; and so a barn was burnt. He had the reputation of being a clever man, had been there some three months waiting for his trial to come on, and would have to wait as much longer; but he was quite domesticated and contented, since he got his board for nothing, and thought that he was well treated.

29   He occupied one window, and I the other; and I saw, that if one stayed there long, his principal business would be to look out the window. I had soon read all the tracts that were left there, and examined where former prisoners had broken out, and where a grate had been sawed off, and heard the history of the various occupants of that room; for I found that even here there was a history and a gossip which never circulated beyond the walls of the jail. Probably this is the only house in the town where verses are composed, which are afterward printed in a circular form, but not published. I was shown quite a long list of verses which were composed by some young men who had been detected in an attempt to escape, who avenged themselves by singing them.

30   I pumped my fellow-prisoner as dry as I could, for fear I should never see him again; but at length he showed me which was my bed, and left me to blow out the lamp.

31   It was like travelling into a far country, such as I had never expected to behold, to lie there for one night. It seemed to me that I never had heard the town-clock strike before, nor the evening sounds of the village; for we slept with the windows open, which were inside the grating. It was to see my native village in the light of the middle ages, and our Concord was turned into a Rhine stream, and visions of knights and castles passed before me. They were the voices of old burghers that I heard in the streets. I was an involuntary spectator and auditor of whatever was done and said in the kitchen of the adjacent village-inn,—a wholly new and rare experience to me. It was a closer view of my native town. I was fairly inside of it. I never had seen its institutions before. This is one of its peculiar institutions; for it is a shire town. I began to comprehend what its inhabitants were about.

32   In the morning, our breakfasts were put through the hole in the door, in small oblong-square tin pans, made to fit, and holding a pint of chocolate, with brown bread, and an iron spoon. When

they called for the vessels again, I was green enough to return what bread I had left; but my comrade seized it, and said that I should lay that up for lunch or dinner. Soon after, he was let out to work at haying in a neighboring field, whither he went every day, and would not be back till noon; so he bade me good-day, saying that he doubted if he should see me again.

When I came out of prison,—for some one interfered, and ³³ paid the tax,—I did not perceive that great changes had taken place on the common, such as he observed who went in a youth, and emerged a tottering and gray-headed man; and yet a change had to my eyes come over the scene,—the town, and State, and country,—greater than any that mere time could effect. I saw yet more distinctly the State in which I lived. I saw to what extent the people among whom I lived could be trusted as good neighbors and friends; that their friendship was for summer weather only; that they did not greatly purpose to do right; that they were a distinct race from me by their prejudices and superstitions, as the Chinamen and Malays are; that, in their sacrifices to humanity, they ran no risks, not even to their property; that, after all, they were not so noble but they treated the thief as he had treated them, and hoped, by a certain outward observance and a few prayers, and by walking in a particular straight though useless path from time to time, to save their souls. This may be to judge my neighbors harshly; for I believe that most of them are not aware that they have such an institution as the jail in their village.

It was formerly the custom in our village, when a poor debtor ³⁴ came out of jail, for his acquaintances to salute him, looking through their fingers, which were crossed to represent the grating of a jail window, "How do ye do?" My neighbors did not thus salute me, but first looked at me, and then at one another, as if I had returned from a long journey. I was put into jail as I was going to the shoemaker's to get a shoe which was mended. When I was let out the next morning, I proceeded to finish my errand, and, having put on my mended shoe, joined a huckleberry party, who were impatient to put themselves under my conduct; and in half an hour,—for the horse was soon tackled,—was in the midst of a huckleberry field, on one of our highest hills, two miles off; and then the State was nowhere to be seen.

35   This is the whole history of "My Prisons."

36   I have never declined paying the highway tax, because I am
as desirous of being a good neighbor as I am of being a bad subject; and, as for supporting schools, I am doing my part to educate
my fellow-countrymen now. It is for no particular item in the tax-
bill that I refuse to pay it. I simply wish to refuse allegiance to the
State, to withdraw and stand aloof from it effectually. I do not care
to trace the course of my dollar, if I could, till it buys a man, or a
musket to shoot one with,—the dollar is innocent,—but I am concerned to trace the effects of my allegiance. In fact, I quietly declare
war with the State, after my fashion, though I will still make what
use and get what advantage of her I can, as is usual in such cases.

37   If others pay the tax which is demanded of me, from a sympathy with the State, they do but what they have already done in
their own case, or rather they abet injustice to a greater extent
than the State requires. If they pay the tax from a mistaken interest in the individual taxed, to save his property or prevent his going to jail, it is because they have not considered wisely how far
they let their private feelings interfere with the public good.

38   This, then, is my position at present. But one cannot be too
much on his guard in such a case, lest his action be biassed by ob-
stinacy, or an undue regard for the opinions of men. Let him see
that he does only what belongs to himself and to the hour.

39   I think sometimes, Why, this people mean well; they are only
ignorant; they would do better if they knew how: why give your
neighbors this pain to treat you as they are not inclined to? But I
think, again, this is no reason why I should do as they do, or permit
others to suffer much greater pain of a different kind. Again, I
sometimes say to myself, When many millions of men, without
heat, without ill-will, without personal feeling of any kind, demand
of you a few shillings only, without the possibility, such is their
constitution, of retracting or altering their present demand, and
without the possibility, on your side, of appeal to any other millions, why expose yourself to this overwhelming brute force? You
do not resist cold and hunger, the winds and the waves, thus ob-
stinately; you quietly submit to a thousand similar necessities.
You do not put your head into the fire. But just in proportion as I

regard this as not wholly a brute force, but partly a human force, and consider that I have relations to those millions as to so many millions of men, and not of mere brute or inanimate things, I see that appeal is possible, first and instantaneously, from them to the Maker of them, and, secondly, from them to themselves. But, if I put my head deliberately into the fire, there is no appeal to fire or to the Maker of fire, and I have only myself to blame. If I could convince myself that I have any right to be satisfied with men as they are, and to treat them accordingly, and not according, in some respects, to my requisitions and expectations of what they and I ought to be, then, like a good Mussulman and fatalist, I should endeavor to be satisfied with things as they are, and say it is the will of God. And, above all, there is this difference between resisting this and a purely brute or natural force, that I can resist this with some effect; but I cannot expect, like Orpheus, to change the nature of the rocks and trees and beasts.

I do not wish to quarrel with any man or nation. I do not wish 40 to split hairs, to make fine distinctions, or set myself up as better than my neighbors. I seek rather, I may say, even an excuse for conforming to the laws of the land. I am but too ready to conform to them. Indeed I have reason to suspect myself on this head; and each year, as the tax-gatherer comes round, I find myself disposed to review the acts and position of the general and state governments, and the spirit of the people, to discover a pretext for conformity. I believe that the State will soon be able to take all my work of this sort out of my hands, and then I shall be no better a patriot than my fellow-countrymen. Seen from a lower point of view, the Constitution, with all its faults, is very good; the law and the courts are very respectable; even this State and this American government are, in many respects, very admirable and rare things, to be thankful for, such as a great many have described them; but seen from a point of view a little higher, they are what I have described them; seen from a higher still, and the highest, who shall say what they are, or that they are worth looking at or thinking of at all?

However, the government does not concern me much, and I 41 shall bestow the fewest possible thoughts on it. It is not many moments that I live under a government, even in this world. If a man is thought-free, fancy-free, imagination-free, that which is *not* never for a long time appearing *to be* to him, unwise rulers or reformers cannot fatally interrupt him.

42   I know that most men think differently from myself; but those whose lives are by profession devoted to the study of these or kindred subjects, content me as little as any. Statesmen and legislators, standing so completely within the institution, never distinctly and nakedly behold it. They speak of moving society, but have no resting-place without it. They may be men of a certain experience and discrimination, and have no doubt invented ingenious and even useful systems, for which we sincerely thank them; but all their wit and usefulness lie within certain not very wide limits. They are wont to forget that the world is not governed by policy and expediency. Webster never goes behind government, and so cannot speak with authority about it. His words are wisdom to those legislators who contemplate no essential reform in the existing government; but for thinkers, and those who legislate for all time, he never once glances at the subject. I know of those whose serene and wise speculations on this theme would soon reveal the limits of his mind's range and hospitality. Yet, compared with the cheap professions of most reformers, and the still cheaper wisdom and eloquence of politicians in general, his are almost the only sensible and valuable words, and we thank Heaven for him. Comparatively, he is always strong, original, and, above all, practical. Still his quality is not wisdom, but prudence. The lawyer's truth is not Truth, but consistency, or a consistent expediency. Truth is always in harmony with herself, and is not concerned chiefly to reveal the justice that may consist with wrong-doing. He well deserves to be called, as he has been called, the Defender of the Constitution. There are really no blows to be given by him but defensive ones. He is not a leader, but a follower. His leaders are the men of '87. "I have never made an effort," he says, "and never propose to make an effort; I have never countenanced an effort, and never mean to countenance an effort, to disturb the arrangement as originally made, by which the various States came into the Union." Still thinking of the sanction which the Constitution gives to slavery, he says, "Because it was a part of the original compact,—let it stand." Notwithstanding his special

acuteness and ability, he is unable to take a fact out of its merely political relations, and behold it as it lies absolutely to be disposed of by the intellect,—what, for instance, it behoves a man to do here in America to-day with regard to slavery, but ventures, or is driven, to make some such desperate answer as the following, while professing to speak absolutely, and as a private man,—from which what new and singular code of social duties might be inferred?—"The manner," says he, "in which the government of those States where slavery exists are to regulate it, is for their own consideration, under their responsibility to their constituents, to the general laws of propriety, humanity, and justice, and to God. Associations formed elsewhere, springing from a feeling of humanity, or any other cause, have nothing whatever to do with it. They have never received any encouragement from me, and they never will."

They who know of no purer sources of truth, who have traced 43 up its stream no higher, stand, and wisely stand, by the Bible and the Constitution, and drink at it there with reverence and humility; but they who behold where it comes trickling into this lake or that pool, gird up their loins once more, and continue their pilgrimage toward its fountain-head.

No man with a genius for legislation has appeared in Amer- 44 ica. They are rare in the history of the world. There are orators, politicians, and eloquent men, by the thousand; but the speaker has not yet opened his mouth to speak, who is capable of settling the much-vexed questions of the day. We love eloquence for its own sake, and not for any truth which it may utter, or any heroism it may inspire. Our legislators have not yet learned the comparative value of free-trade and of freedom, of union, and of rectitude, to a nation. They have no genius or talent for comparatively humble questions of taxation and finance, commerce and manufactures and agriculture. If we were left solely to the wordy wit of legislators in Congress for our guidance, uncorrected by the seasonable experience and the effectual complaints of the people, America would not long retain her rank among the nations. For eighteen hundred years, though perchance I have no right to say it, the New Testament, has been written; yet where is the legislator who has wisdom and practical talent enough to avail himself of the light which it sheds on the science of legislation?

45   The authority of government, even such as I am willing to submit to,—for I will cheerfully obey those who know and can do better than I, and in many things even those who neither know nor can do so well,—is still an impure one: to be strictly just, it must have the sanction and consent of the governed. It can have no pure right over my person and property but what I concede to it. The progress from an absolute to a limited monarchy, from a limited monarchy to a democracy, is a progress toward a true respect for the individual. Is a democracy, such as we know it, the last improvement possible in government? Is it not possible to take a step further towards recognizing and organizing the rights of man? There will never be a really free and enlightened State, until the State comes to recognize the individual as a higher and independent power, from which all its own power and authority are derived, and treats him accordingly. I please myself with imagining a State at last which can afford to be just to all men, and to treat the individual with respect as a neighbor; which even would not think it inconsistent with its own repose, if a few were to live aloof from it, not meddling with it, nor embraced by it, who fulfilled all the duties of neighbors and fellow-men. A State which bore this kind of fruit, and suffered it to drop off as fast as it ripened, would prepare the way for a still more perfect and glorious State, which also I have imagined, but not yet anywhere seen.

1848

Letter from Birmingham City Jail
Martin Luther King, Jr.

1 My dear Fellow Clergymen,
   While confined here in the Birmingham city jail, I came across your recent statement calling our present activities "unwise and

untimely." Seldom, if ever, do I pause to answer criticism of my work and ideas. If I sought to answer all of the criticisms that cross my desk, my secretaries would be engaged in little else in the course of the day, and I would have no time for constructive work. But since I feel that you are men of genuine good will and your criticisms are sincerely set forth, I would like to answer your statement in what I hope will be patient and reasonable terms.

I think I should give the reason for my being in Birmingham, 2 since you have been influenced by the argument of "outsiders coming in." I have the honor of serving as president of the Southern Christian Leadership Conference, an organization operating in every southern state, with headquarters in Atlanta, Georgia. We have some eighty-five affiliate organizations all across the South— one being the Alabama Christian Movement for Human Rights. Whenever necessary and possible we share staff, educational and financial resources with our affiliates. Several months ago our local affiliate here in Birmingham invited us to be on call to engage in a nonviolent direct-action program if such were deemed necessary. We readily consented and when the hour came we lived up to our promises. So I am here, along with several members of my staff, because we were invited here. I am here because I have basic organizational ties here.

Beyond this, I am in Birmingham because injustice is here. 3 Just as the eighth century prophets left their little villages and carried their "thus saith the Lord" far beyond the boundaries of their hometowns; and just as the Apostle Paul left his little village of Tarsus and carried the gospel of Jesus Christ to practically every hamlet and city of the Graeco-Roman world, I too am compelled to carry the gospel of freedom beyond my particular hometown. Like Paul, I must constantly respond to the Macedonian call for aid.

Moreover, I am cognizant of the interrelatedness of all com- 4 munities and states. I cannot sit idly by in Atlanta and not be concerned about what happens in Birmingham. Injustice anywhere is a threat to justice everywhere. We are caught in an inescapable network of mutuality, tied in a single garment of destiny. Whatever affects one directly affects all indirectly. Never again can we afford to live with the narrow, provincial "outside agitator" idea.

Anyone who lives in the United States can never be considered an outsider anywhere in this country.

5   You deplore the demonstrations that are presently taking place in Birmingham. But I am sorry that your statement did not express a similar concern for the conditions that brought the demonstrations into being. I am sure that each of you would want to go beyond the superficial social analyst who looks merely at effects, and does not grapple with underlying causes. I would not hesitate to say that it is unfortunate that so-called demonstrations are taking place in Birmingham at this time, but I would say in more emphatic terms that it is even more unfortunate that the white power structure of this city left the Negro community with no other alternative.

6   In any nonviolent campaign there are four basic steps: (1) collection of the facts to determine whether injustices are alive, (2) negotiation, (3) self-purification, and (4) direct action. We have gone through all of these steps in Birmingham. There can be no gainsaying of the fact that racial injustice engulfs this community.

7   Birmingham is probably the most thoroughly segregated city in the United States. Its ugly record of police brutality is known in every section of this country. Its injust treatment of Negroes in the courts is a notorious reality. There have been more unsolved bombings of Negro homes and churches in Birmingham than any city in this nation. These are the hard, brutal and unbelievable facts. On the basis of these conditions Negro leaders sought to negotiate with the city fathers. But the political leaders consistently refused to engage in good faith negotiation.

8   Then came the opportunity last September to talk with some of the leaders of the economic community. In these negotiating sessions certain promises were made by the merchants—such as the promise to remove the humiliating racial signs from the stores. On the basis of these promises Rev. Shuttlesworth and the leaders of the Alabama Christian Movement for Human Rights agreed to call a moratorium on any type of demonstrations. As the weeks and months unfolded we realized that we were the victims of a broken promise. The signs remained. Like so many experiences of the past we were confronted with blasted hopes, and the dark

shadow of a deep disappointment settled upon us. So we had no
alternative except that of preparing for direct action, whereby we
would present our very bodies as a means of laying our case before the conscience of the local and national community. We were
not unmindful of the difficulties involved. So we decided to go
through a process of self-purification. We started having work-
shops on nonviolence and repeatedly asked ourselves the questions, "Are you able to accept blows without retaliating?" "Are you
able to endure the ordeals of jail?" We decided to set our direct-
action program around the Easter season, realizing that with the
exception of Christmas, this was the largest shopping period of
the year. Knowing that a strong economic withdrawal program
would be the by-product of direct action, we felt that this was the
best time to bring pressure on the merchants for the needed
changes. Then it occurred to us that the March election was ahead
and so we speedily decided to postpone action until after election
day. When we discovered that Mr. Connor was in the run-off, we
decided again to postpone action so that the demonstrations
could not be used to cloud the issues. At this time we agreed to
begin our nonviolent witness the day after the run-off.

This reveals that we did not move irresponsibly into direct 9
action. We too wanted to see Mr. Connor defeated; so we went
through postponement after postponement to aid in this community need. After this we felt that direct action could be delayed
no longer.

You may well ask, "Why direct action? Why sit-ins, marches, 10
etc.? Isn't negotiation a better path?" You are exactly right in your
call for negotiation. Indeed, this is the purpose of direct action.
Nonviolent direct action seeks to create such a crisis and establish
such creative tension that a community that has constantly refused to negotiate is forced to confront the issue. It seeks so to
dramatize the issue that it can no longer be ignored. I just referred
to the creation of tension as a part of the work of the nonviolent
resister. This may sound rather shocking. But I must confess that I
am not afraid of the word tension. I have earnestly worked and
preached against violent tension, but there is a type of constructive nonviolent tension that is necessary for growth. Just as
Socrates felt that it was necessary to create a tension in the mind

so that individuals could rise from the bondage of myths and half-truths to the unfettered realm of creative analysis and objective appraisal, we must see the need of having nonviolent gadflies to create the kind of tension in society that will help men to rise from the dark depths of prejudice and racism to the majestic heights of understanding and brotherhood. So the purpose of the direct action is to create a situation so crisis-packed that it will inevitably open the door to negotiation. We, therefore, concur with you in your call for negotiation. Too long has our beloved Southland been bogged down in the tragic attempt to live in monologue rather than dialogue.

11   One of the basic points in your statement is that our acts are untimely. Some have asked, "Why didn't you give the new administration time to act?" The only answer that I can give to this inquiry is that the new administration must be prodded about as much as the outgoing one before it acts. We will be sadly mistaken if we feel that the election of Mr. Boutwell will bring the millennium to Birmingham. While Mr. Boutwell is much more articulate and gentle than Mr. Connor, they are both segregationists, dedicated to the task of maintaining the status quo. The hope I see in Mr. Boutwell is that he will be reasonable enough to see the futility of massive resistance to desegregation. But he will not see this without pressure from the devotees of civil rights. My friends, I must say to you that we have not made a single gain in civil rights without determined legal and nonviolent pressure. History is the long and tragic story of the fact that privileged groups seldom give up their privileges voluntarily. Individuals may see the moral light and voluntarily give up their unjust posture; but as Reinhold Niebuhr has reminded us, groups are more immoral than individuals.

12   We know through painful experience that freedom is never voluntarily given by the oppressor; it must be demanded by the oppressed. Frankly, I have never yet engaged in a direct action movement that was "well-timed," according to the timetable of those who have not suffered unduly from the disease of segregation. For years now I have heard the words "Wait!" It rings in the ear of every Negro with a piercing familiarity. This "Wait" has almost always meant "Never." It has been a tranquilizing

thalidomide, relieving the emotional stress for a moment, only to give birth to an ill-formed infant of frustration. We must come to see with the distinguished jurist of yesterday that "justice too long delayed is justice denied." We have waited for more than 340 years for our constitutional and God-given rights. The nations of Asia and Africa are moving with jetlike speed toward the goal of political independence, and we still creep at horse and buggy pace toward the gaining of a cup of coffee at a lunch counter. I guess it is easy for those who have never felt the stinging darts of segregation to say, "Wait." But when you have seen vicious mobs lynch your mothers and fathers at will and drown your sisters and brothers at whim; when you have seen hate-filled policemen curse, kick, brutalize and even kill your black brothers and sisters with impunity; when you see the vast majority of your twenty million Negro brothers smothering in an airtight cage of poverty in the midst of an affluent society; when you suddenly find your tongue twisted and your speech stammering as you seek to explain to your six-year-old daughter why she can't go to the public amusement park that has just been advertised on television, and see tears welling up in her little eyes when she is told that Funtown is closed to colored children, and see the depressing clouds of inferiority begin to form in her little mental sky, and see her begin to distort her little personality by unconsciously developing a bitterness toward white people; when you have to concoct an answer for a five-year-old son asking in agonizing pathos: "Daddy, why do white people treat colored people so mean?"; when you take a cross-country drive and find it necessary to sleep night after night in the uncomfortable corners of your automobile because no motel will accept you; when you are humiliated day in and day out by nagging signs reading "white" and "colored"; when your first name becomes "nigger" and your middle name becomes "boy" (however old you are) and your last name becomes "John," and when your wife and mother are never given the respected title "Mrs."; when you are harried by day and haunted by night by the fact that you are a Negro, living constantly at tiptoe stance never quite knowing what to expect next, and plagued with inner fears and outer resentments; when you are forever fighting a degenerating sense of "nobodiness"; then you will understand why we find it difficult to wait. There comes a time when the cup of endurance runs over, and men are no longer willing to be plunged into an abyss of injustice where they experience the blackness of corroding despair. I hope, sirs, you can understand our legitimate and unavoidable impatience.

13   You express a great deal of anxiety over our willingness to break laws. This is certainly a legitimate concern. Since we so diligently urge people to obey the Supreme Court's decision of 1954 outlawing segregation in the public schools, it is rather strange and paradoxical to find us consciously breaking laws. One may well ask, "How can you advocate breaking some laws and obeying others?" The answer is found in the fact that there are two types of laws: there are *just* and there are *unjust* laws. I would agree with Saint Augustine that "An unjust law is no law at all."

14   Now what is the difference between the two? How does one determine when a law is just or unjust? A just law is a man-made code that squares with the moral law or the law of God. An unjust law is a code that is out of harmony with the moral law. To put it in the terms of Saint Thomas Aquinas, an unjust law is a human law that is not rooted in eternal and natural law. Any law that uplifts human personality is just. Any law that degrades human personality is unjust. All segregation statutes are unjust because segregation distorts the soul and damages the personality. It gives the segregator a false sense of superiority, and the segregated a false sense of inferiority. To use the words of Martin Buber, the great Jewish philosopher, segregation substitutes an "I–it" relationship for the "I–thou" relationship, and ends up relegating persons to the status of things. So segregation is not only politically, economically and sociologically unsound, but it is morally wrong and sinful. Paul Tillich has said that sin is separation. Isn't segregation an existential expression of man's tragic separation, an expression of his awful estrangement, his terrible sinfulness? So I can urge men to disobey segregation ordinances because they are morally wrong.

15   Let us turn to a more concrete example of just and unjust laws. An unjust law is a code that a majority inflicts on a minority that is

not binding on itself. This is difference made legal. On the other hand a just law is a code that a majority compels a minority to follow that it is willing to follow itself. This is sameness made legal.

Let me give another explanation. An unjust law is a code inflicted upon a minority which that minority had no part in enacting or creating because they did not have the unhampered right to vote. Who can say that the legislature of Alabama which set up the segregation laws was democratically elected? Throughout the state of Alabama all types of conniving methods are used to prevent Negroes from becoming registered voters and there are some counties without a single Negro registered to vote despite the fact that the Negro constitutes a majority of the population. Can any law set up in such a state be considered democratically structured? 16

These are just a few examples of unjust and just laws. There are some instances when a law is just on its face and unjust in its application. For instance, I was arrested Friday on a charge of parading without a permit. Now there is nothing wrong with an ordinance which requires a permit for a parade, but when the ordinance is used to preserve segregation and to deny citizens the First Amendment privilege of peaceful assembly and peaceful protest, then it becomes unjust. 17

I hope you can see the distinction I am trying to point out. In no sense do I advocate evading or defying the law as the rabid segregationist would do. This would lead to anarchy. One who breaks an unjust law must do it *openly, lovingly* (not hatefully as the white mothers did in New Orleans when they were seen on television screaming, "nigger, nigger, nigger"), and with a willingness to accept the penalty. I submit that an individual who breaks a law that conscience tells him is unjust, and willingly accepts the penalty by staying in jail to arouse the conscience of the community over its injustice, is in reality expressing the very highest respect for law. 18

Of course, there is nothing new about this kind of civil disobedience. It was seen sublimely in the refusal of Shadrach, Meshach and Abednego to obey the laws of Nebuchadnezzar because a higher moral law was involved. It was practiced superbly by the early Christians who were willing to face hungry lions and the excruciating pain of chopping blocks, before sub- 19 mitting to certain unjust laws of the Roman Empire. To a degree academic freedom is a reality today because Socrates practiced civil disobedience.

20   We can never forget that everything Hitler did in Germany was "legal" and everything the Hungarian freedom fighters did in Hungary was "illegal." It was "illegal" to aid and comfort a Jew in Hitler's Germany. But I am sure that if I had lived in Germany during that time I would have aided and comforted my Jewish brothers even though it was illegal. If I lived in a Communist country today where certain principles dear to the Christian faith are suppressed, I believe I would openly advocate disobeying these anti-religious laws. I must make two honest confessions to you, my Christian and Jewish brothers. First, I must confess that over the last few years I have been gravely disappointed with the white moderate. I have almost reached the regrettable conclusion that the Negro's great stumbling block in the stride toward freedom is not the White Citizen's Counciler or the Ku Klux Klanner, but the white moderate who is more devoted to "order" than to justice; who prefers a negative peace which is the absence of tension to a positive peace which is the presence of justice; who constantly says, "I agree with you in the goal you seek, but I can't agree with your methods of direct action"; who paternalistically feels that he can set the timetable for another man's freedom; who lives by the myth of time and who constantly advised the Negro to wait until a "more convenient season." Shallow understanding from people of good will is more frustrating than absolute misunderstanding from people of ill will. Lukewarm acceptance is much more bewildering than outright rejection.

21   I had hoped that the white moderate would understand that law and order exist for the purpose of establishing justice, and that when they fail to do this they become dangerously structured dams that block the flow of social progress. I had hoped that the white moderate would understand that the present tension of the South is merely a necessary phase of the transition from an obnoxious negative peace, where the Negro passively accepted his unjust plight, to a substance-filled positive peace, where all men will respect the dignity and worth of human personality. Actually, we who engage in nonviolent direct action are not the

creators of tension. We merely bring to the surface the hidden tension that is already alive. We bring it out in the open where it can be seen and dealt with. Like a boil that can never be cured as long as it is covered up but must be opened with all its pus-flowing ugliness to the natural medicines of air and light, injustice must likewise be exposed, with all of the tension its exposing creates, to the light of human conscience and the air of national opinion before it can be cured.

In your statement you asserted that our actions, even though 22 peaceful, must be condemned because they precipitate violence. But can this assertion be logically made? Isn't this like condemning the robbed man because his possession of money precipitated the evil act of robbery? Isn't this like condemning Socrates because his unswerving commitment to truth and his philosophical delvings precipitated the misguided popular mind to make him drink the hemlock? Isn't this like condemning Jesus because His unique God-consciousness and never-ceasing devotion to His will precipitated the evil act of crucifixion? We must come to see, as federal courts have consistently affirmed, that it is immoral to urge an individual to withdraw his efforts to gain his basic constitutional rights because the quest precipitates violence. Society must protect the robbed and punish the robber.

I had also hoped that the white moderate would reject the 23 myth of time. I received a letter this morning from a white brother in Texas which said: "All Christians know that the colored people will receive equal rights eventually, but it is possible that you are in too great of a religious hurry. It has taken Christianity almost two thousand years to accomplish what it has. The teachings of Christ take time to come to earth." All that is said here grows out of a tragic misconception of time. It is the strangely irrational notion that there is something in the very flow of time that will inevitably cure all ills. Actually time is neutral. It can be used either destructively or constructively. I am coming to feel that the people of ill will have used time much more effectively than the people of good will. We will have to repent in this generation not merely for the vitriolic words and actions of the bad people, but for the appalling silence of the good people. We must come to see that human progress never rolls in on wheels of inevitability. It comes through the tireless efforts and persistent work of men willing to be co-workers with God, and without this hard work time itself becomes an ally of the forces of social stagnation. We must use time creatively, and forever realize that the time is always ripe to do right. Now is the time to make real the promise of democracy, and transform our pending national elegy into a creative psalm of brotherhood. Now is the time to lift our national policy from the quicksand of racial injustice to the solid rock of human dignity.

24   You spoke of our activity in Birmingham as extreme. At first I was rather disappointed that fellow clergymen would see my nonviolent efforts as those of the extremist. I started thinking about the fact that I stand in the middle of two opposing forces in the Negro community. One is a force of complacency made up of Negroes who, as a result of long years of oppression, have been so completely drained of self-respect and a sense of "somebodiness" that they have adjusted to segregation, and, of a few Negroes in the middle class who, because of a degree of academic and economic security, and because at points they profit by segregation, have unconsciously become insensitive to the problems of the masses. The other force is one of bitterness and hatred, and comes perilously close to advocating violence. It is expressed in the various black nationalist groups that are springing up over the nation, the largest and best known being Elijah Muhammad's Muslim movement. This movement is nourished by the contemporary frustration over the continued existence of racial discrimination. It is made up of people who have lost faith in America, who have absolutely repudiated Christianity, and who have concluded that the white man is an incurable "devil." I have tried to stand between these two forces, saying that we need not follow the "do-nothingism" of the complacent or the hatred and despair of the black nationalist. There is the more excellent way of love and nonviolent protest. I'm grateful to God that, through the Negro church, the dimension of nonviolence entered our struggle. If this philosophy had not emerged, I am convinced that by now many streets of the South would be flowing with floods of blood. And I am further convinced that if our white brothers dismiss us as "rabble-rousers" and "outside agitators" those of us who are

working through the channels of nonviolent direct action and refuse to support our nonviolent efforts, millions of Negroes, out of
frustration and despair, will seek solace and security in black nationalist ideologies, a development that will lead inevitably to a
frightening racial nightmare.

Oppressed people cannot remain oppressed forever. The urge 25
for freedom will eventually come. This is what happened to the
American Negro. Something within has reminded him of his
birthright of freedom; something without has reminded him that
he can gain it. Consciously and unconsciously, he has been swept
in by what the Germans call the *Zeitgeist,* and with his black
brothers of Africa, and his brown and yellow brothers of Asia,
South America and the Caribbean, he is moving with a sense of
cosmic urgency toward the promised land of racial justice. Recognizing this vital urge that has engulfed the Negro community, one
should readily understand public demonstrations. The Negro has
many pent-up resentments and latent frustrations. He has to get
them out. So let him march sometime; let him have his prayer pil-
grimages to the city hall; understand why he must have sit-ins
and freedom rides. If his repressed emotions do not come out in
these nonviolent ways, they will come out in ominous expressions
of violence. This is not a threat; it is a fact of history. So I have not
said to my people "get rid of your discontent." But I have tried to
say that this normal and healthy discontent can be channelized
through the creative outlet of nonviolent direct action. Now this
approach is being dismissed as extremist. I must admit that I was
initially disappointed in being so categorized.

But as I continued to think about the matter I gradually 26
gained a bit of satisfaction from being considered an extremist.
Was not Jesus an extremist in love—"Love your enemies, bless
them that curse you, pray for them that despitefully use you."
Was not Amos an extremist for justice—"Let justice roll down like
waters and righteousness like a mighty stream." Was not Paul an
extremist for the gospel of Jesus Christ—"I bear in my body the
marks of the Lord Jesus." Was not Martin Luther an extremist—
"Here I stand; I can do none other so help me God." Was not John
Bunyan an extremist—"I will stay in jail to the end of my days before I make a butchery of my conscience." Was not Abraham Lin-

coln an extremist—"This nation cannot survive half slave and half free." Was not Thomas Jefferson an extremist—"We hold these truths to be self-evident, that all men are created equal." So the question is not whether we will be extremist but what kind of extremist will we be. Will we be extremists for hate or will we be extremists for love? Will we be extremists for the preservation of injustice—or will we be extremists for the cause of justice? In that dramatic scene on Calvary's hill, three men were crucified. We must not forget that all three were crucified for the same crime—the crime of extremism. Two were extremists for immorality, and thusly fell below their environment. The other, Jesus Christ, was an extremist for love, truth and goodness, and thereby rose above his environment. So, after all, maybe the South, the nation and the world are in dire need of creative extremists.

27   I had hoped that the white moderate would see this. Maybe I was too optimistic. Maybe I expected too much. I guess I should have realized that few members of a race that has oppressed another race can understand or appreciate the deep groans and passionate yearnings of those that have been oppressed and still fewer have the vision to see that injustice must be rooted out by strong, persistent and determined action. I am thankful, however, that some of our white brothers have grasped the meaning of this social revolution and committed themselves to it. They are still all too small in quantity, but they are big in quality. Some like Ralph McGill, Lillian Smith, Harry Golden and James Dabbs have written about our struggle in eloquent, prophetic and understanding terms. Others have marched with us down nameless streets of the South. They have languished in filthy roach-infested jails, suffering the abuse and brutality of angry policemen who see them as "dirty nigger-lovers." They, unlike so many of their moderate brothers and sisters, have recognized the urgency of the moment and sensed the need for powerful "action" antidotes to combat the disease of segregation.

28   Let me rush on to mention my other disappointment. I have been so greatly disappointed with the white church and its leadership. Of course, there are some notable exceptions. I am not unmindful of the fact that each of you has taken some significant stands on this issue. I commend you, Rev. Stallings, for your Christian

stance on this past Sunday, in welcoming Negroes to your worship service on a non-segregated basis. I commend the Catholic leaders of this state for integrating Springhill College several years ago.

But despite these notable exceptions I must honestly reiterate   29
that I have been disappointed with the church. I do not say that as one of the negative critics who can always find something wrong with the church. I say it as a minister of the gospel, who loves the church; who was nurtured in its bosom; who has been sustained by its spiritual blessings and who will remain true to it as long as the cord of life shall lengthen.

I had the strange feeling when I was suddenly catapulted into   30
the leadership of the bus protest in Montgomery several years ago that we would have the support of the white church. I felt that the white ministers, priests and rabbis of the South would be some of our strongest allies. Instead, some have been outright opponents, refusing to understand the freedom movement and misrepresenting its leaders; all too many others have been more cautious than courageous and have remained silent behind the anesthetizing security of the stained-glass windows.

In spite of my shattered dreams of the past, I came to Birm-   31
ingham with the hope that the white religious leadership of this community would see the justice of our cause, and with, deep moral concern, serve as the channel through which our just grievances would get to the power structure. I had hoped that each of you would understand. But again I have been disappointed. I have heard numerous religious leaders of the South call upon their worshippers to comply with a desegregation decision because it is the *law*, but I have longed to hear white ministers say, "Follow this decree because integration is morally *right* and the Negro is your brother." In the midst of blatant injustices inflicted upon the Negro, I have watched white churches stand on the sideline and merely mouth pious irrelevancies and sanctimonious trivialities. In the midst of a mighty struggle to rid our nation of racial and economic injustice, I have heard so many ministers say, "Those are social issues with which the gospel has no real concern," and I have watched so many churches commit themselves to a completely otherwordly religion which made a strange distinction between body and soul, the sacred and the secular.

32   So here we are moving toward the exit of the twentieth century with a religious community largely adjusted to the status quo, standing as a taillight behind other community agencies rather than a headlight leading men to higher levels of justice.

33   I have traveled the length and breadth of Alabama, Mississippi and all the other southern states. On sweltering summer days and crisp autumn mornings I have looked at her beautiful churches with their lofty spires pointing heavenward. I have beheld the impressive outlay of her massive religious education buildings. Over and over again I have found myself asking: "What kind of people worship here? Who is their God? Where were their voices when the lips of Governor Barnett dripped with words of interposition and nullification? Where were they when Governor Wallace gave the clarion call for defiance and hatred? Where were their voices of support when tired, bruised and weary Negro men and women decided to rise from the dark dungeons of complacency to the bright hills of creative protest?"

34   Yes, these questions are still in my mind. In deep disappointment, I have wept over the laxity of the church. But be assured that my tears have been tears of love. There can be no deep disappointment where there is not deep love. Yes, I love the church; I love her sacred walls. How could I do otherwise? I am in the rather unique position of being the son, the grandson and the great-grandson of preachers. Yes, I see the church as the body of Christ. But, oh! How we have blemished and scarred that body through social neglect and fear of being nonconformists.

35   There was a time when the church was very powerful. It was during that period when the early Christians rejoiced when they were deemed worthy to suffer for what they believed. In those days the church was not merely a thermometer that recorded the ideas and principles of popular opinion; it was a thermostat that transformed the mores of society. Wherever the early Christians entered a town the power structure got disturbed and immediately sought to convict them for being "disturbers of the peace" and "outside agitators." But they went on with the conviction that they were "a colony of heaven," and had to obey God rather than man. They were small in number but big in commitment. They were too God-intoxicated to be "astronomically intimidated."

They brought an end to such ancient evils as infanticide and glad-iatorial contest.

Things are different now. The contemporary church is often a 36 weak, ineffectual voice with an uncertain sound. It is so often the arch-supporter of the status quo. Far from being disturbed by the presence of the church, the power structure of the average com-munity is consoled by the church's silent and often vocal sanction of things as they are.

But the judgment of God is upon the church as never before. 37 If the church of today does not recapture the sacrificial spirit of the early church, it will lose its authentic ring, forfeit the loyalty of millions, and be dismissed as an irrelevant social club with no meaning for the twentieth century. I am meeting young people every day whose disappointment with the church has risen to outright disgust.

Maybe again, I have been too optimistic. Is organized religion 38 too inextricably bound to the status quo to save our nation and the world? Maybe I must turn my faith to the inner spiritual church, the church within the church, as the true *ecclesia* and the hope of the world. But again I am thankful to God that some no-ble souls from the ranks of organized religion have broken loose from the paralyzing chains of conformity and joined us as active partners in the struggle for freedom. They have left their secure congregations and walked the streets of Albany, Georgia, with us. They have gone through the highways of the South on tortuous rides for freedom. Yes, they have gone to jail with us. Some have been kicked out of their churches, and lost support of their bish-ops and fellow ministers. But they have gone with the faith that right defeated is stronger than evil triumphant. These men have been the leaven in the lump of the race. Their witness has been the spiritual salt that has preserved the true meaning of the gospel in these troubled times. They have carved a tunnel of hope through the dark mountain of disappointment.

I hope the church as a whole will meet the challenge of this 39 decisive hour. But even if the church does not come to the aid of justice, I have no despair about the future. I have no fear about the outcome of our struggle in Birmingham, even if our motives are presently misunderstood. We will reach the goal of freedom in

Birmingham and all over the nation, because the goal of America is freedom. Abused and scorned though we may be, our destiny is tied up with the destiny of America. Before the Pilgrims landed at Plymouth we were here. Before the pen of Jefferson etched across the pages of history the majestic words of the Declaration of Independence, we were here. For more than two centuries our foreparents labored in this country without wages; they made cotton king; and they built the homes of their masters in the midst of brutal injustice and shameful humiliation—and yet out of a bottomless vitality they continued to thrive and develop. If the inexpressible cruelties of slavery could not stop us, the opposition we now face will surely fail. We will win our freedom because the sacred heritage of our nation and the eternal will of God are embodied in our echoing demands.

40   I must close now. But before closing I am impelled to mention one other point in your statement that troubled me profoundly. You warmly commended the Birmingham police force for keeping "order" and "preventing violence." I don't believe you would have so warmly commended the police force if you had seen its angry violent dogs literally biting six unarmed, nonviolent Negroes. I don't believe you would so quickly commend the policemen if you would observe their ugly and inhuman treatment of Negroes here in the city jail; if you would watch them push and curse old Negro women and young Negro girls; if you would see them slap and kick old Negro men and young boys; if you will observe them, as they did on two occasions, refuse to give us food because we wanted to sing our grace together. I'm sorry that I can't join you in your praise for the police department.

41   It is true that they have been rather disciplined in their public handling of the demonstrators. In this sense they have been rather publicly "nonviolent." But for what purpose? To preserve the evil system of segregation. Over the last few years I have consistently preached that nonviolence demands that the means we use must be as pure as the ends we seek. So I have tried to make it clear that it is wrong to use immoral means to attain moral ends. But now I must affirm that it is just as wrong, or even more so, to use moral means to preserve immoral ends. Maybe Mr. Connor and his policemen have been rather publicly nonviolent, as Chief Pritchett

was in Albany, Georgia, but they have used the moral means of nonviolence to maintain the immoral end of flagrant racial injustice. T. S. Eliot has said that there is no greater treason than to do the right deed for the wrong reason.

I wish you had commended the Negro sit-inners and demon- 42 strators of Birmingham for their sublime courage, their willingness to suffer and their amazing discipline in the midst of the most inhuman provocation. One day the South will recognize its real heroes. They will be the James Merediths, courageously and with a majestic sense of purpose facing jeering and hostile mobs and the agonizing loneliness that characterizes the life of the pioneer. They will be old, oppressed, battered Negro women, symbolized in a seventy-two-year-old woman of Montgomery, Alabama, who rose up with a sense of dignity and with her people decided not to ride the segregated buses, and responded to one who inquired about her tiredness with ungrammatical profundity: "My feet is tired, but my soul is rested." They will be the young high school and college students, young ministers of the gospel and a host of their elders courageously and nonviolently sitting-in at lunch counters and willingly going to jail for conscience's sake. One day the South will know that when these disinherited children of God sat down at lunch counters they were in reality standing up for the best in the American dream and the most sacred values in our Judeo-Christian heritage, and thusly, carrying our whole nation back to those great wells of democracy which were dug deep by the Founding Fathers in the formulation of the Constitution and the Declaration of Independence.

Never before have I written a letter this long (or should I say 43 a book?). I'm afraid that it is much too long to take your precious time. I can assure you that it would have been much shorter if I had been writing from a comfortable desk, but what else is there to do when you are alone for days in the dull monotony of a narrow jail cell other than write long letters, think strange thoughts, and pray long prayers?

If I have said anything in this letter that is an overstatement of 44 the truth and is indicative of an unreasonable impatience, I beg you to forgive me. If I have said anything in this letter that is an understatement of the truth and is indicative of my having a patience that makes me patient with anything less than brotherhood, I beg God to forgive me.

45   I hope this letter finds you strong in the faith. I also hope that circumstances will soon make it possible for me to meet each of you, not as an integrationist or a civil rights leader, but as a fellow clergyman and a Christian brother. Let us all hope that the dark clouds of racial prejudice will soon pass away and the deep fog of misunderstanding will be lifted from our fear-drenched communities and in some not too distant tomorrow the radiant stars of love and brotherhood will shine over our great nation with all of their scintillating beauty.

Yours for the cause of Peace and Brotherhood,
Martin Luther King, Jr.

1963

I Have a Dream
Martin Luther King, Jr.

1   Five score years ago, a great American, in whose symbolic shadow we stand, signed the Emancipation Proclamation. This momentous decree came as a great beacon light of hope to millions of Negro slaves who had been seared in the flames of withering injustice. It came as a joyous daybreak to end the long night of captivity.

2   But one hundred years later, we must face the tragic fact that the Negro is still not free. One hundred years later, the life of the Negro is still sadly crippled by the manacles of segregation and the chains of discrimination. One hundred years later, the Negro lives on a lonely island of poverty in the midst of a vast ocean of material prosperity. One hundred years later, the Negro is still languishing in the corners of American society and finds himself an exile in his own land. So we have come here today to dramatize an appalling condition.

In a sense we have come to our nation's capital to cash a ₃
check. When the architects of our republic wrote the magnificent
words of the Constitution and the Declaration of Independence,
they were signing a promissory note to which every American
was to fall heir. This note was a promise that all men would be
guaranteed the unalienable rights of life, liberty, and the pursuit
of happiness.

It is obvious today that America has defaulted on this prom- ₄
issory note insofar as her citizens of color are concerned. Instead
of honoring this sacred obligation, America has given the Negro
people a bad check; a check which has come back marked "insufficient funds." But we refuse to believe that the bank of justice is
bankrupt. We refuse to believe that there are insufficient funds in
the great vaults of opportunity of this nation. So we have come to
cash this check—a check that will give us upon demand the riches
of freedom and the security of justice. We have also come to this
hallowed spot to remind America of the fierce urgency of *now.*
This is no time to engage in the luxury of cooling off or to take the
tranquilizing drugs of gradualism. *Now* is the time to make real
the promises of Democracy. *Now* is the time to rise from the dark
and desolate valley of segregation to the sunlit path of racial justice. *Now* is the time to open the doors of opportunity to all of
God's children. *Now* is the time to lift our nation from the quick-
sands of racial injustice to the solid rock of brotherhood.

It would be fatal for the nation to overlook the urgency of the ₅
moment and to underestimate the determination of the Negro.
This sweltering summer of the Negro's legitimate discontent will
not pass until there is an invigorating autumn of freedom and
equality. 1963 is not an end, but a beginning. Those who hope that
the Negro needed to blow off steam and will now be content will
have a rude awakening if the nation returns to business as usual.
There will be neither rest nor tranquility in America until the Negro is granted his citizenship rights. The whirlwinds of revolt will
continue to shake the foundations of our nation until the bright
day of justice emerges.

But there is something that I must say to my people who stand ₆
on the warm threshold which leads into the palace of justice. In the

process of gaining our rightful place we must not be guilty of wrongful deeds. Let us not seek to satisfy our thirst for freedom by drinking from the cup of bitterness and hatred. We must forever conduct our struggle on the high plane of dignity and discipline. We must not allow our creative protest to degenerate into physical violence. Again and again we must rise to the majestic heights of meeting physical force with soul force. The marvelous new militancy which has engulfed the Negro community must not lead us to a distrust of all white people, for many of our white brothers, as evidenced by their presence here today, have come to realize that their destiny is tied up with our destiny and their freedom is inextricably bound to our freedom. We cannot walk alone.

7   And as we walk, we must make the pledge that we shall march ahead. We cannot turn back. There are those who are asking the devotees of civil rights, "When will you be satisfied?" We can never be satisfied as long as the Negro is the victim of the unspeakable horrors of police brutality. We can never be satisfied as long as our bodies, heavy with the fatigue of travel, cannot gain lodging in the motels of the highways and the hotels of the cities. We cannot be satisfied as long as the Negro's basic mobility is from a smaller ghetto to a larger one. We can never be satisfied as long as a Negro in Mississippi cannot vote and a Negro in New York believes he has nothing for which to vote. No, no, we are not satisfied, and will not be satisfied until justice rolls down like waters and righteousness like a mighty stream.

8   I am not unmindful that some of you have come here out of great trials and tribulations. Some of you have come fresh from narrow jail cells. Some of you have come from areas where your quest for freedom left you battered by the storms of persecution and staggered by the winds of police brutality. You have been the veterans of creative suffering. Continue to work with the faith that unearned suffering is redemptive.

9   Go back to Mississippi, go back to Alabama, go back to South Carolina, go back to Georgia, go back to Louisiana, go back to the slums and ghettos of our northern cities, knowing that somehow this situation can and will be changed. Let us not wallow in the valley of despair.

I say to you today, my friends, that in spite of the difficulties   10
and frustrations of the moment I still have a dream. It is a dream
deeply rooted in the American dream.

I have a dream that one day this nation will rise up and live   11
out the true meaning of its creed: "We hold these truths to be self-
evident; that all men are created equal."

I have a dream that one day on the red hills of Georgia the   12
sons of former slaves and the sons of former slaveowners will be
able to sit down together at the table of brotherhood.

I have a dream that one day even the state of Mississippi, a   13
desert state sweltering with the heat of injustice and oppression,
will be transformed into an oasis of freedom and justice.

I have a dream that my four little children will one day live in   14
a nation where they will not be judged by the color of their skin
but by the content of their character.

I have a dream today.   15

I have a dream that one day the state of Alabama, whose gov-   16
ernor's lips are presently dripping with the words of interposition
and nullification, will be transformed into a situation where little
black boys and black girls will be able to join hands with little white
boys and white girls and walk together as sisters and brothers.

I have a dream today.   17

I have a dream that one day every valley shall be exalted,   18
every hill and mountain shall be made low, the rough places will be
made plain, and the crooked places will be made straight, and the
glory of the Lord shall be revealed, and all flesh shall see it together.

This is our hope. This is the faith with which I return to the   19
South. With this faith we will be able to hew out of the mountain
of despair a stone of hope. With this faith we will be able to transform the jangling discords of our nation into a beautiful symphony of brotherhood. With this faith we will be able to work
together, to pray together, to struggle together, to go to jail together, to stand up for freedom together, knowing that we will be
free one day.

This will be the day when all of God's children will be able to   20
sing with new meaning

> My country, 'tis of thee,
> Sweet land of liberty,
>   Of thee I sing:
> Land where my fathers died,
> Land of the pilgrims' pride,
> From every mountain-side
>   Let freedom ring.

21   And if America is to be a great nation this must become true. So let freedom ring from the prodigious hilltops of New Hampshire. Let freedom ring from the mighty mountains of New York. Let freedom ring from the heightening Alleghenies of Pennsylvania!

22   Let freedom ring from the snowcapped Rockies of Colorado!

23   Let freedom ring from the curvaceous peaks of California!

24   But not only that; let freedom ring from Stone Mountain of Georgia!

25   Let freedom ring from Lookout Mountain of Tennessee!

26   Let freedom ring from every hill and molehill of Mississippi. From every mountainside, let freedom ring.

27   When we let freedom ring, when we let it ring from every village and every hamlet, from every state and every city, we will be able to speed up that day when all of God's children, black men and white men, Jews and Gentiles, Protestants and Catholics, will be able to join hands and sing in the words of the old Negro spiritual, "Free at last! free at last! thank God almighty, we are free at last!"

1963

Deportations from Western Europe

Hannah Arendt

1   "Ruthless toughness," a quality held in the highest esteem by the rulers of the Third Reich, is frequently characterized in postwar

Germany, which has developed a veritable genius for under-statement with respect to her Nazi past, as being *ungut*—lacking goodness—as though nothing had been wrong with those en-dowed with this quality but a deplorable failure to act according to the exacting standards of Christian charity. In any case, men sent by Eichmann's office to other countries as "advisers on Jewish affairs"—to be attached to the regular diplomatic missions, or to the military staff, or to the local command of the Security Police—were all chosen because they possessed this virtue to the highest degree. In the beginning, during the fall and winter of 1941–42, their main job seems to have been to establish satisfactory rela-tions with the other German officials in the countries concerned, especially with the German embassies in nominally independent countries and with the Reich commissioners in occupied territo-ries; in either case, there was perpetual conflict over jurisdiction in Jewish matters.

In June, 1942, Eichmann recalled his advisers in France, Bel- 2 gium, and Holland in order to lay plans for deportations from these countries. Himmler had ordered that FRANCE be given top priority in "combing Europe from West to East," partly because of the inherent importance of the *nation par excellence,* and partly be-cause the Vichy government had shown a truly amazing "under-standing" of the Jewish problem and had introduced, on its own initiative, a great deal of anti-Jewish legislation; it had even estab-lished a special Department for Jewish Affairs, headed first by Xavier Vallant and somewhat later by Darquier de Pellepoix, both well-known anti-Semites. As a concession to the French brand of anti-Semitism, which was intimately connected with a strong, generally chauvinistic xenophobia in all strata of the population, the operation was to start with foreign Jews, and since in 1942 more than half of France's foreign Jews were stateless—refugees and émigrés from Russia, Germany, Austria, Poland, Rumania, Hungary—that is, from areas that either were under German domination or had passed anti-Jewish legislation before the out-break of war—it was decided to begin by deporting an estimated hundred thousand stateless Jews. (The total Jewish population of the country was now well over three hundred thousand; in 1939, before the influx of refugees from Belgium and Holland in the spring of 1940, there had been about two hundred and seventy thousand Jews, of whom at least a hundred and seventy thousand were foreign or foreign-born.) Fifty thousand each were to be evacuated from the Occupied Zone and from Vichy France with all speed. This was a considerable undertaking, which needed not only the agreement of the Vichy government but the active help of the French police, who were to do the work done in Germany by the Order Police. At first, there were no difficulties whatever, since, as Pierre Laval, Premier under Marshal Pétain, pointed out, "these foreign Jews had always been a problem in France," so that the "French government was glad that a change in the German attitude toward them gave France an opportunity to get rid of them." It must be added that Laval and Pétain thought in terms of these Jews' being resettled in the East; they did not yet know what "resettlement" meant.

3   Two incidents, in particular, attracted the attention of the Jerusalem court, both of which occurred in the summer of 1942, a few weeks after the operation had started. The first concerned a train due to leave Bordeaux on July 15, which had to be canceled because only a hundred and fifty stateless Jews could be found in Bordeaux—not enough to fill the train, which Eichmann had obtained with great difficulty. Whether or not Eichmann recognized this as the first indication that things might not be quite as easy as everybody felt entitled to believe, he became very excited, telling his subordinates that this was "a matter of prestige"—not in the eyes of the French but in those of the Ministry of Transport, which might get wrong ideas about the efficiency of his apparatus—and that he would "have to consider whether France should not be dropped altogether as far as evacuation was concerned" if such an incident was repeated. In Jerusalem, this threat was taken very seriously, as proof of Eichmann's power; if he wished, he could "drop France." Actually, it was one of Eichmann's ridiculous boasts, proof of his "driving power" but hardly "evidence of . . . his status in the eyes of his subordinates," except insofar as he had plainly threatened them with losing their very cozy war jobs. But if the Bordeaux incident was a farce, the second was the basis for one of the most horrible of the many hair-raising stories told at Jerusalem. This was the story of four thousand children,

330   Chapter 5   Government, Power, and Justice

separated from their parents who were already on their way to
Auschwitz. The children had been left behind at the French collection point, the concentration camp at Drancy, and on July 10
Eichmann's French representative, Hauptsturmführer Theodor
Dannecker, phoned him to ask what was to be done with them.
Eichmann took ten days to decide; then he called Dannecker back
to tell him that "as soon as transports could again be dispatched
to the General Government area [of Poland], transports of children could roll." Dr. Servatius pointed out that the whole incident
actually demonstrated that the "persons affected were determined neither by the accused nor by any members of his office."
But what, unfortunately, no one mentioned was that Dannecker
had informed Eichmann that Laval himself had proposed that
children under sixteen be included in the deportations; this meant
that the whole gruesome episode was not even the result of "superior orders" but the outcome of an agreement between France
and Germany, negotiated at the highest level.

    During the summer and fall of 1942, twenty-seven thousand ₄
stateless Jews—eighteen thousand from Paris and nine thousand
from Vichy France—were deported to Auschwitz. Then, when
there were about seventy thousand stateless Jews left in all of
France, the Germans made their first mistake. Confident that the
French had by now become so accustomed to deporting Jews that
they wouldn't mind, they asked for permission to include French
Jews also—simply to facilitate administrative matters. This
caused a complete turnabout; the French were adamant in their
refusal to hand over their own Jews to the Germans. And Himmler, upon being informed of the situation—not by Eichmann or
his men, incidentally, but by one of the Higher S.S. and Police
Leaders—immediately gave in and promised to spare French
Jews. But now it was too late. The first rumors about "resettlement" had reached France, and while French anti-Semites, and
non-anti-Semites too, would have liked to see foreign Jews settle
somewhere else, not even the anti-Semites wished to become ac-
complices in mass murder. Hence, the French now refused to take
a step they had eagerly contemplated only a short time before,
that is, to revoke naturalizations granted to Jews after 1927 (or after 1933), which would have made about fifty thousand more

Jews eligible for deportation. They also started making such endless difficulties with regard to the deportation of stateless and
other foreign Jews that all the ambitious plans for the evacuation
of Jews from France did indeed have to be "dropped." Tens of
thousands of stateless persons went into hiding, while thousands
more fled to the Italian-occupied French zone, the Côte d'Azur,
where Jews were safe, whatever their origin or nationality. In the
summer of 1943, when Germany was declared *judenrein* and the
Allies had just landed in Sicily, no more than fifty-two thousand
Jews, certainly less than twenty per cent of the total, had been deported, and of these no more than six thousand possessed French
nationality. Not even Jewish prisoners of war in the German in-
ternment camps for the French Army were singled out for "special treatment." In April, 1944, two months before the Allies
landed in France, there were still two hundred and fifty thousand
Jews in the country, and they all survived the war. The Nazis, it
turned out, possessed neither the manpower nor the will power to
remain "tough" when they met determined opposition. The truth
of the matter was, as we shall see, that even the members of the
Gestapo and the S.S. combined ruthlessness with softness.

5   At the June, 1942, meeting in Berlin, the figures set for immediate deportations from Belgium and the Netherlands had been
rather low, probably because of the high figure set for France. No
more than ten thousand Jews from Belgium and fifteen thousand
from Holland were to be seized and deported in the immediate
future. In both cases the figures were later significantly enlarged,
probably because of the difficulties encountered in the French operation. The situation of BELGIUM was peculiar in some respects.
The country was ruled exclusively by German military authorities, and the police, as a Belgian government report submitted to
the court pointed out, "did not have the same influence upon the
other German administration services that they enjoyed in other
places." (Belgium's governor, General Alexander von Falken-
hausen, was later implicated in the July, 1944, conspiracy against
Hitler.) Native collaborators were of importance only in Flanders;
the Fascist movement among the French-speaking Walloons,
headed by Degrelle, had little influence. The Belgian police did

not cooperate with the Germans, and the Belgian railway men could not even be trusted to leave deportation trains alone. They contrived to leave doors unlocked or to arrange ambushes, so that Jews could escape. Most peculiar was the composition of the Jewish population. Before the outbreak of war, there were ninety thousand Jews, of whom about thirty thousand were German Jewish refugees, while another fifty thousand came from other European countries. By the end of 1940, nearly forty thousand Jews had fled the country, and among the fifty thousand who remained there were at the most five thousand native-born Belgian citizens. Moreover among those who had fled were all the more important Jewish leaders, most of whom had been foreigners anyway, so that the Jewish Council did not command any authority among native Jews. With this "lack of understanding" on all sides, it is not surprising that very few Belgian Jews were deported. But recently naturalized and stateless Jews—of Czech, Polish, Russian, and German origin, many of whom had only recently arrived—were easily recognizable and most difficult to hide in the small, completely industrialized country. By the end of 1942, fifteen thousand had been shipped to Auschwitz, and by the fall of 1944, when the Allies liberated the country, a total of twenty-five thousand had been killed. Eichmann had his usual "adviser" in Belgium, but the adviser seems not to have been very active in these operations. They were carried out, finally, by the military administration, under increased pressure from the Foreign Office.

As in practically all other countries, the deportations from 6 HOLLAND started with stateless Jews, who in this instance consisted almost entirely of refugees from Germany, whom the prewar Dutch government had officially declared to be "undesirable." There were about thirty-five thousand foreign Jews altogether in a total Jewish population of a hundred and forty thousand. Unlike Belgium, Holland was placed under a civil administration, and, unlike France, the country had no government of its own, since the cabinet, together with the royal family, had fled to London. The small nation was utterly at the mercy of the Germans and of the S.S. Eichmann's "adviser" in Holland was a certain Willi Zöpf (recently arrested in Germany, while the much more efficient adviser in France, Mr. Dannecker, is still at large) but he apparently had very little to say and could hardly do more than keep the Berlin office posted. Deportations and everything connected with them were handled by the lawyer Erich Rajakow- itsch, Eichmann's former legal adviser in Vienna and Prague, who was admitted to the S.S. upon Eichmann's recommendation. He had been sent to Holland by Heydrich in April, 1941, and was di- rectly responsible not to the R.S.H.A. in Berlin but to the local head of the Security Service in The Hague, Dr. Wilhelm Harsten, who in turn was under the command of the Higher S.S. and Police Leader Obergruppenführer Hans Rauter and his assistant in Jew- ish affairs, Ferdinand aus der Fünten. (Rauter and Fünten were condemned to death by a Dutch court; Rauter was executed and Fünten's sentence, allegedly after special intervention from Ade- nauer, was commuted to life imprisonment. Harsten, too, was brought to trial in Holland, sentenced to twelve years' imprison- ment, and released in 1957, whereupon he entered the civil serv- ice of the Bavarian state government. The Dutch authorities are considering proceedings against Rajakowitsch, who seems to live in either Switzerland or Italy. All these details have become known in the last year through the publication of Dutch docu- ments and the report by E. Jacob, Dutch correspondent for the *Basler Nationalzeitung,* a Swiss newspaper.) The prosecution in Jerusalem, partly because it wanted to build up Eichmann at all costs and partly because it got genuinely lost in the intricacies of German bureaucracy, claimed that all these officers had carried out Eichmann's orders. But the Higher S.S. and Police Leaders took orders only directly from Himmler, and that Rajakowitsch was still taking orders from Eichmann at this time is highly un- likely, especially in view of what was then going to happen in Holland. The judgment, without engaging in polemics, quietly corrected a great number of errors made by the prosecution— though probably not all—and showed the constant jockeying for position that went on between the R.S.H.A. and the Higher S.S. and Police Leaders and other offices—the "tenacious, eternal, everlasting negotiations," as Eichmann called them.

7   Eichmann had been especially upset by the arrangements in Holland, because it was clearly Himmler himself who was cutting

him down to size, quite apart from the fact that the zeal of the gentlemen in residence created great difficulties for him in the timing
of his own transports and generally made a mockery of the
importance of the "coordinating center" in Berlin. Thus, right at
the beginning, twenty thousand instead of fifteen thousand Jews
were deported, and Eichmann's Mr. Zöpf, who was far inferior in
rank as well as in position to all others present, was almost forced
to speed up deportations in 1943. Conflicts of jurisdiction in these
matters were to plague Eichmann at all times, and it was in vain
that he explained to anybody who would listen that "it would be
contradictory to the order of the Reichsführer S.S. [i.e., Himmler]
and illogical if at this stage other authorities again were to handle
the Jewish problem." The last clash in Holland came in 1944, and
this time even Kaltenbrunner tried to intervene, for the sake of
uniformity. In Holland, Sephardic Jews, of Spanish origin, had
been exempted, although Jews of that origin had been sent to
Auschwitz from Salonika. The judgment was in error when it ven-
tured that the R.S.H.A. "had the upper hand in this dispute"—for
God knows what reasons, some three hundred and seventy
Sephardic Jews remained unmolested in Amsterdam.

The reason Himmler preferred to work in Holland through [8]
his Higher S.S. and Police Leaders was simple. These men knew
their way around the country, and the problem posed by the
Dutch population was by no means an easy one. Holland had
been the only country in all Europe where students went on strike
when Jewish professors were dismissed and where a wave of
strikes broke out in response to the first deportation of Jews to
German concentration camps—and that deportation, in contrast
to those to extermination camps, was merely a punitive measure,
taken long before the Final Solution had reached Holland. (The
Germans, as de Jong points out, were taught a lesson. From now
on, "the persecution was carried out not with the cudgels of the
Nazi storm troops . . . , but by decrees published in *Verordeningen-
blad* . . . , which the *Joodsche Weekblad* was forced to carry." Police
raids in the streets no longer occurred and there were no strikes
on the part of the population.) However, the widespread hostility
in Holland toward anti-Jewish measures and the relative immu-

nity of the Dutch people to anti-Semitism were held in check by two factors, which eventually proved fatal to the Jews. First, there existed a very strong Nazi movement in Holland, which could be trusted to carry out such police measures as seizing Jews, ferreting out their hiding places, and so on; second, there existed an inordinately strong tendency among the native Jews to draw a line between themselves and the new arrivals, which was probably the result of the very unfriendly attitude of the Dutch government toward refugees from Germany, and probably also because anti-Semitism in Holland, just as in France, focused on foreign Jews. This made it relatively easy for the Nazis to form their Jewish Council, the *Joodsche Raad*, which remained for a long time under the impression that only German and other foreign Jews would be victims of the deportations, and it also enabled the S.S. to enlist, in addition to Dutch police units, the help of a Jewish police force. The result was a catastrophe unparalleled in any Western country; it can be compared only with the extinction, under vastly different and, from the beginning, completely desperate conditions, of Polish Jewry. Although, in contrast with Poland, the attitude of the Dutch people permitted a large number of Jews to go into hiding—twenty to twenty-five thousand, a very high figure for such a small country—yet an unusually large number of Jews living underground, at least half of them, were eventually found, no doubt through the efforts of professional and occasional informers. By July, 1944, a hundred and thirteen thousand Jews had been deported, most of them to Sobibor, a camp in the Lublin area of Poland, by the river Bug, where no selections of able-bodied workers ever took place. Three-fourths of all Jews living in Holland were killed, about two-thirds of these native-born Dutch Jews. The last shipments left in the fall of 1944, when Allied patrols were at the Dutch borders. Of the ten thousand Jews who survived in hiding, about seventy-five per cent were foreigners— a percentage that testifies to the unwillingness of Dutch Jews to face reality.

9   At the Wannsee Conference, Martin Luther, of the Foreign Office, warned of great difficulties in the Scandinavian countries,

notably in Norway and Denmark. (Sweden was never occupied, and Finland, though in the war on the side of the Axis, was the one country the Nazis hardly ever even approached on the Jewish question. This surprising exception of Finland, with some two thousand Jews, may have been due to Hitler's great esteem for the Finns, whom perhaps he did not want to subject to threats and humiliating blackmail.) Luther proposed postponing evacuations from Scandinavia for the time being, and as far as Denmark was concerned, this really went without saying, since the country retained its independent government, and was respected as a neutral state, until the fall of 1943, although it, along with Norway, had been invaded by the German Army in April, 1940. There existed no Fascist or Nazi movement in Denmark worth mentioning, and therefore no collaborators. In Norway, however, the Germans had been able to find enthusiastic supporters; indeed, Vidkun Quisling, leader of the pro-Nazi and anti-Semitic Norwegian party, gave his name to what later became known as a "quisling government." The bulk of Norway's seventeen hundred Jews were stateless, refugees from Germany; they were seized and interned in a few lightning operations in October and November, 1942. When Eichmann's office ordered their deportation to Auschwitz, some of Quisling's own men resigned their government posts. This may not have come as a surprise to Mr. Luther and the Foreign Office, but what was much more serious, and certainly totally unexpected, was that Sweden immediately offered asylum, and sometimes even Swedish nationality, to all who were persecuted. Ernst von Weizsäcker, Undersecretary of State of the Foreign Office, who received the proposal, refused to discuss it, but the offer helped nevertheless. It is always relatively easy to get out of a country illegally, whereas it is nearly impossible to enter the place of refuge without permission and to dodge the immigration authorities. Hence, about nine hundred people, slightly more than half of the small Norwegian community, could be smuggled into Sweden.

It was in Denmark, however, that the Germans found out 10 how fully justified the Foreign Office's apprehensions had been. The story of the Danish Jews is *sui generis*, and the behavior of the

Danish people and their government was unique among all the countries of Europe—whether occupied, or a partner of the Axis, or neutral and truly independent. One is tempted to recommend the story as required reading in political science for all students who wish to learn something about the enormous power potential inherent in non-violent action and in resistance to an opponent possessing vastly superior means of violence. To be sure, a few other countries in Europe lacked proper "understanding of the Jewish question," and actually a majority of them were opposed to "radical" and "final" solutions. Like Denmark, Sweden, Italy, and Bulgaria proved to be nearly immune to anti-Semitism, but of the three that were in the German sphere of influence, only the Danes dared speak out on the subject to their German masters. Italy and Bulgaria sabotaged German orders and indulged in a complicated game of double-dealing and double-crossing, saving their Jews by a tour de force of sheer ingenuity, but they never contested the policy as such. That was totally different from what the Danes did. When the Germans approached them rather cautiously about introducing the yellow badge, they were simply told that the King would be the first to wear it, and the Danish government officials were careful to point out that anti-Jewish measures of any sort would cause their own immediate resignation. It was decisive in this whole matter that the Germans did not even succeed in introducing the vitally important distinction between native Danes of Jewish origin, of whom there were about sixty-four hundred, and the fourteen hundred German Jewish refugees who had found asylum in the country prior to the war and who now had been declared stateless by the German government. This refusal must have surprised the Germans no end, since it appeared so "illogical" for a government to protect people to whom it had categorically denied naturalization and even permission to work. (Legally, the prewar situation of refugees in Denmark was not unlike that in France, except that the general corruption in the Third Republic's civil services enabled a few of them to obtain naturalization papers, through bribes or "connections," and most refugees in France could work illegally, without a permit. But Denmark, like Switzerland, was no country *pour se débrouilller*.) The Danes,

however, explained to the German officials that because the stateless refugees were no longer German citizens, the Nazis could not
claim them without Danish assent. This was one of the few cases
in which statelessness turned out to be an asset, although it was of
course not statelessness per se that saved the Jews but, on the contrary, the fact that the Danish government had decided to protect
them. Thus, none of the preparatory moves, so important for the
bureaucracy of murder, could be carried out, and operations were
postponed until the fall of 1943.

What happened then was truly amazing; compared with what   11
took place in other European countries, everything went topsy-
turvy. In August, 1943—after the German offensive in Russia had
failed, the Afrika Korps had surrendered in Tunisia, and the Allies
had invaded Italy—the Swedish government canceled its 1940
agreement with Germany which had permitted German troops the
right to pass through the country. Thereupon, the Danish workers
decided that they could help a bit in hurrying things up; riots
broke out in Danish shipyards, where the dock workers refused to
repair German ships and then went on strike. The German military
commander proclaimed a state of emergency and imposed martial
law, and Himmler thought this was the right moment to tackle the
Jewish question, whose "solution" was long overdue. What he did
not reckon with was that—quite apart from Danish resistance—the
German officials who had been living in the country for years were
no longer the same. Not only did General von Hannecken, the military commander, refuse to put troops at the disposal of the Reich
plenipotentiary, Dr. Werner Best; the special S.S. units *(Einsatzkom-
mandos)* employed in Denmark very frequently objected to "the
measures they were ordered to carry out by the central agencies"—according to Best's testimony at Nuremberg. And Best himself, an old Gestapo man and former legal adviser to Heydrich,
author of a then famous book on the police, who had worked for
the military government in Paris to the entire satisfaction of his superiors, could no longer be trusted, although it is doubtful that
Berlin ever learned the extent of his unreliability. Still, it was clear
from the beginning that things were not going well, and Eichmann's office sent one of its best men to Denmark—Rolf Günther,

whom no one had ever accused of not possessing the required "ruthless toughness." Günther made no impression on his colleagues in Copenhagen, and now von Hannecken refused even to issue a decree requiring all Jews to report for work.

12   Best went to Berlin and obtained a promise that all Jews from Denmark would be sent to Theresienstadt regardless of their category—a very important concession, from the Nazis' point of view. The night of October 1 was set for their seizure and immediate departure—ships were ready in the harbor—and since neither the Danes nor the Jews nor the German troops stationed in Denmark could be relied on to help, police units arrived from Germany for a door-to-door search. At the last moment, Best told them that they were not permitted to break into apartments, because the Danish police might then interfere, and they were not supposed to fight it out with the Danes. Hence they could seize only those Jews who voluntarily opened their doors. They found exactly 477 people, out of a total of more than 7,800, at home and willing to let them in. A few days before the date of doom, a German shipping agent, Georg F. Duckwitz, having probably been tipped off by Best himself, had revealed the whole plan to Danish government officials, who, in turn, had hurriedly informed the heads of the Jewish community. They, in marked contrast to Jewish leaders in other countries, had then communicated the news openly in the synagogues on the occasion of the New Year services. The Jews had just time enough to leave their apartments and go into hiding, which was very easy in Denmark, because, in the words of the judgment, "all sections of the Danish people, from the King down to simple citizens," stood ready to receive them.

13   They might have remained in hiding until the end of the war if the Danes had not been blessed with Sweden as a neighbor. It seemed reasonable to ship the Jews to Sweden, and this was done with the help of the Danish fishing fleet. The cost of transportation for people without means—about a hundred dollars per person—was paid largely by wealthy Danish citizens, and that was perhaps the most astounding feat of all, since this was a time when Jews were paying for their own deportation, when the rich among them were paying fortunes for exit permits (in Holland,

Slovakia, and, later, in Hungary) either by bribing the local authorities or by negotiating "legally" with the S.S., who accepted
only hard currency and sold exit permits, in Holland, to the tune
of five or ten thousand dollars per person. Even in places where
Jews met with genuine sympathy and a sincere willingness to
help, they had to pay for it, and the chances poor people had of
escaping were nil.

It took the better part of October to ferry all the Jews across 14
the five to fifteen miles of water that separates Denmark from
Sweden. The Swedes received 5,919 refugees, of whom at least
1,000 were of German origin, 1,310 were half-Jews, and 686 were
non-Jews married to Jews. (Almost half the Danish Jews seem to
have remained in the country and survived the war in hiding.)
The non-Danish Jews were better off than ever before, they all
received permission to work. The few hundred Jews whom the
German police had been able to arrest were shipped to Theresienstadt. They were old or poor people, who either had not received
the news in time or had not been able to comprehend its meaning.
In the ghetto, they enjoyed greater privileges than any other
group because of the never-ending "fuss" made about them by
Danish institutions and private persons. Forty-eight persons died,
a figure that was not particularly high, in view of the average age
of the group. When everything was over, it was the considered
opinion of Eichmann that "for various reasons the action against
the Jews in Denmark has been a failure," whereas the curious Dr.
Best declared that "the objective of the operation was not to seize
a great number of Jews but to clean Denmark of Jews, and this objective has now been achieved."

Politically and psychologically, the most interesting aspect of 15
this incident is perhaps the role played by the German authorities
in Denmark, their obvious sabotage of orders from Berlin. It is the
only case we know of in which the Nazis met with *open* native resistance, and the result seems to have been that those exposed to
it changed their minds. They themselves apparently no longer
looked upon the extermination of a whole people as a matter of
course. They had met resistance based on principle, and their
"toughness" had melted like butter in the sun, they had even

been able to show a few timid beginnings of genuine courage. That the ideal of "toughness," except, perhaps, for a few half-demented brutes, was nothing but a myth of self-deception, concealing a ruthless desire for conformity at any price, was clearly revealed at the Nuremberg Trials, where the defendants accused and betrayed each other and assured the world that they "had always been against it" or claimed, as Eichmann was to do, that their best qualities had been "abused" by their superiors. (In Jerusalem, he accused "those in power" of having abused his "obedience." "The subject of a good government is lucky, the subject of a bad government is unlucky. I had no luck.") The atmosphere had changed, and although most of them must have known that they were doomed, not a single one of them had the guts to defend the Nazi ideology. Werner Best claimed at Nuremberg that he had played a complicated double role and that it was thanks to him that the Danish officials had been warned of the impending catastrophe; documentary evidence showed, on the contrary, that he himself had proposed the Danish operation in Berlin, but he explained that this was all part of the game. He was extradited to Denmark and there condemned to death, but he appealed the sentence, with surprising results; because of "new evidence," his sentence was commuted to five years in prison, from which he was released soon afterward. He must have been able to prove to the satisfaction of the Danish court that he really had done his best.

16   ITALY was Germany's only real ally in Europe, treated as an equal and respected as a sovereign independent state. The alliance presumably rested on the very highest kind of common interest, binding together two similar, if not identical, new forms of government, and it is true that Mussolini had once been greatly admired in German Nazi circles. But by the time war broke out and Italy, after some hesitation, joined in the German enterprise, this was a thing of the past. The Nazis knew well enough that they had more in common with Stalin's version of Communism than with Italian Fascism, and Mussolini on his part had neither much confidence in Germany nor much admiration for Hitler. All this, however, belonged among the secrets of the higher-ups, especially in Germany,

and the deep, decisive differences between the totalitarian and the Fascist forms of government were never entirely understood by the world at large. Nowhere did they come more conspicuously into the open than in the treatment of the Jewish question.

Prior to the Badoglio *coup d'état* in the summer of 1943, and the German occupation of Rome and northern Italy, Eichmann and his men were not permitted to be active in the country. They were, however, confronted with the Italian way of *not* solving anything in the Italian-occupied areas of France, Greece, and Yugoslavia, because the persecuted Jews kept escaping into these zones, where they could be sure of temporary asylum. On levels much higher than Eichmann's, Italy's sabotage of the Final Solution had assumed serious proportions, chiefly because of Mussolini's influence on other Fascist governments in Europe—on Pétain's in France, on Horthy's in Hungary, on Antonescu's in Rumania, and even on Franco's in Spain. If Italy could get away with not murdering her Jews, German satellite countries might try to do the same. Thus, Dome Sztojai, the Hungarian Prime Minister whom the Germans had forced upon Horthy, always wanted to know, when it came to anti-Jewish measures, if the same regulations applied to Italy. Eichmann's chief, Gruppenführer Müller, wrote a long letter on the subject to the Foreign Office pointing all this out, but the gentlemen of the Foreign Office could not do much about it, because they always met the same subtly veiled resistance, the same promises and the same failures to fulfill them. The sabotage was all the more infuriating as it was carried out openly, in an almost mocking manner. The promises were given by Mussolini himself or other high-ranking officials, and if the generals simply failed to fulfill them, Mussolini would make excuses for them on the ground of their "different intellectual formation." Only occasionally would the Nazis be met with a flat refusal, as when General Roatta declared that it was "incompatible with the honor of the Italian Army" to deliver the Jews from Italian-occupied territory in Yugoslavia to the appropriate German authorities.

It could be considerably worse when Italians seemed to be fulfilling their promises. One instance of this took place after the Allied landing in French North Africa, when all of France was occupied by the Germans except the Italian Zone in the south, where about fifty thousand Jews had found safety. Under considerable German pressure, an Italian "Commissariat for Jewish Affairs" was established, whose sole function was to register all Jews in this region and expel them from the Mediterranean coast. Twenty-two thousand Jews were indeed seized and removed to the interior of the Italian Zone, with the result, according to Reitlinger, that "a thousand Jews of the poorest class were living in the best hotels of Isère and Savoie." Eichmann thereupon sent Alois Brunner, one of his toughest men, down to Nice and Marseilles, but by the time he arrived, the French police had destroyed all the lists of the registered Jews. In the fall of 1943, when Italy declared war on Germany, the German army could finally move into Nice, and Eichmann himself hastened to the Côte d'Azur. There he was told—and believed—that between ten and fifteen thousand Jews were living in hiding in Monaco (that tiny principality, with some twenty-five thousand residents altogether, whose territory, the *New York Times Magazine* noted, "could fit comfortably inside Central Park"), which caused the R.S.H.A. to start a kind of research program. It sounds like a typically Italian joke. The Jews, in any event, were no longer there; they had fled to Italy proper, and those who were still hiding in the surrounding mountains found their way to Switzerland or to Spain. The same thing happened when the Italians had to abandon their zone in Yugoslavia; the Jews left with the Italian Army and found refuge in Fiume.

19   An element of farce had never been lacking even in Italy's most serious efforts to adjust to its powerful friend and ally. When Mussolini, under German pressure, introduced anti-Jewish legislation in the late thirties he stipulated the usual exemptions—war veterans, Jews with high decorations, and the like—but he added one more category, namely, former members of the Fascist Party, together with their parents and grandparents, their wives and children and grandchildren. I know of no statistics relating to this matter, but the result must have been that the great majority of Italian Jews were exempted. There can hardly have been a Jewish family without at least one member in the Fascist Party, for this happened at a time when Jews, like other Italians, had been flocking for almost twenty years into the Fascist movement, since

positions in the Civil Service were open only to members. And the few Jews who had objected to Fascism on principle, Socialists and Communists chiefly, were no longer in the country. Even convinced Italian anti-Semites seemed unable to take the thing seriously, and Roberto Farinacci, head of the Italian anti-Semitic movement, had a Jewish secretary in his employ. To be sure, such things had happened in Germany too; Eichmann mentioned, and there is no reason not to believe him, that there were Jews even among ordinary S.S. men, but the Jewish origin of people like Heydrich, Milch, and others was a highly confidential matter, known only to a handful of people, whereas in Italy these things were done openly and, as it were, innocently. The key to the riddle was, of course, that Italy actually was one of the few countries in Europe where all anti-Jewish measures were decidedly unpopular, since, in the words of Ciano, they "raised a problem which fortunately did not exist."

Assimilation, that much abused word, was a sober fact in Italy, [20] which had a community of not more than fifty thousand native Jews, whose history reached back into the centuries of the Roman Empire. It was not an ideology, something one was supposed to believe in, as in all German-speaking countries, or a myth and an obvious self-deception, as notably in France. Italian Fascism, not to be outdone in "ruthless toughness," had tried to rid the country of foreign and stateless Jews prior to the outbreak of the war. This had never been much of a success, because of the general unwillingness of the minor Italian officials to get "tough," and when things had become a matter of life and death, they refused, under the pretext of maintaining their sovereignty, to abandon this part of their Jewish population; they put them instead into Italian camps, where they were quite safe until the Germans occupied the country. This conduct can hardly be explained by objective conditions alone—the absence of a "Jewish question"—for these foreigners naturally created a problem in Italy, as they did in every European nation-state based upon the ethnic and cultural homogeneity of its population. What in Denmark was the result of an authentically political sense, an inbred comprehension of the requirements and responsibilities of citizenship and independence—"for the Danes . . . the

Jewish question was a political and not a humanitarian question" (Leni Yahil)—was in Italy the outcome of the almost automatic general humanity of an old and civilized people.

21   Italian humanity, moreover, withstood the test of the terror that descended upon the people during the last year and a half of the war. In December, 1943, the German Foreign Office addressed a formal request for help to Eichmann's boss, Müller: "In view of the lack of zeal shown over the last months by Italian officials in the implementation of anti-Jewish measures recommended by the Duce, we of the Foreign Office deem it urgent and necessary that the implementation . . . be supervised by German officials." Whereupon famous Jew-killers from Poland, such as Odilo Globocnik from the death camps in the Lublin area, were dispatched to Italy; even the head of the military administration was not an Army man but a former governor of Polish Galicia, Gruppenführer Otto Wächter. This put an end to practical jokes. Eichmann's office sent out a circular advising its branches that "Jews of Italian nationality" would at once become subject to "the necessary measures," and the first blow was to fall upon eight thousand Jews in Rome, who were to be arrested by German police regiments, since the Italian police were not reliable. They were warned in time, frequently by old Fascists, and seven thousand escaped. The Germans, yielding, as usual, when they met resistance, now agreed that Italian Jews, even if they did not belong to exempted categories, should not be subject to deportation but should merely be concentrated in Italian camps; this "solution" should be "final" enough for Italy. Approximately thirty-five thousand Jews in northern Italy were caught and put into concentration camps near the Austrian border. In the spring of 1944, when the Red Army had occupied Rumania and the Allies were about to enter Rome, the Germans broke their promise and began shipping Jews from Italy to Auschwitz—about seventy-five hundred people, of whom no more than six hundred returned. Still, this came to considerably less than ten percent of all Jews then living in Italy.

1963

A Modest Proposal

Jonathan Swift

It is a melancholy object to those who walk through this great 1
town[1] or travel in the country, when they see the streets, the roads,
and cabin doors, crowded with beggars of the female sex, followed
by three, four, or six children, all in rags and importuning every
passenger for an alms. These mothers, instead of being able to
work for their honest livelihood, are forced to employ all their
time in strolling to beg sustenance for their helpless infants, who,
as they grow up, either turn thieves for want of work, or leave
their dear native country to fight for the Pretender in Spain,[2] or
sell themselves to the Barbadoes.

I think it is agreed by all parties that this prodigious number 2
of children in the arms, or on the backs, or at the heels of their
mothers, and frequently of their fathers, is in the present deplorable
state of the kingdom a very great additional grievance; and therefore whoever could find out a fair, cheap, and easy method of
making these children sound, useful members of the common-
wealth would deserve so well of the public as to have his statue
set up for a preserver of the nation.

But my intention is very far from being confined to provide 3
only for the children of professed beggars; it is of a much greater
extent, and shall take in the whole number of infants at a certain
age who are born of parents in effect as little able to support them
as those who demand our charity in the streets.

As to my own part, having turned my thoughts for many 4
years upon this important subject, and maturely weighed the
several schemes of other projectors, I have always found them
grossly mistaken in their computation. It is true, a child just
dropped from its dam may be supported by her milk for a solar
year, with little other nourishment; at most not above the value of
two shillings, which the mother may certainly get, or the value in
scraps, by her lawful occupation of begging; and it is exactly at

[1]Dublin, Ireland.
[2]The son James II, whose Catholic sympathies cost him the English throne.

one year old that I propose to provide for them in such a manner as instead of being a charge upon their parents or the parish, or wanting food and raiment for the rest of their lives, they shall on the contrary contribute to the feeding, and partly to the clothing, of many thousands.

5   There is likewise another great advantage in my scheme, that it will prevent those involuntary abortions, and that horrid practice of women murdering their bastard children, alas, too frequent among us, sacrificing the poor innocent babes, I doubt, more to avoid the expense than the shame, which would move tears and pity in the most savage and inhuman breast.

6   The number of souls in this kingdom being usually reckoned one million and a half, of these I calculate there may be about two hundred thousand couples whose wives are breeders, from which number I subtract thirty thousand couples who are able to maintain their own children, although I apprehend there cannot be so many under the present distress of the kingdom; but this being granted, there will remain an hundred and seventy thousand breeders. I again subtract fifty thousand for those women who miscarry, or whose children die by accident or disease within the year. There only remain an hundred and twenty thousand children of poor parents annually born. The question therefore is, how this number shall be reared and provided for, which, as I have already said, under the present situation of affairs, is utterly impossible by all the methods hitherto proposed. For we can neither employ them in handicraft nor agriculture; we neither build houses (I mean in the country) nor cultivate land. They can very seldom pick up livelihood by stealing till they arrive at six years old, except where they are of towardly parts;[3] although I confess they learn the rudiments much earlier, during which time they can however be looked upon only as probationers, as I have been informed by a principal gentleman in the county of Cavan, who protested to me that he never knew above one or two instances under the age of six, even in a part of the kingdom so renowned for the quickest proficiency in that art.

[3]Mature for their age.

I am assured by our merchants that a boy or a girl before 7
twelve years old is no salable commodity; and even when they
come to this age, they will not yield above three pounds, or three
pounds and half a crown at most on the Exchange; which cannot
turn to account either to the parents or the kingdom, the charge of
nutriment and rags having been at least four times that value.

I shall now therefore humbly propose my own thoughts, 8
which I hope will not be liable to the least objection.

I have been assured by a very knowing American of my ac- 9
quaintance in London, that a young healthy child well nursed is
at a year old a most delicious, nourishing, and wholesome food,
whether stewed, roasted, baked, or boiled; and I make no doubt
that it will equally serve in fricasee or a ragout.

I do therefore humbly offer it to public consideration that of 10
the hundred and twenty thousand children, already computed,
twenty thousand may be reserved for breed, whereof only one
fourth part to be males, which is more than we allow to sheep,
black cattle, or swine; and my reason is that these children are
seldom the fruits of marriage, a circumstance not much regarded
by our savages, therefore one male will be sufficient to serve four
females. That the remaining hundred thousand may at a year old
be offered in sale to the persons of quality and fortune through
the kingdom, always advising the mother to let them suck plen-
tifully in the last month, so as to render them plump and fat for a
good table. A child will make two dishes at an entertainment for
friends; and when the family dines alone, the fore or hind quarter will make a reasonable dish, and seasoned with a little pepper
or salt will be very good boiled on the fourth day, especially in
winter.

I have reckoned upon a medium that a child just born will 11
weigh twelve pounds, and in a solar year if tolerably nursed in-
creaseth to twenty-eight pounds.

I grant this food will be somewhat dear, and therefore very 12
proper for landlords, who, as they have already devoured most of
the parents, seem to have the best title to the children.

Infant's flesh will be in season throughout the year, but more 13
plentiful in March, and a little before and after. For we are told by

a grave author, an eminent French physician,[4] that fish being a prolific diet, there are more children born in Roman Catholic countries about nine months after Lent, than at any other season; therefore, reckoning a year after Lent, the markets will be more glutted than usual, because the number of popish infants is at least three to one in this kingdom; and therefore it will have one other collateral advantage, by lessening the number of Papists among us.

14   I have already computed the charge of nursing a beggar's child (in which list I reckon all cottagers, laborers, and four fifths of the farmers) to be about two shillings per annum, rags included; and I believe no gentleman would repine to give ten shillings for the carcass of a good fat child, which, as I have said, will make four dishes of excellent nutritive meat, when he hath only some particular friend or his own family to dine with him. Thus the squire will learn to be a good landlord, and grow popular among the tenants; the mother will have eight shillings net profit, and be fit for work till she produces another child.

15   Those who are more thrifty (as I must confess the times require) may flay the carcass; the skin of which artificially[5] dressed will make admirable gloves for ladies, and summer boots for fine gentlemen.

16   As to our city of Dublin, shambles[6] may be appointed for this purpose in the most convenient parts of it, and butchers we may be assured will not be wanting; although I rather recommend buying the children alive, and dressing them hot from the knife as we do roasting pigs.

17   A very worthy person, a true lover of his country, and whose virtues I highly esteem, was lately pleased in discoursing on this matter to offer a refinement upon my scheme. He said that many gentlemen of his kingdom, having of late destroyed their deer, he conceived that the want of venison might be well supplied by the

[4]François Rabelais, doctor, monk, and scholar, who was also one of the greatest comic writers of the sixteenth century.
[5]Expertly.
[6]Places where animals are butchered.

bodies of young lads and maidens, not exceeding fourteen years of age nor under twelve, so great a number of both sexes in every county being now ready to starve for want of work and service; and these to be disposed of by their parents, if alive, or otherwise by their nearest relations. But with due deference to so excellent a friend and so deserving a patriot, I cannot be altogether in his sentiments; for as to the males, my American acquaintance assured me from frequent experience that their flesh was generally tough and lean, like that of our schoolboys, by continual exercise, and their taste disagreeable; and to fatten them would not answer the charge. Then as to the females, it would, I think with humble submission, be a loss to the public, because they soon would become breeders themselves; and besides, it is not improbable that some scrupulous people might be apt to censure such a practice (although indeed very unjustly) as a little bordering upon cruelty; which, I confess, hath always been with me the strongest objection against any project, how well soever intended.

But in order to justify my friend, he confessed that this expe- 18
dient was put into his head by the famous Psalmanazar,[7] a native of the island Formosa, who came from thence to London above twenty years ago, and in conversation told my friend that in his country when any young person happened to be put to death, the executioner sold the carcass to the persons of quality as a prime dainty; and that in his time the body of a plump girl of fifteen, who was crucified for an attempt to poison the emperor, was sold to his Imperial Majesty's prime minister of state, and other great mandarins of the court, in joints from the gibbet, at four hundred crowns. Neither indeed can I deny that if the same use were made of several plump young girls in this town, who without one single groat to their fortunes cannot stir abroad without a chair,[8] and appear at the playhouse and assemblies in foreign fineries which they never will pay for, the kingdom would not be the worse.

Some persons of a desponding spirit are in great concern 19
about that vast number of poor people who are aged, diseased, or

---

[7]A charlatan who fraudulently claimed to have come from Formosa.
[8]A conveyance carried by servants.

maimed, and I have been desired to employ my thoughts what course may be taken to ease the nation of so grievous an encumbrance. But I am not in the least pain upon that matter, because it is very well known that they are every day dying and rotting by cold and famine, and filth and vermin, as fast as can be reasonably expected. And as to the younger laborers, they are now in almost as hopeful a condition. They cannot get work, and consequently pine away for want of nourishment to a degree that if any time they are accidentally hired to common labor, they have not strength to perform it; and thus the country and themselves are happily delivered from the evils to come.

20   I have too long digressed, and therefore shall return to my subject. I think the advantages by the proposal which I have made are obvious and many, as well as of the highest importance.

21   For first, as I have already observed, it would greatly lessen the number of Papists, with whom we are yearly overrun, being the principal breeders of the nation as well as our most dangerous enemies; and who stay at home on purpose to deliver the kingdom to the Pretender, hoping to take their advantage by the absence of so many good Protestants, who have chosen rather to leave their country than to stay at home and pay tithes against their conscience to an Episcopal curate.

22   Secondly, the poorer tenants will have something valuable of their own, which by law may be made liable to distress,[9] and help to pay their landlord's rent, their corn and cattle being already seized and money a thing unknown.

23   Thirdly, whereas the maintenance of an hundred thousand children, from two years old and upwards, cannot be computed at less than ten shillings a piece per annum, the nation's stock will be thereby increased fifty thousand pounds per annum, besides the profit of a new dish introduced to the tables of all gentlemen of fortune in the kingdom who have any refinement in taste. And the money will circulate among ourselves, the goods being entirely of our own growth and manufacture.

[9]Confiscated as payment for debt.

Fourthly, the constant breeders, besides the gain of eight [24] shillings sterling per annum by the sale of their children, will be rid of the charge for maintaining them after the first year.

Fifthly, this food would likewise bring great custom to tav- [25] erns, where the vintners will certainly be so prudent as to procure the best receipts for dressing it to perfection, and consequently have their houses frequented by all the fine gentlemen, who justly value themselves upon their knowledge in good eating; and a skillful cook, who understands how to oblige his guests, will contrive to make it as expensive as they please.

Sixthly, this would be a great inducement to marriage, which [26] all wise nations have either encouraged by rewards or enforced by laws and penalties. It would increase the care and tenderness of mothers toward their children, when they were sure of a settlement for life to the poor babes, provided in some sort by the public, to their annual profit instead of expense. We should see an honest emulation among the married women, which of them could bring the fattest child to the market. Men would become as fond of their wives during the time of pregnancy as they are now of their mares in foal, their cows in calf, or sows when they are ready to farrow; nor offer to beat or kick them (as is too frequent a practice) for fear of a miscarriage.

Many other advantages might be enumerated. For instance, [27] the addition of some thousand carcasses in our exportation of barreled beef, the propagation of swine's flesh, and improvements in the art of making good bacon, so much wanted among us by the great destruction of pigs, too frequent at our tables, which are no way comparable in taste or magnificence to a well-grown, fat, yearling child, which roasted whole will make a considerable figure at a lord mayor's feast or any other public entertainment. But this and many others I omit, being studious of brevity.

Supposing that one thousand families in this city would be [28] constant customers for infants' flesh, besides others who might have it at merry meetings, particularly weddings and christenings, I compute that Dublin would take off annually about twenty thousand carcasses, and the rest of the kingdom (where probably they will be sold somewhat cheaper) the remaining eighty thousand.

29   I can think of no one objection that will possibly be raised against this proposal, unless it should be urged that the number of people will be thereby much lessened in the kingdom. This I freely own, and it was indeed one principal design in offering it to the world. I desire the reader will observe; that I calculate my remedy for this one individual kingdom of Ireland and for no other that ever was, is, or I think ever can be upon earth. Therefore, let no man talk to me of other expedients: of taxing our absentees at five shillings a pound: of using neither clothes nor household furniture except what is of our own growth and manufacture: of utterly rejecting the materials and instruments that promote foreign luxury: of curing the expensiveness of pride, vanity, idleness, and gaming in our women: of introducing a vein of parsimony, prudence, and temperance: of learning to love our country, in the want of which we differ even from Lowlanders and the inhabitants of Topinamboo:[10] of quitting our animosities and factions, nor acting any longer like the Jews,[11] who were murdering one another at the very moment their city was taken: of being a little cautious not to sell our country and conscience for nothing: of teaching landlords to have at least one degree of mercy toward their tenants: lastly, of putting a spirit of honesty, industry, and skill into our shopkeepers; who, if a resolution could now be taken to buy only our native goods, would immediately unite to cheat and exact upon us in the price, the measure, and the goodness, nor could ever yet be brought to make one fair proposal of just dealing, though often and earnestly invited to it.

30   Therefore, I repeat, let no man talk to me of these and the like expedients, till he hath at least some glimpse of hope that there will ever be some hearty and sincere attempt to put them in practice.

31   But as to myself, having been wearied out for many years with offering vain, idle, visionary thoughts, and at length utterly despairing of success, I fortunately fell upon this proposal, which, as it is wholly new, so it hath something solid and real, of no expense and little trouble, full in our own power, and whereby we can incur no danger in disobliging England. For this kind of

---

[10]In Brazil.
[11]Rome conquered Jerusalem in 70 A.D. during civil war.

commodity will not bear exportation, the flesh being of too tender a consistence to admit a long continuance in salt, although perhaps I could name a country which would be glad to eat up our whole nation without it.

After all, I am not so violently bent upon my own opinion as to reject any offer proposed by wise men, which shall be found equally innocent, cheap, easy, and effectual. But before something of that kind shall be advanced in contradiction to my scheme, and offering a better, I desire the author or authors will be pleased maturely to consider two points. First, as things now stand, how they will be able to find food and raiment for an hundred thousand useless mouths and backs. And secondly, there being a round million of creatures in human figure throughout this kingdom, whose sole subsistence put into a common stock would leave them in debt two millions of pounds sterling, adding those who are beggars by profession to the bulk of farmers, cottagers, and laborers, with their wives and children who are beggars in effect; I desire those politicians who dislike my overture, and may perhaps be so bold to attempt an answer, that they will first ask the parents of these mortals whether they would not at this day think it a great happiness to have been sold for food at a year old in this manner I prescribe, and thereby have avoided such a perpetual scene of misfortunes as they have since gone through by the oppression of landlords, the impossibility of paying rent without money or trade, the want of common sustenance, with neither house nor clothes to cover them from the inclemencies of the weather, and the most inevitable prospect of entailing the like or greater miseries upon their breed forever.

I profess, in the sincerity of my heart, that I have not the least personal interest in endeavoring to promote this necessary work, having no other motive than the public good of my country, by advancing our trade, providing for infants, relieving the poor, and giving some pleasure to the rich. I have no children by which I can propose to get a single penny; the youngest being nine years old, and my wife past childbearing.

1729

Shooting an Elephant

George Orwell

1 In Moulmein, in lower Burma, I was hated by large numbers of people—the only time in my life that I have been important enough for this to happen to me. I was sub-divisional police officer of the town, and in an aimless, petty kind of way anti-European feeling was very bitter. No one had the guts to raise a riot, but if a European woman went through the bazaars alone somebody would probably spit betel juice over her dress. As a police officer I was an obvious target and was baited whenever it seemed safe to do so. When a nimble Burman tripped me up on the football field and the referee (another Burman) looked the other way, the crowd yelled with hideous laughter. This happened more than once. In the end the sneering yellow faces of young men that met me everywhere, the insults hooted after me when I was at a safe distance, got badly on my nerves. The young Buddhist priests were the worst of all. There were several thousands of them in the town and none of them seemed to have anything to do except stand on street corners and jeer at Europeans.

2 All this was perplexing and upsetting. For at that time I had already made up my mind that imperialism was an evil thing and the sooner I chucked up my job and got out of it the better. Theoretically—and secretly, of course—I was all for the Burmese and all against their oppressors, the British. As for the job I was doing, I hated it more bitterly than I can perhaps make clear. In a job like that you see the dirty work of Empire at close quarters. The wretched prisoners huddling in the stinking cages of the lock-ups, the gray, cowed faces of the long-term convicts, the scarred buttocks of the men who had been flogged with bamboos—all these oppressed me with an intolerable sense of guilt. But I could get nothing into perspective. I was young and ill educated and I had had to think out my problems in the utter silence that is imposed on every Englishman in the East. I did not even know that the British Empire is dying, still less did I know that it is a great deal

better than the younger empires that are going to supplant it. All
I knew was that I was stuck between my hatred of the empire I
served and my rage against the evil-spirited little beasts who tried
to make my job impossible. With one part of my mind I thought of
the British Raj as an unbreakable tyranny, as something clamped
down, in *saecula saeculorum,* upon the will of prostrate peoples;
with another part I thought that the greatest joy in the world
would be to drive a bayonet into a Buddhist priest's guts. Feelings
like these are the normal by-products of imperialism; ask any
Anglo-Indian official, if you can catch him off duty.

One day something happened which in a roundabout way 3
was enlightening. It was a tiny incident in itself, but it gave
me a better glimpse than I had had before of the real nature of
imperialism—the real motives for which despotic governments
act. Early one morning the sub-inspector at a police station the
other end of the town rang me up on the phone and said that an
elephant was ravaging the bazaar. Would I please come and do
something about it? I did not know what I could do, but I wanted
to see what was happening and I got on to a pony and started out.
I took my rifle, an old .44 Winchester and much too small to kill an
elephant, but I thought the noise might be useful *in terrorem.* Various Burmans stopped me on the way and told me about the elephant's doings. It was not, of course, a wild elephant, but a tame
one which had gone "must." It had been chained up, as tame elephants always are when their attack of "must" is due, but on the
previous night it had broken its chain and escaped. Its mahout,
the only person who could manage it when it was in that state,
had set out in pursuit, but had taken the wrong direction and was
now twelve hours' journey away, and in the morning the elephant
had suddenly reappeared in the town. The Burmese population
had no weapons and were quite helpless against it. It had already
destroyed somebody's bamboo hut, killed a cow and raided some
fruit-stalls and devoured the stock; also it had met the municipal
rubbish van and, when the driver jumped out and took to his
heels, had turned the van over and inflicted violences upon it.

The Burmese sub-inspector and some Indian constables were 4
waiting for me in the quarter where the elephant had been seen. It
was a very poor quarter, a labyrinth of squalid bamboo huts,

thatched with palm-leaf, winding all over a steep hillside. I remember that it was a cloudy, stuffy morning at the beginning of
the rains. We began questioning the people as to where the elephant had gone and, as usual, failed to get any definite information. That is invariably the case in the East; a story always sounds
clear enough at a distance, but the nearer you get to the scene of
events the vaguer it becomes. Some of the people said that the
elephant had gone in one direction, some said that he had gone in
another, some professed not even to have heard of any elephant. I
had almost made up my mind that the whole story was a pack of
lies, when we heard yells a little distance away. There was a loud,
scandalized cry of "Go away, child! Go away this instant!" and an
old woman with a switch in her hand came round the corner of a
hut, violently shooing away a crowd of naked children. Some
more women followed, clicking their tongues and exclaiming;
evidently there was something that the children ought not to have
seen. I rounded the hut and saw a man's dead body sprawling in
the mud. He was an Indian, a black Dravidian coolie, almost
naked, and he could not have been dead many minutes. The people said that the elephant had come suddenly upon him round the
corner of the hut, caught him with its trunk, put its foot on his
back and ground him into the earth. This was the rainy season
and the ground was soft, and his face had scored a trench a foot
deep and a couple of yards long. He was lying on his belly with
arms crucified and head sharply twisted to one side. His face was
coated with mud, the eyes wide open, the teeth bared and grinning with an expression of unendurable agony. (Never tell me, by
the way, that the dead look peaceful. Most of the corpses I have
seen looked devilish.) The friction of the great beast's foot had
stripped the skin from his back as neatly as one skins a rabbit. As
soon as I saw the dead man I sent an orderly to a friend's house
nearby to borrow an elephant rifle. I had already sent back the
pony, not wanting it to go mad with fright and throw me if it
smelt the elephant.

5   The orderly came back in a few minutes with a rifle and five
cartridges, and meanwhile some Burmans had arrived and told
us that the elephant was in the paddy fields below only a few
hundred yards away. As I started forward practically the whole

population of the quarter flocked out of the houses and followed me. They had seen the rifle and were all shouting excitedly that I was going to shoot the elephant. They had not shown much interest in the elephant when he was merely ravaging their homes, but it was different now that he was going to be shot. It was a bit of fun to them, as it would be to an English crowd; besides they wanted the meat. It made me vaguely uneasy. I had no intention of shooting the elephant—I had merely sent for the rifle to defend myself if necessary—and it is always unnerving to have a crowd following you. I marched down the hill, looking and feeling a fool, with the rifle over my shoulder and an ever-growing army of people jostling at my heels. At the bottom, when you got away from the huts, there was a metalled road and beyond that a miry waste of paddy fields a thousand yards across, not yet ploughed but soggy from the first rains and dotted with coarse grass. The elephant was standing eight yards from the road, his left side toward us. He took not the slightest notice of the crowd's approach. He was tearing up bunches of grass, beating them against his knees to clean them, and stuffing them into his mouth.

I had halted on the road. As soon as I saw the elephant I knew 6 with perfect certainty that I ought not to shoot him. It is a serious matter to shoot a working elephant—it is comparable to destroying a huge and costly piece of machinery—and obviously one ought not to do it if it can possibly be avoided. And at that distance, peacefully eating, the elephant looked no more dangerous than a cow. I thought then and I think now that his attack of "must" was already passing off; in which case he would merely wander harmlessly about until the mahout came back and caught him. Moreover, I did not in the least want to shoot him. I decided that I would watch him for a little while to make sure that he did not turn savage again, and then go home.

But at that moment I glanced round at the crowd that had followed me. It was an immense crowd, two thousand at the least and growing every minute. It blocked the road for a long distance on either side. I looked at the sea of yellow faces above the garish clothes—faces all happy and excited over this bit of fun, all certain that the elephant was going to be shot. They were watching me as they would watch a conjurer about to perform a trick. They did not like me, but with the magical rifle in my hands I was momentarily worth watching. And suddenly I realized that I should have to shoot the elephant after all. The people expected it of me and I had got to do it; I could feel their two thousand wills pressing me forward, irresistibly. And it was at this moment, as I stood there with the rifle in my hands, that I first grasped the hollowness, the futility of the white man's dominion in the East. Here was I, the white man with his gun, standing in front of the unarmed native crowd—seemingly the leading actor of the piece; but in reality I was only an absurd puppet pushed to and fro by the will of those yellow faces behind. I perceived in this moment that when the white man turns tyrant it is his own freedom that he destroys. He becomes a sort of hollow, posing dummy, the conventionalized figure of a sahib. For it is the condition of his rule that he shall spend his life in trying to impress the "natives," and so in every crisis he has got to do what the "natives" expect of him. He wears a mask, and his face grows to fit it. I had got to shoot the elephant. I had committed myself to doing it when I sent for the rifle. A sahib has got to act like a sahib; he has got to appear resolute, to know his own mind and do definite things. To come all that way, rifle in hand, with two thousand people marching at my heels, and then to trail feebly away, having done nothing—no, that was impossible. The crowd would laugh at me. And my whole life, every white man's life in the East, was one long struggle not to be laughed at.

8   But I did not want to shoot the elephant. I watched him beating his bunch of grass against his knees with that preoccupied grandmotherly air that elephants have. It seemed to me that it would be murder to shoot him. At that age I was not squeamish about killing animals, but I had never shot an elephant and never wanted to. (Somehow it always seems worse to kill a *large* animal.) Besides, there was the beast's owner to be considered. Alive, the elephant was worth at least a hundred pounds; dead, he would only be worth the value of his tusks, five pounds, possibly. But I had got to act quickly. I turned to some experienced-looking Burmans who had been there when we arrived, and asked them

how the elephant had been behaving. They all said the same thing: he took no notice of you if you left him alone, but he might charge if you went too close to him.

It was perfectly clear to me what I ought to do. I ought to 9 walk up to within say, twenty-five yards of the elephant and test his behavior. If he charged, I could shoot; if he took no notice of me, it would be safe to leave him until the mahout came back. But also I knew that I was going to do no such thing. I was a poor shot with a rifle and the ground was soft mud into which one would sink at every step. If the elephant charged and I missed him, I should have about as much chance as a toad under a steam-roller. But even then I was not thinking particularly of my own skin, only of the watchful yellow faces behind. For at that moment, with the crowd watching me, I was not afraid in the ordinary sense, as I would have been if I had been alone. A white man mustn't be frightened in front of "natives," and so, in general, he isn't frightened. The sole thought in my mind was that if anything went wrong those two thousand Burmans would see me pursued, caught, trampled on, and reduced to a grinning corpse like that Indian up the hill. And if that happened it was quite probable that some of them would laugh. That would never do. There was only one alternative. I shoved the cartridges into the magazine and lay down on the road to get a better aim.

The crowd grew very still, and a deep, low, happy sigh, as of 10 people who see the theater curtain go up at last, breathed from innumerable throats. They were going to have their bit of fun after all. The rifle was a beautiful German thing with cross-hair sights. I did not then know that in shooting an elephant one would shoot to cut an imaginary bar running from ear-hole to ear-hole. I ought, therefore, as the elephant was sideways on, to have aimed straight at his ear-hole, actually I aimed several inches in front of this, thinking the brain would be further forward.

When I pulled the trigger I did not hear the bang or feel the 11 kicks—one never does when a shot goes home—but I heard the devilish roar of glee that went up from the crowd. In that instant, in too short a time, one would have thought, even for the bullet to get there, a mysterious, terrible change had come over the elep.. nt. He ne '..er stirred nor fell, but every line of his body had altered. He looked suddenly stricken, shrunken, immensely old, as though the frightful impact of the bullet had paralyzed him without knocking him down. At last, after what seemed a long time—it might have been five seconds, I dare say—he sagged flabbily to his knees. His mouth slobbered. An enormous senility seemed to have settled upon him. One could have imagined him thousands of years old. I fired again into the same spot. At the second shot he did not collapse but climbed with desperate slow-ness to his feet and stood weakly upright, with legs sagging and head drooping. I fired a third time. That was the shot that did for him. You could see the agony of it jolt his whole body and knock the last remnant of strength from his legs. But in falling he seemed for a moment to rise, for as his hind legs collapsed beneath him he seemed to tower upward like a huge rock toppling, his trunk reaching skyward like a tree. He trumpeted, for the first and only time. And then down he came, his belly toward me with a crash that seemed to shake the ground even where I lay.

12   I got up. The Burmans were already racing past me across the mud. It was obvious that the elephant would never rise again, but he was not dead. He was breathing very rhythmically with long rattling gasps, his great mound of a side painfully rising and falling. His mouth was wide open—I could see far down into cav-erns of pale pink throat. I waited a long time for him to die, but his breathing did not weaken. Finally I fired my two remaining shots into the spot where I thought his heart must be. The thick blood welled out of him like red velvet, but still he did not die. His body did not even jerk when the shots hit him, the tortured breathing continued without a pause. He was dying, very slowly and in great agony, but in some world remote from me where not even a bullet could damage him further. I felt that I had got to put an end to that dreadful noise. It seemed dreadful to see the great beast lying powerless to move and yet powerless to die, and not even to be able to finish him. I sent back for my small rifle and poured shot after shot into his heart and down his throat. They seemed to make no impression. The tortured gasps continued as steadily as the ticking of a clock.

In the end I could not stand it any longer and went away. I   13
heard later that it took him half an hour to die. Burmans were
bringing dahs and baskets even before I left, and I was told they
had stripped his body almost to the bones by the afternoon.

Afterward, of course, there were endless discussions about   14
the shooting of the elephant. The owner was furious, but he was
only an Indian and could do nothing. Besides, legally I had done
the right thing, for a mad elephant has to be killed, like a mad
dog, if its owner fails to control it. Among the Europeans opinion
was divided. The older men said I was right, the younger men
said it was a damn shame to shoot an elephant for killing a
coolie, because an elephant was worth more than any damn Cor-
inghee coolie. And afterward I was very glad that the coolie had
been killed; it put me legally in the right and it gave me a sufficient pretext for shooting the elephant. I often wondered whether
any of the others grasped that I had done it solely to avoid looking a fool.

1936

The Meaning of Democracy

E. B. White

We received a letter from the Writers' War Board the other day ask-   1
ing for a statement on "The Meaning of Democracy." It presumably is our duty to comply with such a request, and it is certainly
our pleasure.

Surely the Board knows what democracy is. It is the line that   2
forms on the right. It is the don't in Don't Shove. It is the hole in
the stuffed shirt through which the sawdust slowly trickles; it is
the dent in the high hat. Democracy is the recurrent suspicion that
more than half of the people are right more than half of the time.
It is the feeling of privacy in the voting booths, the feeling of communion in the libraries, the feeling of vitality everywhere. Democ-

racy is the score at the beginning of the ninth. It is an idea which hasn't been disproved yet, a song the words of which have not gone bad. It's the mustard on the hot dog and the cream in the rationed coffee. Democracy is a request from a War Board, in the middle of a morning in the middle of a war, wanting to know what democracy is.

1944

Chapter

Economics, Work, and Consumer Culture

"The great affair, we always find, is to get money," observes the eighteenth-century philosopher Adam Smith, in his book *The Wealth of Nations*. An ardent capitalist and moral philosopher known for his tightly reasoned arguments, Smith's views that citizens' unencumbered acquisition of wealth will drive the wealth of the whole nation continue to be widely held today. He advocated free trade, proposed that currency itself was not as sure a measure of wealth as the abundance or scarcity of consumable goods, and gave voice to the theory of supply and demand. While Smith addressed a nation's acquisition of wealth, Benjamin Franklin contemplates the "Way to Wealth" for the individual. Through the persona of Richard Saunders in *Poor Richard's Almanac*, Franklin puts forward the principles of thrift, hard work, and personal industry. He admonished that it is the extravagant consumption of goods that is most to blame for the loss of an individual's wealth; but as is his hallmark, Franklin ends his homegrown advice with humor: "The people heard it, and approved the doctrine, and immediately practiced the contrary." Buying and selling is at the heart of our economy, but abundance can be had at too high a human cost, as Patricia J. Williams chillingly brings home when she finds the bill of sale for her great-great grandmother—sold as a slave at age eleven. Jesse Jackson also looks at the human cost of globalization in "Who Makes the Clothes We Wear?" Studs Terkel offers another take on production and consumption in his unsentimental interview with a steelworker,

365

Mike Lefevre, and Barbara Ehrenreich examines the service work that is invisible in our culture in "Nickel-and-Dimed." Russell Baker's "Work in Corporate America" postulates that the middle class, on the other hand, "produces nothing but paper." Consumption is now a national product in itself. James Q. Wilson in his "Cars and Their Enemies" reflects on the preference for cars over public transportation. Gloria Steinem in "Sex, Lies, and Advertising" and James B. Twitchell in "But First a Word from Our Sponsors" look at engineering consumption from the point of view of advertisers, and note how advertisement not only sells products but undermines the quality of public debate. Dave Barry concludes with a case study of "retail patriotism." He notes that wrapping consumption in patriotism is as tried and true in effective advertising as red, white, and "beer."

Of the Principle of the Commercial, or Mercantile System

Adam Smith

1   That wealth consists in money, or in gold and silver, is a popular notion which naturally arises from the double function of money, as the instrument of commerce and as the measure of value. In consequence of its being the instrument of commerce, when we have money we can more readily obtain whatever else we have occasion for than by means of any other commodity. The great affair, we always find, is to get money. When that is obtained, there is no difficulty in making any subsequent purchase. In consequence of its being the measure of value, we estimate that of all other commodities by the quantity of money which they will exchange for. We say of a rich man that he is worth a great deal, and of a poor man that he is worth very little money. A frugal man, or a man eager to be rich, is said to love money; and a careless, a generous, or a profuse man, is said to be indifferent about it. To grow rich is to get money; and wealth and money, in short, are, in common language, considered as in every respect synonymous.

2   A rich country, in the same manner as a rich man, is supposed to be a country abounding in money; and to heap up gold and silver in any country is supposed to be the readiest way to enrich it. For some time after the discovery of America, the first inquiry of the Spaniards, when they arrived upon any unknown coast, used to be, if there was any gold or silver to be found in the neighbourhood. By the information which they received, they judged whether it was worth while to make a settlement there, or if the country was worth the conquering. Plano Carpino, a monk, sent ambassador from the King of France to one of the sons of the famous Gengis Khan, says that the Tartars used frequently to ask him if there was plenty of sheep and oxen in the kingdom of France? Their inquiry had the same object with that of the Spaniards. They wanted to know if the country was rich enough

to be worth the conquering. Among the Tartars, as among all other nations of shepherds, who are generally ignorant of the use of money, cattle are the instruments of commerce and the measures of value. Wealth, therefore, according to them, consisted in cattle, as according to the Spaniards it consisted in gold and silver. Of the two, the Tartar notion, perhaps, was the nearest to the truth.

Mr. Locke remarks a distinction between money and other movable goods. All other movable goods, he says, are of so consumable a nature that the wealth which consists in them cannot be much depended on, and a nation which abounds in them one year may, without any exportation, but merely by their own waste and extravagance, be in great want of them the next. Money, on the contrary, is a steady friend, which, though it may travel about from hand to hand, yet if it can be kept from going out of the country, is not very liable to be wasted and consumed. Gold and silver, therefore, are, according to him, the most solid and substantial part of the movable wealth of a nation, and to multiply those metals ought, he thinks, upon that account, to be the great object of its political economy. 3

Others admit that if a nation could be separated from all the world, it would be of no consequence how much, or how little money circulated in it. The consumable goods which were circulated by means of this money would only be exchanged for a greater or a smaller number of pieces; but the real wealth or poverty of the country, they allow, would depend altogether upon the abundance or scarcity of those consumable goods. But it is otherwise, they think, with countries which have connections with foreign nations, and which are obliged to carry on foreign wars, and to maintain fleets and armies in distant countries. This, they say, cannot be done, but by sending abroad money to pay them with; and a nation cannot send much money abroad unless it has a good deal at home. Every such nation, therefore, must endeavour in time of peace to accumulate gold and silver that, when occasion requires, it may have wherewithal to carry on foreign wars. 4

In consequence of these popular notions, all the different nations of Europe have studied, though to little purpose, every possible means of accumulating gold and silver in their respective countries. Spain and Portugal, the proprietors of the principal 5

mines which supply Europe with those metals, have either prohibited their exportation under the severest penalties, or subjected
it to a considerable duty. The like prohibition seems anciently to
have made a part of the policy of most other European nations. It
is even to be found, where we should least of all expect to find it,
in some old Scotch acts of parliament, which forbid under heavy
penalties the carrying gold or silver *forth of the kingdom*. The like
policy anciently took place both in France and England.

6   When those countries became commercial, the merchants
found this prohibition, upon many occasions, extremely inconvenient. They could frequently buy more advantageously with
gold and silver than with any other commodity the foreign goods
which they wanted, either to import into their own, or to carry to
some other foreign country. They remonstrated, therefore, against
this prohibition as hurtful to trade.

7   They represented, first, that the exportation of gold and silver
in order to purchase foreign goods, did not always diminish the
quantity of those metals in the kingdom. That, on the contrary, it
might frequently increase that quantity; because, if the consumption of foreign goods was not thereby increased in the country,
those goods might be re-exported to foreign countries, and, being
there sold for a large profit, might bring back much more treasure
than was originally sent out to purchase them. Mr. Mun compares
this operation of foreign trade to the seed-time and harvest of
agriculture. "If we only behold," says he, "the actions of the husbandman in the seed-time, when he casteth away much good corn
into the ground, we shall account him rather a madman than a
husbandman. But when we consider his labours in the harvest,
which is the end of his endeavours, we shall find the worth and
plentiful increase of his actions."

8   They represented, secondly, that this prohibition could not
hinder the exportation of gold and silver, which, on account of the
smallness of their bulk in proportion to their value, could easily
be smuggled abroad. That this exportation could only be prevented by a proper attention to, what they called, the balance of
trade. That when the country exported to a greater value than it
imported, a balance became due to it from foreign nations, which
was necessarily paid to it in gold and silver, and thereby increased

the quantity of those metals in the kingdom. But that when it imported to a greater value than it exported, a contrary balance became due to foreign nations, which was necessarily paid to them in the same manner, and thereby diminished that quantity. That in this case to prohibit the exportation of those metals could not prevent it, but only, by making it more dangerous, render it more expensive. That the exchange was thereby turned more against the country which owed the balance than it otherwise might have been; the merchant who purchased a bill upon the foreign country being obliged to pay the banker who sold it, not only for the natural risk, trouble, and expense of sending the money thither, but for the extraordinary risk arising from the prohibition. But that the more the exchange was against any country, the more the balance of trade became necessarily against it; the money of that country becoming necessarily of so much less value in comparison with that of the country to which the balance was due. That if the exchange between England and Holland, for example, was five per cent against England, it would require a hundred and five ounces of silver in England to purchase a bill for a hundred ounces of silver in Holland: that a hundred and five ounces of silver in England, therefore, would be worth only a hundred ounces of silver in Holland, and would purchase only a proportionable quantity of Dutch goods; but that a hundred ounces of silver in Holland, on the contrary, would be worth a hundred and five ounces in England, and would purchase a proportionable quantity of English goods: that the English goods which were sold to Holland would be sold so much cheaper; and the Dutch goods which were sold to England so much dearer by the difference of the exchange; that the one would draw so much less Dutch money to England, and the other so much more English money to Holland, as this difference amounted to: and that the balance of trade, therefore, would necessarily be so much more against England, and would require a greater balance of gold and silver to be exported to Holland.

   Those arguments were partly solid and partly sophistical. [9] They were solid so far as they asserted that the exportation of gold and silver in trade might frequently be advantageous to the country. They were solid, too, in asserting that no prohibition could prevent their exportation when private people found any advantage in exporting them. But they were sophistical in supposing that either to preserve or to augment the quantity of those metals required more the attention of government than to preserve or to augment the quantity of any other useful commodities, which the freedom of trade, without any such attention, never fails to supply in the proper quantity. They were sophistical too, perhaps, in asserting that the high price of exchange necessarily increased what they called the unfavourable balance of trade, or occasioned the exportation of a greater quantity of gold and silver. That high price, indeed, was extremely disadvantageous to the merchants who had any money to pay in foreign countries. They paid so much dearer for the bills which their bankers granted them upon those countries. But though the risk arising from the prohibition might occasion some extraordinary expense to the bankers, it would not necessarily carry any more money out of the country. This expense would generally be all laid out in the country, in smuggling the money out of it, and could seldom occasion the exportation of a single sixpence beyond the precise sum drawn for. The high price of exchange too would naturally dispose the merchants to endeavour to make their exports nearly balance their imports, in order that they might have this high exchange to pay upon as small a sum as possible. The high price of exchange, besides, must necessarily have operated as a tax, in raising the price of foreign goods, and thereby diminishing their consumption. It would tend, therefore, not to increase but to diminish what they called the unfavourable balance of trade, and consequently the exportation of gold and silver.

10   Such as they were, however, those arguments convinced the people to whom they were addressed. They were addressed by merchants to parliaments and to the councils of princes, to nobles and to country gentlemen, by those who were supposed to understand trade to those who were conscious to themselves that they knew nothing about the matter. That foreign trade enriched the country, experience demonstrated to the nobles and country gentlemen as well as to the merchants; but how, or in what manner, none of them well knew. The merchants knew perfectly in what manner it enriched themselves. It was their business to know it. But to know in what manner it enriched the country was

no part of their business. This subject never came into their consideration but when they had occasion to apply to their country for some change in the laws relating to foreign trade. It then became necessary to say something about the beneficial effects of foreign trade, and the manner in which those effects were obstructed by the laws as they then stood. To the judges who were to decide the business it appeared a most satisfactory account of the matter, when they were told that foreign trade brought money into the country, but that the laws in question hindered it from bringing so much as it otherwise would do. Those arguments therefore produced the wished-for effect. The prohibition of exporting gold and silver was in France and England confined to the coin of those respective countries. The exportation of foreign coin and of bullion was made free. In Holland, and in some other places, this liberty was extended even to the coin of the country. The attention of government was turned away from guarding against the exportation of gold and silver to watch over the balance of trade as the only cause which could occasion any augmentation or diminution of those metals. From one fruitless care it was turned away to another care much more intricate, much more embarrassing, and just equally fruitless. The title of Mun's book, *England's Treasure in Foreign Trade,* became a fundamental maxim in the political economy, not of England only, but of all other commercial countries. The inland or home trade, the most important of all, the trade in which an equal capital affords the greatest revenue, and creates the greatest employment to the people of the country, was considered as subsidiary only to foreign trade. It neither brought money into the country, it was said, nor carried any out of it. The country, therefore, could never become either richer or poorer by means of it, except so far as its prosperity or decay might indirectly influence the state of foreign trade.

A country that has no mines of its own must undoubtedly 11 draw its gold and silver from foreign countries in the same manner as one that has no vineyards of its own must draw its wines. It does not seem necessary, however, that the attention of government should be more turned towards the one than towards the other object. A country that has wherewithal to buy wine will always get the wine which it has occasion for; and a country that has wherewithal to buy gold and silver will never be in want of those metals. They are to be bought for a certain price like all other commodities, and as they are the price of all other commodities, so all other commodities are the price of those metals. We trust with perfect security that the freedom of trade, without any attention of government, will always supply us with the wine which we have occasion for: and we may trust with equal security that it will always supply us with all the gold and silver which we can afford to purchase or to employ, either in circulating our commodities, or in other uses.

12   The quantity of every commodity which human industry can either purchase or produce naturally regulates itself in every country according to the effectual demand, or according to the demand of those who are willing to pay the whole rent, labour, and profits which must be paid in order to prepare and bring it to market. But no commodities regulate themselves more easily or more exactly according to this effectual demand than gold and silver; because, on account of the small bulk and great value of those metals, no commodities can be more easily transported from one place to another, from the places where they are cheap to those where they are dear, from the places where they exceed to those where they fall short of this effectual demand. If there were in England, for example, an effectual demand for an additional quantity of gold, a packet-boat could bring from Lisbon, or from wherever else it was to be had, fifty tons of gold, which could be coined into more than five millions of guineas. But if there were an effectual demand for grain to the same value, to import it would require, at five guineas a ton, a million of tons of shipping, or a thousand ships of a thousand tons each. The navy of England would not be sufficient.

13   When the quantity of gold and silver imported into any country exceeds the effectual demand, no vigilance of government can prevent their exportation. All the sanguinary laws of Spain and Portugal are not able to keep their gold and silver at home. The continual importations from Peru and Brazil exceed the effectual demand of those countries, and sink the price of those metals there below that in the neighbouring countries. If, on the contrary, in any particular country their quantity fell short of the effectual

demand, so as to raise their price above that of the neighbouring countries, the government would have no occasion to take any pains to import them. If it were even to take pains to prevent their importation, it would not be able to effectuate it. Those metals, when the Spartans had got wherewithal to purchase them, broke through all the barriers which the laws of Lycurgus opposed to their entrance into Lacedemon. All the sanguinary laws of the customs are not able to prevent the importation of the teas of the Dutch and Gottenburgh East India companies, because somewhat cheaper than those of the British company. A pound of tea, however, is about a hundred times the bulk of one of the highest prices, sixteen shillings, that is commonly paid for it in silver, and more than two thousand times the bulk of the same price in gold, and consequently just so many times more difficult to smuggle.

It is partly owing to the easy transportation of gold and silver 14 from the places where they abound to those where they are wanted that the price of those metals does not fluctuate continually like that of the greater part of other commodities, which are hindered by their bulk from shifting their situation when the market happens to be either over or under-stocked with them. The price of those metals, indeed, is not altogether exempted from variation, but the changes to which it is liable are generally slow, gradual, and uniform. In Europe, for example, it is supposed, without much foundation, perhaps, that during the course of the present and preceding century they have been constantly, but gradually, sinking in their value, on account of the continual importations from the Spanish West Indies. But to make any sudden change in the price of gold and silver, so as to raise or lower at once, sensibly and remarkably, the money price of all other commodities, requires such a revolution in commerce as that occasioned by the discovery of America.

If, notwithstanding all this, gold and silver should at any time 15 fall short in a country which has wherewithal to purchase them, there are more expedients for supplying their place than that of almost any other commodity. If the materials of manufacture are wanted, industry must stop. If provisions are wanted, the people must starve. But if money is wanted, barter will supply its place, though with a good deal of inconveniency. Buying and selling upon credit, and the different dealers compensating their credits with one another, once a month or once a year, will supply it with less inconveniency. A well-regulated paper money will supply it, not only without any inconveniency, but, in some cases, with some advantages. Upon every account, therefore, the attention of government never was so unnecessarily employed as when directed to watch over the preservation or increase of the quantity of money in any country.

16   No complaint, however, is more common than that of a scarcity of money. Money, like wine, must always be scarce with those who have neither wherewithal to buy it nor credit to borrow it. Those who have either will seldom be in want either of the money or of the wine which they have occasion for. This complaint, however, of the scarcity of money is not always confined to improvident spendthrifts. It is sometimes general through a whole mercantile town and the country in its neighbourhood. Over-trading is the common cause of it. Sober men, whose projects have been disproportioned to their capitals, are as likely to have neither wherewithal to buy money nor credit to borrow it, as prodigals whose expense has been disproportioned to their revenue. Before their projects can be brought to bear, their stock is gone, and their credit with it. They run about everywhere to borrow money, and everybody tells them that they have none to lend. Even such general complaints of the scarcity of money do not always prove that the usual number of gold and silver pieces are not circulating in the country, but that many people want those pieces who have nothing to give for them. When the profits of trade happen to be greater than ordinary, over-trading becomes a general error both among great and small dealers. They do not always send more money abroad than usual, but they buy upon credit, both at home and abroad, an unusual quantity of goods, which they send to some distant market in hopes that the returns will come in before the demand for payment. The demand comes before the returns, and they have nothing at hand with which they can either purchase money, or give solid security for borrowing. It is not any scarcity of gold and silver, but the difficulty

which such people find in borrowing, and which their creditors find in getting payment, that occasions the general complaint of the scarcity of money.

It would be too ridiculous to go about seriously to prove that 17 wealth does not consist in money, or in gold and silver; but in what money purchases, and is valuable only for purchasing. Money, no doubt, makes always a part of the national capital; but it has already been shown that it generally makes but a small part, and always the most unprofitable part of it.

It is not because wealth consists more essentially in money 18 than in goods that the merchant finds it generally more easy to buy goods with money than to buy money with goods; but because money is the known and established instrument of commerce, for which everything is readily given in exchange, but which is not always with equal readiness to be got in exchange for everything. The greater part of goods, besides, are more perishable than money, and he may frequently sustain a much greater loss by keeping them. When his goods are upon hand, too, he is more liable to such demands for money as he may not be able to answer than when he has got their price in his coffers. Over and above all this, his profit arises more directly from selling than from buying, and he is upon all these accounts generally much more anxious to exchange his goods for money than his money for goods. But though a particular merchant, with abundance of goods in his warehouse, may sometimes be ruined by not being able to sell them in time, a nation or country is not liable to the same accident. The whole capital of a merchant frequently consists in perishable goods destined for purchasing money. But it is but a very small part of the annual produce of the land and labour of a country which can ever be destined for purchasing gold and silver from their neighbours. The far greater part is circulated and consumed among themselves; and even of the surplus which is sent abroad, the greater part is generally destined for the purchase of other foreign goods. Though gold and silver, therefore, could not be had in exchange for the goods destined to purchase them, the nation would not be ruined. It might, indeed, suffer some loss and inconveniency, and be forced upon some of those expedients which are necessary for supplying the place of money. The annual produce of its land and labour, however, would be the same, or very nearly the same, as usual, because the same, or very nearly the same, consumable capital would be employed in maintaining it. And though goods do not always draw money so readily as money draws goods, in the long run they draw it more necessarily than even it draws them. Goods can serve many other purposes besides purchasing money, but money can serve no other purpose besides purchasing goods. Money, therefore, necessarily runs after goods, but goods do not always or necessarily run after money. The man who buys does not always mean to sell again, but frequently to use or to consume; whereas he who sells always means to buy again. The one may frequently have done the whole, but the other can never have done more than the one-half of his business. It is not for its own sake that men desire money, but for the sake of what they can purchase with it.

1776

The Way to Wealth
Benjamin Franklin

PREFACE TO POOR RICHARD IMPROVED

Courteous Reader,

1 I have heard that nothing gives an author so great pleasure, as to find his works respectfully quoted by other learned authors. This pleasure I have seldom enjoyed; for though I have been, if I may say it without vanity, an eminent author of almanacs annually now a full quarter of a century, my brother authors in the same way, for what reason I know not, have ever been very sparing in their applauses, and no other author has taken the least notice of me, so that did not my writings produce me some solid pudding, the great deficiency of praise would have quite discouraged me.

I concluded at length, that the people were the best judges of   2
my merit; for they buy my works; and besides, in my rambles,
where I am not personally known, I have frequently heard one or
other of my adages repeated, with "as Poor Richard says" at the
end on 't; this gave me some satisfaction, as it showed not only
that my instructions were regarded, but discovered likewise some
respect for my authority; and I own, that to encourage the practice
of remembering and repeating those wise sentences, I have sometimes quoted myself with great gravity.

Judge, then, how much I must have been gratified by an inci-   3
dent I am going to relate to you. I stopped my horse lately where
a great number of people were collected at a vendue[1] of merchant
goods. The hour of sale not being come, they were conversing on
the badness of the times and one of the company called to a plain
clean old man, with white locks, "Pray, Father Abraham, what
think you of the times? Won't these heavy taxes quite ruin the
country? How shall we be ever able to pay them? What would
you advise us to?" Father Abraham stood up, and replied, "If
you'd have my advice, I'll give it you in short, for a *word to the
wise is enough, and many words won't fill a bushel,* as Poor Richard
says." They joined in desiring him to speak his mind, and gathering round him, he proceeded as follows:

"Friends," says he, "and neighbors, the taxes are indeed very   4
heavy, and if those laid on by the government were the only ones
we had to pay, we might more easily discharge them; but we have
many others, and much more grievous to some of us. We are
taxed twice as much by our idleness, three times as much by our
pride, and four times as much by our folly; and from these taxes
the commissioners cannot ease or deliver us by allowing an abate-
ment. However, let us hearken to good advice, and something
may be done for us; *God helps them that help themselves,* as Poor
Richard says, in his Almanack of 1733.

"It would be thought a hard government that should tax its   5
people one-tenth part of their time, to be employed in its service.
But idleness taxes many of us much more, if we reckon all that is
spent in absolute sloth, or doing of nothing, with that which is
spent in idle employments or amusements, that amount to nothing.

[1]A place where merchandise is sold.

Sloth, by bringing on diseases, absolutely shortens life. *Sloth, like rust, consumes faster than labor wears; while the used key is always bright,* as Poor Richard says. *But dost thou love life, then do not squander time, for that's the stuff life is made of,* as Poor Richard says. How much more than is necessary do we spend in sleep, forgetting that *the sleeping fox catches no poultry* and that *there will be sleeping enough in the grave,* as Poor Richard says.

6   "*If time be of all things the most precious, wasting time must be,* as Poor Richard says, *the greatest prodigality;* since, as he elsewhere tells us, *lost time is never found again; and what we call time enough, always proves little enough;* let us then up and be doing, and doing to the purpose; so by diligence shall we do more with less perplexity. *Sloth makes all things difficult, but industry all easy,* as Poor Richard says; *and he that riseth late must trot all day, and shall scarce overtake his business at night;* while *laziness travels so slowly, that soon overtakes him,* as we read in Poor Richard, who adds, *drive thy business, let not that drive thee,* and *early to bed, and early to rise, makes a man healthy, wealthy, and wise.*

7   "So what signifies wishing and hoping for better times. We may make these times better, if we bestir ourselves. *Industry need not wish,* as Poor Richard says, *and he that lives upon hope will die fasting. There are no gains, without pains; then help hands, for I have no lands,* or if I have, they are smartly taxed. And, as Poor Richard likewise observes, *he that hath a trade hath an estate, and he that hath a calling, hath an office of profit and honor;* but then the trade must be worked at, and the calling well followed, or neither the estate nor the office will enable us to pay our taxes. If we are industrious, we shall never starve, for, as Poor Richard says, *at the workingman's house hunger looks in, but dares not enter.* Nor will the bailiff nor the constable enter, for *industry pays debts, while despair encreaseth them,* says Poor Richard. What though you have found no treasure, nor has any rich relation left you a legacy, *diligence is the mother of good luck,* as Poor Richard says, and *God gives all things to industry. Then plough deep, while sluggards sleep, and you shall have corn to sell and to keep,* says Poor Dick. Work while it is called today, for you know not how much you may be hindered tomorrow, which makes Poor Richard say, *one today is worth two tomorrows,* and farther, *have you somewhat to do tomorrow, do it today.* If you were a servant, would you not be ashamed that a good master should catch you

idle? Are you then your own master, *be ashamed to catch yourself idle*, as Poor Dick says. When there is so much to be done for yourself, your family, your country, and your gracious king, be up by peep of day; *let not the sun look down and say, inglorious here he lies.* Handle your tools without mittens; remember that *the cat in gloves catches no mice*, as Poor Richard says. 'Tis true there is much to be done, and perhaps you are weak-handed, but stick to it steadily; and you will see great effects, for *constant dropping wears away stones*, and *by diligence and patience the mouse ate in two the cable;* and *little strokes fell great oaks*, as Poor Richard says in his Almanack, the year I cannot just now remember.

"Methinks I hear some of you say, 'must a man afford himself   8
no leisure?' I will tell thee, my friend, what Poor Richard says, *employ thy time well, if thou meanest to gain leisure; and, since thou art not sure of a minute, throw not away an hour.* Leisure is time for doing something useful; this leisure the diligent man will obtain, but the lazy man never; so that, as Poor Richard says, *a life of leisure and a life of laziness are two things.* Do you imagine that sloth will afford you more comfort than labor? No, for as Poor Richard says, *trouble springs from idleness, and grievous toil from needless ease. Many without labor would live by their wits only, but they break for want of stock.* Whereas industry gives comfort, and plenty, and respect: *fly pleasures, and they'll follow you. The diligent spinner has a large shift,*[2] *and now I have a sheep and a cow, everybody bids me good morrow,* all which is well said by Poor Richard.

"But with our industry, we must likewise be steady, settled,   9
and careful, and oversee our own affairs with our own eyes, and not trust too much to others; for, as Poor Richard says,

> *I never saw an oft-removed tree,*
> *Nor yet an oft-removed family,*
> *That throve so well as those that settled be.*

And again, *three removes*[3] *is as bad as a fire*, and again, *keep thy shop, and thy shop will keep thee;* and again, *if you would have your business done, go; if not, send.* And again,

---

[2]Supply of clothing.
[3]Changes of address, moves from one home to a new one.

> *He that by the plough would thrive,*
> *Himself must either hold or drive.*

And again, *the eye of a master will do more work than both his hands;* and again, *want of care does us more damage than want of knowledge;* and again, *not to oversee workmen is to leave them your purse open.* Trusting too much to others' care is the ruin of many; for, as the Almanack says, *in the affairs of this world, men are saved, not by faith, but by the want of it;* but a man's own care is profitable; for, saith Poor Dick, *learning is to the studious,* and *riches to the careful,* as well as *power to the bold,* and *heaven to the virtuous,* and farther, *if you would have a faithful servant, and one that you like, serve yourself.* And again, he adviseth to circumspection and care, even in the smallest matters, because sometimes *a little neglect may breed great mischief;* adding, *for want of a nail the shoe was lost; for want of a shoe the horse was lost; and for want of a horse the rider was lost, being overtaken and slain by the enemy; all for want of care about a horseshoe nail.*

10   "So much for industry, my friends, and attention to one's own business; but to these we must add frugality, if we would make our industry more certainly successful. A man may, if he knows not how to save as he gets, keep his nose all his life to the grindstone, and die not worth a groat[4] at last. A *fat kitchen makes a lean will*, as Poor Richard says; and,

> *Many estates are spent in the getting,*
> *Since women for tea forsook spinning and knitting,*
> *And men for punch forsook hewing and splitting.*

If you would be wealthy, says he, in another Almanack, *think of saving as well as of getting: the Indies have not made Spain rich, because her outgoes are greater than her incomes.*

11   "Away then with your expensive follies, and you will not then have so much cause to complain of hard times, heavy taxes, and chargeable families; for, as Poor Dick says,

> *Women and wine, game and deceit,*
> *Make the wealth small and the wants great.*

And farther, *what maintains one vice would bring up two children.* You may think perhaps, that a little tea, or a little punch now and

---

[4]A coin of small value no longer in use.

then, diet a little more costly, clothes a little finer, and a little entertainment now and then, can be no great matter; but remember what Poor Richard says, *many a little makes a mickle,*[5] and farther, *Beware of little expenses; a small leak will sink a great ship;* and again, *who dainties love, shall beggars prove;* and moreover, *fools make feasts, and wise men eat them.*

"Here you are all got together at this vendue of fineries and   12
knicknacks. You call them goods; but if you do not take care, they will prove evils to some of you. You expect they will be sold cheap, and perhaps they may for less than they cost; but if you have no occasion for them, they must be dear to you. Remember what Poor Richard says; *buy what thou hast no need of, and ere long thou shalt sell thy necessaries.* And again, *at a great pennyworth pause a while:* he means, that perhaps the cheapness is apparent only, and not real; or the bargain, by straightening thee in thy business, may do thee more harm than good. For in another place he says, *many have been ruined by buying good pennyworths.* Again, Poor Richard says, *'tis foolish to lay our money in a purchase of repentance;* and yet this folly is practiced every day at vendues, for want of minding the Almanack. *Wise men,* as Poor Dick says, *learn by others' harms, fools scarcely by their own;* but *felix quem faciunt aliena pericula cautum.*[6] Many a one, for the sake of finery on the back, have gone with a hungry belly, and half-starved their families. *Silks and satins, scarlet and velvets,* as Poor Richard says, *put out the kitchen fire.*

"These are not the necessaries of life; they can scarcely be   13
called the conveniences; and yet only because they look pretty, how many want to have them! The artificial wants of mankind thus become more numerous than the natural; and, as Poor Dick says, *for one poor person, there are an hundred indigent.* By these, and other extravagancies, the genteel are reduced to poverty, and forced to borrow of those whom they formerly despised, but who through industry and frugality have maintained their standing; in which case it appears plainly, that *a plowman on his legs is higher than a gentleman on his knees,* as Poor Richard says.

[5]Much.
[6]This saying in Latin.

Perhaps they have had a small estate left them, which they knew not the getting of; they think 'Tis day, and will never be night'; that a little to be spent out of so much is not worth minding; *a child and a fool*, as Poor Richard says, *imagine twenty shillings and twenty years can never be spent* but, *always taking out of the meal-tub, and never putting in, soon comes to the bottom;* as Poor Dick says, *when the well's dry, they know the worth of water.* But this they might have known before, if they had taken his advice; *if you would know the value of money, go and try to borrow some; for, he that goes a-borrowing goes a-sorrowing;* and indeed so does he that lends to such people, when he goes to get it in again. Poor Dick farther advises, and says,

> *Fond pride of dress, is sure a very curse;*
> *E'er fancy you consult, consult your purse.*

And again, *pride is as loud a beggar as want, and a great deal more saucy.* When you have bought one fine thing, you must buy ten more, that your appearance may be all of a piece; but Poor Dick says, *'tis easier to suppress the first desire than to satisfy all that follow it.* And 'tis as truly folly for the poor to ape the rich, as for the frog to swell, in order to equal the ox.

> *Great estates may venture more,*
> *But little boats should keep near shore.*

'Tis, however, a folly soon punished; for *pride that dines on vanity sups on contempt*, as Poor Richard says. And in another place, *pride breakfasted with plenty, dined with poverty, and supped with infamy.* And after all, of what use is this pride of appearance, for which so much is risked, so much is suffered? It cannot promote health; or ease pain; it makes no increase of merit in the person, it creates envy, it hastens misfortune.

> *What is a butterfly? At best*
> *He's but a caterpillar dressed.*
> *The gaudy fop's his picture just,*

[14] as Poor Richard says.

"But what madness must it be to run in debt for these super-fluities! We are offered, by the terms of this vendue, *six months' credit;* and that perhaps has induced some of us to attend it, because we cannot spare the ready money, and hope now to be fine without it. But, ah, think what you do when you run in debt; you give to another power over your liberty. If you cannot pay at the time, you will be ashamed to see your creditor; you will be in fear when you speak to him; you will make poor pitiful sneaking excuses, and by degrees come to lose your veracity, and sink into base downright lying; for, as Poor Richard says, *the second vice is lying, the first is running in debt.* And again, to the same purpose, *lying rides upon debt's back.* Whereas a free-born Englishman ought not to be ashamed or afraid to see or speak to any man living. But poverty often deprives a man of all spirit and virtue: *'tis hard for an empty bag to stand upright,* as Poor Richard truly says.

"What would you think of that prince, or that government, 15 who should issue an edict forbidding you to dress like a gentleman or a gentlewoman, on pain of imprisonment or servitude? Would you not say, that you are free, have a right to dress as you please, and that such an edict would be a breach of your privileges, and such a government tyrannical? And yet you are about to put yourself under that tyranny, when you run in debt for such dress! Your creditor has authority at his pleasure to deprive you of your liberty, by confining you in gaol for life, or to sell you for a servant, if you should not be able to pay him! When you have got your bargain, you may, perhaps, think little of payment; but *creditors,* Poor Richard tells us, *have better memories than debtors;* and in another place says, *creditors are a superstitious sect, great observers of set days and times.* The day comes round before you are aware, and the demand is made before you are prepared to satisfy it, or if you bear your debt in mind, the term which at first seemed so long, will, as it lessens, appear extremely short. Time will seem to have added wings to his heels as well as shoulders. *Those have a short Lent,* said Poor Richard, *who owe money to be paid at Easter.* Then since, as he says, *The borrower is a slave to the lender, and the debtor to the creditor,* disdain the chain, preserve your freedom; and maintain your independency: be industrious and free; be frugal and free. At present, perhaps, you may think yourself in thriving circumstances, and that you can bear a little extravagance without injury; but,

> *For age and want, save while you may;*
> *No morning sun lasts a whole day,*

as Poor Richard says. Gain may be temporary and uncertain, but ever while you live, expense is constant and entire; and *'tis easier to build two chimneys than to keep one in fuel*, as Poor Richard says. So, *rather go to bed supperless than rise in debt*.

> *Get what you can, and what you get hold;*
> *'Tis the stone that will turn all your lead into gold,*

as Poor Richard says. And when you have got the philosopher's stone,[7] sure you will no longer complain of bad times, or the difficulty of paying taxes.

16   "This doctrine, my friends, is reason and wisdom; but after all, do not depend too much upon your own industry, and frugality, and prudence, though excellent things, for they may all be blasted without the blessing of heaven; and therefore, ask that blessing humbly, and be not uncharitable to those that at present seem to want it, but comfort and help them. Remember, Job suffered, and was afterwards prosperous.

17   "And now to conclude, *experience keeps a dear school, but fools will learn in no other, and scarce in that;* for it is true, *we may give advice, but we cannot give conduct,* as Poor Richard says: however, remember this, *they that won't be counseled, can't be helped,* as Poor Richard says: and farther, that, *if you will not hear reason, she'll surely rap your knuckles.*"

18   Thus the old gentleman ended his harangue. The people heard it, and approved the doctrine, and immediately practiced the contrary, just as if it had been a common sermon; for the vendue opened, and they began to buy extravagantly, notwithstanding all his cautions, and their own fear of taxes. I found the good man had thoroughly studied my almanacs, and digested all I had dropped on those topics during the course of five and twenty years. The frequent mention he made of me must have tired any one else, but my vanity was wonderfully delighted

---

[7] Said to turn metals into gold.

with it, though I was conscious that not a tenth part of the wisdom was my own, which he ascribed to me, but rather the gleanings I had made of the sense of all ages and nations. However, I resolved to be the better for the echo of it; and though I had at first determined to buy stuff for a new coat, I went away resolved to wear my old one a little longer. Reader, if thou wilt do the same, thy profit will be as great as mine. I am, as ever, thine to serve thee,

Richard Saunders
July 7, 1757

Gilded Lilies and Liberal Guilt

Patricia J. Williams

The original vehicle for my interest in the intersection of commerce and the Constitution was my family history. A few years ago, I came into the possession of what may have been the contract of sale for my great-great-grandmother. It is a very simple but lawyerly document, describing her as "one female" and revealing her age as eleven; no price is specified, merely "value exchanged." My sister also found a county census record taken two years later; on a list of one Austin Miller's personal assets she appears again, as "slave, female"—thirteen years old now with an eight-month infant.

Since then I have tried to piece together what it must have been like to be my great-great-grandmother. She was purchased, according to matrilineal recounting, by a man who was extremely temperamental and quite wealthy. I try to imagine what it would have been like to have a discontented white man buy me, after a fight with his mother about prolonged bachelorhood. I wonder what it would have been like to have a thirty-five-year-old man own the secrets of my puberty, which he bought to prove himself sexually as well as to increase his livestock of slaves. I imagine trying to please, with the yearning of adolescence, a man who

truly did not know I was human, whose entire belief system resolutely defined me as animal, chattel, talking cow. I wonder what
it would have been like to have his child, pale-faced but also animal, before I turned thirteen. I try to envision being casually
threatened with sale from time to time, teeth and buttocks bared
to interested visitors.

3   Family legend has it that my great-great-grandmother was
very lazy, that she sat on the bank of the river all day and fished.
According to the census, she was at least two decades younger
than any other slave on the estate; family legend says that no one
liked her. What could it have been like for my stunned, raped
great-great-grandmother—an unwed teenage mother in today's
parlance—so disliked and isolated from even her own children
that the stones they purveyed were of her laziness? Her children
were the exclusive property of their father (though that's not what
they called him). They grew up in his house, taken from her as she
had been taken from her mother. They became haughty, favored,
frightened house servants who were raised playing with, caring
for, and envying this now-married man's legitimate children,
their half brothers and sister. Her children grew up reverent of
and obedient to this white man—my great-great-grandfather—
and his other children, to whom they were taught they owed the
debt of their survival. It was a mistake from which the Emancipation Proclamation never fully freed any of them.

4   Her children must have been something of an ultimate betrayal; it could not have been easy to see in them the hope of her
own survival. Freed from slavery by the Civil War, they went on
to establish respected black Episcopal churches and to learn to
play the piano. They grew up clever and well-bred. They grew up
to marry other frightened, refined, master-blooded animals; they
grew up good people, but alien.

5   Austin Miller, one of Tennessee's finest lawyers according to
other records, went on to become a judge; and the sons by his wife
went on to become lawyers as well. There is no surviving record
of what happened to my great-great-grandmother, no account of
how or when she died.

6   This story is what inspired my interest in the interplay of notions of public and private, of family and market; of male and female, of molestation and the law. I track meticulously the

dimension of meaning in my great-great-grandmother as chattel: the meaning of money; the power of consumerist world view, the deaths of those we label the unassertive and the inefficient. I try to imagine where and who she would be today. I am engaged in a long-term project of tracking his words—through his letters and opinions—and those of his sons who were also lawyers and judges, of finding the shape described by her absence in all this.

I see her shape and his hand in the vast networking of our so- 7
ciety, and in the evils and oversights that plague our lives and laws. The control he had over her body. The force he was in her life, in the shape of my life today. The power he exercised in the choice to breed her or not. The choice to breed slaves in his image, to choose her mate and be that mate. In his attempt to own what no man can own, the habit of his power and the absence of her choice.

I look for her shape and his hand.   8

1991

Who Makes the Clothes We Wear?

Jesse Jackson

Would you spend $20 for a stylish Gap T-shirt if you knew it was 1
made by teen-age girls in El Salvador forced to work 18 hours a day in a sweatshop for about 16 cents a shirt?

Would you pay top dollar for designer fashions at Neiman 2
Marcus that were made by immigrant Thai women imprisoned behind barbed wire in forced-labor conditions?

Would you give Nike $80 for a pair of athletic shoes if you 3
knew they were made by teen-age girls in Indonesia working 60-hour weeks for less than Indonesia's miserable minimum wage? Would you buy them if you knew that one young woman who or-

ganized a strike to demand that Nike pay the statutory minimum wage in Indonesia was abducted, raped and murdered?

4   Across the world—including in the United States, the sweat-shop is back in the press. High-profit, high-profile, high-priced re-tailers have grown callous and uncaring about the inhuman working conditions of the desperate—here and abroad—who make their products. Private companies turn their backs as their subcontractors routinely trample the basic rights of their work-ers—speech, association, the right to organize, the right to a living wage, the right to a bathroom break, to healthy and safe work conditions, to overtime, the prohibition of child and slave labor. Desperate workers have been too weak to resist.

5   Look, for instance, at the conditions in El Monte, Calif. On Aug. 2, government officials raided a sweatshop filled with immi-grant Thai women laboring for as little as 59 cents per hour for 16 to 22 hours a day. Discipline was enforced by threats of rape and beatings. The women were locked up day and night as they pro-duced garments for Neiman Marcus, J.C. Penney and other U.S. retailers and manufacturers.

6   As these outrages have gained public attention, manufactur-ers and retailers are getting nervous. The $200 million or so that Nike spends each year to paste its symbol on everything from Pete Sampras at the U.S. Open to the Dallas Cowboy uniforms can be wasted by one powerful scandal that ignites consumers' moral sensibilities. "Just do it" is Nike's multimillion-dollar slogan. But many Americans, if informed of these sweatshop realities, just might not do it; and that has major clothing and shoe manufac-turers terrified. A consumer time bomb has begun to tick.

7   Republicans are out of step with this growing popular con-cern. They are busy gutting what few government protections ex-ist for working people. The budget to enforce U.S. labor laws and workplace health and safety is being slashed. Republicans are blocking efforts to codify minimal labor and environmental stan-dards in global trade treaties and develop international investiga-tion and reporting.

8   Their opposition isn't just about trimming "big government." They also oppose legislation that would empower workers to elect

their own representatives to monitor workplace safety. Even House Speaker Newt Gingrich—self-styled Third Wave revolutionary—has had little to say about the growing consumer reaction.

Unions, consumer groups, and human-rights organizations 9 are expanding their monitoring of labor conditions here and abroad. Many citizens would happily join a groundswell to hold one of these global corporate behemoths accountable for how they treat the least of their workers. If consumers spurn just one popular brand name, the other companies will rush to clean up their act.

Then the companies will push for government regulation and 10 policing as insulation against independent consumer movements. Gingrich will scurry to get in front of the parade. Conservatives will shelve opposition to big government and line up to pass the laws and codes of conduct that businesses want.

Practices like those in El Monte aren't about reasonable profit; 11 they are about greed. These companies have grown arrogant in their global reach. Like true cynics, they know the price of everything and the value of nothing. In 1993, the labor cost to Nike for a pair of $80 sneakers was 12 cents; in 1994, the company had more than $4.3 billion in sales. Nike paid more to give shoes away in promotions than to pay 12,000 women in Indonesia who make them. Organizers estimate that 1% of the Nike advertising budget could double the wages paid to the women and lift them above the poverty line.

Nike can afford minimal rights for their workers. Now in- 12 formed consumers may begin to make the trampling of basic decency a whole lot more expensive than the cost of respecting it.

1995

Who Built the Pyramids? Mike Lefevre

Studs Terkel

Who built the seven towers of Thebes?
The books are filled with the names of kings.
Was it kings who hauled the craggy blocks of stone? . . .

In the evening when the Chinese wall was finished
Where did the masons go? . . .

—BERTOLT BRECHT

1   *It is a two-flat dwelling, somewhere in Cicero, on the outskirts of*
Chicago. He is thirty-seven. He works in a steel mill. On occasion, his
wife Carol works as a waitress in a neighborhood restaurant; otherwise,
she is at home, caring for their two small children, a girl and a boy.

2   *At the time of my first visit, a sculpted statuette of Mother and*
Child was on the floor, head severed from body. He laughed softly as he
indicated his three-year-old daughter: "She Doctor Spock'd it."

3   I'm a dying breed. A laborer. Strictly muscle work . . . pick it
up, put it down, pick it up, put it down. We handle between forty
and fifty thousand pounds of steel a day. (Laughs.) I know this is
hard to believe—from four hundred pounds to three- and four-
pound pieces. It's dying.

4   You can't take pride any more. You remember when a guy
could point to a house he built, how many logs he stacked. He built
it and he was proud of it. I don't really think I could be proud if a
contractor built a home for me. I would be tempted to get in there
and kick the carpenter in the ass (laughs), and take the saw away
from him. 'Cause I would have to be part of it, you know.

5   It's hard to take pride in a bridge you're never gonna cross, in
a door you're never gonna open. You're mass-producing things
and you never see the end result of it. (Muses.) I worked for a
trucker one time. And I got this tiny satisfaction when I loaded a
truck. At least I could see the truck depart loaded. In a steel mill,
forget it. You don't see where nothing goes.

6   I got chewed out by my foreman once. He said, "Mike, you're
a good worker but you have a bad attitude." My attitude is that I
don't get excited about my job. I do my work but I don't say
whoopee-doo. The day I get excited about my job is the day I go
to a head shrinker. How are you gonna get excited about pullin'
steel? How are you gonna get excited when you're tired and want
to sit down?

7   It's not just the work. Somebody built the pyramids. Somebody's going to build something. Pyramids, Empire State Building—these things just don't happen. There's hard work behind it.
I would like to see a building, say, the Empire State, I would like

to see on one side of it a foot-wide strip from top to bottom with the name of every bricklayer, the name of every electrician, with all the names. So when a guy walked by, he could take his son and say, "See, that's me over there on the forty-fifth floor. I put the steel beam in." Picasso can point to a painting. What can I point to? A writer can point to a book. Everybody should have something to point to.

It's the not-recognition by other people. To say a woman is 8 *just* a housewife is degrading right? Okay. *Just* a housewife. It's also degrading to say *just* a laborer. The difference is that a man goes out and maybe gets smashed.

When I was single, I could quit, just split. I wandered all over 9 the country. You worked just enough to get a poke, money in your pocket. Now I'm married and I got two kids . . . (trails off). I worked on a truck dock one time and I was single. The foreman came over and he grabbed my shoulder, kind of gave me a shove. I punched him and knocked him off the dock. I said, "Leave me alone. I'm doing my work, just stay away from me, just don't give me the with-the-hands business."

Hell, if you whip a damn mule he might kick you. Stay out of 10 my way, that's all. Working is bad enough, don't bug me. I would rather work my ass off for eight hours a day with nobody watching me than five minutes with a guy watching me. Who you gonna sock? You can't sock General Motors, you can't sock anybody in Washington, you can't sock a system.

A mule, an old mule, that's the way I feel. Oh yeah. See. 11 (Shows black and blue marks on arms and legs, burns.) You know what I heard from more than one guy at work? "If my kid wants to work in a factory, I am going to kick the hell out of him." I want my kid to be an effete snob. Yeah, mm-hmm. (Laughs.) I want him to be able to quote Walt Whitman, to be proud of it.

If you can't improve yourself, you improve your posterity. 12 Otherwise life isn't worth nothing. You might as well go back to the cave and stay there. I'm sure the first caveman who went over the hill to see what was on the other side—I don't think he went there wholly out of curiosity. He went there because he wanted to get his son out of the cave. Just the same way I want to send my kid to college.

13   I work so damn hard and want to come home and sit down and lay around. *But I gotta get it out.* I want to be able to turn around to somebody and say, "Hey, fuck you." You know? (Laughs.) The guy sitting next to me on the bus too. 'Cause all day I wanted to tell my foreman to go fuck himself, but I can't.

14   So I find a guy in a tavern. To tell him that. And he tells me too. I've been in brawls. He's punching me and I'm punching him, because we actually want to punch somebody else. The most that'll happen is the bartender will bar us from the tavern. But at work, you lose your job.

15   This one foreman I've got, he's a kid. He's a college graduate. He thinks he's better than everybody else. He was chewing me out and I was saying, "Yeah, yeah, yeah." He said, "What do you mean, yeah, yeah, yeah. Yes, *sir.*" I told him, "Who the hell are you, Hitler? What is this *'Yes, sir'* bullshit? I came here to work, I didn't come here to crawl. There's a fuckin' difference." One word led to another and I lost.

16   I got broke down to a lower grade and lost twenty-five cents an hour, which is a hell of a lot. It amounts to about ten dollars a week. He came over—after breaking me down. The guy comes over and smiles at me. I blew up. He didn't know it, but he was about two seconds and two feet away from a hospital. I said, "Stay the fuck away from me." He was just about to say something and was pointing his finger. I just reached my hand up and just grabbed his finger because I'm married. If I'd a been single, I'd a grabbed his head. That's the difference.

17   You're doing this manual labor and you know that technology can do it. (Laughs.) Let's face it, a machine can do the work of a man; otherwise they wouldn't have space probes. Why can we send a rocket ship that's unmanned and yet send a man in a steel mill to do a mule's work?

18   Automation? Depends how it's applied. It frightens me if it puts me out on the street. It doesn't frighten me if it shortens my workweek. You read that little thing: what are you going to do when this computer replaces you? Blow up computers. (Laughs.) Really. Blow up computers. I'll be goddamned if a computer is gonna eat before I do! I want milk for my kids and beer for me. Machines can either liberate man or enslave 'im, because they're

pretty neutral. It's man who has the bias to put the thing one place or another.

If I had a twenty-hour workweek, I'd get to know my kids 19 better, my wife better. Some kid invited me to go on a college campus. On a Saturday. It was summertime. Hell, if I have a choice of taking my wife and kids to a picnic or going to a college campus, it's gonna be the picnic. But if I worked a twenty-hour week, I could go do both. Don't you think with that extra twenty hours people could really expand? Who's to say? There are some people in factories just by force of circumstance. I'm just like the colored people. Potential Einsteins don't have to be white. They could be in cotton fields, they could be in factories.

The twenty-hour week is a possibility today. The intellectuals, 20 they always say there are potential Lord Byrons, Walt Whitmans, Roosevelts, Picassos working in construction or steel mills or factories. But I don't think they believe it. I think what they're afraid of is the potential Hitlers and Stalins that are there too. The people in power fear the leisure man. Not just the United States. Russia's the same way.

What do you think would happen in this country if, for one 21 year, they experimented and gave everybody a twenty-hour week? How do they know that the guy who digs Wallace[1] today doesn't try to resurrect Hitler tomorrow? Or the guy who is mildly disturbed at pollution doesn't decide to go to General Motors and shit on the guy's desk? You can become a fanatic if you had the time. The whole thing is time. That is, I think, one reason rich kids tend to be fanatic about politics: they have time. Time, that's the important thing.

It isn't that the average working guy is dumb. He's tired, 22 that's all. I picked up a book on chess one time. That thing laid in the drawer for two or three weeks, you're too tired. During the weekends you want to take your kids out. You don't want to sit there and the kid comes up: "Daddy, can I go to the park?" You got your nose in a book? Forget it.

I know a guy fifty-seven years old. Know what he tells me? 23 "Mike, I'm old and tired *all* the time." The first thing happens at

[1]George Wallace, former governor of Alabama, who advocated segregation.

work: when the arms start moving, the brain stops. I punch in about ten minutes to seven in the morning. I say hello to a couple of guys I like, I kid around with them. One guy says good morning to you and you say good morning. To another guy you say fuck you. The guy you say fuck you to is your friend.

24   I put on my hard hat, change into my safety shoes, put on my safety glasses, go to the bonderizer. It's the thing I work on. They rake the metal, they wash it, they dip it in a paint solution, and we take it off. Put it on, take it off, put it on, take it off, put it on, take it off . . .

25   I say hello to everybody but my boss. At seven it starts. My arms get tired about the first half-hour. After that, they don't get tired any more until maybe the last half-hour at the end of the day. I work from seven to three thirty. My arms are tired at seven thirty and they're tired at three o'clock. I hope to God I never get broke in, because I always want my arms to be tired at seven thirty and three o'clock. (Laughs.) 'Cause that's when I know that there's a beginning and there's an end. That I'm not brainwashed. In between, I don't even try to think.

26   If I were to put you in front of a dock and I pulled up a skid in front of you with fifty hundred-pound sacks of potatoes and there are fifty more skids just like it, and this is what you're gonna do all day, what would you think about—potatoes? Unless a guy's a nut, he never thinks about work or talks about it. Maybe about baseball or about getting drunk the other night or he got laid or he didn't get laid. I'd say one out of a hundred will actually get excited about work.

27   Why is it that the communists always say they're for the workingman, and as soon as they set up a country, you got guys singing to tractors? They're singing about how they love the factory. That's where I couldn't buy communism. It's the intellectuals' utopia, not mine. I cannot picture myself singing to a tractor, I just can't. (Laughs.) Or singing to steel. (Singsongs.) Oh whoop-dee-doo, I'm at the bonderizer, oh how I love this heavy steel. No thanks. Never happen.

28   Oh yeah, I daydream. I fantasize about a sexy blond in Miami who's got my union dues. (Laughs.) I think of the head of the union the way I think of the head of my company. Living it up. I

think of February in Miami. Warm weather, a place to lay in. When I hear a college kid say, "I'm oppressed," I don't believe him. You know what I'd like to do for one year? Live like a college kid. Just for one year. I'd love to. Wow! (Whispers.) Wow! Sports car! Marijuana! (Laughs.) Wild, sexy broads. I'd love that, hell yes, I would.

Somebody has to do this work. If my kid ever goes to college, 29 I just want him to have a little respect, to realize that his dad is one of those somebodies. This is why even on—(muses) yeah, I guess, sure—on the black thing . . . (Sighs heavily.) I can't really hate the colored fella that's working with me all day. The black intellectual I got no respect for. The white intellectual I got no use for. I got no use for the black militant who's gonna scream three hundred years of slavery to me while I'm busting my ass. You know what I mean? (Laughs.) I have one answer for that guy: go see Rocke-feller. See Harriman. Don't bother me. We're in the same cotton field. So just don't bug me. (Laughs.)

After work I usually stop off at a tavern. Cold beer. Cold beer 30 right away. When I was single, I used to go into hillbilly bars, get in a lot of brawls. Just to explode. I got a thing on my arm here (in-dicates scar). I got slapped with a bicycle chain. Oh, wow! (Softly) Mmm. I'm getting older. (Laughs.) I don't explode as much. You might say I'm broken in. (Quickly) No, I'll never be broken in. (Sighs.) When you get a little older, you exchange the words. When you're younger, you exchange the blows.

When I get home, I argue with my wife a little bit. Turn on TV, 31 get mad at the news. (Laughs.) I don't even watch the news that much. I watch Jackie Gleason. I look for any alternative to the ten o'clock news. I don't want to go to bed angry. Don't hit a man with anything heavy at five o'clock. He just can't be bothered. This is his time to relax. The heaviest thing he wants is what his wife has to tell him.

When I come home, know what I do for the first twenty min- 32 utes? Fake it. I put on a smile. I got a kid three years old. Some-times she says, "Daddy, where've you been?" I say, "Work." I could have told her I'd been in Disneyland. What's work to a three-year-old kid? If I feel bad, I can't take it out on the kids. Kids are born innocent of everything but birth. You can't take it out on

your wife either. This is why you go to a tavern. You want to release it there rather than do it at home. What does an actor do
when he's got a bad movie? I got a bad movie every day.

33   I don't even need the alarm clock to get up in the morning. I
can go out drinking all night, fall asleep at four, and bam! I'm up at
six—no matter what I do. (Laughs.) It's a pseudo-death, more or
less. Your whole system is paralyzed and you give all the appearance of death. It's an ingrown clock. It's a thing you just get used to.
The hours differ. It depends. Sometimes my wife wants to do something crazy like play five hundred rummy or put a puzzle together.
It could be midnight, could be ten o'clock, could be nine thirty.

34   *What do you do weekends?*

35   Drink beer, read a book. See that one? *Violence in America.* It's
one of them studies from Washington. One of them committees
they're always appointing. A thing like that I read on a weekend.
But during the weekdays, gee . . . I just thought about it. I don't do
that much reading from Monday through Friday. Unless it's a
horny book. I'll read it at work and go home and do my homework. (Laughs.) That's what the guys at the plant call it—homework. (Laughs.) Sometimes my wife works on Saturday and I
drink beer at the tavern.

36   I went out drinking with one guy, oh, a long time ago. A college boy. He was working where I work now. Always preaching
to me about how you need violence to change the system and all
that garbage. We went into a hillbilly joint. Some guy there, I didn't
know him from Adam, he said, "You think you're smart." I said,
"What's your pleasure?" (Laughs.) He said, "My pleasure's to
kick your ass." I told him I really can't be bothered. He said,
"What're you, chicken?" I said, "No, I just don't want to be bothered." He came over and said something to me again. I said, "I
don't beat women, drunks, or fools. Now leave me alone."

37   The guy called his brother over. This college boy that was
with me, he came nudging my arm, "Mike, let's get out of here." I
said, "What are you worried about?" (Laughs.) This isn't unusual.
People will bug you. You fend it off as much as you can with your
mouth and when you can't, you punch the guy out.

38   It was close to closing time and we stayed. We could have left,
but when you go into a place to have a beer and a guy challenges

you—if you expect to go in that place again, you don't leave. If you have to fight the guy, you fight.

I got just outside the door and one of these guys jumped on me and grabbed me around the neck. I grabbed his arm and flung him against the wall. I grabbed him here (indicates throat), and jiggled his head against the wall quite a few times. He kind of slid down a little bit. This guy who said he was his brother took a swing at me with a garrison belt. He just missed and hit the wall. I'm looking around for my junior Stalin (laughs), who loves violence and everything. He's gone. Split. (Laughs.) Next day I see him at work. I couldn't get mad at him, he's a baby.

He saw a book in my back pocket one time and he was amazed. He walked up to me and he said, "You read?" I said, "What do you mean, I read?" He said, "All these dummies read the sports pages around here. What are you doing with a book?" I got pissed off at the kid right away. I said, "What do you mean, all these dummies? Don't knock a man who's paying somebody else's way through college." He was a nineteen-year-old effete snob.

Yet you want your kid to be an effete snob?

Yes. I want my kid to look at me and say, "Dad, you're a nice guy, but you're a fuckin' dummy." Hell yes, I want my kid to tell me that he's not gonna be like me . . .

If I were hiring people to work, I'd try naturally to pay them a decent wage. I'd try to find out their first names, their last names, keep the company as small as possible, so I could personalize the whole thing. All I would ask a man is a handshake, see you in the morning. No applications, nothing. I wouldn't be interested in the guy's past. Nobody ever checks the pedigree on a mule, do they? But they do on a man. Can you picture walking up to a mule and saying, "I'd like to know who his granddaddy was?"

I'd like to run a combination bookstore and tavern. (Laughs.) I would like to have a place where college kids came and a steelworker could sit down and talk. Where a workingman could not be ashamed of Walt Whitman and where a college professor could not be ashamed that he painted his house over the weekend.

If a carpenter built a cabin for poets, I think the least the poets owe the carpenter is just three or four one-liners on the wall. A little plaque: Though we labor with our minds, this place we can relax in was built by someone who can work with his hands. And his work is as noble as ours. I think the poet owes something to the guy who builds the cabin for him.

46   I don't think of Monday. You know what I'm thinking about on Sunday night? Next Sunday. If you work real hard, you think of a perpetual vacation. Not perpetual sleep . . . What do I think of on a Sunday night? Lord, I wish the fuck I could do something else for a living.

47   I don't know who the guy is who said there is nothing sweeter than an unfinished symphony. Like an unfinished painting and an unfinished poem. If he creates this thing one day—let's say, Michelangelo's Sistine Chapel. It took him a long time to do this, this beautiful work of art. But what if he had to create this Sistine Chapel a thousand times a year? Don't you think that would even dull Michelangelo's mind? Or if da Vinci had to draw his anatomical charts thirty, forty, fifty, sixty, eighty, ninety, a hundred times a day? Don't you think that would even bore da Vinci?

48   *Way back, you spoke of the guys who built the pyramids, not the pharaohs, the unknowns. You put yourself in their category?*

49   Yes. I want my signature on 'em, too. Sometimes, out of pure meanness, when I make something, I put a little dent in it. I like to do something to make it really unique. Hit it with a hammer. I deliberately fuck it up to see if it'll get by, just so I can say I did it. It could be anything. Let me put it this way: I think God invented the dodo bird so when we get up there we could tell Him, "Don't you ever make mistakes?" and He'd say, "Sure, look." (Laughs.) I'd like to make my imprint. My dodo bird. A mistake, *mine.* Let's say the whole building is nothing but red bricks. I'd like to have just the black one or the white one or the purple one. Deliberately fuck up.

50   This is gonna sound square, but my kid is my imprint. He's my freedom. There's a line in one of Hemingway's books. I think it's from *For Whom the Bell Tolls.* They're behind the enemy lines, somewhere in Spain, and she's pregnant. She wants to stay with him. He tells her no. He says, "if you die, I die," knowing he's gonna die. But if you go, I go. Know what I mean? The mystics call it the brass bowl. Continuum. You know what I mean? This is why I work. Every time I see a young guy walk by with a shirt and tie and dressed up real sharp, I'm lookin' at my kid, you know? That's it.

1972

Nickel-and-Dimed
On (not) getting by in America

Barbara Ehrenreich

At the beginning of June 1998 I leave behind everything that nor-   1
mally soothes the ego and sustains the body—home, career, companion, reputation, ATM card—for a plunge into the low-wage
workforce. There, I become another, occupationally much diminished "Barbara Ehrenreich"—depicted on job-application forms
as a divorced homemaker whose sole work experience consists of
housekeeping in a few private homes. I am terrified, at the beginning, of being unmasked for what I am: a middle-class journalist setting out to explore the world that welfare mothers are
entering, at the rate of approximately 50,000 a month, as welfare
reform kicks in. Happily, though, my fears turn out to be entirely
unwarranted: during a month of poverty and toil, my name goes
unnoticed and for the most part unuttered. In this parallel universe where my father never got out of the mines and I never got
through college, I am "baby," "honey," "blondie," and, most
commonly, "girl."

My first task is to find a place to live. I figure that if I can earn   2
$7 an hour—which, from the want ads, seems doable—I can afford
to spend $500 on rent, or maybe, with severe economies, $600. In
the Key West area, where I live, this pretty much confines me to
flophouses and trailer homes—like the one, a pleasing fifteen-
minute drive from town, that has no air-conditioning, no screens,
no fans, no television, and, by way of diversion, only the challenge
of evading the landlord's Doberman pinscher. The big problem
with this place, though, is the rent, which at $675 a month is well
beyond my reach. All right, Key West is expensive. But so is New
York City, or the Bay Area, or Jackson Hole, or Telluride, or Boston,
or any other place where tourists and the wealthy compete for living space with the people who clean their toilets and fry their hash
browns.[1] Still, it is a shock to realize that "trailer trash" has become, for me, a demographic category to aspire to.

3   So I decide to make the common trade-off between afford-ability and convenience, and go for a $500-a-month efficiency thirty miles up a two-lane highway from the employment oppor-tunities of Key West, meaning forty-five minutes if there's no road construction and I don't get caught behind some sun-dazed Canadian tourists. I hate the drive, along a roadside studded with white crosses commemorating the more effective head-on colli-sions, but it's a sweet little place—a cabin, more or less, set in the swampy back yard of the converted mobile home where my land-lord, an affable TV repairman, lives with his bartender girlfriend. Anthropologically speaking, a bustling trailer park would be preferable, but here I have a gleaming white floor and a firm mat-tress, and the few resident bugs are easily vanquished.

4   Besides, I am not doing this for the anthropology. My aim is nothing so mistily subjective as to "experience poverty" or find out how it "really feels" to be a long-term low-wage worker. I've had enough unchosen encounters with poverty and the world of low-wage work to know it's not a place you want to visit for touristic purposes; it just smells too much like fear. And with all my real-life assets—bank account, IRA, health insurance, multiroom home—waiting indulgently in the background, I am, of course, thoroughly insulated from the terrors that afflict the genuinely poor.

5   No, this is a purely objective, scientific sort of mission. The humanitarian rationale for welfare reform—as opposed to the more punitive and stingy impulses that may actually have moti-vated it—is that work will lift poor women out of poverty while simultaneously inflating their self-esteem and hence their future value in the labor market. Thus, whatever the hassles involved in finding child care, transportation, etc., the transition from welfare to work will end happily, in greater prosperity for all. Now there

[1]According to the Department of Housing and Urban Development, the "fair-market rent" for an efficiency is $551 here in Monroe County, Florida. A compara-ble rent in the five boroughs of New York City is $704; in San Francisco, $713; and in the heart of Silicon Valley, $808. The fair-market rent for an area is defined as the amount that would be needed to pay rent plus utilities for "privately owned, decent, safe, and sanitary rental housing of a modest (non-luxury) nature with suitable amenities."

are many problems with this comforting prediction, such as the fact that the economy will inevitably undergo a downturn, eliminating many jobs. Even without a downturn, the influx of a million former welfare recipients into the low-wage labor market could depress wages by as much as 11.9 percent, according to the Economic Policy Institute (EPI) in Washington, D.C.

But is it really possible to make a living on the kinds of jobs 6 currently available to unskilled people? Mathematically, the answer is no, as can be shown by taking $6 to $7 an hour, perhaps subtracting a dollar or two an hour for child care, multiplying by 160 hours a month, and comparing the result to the prevailing rents. According to the National Coalition for the Homeless, for example, in 1998 it took, on average nationwide, an hourly wage of $8.89 to afford a one-bedroom apartment, and the Preamble Center for Public Policy estimates that the odds against a typical welfare recipient's landing a job at such a "living wage" are about 97 to 1. If these numbers are right, low-wage work is not a solution to poverty and possibly not even to homelessness.

It may seem excessive to put this proposition to an experi- 7 mental test. As certain family members keep unhelpfully reminding me, the viability of low-wage work could be tested, after a fashion, without ever leaving my study. I could just pay myself $7 an hour for eight hours a clay, charge myself for room and board, and total up the numbers after a month. Why leave the people and work that I love? But I am an experimental scientist by training. In that business, you don't just sit at a desk and theorize; you plunge into the everyday chaos of nature, where surprises lurk in the most mundane measurements. Maybe, when I got into it, I would discover some hidden economies in the world of the low-wage worker. After all, if 30 percent of the workforce toils for less than $8 an hour, according to the EPI, they may have found some tricks as yet unknown to me. Maybe—who knows?—I would even be able to detect in myself the bracing psychological effects of getting out of the house, as promised by the welfare wonks at places like the Heritage Foundation. Or, on the other hand, maybe there would be unexpected costs—physical, mental, or financial— to throw off all my calculations. Ideally, I should do this with two small children in tow, that being the welfare average, but mine are grown and no one is willing to lend me theirs for a month-long vacation in penury. So this is not the perfect experiment, just a test of the best possible case: an unencumbered woman, smart and even strong, attempting to live more or less off the land.

8   On the morning of my first full day of job searching, I take a red pen to the want ads, which are auspiciously numerous. Everyone in Key West's booming "hospitality industry" seems to be looking for someone like me—trainable, flexible, and with suitably humble expectations as to pay. I know I possess certain traits that might be advantageous—I'm white and, I like to think, well-spoken and poised—but I decide on two rules: One, I cannot use any skills derived from my education or usual work—not that there are a lot of want ads for satirical essayists anyway. Two, I have to take the best-paid job that is offered me and of course do my best to hold it; no Marxist rants or sneaking off to read novels in the ladies' room. In addition, I rule out various occupations for one reason or another: Hotel front-desk clerk, for example, which to my surprise is regarded as unskilled and pays around $7 an hour, gets eliminated because it involves standing in one spot for eight hours a day. Waitressing is similarly something I'd like to avoid, because I remember it leaving me bone tired when I was eighteen, and I'm decades of varicosities and back pain beyond that now. Telemarketing, one of the first refuges of the suddenly indigent, can be dismissed on grounds of personality. This leaves certain supermarket jobs, such as deli clerk, or housekeeping in Key West's thousands of hotel and guest rooms. Housekeeping is especially appealing, for reasons both atavistic and practical: it's what my mother did before I came along, and it can't be too different from what I've been doing part-time, in my own home, all my life.

9   So I put on what I take to be a respectful-looking outfit of ironed Bermuda shorts and scooped-neck T-shirt and set out for a tour of the local hotels and supermarkets. Best Western, Econo Lodge, and HoJo's all let me fill out application forms, and these are, to my relief, interested in little more than whether I am a legal resident of the United States and have committed any felonies.

My next stop is Winn-Dixie, the supermarket, which turns out to have a particularly onerous application process, featuring a fifteen-minute "interview" by computer since, apparently, no human on the premises is deemed capable of representing the corporate point of view. I am conducted to a large room decorated with posters illustrating how to look "professional" (it helps to be white and, if female, permed) and warning of the slick promises that union organizers might try to tempt me with. The interview is multiple choice: Do I have anything, such as child-care problems, that might make it hard for me to get to work on time? Do I think safety on the job is the responsibility of management? Then, popping up cunningly out of the blue: How many dollars' worth of stolen goods have I purchased in the last year? Would I turn in a fellow employee if I caught him stealing? Finally, "Are you an honest person?"

Apparently, I ace the interview, because I am told that all I 10 have to do is show up in some doctor's office tomorrow for a urine test. This seems to be a fairly general rule: if you want to stack Cheerio boxes or vacuum hotel rooms in chemically fascist America, you have to be willing to squat down and pee in front of some health worker (who has no doubt had to do the same thing herself). The wages Winn-Dixie is offering—$6 and a couple of dimes to start with—are not enough, I decide, to compensate for this indignity.[2]

I lunch at Wendy's, where $4.99 gets you unlimited refills at the 11 Mexican part of the Superbar, a comforting surfeit of refried beans and "cheese sauce." A teenage employee, seeing me studying the want ads, kindly offers me an application form, which I fill out,

[2]According to the *Monthly Labor Review* (November 1996), 28 percent of work sites surveyed in the service industry conduct drug tests (corporate workplaces have much higher rates), and the incidence of testing has risen markedly since the Eighties. The rate of testing is highest in the South (56 percent of work sites polled), with the Midwest in second place (50 percent). The drug most likely to be detected—marijuana, which can be detected in urine for weeks—is also the most innocuous, while heroin and cocaine are generally undetectable three days after use. Prospective employees sometimes try to cheat the tests by consuming excessive amounts of liquids and taking diuretics and even masking substances available through the Internet.

though here, too, the pay is just $6 and change an hour. Then it's off for a round of the locally owned inns and guesthouses. At "The Palms," let's call it, a bouncy manager actually takes me around to see the rooms and meet the existing housekeepers, who, I note with satisfaction, look pretty much like me—faded ex-hippie types in shorts with long hair pulled back in braids. Mostly, though, no one speaks to one or even looks at me except to proffer an application form. At my last stop, a palatial B&B, I wait twenty minutes to meet "Max," only to be told that there are no jobs now but there should be one soon, since "nobody lasts more than a couple weeks." (Because none of the people I talked to knew I was a reporter, I have changed their names to protect their privacy and, in some cases perhaps, their jobs.)

12   Three days go by like this, and, to my chagrin, no one out of the approximately twenty places I've applied calls me for an interview. I had been vain enough to worry about coming across as too educated for the jobs I sought, but no one even seems interested in finding out how overqualified I am. Only later will I realize that the want ads are not a reliable measure of the actual jobs available at any particular time. They are, as I should have guessed from Max's comment, the employers' insurance policy against the relentless turnover of the low-wage workforce. Most of the big hotels run ads almost continually, just to build a supply of applicants to replace the current workers as they drift away or are fired, so finding a job is just a matter of being at the right place at the right time and flexible enough to take whatever is being offered that day. This finally happens to me at a one of the big discount hotel chains, where I go, as usual, for housekeeping and am sent, instead, to try out as a waitress at the attached "family restaurant," a dismal spot with a counter and about thirty tables that looks out on a parking garage and features such tempting fare as "Pollish [sic] sausage and BBQ sauce" on 95-degree days. Phillip, the dapper young West Indian who introduces himself as the manager, interviews me with about as much enthusiasm as if he were a clerk processing me for Medicare, the principal questions being what shifts can I work and when can I start. I mutter something about being woefully out of practice as a waitress, but

he's already on to the uniform: I'm to show up tomorrow wearing black slacks and black shoes; he'll provide the rust-colored polo shirt with HEARTHSIDE embroidered on it, though I might want to wear my own shirt to get to work, ha ha. At the word "tomorrow," something between fear and indignation rises in my chest. I want to say, "Thank you for your time, sir, but this is just an experiment, you know, not my actual life."

So begins my career at the Hearthside, I shall call it, one small 13 profit center within a global discount hotel chain, where for two weeks I work from 2:00 till 10:00 P.M. for $2.43 an hour plus tips.[3] In some futile bid for gentility, the management has barred employees from using the front door, so my first day I enter through the kitchen, where a red-faced man with shoulder-length blond hair is throwing frozen steaks against the wall and yelling, "Fuck this shit!" "That's just Jack," explains Gail, the wiry middle-aged waitress who is assigned to train me. "He's on the rag again"—a condition occasioned, in this instance, by the fact that the cook on the morning shift had forgotten to thaw out the steaks. For the next eight hours, I run after the agile Gail, absorbing bits of instruction along with fragments of personal tragedy. All food must be trayed, and the reason she's so tired today is that she woke up in a cold sweat thinking of her boyfriend, who killed himself recently in an upstate prison. No refills on lemonade. And the reason he was in prison is that a few DUIs caught up with him, that's all, could have happened to anyone. Carry the creamers to the table in a monkey bowl, never in your hand. And after he was gone she spent several months living in her truck, peeing in a plastic pee bottle and reading by candlelight at night, but you can't live in a truck in the summer, since you need to have the windows down, which means anything can get in, from mosquitoes on up.

At least Gail puts to rest any fears I had of appearing 14 overqualified. From the first day on, I find that of all the things I

[3]According to the Fair Labor Standards Act, employers are not required to pay "tipped employees," such as restaurant servers, more than $2.13 an hour in direct wages. However, if the sum of tips plus $2.13 an hour falls below the minimum wage, or $5.15 an hour, the employer is required to make up the difference. This fact was not mentioned by managers or otherwise publicized at either of the restaurants where I worked.

have left behind, such as home and identity, what I miss the most is competence. Not that I have ever felt utterly competent in the writing business, in which one day's success augurs nothing at all for the next. But in my writing life, I at least have some notion of procedure: do the research, make the outline, rough out a draft, etc. As a server, though, I am beset by requests like bees: more iced tea here, ketchup over there, a to-go box for table fourteen, and where are the high chairs, anyway? Of the twenty-seven tables, up to six are usually mine at any time, though on slow afternoons or if Gail is off, I sometimes have the whole place to myself. There is the touch-screen computer-ordering system to master, which is, I suppose, meant to minimize server–cook contact, but in practice requires constant verbal fine-tuning: "That's gravy on the mashed, okay? None on the meatloaf," and so forth—while the cook scowls as if I were inventing these refinements just to torment him. Plus, something I had forgotten in the years since I was eighteen: about a third of a server's job is "side work" that's invisible to customers—sweeping, scrubbing, slicing, refilling, and restocking. If it isn't all done, every little bit of it, you're going to face the 6:00 P.M. dinner rush defenseless and probably go down in flames. I screw up dozens of times at the beginning, sustained in my shame entirely by Gail's support—"It's okay, baby, everyone does that sometime"—because, to my total surprise and despite the scientific detachment I am doing my best to maintain, I care.

15   The whole thing would be a lot easier if I could just skate through it as Lily Tomlin in one of her waitress skits, but I was raised by the absurd Booker T. Washingtonian precept that says: If you're going to do something, do it well. In fact, "well" isn't good enough by half. Do it better than anyone has ever done it before. Or so said my father, who must have known what he was talking about because he managed to pull himself, and us with him, up from the mile-deep copper mines of Butte to the leafy suburbs of the Northeast, ascending from boilermakers to martinis before booze beat out ambition. As in most endeavors I have encountered in my life, doing it "better than anyone" is not a reasonable goal. Still, when I wake up at 4:00 A.M. in my own cold sweat, I am not thinking about the writing deadlines I'm neglecting; I'm thinking about the table whose order I screwed up so that one of

the boys didn't get his kiddie meal until the rest of the family had moved on to their Key Lime pies. That's the other powerful motivation I hadn't expected—the customers, or "patients," as I can't help thinking of them on account of the mysterious vulnerability that seems to have left them temporarily unable to feed themselves. After a few days at the Hearthside, I feel the service ethic kick in like a shot of oxytocin, the nurturance hormone. The plurality of my customers are hard-working locals—truck drivers, construction workers, even housekeepers from the attached hotel—and I want them to have the closest to a "fine dining" experience that the grubby circumstances will allow. No "you guys" for me; everyone over twelve is "sir" or "ma'am." I ply them with iced tea and coffee refills; I return, mid-meal, to inquire how everything is; I doll up their salads with chopped raw mushrooms, summer squash slices, or whatever bits of produce I can find that have survived their sojourn in the cold-storage room mold-free.

There is Benny, for example, a short, tight-muscled sewer re- 16 pairman, who cannot even think of eating until he has absorbed a half hour of air-conditioning and ice water. We chat about hyperthermia and electrolytes until he is ready to order some finicky combination like soup of the day, garden salad, and a side of grits. There are the German tourists who are so touched by my pidgin "Willkommen" and "Ist alles gut?" that they actually tip. (Europeans, spoiled by their trade-union-ridden, high-wage welfare states, generally do not know that they are supposed to tip. Some restaurants, the Hearthside included, allow servers to "grat" their foreign customers, or add a tip to the bill. Since this amount is added before the customers have a chance to tip or not tip, the practice amounts to an automatic penalty for imperfect English.) There are the two dirt-smudged lesbians, just off their construction shift, who are impressed enough by my suave handling of the fly in the pina colada that they take the time to praise me to Stu, the assistant manager. There's Sam, the kindly retired cop, who has to plug up his tracheotomy hole with one finger in order to force the cigarette smoke into his lungs.

Sometimes I play with the fantasy that I am a princess who, in 17 penance for some tiny transgression, has undertaken to feed each of her subjects by hand. But the non-princesses working with me are just as indulgent, even when this means flouting management rules—concerning, for example, the number of croutons that can go on a salad (six). "Put on all you want," Gail whispers, "as long as Stu isn't looking." She dips into her own tip money to buy biscuits and gravy for an out-of-work mechanic who's used up all his money on dental surgery, inspiring me to pick up the tab for his milk and pie. Maybe the same high levels of agape can be found throughout the "hospitality industry." I remember the poster decorating one of the apartments I looked at, which said "If you seek happiness for yourself you will never find it. Only when you seek happiness for others will it come to you," or words to that effect—an odd sentiment, it seemed to me at the time, to find in the dank one-room basement apartment of a bellhop at the Best Western. At the Hearthside, we utilize whatever bits of autonomy we have to ply our customers with the illicit calories that signal our love. It is our job as servers to assemble the salads and desserts, pouring the dressings and squirting the whipped cream. We also control the number of butter patties our customers get and the amount of sour cream on their baked potatoes. So if you wonder why Americans are so obese, consider the fact that waitresses both express their humanity and earn their tips through the covert distribution of fats.

18   Ten days into it, this is beginning to look like a livable lifestyle. I like Gail, who is "looking at fifty" but moves so fast she can alight in one place and then another without apparently being anywhere between them. I clown around with Lionel, the teenage Haitian busboy, and catch a few fragments of conversation with Joan, the svelte fortyish hostess and militant feminist who is the only one of us who dares to tell Jack to shut the fuck up. I even warm up to Jack when, on a slow night and to make up for a particularly unwarranted attack on my abilities, or so I imagine, he tells me about his glory days as a young man at "coronary school"—or do you say "culinary"?—in Brooklyn, where he dated a knock-out Puerto Rican chick and learned everything there is to know about food. I finish up at 10:00 or 10:30, depending on how much side work I've been able to get done during the shift, and cruise home to the tapes I snatched up at random when I left my

real home—Marianne Faithfull, Tracy Chapman, Enigma, King
Sunny Ade, the Violent Femmes—just drained enough for the
music to set my cranium resonating but hardly dead. Midnight
snack is Wheat Thins and Monterey Jack, accompanied by cheap
white wine on ice and whatever AMC has to offer. To bed by 1:30
or 2:00, up at 9:00 or 10:00, read for an hour while my uniform
whirls around in the landlord's washing machine, and then it's
another eight hours spent following Mao's central instruction, as
laid out in the Little Red Book, which was: Serve the people.

I could drift along like this, in some dreamy proletarian idyll, 19
except for two things. One is management. If I have kept this subject on the margins thus far it is because I still flinch to think that I
spent all those weeks under the surveillance of men (and later
women) whose job it was to monitor my behavior for signs of
sloth, theft, drug abuse, or worse. Not that managers and especially "assistant managers" in low-wage settings like this are exactly the class enemy. In the restaurant business, they are mostly
former cooks or servers, still capable of pinch-hitting in the
kitchen or on the floor, just as in hotels they are likely to be former
clerks, and paid a salary of only about $400 a week. But everyone
knows they have crossed over to the other side, which is, crudely
put, corporate as opposed to human. Cooks want to prepare tasty
meals; servers want to serve them graciously; but managers are
there for only one reason—to make sure that money is made for
some theoretical entity that exists far away in Chicago or New
York, if a corporation can be said to have a physical existence at
all. Reflecting on her career, Gail tells me ruefully that she had
sworn, years ago, never to work for a corporation again. "They
don't cut you no slack. You give and you give, and they take."

Managers can sit—for hours at a time if they want—but it's 20
their job to see that no one else ever does, even when there's nothing to do, and this is why, for servers, slow times can be as exhausting as rushes. You start dragging out each little chore,
because if the manager on duty catches you in an idle moment, he
will give you something far nastier to do. So I wipe, I clean, I con-
solidate ketchup bottles and recheck the cheesecake supply, even
tour the tables to make sure the customer evaluation forms are all

standing perkily in their places—wondering all the time how many calories I burn in these strictly theatrical exercises. When, on a particularly dead afternoon, Stu finds me glancing at a *USA Today* a customer has left behind, he assigns me to vacuum the entire floor with the broken vacuum cleaner that has a handle only two feet long, and the only way to do that without incurring orthopedic damage is to proceed from spot to spot on your knees.

21   On my first Friday at the Hearthside there is a "mandatory meeting for all restaurant employees," which I attend, eager for insight into our overall marketing strategy and the niche (your basic Ohio cuisine with a tropical twist?) we aim to inhabit. But there is no "we" at this meeting. Phillip, our top manager except for an occasional "consultant" sent out by corporate headquarters, opens it with a sneer: "The break room—it's disgusting. Butts in the ashtrays, newspapers lying around, crumbs." This windowless little room, which also houses the time clock for the entire hotel, is where we stash our bags and civilian clothes and take our half-hour meal breaks. But a break room is not a right, he tells us. It can be taken away. We should also know that the lockers in the break room and whatever is in them can be searched at any time. Then comes gossip; there has been gossip; gossip (which seems to mean employees talking among themselves) must stop. Off-duty employees are henceforth barred from eating at the restaurant, because "other servers gather around them and gossip." When Phillip has exhausted his agenda of rebukes, Joan complains about the condition of the ladies' room and I throw in my two bits about the vacuum cleaner. But I don't see any backup coming from my fellow servers, each of whom has subsided into her own personal funk; Gail, my role model, stares sorrowfully at a point six inches from her nose. The meeting ends when Andy, one of the cooks, gets up, muttering about breaking up his day off for this almighty bullshit.

22   Just four days later we are suddenly summoned into the kitchen at 3:30 P.M., even though there are live tables on the floor. We all—about ten of us—stand around Phillip, who announces grimly that there has been a report of some "drug activity" on the night shift and that, as a result, we are now to be a "drug-free" workplace, meaning that all new hires will be tested, as will possibly current employees on a random basis. I am glad that this

part of the kitchen is so dark, because I find myself blushing as hard as if I had been caught toking up in the ladies' room myself: I haven't been treated this way—lined up in the corridor, threatened with locker searches, peppered with carelessly aimed accusations—since junior high school. Back on the floor, Joan cracks, "Next they'll be telling us we can't have sex on the job." When I ask Stu what happened to inspire the crackdown, he just mutters about "management decisions" and takes the opportunity to upbraid Gail and me for being too generous with the rolls. From now on there's to be only one per customer, and it goes out with the dinner, not with the salad. He's also been riding the cooks, prompting Andy to come out of the kitchen and observe—with the serenity of a man whose customary implement is a butcher knife—that "Stu has a death wish today."

Later in the evening, the gossip crystallizes around the theory 23 that Stu is himself the drug culprit, that he uses the restaurant phone to order up marijuana and sends one of the late servers out to fetch it for him. The server was caught, and she may have ratted Stu out or at least said enough to cast some suspicion on him, thus accounting for his pissy behavior. Who knows? Lionel, the busboy, entertains us for the rest of the shift by standing just behind Stu's back and sucking deliriously on an imaginary joint.

The other problem, in addition to the less-than-nurturing 24 management style, is that this job shows no sign of being financially viable. You might imagine, from a comfortable distance, that people who live, year in and year out, on $6 to $10 an hour have discovered some survival stratagems unknown to the middle class. But no. It's not hard to get my co-workers to talk about their living situations, because housing, in almost every case, is the principal source of disruption in their lives, the first thing they fill you in on when they arrive for their shifts. After a week, I have compiled the following survey:

- Gail is sharing a room in a well-known downtown flophouse 25 for which she and a roommate pay about $250 a week. Her roommate, a male friend, has begun hitting on her, driving her nuts, but the rent would be impossible alone.

26 • Claude, the Haitian cook, is desperate to get out of the two-room apartment he shares with his girlfriend and two other, unrelated, people. As far as I can determine, the other Haitian men (most of whom only speak Creole) live in similarly crowded situations.

27 • Annette, a twenty-year-old server who is six months pregnant and has been abandoned by her boyfriend, lives with her mother, a postal clerk.

28 • Marianne and her boyfriend are paying $170 a week for a one-person trailer.

29 • Jack, who is, at $10 an hour, the wealthiest of us, lives in the trailer he owns, paying only the $400-a-month lot fee.

30 • The other white cook, Andy, lives on his dry-docked boat, which, as far as I can tell from his loving descriptions, can't be more than twenty feet long. He offers to take me out on it, once it's repaired, but the offer comes with inquiries as to my marital status, so I do not follow up on it.

31 • Tina and her husband are paying $60 a night for a double room in a Days Inn. This is because they have no car and the Days Inn is within walking distance of the Hearthside. When Marianne, one of the breakfast servers, is tossed out of her trailer for subletting (which is against the trailer-park rules), she leaves her boyfriend and moves in with Tina and her husband.

32 • Joan, who had fooled me with her numerous and tasteful outfits (hostesses wear their own clothes), lives in a van she parks behind a shopping center at night and showers in Tina's motel room. The clothes are from thrift shops.[4]

33   It strikes me, in my middle-class solipsism, that there is gross improvidence in some of these arrangements. When Gail and I are wrapping silverware in napkins—the only task for which we are permitted to sit—she tells me she is thinking of escaping from her

---

[4]I could find no statistics on the number of employed people living in cars or vans, but according to the National Coalition for the Homeless's 1997 report "Myths and Facts About Homelessness," nearly one in five homeless people (in twenty-nine cities across the nation) is employed in a full- or part-time job.

roommate by moving into the Days Inn herself. I am astounded: How can she even think of paying between $40 and $60 a day? But if I was afraid of sounding like a social worker, I come out just sounding like a fool. She squints at me in disbelief, "And where am I supposed to get a month's rent and a month's deposit for an apartment?" I'd been feeling pretty smug about my $500 efficiency, but of course it was made possible only by the $1,300 I had allotted myself for start-up costs when I began my low-wage life: $1,000 for the first month's rent and deposit, $100 for initial groceries and cash in my pocket, $200 stuffed away for emergencies. In poverty, as in certain propositions in physics, starting conditions are everything.

There are no secret economies that nourish the poor; on the   34
contrary, there are a host of special costs. If you can't put up the two months' rent you need to secure an apartment, you end up paying through the nose for a room by the week. If you have only a room, with a hot plate at best, you can't save by cooking up huge lentil stews that can be frozen for the week ahead. You eat fast food, or the hot dogs and styrofoam cups of soup that can be microwaved in a convenience store. If you have no money for health insurance—and the Hearthside's niggardly plan kicks in only after three months—you go without routine care or prescription drugs and end up paying the price. Gail, for example, was fine until she ran out of money for estrogen pills. She is supposed to be on the company plan by now, but they claim to have lost her application form and need to begin the paperwork all over again. So she spends $9 per migraine pill to control the headaches she wouldn't have, she insists, if her estrogen supplements were covered. Similarly, Marianne's boyfriend lost his job as a roofer because he missed so much time after getting a cut on his foot for which he couldn't afford the prescribed antibiotic.

My own situation, when I sit down to assess it after two   35
weeks of work, would not be much better if this were my actual life. The seductive thing about waitressing is that you don't have to wait for payday to feel a few bills in your pocket, and my tips usually cover meals and gas, plus something left over to stuff into the kitchen drawer I use as a bank. But as the tourist business slows in the summer heat, I sometimes leave work with only $20 in tips (the gross is higher, but servers share about 15 percent of

their tips with the busboys and bartenders). With wages included, this amounts to about the minimum wage of $5.15 an hour. Although the sum in the drawer is piling up, at the present rate of accumulation it will be more than a hundred dollars short of my rent when the end of the month comes around. Nor can I see any expenses to cut. True, I haven't gone the lentil-stew route yet, but that's because I don't have a large cooking pot, pot holders, or a ladle to stir with (which cost about $30 at Kmart, less at thrift stores), not to mention onions, carrots, and the indispensable bay leaf. I do make my lunch almost every day—usually some slow-burning, high-protein combo like frozen chicken patties with melted cheese on top and canned pinto beans on the side. Dinner is at the Hearthside, which offers its employees a choice of BLT, fish sandwich, or hamburger for only $2. The burger lasts longest, especially if it's heaped with gut-puckering jalapeños, but by midnight my stomach is growling again.

36   So unless I want to start using my car as a residence, I have to find a second, or alternative, job. I call all the hotels where I filled out housekeeping applications weeks ago—the Hyatt, Holiday Inn, Econo Lodge, HoJo's, Best Western, plus a half dozen or so locally run guesthouses. Nothing. Then I start making the rounds again, wasting whole mornings waiting for some assistant manager to show up, even dipping into places so creepy that the front-desk clerk greets you from behind bulletproof glass and sells pints of liquor over the counter. But either someone has exposed my real-life housekeeping habits—which are, shall we say, mellow—or I am at the wrong end of some infallible ethnic equation: most, but by no means all, of the working housekeepers I see on my job searches are African Americans, Spanish-speaking, or immigrants from the Central European post-Communist world, whereas servers are almost invariably white and monolingually English-speaking. When I finally get a positive response, I have been identified once again as server material. Jerry's, which is part of a well-known national family restaurant chain and physically attached here to another budget hotel chain, is ready to use me at once. The prospect is both exciting and terrifying, because, with about the same number of tables and counter seats, Jerry's attracts three or four times the volume of customers as the gloomy old Hearthside.

Picture a fat person's hell, and I don't mean a place with no 37
food. Instead there is everything you might eat if eating had no
bodily consequences—cheese fries, chicken-fried steaks, fudge-
laden desserts—only here every bite must be paid for, one way or
another, in human discomfort. The kitchen is a cavern, a stomach
leading to the lower intestine that is the garbage and dishwashing
area, from which issue bizarre smells combining the edible and
the offal: creamy carrion, pizza barf, and that unique and enig-
matic Jerry's scent—citrus fart. The floor is slick with spills, forcing us to walk through the kitchen with tiny steps, like Susan
McDougal in leg irons. Sinks everywhere are clogged with scraps
of lettuce, decomposing lemon wedges, waterlogged toast crusts.
Put your hand down on any counter and you risk being stuck to it
by the film of ancient syrup spills, and this is unfortunate, because
hands are utensils here, used for scooping up lettuce onto salad
plates, lifting out pie slices, and even moving hash browns from
one plate to another. The regulation poster in the single unisex
restroom admonishes us to wash our hands thoroughly and even
offers instructions for doing so, but there is always some vital substance missing—soap, paper towels, toilet paper—and I never find
all three at once. You learn to stuff your pockets with napkins before going in there, and too bad about the customers, who must eat,
though they don't realize this, almost literally out of our hands.

The break room typifies the whole situation: there is none, be- 38
cause there are no breaks at Jerry's. For six to eight hours in a row,
you never sit except to pee. Actually, there are three folding chairs
at a table immediately adjacent to the bathroom, but hardly anyone ever sits here, in the very rectum of the gastro-architectural
system. Rather, the function of the peritoilet area is to house the
ashtrays in which servers and dishwashers leave their cigarettes
burning at all times, like votive candles, so that they don't have to
waste time lighting up again when they dash back for a puff. Almost everyone smokes as if his or her pulmonary well-being depended on it—the multinational mélange of cooks, the Czech
dishwashers, the servers, who are all American natives—creating
an atmosphere in which oxygen is only an occasional pollutant.
My first morning at Jerry's, when the hypoglycemic shakes set in,
I complain to one of my fellow servers that I don't understand
how she can go so long without food. "Well, I don't understand

how you can go so long without a cigarette," she responds in a tone of reproach—because work is what you do for others; smoking is what you do for yourself. I don't know why the antismoking crusaders have never grasped the element of defiant self-nurturance that makes the habit so endearing to its victims— as if, in the American workplace, the only thing people have to call their own is the tumors they are nourishing and the spare moments they devote to feeding them.

39   Now, the Industrial Revolution is not an easy transition, especially when you have to zip through it in just a couple of days. I have gone from craft work straight into the factory, from the air-conditioned morgue of the Hearthside directly into the flames. Customers arrive in human waves, sometimes disgorged fifty at a time from their tour buses, peckish and whiny. Instead of two "girls" on the floor at once, there can be as many as six of us running around in our brilliant pink-and-orange Hawaiian shirts. Conversations, either with customers or fellow employees, seldom last more than twenty seconds at a time. On my first day, in fact, I am hurt by my sister servers' coldness. My mentor for the day is an emotionally uninflected twenty-three-year-old, and the others, who gossip a little among themselves about the real reason someone is out sick today and the size of the bail bond someone else has had to pay, ignore me completely. On my second day, I find out why. "Well, it's good to see you again," one of them says in greeting. "Hardly anyone comes back after the first day." I feel powerfully vindicated—a survivor—but it would take a long time, probably months, before I could hope to be accepted into this sorority.

40   I start out with the beautiful, heroic idea of handling the two jobs at once, and for two days I almost do it: the breakfast/lunch shift at Jerry's, which goes till 2:00, arriving at the Hearthside at 2:10, and attempting to hold out until 10:00. In the ten minutes between jobs, I pick up a spicy chicken sandwich at the Wendy's drive-through window, gobble it down in the car, and change from khaki slacks to black, from Hawaiian to rust polo. There is a problem, though. When during the 3:00 to 4:00 P.M. dead time I finally sit down to wrap silver, my flesh seems to bond to the seat. I try to refuel with a purloined cup of soup, as I've seen Gail and Joan do dozens of times, but a manager catches me and hisses

"No eating!" though there's not a customer around to be offended by the sight of food making contact with a server's lips. So I tell Gail I'm going to quit, and she hugs me and says she might just follow me to Jerry's herself.

But the chances of this are minuscule. She has left the flop- 41 house and her annoying roommate and is back to living in her beat-up old truck. But guess what? She reports to me excitedly later that evening: Phillip has given her permission to park overnight in the hotel parking lot, as long as she keeps out of sight, and the parking lot should be totally safe, since it's patrolled by a hotel security guard! With the Hearthside offering benefits like that, how could anyone think of leaving?

Gail would have triumphed at Jerry's, I'm sure, but for me it's 42 a crash course in exhaustion management. Years ago, the kindly fry cook who trained me to waitress at a Los Angeles truck stop used to say: Never make an unnecessary trip; if you don't have to walk fast, walk slow; if you don't have to walk, stand. But at Jerry's the effort of distinguishing necessary from unnecessary and urgent from whenever would itself be too much of an energy drain. The only thing to do is to treat each shift as a one-time-only emergency: you've got fifty starving people out there, lying scattered on the battlefield, so get out there and feed them! Forget that you will have to do this again tomorrow, forget that you will have to be alert enough to dodge the drunks on the drive home tonight—just burn, burn, burn! Ideally, at some point you enter what servers call "a rhythm" and psychologists term a "flow state," in which signals pass from the sense organs directly to the muscles, bypassing the cerebral cortex, and a Zen-like emptiness sets in. A male server from the Hearthside's morning shift tells me about the time he "pulled a triple"—three shifts in a row, all the way around the clock—and then got off and had a drink and met this girl, and maybe he shouldn't tell me this, but they had sex right then and there, and it was like, beautiful.

But there's another capacity of the neuromuscular system, 43 which is pain. I start tossing back drugstore-brand ibuprofen pills as if they were vitamin C, four before each shift, because an old mouse-related repetitive-stress injury in my upper back has come back to full-spasm strength, thanks to the tray carrying. In my ordinary life, this level of disability might justify a day of ice packs and stretching. Here I comfort myself with the Aleve commercial in which the cute blue-collar guy asks: If you quit after working four hours, what would your boss say? And the not-so-cute blue-collar guy, who's lugging a metal beam on his back, answers: He'd fire me, that's what. But fortunately, the commercial tells us, we workers can exert the same kind of authority over our painkillers that our bosses exert over us. If Tylenol doesn't want to work for more than four hours, you just fire its ass and switch to Aleve.

44   True, I take occasional breaks from this life, going home now and then to catch up on e-mail and for conjugal visits (though I am careful to "pay" for anything I eat there), seeing *The Truman Show* with friends and letting them buy my ticket. And I still have those what-am-I-doing-here moments at work, when I get so homesick for the printed word that I obsessively reread the six-page menu. But as the days go by, my old life is beginning to look exceedingly strange. The e-mails and phone messages addressed to my former self come from a distant race of people with exotic concerns and far too much time on their hands. The neighborly market I used to cruise for produce now looks forbiddingly like a Manhattan yuppie emporium. And when I sit down one morning in my real home to pay bills from my past life, I am dazzled at the two- and three-figure sums owed to outfits like Club BodyTech and Amazon.com.

45   Management at Jerry's is generally calmer and more "professional" than at the Hearthside, with two exceptions. One is Joy, a plump, blowsy woman in her early thirties, who once kindly devoted several minutes to instructing me in the correct one-handed method of carrying trays but whose moods change disconcertingly from shift to shift and even within one. Then there's B. J., a.k.a. B. J.-the-bitch, whose contribution is to stand by the kitchen counter and yell, "Nita, your order's up, move it!" or, "Barbara, didn't you see you've got another table out there? Come on, girl!" Among other things, she is hated for having replaced the whipped-cream squirt cans with big plastic whipped-cream-filled baggies that have to be squeezed with both hands—because, reportedly, she saw or thought she saw employees trying to inhale the propellant gas from the squirt cans, in the hope that it might be nitrous oxide. On my third night, she pulls me aside abruptly

and brings her face so close that it looks as if she's planning to
butt me with her forehead. But instead of saying, "You're fired,"
she says, "You're doing fine." The only trouble is I'm spending
time chatting with customers: "That's how they're getting you."
Furthermore I am letting them "run me," which means harassment by sequential demands: you bring the ketchup and they decide they want extra Thousand Island; you bring that and they
announce they now need a side of fries; and so on into distraction.
Finally she tells me not to take her wrong. She tries to say things
in a nice way, but you get into a mode, you know, because everything has to move so fast.[5]

I mumble thanks for the advice, feeling like I've just been　46
stripped naked by the crazed enforcer of some ancient sumptuary
law: No chatting for you, girl. No fancy service ethic allowed for
the serfs. Chatting with customers is for the beautiful young college-educated servers in the downtown carpaccio joints, the kids
who can make $70 to $100 a night. What had I been thinking? My
job is to move orders from tables to kitchen and then trays from
kitchen to tables. Customers are, in fact, the major obstacle to the
smooth transformation of information into food and food into
money—they are, in short, the enemy. And the painful thing is
that I'm beginning to see it this way myself. There are the traditional asshole types—frat boys who down multiple Buds and then
make a fuss because the steaks are so emaciated and the fries so
sparse—as well as the variously impaired—due to age, diabetes,
or literacy issues—who require patient nutritional counseling.
The worst, for some reason, are the Visible Christians—like the
ten-person table, all jolly and sanctified after Sunday-night service,
who run me mercilessly and then leave me $1 on a $92 bill. Or the
guy with the crucifixion T-shirt (SOMEONE TO LOOK UP TO)
who complains that his baked potato is too hard and his iced tea
too icy (I cheerfully fix both) and leaves no tip. As a general rule,

[5]In *Workers in a Lean World: Unions in the International Economy* (Verso, 1997), Kim
Moody cites studies finding an increase in stress-related workplace injuries and
illness between the mid-1980s and the early 1990s. He argues that rising stress
levels reflect a new system of "management by stress," in which workers in a
variety of industries are being squeezed to extract maximum productivity, to the
detriment of their health.

people wearing crosses or WWJD? (What Would Jesus Do?) buttons look at us disapprovingly no matter what we do, as if they
were confusing waitressing with Mary Magdalene's original profession.

47   I make friends, over time, with the other "girls" who work my
shift: Nita, the tattooed twenty-something who taunts us by going
around saying brightly, "Have we started making money yet?"
Ellen, whose teenage son cooks on the graveyard shift and who
once managed a restaurant in Massachusetts but won't try out for
management here because she prefers being a "common worker"
and not "ordering people around." Easy-going fiftyish Lucy, with
the raucous laugh, who limps toward the end of the shift because
of something that has gone wrong with her leg, the exact nature of
which cannot be determined without health insurance. We talk
about the usual girl things—men, children, and the sinister allure
of Jerry's chocolate peanut-butter cream pie—though no one, I notice, ever brings up anything potentially expensive, like shopping
or movies. As at the Hearthside, the only recreation ever referred
to is partying, which requires little more than some beer, a joint,
and a few close friends. Still, no one here is homeless, or cops to it
anyway, thanks usually to a working husband or boyfriend. All in
all, we form a reliable mutual-support group: If one of us is feeling sick or overwhelmed, another one will "bev" a table or even
carry trays for her. If one of us is off sneaking a cigarette or a pee,[6]
the others will do their best to conceal her absence from the en-
forcers of corporate rationality.

[6]Until April 1998, there was no federally mandated right to bathroom breaks. According to Marc Linder and Ingrid Nygaard, authors of *Void Where Prohibited:
Rest Breaks and the Right to Urinate on Company Time* (Cornell University Press,
1997), "The right to rest and void at work is not high on the list of social or political causes supported by professional or executive employees, who enjoy personal
workplace liberties that millions of factory workers can only daydream about. . . .
While we were dismayed to discover that workers lacked an acknowledged legal
right to void at work, [the workers] were amazed by outsiders' naive belief that
their employers would permit them to perform this basic bodily function when
necessary. . . . A factory worker, not allowed a break for six-hour stretches, voided
into pads worn inside her uniform; and a kindergarten teacher in a school without aides had to take all twenty children with her to the bathroom and line them
up outside the stall door when she voided."

But my saving human connection—my oxytocin receptor, as it 48
were—is George, the nineteen-year-old, fresh-off-the-boat Czech
dishwasher. We get to talking when he asks me, tortuously, how
much cigarettes cost at Jerry's. I do my best to explain that they cost
over a dollar more here than at a regular store and suggest that he
just take one from the half-filled packs that are always lying around
on the break table. But that would be unthinkable. Except for the
one tiny earring signaling his allegiance to some vaguely alternative point of view, George is a perfect straight arrow—crew-cut,
hardworking, and hungry for eye contact. "Czech Republic," I ask,
"or Slovakia?" and he seems delighted that I know the difference.
"Václav Havel," I try. "Velvet Revolution, Frank Zappa?" "Yes, yes,
1989," he says, and I realize we are talking about history.

My project is to teach George English. "How are you today, 49
George?" I say at the start of each shift. "I am good, and how are
you today, Barbara?" I learn that he is not paid by Jerry's but by
the "agent" who shipped him over—$5 an hour, with the agent
getting the dollar or so difference between that and what Jerry's
pays dishwashers. I learn also that he shares an apartment with a
crowd of other Czech "dishers," as he calls them, and that he cannot sleep until one of them goes off for his shift, leaving a vacant
bed. We are having one of our ESL sessions late one afternoon
when B.J. catches us at it and orders "Joseph" to take up the rubber
mats on the floor near the dishwashing sinks and mop underneath. "I thought your name was George," I say loud enough for
B.J. to hear as she strides off back to the counter. Is she embarrassed? Maybe a little, because she greets me back at the counter
with "George, Joseph—there are so many of them!" I say nothing,
neither nodding nor smiling, and for this I am punished later
when I think I am ready to go and she announces that I need to roll
fifty more sets of silverware and isn't it time I mixed up a fresh
four-gallon batch of blue-cheese dressing? May you grow old in
this place, B.J., is the curse I beam out at her when I am finally permitted to leave. May the syrup spills glue your feet to the floor.

I make the decision to move closer to Key West. First, because 50
of the drive. Second and third, also because of the drive: gas is eating up $4 to $5 a day, and although Jerry's is as high-volume as
you can get, the tips average only 10 percent, and not just for a

newbie like me. Between the base pay of $2.15 an hour and the obligation to share tips with the busboys and dishwashers, we're averaging only about $7.50 an hour. Then there is the $30 I had to spend on the regulation tan slacks worn by Jerry's servers—a setback it could take weeks to absorb. (I had combed the town's two downscale department stores hoping for something cheaper but decided in the end that these marked-down Dockers, originally $49, were more likely to survive a daily washing.) Of my fellow servers, everyone who lacks a working husband or boyfriend seems to have a second job: Nita does something at a computer eight hours a day; another welds. Without the forty-five-minute commute, I can picture myself working two jobs and having the time to shower between them.

51   So I take the $500 deposit I have coming from my landlord, the $400 I have earned toward the next month's rent, plus the $200 reserved for emergencies, and use the $1,100 to pay the rent and deposit on trailer number 46 in the Overseas Trailer Park, a mile from the cluster of budget hotels that constitute Key West's version of an industrial park. Number 46 is about eight feet in width and shaped like a barbell inside, with a narrow region—because of the sink and the stove—separating the bedroom from what might optimistically be called the "living" area, with its two-person table and half-sized couch. The bathroom is so small my knees rub against the shower stall when I sit on the toilet, and you can't just leap out of the bed, you have to climb down to the foot of it in order to find a patch of floor space to stand on. Outside, I am within a few yards of a liquor store, a bar that advertises "free beer tomorrow," a convenience store, and a Burger King—but no supermarket or, alas, laundromat. By reputation, the Overseas park is a nest of crime and crack, and I am hoping at least for some vibrant, multicultural street life. But desolation rules night and day, except for a thin stream of pedestrian traffic heading for their jobs at the Sheraton or 7-Eleven. There are not exactly people here but what amounts to canned labor, being preserved from the heat between shifts.

52   In line with my reduced living conditions, a new form of ugliness arises at Jerry's. First we are confronted—via an announcement on the computers through which we input orders—with the

new rule that the hotel bar is henceforth off-limits to restaurant employees. The culprit, I learn through the grapevine, is the ultra-efficient gal who trained me—another trailer-home dweller and a mother of three. Something had set her off one morning, so she slipped out for a nip and returned to the floor impaired. This mostly hurts Ellen, whose habit it is to free her hair from its rubber band and drop by the bar for a couple of Zins before heading home at the end of the shift, but all of us feel the chill. Then the next day, when I go for straws, for the first time I find the dry-storage room locked. Ted, the portly assistant manager who opens it for me, explains that he caught one of the dishwashers attempting to steal something, and, unfortunately, the miscreant will be with us until a replacement can be found—hence the locked door. I neglect to ask what he had been trying to steal, but Ted tells me who he is—the kid with the buzz cut and the earring. You know, he's back there right now.

I wish I could say I rushed back and confronted George to get 53 his side of the story. I wish I could say I stood up to Ted and insisted that George be given a translator and allowed to defend himself, or announced that I'd find a lawyer who'd handle the case pro bono. The mystery to me is that there's not much worth stealing in the dry-storage room, at least not in any fenceable quantity: "Is Gyorgi here, and am having 200—maybe 250—ketchup packets. What do you say?" My guess is that he had taken—if he had taken anything at all—some Saltines or a can of cherry-pie mix, and that the motive for taking it was hunger.

So why didn't I intervene? Certainly not because I was held 54 back by the kind of moral paralysis that can pass as journalistic objectivity. On the contrary, something new—something loathsome and servile—had infected me, along with the kitchen odors that I could still sniff on my bra when I finally undressed at night. In real life I am moderately brave, but plenty of brave people shed their courage in concentration camps, and maybe something similar goes on in the infinitely more congenial milieu of the low-wage American workplace. Maybe, in a month or two more at Jerry's, I might have regained my crusading spirit. Then again, in a month or two I might have turned into a different person altogether—say, the kind of person who would have turned George in.

55   But this is not something I am slated to find out. When my month-long plunge into poverty is almost over, I finally land my dream job—housekeeping. I do this by walking into the personnel office of the only place I figure I might have some credibility, the hotel attached to Jerry's, and confiding urgently that I have to have a second job if I am to pay my rent and, no, it couldn't be front-desk clerk. "All right," the personnel lady fairly spits, "So it's housekeeping," and she marches me back to meet Maria, the housekeeping manager, a tiny, frenetic Hispanic woman who greets me as "babe" and hands me a pamphlet emphasizing the need for a positive attitude. The hours are nine in the morning till whenever, the pay is $6.10 an hour, and there's one week of vacation a year. I don't have to ask about health insurance once I meet Carlotta; the middle-aged African-American woman who will be training me. Carla, as she tells me to call her, is missing all of her top front teeth.

56   On that first day of housekeeping and last day of my entire project—although I don't yet know it's the last—Carla is in a foul mood. We have been given nineteen rooms to clean, most of them "checkouts," as opposed to "stay-overs," that require the whole enchilada of bed-stripping, vacuuming, and bathroom-scrubbing. When one of the rooms that had been listed as a stay-over turns out to be a checkout, Carla calls Maria to complain, but of course to no avail. "So make up the motherfucker," Carla orders me, and I do the beds while she sloshes around the bathroom. For four hours without a break I strip and remake beds, taking about four and a half minutes per queen-sized bed, which I could get down to three if there were any reason to. We try to avoid vacuuming by picking up the larger specks by hand, but often there is nothing to do but drag the monstrous vacuum cleaner—it weighs about thirty pounds—off our cart and try to wrestle it around the floor. Sometimes Carla hands me the squirt bottle of "BAM" (an acronym for something that begins, ominously, with "butyric"; the rest has been worn off the label) and lets me do the bathrooms. No service ethic challenges me here to new heights of performance. I just concentrate on removing the pubic hairs from the bathtubs, or at least the dark ones that I can see.

I had looked forward to the breaking-and-entering aspect of 57
cleaning the stay-overs, the chance to examine the secret, physical
existence of strangers. But the contents of the rooms are always
banal and suprisingly neat—zipped-up shaving kits, shoes lined
up against the wall (there are no closets), flyers for snorkeling
trips, maybe an empty wine bottle or two. It is the TV that keeps
us going, from *Jerry* to *Sally* to *Hawaii Five-O* and then on to the
soaps. If there's something especially arresting, like "Won't Take
No for an Answer" on *Jerry*, we sit down on the edge of a bed and
giggle for a moment as if this were a pajama party instead of a terminally dead-end job. The soaps are the best, and Carla turns the
volume up full blast so that she won't miss anything from the
bathroom or while the vacuum is on. In room 503, Marcia confronts Jeff about Lauren. In 505, Lauren taunts poor cuckolded
Marcia. In 511, Helen offers Amanda $10,000 to stop seeing Eric,
prompting Carla to emerge from the bathroom to study Amanda's
troubled face. "You take it, girl," she advises. "I would for sure."

The tourists' rooms that we clean and, beyond them, the far 58
more expensively appointed interiors in the soaps, begin after a
while to merge. We have entered a better world—a world of comfort where every day is a day off, waiting to be filled up with sexual intrigue. We, however, are only gatecrashers in this fantasy,
forced to pay for our presence with backaches and perpetual
thirst. The mirrors, and there are far too many of them in hotel
rooms, contain the kind of person you would normally find pushing a shopping cart down a city street—bedraggled, dressed in a
damp hotel polo shirt two sizes too large, and with sweat drib-
bling down her chin like drool. I am enormously relieved when
Carla announces a half-hour meal break, but my appetite fades
when I see that the bag of hot-dog rolls she has been carrying
around on our cart is not trash salvaged from a checkout but what
she has brought for her lunch.

When I request permission to leave at about 3:30, another 59
housekeeper warns me that no one has so far succeeded in combining housekeeping at the hotel with serving at Jerry's: "Some kid
did it once for five days, and you're no kid." With that helpful information in mind, I rush back to number 46, down four Advils
(the name brand this time), shower, stooping to fit into the stall,

and attempt to compose myself for the oncoming shift. So much
for what Marx termed the "reproduction of labor power," meaning
the things a worker has to do just so she'll be ready to work again.
The only unforeseen obstacle to the smooth transition from job to
job is that my tan Jerry's slacks, which had looked reasonably clean
by 40-watt bulb last night when I handwashed my Hawaiian shirt,
prove by daylight to be mottled with ketchup and ranch-dressing
stains. I spend most of my hour-long break between jobs attempting to remove the edible portions with a sponge and then drying
the slacks over the hood of my car in the sun.

60   I can do this two-job thing, is my theory, if I can drink enough
caffeine and avoid getting distracted by George's ever more obvious suffering.[7] The first few days after being caught he seemed
not to understand the trouble he was in, and our chirpy little conversations had continued. But the last couple of shifts he's been
listless and unshaven, and tonight he looks like the ghost we all
know him to be, with dark half-moons hanging from his eyes. At
one point, when I am briefly immobilized by the task of filling little paper cups with sour cream for baked potatoes, he comes over
and looks as if he'd like to explore the limits of our shared vocabulary, but I am called to the floor for a table. I resolve to give him
all my tips that night and to hell with the experiment in low-wage
money management. At eight, Ellen and I grab a snack together
standing at the mephitic end of the kitchen counter, but I can only
manage two or three mozzarella sticks and lunch had been a mere
handful of McNuggets. I am not tired at all, I assure myself,
though it may be that there is simply no more "I" left to do the
tiredness monitoring. What I would see, if I were more alert to the
situation, is that the forces of destruction are already massing
against me. There is only one cook on duty, a young man named
Jesus ("Hay-Sue," that is) and he is new to the job. And there is

[7]In 1996, the number of persons holding two or more jobs averaged 7.8 million,
or 6.2 percent of the workforce. It was about the same rate for men and for
women (6.1 versus 6.2), though the kinds of jobs differ by gender. About two
thirds of multiple jobholders work one job full-time and the other part-time.
Only a heroic minority—4 percent of men and 2 percent of women—work two
full-time jobs simultaneously. (From John F. Stinson Jr., "New Data on Multiple
Jobholding Available from the CPS," in the *Monthly Labor Review,* March 1997.)

Joy, who shows up to take over in the middle of the shift, wearing high heels and a long, clingy white dress and fuming as if she'd just been stood up in some cocktail bar.

Then it comes, the perfect storm. Four of my tables fill up at once. Four tables is nothing for me now, but only so long as they are obligingly staggered. As I bev table 27, tables 25, 28, and 24 are watching enviously. As I bev 25, 24 glowers because their bevs haven't even been ordered. Twenty-eight is four yuppyish types, meaning everything on the side and agonizing instructions as to the chicken Caesars. Twenty-five is a middle-aged black couple, who complain, with some justice, that the iced tea isn't fresh and the tabletop is sticky. But table 24 is the meteorological event of the century: ten British tourists who seem to have made the decision to absorb the American experience entirely by mouth. Here everyone has at least two drinks—iced tea and milk shake, Michelob and water (with lemon slice, please)—and a huge promiscuous orgy of breakfast specials, mozz sticks, chicken strips, quesadillas, burgers with cheese and without, sides of hash browns with cheddar, with onions, with gravy, seasoned fries, plain fries, banana splits. Poor Jesus! Poor me! Because when I arrive with their first tray of food—after three prior trips just to refill bevs—Princess Di refuses to eat her chicken strips with her pancake-and-sausage special, since, as she now reveals, the strips were meant to be an appetizer. Maybe the others would have accepted their meals, but Di, who is deep into her third Michelob, insists that everything else go back while they work on their "starters." Meanwhile, the yuppies are waving me down for more decaf and the black couple looks ready to summon the NAACP.

Much of what happened next is lost in the fog of war. Jesus starts going under. The little printer on the counter in front of him is spewing out orders faster than he can rip them off, much less produce the meals. Even the invincible Ellen is ashen from stress. I bring table 24 their reheated main courses, which they immediately reject as either too cold or fossilized by the microwave. When I return to the kitchen with their trays (three trays in three trips), Joy confronts me with arms akimbo: "What is this?" She means the food—the plates of rejected pancakes, hash browns in assorted flavors, toasts, burgers, sausages, eggs. "Uh, scrambled with cheddar," I try, "and that's . . ." "NO," she screams in my face.

"Is it a traditional, a super-scramble, an eye-opener?" I pretend to study my check for a clue, but entropy has been up to its tricks, not only on the plates but in my head, and I have to admit that the original order is beyond reconstruction. "You don't know an eye-opener from a traditional?" she demands in outrage. All I know, in fact, is that my legs have lost interest in the current venture and have announced their intention to fold. I am saved by a yuppie (mercifully not one of mine) who chooses this moment to charge into the kitchen to bellow that his food is twenty-five minutes late. Joy screams at him to get the hell out of her kitchen, please, and then turns on Jesus in a fury, hurling an empty tray across the room for emphasis.

63   I leave. I don't walk out, I just leave. I don't finish my side work or pick up my credit-card tips, if any, at the cash register or, of course, ask Joy's permission to go. And the surprising thing is that you *can* walk out without permission, that the door opens, that the thick tropical night air parts to let me pass, that my car is still parked where I left it. There is no vindication in this exit, no fuck-you surge of relief, just an overwhelming, dank sense of failure pressing down on me and the entire parking lot. I had gone into this venture in the spirit of science, to test a mathematical proposition, but somewhere along the line, in the tunnel vision imposed by long shifts and relentless concentration, it became a test of myself, and clearly I have failed. Not only had I flamed out as a housekeeper/server, I had even forgotten to give George my tips, and, for reasons perhaps best known to hardworking, generous people like Gail and Ellen, this hurts. I don't cry, but I am in a position to realize, for the first time in many years, that the tear ducts are still there, and still capable of doing their job.

64   When I moved out of the trailer park, I gave the key to number 46 to Gail and arranged for my deposit to be transferred to her. She told me that Joan is still living in her van and that Stu had been fired from the Hearthside. I never found out what happened to George.

65   In one month, I had earned approximately $1,040 and spent $517 on food, gas, toiletries, laundry, phone, and utilities. If I had remained in my $500 efficiency, I would have been able to pay the rent and have $22 left over (which is $78 less than the cash I had in my pocket at the start of the month). During this time I bought no

clothing except for the required slacks and no prescription drugs
or medical care (I did finally buy some vitamin B to compensate
for the lack of vegetables in my diet). Perhaps I could have saved
a little on food if I had gotten to a supermarket more often, instead of convenience stores, but it should be noted that I lost almost four pounds in four weeks, on a diet weighted heavily
toward burgers and fries.

How former welfare recipients and single mothers will (and   66
do) survive in the low-wage workforce, I cannot imagine. Maybe
they will figure out how to condense their lives—including child-
raising, laundry, romance, and meals—into the couple of hours
between fulltime jobs. Maybe they will take up residence in their
vehicles, if they have one. All I know is that I couldn't hold two
jobs and I couldn't make enough money to live on with one. And
I had advantages unthinkable to many of the long-term poor—
health, stamina, a working car, and no children to care for and
support. Certainly nothing in my experience contradicts the conclusion of Kathryn Edin and Laura Lein, in their recent book *Making Ends Meet: How Single Mothers Survive Welfare and Low-Wage
Work,* that low-wage work actually involves more hardship and
deprivation than life at the mercy of the welfare state. In the coming months and years, economic conditions for the working poor
are bound to worsen, even without the almost inevitable reces-
sion. As mentioned earlier, the influx of former welfare recipients
into the low-skilled workforce will have a depressing effect on
both wages and the number of jobs available. A general economic
downturn will only enhance these effects, and the working poor
will of course be facing it without the slight, but nonetheless often
saving, protection of welfare as a backup.

The thinking behind welfare reform was that even the hum-   67
blest jobs are morally uplifting and psychologically buoying. In reality they are likely to be fraught with insult and stress. But I did
discover one redeeming feature of the most abject low-wage
work—the camaraderie of people who are, in almost all cases, far
too smart and funny and caring for the work they do and the wages
they're paid. The hope, of course, is that someday these people will
come to know what they're worth, and take appropriate action.

1999

Work in Corporate America
Russell Baker

1   It is not surprising that modern children tend to look blank and dispirited when informed that they will someday have to "go to work and make a living." The problem is that they cannot visualize what work is in corporate America.

2   Not so long ago, when a parent said he was off to work, the child knew very well what was about to happen. His parent was going to make something or fix something. The parent could take his offspring to his place of business and let him watch while he repaired a buggy or built a table.

3   When a child asked, "What kind of work do you do, Daddy?" his father could answer in terms that a child could come to grips with. "I fix steam engines." "I make horse collars."

4   Well, a few fathers still fix steam engines and build tables, but most do not. Nowadays, most fathers sit in glass buildings doing things that are absolutely incomprehensible to children. The answers they give when asked, "What kind of work do you do, Daddy?" are likely to be utterly mystifying to a child.

5   "I sell space." "I do market research." "I am a data processor." "I am in public relations." "I am a systems analyst." Such explanations must seem nonsense to a child. How can he possibly envision anyone analyzing a system or researching a market?

6   Even grown men who do market research have trouble visualizing what a public relations man does with his day, and it is a safe bet that the average systems analyst is as baffled about what a space salesman does at the shop as the average space salesman is about the tools needed to analyze a system.

7   In the common everyday job, nothing is made any more. Things are now made by machines. Very little is repaired. The machines that make things make them in such a fashion that they will quickly fall apart in such a way that repairs will be prohibitively expensive. Thus the buyer is encouraged to throw the thing away and buy a new one. In effect, the machines are making junk.

8   The handful of people remotely associated with these machines can, of course, tell their inquisitive children "Daddy makes

junk." Most of the work force, however, is too remote from junk production to sense any contribution to the industry. What do these people do?

Consider the typical twelve-story glass building in the typical American city. Nothing is being made in this building and nothing is being repaired, including the building itself. Constructed as a piece of junk, the building will be discarded when it wears out, and another piece of junk will be set in its place. 9

Still, the building is filled with people who think of themselves as working. At any given moment during the day perhaps one-third of them will be talking into telephones. Most of these conversations will be about paper, for paper is what occupies nearly everyone in this building. 10

Some jobs in the building require men to fill paper with words. There are persons who type neatly on paper and persons who read paper and jot notes in the margins. Some persons make copies of paper and other persons deliver paper. There are persons who file paper and persons who unfile paper. 11

Some persons mail paper. Some persons telephone other persons and ask that paper be sent to them. Others telephone to ascertain the whereabouts of paper. Some persons confer about paper. In the grandest offices, men approve of some paper and disapprove of other paper. 12

The elevators are filled throughout the day with young men carrying paper from floor to floor and with vital men carrying paper to be discussed with other vital men. 13

What is a child to make of all this? His father may be so eminent that he lunches with other men about paper. Suppose he brings his son to work to give the boy some idea of what work is all about. What does the boy see happening? 14

His father calls for paper. He reads paper. Perhaps he scowls at paper. Perhaps he makes an angry red mark on paper. He telephones another man and says they had better lunch over paper. 15

At lunch they talk about paper. Back at the office, the father orders the paper retyped and reproduced in quintuplicate, and then sent to another man for comparison with paper that was reproduced in triplicate last year. 16

17   Imagine his poor son afterwards mulling over the mysteries of work with a friend, who asks him, "What's your father do?" What can the boy reply? "It beats me," perhaps, if he is not very observant. Or if he is, "Something that has to do with making junk, I think. Same as everybody else."

1971

Cars and Their Enemies

James Q. Wilson

1 Imagine the country we now inhabit—big, urban, prosperous—with one exception: the automobile has not been invented. We have trains and bicycles, and some kind of self-powered buses and trucks, but no private cars driven by their owners for business or pleasure. Of late, let us suppose, someone has come forward with the idea of creating the personal automobile. Consider how we would react to such news.

2   Libertarians might support the idea, but hardly anyone else. Engineers would point out that such cars, if produced in any significant number, would zip along roads just a few feet—perhaps even a few inches—from one another; the chance of accidents would not simply be high, it would be certain. Public-health specialists would estimate that many of these accidents would lead to serious injuries and deaths. No one could say in advance how common they would be, but the best experts might guess that the number of people killed by cars would easily exceed the number killed by murderers. Psychologists would point out that if any young person were allowed to operate a car, the death rate would be even higher, as youngsters—those between the ages of sixteen and twenty-four—are much more likely than older persons to be impulsive risk-takers who find pleasure in reckless bravado. Educators would explain that, though they might try by training to reduce this youthful death rate, they could not be optimistic they would succeed.

3   Environmentalists would react in horror to the idea of automobiles powered by the internal combustion engine, apparently

the most inexpensive method. Such devices, because they burn fuel incompletely, would eject large amounts of unpleasant gases into the air, such as carbon monoxide, nitrogen oxide, and sulfur dioxide. Other organic compounds, as well as clouds of particles, would also enter the atmosphere to produce unknown but probably harmful effects. Joining in this objection would be people who would not want their view spoiled by the creation of a network of roads.

Big-city mayors would add their own objections, though 4 these would reflect their self-interest as much as their wisdom. If people could drive anywhere from anywhere, they would be able to live wherever they wished. This would produce a vast exodus from the large cities, led in all likelihood by the most prosperous—and thus the most tax-productive—citizens. Behind would remain people who, being poorer, were less mobile. Money would depart but problems remain.

Governors, pressed to keep taxes down and still fund costly 5 health, welfare, educational, and criminal-justice programs, would wonder who would pay for the vast networks of roads that would be needed to carry automobiles. Their skepticism would be reinforced by the worries of police officials fearful of motorized thieves evading apprehension, and by the opposition of railroad executives foreseeing the collapse of their passenger business as people abandoned trains for cars.

Energy experts would react in horror at the prospect of sup- 6 plying the gasoline stations and the vast quantities of petroleum necessary to fuel automobiles which, unlike buses and trucks, would be stored at home and not at a central depot and would burn much more fuel per person carried than some of their mass-transit alternatives.

In short, the automobile, the device on which most Americans 7 rely for not only transportation but mobility, privacy, and fun would not exist if it had to be created today. Of course, the car does exist, and has powerfully affected the living, working, and social spaces of America. But the argument against it persists. That argument dominates the thinking of academic experts on urban transportation and much of city planning. It can be found in countless books complaining of dreary suburban architecture, endless trips to and from work, the social isolation produced by solo auto trips, and the harmful effects of the car on air quality, noise levels, petroleum consumption, and road congestion.

8   In her recent book, *Asphalt Nation: How the Automobile Took Over America and How We Can Take It Back,* Jane Holtz Kay, the architecture critic for the *Nation,* assails the car unmercifully. It has, she writes, "strangled" our lives and landscape, imposing on us "the costs of sprawl, of pollution, of congestion, of commuting." For this damage to be undone, the massively subsidized automobile will have to be sharply curtailed, by investing heavily in public transportation and imposing European-like taxes on gasoline. (According to Kay, if we cut highway spending by a mere $10 million, we could buy bicycles for all 93,000 residents of Eugene, Oregon, over the age of eleven.) What is more, people ought to live in cities with high population densities, since "for mass transit," as Kay notes, "you need mass." Housing should be built within a short walk of the corner store, and industries moved back downtown.

9   In Kay's book, hostility to the car is linked inextricably to hostility to the low-density suburb. Her view is by no means one that is confined to the political Left. Thus, Karl Zinsmeister, a conservative, has argued in the *American Enterprise* that we have become "slaves to our cars" and that, by using them to live in suburbs, we have created "inhospitable places for individualism and community life." Suburbs, says Zinsmeister, encourage "rootlessness," and are the enemy of the "traditional neighborhood" with its "easy daily interactions."

10   The same theme has been taken up by Mark Gauvreau Judge in the *Weekly Standard.* Emerging from his home after a heavy snowfall, Judge, realizing that the nearest tavern was four miles away, concluded that he had to leave the suburbs. He repeats Zinsmeister's global complaint. Suburbanization, he writes, has fed, and sometimes caused,

> hurried life, the disappearance of family time, the weakening of generational links, our ignorance of history, our lack of local ties, an exaggerated focus on money, the anonymity of community life, the rise of radical feminism, the decline of civic action, the tyrannical dominance of TV and pop culture over leisure time.

Wow.   11

These people must live in or near very odd suburbs. The one   12
in which I lived while my children were growing up, and the different ones in which my married daughter and married son now
live, are not inhospitable, rootless, isolated, untraditional, or lacking in daily interactions. The towns are small. Life is organized
around the family, for which there is a lot of time. Money goes farther for us than for Manhattanites struggling to get their children
into the nursery school with the best link to Harvard. Television is
less important than in big cities, where the streets are far less safe
and TV becomes a major indoor activity. In most cases you can
walk to a store. You know your neighbors. There is a Memorial
Day parade. People care passionately and argue intensely about
school policies and land-use controls. Of course, these are only my
personal experiences—but unlike the critics, I find it hard to convert personal beliefs into cosmic generalizations.

Now I live in a suburb more remote from a big city than the   13
one where my children were raised. Because population density is
much lower, my wife and I walk less and drive more. But as I
write this, my wife is at a neighborhood meeting where she will
be joined by a travel agent, a retired firefighter, a hospital manager, and two housewives who are trying to decide how best to
get the city to fix up a road intersection, prevent a nearby land development, and induce our neighbors to prepare for the fire season. On the way back, she will stop at the neighborhood mail
station where she may talk to other friends, and then go on to the
market where she will deal with people she has known for many
years. She will do so by car.

And so back to our theme. Despite the criticisms of Kay and   14
others, the use of the automobile has grown. In 1960, one-fifth of
all households owned no car and only one-fifth owned two; by
1990, only one-tenth owned no car and over one-third owned
two. In 1969, 80 percent of all urban trips involved a car and only
one-twentieth involved public transport; by 1990, car use had
risen to 84 percent and public transit had fallen to less than 3 percent. In 1990, three-fourths or more of the trips to and from work

in nineteen out of our twenty largest metropolitan areas were by a single person in an automobile. The exception was the New York metropolitan region, but even there—with an elaborate mass-transit system and a residential concentration high enough to make it possible for some people to walk to work—solo car use made up over half of all trips to work.

15   Some critics explain this American fascination with the car as the unhappy consequence of public policies that make auto use more attractive than the alternatives. To Jane Holtz Kay, if only we taxed gasoline at a high enough rate to repay society for the social costs of automobiles, if only we had an elaborate mass-transit system that linked our cities, if only we placed major restraints on building suburbs on open land, if only we placed heavy restrictions on downtown parking, then things would be better.

16   Would they? Charles Lave, an economist at the University of California at Irvine, has pointed out that most of Western Europe has long had just these sorts of anti-auto policies in effect. The result? Between 1965 and 1987, the growth in the number of autos per capita has been three times faster in Western Europe than in the United States. Part of the reason for the discrepancy is that the American auto market is approaching saturation: we now have roughly one car in existence for every person of driving age. But if this fact helps explain why the car market here is not growing rapidly, it does not explain the growth in Europe, which is the real story. Despite policies that penalize car use, make travel very expensive, and restrict parking spaces, Europeans, once they can afford to do so, buy cars, and drive them; according to Lave, the average European car is driven about two-thirds as many miles per year as the average American car. One result is obvious: the heavily subsidized trains in Europe are losing business to cars, and governments there must pay an even larger share of the running cost to keep the trains moving.

17   In fact, the United States *has* tried to copy the European investment in mass transit. Relentlessly, transportation planners have struggled to find ways of getting people out of their cars and into buses, trains, and subways (and car pools). Relentlessly, and

unsuccessfully. Despite spending about $100 billion, Washington has yet to figure out how to do it.

New subway systems have been built, such as the BART system in San Francisco and the Metro system in Washington, D.C. But BART, in the words of the transportation economist Charles L. Wright, "connects almost nothing to little else." The Metro is still growing, and provides a fine (albeit expensive) route for people moving about the city; but only 7 percent of all residential land area in Washington is within a mile of a Metro station, which means that people must either walk a long way to get to a stop or continue to travel by car. Between 1980 and 1990, while the Washington Metrorail system grew from 30 to 73 miles of line and opened an additional 30 stations, the number of people driving to work increased from 980,000 to 1,394,000, and the transit share of all commutes declined. [18]

The European experience should explain why this is so: if people can afford it, they will want to purchase convenience, flexibility, and privacy. These facts are as close to a Law of Nature as one can get in the transportation business. When the industrial world became prosperous, people bought cars. It is unstoppable. [19]

Suppose, however, that the anti-car writers were to win over the vastly more numerous pro-car drivers. Let us imagine what life would be like in a carless nation. People would have to live very close together so they could walk or, for healthy people living in sunny climes, bicycle to mass-transit stops. Living in close quarters would mean life as it is now lived in Manhattan. There would be few freestanding homes, many row houses, and lots of apartment buildings. There would be few private gardens except for flowerpots on balconies. The streets would be congested by pedestrians, trucks, and buses, as they were at the turn of the century before automobiles became common. [20]

Moving about outside the larger cities would be difficult. People would be able to take trains to distant sites, but when they arrived at some attractive locale it would turn out to be another city. They could visit the beach, but only (of necessity) crowded parts of it. They could go to a national park, but only the built-up section of it. They could see the countryside, but (mostly) through a [21] train window. More isolated or remote locations would be accessible, but since public transit would provide the only way of getting there, the departures would be infrequent and the transfers frequent.

22   In other words, you could see the United States much as most Europeans saw their countryside before the automobile became an important means of locomotion. A train from London or Paris would take you to "the country" by way of a long journey through ugly industrial areas to those rural parts where either you had a home (and the means to ferry yourself to it) or there was a resort (that would be crowded enough to support a nearby train stop).

23   All this is a way of saying that the debate between car defenders and car haters is a debate between private benefits and public goods. List the characteristics of travel that impose few costs on society and, in general, walking, cycling, and some forms of public transit will be seen to be superior. Non-car methods generate less pollution, use energy a bit more efficiently, produce less noise, and (with some exceptions) are safer. But list the characteristics of travel that are desired by individuals, and (with some exceptions) the car is clearly superior. The automobile is more flexible, more punctual, supplies greater comfort, provides for carrying more parcels, creates more privacy, enables one to select fellow passengers, and, for distances over a mile or more, requires less travel time.

24   As a practical matter, of course, the debate between those who value private benefits and those who insist on their social costs is no real debate at all, since people select modes of travel based on individual, not social, preferences. That is why in almost every country in the world, the automobile has triumphed, and much of public policy has been devoted to the somewhat inconsistent task of subsidizing individual choices while attempting to reduce the costs attached to them. In the case of the automobile, governments have attempted to reduce exhaust pollution, make roadways safer, and restrict use (by tolls, speed bumps, pedestrian-only streets, and parking restrictions) in neighborhoods that attach a high value to pedestrian passage. Yet none of these efforts can alter the central fact that people have found cars to be the best means for getting about.

Take traffic congestion. Television loves to focus on grim 25
scenes of gridlocked highways and angry motorists, but in fact
people still get to work faster by car than by public transit. And
the reason is not that car drivers live close to work and transit
users travel a greater distance. According to the best estimates,
cars outperform public transit in getting people quickly from
their front doors to their work places. This fact is sometimes lost
on car critics. Kay, for example, writes that "the same number of
people who spend an hour driving sixteen lanes of highway can
travel on a two-track train line." Wrong. Train travel is efficient
over a fixed, permanent route, but people have to find some way to
get to where the train starts and get to their final destination after
the train stops. The *full* cost of moving people from home to work
and back to the home is lower for cars than for trains. Moreover,
cars are not subject to union strikes. The Long Island railroad or
the bus system may shut down when workers walk off the job;
cars do not.

The transportation argument rarely seems to take cognizance 26
of the superiority of cars with respect to individual wants. Whenever there is a discussion about how best to move people about,
mass-transit supporters typically overestimate, usually by a wide
margin, how many people will leave their cars and happily hop
onto trains or buses. According to one study, by Don Pickerell, the
vast majority of American rail-transportation proposals greatly
exaggerate the number of riders to be attracted; the actual rider-
ship turns out to be about a third of the predicted level. For this
reason, urban public transport almost never recovers from the fare
box more than a fraction of the actual cost of moving people. Os-
aka, Japan, seems to be the only large city in the world that gets
back from passengers what it spends; in Atlanta, Detroit, and
Houston, public transit gets from passengers no more than a third
of their cost.

So the real debate ought not be one between car enthusiasts 27
and mass-transit advocates, but about ways of moderating the inevitable use of cars in order to minimize their deleterious effects.

One such discussion has already had substantial effects. Auto- 28
exhaust pollution has been dramatically reduced in this country

by redesigning engines, changing fuels (largely by removing lead), and imposing inspection requirements.

29   Since the mid-1960's, auto emissions have been reduced by about 95 percent. Just since 1982, ten years after the Clean Air Act was passed, carbon-monoxide levels have fallen by 40 percent and nitrogen-oxide levels by 25 percent. I live in the Los Angeles area and know from personal experience how irritating smog was in the 1950's. I also know that smog has decreased dramatically for most (but not all) of the region. The number of "smog alert" days called by the South Coast Air Quality Management District (AQMD) declined from 121 in the mid-1970's to seven in 1996. AQMD now predicts that by the year 2000 the number may fall to zero.

30   Nationally, very little of this improvement has come about from moving people from solo cars into car pools or onto mass transit. What experts call "Transportation Control Measures" (TCM's)—the combined effect of mass transit, car pools, telecommuting, and the like—have produced small reductions in smog levels. Transit expansion has decreased carbon monoxide by six-tenths of 1 percent and car pools by another seven-tenths of 1 percent. Adding BART to San Francisco has had only trivial effects on pollution. The Environmental Protection Agency (in the Clinton administration) has issued a report that puts it bluntly: "Efforts to reduce emissions through traditional TCM's have not generated significant air-quality benefits." The methods that *have* reduced pollution significantly are based on markets, not capital investments, and include smog fees, congestion pricing, gas taxes, and higher parking charges.

31   There is still more pollution to eliminate, but the anti-car enthusiasts rarely approach the task rationally. General Motors now leases electric cars, but they are very expensive and require frequent recharging from scarce power outlets. The electric car is an impressive engineering achievement, but not if you want to travel very far.

We could pass laws that would drive down even further the
32 pollution output of cars, but this would impose huge costs on manufacturers and buyers without addressing the real source of auto pollution—a small percentage of older or modified cars that generate huge amounts of exhaust. Devices now exist for measuring the pollution of cars as they move on highways and then ticketing the

offenders, but only recently has there been a large-scale trial of this method, and the results are not yet in. The method has the virtue of targeting enforcement on real culprits, but the defect (for car critics) of not requiring a "tough new law" aimed at every auto owner.

As for traffic congestion, that has indeed become worse— 33 because highway construction has not kept pace with the growth of automobile use. But it is not as bad as some imagine—the average commuting time was the same in 1990 as in 1980—and it is not bad where it is often assumed to be bad. A road is officially called "congested" if its traffic volume exceeds 80 percent of its designed capacity. By this measure, the most congested highways are in and around Washington, D.C., and San Francisco. But if you drive these roads during rush hour, as I have, you will acquire a very different sense of things. The highways into Washington and San Francisco do produce blockages, usually at familiar intersections, bridges, or merges. They rarely last very long and, on most days, one can plan around them.

Indeed, the fact and consequences of auto congestion are 34 greatly exaggerated in most large cities. During rush hour, I have driven into and out of Dallas, Kansas City, Phoenix, St. Louis, and San Diego without much more than an occasional slowdown. Moreover, despite the massive reliance on cars and a short-term decline in the economic vitality of their downtown areas, most of these cities have restored their central areas. Kansas City is bleak in the old downtown, but the shopping area (built 75 years ago!) called Country Club Plaza is filled with people, stores, and restaurants. San Diego and San Francisco have lively downtowns. Los Angeles even managed to acquire a downtown (actually, several downtowns) after it grew up without much of one—and this in a city allegedly "built around the car."[1] Phoenix is restoring its downtown and San Diego never really lost its center.

[1]Allegedly. In fact, Los Angeles grew up around a massive rail-based mass-transit system that used streetcars to move people along hundreds of miles of tracks built down the center of broad roads. When rail transit lost popularity to the car, the tracks were pulled up or paved over, leaving behind the wide roads on which cars could move. The region once had more rail transit than any other place in the country.

35   *Real* congestion, by contrast, is found in New York City, Chicago, and Boston, where almost any movement on any downtown street is extremely difficult. From the moment you enter a car or taxi, you are in a traffic jam. Getting to the airport by car from Manhattan or Boston is vastly more difficult than getting there from San Francisco, Los Angeles, or Washington.

36   But the lesson in this should be disturbing to car critics: *car travel is most congested in cities that have the oldest and most highly developed rail-based transit systems.* One reason is historical: having subways from their early days, these cities built up to high levels of residential and commercial concentration. A car added to this mix has to navigate through streets surrounded by high office buildings and tall apartment towers. When many people in those buildings take cars or taxis, the congestion can be phenomenal.

37   But there is another reason as well. Even where rail transportation exists, people will not use it enough to relieve congestion. There is, for example, an excellent rail line from O'Hare Airport to downtown Chicago, and some people use it. But it has done little or nothing to alleviate congestion on the parallel highway. People do not like dragging suitcases on and off trains. And the train does not stop where people want to go—namely, where they live. It stops at busy street corners, sometimes in dangerous neighborhoods. If you take the train, you still must shift to a car at the end, and finding one is not always easy. This is why taking a car from the Los Angeles airport, though it will place you in a few pockets of congestion, gets you to your home faster (and with all of your belongings) than taking a train and taxi a comparable distance from O'Hare.

38   A great deal can still be done to moderate the social costs of automobile traffic. More toll roads can be built with variable rates that will allow people to drive—at different prices, depending on the level of congestion—to and from cities. Bridges into cities can charge tolls to ensure that only highly motivated people consume scarce downtown road space. (A friend of mine, a distinguished economist, was once asked, in derision, whether he would buy the Brooklyn Bridge. "I would if I could charge tolls on it," he

replied.) Cars can be banned from streets that are capable of being pedestrian malls—though there are not many such places. (A number of such malls were created for the purpose of keeping people downtown who did not want to be downtown, and were doomed to failure from the start.)

Other measures are also possible. More bicycle pathways can 39 be created, though these are rarely alternatives to auto transportation; some people do ride a bike to work, but few do so often. Street patterns in residential areas can be arranged to minimize the amount of through road traffic they must endure. Gasoline taxes can be set high enough to recover more of the social costs of operating automobiles. (This will not happen in a society as democratic as ours, but it is a good idea, and maybe someday a crisis will create an opportunity.)

Portland, Oregon, has become well-known among American 40 cities for having adopted a law—the Urban Growth Boundary— that denies people the right to build almost any new structure in a green belt starting about twenty minutes from downtown. This means that new subdivisions to which one must travel by car cannot be created outside the line. The nice result is that outside the city, you can drive through unspoiled farm land.

The mayor and downtown business leaders like what they 41 have created. So do environmentalists, social-service organizations, and many ordinary citizens. The policy, described in a recent issue of *Governing* magazine, is called the New Urbanism, and has attracted interest from all over the country. But the policy also has its costs. As the city's population grows, more people must be squeezed into less space. Housing density is up. Before the Urban Growth Boundary, the average Portland house was built on a lot about 13,000 feet square and row houses made up only 3 percent of all dwelling units. Now, the average lot size has fallen to 8,700 square feet and row houses make up 12 percent of the total. And housing prices are also up. Six years ago, Portland was the nation's 55th most affordable city; today, it is the 165th.

As density goes up in Portland, so will the problems associ- 42 ated with density, such as crime. Reserving land out of a city for scenic value is an important goal, but it must be balanced with supplying affordable housing. Portland will work out the balance, once people begin to yearn for lower density.

43   But even if we do all the things that can be done to limit the social costs of cars, the campaign against them will not stop. It will not stop because so many of the critics dislike everything the car stands for and everything that society constructs to serve the needs of its occupants.

44   Cars are about privacy; critics say privacy is bad and prefer group effort. (Of course, one rarely meets these critics in groups. They seem to be too busy rushing about being critics.) Cars are about autonomy; critics say that the pursuit of autonomy destroys community. (Actually, cars allow people to select the kind of community in which they want to live.) Cars are about speed; critics abhor the fatalities they think speed causes. (In fact, auto fatalities have been declining for decades, including after the 55-mile-per-hour national speed limit was repealed. Charles Lave suggests that this is because higher speed limits reduce the variance among cars in their rates of travel, thereby producing less passing and overtaking, two dangerous highway maneuvers.) Cars are about the joyous sensation of driving on beautiful country roads; critics take their joy from politics. (A great failing of the intellectual life of this country is that so much of it is centered in Manhattan, where one finds the highest concentration of non-drivers in the country.) Cars make possible Wal-Mart, Home Depot, the Price Club, and other ways of allowing people to shop for rock-bottom prices; critics want people to spend their time gathering food at downtown shops (and paying the much higher prices that small stores occupying expensive land must charge). Cars make California possible; critics loathe California. (But they loathe it for the wrong reason. The state is not the car capital of the nation; 36 states have more cars per capita, and their residents drive more miles.)

45   Life in California would be very difficult without cars. This is not because the commute to work is so long; in Los Angeles, according to Charles Lave, the average trip to work in 1994 was 26 minutes, five minutes *shorter* than in New York City. Rather, a carless state could not be enjoyed. You could not see the vast areas of

farm land, the huge tracts of empty mountains and deserts, the miles of deserted beaches and forests.

No one who visits Los Angeles or San Francisco can imagine 46 how much of California is, in effect, empty, unsettled. It is an empire of lightly used roads, splendid vistas, and small towns, intersected by a highway system that, should you be busy or foolish enough to use it, will speed you from San Francisco to Los Angeles or San Diego. Off the interstate, it is a kaleidoscope of charming places to be alone.

Getting there in order to be alone is best done in one of the re- 47 markably engineered, breathtakingly fast, modern cars that give to the driver the deepest sense of what the road can offer: the beauty of its views, the excitement of command, the passion of engagement.

I know the way. If you are a friend, you need only ask.   48

1997

Sex, Lies, and Advertising

Gloria Steinem

About three years ago, as *glasnost* was beginning and *Ms.* seemed 1 to be ending, I was invited to a press lunch for a Soviet official. He entertained us with anecdotes about new problems of democracy in his country. Local Communist leaders were being criticized in their media for the first time, he explained, and they were angry.

"So I'll have to ask my American friends," he finished point- 2 edly, "how more *subtly* to control the press." In the silence that followed, I said, "Advertising."

The reporters laughed, but later, one of them took me aside: 3 How *dare* I suggest that freedom of the press was limited? How dare I imply that his newsweekly could be influenced by ads?

I explained that I was thinking of advertising's mediawide in- 4 fluence on most of what we read. Even newsmagazines use "soft" cover stories to sell ads, confuse readers with "advertorials," and occasionally self-censor on subjects known to be a problem with big advertisers.

5   But, I also explained, I was thinking especially of women's magazines. There, it isn't just a little content that's devoted to attracting ads, it's almost all of it. That's why advertisers—not readers—have always been the problem for *Ms.* As the only women's magazine that didn't supply what the ad world euphemistically describes as "supportive editorial atmosphere" or "complementary copy" (for instance, articles that praise food/fashion/beauty subjects to "support" and "complement" food/fashion/beauty ads), *Ms.* could never attract enough advertising to break even.

6   "Oh, *women's* magazines," the journalist said with contempt. "Everybody knows they're catalogs—but who cares? They have nothing to do with journalism."

7   I can't tell you how many times I've had this argument in 25 years of working for many kinds of publications. Except as moneymaking machines—"cash cows" as they are so elegantly called in the trade—women's magazines are rarely taken seriously. Though changes being made by women have been called more far-reaching than the industrial revolution—and though many editors try hard to reflect some of them in the few pages left to them after all the ad-related subjects have been covered—the magazines serving the female half of this country are still far below the journalistic and ethical standards of news and general interest publications. Most depressing of all, this doesn't even rate an exposé.

8   If *Time* and *Newsweek* had to lavish praise on cars in general and credit General Motors in particular to get GM ads, there would be a scandal—maybe a criminal investigation. When women's magazines from *Seventeen* to *Lear's* praise beauty products in general and credit Revlon in particular to get ads, it's just business as usual.

I.

9 When *Ms.* began, we didn't consider *not* taking ads. The most important reason was keeping the price of a feminist magazine low

enough for most women to afford. But the second and almost equal reason was providing a forum where women and advertisers could talk to each other and improve advertising itself. After all, it was (and still is) as potent a source of information in this country as news or TV and movie dramas.

We decided to proceed in two stages. First, we would con- 10 vince makers of "people products" used by both men and women but advertised mostly to men—cars, credit cards, insurance, sound equipment, financial services, and the like—that their ads should be placed in a women's magazine. Since they were accustomed to the division between editorial and advertising in news and general interest magazines, this would allow our editorial content to be free and diverse. Second, we would add the best ads for whatever traditional "women's products" (clothes, shampoo, fragrance, food, and so on) that surveys showed *Ms.* readers used. But we would ask them to come in *without* the usual quid pro quo of "complementary copy."

We knew the second step might be harder. Food advertisers 11 have always demanded that women's magazines publish recipes and articles on entertaining (preferably ones that name their products) in return for their ads; clothing advertisers expect to be surrounded by fashion spreads (especially ones that credit their designers); and shampoo, fragrance, and beauty products in general usually insist on positive editorial coverage of beauty subjects, plus photo credits besides. That's why women's magazines look the way they do. But if we could break this link between ads and editorial content, then we wanted good ads for "women's products," too.

By playing their part in this unprecedented mix of *all* the 12 things our readers need and use, advertisers also would be rewarded: ads for products like cars and mutual funds would find a new growth market; the best ads for women's products would no longer be lost in oceans of ads for the same category; and both would have access to a laboratory of smart and caring readers whose response would help create effective ads for other media as well.

I thought then that our main problem would be the imagery 13 in ads themselves. Carmakers were still draping blondes in evening gowns over the hoods like ornaments. Authority figures were almost always male, even in ads for products that only women used. Sadistic, he-man campaigns even won industry praise. (For instance, *Advertising Age* had hailed the infamous Silva Thin cigarette theme, "How to Get a Woman's Attention: Ignore Her," as "brilliant.") Even in medical journals, tranquilizer ads showed depressed housewives standing beside piles of dirty dishes and promised to get them back to work.

14   Obviously, *Ms.* would have to avoid such ads and seek out the best ones—but this didn't seem impossible. *The New Yorker* had been selecting ads for aesthetic reasons for years, a practice that only seemed to make advertisers more eager to be in its pages. *Ebony* and *Essence* were asking for ads with positive black images, and though their struggle was hard, they weren't being called unreasonable.

15   Clearly, what *Ms.* needed was a very special publisher and ad sales staff. I could think of only one woman with experience on the business side of magazines—Patricia Carbine, who recently had become a vice president of *McCall's* as well as its editor in chief—and the reason I knew her name was a good omen. She had been managing editor at *Look* (really *the* editor, but its owner refused to put a female name at the top of his masthead) when I was writing a column there. After I did an early interview with Cesar Chavez, then just emerging as a leader of migrant labor, and the publisher turned it down because he was worried about ads from Sunkist, Pat was the one who intervened. As I learned later, she had told the publisher she would resign if the interview wasn't published. Mainly because *Look* couldn't afford to lose Pat, it *was* published (and the ads from Sunkist never arrived).

16   Though I barely knew this woman, she had done two things I always remembered: put her job on the line in a way that editors often talk about but rarely do, and been so loyal to her colleagues that she never told me or anyone outside *Look* that she had done so.

17   Fortunately, Pat did agree to leave *McCall's* and take a huge cut in salary to become publisher of *Ms.* She became responsible for training and inspiring generations of young women who joined the *Ms.* ad sales force, many of whom went on to become "firsts" at the top of publishing. When *Ms.* first started, however, there were so few women with experience selling space that Pat

and I made the rounds of ad agencies ourselves. Later, the fact that *Ms.* was asking companies to do business in a different way meant our saleswomen had to make many times the usual number of calls—first to convince agencies and then client companies besides—and to present endless amounts of research. I was often asked to do a final ad presentation, or see some higher decision-maker, or speak to women employees so executives could see the interest of women they worked with. That's why I spent more time persuading advertisers than editing or writing for *Ms.* and why I ended up with an unsentimental education in the seamy underside of publishing that few writers see (and even fewer magazines can publish).

Let me take you with us through some experiences, just as they happened: 18

• Cheered on by early support from Volkswagen and one or two other car companies, we scrape together time and money to put on a major reception in Detroit. We know U.S. carmakers firmly believe that women choose the upholstery, not the car, but we are armed with statistics and reader mail to prove the contrary: a car is an important purchase for women, one that symbolizes mobility and freedom. 19

But almost nobody comes. We are left with many pounds of shrimp on the table, and quite a lot of egg on our face. We blame ourselves for not guessing that there would be a baseball pennant play-off on the same day, but executives go out of their way to explain they wouldn't have come anyway. Thus begins ten years of knocking on hostile doors, presenting endless documentation, and hiring a full-time saleswoman in Detroit—all necessary before *Ms.* gets any real results. 20

This long saga has a semihappy ending: foreign and, later, domestic carmakers eventually provided *Ms.* with enough advertising to make cars one of our top sources of ad revenue. Slowly, Detroit began to take the women's market seriously enough to put car ads in other women's magazines, too, thus freeing a few pages from the hothouse of fashion–beauty–food ads. 21

But long after figures showed a third, even a half, of many car models being bought by women, U.S. makers continued to be uncomfortable addressing women. Unlike foreign carmakers, 22

Detroit never quite learned the secret of creating intelligent ads that exclude no one, and then placing them in women's magazines to overcome past exclusion. (*Ms.* readers were so grateful for a routine Honda ad featuring rack and pinion steering, for instance, that they sent fan mail.) Even now, Detroit continues to ask, "Should we make special ads for women?" Perhaps that's why some foreign cars still have a disproportionate share of the U.S. women's market.

23 •   In the *Ms.* Gazette, we do a brief report on a congressional hearing into chemicals used in hair dyes that are absorbed through the skin and may be carcinogenic. Newspapers report this too, but Clairol, a Bristol-Myers subsidiary that makes dozens of products—a few of which have just begun to advertise in *Ms.*—is outraged. Not at newspapers or newsmagazines, just at us. It's bad enough that *Ms.* is the only women's magazine refusing to provide the usual "complementary" articles and beauty photos, but to criticize one of their categories—*that* is going too far.

24   We offer to publish a letter from Clairol telling its side of the story. In an excess of solicitousness, we even put this letter in the Gazette, not in Letters to the Editors where it belongs. Nonetheless—and in spite of surveys that show *Ms.* readers are active women who use more of almost everything Clairol makes than do the readers of any other women's magazine—*Ms.* gets almost none of these ads for the rest of its natural life.

25   Meanwhile, Clairol changes its hair coloring formula, apparently in response to the hearings we reported.

26 •   Our saleswomen set out early to attract ads for consumer electronics: sound equipment, calculators, computers, VCRs, and the like. We know that our readers are determined to be included in the technological revolution. We know from reader surveys that *Ms.* readers are buying this stuff in numbers as high as those of magazines like *Playboy,* or "men 18 to 34," the prime targets of the consumer electronics industry. Moreover, unlike traditional women's products that our readers buy but don't need to read articles about, these are subjects they want covered in our pages. There actually is a supportive editorial atmosphere.

"But women don't understand technology," say executives at   27
the end of ad presentations. "Maybe not," we respond, "but neither do men—and we all buy it."

"If women *do* buy it," say the decision-makers, "they're ask-   28
ing their husbands and boyfriends what to buy first." We produce letters from *Ms.* readers saying how turned off they are
when salesmen say things like "Let me know when you husband
can come in."

After several years of this, we get a few ads for compact   29
sound systems. Some of them come from JVC, whose vice president, Harry Elias, is trying to convince his Japanese bosses that
there is something called a women's market. At his invitation, I
find myself speaking at huge trade shows in Chicago and Las
Vegas, trying to persuade JVC dealers that showrooms don't
have to be locker rooms where women are made to feel unwel-
come. But as it turns out, the shows themselves are part of the
problem. In Las Vegas, the only women around the technology
displays are seminude models serving champagne. In Chicago,
the big attraction is Marilyn Chambers, who followed Linda
Lovelace of *Deep Throat* fame as Chuck Traynor's captive and/or
employee. VCRs are being demonstrated with her porn videos.

In the end, we get ads for a car stereo now and then, but no   30
VCRs; some IBM personal computers, but no Apple or Japanese
ones. We notice that office magazines like *Working Woman* and
Savvy don't benefit as much as they should from office equipment
ads either. In the electronics world, women and technology seem
mutually exclusive. It remains a decade behind even Detroit.

• Because we get letters from little girls who love toy trains,   31
and who ask our help in changing ads and box-top photos that
feature little boys only, we try to get toy-train ads from Lionel.
It turns out that Lionel executives *have* been concerned about
little girls. They made a pink train, and were surprised when it
didn't sell.

Lionel bows to consumer pressure with a photograph of a boy   32
and a girl—but only on some of their boxes. They fear that, if
trains are associated with girls, they will be devalued in the
minds of boys. Needless to say, *Ms.* gets no train ads, and little

girls remain a mostly unexplored market. By 1986, Lionel is put up for sale.

33   But for different reasons, we haven't had much luck with other kinds of toys either. In spite of many articles on child-rearing; an annual listing of nonsexist, multi-racial toys by Letty Cottin Pogrebin; Stories for Free Children, a regular feature also edited by Letty; and other prizewinning features for or about children, we get virtually no toy ads. Generations of *Ms.* sales-women explain to toy manufacturers that a larger proportion of *Ms.* readers have preschool children than do the readers of other women's magazines, but this industry can't believe feminists have or care about children.

34   •   When *Ms.* begins, the staff decides not to accept ads for femi-nine hygiene sprays or cigarettes: they are damaging and carry no appropriate health warnings. Though we don't think we should tell our readers what to do, we do think we should pro-vide facts so they can decide for themselves. Since the antismok-ing lobby has been pressing for health warnings on cigarette ads, we decided to take them only as they comply.

        Philip Morris is among the first to do so. One of its brands,
35   Virginia Slims, is also sponsoring women's tennis and the first national polls of women's opinions. On the other hand, the Vir-ginia Slims theme, "You've come a long way, baby," has more than a "baby" problem. It makes smoking a symbol of progress for women.

36   We explain to Philip Morris that this slogan won't do well in our pages, but they are convinced its success with some women means it will work with *all* women. Finally, we agree to publish an ad for a Virginia Slims calendar as a test. The letters from readers are critical—and smart. For instance: Would you show a black man picking cotton, the same man in a Cardin suit, and symbolize the antislavery and civil rights movements by smok-ing? Of course not. But instead of honoring the test results, the Philip Morris people seem angry to be proven wrong. They take away ads for *all* their many brands.

37   This costs *Ms.* about $250,000 the first year. After five years, we can no longer keep track. Occasionally, a new set of executives

listens to *Ms.* saleswomen, but because we won't take Virginia
Slims, not one Philip Morris product returns to our pages for the
next 16 years.

Gradually, we also realize our naiveté in thinking we *could*   38
decide against taking cigarette ads. They became a disproportionate support of magazines the moment they were banned on
television, and few magazines could compete and survive without them; certainly not *Ms.*, which lacks so many other categories. By the time statistics in the 1980s showed the women's
rate of lung cancer was approaching men's, the necessity of taking cigarette ads has become a kind of prison.

• General Mills, Pillsbury, Carnation, DelMonte, Dole, Kraft,   39
Stouffer, Hormel, Nabisco: you name the food giant, we try it.
But no matter how desirable the *Ms.* readership, our lack of
recipes is lethal.

We explain to them that placing food ads *only* next to recipes   40
associates food with work. For many women, it is a negative that
works *against* the ads. Why not place food ads in diverse media
without recipes (thus reaching more men, who are now a third of
the shoppers in supermarkets anyway), and leave the recipes to
specialty magazines like *Gourmet* (a third of whose readers are
also men)?

These arguments elicit interest, but except for an occasional   41
ad for a convenience food, instant coffee, diet drinks, yogurt, or
such extras as avocados and almonds, this mainstay of the publishing industry stays closed to us. Period.

• Traditionally, wines and liquors didn't advertise to women: 42
men were thought to make the brand decisions, even if women
did the buying. But after endless presentations, we begin to
make a dent in this category. Thanks to the unconventional
Michel Roux of Carillon Importers (distributors of Grand
Marnier, Absolut Vodka, and others), who assumes that food and
drink have no gender, some ads are leaving their men's club.

Beermakers are still selling masculinity. It takes *Ms.* fully   43
eight years to get its first beer ad (Michelob). In general, however, liquor ads are less stereotyped in their imagery—and far
less controlling of the editorial content around them—than are

women's products. But given the underrepresentation of other categories, these very facts tend to create a disproportionate number of alcohol ads in the pages of *Ms.* This in turn dismays readers worried about women and alcoholism.

44 • We hear in 1980 that women in the Soviet Union have been producing feminist *samizdat* (underground, self-published books) and circulating them throughout the country. As punishment, four of the leaders have been exiled. Though we are operating on our usual shoestring, we solicit individual contributions to send Robin Morgan to interview these women in Vienna.

45 The result is an exclusive cover story that includes the first news of a populist peace movement against the Afghanistan occupation, a prediction of *glasnost* to come, and a grass-roots, intimate view of Soviet women's lives. From the popular press to women's studies courses, the response is great. The story wins a Front Page award.

46 Nonetheless, this journalistic coup undoes years of efforts to get an ad schedule from Revlon. Why? Because the Soviet women on our cover *are not wearing makeup.*

47 • Four years of research and presentations go into convincing airlines that women now make travel choices and business trips. United, the first airline to advertise in *Ms.,* is so impressed with the response from our readers that one of its executives appears in a film for our ad presentations. As usual, good ads get great results.

48 But we have problems unrelated to such results. For instance: because American Airlines flight attendants include among their labor demands the stipulation that they could choose to have their last names preceded by "Ms." on their name tags—in a long-delayed revolt against the standard, "I am your pilot, Captain Rothgart, and this is your flight attendant, Cindy Sue"—American officials seem to hold the magazine responsible. We get no ads.

49 There is still a different problem at Eastern. A vice president cancels subscriptions for thousands of copies on Eastern flights. Why? Because he is offended by ads for lesbian poetry journals in the *Ms.* Classified. A "family airline," as he explains to me coldly on the phone, has to "draw the line somewhere."

It's obvious that *Ms.* can't exclude lesbians and serve women. 50
We've been trying to make that point ever since our first issue included an article by and about lesbians, and both Suzanne
Levine, our managing editor, and I were lectured by such heavy
hitters as Ed Kosner, then editor of *Newsweek* (and now of *New
York Magazine*), who insisted that *Ms.* should "position" itself
against lesbians. But our advertisers have paid to reach a guaranteed number of readers, and soliciting new subscriptions to compensate for Eastern would cost $150,000 plus rebating money in
the meantime.

Like almost everything ad-related, this presents an elaborate 51
organizing problem. After days of searching for sympathetic
members of the Eastern board, Frank Thomas, president of the
Ford Foundation, kindly offers to call Roswell Gilpatrick, a director of Eastern. I talk with Mr. Gilpatrick, who calls Frank Borman, then the president of Eastern. Frank Borman calls me to say
that his airline is not in the business of censoring magazines: *Ms.*
will be returned to Eastern flights.

• Women's access to insurance and credit is vital, but with the 52
exception of Equitable and a few other ad pioneers, such financial
services address men. For almost a decade after the Equal Credit
Opportunity Act passes in 1974, we try to convince American Express that women are a growth market—but nothing works.

Finally, a former professor of Russian named Jerry Welsh be- 53
comes head of marketing. He assumes that women should be
cardholders, and persuades his colleagues to feature women in a
campaign. Thanks to this 1980s series, the growth rate for female
cardholders surpasses that for men.

For this article, I asked Jerry Welsh if he would explain why 54
American Express waited so long. "Sure," he said, "they were
afraid of having a 'pink' card."

• Women of color read *Ms.* in disproportionate numbers. This 55
is a source of pride to *Ms.* staffers, who are also more racially
representative than the editors of other women's magazines. But
this reality is obscured by ads filled with enough white women
to make a reader snowblind.

56   Pat Carbine remembers mostly "astonishment" when she re-
quested African American, Hispanic, Asian, and other diverse
images. Marcia Ann Gillespie, a *Ms.* editor who was previously
the editor in chief of *Essence*, witnesses ad bias a second time:
having tried for *Essence* to get white advertisers to use black images (Revlon did so eventually, but L'Oréal, Lauder, Chanel, and
other companies never did), she sees similar problems getting integrated ads for an integrated magazine. Indeed, the ad world
often creates black and Hispanic ads only for black and Hispanic
media. In an exact parallel of the fear that marketing a product to
women will endanger its appeal to men, the response is usually,
"But your [white] readers won't identify."

57   In fact, those we are able to get—for instance, a Max Factor
ad made for *Essence* that Linda Wachner gives us after she becomes president—are praised by white readers, too. But there are
pathetically few such images.

58 •   By the end of 1986, production and mailing costs have risen
astronomically, ad income is flat, and competition for ads is
stiffer than ever. The 60/40 preponderance of edit over ads that
we promised to readers becomes 50/50; children's stories, most
poetry, and some fiction are casualties of less space; in order to
get variety into limited pages, the length (and sometimes the
depth) of articles suffers; and, though we do refuse most of the
ads that would look like a parody in our pages, we get so worn
down that some slip through. (See this issue's No Comment.)
Still, readers perform miracles. Though we haven't been able to
afford a subscription mailing in two years, they maintain our
guaranteed circulation of 450,000.

59   Nonetheless, media reports on *Ms.* often insist that our un-
profitability must be due to reader disinterest. The myth that advertisers simply follow readers is very strong. Not one reporter
notes that other comparable magazines our size (say, *Vanity Fair*
or *The Atlantic*) have been losing more money in one year than *Ms.*
has lost in 16 years. No matter how much never-to-be-recovered
cash is poured into starting a magazine or keeping one going, appearances seem to be all that matter. (Which is why we haven't

been able to explain our fragile state in public. Nothing causes ad-flight like the smell of nonsuccess.)

My healthy response is anger. My not-so-healthy response is 60
constant worry. Also an obsession with finding one more rescue. There is hardly a night when I don't wake up with sweaty palms and pounding heart, scared that we won't be able to pay the printer or the post office; scared most of all that closing our doors will hurt the women's movement.

Out of chutzpah and desperation, I arrange a lunch with 61
Leonard Lauder, president of Estée Lauder. With the exception of Clinique (the brainchild of Carol Phillips), none of Lauder's hundreds of products has been advertised in *Ms.* A year's schedule of ads for just three or four of them could save us. Indeed, as the scion of a family-owned company whose ad practices are followed by the beauty industry, he is one of the few men who could liberate many pages in all women's magazines just by changing his mind about "complementary copy."

Over a lunch that costs more than we can pay for some arti- 62
cles, I explain the need for his leadership. I also lay out the record of *Ms.:* more literary and journalistic prizes won, more new issues introduced into the mainstream, new writers discovered, and impact on society than any other magazine; more articles that became books, stories that became movies, ideas that became television series, and newly advertised products that became profitable; and, most important for him, a place for his ads to reach women who aren't reachable through any other women's magazine. Indeed, if there is one constant characteristic of the ever-changing *Ms.* readership, it is their impact as leaders. Whether it's waiting until later to have first babies, or pioneering PABA as sun protection in cosmetics, *whatever* they are doing today, a third to a half of American women will be doing three to five years from now. It's never failed.

But, he says, *Ms.* readers are not *our* women. They're not in- 63
terested in things like fragrance and blush-on. If they were, *Ms.* would write articles about them.

On the contrary, I explain, surveys show they are more likely 64
to buy such things than the readers of, say, *Cosmopolitan* or *Vogue.* They're good customers because they're out in the world enough

to need several sets of everything: home, work, purse, travel, gym, and so on. They just don't need to read articles about these things. Would he ask a men's magazine to publish monthly columns on how to shave before he advertised Aramis products (his line for men)?

65   He concedes that beauty features are often concocted more for advertisers than readers. But *Ms.* isn't appropriate for his ads anyway, he explains. Why? Because Estée Lauder is selling "a kept-woman mentality."

66   I can't quite believe this. Sixty percent of the users of his products are salaried, and generally resemble *Ms.* readers. Besides, his company has the appeal of having been started by a creative and hardworking woman, his mother, Estée Lauder.

67   That doesn't matter, he says. He knows his customers, and they would *like* to be kept women. That's why he will never advertise in *Ms.*

68   In November 1987, by vote of the Ms. Foundation for Education and Communication (*Ms.*'s owner and publisher, the media subsidiary of the Ms. Foundation for Women), *Ms.* was sold to a company whose officers, Australian feminists Sandra Yates and Anne Summers, raised the investment money in their country that *Ms.* couldn't find in its own. They also started *Sassy* for teenage women.

69   In their two year tenure, circulation was raised to 550,000 by investment in circulation mailings, and, to the dismay of some readers, editorial features on clothes and new products made a more traditional bid for ads. Nonetheless, ad pages fell below previous levels. In addition, *Sassy*, whose fresh voice and sexual frankness were an unprecedented success with young readers, was targeted by two mothers from Indiana who began, as one of them put it, "calling every Christian organization I could think of." In response to this controversy, several crucial advertisers pulled out.

70   Such links between ads and editorial content were a problem in Australia, too, but to a lesser degree. "Our readers pay two times more for their magazines," Anne explained, "so advertisers have less power to threaten a magazine's viability."

"I was shocked," said Sandra Yates with characteristic direct-   71
ness. "In Australia, we think you have freedom of the press—but
you don't."

Since Anne and Sandra had not met their budget's projections   72
for ad revenue, their investors forced a sale. In October 1989, *Ms.*
and *Sassy* were bought by Dale Lang, owner of *Working Mother,*
Working Woman, and one of the few independent publishing
companies left among the conglomerates. In response to a request from the original *Ms.* staff—as well as to reader letters urg-
ing that *Ms.* continue, plus his own belief that *Ms.* would benefit
his other magazines by blazing a trail—he agreed to try the ad-
free, reader-supported *Ms.* you hold now and to give us complete
editorial control.

II.

Do you think, as I once did, that advertisers make decisions based   73
on solid research? Well, think again. "Broadly speaking," says
Joseph Smith of Oxtoby-Smith, Inc., a consumer research firm,
"there is no persuasive evidence that the editorial context of
an ad matters."

Advertisers who demand such "complementary copy," even   74
in the absence of respectable studies, clearly are operating under
a double standard. The same food companies place ads in *People*
with no recipes. Cosmetics companies support *The New Yorker*
with no regular beauty columns. So where does this habit of controlling the content of women's magazines come from?

Tradition. Ever since *Ladies Magazine* debuted in Boston in 1828,   75
editorial copy directed to women has been informed by something
other than its readers' wishes. There were no ads then, but in an age
when married women were legal minors with no right to their own
money, there was another revenue source to be kept in mind: husbands. "Husbands may rest assured," wrote editor Sarah Joseph
Hale, "that nothing found in these pages shall cause her [his wife]
to be less assiduous in preparing for his reception or encourage her
to 'usurp station' or encroach upon prerogatives of men."

76   Hale went on to become the editor of *Godey's Lady's Book*, a magazine featuring "fashion plates": engravings of dresses for readers to take to their seamstresses or copy themselves. Hale added "how to" articles, which set the tone for women's service magazines for years to come: how to write politely, avoid sunburn, and—in no fewer than 1,200 words—how to maintain a goose quill pen. She advocated education for women but avoided controversy. Just as most women's magazines now avoid politics, poll their readers on issues like abortion but rarely take a stand, and praise socially approved lifestyles, Hale saw to it that *Godey's* avoided the hot topics of its day: slavery, abolition, and women's suffrage.

77   What definitively turned women's magazines into catalogs, however, were two events: Ellen Butterick's invention of the clothing pattern in 1863 and the mass manufacture of patent medicines containing everything from colored water to cocaine. For the first time, readers could purchase what magazines encouraged them to want. As such magazines became more profitable, they also began to attract men as editors. (Most women's magazines continued to have men as top editors until the feminist 1970s.) Edward Bok, who became editor of *The Ladies' Home Journal* in 1889, discovered the power of advertisers when he rejected ads for patent medicines and found that other advertisers canceled in retribution. In the early 20th century, *Good Housekeeping* started its Institute to "test and approve" products. Its Seal of Approval became the grandfather of current "value added" programs that offer advertisers such bonuses as product sampling and department store promotions.

78   By the time suffragists finally won the vote in 1920, women's magazines had become too entrenched as catalogs to help women learn how to use it. The main function was to create a desire for products, teach how to use products, and make products a crucial part of gaining social approval, pleasing a husband, and performing as a homemaker. Some unrelated articles and short stories were included to persuade women to pay for these catalogs. But articles were neither consumerist nor rebellious. Even fiction was usually subject to formula: if a woman had any sexual life outside marriage, she was supposed to come to a bad end.

In 1965, Helen Gurley Brown began to change part of that for- 79
mula by bring "the sexual revolution" to women's magazines—
but in an ad-oriented way. Attracting multiple men required even
more consumerism, as the Cosmo Girl made clear, than finding
one husband.

In response to the workplace revolution of the 1970s, tradi- 80
tional women's magazines—that is, "trade books" for women
working at home—were joined by *Savvy, Working Woman,* and
other trade books for women working in offices. But by keeping
the fashion/beauty/entertaining articles necessary to get traditional ads and then adding career articles besides, they inadvertently produced the antifeminist stereotype of Super Woman. The
male-imitative, dress-for-success woman carrying a briefcase became the media image of a woman worker, even though a blue-
collar woman's salary was often higher than her glorified
secretarial sister's, and though women at a real briefcase level are
statistically rare. Needless to say, these dress-for-success women
were also thin, white, and beautiful.

In recent years, advertisers' control over the editorial content 81
of women's magazines has become so institutionalized that it is
written into "insertion orders" or dictated to ad salespeople as official policy. The following are recent typical orders to women's
magazines:

• Dow's Cleaning Products stipulates that ads for its Vivid and 82
Spray 'n Wash products should be adjacent to "children or fashion editorial"; ads for Bathroom Cleaner should be next to
"home furnishing/family" features; and so on for other brands.
"If a magazine fails for ½ the brands or more," the Dow order
warns, "it will be omitted from further consideration."

• Bristol-Myers, the parent of Clairol, Windex, Drano, Bufferin, 83
and much more, stipulates that ads be placed next to "a full page
of compatible editorial."

• S.C. Johnson & Son, makers of Johnson Wax, lawn and laundry 84
products, insect sprays, hair sprays, and so on orders that its ads
*"should not be opposite extremely controversial features or material anti-
thetical to the nature/copy of the advertised product."* (Italics theirs.)

85 • Maidenform, manufacturer of bras and other apparel, leaves
a blank for the particular product and states: "The creative concept of the _____ campaign, and the very nature of the product
itself appeal to the positive emotions of the reader/consumer.
Therefore, it is imperative that all editorial adjacencies reflect
that same positive tone. The editorial must not be negative in
content or lend itself contrary to the _____ product imagery/mes-
sage (e.g. _editorial relating to illness, disillusionment, large size fashion, etc._)." (Italics mine.)

86 • The De Beers diamond company, a big seller of engagement
rings, prohibits magazines from placing its ads with "adjacencies
to hard news or anti/love-romance themed editorial."

87 • Procter & Gamble, one of this country's most powerful and
diversified advertisers, stands out in the memory of Anne Summers and Sandra Yates (no mean feat in this context): its products were not to be placed in _any_ issue that included _any_ material
on gun control, abortion, the occult, cults, or the disparagement
of religion. Caution was also demanded in any issue covering
sex or drugs, even for educational proposes.

88   Those are the most obvious chains around women's magazines. There are also rules so clear they needn't be written down:
for instance, an overall "look" compatible with beauty and fashion
ads. Even "real" nonmodel women photographed for a woman's
magazine are usually made up, dressed in credited clothes, and re-
touched out of all reality. When editors do include articles on less-
than-cheerful subjects (for instance, domestic violence), they tend
to keep them short and unillustrated. The point is to be "upbeat."
Just as women in the street are asked, "Why don't you smile,
honey?" women's magazines acquire an institutional smile.

       Within the text itself, praise for advertisers' products has be-
89 come so ritualized that fields like "beauty writing" have been invented. One of its frequent practitioners explained seriously that
"It's a difficult art. How many new adjectives can you find? How
much greater can you make a lipstick sound? The FDA restricts
what companies can say on labels, but we create illusion. And ad
agencies are on the phone all the time pushing you to get their

product in. A lot of them keep the business based on how many editorial clippings they produce every month. The worst are products," like Lauder's as the writer confirmed, "with their own name involved. It's all ego."

Often, editorial becomes one giant ad. Last November, for instance, *Lear's* featured an elegant woman executive on the cover. 90 On the contents page, we learned she was wearing Guerlian makeup and Samsara, a new fragrance by Guerlain. Inside were full-page ads for Samsara and Guerlain antiwrinkle cream. In the cover profile, we learned that this executive was responsible for launching Samsara and is Guerlain's director of public relations. When the *Columbia Journalism Review* did one of the few articles to include women's magazines in coverage of the influence of ads, editor Frances Lear was quoted as defending her magazine because "this kind of thing is done all the time."

Often, advertisers also plunge odd-shaped ads into the text, no matter what the cost to the readers. At *Woman's Day*, a maga- 91 zine originally founded by a supermarket chain, editor in chief Ellen Levine said, "The day the copy had to rag around a chicken leg was not a happy one."

Advertisers are also adamant about where in a magazine their ads appear. When Revlon was not placed as the first beauty ad in 92 one Hearst magazine, for instance, Revlon pulled its ads from *all* Hearst magazines. Ruth Whitney, editor in chief of *Glamour*, attributes some of these demands to "ad agencies wanting to prove to a client that they've squeezed the last drop of blood out of a magazine." She also is, she says, "sick and tired of hearing that women's magazines are controlled by cigarette ads." Relatively speaking, she's right. To be as censoring as are many advertisers for women's products, tobacco companies would have to demand articles in praise of smoking and expect glamorous photos of beautiful women smoking their brands.

I don't mean to imply that the editors I quote here share my objections to ads: most assume that women's magazines have to 93 be the way they are. But it's also true that only former editors can be completely honest. "Most of the pressure came in the form of direct project mentions," explains Sey Chassler, who was editor in chief of *Redbook* from the sixties to the eighties. "We got threats from the big guys, the Revlons, blackmail threats. They wouldn't run ads unless we credited them.

"But it's not fair to single out the beauty advertisers because
94 these pressures came from everybody. Advertisers want to know two things: What are you going to charge me? What *else* are you going to do for me? It's a holdup. For instance, management felt that fiction took up too much space. They couldn't put any advertising in that. For the last ten years, the number of fiction entries into the National Magazine Awards has declined.

"And pressures are getting worse. More magazines are more
95 bottom-line oriented because they have been taken over by companies with no interest in publishing.

"I also think advertisers do this to women's magazines espe-
96 cially," he concluded, "because of the general disrespect they have for women."

Even media experts who don't give a damn about women's
97 magazines are alarmed by the spread of this ad–edit linkage. In a climate *The Wall Street Journal* describes as an unacknowledged Depression for media, women's products are increasingly able to take their low standards wherever they go. For instance: newsweeklies publish uncritical stories on fashion and fitness. *The New York Times Magazine* recently ran an article on "firming creams," complete with mentions of advertisers. *Vanity Fair* published a profile of one major advertiser, Ralph Lauren, illustrated by the same photographer who does his ads, and turned the lifestyle of another, Calvin Klein, into a cover story. Even the outrageous *Spy* has toned down since it began to go after fashion ads.

And just to make us really worry, films and books, the last
98 media that go directly to the public without having to attract ads first, are in danger, too. Producers are beginning to depend on payments for displaying products in movies, and books are now being commissioned by companies like Federal Express.

But the truth is that women's products—like women's maga-
99 zines —have never been the subjects of much serious reporting anyway. News and general interest publications, including the "style" or "living" sections of newspapers, write about food and clothing as cooking and fashion, and almost never evaluate such

products by brand name. Though chemical additives, pesticides, and animal fats are major health risks in the United States, and clothes, shoddy or not, absorb more consumer dollars than cars, this lack of information is serious. So is ignoring the contents of beauty products that are absorbed into our bodies through our skins, and that have profit margins so big they would make a loan shark blush.

III

What could women's magazines be like if they were as free as   100
books? as realistic as newspapers? as creative as films? as diverse as women's lives? We don't know.

But we'll only find out if we take women's magazines seri-   101
ously. If readers were to act in a concerted way to change traditional practices of *all* women's magazines and the marketing of *all* women's products, we could do it. After all, they are operating on our consumer dollars, money that we now control. You and I could:

- write to editors and publishers (with copies to advertisers) that we're willing to pay *more* for magazines with editorial independence, but will *not* continue to pay for those that are just editorial extensions of ads;
- write to advertisers (with copies to editors and publishers) that we want fiction, political reporting, consumer reporting—whatever is, or is not, supported by their ads;
- put as much energy into breaking advertising's control over content as into changing the images in ads, or protesting ads for harmful products like cigarettes;
- support only those women's magazines and products that take *us* seriously as readers and consumers.

Those of us in the magazine world can also use the carrot-and-   102
stick technique. For instance: pointing out that, if magazines were a regulated medium like television, the demands of advertisers would be against FCC rules. Payola and extortion could be punished. As it is, there are probably illegalities. A magazine's postal rates are determined by the ratio of ad to edit pages, and the former costs more than the latter. So much for the stick.

103   The carrot means appealing to enlightened self-interest. For instance: there are many studies showing that the greatest factor in determining an ad's effectiveness is the credibility of its surroundings. The "higher the rating of editorial believability," concluded a 1987 survey by the *Journal of Advertising Research*, "the higher the rating of the advertising." Thus, an impenetrable wall between edit and ads would also be in the best interest of advertisers.

104   Unfortunately, few agencies or clients hear such arguments. Editors often maintain the false purity of refusing to talk to them at all. Instead, they see ad salespeople who know little about editorial, are trained in business as usual, and are usually paid by commission. Editors might also band together to take on controversy. That happened once when all the major women's magazines did articles in the same month on the Equal Rights Amendment. It could happen again.

105   It's almost three years away from life between the grindstones of advertising pressures and readers' needs. I'm just beginning to realize how edges got smoothed down—in spite of all our resistance.

106   I remember feeling put upon when I changed "Porsche" to "car" in a piece about Nazi imagery in German pornography by Andrea Dworkin—feeling sure Andrea would understand that Volkswagen, the distributor of Porsche and one of our few supportive advertisers, asked only to be far away from Nazi subjects. It's taken me all this time to realize that Andrea was the one with a right to feel put upon.

107   Even as I write this, I get a call from a writer for *Elle*, who is doing a whole article on where women part their hair. Why, she wants to know, do I part mine in the middle?

108   It's all so familiar. A writer trying to make something of a nothing assignment; an editor laboring to think of new ways to attract ads; readers assuming that other women must want this ridiculous stuff; more women suffering for lack of information, insight, creativity, and laughter that could be on these same pages.

109   I ask you: Can't we do better than this?

1990

"But First, a Word from Our Sponsor"

James B. Twitchell

Whenever a member of my paunchy fifty-something set pulls me   1
aside and complains of the dumbing down of American culture, I
tell him that if he doesn't like it, he should quit moaning and go
buy a lot of Fast-Moving Consumer Goods. And every time he
buys soap, toothpaste, beer, gasoline, bread, aspirin, and the like,
he should make it a point to buy a different brand. He should im-
plore his friends to do likewise. At the same time, he should quit
giving so much money to his kids. That, I'm sorry to say, is his
only hope.

Here's why. The culture we live in is carried on the back of ad-   2
vertising. Now I mean that literally. If you cannot find commercial
support for what you have to say, it will not be transported. Much
of what we share, and what we know, and even what we treasure,
is carried to us each second in a plasma of electrons, pixels, and
ink, underwritten by multinational advertising agencies dedicated to attracting our attention for entirely nonaltruistic reasons.
These agencies, gathered up inside worldwide conglomerates
with weird, sci-fi names like WPP, Omnicom, Saatchi & Saatchi,
Dentsu, and Euro RSCG, are usually collections of established
shops linked together to provide "full service" to their global
clients. Their service is not moving information or creating entertainment, but buying space and inserting advertising. They essentially rent our concentration to other companies—sponsors—for
the dubious purpose of informing us of something that we've
longed for all our lives even though we've never heard of it before. Modern selling is not about trading information, as it was in
the 19th century, as much as about creating an infotainment culture with sufficient allure to enable other messages—commercials—to get through. In the spirit of the enterprise, I call this new
culture Adcult.

Adcult is there when we blink, it's there when we listen, it's   3
there when we touch, it's even there to be smelled in scent strips

when we open a magazine. There is barely a space in our culture not already carrying commercial messages. Look anywhere: in schools there is Channel One; in movies there is product place-ment; ads are in urinals, played on telephone hold, in alphanu-meric displays in taxis, sent unannounced to fax machines, inside catalogs, on the video in front of the Stairmaster at the gym, on T-shirts, at the doctor's office, on grocery carts, on parking meters, on tees at golf holes, on inner-city basketball backboards, piped in along with Muzak . . . ad nauseam (and yes, even on airline vomit bags). We have to shake magazines like rag dolls to free up their pages from the "blow-in" inserts and then wrestle out the stapled-or glued-in ones before reading can begin. We now have to fast-forward through some five minutes of advertising that opens rental videotapes. President Bill Clinton's inaugural parade fea-tured a Budweiser float. At the Smithsonian, the Orkin Pest Con-trol Company sponsored an exhibit on exactly what it advertises it kills: insects. No venue is safe. Is there a blockbuster museum show not decorated with corporate logos? The Public Broadcast-ing Service is littered with "underwriting announcements" that look and sound almost exactly like what PBS claims they are not: commercials.

4   Okay, you get the point. Commercial speech is so powerful that it drowns out all other sounds. But sounds are always con-veyed in a medium. The media of modern culture are these: print, sound, pictures, or some combination of each. Invariably, conver-sations about dumbing down focus on the supposed corruption of these media, as demonstrated by the sophomoric quality of most movies, the fall from the golden age of television, the mindlessness of most best-sellers, and the tarting-up of the news, be it in or on *USA Today, Time,* ABC, or *Inside Edition.* The media make especially convenient whipping boys because they are now all conglomer-ated into huge worldwide organizations such as Time Warner, General Electric, Viacom, Bertelsmann, and Sony. But, alas, as much fun as it is to blame the media, they have very little to do with the explanation for whatever dumbing down has occurred.

5   The explanation is, I think, more fundamental, more economic in nature. These media are delivered for a price. We have to pay for

them, either by spending money or by spending time. Given a choice, we prefer to spend time. We spend our time paying attention to ads, and in exchange we are given infotainment. This trade is central to Adcult. Economists call this "cost externalization." If you want to see it at work, go to McDonald's. You order. You carry your food to the table. You clean up. You pay less. Want to see it elsewhere? Buy gas. Just as the "work" you do at the self-service gas station lowers the price of gas, so consuming ads is the "work" you do that lowers the price of delivering the infotainment. In Adcult, the trade is more complex. True, you are entertained at lower cost, but you are also encultured in the process.

So far, so good. The quid pro quo of modern infotainment culture is that if you want it, you'll get it—no matter what it is—as long as there are enough of you who (1) are willing to spend some energy along the way hearing "a word from our sponsor" and (2) have sufficient disposable income possibly to buy some of the advertised goods. In Adcult you pay twice: once with the ad and once with the product. So let's look back a step to examine these products because—strange as it may seem—they are at the center of the dumbing down of American culture.

Before all else, we must realize that modern advertising is tied primarily to things, and only secondarily to services. Manufacturing both things *and* their meanings is what American culture is all about. If Greece gave the world philosophy, Britain drama, Austria music, Germany politics, and Italy art, then America gave mass-produced objects. "We bring good things to life" is no offhand claim. Most of these "good things" are machine made and hence interchangeable. Such objects, called parity items, constitute most of the stuff that surrounds us, from bottled water to toothpaste to beer to cars. There is really no great difference between Evian and Mountain Spring, Colgate and Crest, Miller and Budweiser, Ford and Chevrolet. Often, the only difference is in the advertising. Advertising is how we talk about these fungible things, how we know their supposed differences, how we recognize them. We don't consume the products as much as we consume the advertising.

For some reason, we like it this way. Logically, we should all read *Consumer Reports* and then all buy the most sensible product. But we don't. So why do we waste our energy (and billions of dollars) entertaining fraudulent choice? I don't know. Perhaps just as we drink the advertising, not the beer, we prefer the illusion of choice to the reality of decision. How else to explain the appearance of so much superfluous choice? A decade ago, grocery stores carried about 9,000 items; they now stock about 24,000. Revlon makes 158 shades of lipstick. Crest toothpaste comes in 36 sizes and shapes and flavors. We are even eager to be offered choice where there is none to speak of. AT&T offers "the right choice"; Wendy's asserts that "there is no better choice"; Pepsi is "the choice of a new generation"; Taster's Choice is "the choice for taste." Even advertisers don't understand the phenomenon. Is there a relationship between the number of soft drinks and television channels—about 27? What's going to happen when the information pipe carries 500?

9   I have no idea. But I do know this: human beings like things. We buy things. We like to exchange things. We steal things. We donate things. We live through things. We call these things "goods," as in "goods and services." We do not call them "bads." This sounds simplistic, but it is crucial to understanding the power of Adcult. The still-going-strong Industrial Revolution produces more and more things, not because production is what machines do and not because nasty capitalists twist their handlebar mustaches and mutter, "More slop for the pigs," but because we are powerfully attracted to the world of things. Advertising, when it's lucky, supercharges some of this attraction.

10   This attraction to the inanimate happens all over the world. Berlin Walls fall because people want things, and they want the culture created by things. China opens its doors not so much because it wants to get out, but because it wants to get things in. We were not suddenly transformed from customers to consumers by wily manufacturers eager to unload a surplus of products. We have created a surfeit of things because we enjoy the process of "getting and spending." The consumption ethic may have started in the early 1900s, but the desire is ancient. Kings and princes once thought they could solve problems by amassing things. We now join them.

11   The Marxist balderdash of cloistered academics aside, human beings did not suddenly become materialistic. We have always been desirous of things. We have just not had many of them until quite recently, and, in a few generations, we may return to having

fewer and fewer. Still, while they last, we enjoy shopping for things and see both the humor and the truth reflected in the aphoristic "born to shop," "shop 'til you drop," and "when the going gets tough, the tough go shopping." Department store windows, whether on the city street or inside a mall, did not appear by magic. We enjoy looking through them to another world. It is voyeurism for capitalists. Our love of things is the *cause* of the Industrial Revolution, not the consequence. We are not only *homo sapiens,* or *homo ludens,* or *homo faber,* but also *homo emptor.*

Mid-20th-century American culture is often criticized for being too materialistic. Ironically, we are not too materialistic. We are not materialistic enough. If we craved objects *and* knew what they meant, there would be no need to add meaning through advertising. We would gather, use, toss out, or hoard based on some *inner* sense of value. But we don't. We don't know what to gather, we like to trade what we have gathered, and we need to know how to evaluate objects of little practical use. What is clear is that most things in and of themselves simply do not mean enough. In fact, what we crave may not be objects at all but their meaning. For whatever else advertising "does," one thing is certain: by adding value to material, by adding meaning to objects, by branding things, advertising performs a role historically associated with religion. The Great Chain of Being, which for centuries located value above the horizon in the world Beyond, has been reforged to settle value into the objects of the Here and Now . . .

We are now closing in on why the dumbing down of American culture has occurred with such startling suddenness in the last 30 years. We are also closing in on why the big complainers about dumbing down are me and my paunchy pals. The people who want things the most and have the best chance to acquire them are the young. They are also the ones who have not yet decided which brands of objects they wish to consume. In addition, they have a surplus of two commodities: time and money, especially the former. If you can make a sale to these twentysomethings, if you can "brand" them with your product, you may have them for life. But to do this you have to be able to speak to them, and to do that you have to go to where you will be heard.

14   The history of mass media can be summarized in a few words: if it can't carry advertising, it won't survive . . .

15   We need not be reminded of what is currently happening to television to realize the direction of the future. MTV, the infomercial, and the home-shopping channels are not flukes but the predictable continuation of this medium. Thanks to the remote-control wand and the coaxial (soon to be fiber-optic) cable, commercials will disappear. They will become the programming. Remember, the first rule of Adcult is this: given the choice between paying money or paying attention, we prefer to pay attention.

16   What all this means is that if you think things are bad now, just wait. There are few gatekeepers left. Most of them reside on Madison Avenue. Just as the carnival barker doesn't care what is behind the tent flap, only how long the line is in front, the poobahs of Adcult care only about who's looking, not what they are looking at. The best-seller lists, the box office, the Nielsens, the various circulation figures for newspapers and magazines, are the meters. They decide what gets through. Little wonder that so much of our popular culture is derivative of itself, that prequels and sequels and spin-offs are the order of the day, that celebrity is central, and that innovation is the cross to the vampire. Adcult is recombinant culture. This is how it has to be if advertisers are to be able to direct their spiels at the appropriate audiences for their products. It's simply too expensive to be any other way.

17   Will Adcult continue? Will there be some new culture to "afflict the comfortable and comfort the afflicted"? Will advertising, on its own terms, lose *it*? Who knows? Certainly, signs of stress are showing. Here are a few: (1) The kids are passing through "prime-branding time" like a rabbit in the python, and as they get older things may settle down. The supposedly ad-proof Generation X may be impossible to reach and advertisers will turn to older audiences by default. (2) The media are so clogged and cluttered that companies may move to other promotional highways, such as direct mail, point-of-purchase displays, and couponing, leaving the traditional avenues targeted at us older folks. (3) Branding, the heart of advertising, may become problematic if generics or store brands become as popular in this country as they

have in Europe. After all, the much-vaunted brand extension whereby Coke becomes Diet Coke which becomes Diet Cherry Coke does not always work, as Kodak Floppy Disks, Milky Way Ice Cream, Arm & Hammer antiperspirant, Life Saver Gum, and even EuroDisney have all shown. And (4)—the unthinkable— mass consumption may become too expensive. Advertising can flourish only in times of surplus, and no one can guarantee that our society will always have more than it needs.

But by no means am I predicting Adcult's imminent demise. 18 As long as goods are interchangeable and in surplus quantities, as long as producers are willing to pay for short-term advantages (especially for new products), and as long as consumers have plenty of disposable time and money so that they can consume both the ad and the product, Adcult will remain the dominant meaning-making system of modern life. I don't think you can roll this tape backwards. Adcult is the application of capitalism to culture: dollars voting. And so I say to my melancholy friends who bemoan the passing of a culture once concerned with the arts and the humanities that the only way they can change this situation is if they buy more Fast-Moving Consumer Goods, change brands capriciously, and cut the kids' allowances. Good luck.

1996

Red, White, and Beer

Dave Barry

Lately I've been feeling very patriotic, especially during commer- 1 cials. Like, when I see those strongly pro-American Chrysler commercials, the ones where the winner of the Bruce Springsteen Sound-Alike Contest sings about how The Pride Is Back, the ones where Lee Iacocca himself comes striding out and practically challenges the president of Toyota to a knife fight, I get this warm, proud feeling inside, the same kind of feeling I get whenever we hold routine naval maneuvers off the coast of Libya.

2   But if you want to talk about *real* patriotism, of course, you have to talk about beer commercials. I would have to say that Miller is the most patriotic brand of beer. I grant you it tastes like rat saliva, but we are not talking about taste here. What we are talking about, according to the commercials, is that Miller is by God an *American* beer, "born and brewed in the U.S.A.," and the men who drink it are American men, the kind of men who aren't afraid to perspire freely and shake a man's hand. That's mainly what happens in Miller commercials: Burly American men go around, drenched in perspiration, shaking each other's hands in a violent and patriotic fashion.

3   You never find out exactly why these men spend so much time shaking hands. Maybe shaking hands is just their simple straight-forward burly masculine American patriotic way of saying to each other: "Floyd, I am truly sorry I drank all that Miller beer last night and went to the bathroom in your glove compartment." Another possible explanation is that, since there are never any women in the part of America where beer commercials are made, the burly men have become lonesome and desperate for any form of physical contact. I have noticed that sometimes, in addition to shaking hands, they hug each other. Maybe very late at night, after the David Letterman show, there are Miller commercials in which the burly men engage in slow dancing. I don't know.

4   I do know that in one beer commercial, I think this is for Miller—although it could be for Budweiser, which is also a very patriotic beer—the burly men build a house. You see them all getting together and pushing up a brand-new wall. Me, I worry some about a house built by men drinking beer. In my experience, you run into trouble when you ask a group of beer-drinking men to perform any task more complex than remembering not to light the filter ends of cigarettes.

5   For example, in my younger days, whenever anybody in my circle of friends wanted to move, he'd get the rest of us to help, and, as an inducement, he'd buy a couple of cases of beer. This almost always produced unfortunate results, such as the time we were trying to move Dick "The Wretch" Curry from a horrible fourth-floor walk-up apartment in Manhattan's Lower East Side to another horrible fourth-floor walk-up apartment in Manhattan's Lower East Side, and we hit upon the labor-saving concept of,

instead of carrying The Wretch's possessions manually down the stairs, simply dropping them out the window, down onto the street, where The Wretch was racing around, gathering up the broken pieces of his life and shrieking at us to stop helping him move, his emotions reaching a fever pitch when his bed, which had been swinging wildly from a rope, entered the apartment two floors below his through what had until seconds earlier been a window.

This is the kind of thinking you get, with beer. So I figure 6 what happens, in the beer commercial where the burly men are building the house, is they push the wall up so it's vertical, and then, after the camera stops filming them, they just keep pushing, and the wall crashes down on the other side, possibly onto somebody's pickup truck. And then they all shake hands.

But other than that, I'm in favor of the upsurge in retail patri- 7 otism, which is lucky for me because the airwaves are saturated with pro-American commercials. Especially popular are commercials in which the newly restored Statue of Liberty—and by the way, I say Lee Iacocca should get some kind of medal for that, or at least be elected president—appears to be endorsing various products, as if she were Mary Lou Retton or somebody. I saw one commercial strongly suggesting that the Statue of Liberty uses Sure brand underarm deodorant.

I have yet to see a patriotic laxative commercial, but I imagine 8 it's only a matter of time. They'll show some actors dressed up as hard-working country folk, maybe at a church picnic, smiling at each other and eating pieces of pie. At least one of them will be a black person. The Statue of Liberty will appear in the background. Then you'll hear a country-style singer singing:

> Folks 'round here they love this land;
> They stand by their beliefs;
> An' when they git themselves stopped up;
> They want some quick relief.

Well, what do you think? Pretty good commercial concept, huh? 9

Nah, you're right. They'd never try to pull something like 10 that. They'd put the statue in the *foreground*.

1997

7

Philosophy, Ethics, and the Value of Life

What is good? What is valuable? What does it mean to be human? The decisions we routinely make regarding what is worth living— or dying—for create the answer to the most primal questions about the quality of the life we lead and the society we live in. Taken from Plato's political treatise *The Republic*, which was written when Athens was ruled by tyrants, "The Allegory of the Cave" is a touchstone of Western philosophy and a meditation on the nature of reality. In it, Plato frames the question of how we know what is good, indicating the good "is the power upon which he who would act rationally either in public or private life must have his eye fixed." For Plato, however, the difficulty is that we understand truths only darkly, as shadows that are illuminated by a pure and essential truth that exists outside human physical reality. In this section, a variety of arguments explore the good and how we make life and death decisions as a society. William J. Bennett's "America at Risk: Can We Survive Without Moral Values?" argues that principled living elevates the human life and its spirit and that a society not based on the constancy of certain moral principles will lead to the diminution of the quality and value of life. Edward I. Koch's "Death and Justice" also looks at how a society values life in his argument for capital punishment. Such appeals to the rule of law or morality can provide clarity, comfort, and guidance in their ideal for the good of society. The moral choices for James Rachels and Sallie Tisdale, however, are relative not to an abstract good outside of an individual's

experience but to alleviating an individual's suffering. James
Rachels examines what he finds hypocritical in the principles promoted by the medical establishment in "Active and Passive Euthanasia." He argues that passive euthanasia, refusing help, is as
much an action as active euthanasia, mercy killing—and that
mercy killing can often be the more humane action. Sallie Tisdale,
a nurse, provides an unflinching account of an abortion clinic and
the abject conditions that create the need for abortion. She recounts the ruthless reality of the procedure as well as the psychological situation, where many teenage girls ask, what is it—a boy
or a girl?. . . when they still don't know exactly how they got pregnant. What is right and what is wrong under circumstances this
extreme? Is there a principle or law that can consistently and hu-
manely be applied in every situation? Is there a platonic ideal of
absolute good that might help navigate such moral ambiguity?
Such principled notions have no place in the "Dumpster Diving"
world of Lars Eighner, accomplished writer and homeless person, who objectively discusses scavenging for food in a way that
maintains his own dignity and by extension the dignity of those
who are in similar straits. Eighner has no room for the "abstract"
in the privations of his life; and neither may Nancy Mairs, who
movingly describes what is a heroic life in the face of multiple
sclerosis. It is, after all, our imperfection that makes us human.
What makes us human is also that we are part of a greater cycle of
life and death. Virginia Woolf's "The Death of the Moth"
poignantly depicts the moment of death and what is precious in
what is ordinary and commonplace. In the death of a moth, Woolf
finds the beauty of our transitory state.

Allegory of the Cave

Plato

1   And now, I said, let me show in a figure how far our nature is enlightened or unenlightened: Behold! human beings living in an underground den, which has a mouth open towards the light and reaching all along the den; here, they have been from their childhood, and have their legs and necks chained so that they cannot move, and can only see before them, being prevented by the chains from turning round their heads. Above and behind them a fire is blazing at a distance, and between the fire and the prisoners there is a raised way; and you will see, if you look, a low wall built along the way, like the screen which marionette players have in front of them, over which they show the puppets.

2   I see.

3   And do you see, I said, men passing along the wall carrying all sorts of vessels, and statues and figures of animals made of wood and stone and various materials, which appear over the wall? Some of them are talking, others silent.

4   You have shown me a strange image, and they are strange prisoners.

5   Like ourselves, I replied; and they see only their own shadows, or the shadows of one another, which the fire throws on the opposite wall of the cave?

6   True, he said; how could they see anything but the shadows if they were never allowed to move their heads?

7   And of the objects which are being carried in like manner they would only see the shadows?

8   Yes, he said.

9   And if they were able to converse with one another, would they not suppose that they were naming what was actually before them?

10   Very true.

11   And suppose further that the prison had an echo which came from the other side, would they not be sure to fancy when one of the passers-by spoke that the voice which they heard came from the passing shadow?

No question, he replied.   12

To them, I said, the truth would be literally nothing but the   13
shadows of the images.

That is certain.   14

And now look again, and see what will naturally follow if the   15
prisoners are released and disabused of their error. At first, when
any of them is liberated and compelled suddenly to stand up and
turn his neck round and walk and look towards the light, he will
suffer sharp pains; the glare will distress him and he will be unable to see the realities of which in his former state he had seen the
shadows; and then conceive some one saying to him, that what he
saw before was an illusion, but that now, when he is approaching
nearer to being and his eye is turned towards more real existence,
he has a clearer vision—what will be his reply? And you may further imagine that his instructor is pointing to the objects as they
pass and requiring him to name them—will he not be perplexed?
Will he not fancy that the shadows which he formerly saw are
truer than the objects which are now shown to him?

Far truer.   16

And if he is compelled to look straight at the light, will he not   17
have a pain in his eyes which will make him turn away to take
refuge in the objects of vision which he can see, and which he will
conceive to be in reality clearer than the things which are now
being shown to him?

True, he said.   18

And suppose once more, that he is reluctantly dragged up a   19
steep and rugged ascent, and held fast until he is forced into the
presence of the sun himself, is he not likely to be pained and irritated? When he approaches the light his eyes will be dazzled and
he will not be able to see anything at all of what are now called
realities.

Not all in a moment, he said.   20

He will require to grow accustomed to the sight of the upper   21
world. And first he will see the shadows best, next the reflections
of men and other objects in the water, and then the objects themselves; then he will gaze upon the light of the moon and the stars
and the spangled heaven; and he will see the sky and the stars by
night better than the sun or the light of the sun by day?

22   Certainly.

23   Last of all he will be able to see the sun, and not mere reflections of him in the water, but he will see him in his own proper
place, and not in another; and he will contemplate him as he is.

24   Certainly.

25   He will then proceed to argue that this is he who gives the
season and the years, and is the guardian of all that is in the visible world, and in a certain way the cause of all things which he
and his fellows have been accustomed to behold?

26   Clearly, he said, he would first see the sun and then reason
about him.

27   And when he remembered his old habitation, and the wisdom of the den and his fellow-prisoners, do you not suppose that
he would felicitate himself on the change, and pity them?

28   Certainly, he would.

29   And if they were in the habit of conferring honors among
themselves on those who were quickest to observe the passing
shadows and to remark which of them went before, and which
followed after, and which were together; and who were therefore
best able to draw conclusions as to the future, do you think that he
would care for such honors and glories, or envy the possessors of
them? Would he not say with Homer,

Better to be the poor servant of a poor master,

and to endure anything, rather than think as they do and live after their manner?

30   Yes, he said, I think that he would rather suffer anything than
entertain these false notions and live in this miserable manner.

31   Imagine once more, I said, such a one coming suddenly out of
the sun to be replaced in his old situation; would he not be certain
to have his eyes full of darkness?

32   To be sure, he said.

33   And if there were a contest, and he had to compete in measuring the shadows with the prisoners who had never moved out
of the den, while his sight was still weak, and before his eyes had
become steady (and the time which would be needed to acquire
this new habit of sight might be very considerable) would he not
be ridiculous? Men would say of him that up he went and down

he came without his eyes; and that it was better not even to think of ascending; and if any one tried to loose another and lead him up to the light, let them only catch the offender, and they would put him to death.

No question, he said. 34

This entire allegory, I said, you may now append, dear Glau- 35 con, to the previous argument; the prison-house is the world of sight, the light of fire is the sun, and you will not misapprehend me if you interpret the journey upwards to be the ascent of the soul into the intellectual world according to my poor belief, which, at your desire, I have expressed—whether rightly or wrongly God knows. But, whether true or false, my opinion is that in the world of knowledge the idea of good appears last of all, and is seen only with an effort; and, when seen, is also inferred to be the universal author of all things beautiful and right, parent of light and of the lord of light in this visible world, and the immediate source of reason and truth in the intellectual; and that this is the power upon which he who would act rationally either in public or private life must have his eye fixed.

I agree, he said, as far as I am able to understand you. 36

Moreover, I said, you must not wonder that those who attain 37 to this beatific vision are unwilling to descend to human affairs; for their souls are ever hastening into the upper world where they desire to dwell; which desire of theirs is very natural, if our allegory may be trusted.

Yes, very natural. 38

And is there anything surprising in one who passes from di- 39 vine contemplations to the evil state of man, misbehaving himself in a ridiculous manner; if, while his eyes are blinking and before he has become accustomed to the surrounding darkness, he is compelled to fight in courts of law, or in other places, about the images or the shadows of images of justice, and is endeavoring to meet the conceptions of those who have never yet seen absolute justice?

Anything but surprising, he replied. 40

Any one who has common sense will remember that the bewil- 41 derments of the eyes are of two kinds, and arise from two causes, either from coming out of the light or from going into the light, which is true of the mind's eye, quite as much as of the bodily eye; and he who remembers this when he sees any one whose vision is perplexed and weak, will not be too ready to laugh; he will first ask whether that soul of man has come out of the brighter light, and is unable to see because unaccustomed to the dark, or having turned from darkness to the day is dazzled by excess of light. And he will count the one happy in his condition and state of being, and he will pity the other; or, if he have a mind to laugh at the soul which comes from below into the light, there will be more reason in this than the laugh which greets him who returns from above out of the light into the den.

42   That, he said, is a very just distinction.

Fourth Century BCE

America at Risk: Can We Survive without Moral Values?

William J. Bennett

1   Novelist Walker Percy once was asked what concerned him most about the future of America. He responded: "Probably the fear of seeing America, with all its great strength and beauty and freedom gradually subside into decay through default and be defeated, not by the Communist movement but from within by weariness, boredom, cynicism, greed and in the end helplessness before its great problems."

2   The social science data confirm Percy's concerns. They are uncomfortably close to becoming reality.

3   Since 1960, the U.S. population has grown 41%, the gross domestic product nearly has tripled, and total levels of social spending by all levels of government (measured in constant 1990 dollars) have risen from $143,730,000,000 to $787,000,000,000—

more than a fivefold increase. During the same 34-year period, there has been a more than 500% rise in violent crime; a greater than 400% hike in illegitimate births; a tripling of the percentage of children living in single-parent homes; a threefold increase in teenage suicides; a doubling in the divorce rate; and a drop of almost 75 points in SAT scores.

No institution has suffered more during this period than the 4 American family. Today, 30% of all births and almost 70% of all black births are to unmarried females. By the end of the century, according to the most reliable projections, 40% of all births and 80% of minority births will be out of wedlock. In a few years, illegitimacy will surpass divorce as the main cause of fatherlessness in the U.S.

These figures have frightening social implications, but should 5 not cause Americans to despair. Instead, they should stir the nation.

There are three brief explanations for what accounts for Amer- 6 ica's social regression. The first has to do with a marked shift in the public's attitudes. According to social scientist James Q. Wilson, "The powers exercised by the institutions of social control have been constrained, and people, especially young people, have embraced an ethos that values self-expression over self-control."

During the last quarter-century, the American people increas- 7 ingly have abandoned time-honored moral codes. The U.S. now is seeing the results being played out on urban streets and in hospital emergency rooms, the courts, and classrooms.

A second is that a number of pernicious ideas made their way 8 into the mainstream of American life. It became unfashionable to make value judgments. The nation witnessed an expansive notion of "rights" and an attenuated sense of personal responsibility. "If it feels good, do it"; "Do your own thing"; and "You only go around once in life, so you have to grab all the gusto you can" became words to live by. These seemingly innocuous phrases masked a destructive underlying philosophy that eventually found its way into public policy.

A third explanation has to do with the failures of contemporary 9 liberalism—an ideology that dominates the national Democratic Party. A series of misguided social policies were championed. In the area of criminal justice, an anti-incarceration outlook took hold that

said, in effect, society's response to criminal behavior should be re-
habilitation, not punishment. Schools replaced moral education
with "values clarification," standards were abandoned, and homework was forgotten. Having a child out of wedlock was rewarded
with government subsidies in the form of welfare checks.

10   Through the National Endowment for the Arts, government
got into the business of subsidizing pornography and obscenity.
Abortion, for any reason, at any point in pregnancy, was elevated
to a constitutional right. Tax policies penalized the traditional nuclear family. No-fault divorce laws made a mockery of the belief
that marriage is a sacred covenant. Racial relations deteriorated
as, in law and policy, people began to be judged not by the content
of their character, but by the color of their skin (i.e., quotas, race-
norming, and set-asides).

11   These policies effectively tore down cultural guardrails. Not
surprisingly, individual casualties followed.

12   . . . Republicans should hammer home the point of how much
better American life would be if a sweeping, reform-minded, and
humane social agenda were implemented that included:

- A more effective and tough-minded criminal justice system,
  including more prisons, judges, and prosecutors.
- Reform of the juvenile criminal justice system (including try-
  ing as adults juveniles who commit violent crimes).
- Increased attention to victims' rights and roles in the criminal
  justice process.
- Reform of parole.
- Enactment of "truth in sentencing" guidelines.
- Alternative forms of punishment, such as boot camps.
- An integrated anti-drug strategy.
- The fundamental reform of education through national standards, merit pay, alternative certification, and, most important, allowing parents to choose the public, private, or
  religious schools to which they can send their children.
- Removal of the economic barriers that keep the underclass in
  poverty by providing tax incentives for businesses to locate
  in urban enterprise zones, as well as such items as tenant
  ownership and investment in low-income housing.

- Support for families by increasing the Federal personal income tax dependent exemption.
- Removal of major obstacles to adoption and increasing residential schools, congregate care facilities, and orphanages for abandoned and abused children.

It is well-known that there is some skittishness among Republicans in dealing with social issues. My response is: Philosophers from Aristotle on have understood that there is no more important political consideration than the moral precepts that underlie society and the policies that flow from them. No serious political party can duck these issues. Republicans simply must make sure that public officials deal with them in a responsible, thoughtful and constructive manner.   13

As Republicans address the set of issues that travel under the banner of "values," they need to recognize that many of the problems afflicting society today are manifestly moral. Therefore, they are remarkably resistant to government cures, so there are limits to the degree to which public policies can cure what ails the U.S.   14

The Republican Party needs to point out that not only are there some tasks that government cannot do, in a nation of free and sovereign people, there are some tasks it should not do. The more Americans have asked of government, the less they have asked of themselves. A compelling message might be this: The Republican philosophy is to say to the Federal government, "Give us back our money—and with it, our sense of responsibility."   15

During the last decade of the 20th century, the failures of contemporary liberalism are all around. It is an intellectually and morally bankrupt ideology, one that no longer has the power to inspire people. A confident Republican Party, therefore, should offer a fundamentally different governing philosophy and set of solutions.   16

The GOP's task is to link the values debate to a specific set of policies, insist that moral common sense once again become the touchstone of social policy, and oppose the radical social agenda of the Clinton Administration in a principled, vigorous, and determined manner—all the while recognizing that this debate must be conducted in a calm, civilized, and reasoned voice.   17

18   If Republicans do, their voices will be heard, their philosophy
will prevail, and their prospects as a party will continue to brighten.
The opportunities are there—if Republicans have the courage and
the wisdom to seize them.

1994

Death and Justice
Edward I. Koch

1 Last December a man named Robert Lee Willie, who had been
convicted of raping and murdering an 18-year-old woman, was
executed in the Louisiana state prison. In a statement issued several minutes before his death, Mr. Willie said: "Killing people is
wrong . . . . It makes no difference whether it's citizens, countries,
or governments. Killing is wrong." Two weeks later in South Carolina, an admitted killer named Joseph Carl Shaw was put to
death for murdering two teenagers. In an appeal to the governor
for clemency, Mr. Shaw wrote: "Killing is wrong when I did it.
Killing is wrong when you do it. I hope you have the courage and
moral strength to stop the killing."

2   It is a curiosity of modern life that we find ourselves being
lectured on morality by cold-blooded killers. Mr. Willie previously had been convicted of aggravated rape, aggravated kidnapping, and the murders of a Louisiana deputy and a man from
Missouri. Mr. Shaw committed another murder a week before the
two for which he was executed, and admitted mutilating the body
of the 14-year-old girl he killed. I can't help wondering what
prompted these murderers to speak out against killing as they entered the death-house door. Did their newfound reverence for life
stem from the realization that they were about to lose their own?

3   Life is indeed precious, and I believe the death penalty helps
to affirm this fact. Had the death penalty been a real possibility in
the minds of these murderers, they might well have stayed their

hand. They might have shown moral awareness before their victims died, and not after. Consider the tragic death of Rosa Velez, who happened to be home when a man named Luis Vera burglarized her apartment in Brooklyn. "Yeah, I shot her," Vera admitted. "She knew me, and I knew I wouldn't go to the chair."

During my 22 years in public service, I have heard the pros 4 and cons of capital punishment expressed with special intensity. As a district leader, councilman, congressman, and mayor, I have represented constituencies generally thought of as liberal. Because I support the death penalty for heinous crimes of murder, I have sometimes been the subject of emotional and outraged attacks by voters who find my position reprehensible or worse. I have listened to their ideas. I have weighed their objections carefully. I still support the death penalty. The reasons I maintain my position can be best understood by examining the arguments most frequently heard in opposition.

(1) *The death penalty is "barbaric."* Sometimes opponents of 5 capital punishment horrify with tales of lingering death on the gallows, of faulty electric chairs, or of agony in the gas chamber. Partly in response to such protests, several states such as North Carolina and Texas switched to execution by lethal injection. The condemned person is put to death painlessly, without ropes, voltage, bullets, or gas. Did this answer the objections of death penalty opponents? Of course not. On June 22, 1984, *The New York Times* published an editorial that sarcastically attacked the new "hygienic" method of death by injection, and stated that "execution can never be made humane through science." So it's not the method that really troubles opponents. It's the death itself they consider barbaric.

Admittedly, capital punishment is not a pleasant topic. How- 6 ever, one does not have to like the death penalty in order to support it any more than one must like radical surgery, radiation, or chemotherapy in order to find necessary these attempts at curing cancer. Ultimately we may learn how to cure cancer with a simple pill. Unfortunately, that day has not yet arrived. Today we are faced with the choice of letting the cancer spread or trying to cure it with the methods available, methods that one day will almost c͟ ͙tainly be ͙ ͙ nsidered barbaric. But to give up and do nothing would be far more barbaric and would certainly delay the discovery of an eventual cure. The analogy between cancer and murder is imperfect, because murder is not the "disease" we are trying to cure. The disease is injustice. We may not like the death penalty, but it must be available to punish crimes of cold-blooded murder, cases in which any other form of punishment would be inadequate and, therefore, unjust. If we create a society in which injustice is not tolerated, incidents of murder—the most flagrant form of injustice—will diminish.

7   (2) *No other major democracy uses the death penalty.* No other major democracy—in fact, few other countries of any description— are plagued by a murder rate such as that in the United States. Fewer and fewer Americans can remember the days when unlocked doors were the norm and murder was a rare and terrible offense. In America the murder rate climbed 122 percent between 1963 and 1980. During that same period, the murder rate in New York City increased by almost 400 percent, and the statistics are even worse in many other cities. A study at M.I.T. showed that based on 1970 homicide rates a person who lived in a large American city ran a greater risk of being murdered than an American soldier in World War II ran of being killed in combat. It is not surprising that the laws of each country differ according to differing conditions and traditions. If other countries had our murder problem, the cry for capital punishment would be just as loud as it is here. And I daresay that any other major democracy where 75 percent of the people supported the death penalty would soon enact it into law.

8   (3) *An innocent person might be executed by mistake.* Consider the work of Adam Bedau, one of the most implacable foes of capital punishment in this country. According to Mr. Bedau, it is "false sentimentality to argue that the death penalty should be abolished because of the abstract possibility that an innocent person might be executed." He cites a study of the 7,000 executions in this country from 1893 to 1971, and concludes that the record fails to show that such cases occur. The main point, however, is this. If government functioned only when the possibility of error didn't exist, government wouldn't function at all. Human life deserves special

protection, and one of the best ways to guarantee that protection is to assure that convicted murderers do not kill again. Only the death penalty can accomplish this end. In a recent case in New Jersey, a man named Richard Biegenwald was freed from prison after serving 18 years for murder; since his release he has been convicted of committing four murders. A prisoner named Lemuel Smith, who, while serving four life sentences for murder (plus two life sentences for kidnapping and robbery) in New York's Green Haven Prison, lured a woman corrections officer into the chaplain's office and strangled her. He then mutilated and dismembered her body. An additional life sentence for Smith is meaningless. Because New York has no death penalty statute, Smith has effectively been given a license to kill.

But the problem of multiple murder is not confined to the nation's penitentiaries. In 1981, 91 police officers were killed in the line of duty in this country. Seven percent of those arrested in the cases that have been solved had a previous arrest for murder. In New York City in 1976 and 1977, 85 persons arrested for homicide had a previous arrest for murder. Six of these individuals had two previous arrests for murder, and one had four previous murder arrests. During those two years the New York police were arresting for murder persons with a previous arrest for murder on the average of one every 8.5 days. This is not surprising when we learn that in 1975, for example, the median time served in Massachusetts for homicide was less than two-and-a-half years. In 1976 a study sponsored by the Twentieth Century Fund found that the average time served in the United States for first-degree murder is ten years. The median time served may be considerably lower. 9

(4) *Capital punishment cheapens the value of human life.* On the contrary, it can be easily demonstrated that the death penalty strengthens the value of human life. If the penalty for rape were lowered, clearly it would signal a lessened regard for the victims' suffering, humiliation, and personal integrity. It would cheapen their horrible experience, and expose them to an increased danger of recurrence. When we lower the penalty for murder, it signals a lessened regard for the value of the victim's life. Some critics of capital punishment, such as columnist Jimmy Breslin, 10

have suggested that a life sentence is actually a harsher penalty for murder than death. This is sophistic nonsense. A few killers may decide not to appeal a death sentence, but the overwhelming majority make every effort to stay alive. It is by exacting the highest penalty for the taking of human life that we affirm the highest value of human life.

11   (5) *The death penalty is applied in a discriminatory manner.* This factor no longer seems to be the problem it once was. The appeals process for a condemned prisoner is lengthy and painstaking. Every effort is made to see that the verdict and sentence were fairly arrived at. However, assertions of discrimination are not an argument for ending the death penalty but for extending it. It is not justice to exclude everyone from the penalty of the law if a few are found to be so favored. Justice requires that the law be applied equally to all.

12   (6) *Thou Shalt Not Kill.* The Bible is our greatest source of moral inspiration. Opponents of the death penalty frequently cite the sixth of the Ten Commandments in an attempt to prove that capital punishment is divinely proscribed. In the original Hebrew, however, the Sixth Commandment reads, "Thou Shalt Not Commit Murder," and the Torah specifies capital punishment for a variety of offenses. The biblical viewpoint has been upheld by philosophers throughout history. The greatest thinkers of the 19th century—Kant, Locke, Hobbes, Rousseau, Montesquieu, and Mill—agreed that natural law properly authorizes the sovereign to take life in order to vindicate justice. Only Jeremy Bentham was ambivalent. Washington, Jefferson, and Franklin endorsed it. Abraham Lincoln authorized executions for deserters in wartime. Alexis de Tocqueville, who expressed profound respect for American institutions, believed that the death penalty was indispensable to the support of social order. The United States Constitution, widely admired as one of the seminal achievements in the history of humanity, condemns cruel and inhuman punishment, but does not condemn capital punishment.

13   (7) *The death penalty is state-sanctioned murder.* This is the defense with which Messrs. Willie and Shaw hoped to soften the resolve of those who sentenced them to death. By saying in effect, "You're no better than I am," the murderer seeks to bring his

accusers down to his own level. It is also a popular argument among opponents of capital punishment, but a transparently false one. Simply put, the state has rights that the private individual does not. In a democracy, those rights are given to the state by the electorate. The execution of a lawfully condemned killer is no more an act of murder than is legal imprisonment an act of kidnapping. If an individual forces a neighbor to pay him money under threat of punishment, it's called extortion. If the state does it, it's called taxation. Rights and responsibilities surrendered by the individual are what give the state its power to govern. This contract is the foundation of civilization itself.

Everyone wants his or her rights, and will defend them jealously. Not everyone, however, wants responsibilities, especially the painful responsibilities that come with law enforcement. Twenty-one years ago a woman named Kitty Genovese was assaulted and murdered on a street in New York. Dozens of neighbors heard her cries for help but did nothing to assist her. They didn't even call the police. In such a climate the criminal understandably grows bolder. In the presence of moral cowardice, he lectures us on our supposed failings and tries to equate his crimes with our quest for justice. 14

The death of anyone—even a convicted killer—diminishes us all. But we are diminished even more by a justice system that fails to function. It is an illusion to let ourselves believe that doing away with capital punishment removes the murderer's deed from our conscience. The rights of society are paramount. When we protect guilty lives, we give up innocent lives in exchange. When opponents of capital punishment say to the state: "I will not let you kill in my name," they are also saying to murderers: "You can kill in your *own* name as long as I have an excuse for not getting involved." 15

It is hard to imagine anything worse than being murdered while neighbors do nothing. But something worse exists. When those same neighbors shrink back from justly punishing the murderer, the victim dies twice. 16

1985

Active and Passive Euthanasia

James Rachels

1   The distinction between active and passive euthanasia is thought to be crucial for medical ethics. The idea is that it is permissible, at least in some cases, to withhold treatment and allow a patient to die, but it is never permissible to take any direct action designed to kill the patient. This doctrine seems to be accepted by most doctors, and it is endorsed in a statement adopted by the House of Delegates of the American Medical Association on December 4, 1973:

> The intentional termination of the life of one human being by another—mercy killing—is contrary to that for which the medical profession stands and is contrary to the policy of the American Medical Association. The cessation of the employment of extraordinary means to prolong the life of the body when there is irrefutable evidence that biological death is imminent is the decision of the patient and/or his immediate family. The advice and judgment of the physician should be freely available to the patient and/or his immediate family.

However, a strong case can be made against this doctrine. In what follows I will set out some of the relevant arguments, and urge doctors to reconsider their views on this matter.

2   To begin with a familiar type of situation, a patient who is dying of incurable cancer of the throat is in terrible pain, which can no longer be satisfactorily alleviated. He is certain to die within a few days, even if present treatment is continued, but he does not want to go on living for those days since the pain is unbearable. So he asks the doctor for an end to it, and his family joins in the request.

3   Suppose the doctor agrees to withhold treatment, as the conventional doctrine says he may. The justification for his doing so is that the patient is in terrible agony, and since he is going to die anyway, it would be wrong to prolong his suffering needlessly. But now notice this. If one simply withholds treatment, it may take the patient longer to die, and so he may suffer more than he would if more direct action were taken and a lethal injection given. This fact provides strong reason for thinking that, once the

initial decision not to prolong his agony has been made, active euthanasia is actually preferable to passive euthanasia, rather than
the reverse. To say otherwise is to endorse the option that leads to
more suffering rather than less, and is contrary to the humanitarian impulse that prompts the decision not to prolong his life in the
first place.

Part of my point is that the process of being "allowed to die" ₄
can be relatively slow and painful, whereas being given a lethal
injection is relatively quick and painless. Let me give a different
sort of example. In the United States about one in six hundred
babies is born with Down's syndrome. Most of these babies are
otherwise healthy—that is, with only the usual pediatric care,
they will proceed to an otherwise normal infancy. Some, however,
are born with congenital defects such as intestinal obstructions
that require operations if they are to live. Sometimes, the parents
and the doctor will decide not to operate, and let the infant die.
Anthony Shaw describes what happens then:

> When surgery is denied [the doctor] must try to keep the infant
> from suffering while natural forces sap the baby's life away. As
> a surgeon whose natural inclination is to use the scalpel to fight
> off death, standing by and watching a salvageable baby die is
> the most emotionally exhausting experience I know. It is easy at
> a conference, in a theoretical discussion to decide that such in-
> fants should be allowed to die. It is altogether different to stand
> by in the nursery and watch as dehydration and infection
> wither a tiny being over hours and days. This is a terrible ordeal
> for me and the hospital staff—much more so than for the par-
> ents who never set foot in the nursery.[1]

I can understand why some people are opposed to all euthanasia,
and insist that such infants must be allowed to live. I think I can
also understand why other people favor destroying these babies
quickly and painlessly. But why should anyone favor letting "de-
hydration and infection wither a tiny being over hours and
days"? The doctrine that says that a baby may be allowed to de-
hydrate and wither, but may not be given an injection that would

---

[1]Anthony Shaw, "Doctor Do We Have a Choice?" *New York Times Magazine,*
January 30, 1972, p. 54.

end its life without suffering, seems so patently cruel as to require no further refutation. The strong language is not intended to offend, but only to put the point in the clearest possible way.

5   My second argument is that the conventional doctrine leads to decisions concerning life and death made on irrelevant grounds.

6   Consider again the case of the infants with Down's syndrome who need operations for congenital defects unrelated to the syndrome to live. Sometimes, there is no operation, and the baby dies, but when there is no such defect, the baby lives on. Now, an operation such as that to remove an intestinal obstruction is not prohibitively difficult. The reason why such operations are not performed in these cases is, clearly, that the child has Down's syndrome and the parents and the doctor judge that because of that fact it is better for the child to die.

7   But notice that this situation is absurd, no matter what view one takes of the lives and potentials of such babies. If the life of such an infant is worth preserving, what does it matter if it needs a simple operation? Or, if one thinks it better that such a baby should not live on, what difference does it make that it happens to have an unobstructed intestinal tract? In either case, the matter of life and death is being decided on irrelevant grounds. It is the Down's syndrome, and not the intestines, that is the issue. The matter should be decided, if at all, on that basis, and not be allowed to depend on the essentially irrelevant question of whether the intestinal tract is blocked.

8   What makes this situation possible, of course, is the idea that when there is an intestinal blockage, one can "let the baby die," but when there is no such defect there is nothing that can be done, for one must not "kill" it. The fact that this idea leads to such results as deciding life or death on irrelevant grounds is another good reason why the doctrine would be rejected.

9   One reason why so many people think that there is an important moral difference between active and passive euthanasia is that they think killing someone is morally worse than letting someone die. But is it? Is killing, in itself, worse than letting die? To investigate this issue, two cases may be considered that are exactly alike except that one involves killing whereas the other involves letting someone die. Then, it can be asked whether this difference makes

any difference to the moral assessments. It is important that the cases be exactly alike, except for this one difference, since otherwise one cannot be confident that it is this difference and not some other that accounts for any variation in the assessments of the two cases. So, let us consider this pair of cases:

In the first, Smith stands to gain a large inheritance if any- 10 thing should happen to his six-year-old cousin. One evening while the child is taking his bath, Smith sneaks into the bathroom and drowns the child, and then arranges things so that it will look like an accident.

In the second, Jones also stands to gain if anything should 11 happen to his six-year-old cousin. Like Smith, Jones sneaks in planning to drown the child in his bath. However, just as he enters the bathroom Jones sees the child slip and hit his head, and fall face down in the water. Jones is delighted; he stands by, ready to push the child's head back under if it is necessary, but it is not necessary. With only a little thrashing about, the child drowns all by himself, "accidentally," as Jones watches and does nothing.

Now Smith killed the child, whereas Jones "merely" let the 12 child die. That is the only difference between them. Did either man behave better, from a moral point of view? If the difference between killing and letting die were in itself a morally important matter, one should say that Jones's behavior was less reprehensible than Smith's. But does one really want to say that? I think not. In the first place, both men acted from the same motive, personal gain, and both had exactly the same end in view when they acted. It may be inferred from Smith's conduct that he is a bad man, although the judgment may be withdrawn or modified if certain further facts are learned about him—for example, that he is mentally deranged. But would not the very same thing be inferred about Jones from his conduct? And would not the same further considerations also be relevant to any modification of this judgment? Moreover, suppose Jones pleaded, in his own defense, "After all, I didn't do anything except just stand there and watch the child drown. I didn't kill him; I only let him die." Again, if letting die were in itself less bad than killing, this defense should have at least some weight. But it does not. Such a "defense" can only be regarded as a grotesque perversion of moral reasoning. Morally speaking, it is no defense at all.

13   Now, it may be pointed out, quite properly, that the cases of euthanasia with which doctors are concerned are not like this at all. They do not involve personal gain or the destruction of normal healthy children. Doctors are concerned only with cases in which the patient's life is of no further use to him, or in which the patient's life has become or will soon become a terrible burden. However, the point is the same in these cases: The bare difference between killing and letting die does not, in itself, make a moral difference. If a doctor lets a patient die, for humane reasons, he is in the same moral position as if he had given the patient a lethal injection for humane reasons. If his decision was wrong—if, for example, the patient's illness was in fact curable—the decision would be equally regrettable no matter which method was used to carry it out. And if the doctor's decision was the right one, the method used is not in itself important.

14   The AMA policy statement isolates the crucial issue very well; the crucial issue is "the intentional termination of the life of one human being by another." But after identifying this issue, and for-bidding "mercy killing," the statement goes on to deny that the cessation of treatment is the intentional termination of life. This is where the mistake comes in, for what is the cessation of treatment, in these circumstances, if it is not "the intentional termination of life of one human being by another"? Of course it is exactly that, and if it were not, there would be no point to it.

15   Many people will find this judgment hard to accept. One reason, I think, is that it is very easy to conflate the question of whether killing is, in itself, worse than letting die, with the very different question of whether most actual cases of killing are more reprehensible than most actual cases of letting die. Most actual cases of killing are clearly terrible (think, for example, of all the murders reported in the newspapers), and one hears of such cases every day. On the other hand, one hardly ever hears of a case of letting die, except for the actions of doctors who are motivated by humanitarian reasons. So one learns to think of killing in a much worse light than of letting die. But this does not mean that there is something about killing that makes it in itself worse than letting die, for it is not the bare difference between killing and letting die that makes the difference in these cases. Rather, the other factors— the murderer's motive of personal gain, for example, contrasted

with the doctor's humanitarian motivation—account for different reactions to the different cases.

I have argued that killing is not in itself any worse than letting 16 die; if my contention is right, it follows that active euthanasia is not any worse than passive euthanasia. What arguments can be given on the other side? The most common, I believe, is the following:

> The important difference between active and passive euthanasia is that, in passive euthanasia, the doctor does not do anything to bring about the patient's death. The doctor does nothing, and the patient dies of whatever ills already afflict him. In active euthanasia, however, the doctor does something to bring about the patient's death: He kills him. The doctor who gives the patient with cancer a lethal injection has himself caused his patient's death; whereas if he merely ceases treatment, the cancer is the cause of the death.

A number of points need to be made here. This first is that it is not exactly correct to say that in passive euthanasia the doctor does nothing, for he does do one thing that is very important: He lets the patient die. "Letting someone die" is certainly different, in some respects, from other types of action—mainly in that it is a kind of action that one may perform by way of not performing certain other actions. For example, one may let a patient die by way of not giving medication, just as one may insult someone by way of not shaking his hand. But for any purpose of moral assessment, it is a type of action nonetheless. The decision to let a patient die is subject to moral appraisal in the same way that a decision to kill him would be subject to moral appraisal: It may be assessed as wise or unwise, compassionate or sadistic, right or wrong. If a doctor deliberately let a patient die who was suffering from a routinely curable illness, the doctor would certainly be to blame for what he had done, just as he would be to blame if he had needlessly killed the patient. Charges against him would then be appropriate. If so, it would be no defense at all for him to insist that he didn't "do anything." He would have done something very serious indeed, for he let his patient die.

Fixing the cause of death may be very important from a legal 17 point of view, for it may determine whether criminal charges are brought against the doctor. But I do not think that this notion can be used to show a moral difference between active and passive euthanasia. The reason why it is considered bad to be the cause of someone's death is that death is regarded as a great evil—and so it is. However, if it has been decided that euthanasia—even passive euthanasia—is desirable in a given case, it has also been decided that in this instance death is not greater an evil than the patient's continued existence. And if this is true, the usual reason for not wanting to be the cause of someone's death simply does not apply.

18   Finally, doctors may think that all of this is only of academic interest—the sort of thing that philosophers may worry about but that has no practical bearing on their own work. After all, doctors must be concerned about the legal consequences of what they do, and active euthanasia is clearly forbidden by the law. But even so, doctors should also be concerned with the fact that the law is forcing upon them a moral doctrine that may be indefensible, and has a considerable effect on their practices. Of course, most doctors are not now in the position of being coerced in this matter, for they do not regard themselves as merely going along with what the law requires. Rather, in statements such as the AMA policy statement that I have quoted, they are endorsing this doctrine as a central point of medical ethics. In that statement, active euthanasia is condemned not merely as illegal but as "contrary to that for which the medical profession stands," whereas passive euthanasia is approved. However, the preceding considerations suggest that there is really no moral difference between the two, considered in themselves (there may be important moral differences in some cases in their *consequences,* but, as I pointed out, these differences may make active euthanasia, and not passive euthanasia, the morally preferable option). So, whereas doctors may have to discriminate between active and passive euthanasia to satisfy the law, they should not do any more than that. In particular, they should not give the distinction any added authority and weight by writing it into official statements of medical ethics.

1975

We Do Abortions Here

Sallie Tisdale

We do abortions here; that is all we do. There are weary, grim mo- 1
ments when I think I cannot bear another basin of bloody remains, utter another kind phrase of reassurance. So I leave the
procedure room in the back and reach for a new chart. Soon I am
talking to an eighteen-year-old woman pregnant for the fourth
time. I push up her sleeve to check her blood pressure and find
row upon row of needle marks, neat and parallel and discolored.
She has been so hungry for her drug for so long that she has taken
to using the loose skin of her upper arms; her elbows are already
a permanent ruin of bruises. She is surprised to find herself nearly
four months pregnant. I suspect she is often surprised, in a mild
way, by the blows she is dealt. I prepare myself for another basin,
another brief and chafing loss.

"How can you stand it?" Even the clients ask. They see the 2
machine, the strange instruments, the blood, the final stroke that
wipes away the promise of pregnancy. Sometimes I see that too: I
watch a woman's swollen abdomen sink to softness in a few stut-
tering moments and my own belly flip-flops with sorrow. But all
it takes for me to catch my breath is another interview, one more
story that sounds so much like the last one. There is a numbing
sameness lurking in this job: the same questions, the same answers, even the same trembling tone in the voices. The worst is
the sameness of human failure, of inadequacy in the face of each
day's dull demands.

In describing this work, I find it difficult to explain how much 3
I enjoy it most of the time. We laugh a lot here, as friends and as
professional peers. It's nice to be with women all day. I like the
sudden, transient bonds I forge with some clients: moments when
I am in my strength, remembering weakness, and a woman in
weakness reaches out for my strength. What I offer is not power,
but solidness, offered almost eagerly. Certain clients waken in me
every tender urge I have—others make me wince and bite my

tongue. Both challenge me to find a balance. It is a sweet brutality we practice here, a stark and loving dispassion.

4   I look at abortion as if I am standing on a cliff with a telescope, gazing at some great vista. I can sweep the horizon with both eyes, survey the scene in all its distance and size. Or I can put my eye to the lens and focus on the small details, suddenly so close. In abortion the absolute must always be tempered by the contextual, because both are real, both valid, both hard. How can we do this? How can we refuse? Each abortion is a measure of our failure to protect, to nourish our own. Each basin I empty is a promise—but a promise broken a long time ago.

5   I grew up on the great promise of birth control. Like many women my age, I took the pill as soon as I was sexually active. To risk pregnancy when it was so easy to avoid seemed stupid, and my contraceptive success, as it were, was part of the promise of social enlightenment. But birth control fails, far more frequently than laboratory trials predict. Many of our clients take the pill; its failure to protect them is a shocking realization. We have clients who have been sterilized, whose husbands have had vasectomies; each one is a statistical misfit, fine print come to life. The anger and shame of these women I hold in one hand, and the basin in the other. The distance between the two, the length I pace and try to measure, is the size of an abortion.

6   The procedure is disarmingly simple. Women are surprised, as though the mystery of conception, a dark and hidden genesis, requires an elaborate finale. In the first trimester of pregnancy, it's a mere few minutes of vacuuming, a neat tidying up. I give a woman a small yellow Valium, and when it has begun to relax her, I lead her into the back, into bareness, the stirrups. The doctor reaches in her, opening the narrow tunnel to the uterus with a succession of slim, smooth bars of steel. He inserts a plastic tube and hooks it to a hose on the machine. The woman is framed against white paper that crackles as she moves, the light bright in her eyes. Then the machine rumbles low and loud in the small windowless room; the doctor moves the tube back and forth with an efficient rhythm, and the long tail of it fills with blood that spurts and stumbles along into a jar. He is usually finished in a few minutes. They are long minutes for the woman; her uterus

frequently reacts to its abrupt emptying with a powerful, unceasing cramp, which cuts off the blood vessels and enfolds the irritated, bleeding tissue.

I am learning to recognize the shadows that cross the faces of 7 the women I hold. While the doctor works between her spread legs, the paper drape hiding his intent expression, I stand beside the table. I hold the woman's hands in mine, resting them just below her ribs. I watch her eyes, finger her necklace, stroke her hair. I ask about her job, her family; in a haze she answers me; we chatter, faces close, eyes meeting and sliding apart.

I watch the shadows that creep up unnoticed and suddenly 8 darken her face as she screws up her features and pushes a tear out each side to slide down her cheeks. I have learned to anticipate the quiver of chin, the rapid intake of breath and the surprising sobs that rise soon after the machine starts to drum. I know this is when the cramp deepens, and the tears are partly the tears that follow pain—the sharp, childish crying when one bumps one's head on a cabinet door. But a well of woe seems to open beneath many women when they hear that thumping sound. The anticipation of the moment has finally come to fruit; the moment has arrived when the loss is no longer an imagined one. It has come true.

I am struck by the sameness and I am struck every day by the 9 variety here—how this commonplace dilemma can so display the differences of women. A twenty-one-year-old woman, unemployed, uneducated, without family, in the fifth month of her fifth pregnancy. A forty-two-year-old mother of teenagers, shocked by her condition, refusing to tell her husband. A twenty-three-year-old mother of two having her seventh abortion, and many women in their thirties having their first. Some are stoic, some hysterical, a few giggle uncontrollably, many cry.

I talk to a sixteen-year-old uneducated girl who was raped. 10 She has gonorrhea. She describes blinding headaches, attacks of breathlessness, nausea. "Sometimes I feel like two different people," she tells me with a calm smile, "and I talk to myself."

I pull out my plastic models. She listens patiently for a time, 11 and then holds her hands wide in front of her stomach.

"When's the baby going to go up into my stomach?" she asks. 12

13   I blink. "What do you mean?"

14   "Well," she says, still smiling, "when women get so big, isn't the baby in your stomach? Doesn't it hatch out of an egg there?"

15   My first question in an interview is always the same. As I walk down the hall with the woman, as we get settled in chairs and I glance through her files, I am trying to gauge her, to get a sense of the words, and the tone, I should use. With some I joke, with others I chat, sometimes I fall into a brisk, business-like patter. But I ask every woman, "Are you sure you want to have an abortion?" Most nod with grim knowing smiles. "Oh yes," they sigh. Some seek forgiveness, offer excuses. Occasionally a woman will flinch and say, "Please don't use that word."

16   Later I describe the procedure to come, using care with my language. I don't say "pain" any more than I would say "baby." So many are afraid to ask how much it will hurt. "My sister told me—" I hear. "A friend of mine said—" and the dire expectations unravel. I prick the index finger of a woman for a drop of blood to test, and as the tiny lancet approaches the skin she averts her eyes, holding her trembling hand out to me and jumping at my touch.

17   It is when I am holding a plastic uterus in one hand, a suction tube in the other, moving them together in imitation of the scrubbing to come, that women ask the most secret question. I am speaking in a matter-of-fact voice about "the tissue" and "the contents" when the woman suddenly catches my eye and asks, "How big is the baby now?" These words suggest a quiet need for a definition of the boundaries being drawn. It isn't so odd, after all, that she feels relief when I describe the growing bud's bulbous shape, its miniature nature. Again I gauge, and sometimes lie a little, weaseling around its infantile features until its clinging power slackens.

18   But when I look in the basin, among the curdlike blood clots, I see an elfin thorax, attenuated, its pencilline ribs all in parallel rows with tiny knobs of spine rounding upwards. A translucent arm and hand swim beside.

19   A sleepy-eyed girl, just fourteen, watched me with a slight and goofy smile all through her abortion. "Does it have little feet and little fingers and all?" she'd asked earlier. When the suction

was over she sat up woozily at the end of the table and murmured, "Can I see it?" I shook my head firmly.

"It's not allowed," I told her sternly, because I knew she didn't 20 really want to see what was left. She accepted this statement of authority, and a shadow of confused relief crossed her plain, pale face.

Privately, even grudgingly, my colleagues might admit the 21 power of abortion to provoke emotion. But they seem to prefer the broad view and disdain the telescope. Abortion is a matter of choice, privacy, control. Its uncertainty lies in specific cases: retarded women and girls too young to give consent for surgery, women who are ill or hostile or psychotic. Such common dilemmas are met with both compassion and impatience: they slow things down. We are too busy to chew over ethics. One person might discuss certain concerns, behind closed doors, or describe a particularly disturbing dream. But generally there is to be no ambivalence.

Every day I take calls from women who are annoyed that we 22 cannot see them, cannot do their abortion today, this morning, now. They argue the price, demand that we stay after hours to accommodate their job or class schedule. Abortion is so routine that one expects it to be like a manicure: quick, cheap, and painless.

Still, I've cultivated a certain disregard. It isn't negligence, but 23 I don't always pay attention. I couldn't be here if I tried to judge each case on its merits; after all, we do over a hundred abortions a week. At some point each individual in this line of work draws a boundary and adheres to it. For one physician the boundary is a particular week of gestation; for another, it is a certain number of repeated abortions. But these boundaries can be fluid too: one physician overruled his own limit to abort a mature but severely malformed fetus. For me, the limit is allowing my clients to carry their own burden, shoulder the responsibility themselves. I shoulder the burden of trying not to judge them.

This city has several "crisis pregnancy centers" advertised in 24 the Yellow Pages. They are small offices staffed by volunteers, and they offer free pregnancy testing, glossy photos of dead fetuses, and movies. I had a client recently whose mother is active in the anti-abortion movement. The young woman went to the local crisis center and was told that the doctor would make her touch her dismembered baby, that the pain would be the most horrible she could imagine, and that she might, after an abortion, never be able to have children. All lies. They called her at home and at work, over and over and over, but she had been wise enough to give a false name. She came to us a fugitive. We who do abortions are marked, by some, as impure. It's dirty work.

25   When a deliveryman comes to the sliding glass window by the reception desk and tilts a box toward me, I hesitate. I read the packing slip, assess the shape and weight of the box in light of its supposed contents. We request familiar faces. The doors are carefully locked; I have learned to half glance around at bags and boxes, looking for a telltale sign. I register with security when I arrive, and I am careful not to bang a door. We are all a little on edge here.

26   Concern about size and shape seems to be natural, and so is the relief that follows. We make the powerful assumption that the fetus is different from us, and even when we admit the similarities, it is too simplistic to be seduced by form alone. But the form is enormously potent—humanoid, powerless, palm-sized, and pure, it evokes an almost fierce tenderness when viewed simply as what it appears to be. But appearance, and even potential, aren't enough. The fetus, in becoming itself, can ruin others; its utter dependence has a sinister side. When I am stuck in the moment by the contents in the basin, I am careful to remember the context, to note the tearful teenager and the woman sighing with something more than relief. One kind of question, though, I find considerably trickier.

27   "Can you tell what it is?" I am asked, and this means gender. This question is asked by couples, not women alone. Always couples would abort a girl and keep a boy. I have been asked about twins, and even if I could tell what race the father was.

28   An eighteen-year-old woman with three daughters brought her husband to the interview. He glared first at me, then at his wife, as he sank lower and lower in the chair, picking his teeth with a toothpick. He interrupted a conversation with his wife to ask if I could tell whether the baby would be a boy or a girl. I told him I could not.

"Good," he replied in a slow and strangely malevolent voice, 29 "'cause if it was a boy I'd wring her neck."

In a literal sense, abortion exists because we are able to ask 30 such questions, able to assign a value to the fetus which can shift with changing circumstances. If the human bond to a child were as primitive and unflinchingly narrow as that of other animals, there would be no abortion. There would be no abortion because there would be nothing more important than caring for the young and perpetuating the species, no reason for sex but to make babies. I sense this sometimes, this wordless organic duty, when I do ultrasounds.

We do ultrasound, a sound-wave test that paints a faint, gray 31 picture of the fetus, whenever we're uncertain of gestation. Age is measured by the width of the skull and confirmed by the length of the femur or thighbone; we speak of a pregnancy as being a certain "femur length" in weeks. The usual concern is whether a pregnancy is within the legal limit for an abortion. Women this far along have bellies which swell out round and tight like trim muscles. When they lie flat, the mound rises softly above the hips, pressing the umbilicus upward.

It takes practice to read an ultrasound picture, which is grainy 32 and etched as though in strokes of charcoal. But suddenly a rapid rhythmic motion appears—the beating heart. Nearby is a soft oval, scratched with lines—the skull. The leg is harder to find, and then suddenly the fetus moves, bobbing in the surf. The skull turns away, an arm slides across the screen, the torso rolls. I know the weight of a baby's head on my shoulder, the whisper of lips on ears, the delicate curve of a fragile spine in my hand. I know how heavy and correct a newborn cradled feels. The creature I watch in secret requires nothing from me but to be left alone, and that is precisely what won't be done.

These inadvertently made beings are caught in a twisting web 33 of motive and desire. They are at least inconvenient, sometimes quite literally dangerous in the womb, but most often they fall somewhere in between—consequences never quite believed in come to roost. Their virtue rises and falls outside their own nature: they become only what we make them. A fetus created by accident is the most absolute kind of surprise. Whether the blame lies in a failed IUD, a slipped condom, or a false impression of safety, that fetus is a thing whose creation has been actively worked against. Its existence is an error. I think this is why so few women, even late in a pregnancy, will consider giving a baby up for adoption. To do so means making the fetus real—imagining it as something whole and outside oneself. The decision to terminate a pregnancy is sometimes so difficult and confounding that it creates an enormous demand for immediate action. The decision is a rejection; the pregnancy has become something to be rid of, a condition to be ended. It is a burden, a weight, a thing separate.

34   Women have abortions because they are too old, and too young, too poor, and too rich, too stupid, and too smart. I see women who berate themselves with violent emotions for their first and only abortion, and others who return three times, five times, hauling two or three children, who cannot remember to take a pill or where they put the diaphragm. We talk glibly about choice. But the choice for what? I see all the broken promises in lives lived like a series of impromptu obstacles. There are the sweet, light promises of love and intimacy, the glittering promise of education and progress, the warm promise of safe families, long years of innocence and community. And there is the promise of freedom: freedom from failure, from faithlessness. Freedom from biology. The early feminist defense of abortion asked many questions, but the one I remember is this: Is biology destiny? And the answer is yes, sometimes it is. Women who have the fewest choices of all exercise their right to abortion the most.

35   Oh, the ignorance. I take a woman to the back room and ask her to undress; a few minutes later I return and find her positioned discreetly behind a drape, still wearing underpants. "Do I have to take these off too?" she asks, a little shocked. Some swear they have not had sex, many do not know what a uterus is, how sperm and egg meet, how sex makes babies. Some late seekers do not believe themselves pregnant; they believe themselves *impregnable*. I was chastised when I began this job for referring to some clients as girls: it is a feminist heresy. They come so young, snapping gum, sockless and sneakered, and their shakily applied eyeliner smears when they cry. I call them girls with maternal benignity. I cannot imagine them as mothers.

The doctor seats himself between the woman's thighs and 36
reaches into the dilated opening of a five-month pregnant uterus.
Quickly he grabs and crushes the fetus in several places, and the
room is filled with a low clatter and snap of forceps, the click of
the tanaculum, and a pulling, sucking sound. The paper crinkles
as the drugged and sleepy woman shifts, the nurse's low, honey-
brown voice explains each step in delicate words.

I have fetus dreams, we all do here: dreams of abortions one 37
after the other; of buckets of blood splashed on the walls; trees full
of crawling fetuses. I dreamed that two men grabbed me and began to drag me away. "Let's do an abortion," they said with a sick-
ening leer, and I began to scream, plunged into a vision of sucking,
scraping pain, of being spread and torn by impartial instruments
that do only what they are bidden. I woke from this dream barely
able to breathe and thought of kitchen tables and coat hangers,
knitting needles striped with blood, and women all alone clutch-
ing a pillow in their teeth to keep the screams from piercing the
apartment-house walls. Abortion is the narrowest edge between
kindness and cruelty. Done as well as it can be, it is still violence—
merciful violence, like putting a suffering animal to death.

Maggie, one of the nurses, received a call at midnight not long 38
ago. It was a woman in her twentieth week of pregnancy; the necessarily gradual process of cervical dilation begun the day before
had stimulated labor, as it sometimes does. Maggie and one of the
doctors met the woman at the office in the night. Maggie helped her
onto the table, and as she lay down the fetus was delivered into
Maggie's hands. When Maggie told me about it the next day, she
cupped her hands into a small bowl—"It was just like a little kit-
ten," she said softly, wonderingly. "Everything was still attached."

At the end of the day I clean out the suction jars, pouring 39
blood into the sink, splashing the sides with flecks of tissue. From
the sink rises a rich and humid smell, hot, earthy, and moldering;
it is the smell of something recently alive beginning to decay. I
take care of the plastic tub on the floor, filled with pieces too big to
be trusted to the trash. The law defines the contents of the bucket
I hold protectively against my chest as "tissue." Some would say
my complicity in filling that bucket gives me no right to call it

anything else. I slip the tissue gently into a bag and place it in the freezer, to be burned at another time. Abortion requires of me an entirely new set of assumptions. It requires a willingness to live with conflict, fearlessness, and grief. As I close the freezer door, I imagine a world where this won't be necessary, and then return to the world where it is.

1990

On Dumpster Diving

Lars Eighner

1 Long before I began Dumpster diving I was impressed with Dumpsters, enough so that I wrote the Merriam-Webster research service to discover what I could about the word *Dumpster*. I learned from them that it is a proprietary word belonging to the Dempster Dumpster company. Since then I have dutifully capitalized the word, although it was lowercased in almost all the citations Merriam-Webster photocopied for me. Dempster's word is too apt. I have never heard these things called anything but Dumpsters. I do not know anyone who knows the generic name for these objects. From time to time I have heard a wino or hobo give some corrupted credit to the original and call them Dipsy Dumpsters.

2   I began Dumpsters diving about a year before I became homeless.

3   I prefer the word *scavenging* and use the word *scrounging* when I mean to be obscure. I have heard people, evidently meaning to be polite, use the word *foraging,* but I prefer to reserve that word for gathering nuts and berries and such, which I do also according to the season and the opportunity. *Dumpster diving* seems to me to be a little too cute and, in my case, inaccurate because I lack the athletic ability to lower myself into the Dumpsters as the true divers do, much to their increased profit.

I like the frankness of the word *scavenging*, which I can hardly 4
think of without picturing a big black snail on an aquarium wall.
I live from the refuse of others. I am a scavenger. I think it a
sound and honorable niche, although if I could I would naturally
prefer to live the comfortable consumer life, perhaps—and only
perhaps—as a slightly less wasteful consumer, owing to what I
have learned as a scavenger.

While Lizbeth [Eighner's dog] and I were still living in the 5
shack on Avenue B as my savings ran out, I put almost all my spo-
radic income into rent. The necessities of daily life I began to extract from Dumpsters. Yes, we ate from them. Except for jeans, all
my clothes came from Dumpsters. Boom boxes, candles, bedding,
toilet paper, a virgin male love doll, medicine, books, a typewriter,
dishes, furnishing, and change, sometimes amounting to many
dollars—I acquired many things from the Dumpsters.

I have learned much as a scavenger. I mean to put some of 6
what I have learned down here, beginning with the practical art of
Dumpster diving and proceeding to the abstract.

What is safe to eat?   7

After all, the finding of objects is becoming something of an 8
urban art. Even respectable employed people will sometimes find
something tempting sticking out of a Dumpster or standing beside one. Quite a number of people, not all of them of the bo-
hemian type, are willing to brag that they found this or that piece
in the trash. But eating from Dumpsters is what separates the
dilettanti from the professionals. Eating safely from the Dumpsters
involves three principles: using the senses and common sense to
evaluate the condition of the found materials, knowing the Dumpsters of a given area and checking them regularly, and seeking always to answer the question "Why was this discarded?"

Perhaps everyone who has a kitchen and a regular supply of 9
groceries has, at one time or another, made a sandwich and eaten
half of it before discovering mold on the bread or got a mouthful
of milk before realizing the milk had turned. Nothing of the sort is
likely to happen to a Dumpster diver because he is constantly reminded that most food is discarded for a reason. Yet a lot of perfectly good food can be found in Dumpsters.

10   Canned goods, for example, turn up fairly often in the Dumpsters I frequent. All except the most phobic people would be willing to eat from a can, even if it came from a Dumpster. Canned goods are among the safest of foods to be found in Dumpsters but are not utterly foolproof.

11   Although very rare with modern canning methods, botulism is a possibility. Most other forms of food poisoning seldom do lasting harm to a healthy person, but botulism is almost certainly fatal and often the first symptom is death. Except for carbonated beverages, all canned goods should contain a slight vacuum and suck air when first punctured. Bulging, rusty, and dented cans and cans that spew when punctured should be avoided, especially when the contents are not very acidic or syrupy.

12   Heat can break down the botulin, but this requires much more cooking than most people do to canned goods. To the extent that botulism occurs at all, of course, it can occur in cans on pantry shelves as well as in cans from Dumpsters. Need I say that home-canned goods are simply too risky to be recommended.

13   From time to time one of my companions, aware of the source of my provisions, will ask, "Do you think these crackers are really safe to eat?" For some reason it is most often the crackers they ask about.

14   This question has always made me angry. Of course I would not offer my companion anything I had doubts about. But more than that, I wonder why he cannot evaluate the condition of the crackers for himself. I have no special knowledge and I have been wrong before. Since he knows where the food comes from, it seems to me he ought to assume some of the responsibility for deciding what he will put in his mouth. For myself I have few qualms about dry foods such as crackers, cookies, cereal, chips, and pasta if they are free of visible contaminates and still dry and crisp. Most often such things are found in the original packaging, which is not so much a positive sign as it is the absence of a negative one.

15   Raw fruits and vegetables with intact skins seem perfectly safe to me, excluding of course the obviously rotten. Many are discarded for minor imperfections that can be pared away. Leafy vegetables, grapes, cauliflower, broccoli, and similar things may be contaminated by liquids and may be impractical to wash.

Candy, especially hard candy, is usually safe if it has not 16
drawn ants. Chocolate is often discarded only because it has become discolored as the cocoa butter de-emulsified. Candying, after all, is one method of food preservation because pathogens do
not like very sugary substances.

All of these foods might be found in any Dumpster and can 17
be evaluated with some confidence largely on the basis of appearance. Beyond these are foods that cannot be correctly evaluated
without additional information.

I began scavenging by pulling pizzas out of the Dumpster be- 18
hind a pizza delivery shop. In general, prepared food requires
caution, but in this case I knew when the shop closed and went to
the Dumpster as soon as the last of the help left.

Such shops often get prank orders; both the orders and the 19
products made to fill them are called *bogus*. Because help seldom
stays long at these places, pizzas are often made with the wrong
topping, refused on delivery for being cold, or baked incorrectly.
The products to be discarded are boxed up because inventory is
kept by counting boxed: A boxed pizza can be written off; an un-
boxed pizza does not exist.

I never placed a bogus order to increase the supply of pizzas 20
and I believe no one else was scavenging in this Dumpster. But the
people in the shop became suspicious and began to retain their
garbage in the shop overnight. While it lasted I had a steady supply of fresh, sometimes warm pizza. Because I knew the Dumpster
I knew the source of the pizza, and because I visited the dumpster
regularly I knew what was fresh and what was yesterday's.

The area I frequent is inhabited by many affluent college stu- 21
dents. I am not here by chance; the Dumpsters in this area are
very rich. Students throw out many good things, including food.
In particular they tend to throw everything out when they move
at the end of a semester, before and after breaks, and around
midterm, when many of them despair of college. So I find it advantageous to keep an eye on the academic calendar.

Students throw food away around breaks because they do not 22
know whether it has spoiled or will spoil before they return. A
typical discard is a half jar of peanut butter. In fact, nonorganic
peanut butter does not require refrigeration and is unlikely to

spoil in any reasonable time. The student does not know that, and since it is Daddy's money, the student decides not to take a chance. Opened containers require caution and some attention to the question "Why was this discarded?" But in the case of discards from student apartments, the answer may be that the item was thrown out through carelessness, ignorance, or wastefulness. This can sometimes be deduced when the item is found with many others, including some that are obviously perfectly good.

23   Some students, and others, approach defrosting a freezer by chucking out the whole lot. Not only do the circumstances of such a find tell the story, but also the mass of frozen goods stays cold for a long time and items may be found still frozen or freshly thawed.

24   Yogurt, cheese, and sour cream are items that are often thrown out while they are still good. Occasionally I find a cheese with a spot of mold, which of course I just pare off, and because it is obvious why such a cheese was discarded, I treat it with less suspicion than an apparently perfect cheese found in similar circumstances. Yogurt is often discarded, still sealed, only because the expiration date on the carton had passed. This is one of my favorite finds because yogurt will keep for several days, even in warm weather.

25   Students throw out canned goods and staples at the end of semesters and when they give up college at midterm. Drugs, pornography, spirits, and the like are often discarded when parents are expected—Dad's Day, for example. And spirits also turn up after big party weekends, presumably discarded by the newly reformed. Wine and spirits, of course, keep perfectly well even once opened, but the same cannot be said of beer.

26   My test for carbonated soft drinks is whether they still fizz vigorously. Many juices or other beverages are too acidic or too syrupy to cause much concern, provided they are not visibly contaminated. I have discovered nasty molds in vegetables juices, even when the product was found under its original seal; I recommend that such products be decanted slowly into a clear glass. Liquids always require some care. One hot day I found a large jug of Pat O'Brien's Hurricane mix. The jug had been opened but was still ice cold. I drank three large glasses before it became apparent to me that someone had added the rum to the mix, and not a little

rum. I never tasted the rum, and by the time I began to feel the effects I had already ingested a very large quantity of the beverage. Some divers would have considered this a boon, but being suddenly intoxicated in a public place in the early afternoon is not my idea of a good time.

I have heard of people maliciously contaminating discarded 27 food and even handouts, but mostly I have heard of this from people with vivid imaginations who have had no experience with the Dumpsters themselves. Just before the pizza shop stopped discarding its garbage at night, jalapeños began showing up on most of the thrown-out pizzas. If indeed this was meant to discourage me, it was a wasted effort because I am a native Texan.

For myself, I avoid game, poultry, pork, and egg-based foods, 28 whether I find them raw or cooked. I seldom have the means to cook what I find, but when I do I avail myself of plentiful supplies of beef, which is often in very good condition. I suppose fish becomes disagreeable before it becomes dangerous. Lizbeth is happy to have any such thing that is past its prime and, in fact, does not recognize fish as food until it is quite strong.

Home leftovers, as opposed to surpluses from restaurants, are 29 very often bad. Evidently, especially among students, there is a common type of personality that carefully wraps up even the smallest leftover and shoves it into the back of the refrigerator for six months or so before discarding it. Characteristic of this type are the reused jars and margarine tubs to which the remains are committed. I avoid ethnic foods I am unfamiliar with. If I do not know what it is supposed to look like when it is good, I cannot be certain I will be able to tell if it is bad.

No matter how careful I am I still get dysentery at least once a 30 month, oftener in warm weather. I do not want to paint too romantic a picture. Dumpster diving has serious drawbacks as a way of life.

I learned to scavenge gradually, on my own. Since then I have 31 initiated several companions into the trade. I have learned that there is a predictable series of stages a person goes through in learning to scavenge.

At first the new scavenger is filled with disgust and self-loathing. 32 He is ashamed of being seen and may lurk around, trying to duck behind things, or he may dry to dive at night. (In fact, most people instinctively look away from a scavenger. By skulking around, the novice calls attention to himself and arouses suspicion. Diving at night is ineffective and needlessly messy.)

33   Every grain of rice seems to be a maggot. Everything seems to stink. He can wipe the egg yolk off the found can, but he cannot erase from his mind the stigma of eating garbage.

34   That stage passes with experience. The scavenger finds a pair of running shoes that fit and look and smell brand-new. He finds a pocket calculator in perfect working order. He finds pristine ice cream, still frozen, more than he can eat or keep. He begins to understand: People throw away perfectly good stuff, a lot of perfectly good stuff.

35   At this stage, Dumpster shyness begins to dissipate. The diver, after all, has the last laugh. He is finding all manner of good things that are his for the taking. Those who disparage his profession are the fools, not he.

36   He may begin to hang on to some perfectly good things for which he has neither a use nor a market. Then he begins to take note of the things that are not perfectly good but are nearly so. He mates a Walkman with broken earphones and one that is missing a battery cover. He picks up things that he can repair.

37   At this stage he may become lost and never recover. Dumpsters are full of things of some potential value to someone and also of things that never have much intrinsic value but are interesting. All the Dumpster divers I have known come to the point of trying to acquire everything they touch. Why not take it, they reason, since it is all free? This is, of course, hopeless. Most divers come to realize that they must restrict themselves to items of relatively immediate utility. But in some cases the diver simply cannot control himself. I have met several of these pack-rat types. Their ideas of the values of various pieces of junk verge on the psychotic. Every bit of glass may be a diamond, they think, and all that glistens, gold.

38   I tend to gain weight when I am scavenging. Partly this is because I always find far more pizza and doughnuts than water-packed tuna, nonfat yogurt, and fresh vegetables. Also I have not developed much faith in the reliability of Dumpsters as a food source, although it has been proven to me many times. I tend to eat as if I have no idea where my next meal is coming from. But mostly

I just hate to see food go to waste and so I eat much more than I should. Something like this drives the obsession to collect junk.

As for collecting objects, I usually restrict myself to collecting 39 one kind of small object at a time, such as pocket calculators, sunglasses, or campaign buttons. To live on the street I must anticipate my needs to a certain extent: I must pick up and save warm bedding I find in August because it will not be found in Dumpsters in November. As I have no access to health care, I often hoard essential drugs, such as antibiotics and antihistamines. (This course can be recommended only to those with some grounding in pharmacology. Antibiotics, for example, even when indicated are worse than useless if taken in insufficient amounts.) But even if I had a home with extensive storage space, I could not save everything that might be valuable in some contingency.

I have proprietary feelings about my Dumpsters. As I have 40 mentioned, it is no accident that I scavenge from ones where good finds are common. But my limited experience with Dumpsters in other areas suggests to me that even in poorer areas, Dumpsters, if attended with sufficient diligence, can be made to yield a livelihood. The rich students discard perfectly good kiwifruit; poorer people discard perfectly good apples. Slacks and Polo shirts are found in the one place; jeans and T-shirts in the other. The population of competitors rather than the affluence of the dumpers most affects the feasibility of survival by scavenging. The large number of competitors is what puts me off the idea of trying to scavenge in places like Los Angeles.

Curiously, I do not mind my direct competition, other scav- 41 engers, so much as I hate the can scroungers.

People scrounge cans because they have to have a little cash. I 42 have tried scrounging cans with an able-bodied companion. Afoot a can scrounger simply cannot make more than a few dollars a day. One can extract the necessities of life from the Dumpsters directly with far less effort than would be required to accumulate the equivalent value in cans. (These observations may not hold in places with container redemption laws.)

Can scroungers, then, are people who must have small 43 amounts of cash. These are drug addicts and winos, mostly the latter because the amounts are so small. Spirits and drugs do, like all other commodities, turn up in Dumpsters and the scavenger will from time to time have a half bottle of a rather good wine with his dinner. But the wino cannot survive on these occasional finds; he must have his daily dose to stave off the DTs. All the cans he can carry will buy about three bottles of Wild Irish Rose.

44   I do not begrudge them the cans, but can scroungers tend to tear up the Dumpsters, mixing the contents and littering the area. They become so specialized that they can see only cans. They earn my contempt by passing up change, canned goods, and readily hockable items.

45   There are precious few courtesies among scavengers. But it is common practice to set aside surplus items: pairs of shoes, clothing, canned goods, and such. A true scavenger hates to see good stuff go to waste, and what he cannot use he leaves in good condition in plain sight.

46   Can scroungers lay waste to everything in their path and will stir one of a pair of good shoes to the bottom of a Dumpster, to be lost or ruined in the muck. Can scroungers will even go through individual garbage cans, something I have never seen a scavenger do.

47   Individual garbage cans are set out on the public easement only on garbage days. On other days going through them requires trespassing close to a dwelling. Going through individual garbage cans without scattering litter is almost impossible. Litter is likely to reduce the public's tolerance of scavenging. Individual cans are simply not as productive as Dumpsters; people in houses and duplexes do not move so often and for some reason do not tend to discard as much useful material. Moreover, the time required to go through one garbage can that serves one household is not much less than the time required to go through a Dumpster that contains the refuse of twenty apartments.

48   But my strongest reservation about going through individual garbage cans is that this seems to me a very personal kind of invasion to which I would object if I were a householder. Although many things in Dumpsters are obviously meant never to come to light, a Dumpster is somehow less personal.

49   I avoid trying to draw conclusions about the people who dump in the Dumpsters I frequent. I think it would be unethical to do so, although I know many people will find the idea of scavenger ethics too funny for words.

Dumpsters contain bank statements, correspondence, and 50
other documents, just as anyone might expect. But there are less
obvious sources of information. Pill bottles, for example. The labels bear the name of the patient, the name of the doctor, and the
name of the drug. AIDS drugs and antipsychotic medicines, to
name but two groups, are specific and are seldom prescribed for
any other disorders. The plastic compacts for birth-control pills
usually have complete label information.

Despite all of this sensitive information, I have had only one 51
apartment resident object to my going through the Dumpster. In
that case it turned out the resident was a university athlete who was
taking bets and who was afraid I would turn up his wager slips.

Occasionally a find tells a story. I once found a small paper 52
bag containing some unused condoms, several partial tubes of fla-
vored sexual lubricants, a partially used compact of birth-control
pills, and the torn pieces of a picture of a young man. Clearly she
was through with him and planning to give up sex altogether.

Dumpster things are often sad—abandoned teddy bears, 53
shredded wedding books, despaired-of sales kits. I find many
pets lying in state in Dumpsters. Although I hope to get off the
streets so that Lizbeth can have a long and comfortable old age, I
know this hope is not very realistic. So I suppose when her time
comes she too will go into a Dumpster. I will have no better place
for her. And after all, it is fitting, since for most of her life her
livelihood has come from the Dumpster. When she finds something I think is safe that has been spilled from a Dumpster, I let
her have it. She already knows the route around the best ones. I
like to think that if she survives me she will have a chance of evading the dog catcher and of finding her sustenance on the route.

Silly vanities also come to rest in the Dumpsters. I am a rather 54
accomplished needleworker. I get a lot of material from the
Dumpsters. Evidently sorority girls, hoping to impress someone,
perhaps themselves, with their mastery of a womanly art, buy a
lot of embroider-by-number kits, work a few stitches horribly, and
eventually discard the whole mess. I pull out their stitches, turn
the canvas over and work an original design. Do not think I refrain from chuckling as I make gifts from these kits.

55   I find diaries and journals. I have often thought of compiling a book of literary found objects. And perhaps I will one day. But what I find is hopelessly commonplace and bad without being, even unconsciously, camp. College students also discard their papers. I am horrified to discover the kind of paper that now merits an A in an undergraduate course. I am grateful, however, for the number of good books and magazines the students throw out.

56   In the area I know best I have never discovered vermin in the Dumpsters, but there are two kinds of kitty surprise. One is alley cats whom I meet as they leap, claws first, out of Dumpsters. This is especially thrilling when I have Lizbeth in tow. The other kind of kitty surprise is a plastic garbage bag filled with some ponderous, amorphous mass. This always proves to be used cat litter.

57   City bees harvest doughnut glaze and this makes the Dumpster at the doughnut shop more interesting. My faith in the instinctive wisdom of animals is always shaken whenever I see Lizbeth attempt to catch a bee in her mouth, which she does wherever bees are present. Evidently some birds find Dumpsters profitable, for birdie surprise is almost as common as kitty surprise of the first kind. In hunting season all kinds of small game turn up in Dumpsters, some of it, sadly, not entirely dead. Curiously, summer and winter, maggots are uncommon.

58   The worst of the living and near-living hazards of the Dumpsters are the fire ants. The food they claim is not much of a loss, but they are vicious and aggressive. It is very easy to brush against some surface of the Dumpster and pick up half a dozen or more fire ants, usually in some sensitive area such as the underarm. One advantage of bringing Lizbeth along as I make Dumpster rounds is that, for obvious reasons, she is very alert to ground-based fire ants. When Lizbeth recognizes a fire-ant infestation around our feet, she does the Dance of the Zillion Fire Ants. I have learned not to ignore this warning from Lizbeth, whether I perceive the tiny ants or not, but to remove ourselves at Lizbeth's first pas de bourée. All the more so because the ants are the worst in the summer months when I wear flip-flops if I have them. (Perhaps someone will misunderstand this. Lizbeth does the Dance of the Zillion Fire Ants when she recognizes more fire ants than she

cares to eat, not when she is being bitten. Since I have learned to react promptly, she does not get bitten at all. It is the isolated patrol of fire ants that falls in Lizbeth's range that deserves pity. She finds them quite tasty.)

By far the best way to go through a Dumpster is to lower 59 yourself into it. Most of the good stuff tends to settle at the bottom because it is usually weightier than the rubbish. My more athletic companions have often demonstrated to me that they can extract much good material from a Dumpster I have already been over.

To those psychologically or physically unprepared to enter a 60 Dumpster, I recommend a stout stick, preferably with some barb or hook at one end. The hook can be used to grab plastic garbage bags. When I find canned goods or other objects loose at the bottom of a Dumpster I lower a bag into it, roll the desired object into the bag, and then hoist the bag out—a procedure more easily described than executed. Much Dumpster diving is a matter of experience for which nothing will do except practice.

Dumpster diving is outdoor work, often surprisingly pleas- 61 ant. It is not entirely predictable; things of interest turn up every day and some days there are finds of great value. I am always very pleased when I can turn up exactly the thing I most wanted to find. Yet in spite of the element of chance, scavenging more than most other pursuits tends to yield returns in some proportion to the effort and intelligence brought to bear. It is very sweet to turn up a few dollars in change from a Dumpster that has just been gone over by a wino.

The land is now covered with cities. The cities are full of Dump- 62 sters. If a member of the canine race is ever able to know what it is doing, then Lizbeth knows that when we go around to the Dumpsters, we are hunting. I think of scavenging as a modern form of self-reliance. In any event, after having survived nearly ten years of government service, where everything is geared to the lowest common denominator, I find it refreshing to have work that rewards initiative and effort. Certainly I would be happy to have a sinecure again, but I am no longer heartbroken that I left one.

I find from the experience of scavenging two rather deep les- 63 sons. The first is to take what you can use and let the rest go by. I have come to think that there is no value in the abstract. A thing I cannot use or make useful, perhaps by trading, has no value however rare or fine it may be. I mean useful in a broad sense—some art I would find useful and some otherwise.

64   I was shocked to realize that some things are not worth acquiring, but now I think it is so. Some material things are white elephants that eat up the possessor's substance. The second lesson is the transience of material being. This has not quite converted me to a dualist, but it has made some headway in that direction. I do not suppose that ideas are immortal, but certainly mental things are longer lived than other material things.

65   Once I was the sort of person who invests objects with sentimental value. Now I no longer have those objects, but I have the sentiments yet.

66   Many times in our travels I have lost everything but the clothes I was wearing and Lizbeth. The things I find in Dumpsters, the love letters and rag dolls of so many lives, remind me of this lesson. Now I hardly pick up a thing without envisioning the time I will cast it aside. This I think is a healthy state of mind. Almost everything I have now has already been cast out at least once, proving that what I own is valueless to someone.

67   Anyway, I find my desire to grab for the gaudy bauble has been largely sated. I think this is an attitude I share with the very wealthy—we both know there is plenty more where what we have came from. Between us are the rat-race millions who nightly scavenge the cable channels looking for they know not what.

68   I am sorry for them.

1993

On Being a Cripple

Nancy Mairs

1   The other day I was thinking of writing an essay on being a cripple. I was thinking hard in one of the stalls of the women's room

in my office building, as I was shoving my shirt into my jeans and tugging up my zipper. Preoccupied, I flushed, picked up my book bag, took my cane down from the hook, and unlatched the door. So many movements unbalanced me, and as I pulled the door open I fell over backward, landing fully clothed on the toilet seat with my legs splayed in front me: the old beetle-on-its back routine. Saturday afternoon, the building deserted, I was free to laugh aloud as I wriggled back to my feet, my voice bouncing off the yellowish tiles from all directions. Had anyone been there with me, I'd have been still and faint and hot with chagrin. I decided that it was high time to write the essay.

First, the matter of semantics. I am a cripple. I choose this 2 word to name me. I choose from among several possibilities, the most common of which are "handicapped" and "disabled." I made the choice a number of years ago, without thinking, unaware of my motives for doing so. Even now, I'm not sure what those motives are, but I recognize that they are complex and not entirely flattering. People—crippled or not—wince at the word "cripple," as they do not at "handicapped" or "disabled." Perhaps I want them to wince. I want them to see me as a tough customer, one to whom the fates/gods/viruses have not been kind, but who can face the brutal truth of her existence squarely. As a cripple, I swagger.

But, to be fair to myself, a certain amount of honesty underlies 3 my choice. "Cripple" seems to me a clean word, straightforward and precise. It has an honorable history, having made its first appearance in the Lindisfarne Gospel in the tenth century. As a lover of words, I like the accuracy with which it describes my condition: I have lost the full use of my limbs. "Disabled," by contrast, suggests an incapacity, physical or mental. And I certainly don't like "handicapped," which implies that I have deliberately been put at a disadvantage, by whom I can't imagine (my God is not a Handicapper General), in order to equalize chances in the great race of life. These words seem to me to be moving away from my condition, to be widening the gap between word and reality. Most remote is the recently coined euphemism "differently abled," which partakes of the same semantic hopefulness that transformed countries from "undeveloped" to "underdeveloped," then to "less developed," and finally to "developing" nations. People have continued to starve in those countries during the shift. Some realities do not obey the dictates of language.

4   Mine is one of them. Whatever you call me, I remain crippled. But I don't care what you call me, so long as it isn't "differently abled," which strikes me as pure verbal garbage designed, by its ability to describe anyone, to describe no one. I subscribe to George Orwell's thesis that "the slovenliness of our language makes it easier for us to have foolish thoughts." And I refuse to participate in the degeneration of the language to the extent that I deny that I have lost anything in the course of this calamitous disease; I refuse to pretend that the only differences between you and me are the various ordinary ones that distinguish any one person from another. But call me "disabled" or "handicapped" if you like. I have long since grown accustomed to them; and if they are vague, at least they hint at the truth. Moreover, I use them myself. Society is no readier to accept crippledness than to accept death, war, sex, sweat, or wrinkles. I would never refer to another person as a cripple. It is the word I use to name only myself.

5   I haven't always been crippled, a fact for which I am soundly grateful. To be whole of limb is, I know from experience, infinitely more pleasant and useful than to be crippled; and if that knowledge leaves me open to bitterness at my loss, the physical soundness I once enjoyed (though I did not enjoy it half enough) is well worth the occasional stab of regret. Though never any good at sports, I was a normally active child and young adult. I climbed trees, played hopscotch, jumped rope, skated, swam, rode my bicycle, sailed. I despised team sports, spending some of the wretchedest afternoons of my life sweaty and humiliated, behind a field-hockey stick and under a basketball hoop. I tramped alone for miles along the bridle paths that webbed the woods behind the house I grew up in. I swayed through countless dim hours in the arms of one man or another under the scattered shot of light from mirrored balls, and gyrated through countless more as Tab Hunter and Johnny Mathis gave way to the Rolling Stones, Creedence Clearwater Revival, Cream. I walked down the aisle. I pushed baby carriages, changed tires in the rain, marched for peace.

6   When I was twenty-eight I started to trip and drop things. What at first seemed my natural clumsiness soon became too pronounced to shrug off. I consulted a neurologist, who told me that I

had a brain tumor. A battery of tests, increasingly disagreeable, revealed no tumor. About a year and a half later I developed a blurred spot in one eye. I had, at last, the episodes "disseminated in space and time" requisite for a diagnosis: multiple sclerosis. I have never been sorry for the doctor's initial misdiagnosis, however. For almost a week, until the negative results of the tests were in, I thought that I was going to die right away. Every day for the past nearly ten years, then, has been a kind of gift; I accept all gifts.

Multiple sclerosis is a chronic degenerative disease of the central nervous system, in which the myelin that sheathes the nerves is somehow eaten away and scar tissue forms in its place, interrupting the nerves' signals. During its course, which is unpredictable and uncontrollable, one may lose vision, hearing, speech, the ability to walk, control of bladder and/or bowels, strength in any or all extremities, sensitivity to touch, vibration, and/or pain, potency, coordination of movements—the list of possibilities is lengthy and yes, horrifying. One may also lose one's sense of humor. That's the easiest to lose and the hardest to survive without. 7

In the past ten years, I have sustained some of these losses. Characteristic of MS are sudden attacks, called exacerbations, followed by remissions, and these I have not had. Instead, my disease has been slowly progressive. My left leg is now so weak that I walk with the aid of a brace and a cane; and for distances I use an Amigo, a variation on the electric wheelchair that looks rather like an electrified kiddie car. I no longer have much use of my left hand. Now my right side is weakening as well. I still have the blurred spot in my right eye. Overall, though, I've been lucky so far. My world has, of necessity, been circumscribed by my losses, but the terrain left me has been ample enough for me to continue many of the activities that absorb me: writing, teaching, raising children and cats and plants and snakes, reading, speaking publicly about MS and depression, even playing bridge with people patient and honorable enough to let me scatter cards every which way without sneaking a peek. 8

Lest I begin to sound like Pollyanna, however, let me say that I don't like having MS. I hate it. My life holds realities—harsh ones, some of them—that no right-minded human being ought to accept without grumbling. One of them is fatigue. I know of no 9 one with MS who does not complain of bone-weariness; in a disease that presents an astonishing variety of symptoms, fatigue seems to be a common factor. I wake up in the morning feeling the way most people do at the end of a bad day, and I take it from there. As a result, I spend a lot of time *in extremis* and, impatient with limitation, I tend to ignore my fatigue until my body breaks down in some way and forces rest. Then I miss picnics, dinner parties, poetry readings, the brief visits of old friends from out of town. The offspring of a puritanical tradition of exceptional venerability, I cannot view these lapses without shame. My life often seems a series of small failures to do as I ought.

10   I lead, on the whole, an ordinary life, probably rather like the one I would have led had I not had MS. I am lucky that my predilections were already solitary, sedentary, and bookish—unlike the world-famous French cellist I have read about, or the young woman I talked with one long afternoon who wanted only to be a jockey. I had just begun graduate school when I found out something was wrong with me, and I have remained, interminably, a graduate student. Perhaps I would not have if I'd thought I had the stamina to return to a full-time job as a technical editor; but I've enjoyed my studies.

11   In addition to studying, I teach writing courses. I also teach medical students how to give neurological examinations. I pick up freelance editing jobs here and there. I have raised a foster son and sent him into the world, where he has made me two grandbabies, and I am still escorting my daughter and son through adolescence. I go to Mass every Saturday. I am a superb, if messy, cook. I am also an enthusiastic laundress, capable of sorting a hamper full of clothes into five subtly differentiated piles, but a terrible housekeeper. I can do italic writing and, in an emergency, bathe an oil-soaked cat. I play a fiendish game of Scrabble. When I have the time and the money, I like to sit on my front steps with my husband, drinking Amaretto and smoking a cigar, as we imagine our counterparts in Leningrad and make sure that the sun gets down once more behind the sharp childish scrawl of the Tucson Mountains.

12   This lively plenty has its bleak complement, of course, in all the things I can no longer do. I will never run again, except in dreams,

and one day I may have to write that I will never walk again. I like to go camping, but I can't follow George and the children along the trails that wander out of a campsite through the desert or into the mountains. In fact, even on the level I've learned never to check the weather or try to hold a coherent conversation: I need all my attention for my wayward feet. Of late, I have begun to catch myself wondering how people can propel themselves without canes. With only one usable hand, I have to select my clothing with care not so much for style as for ease of ingress and egress, and even so, dressing can be laborious. I can no longer do fine stitchery, pick up babies, play the piano, braid my hair. I am immobilized by acute attacks of depression, which may or may not be physiologically related to MS but are certainly its logical concomitant.

These two elements, the plenty and the privation, are never 13 pure, nor are the delight and wretchedness that accompany them. Almost every pickle that I get into as a result of my weakness and clumsiness—and I get into plenty—is funny as well as maddening and sometimes painful. I recall one May afternoon when a friend and I were going out for a drink after finishing up at school. As we were climbing into opposite sides of my car, chatting, I tripped and fell, flat and hard, onto the asphalt parking lot, my abrupt departure interrupting him in mid-sentence. "Where'd you go?" he called as he came around the back of the car to find me hauling myself up by the door frame. "Are you all right?" Yes, I told him, I was fine, just a bit rattly, and we drove off to find a shady patio and some beer. When I got home an hour or so later, my daughter greeted me with "What have you done to yourself?" I looked down. One elbow of my white turtleneck with the green froggies, one knee of my white trousers, one white kneesock were blood-soaked. We peeled off the clothes and inspected the damage, which was nasty enough but not alarming. That part wasn't funny: The abrasions took a long time to heal, and one got a little infected. Even so, when I think of my friend talking earnestly, suddenly, to the hot thin air while I dropped from his view as though through a trap door, I find the image as silly as something from a Marx Brothers movie.

I may find it easier than other cripples to amuse myself be- 14 cause I live propped by the acceptance and the assistance and, sometimes, the amusement of those around me. Grocery clerks tear my checks out of my checkbook for me, and sales clerks find chairs to put into dressing rooms when I want to try on clothes. The people I work with make sure I teach at times when I am least likely to be fatigued, in places I can get to, with the materials I need. My students, with one anonymous exception (in an end-of-the-semester evaluation), have been unperturbed by my disability. Some even like it. One was immensely cheered by the information that I paint my own fingernails; she decided, she told me, that if I could go to such trouble over fine details, she could keep on writing essays. I suppose I became some sort of bright-fingered muse. She wrote good essays, too.

15   The most important struts in the framework of my existence, of course, are my husband and children. Dismayingly few marriages survive the MS test, and why should they? Most twenty-two- and nineteen-year-olds, like George and me, can vow in clear conscience, after a childhood of chickenpox and summer colds, to keep one another in sickness and in health so long as they both shall live. Not many are equipped for catastrophe: the dismay, the depression, the extra work, the boredom that a degenerative disease can insinuate into a relationship. And our society, with its emphasis on fun and its association of fun with physical performance, offers little encouragement for a whole spouse to stay with a crippled partner. Children experience similar stresses when faced with a crippled parent, and they are more helpless, since parents and children can't usually get divorced. They hate, of course, to be different from their peers, and the child whose mother is tacking down the aisle of a school auditorium packed with proud parents like a Cape Cod dinghy in stiff breeze jolly well stands out in a crowd. Deprived of legal divorce, the child can at least deny the mother's disability, even her existence, forgetting to tell her about recitals and PTA meetings, refusing to accompany her to stores or church or the movies, never inviting friends to the house. Many do.

16   But I've been limping along for ten years now, and so far George and the children are still at my left elbow, holding tight. Ann and Matthew vacuum floors and dust furniture and haul trash and rake up dog droppings and button my cuffs and bake

lasagne and Toll House cookies with just enough grumbling so I know that they don't have brain fever. And far from hiding me, they're forever dragging me by racks of fancy clothes or through teeming school corridors, or welcoming gaggles of friends while I'm wandering through the house in Anne's filmy pink babydoll pajamas. George generally calls before he brings someone home, but he does just as many dumb thankless chores as the children. And they all yell at me, laugh at some of my jokes, write me funny letters when we're apart—in short, treat me as an ordinary human being for whom they have some use. I think they like me. Unless they're faking. . . .

Faking. There's the rub. Tugging at the fringes of my con- 17 sciousness always is the terror that people are kind to me only because I'm a cripple. My mother almost shattered me once, with that instinct mothers have—blind, I think, in this case, but unerring nonetheless—for striking blows along the fault-lines of their children's hearts, by telling me, in an attack on my selfishness, "We all have to make allowances for you, of course, because of the way you are." From the distance of a couple of years, I have to admit that I haven't any idea just what she meant, and I'm not sure that she knew either. She was awfully angry. But at the time, as the words thudded home, I felt my worst fear, suddenly realized. I could bear being called selfish: I am. But I couldn't bear the corroboration that those around me were doing in fact what I'd always suspected them of doing, professing fondness while silently putting up with me because of the way I am. A cripple. I've been a little cracked ever since.

Along with this fear that people are secretly accepting shoddy 18 goods comes a relentless pressure to please—to prove myself worth the burdens I impose, I guess, or to build a substantial account of goodwill against which I may write drafts in times of need. Part of the pressure arises from social expectations. In our society, anyone who deviates from the norm had better find some way to compensate. Like fat people, who are expected to be jolly, cripples must bear their lot meekly and cheerfully. A grumpy cripple isn't playing by the rules. And much of the pressure is self-generated. Early on I vowed that, if I had to have MS, by God I was going to do it well. This a class act, ladies and gentlemen. No tears, no recriminations, no faint-heartedness.

19   One way and another, then, I wind up feeling like Tiny Tim, peering over the edge of the table at the Christmas goose, waving my crutch, piping down God's blessing on us all. Only sometimes I don't want to play Tiny Tim. I'd rather be Caliban, a most scurvy monster. Fortunately, at home no one much cares whether I'm a good cripple or a bad cripple as long as I make vichyssoise with fair regularity. One evening several years ago, Anne was reading at the dining-room table while I cooked dinner. As I opened a can of tomatoes, the can slipped in my left hand and juice spattered me and the counter with bloody spots. Fatigued and infuriated, I bellowed, "I'm so sick of being crippled!" Anne glanced at me over the top of her book. "There now," she said, "do you feel better?" "Yes," I said, "yes, I do." She went back to her reading. I felt better. That's about all the attention my scurviness ever gets.

20   Because I hate being crippled, I sometimes hate myself for being a cripple. Over the years I have come to expect—even accept—attacks of violent self-loathing. Luckily, in general our society no longer connects deformity and disease directly with evil (though a charismatic once told me that I have MS because a devil is in me) and so I'm allowed to move largely at will, even among small children. But I'm not sure that this revision of attitude has been particularly helpful. Physical imperfection, even freed of moral disapprobation, still defies and violates the ideal, especially for women, whose confinement in their bodies as objects of desire is far from over. Each age, of course, has its ideal, and I doubt that ours is any better or worse than any other. Today's ideal woman, who lives on the glossy pages of dozens of magazines, seems to be between the ages of eighteen and twenty-five; her hair has body, her teeth flash white, her breath smells minty, her underarms are dry; she has a career but is still a fabulous cook, especially of meals that take less than twenty minutes to prepare; she does not ordinarily appear to have a husband or children; she is trim and deeply tanned; she jogs, swims, plays tennis, rides a bicycle, sails, but does not bowl; she travels widely, even to out-of-the-way places like Finland and Samoa, always in the company of the ideal man, who possesses a nearly identical set of characteristics. There are a few exceptions. Though usually white and often blonde, she may be black, Hispanic, Asian, or Native American, so long as she is unusually sleek. She may be old,

provided she is selling a laxative or is Lauren Bacall. If she is selling a detergent, she may be married and have a flock of strikingly
messy children. But she is never a cripple.

Like many women I know, I have always had an uneasy rela-   21
tionship with my body. I was not a popular child, largely, I think
now, because I was peculiar: intelligent, intense, moody, shy,
given to unexpected actions and inexplicable notions and emotions. But as I entered adolescence, I believed myself unpopular
because I was homely: my breasts too flat, my mouth too wide,
my hips too narrow, my clothing never quite right in fit or style. I
was not, in fact, particularly ugly, old photographs inform me,
though I was well off the ideal; but I carried this sense of self-
alienation with me into adulthood, where it regenerated in response to the depredations of MS. Even with my brace I walk
with a limp so pronounced that, seeing myself on the videotape of
a television program on the disabled, I couldn't believe that anything but an inchworm could make progress humping along like
that. My shoulders droop and my pelvis thrusts forward as I try
to balance myself upright, throwing my frame into a bony S. As a
result of contractures, one shoulder is higher than the other and I
carry one arm bent in front of me, the fingers curled into a claw.
My left arm and leg have wasted into pipe-stems, and I try always
to keep them covered. When I think about how my body must
look to others, especially to men, to whom I have been trained to
display myself, I feel ludicrous, even loathsome.

At my age, however, I don't spend much time thinking about   22
my appearance. The burning egocentricity of adolescence, which
assures one that all the world is looking all the time, has passed,
thank God, and I'm generally too caught up in what I'm doing to
step back, as I used to, and watch myself as though upon a stage.
I'm also too old to believe in the accuracy of self-image. I know
that I'm not a hideous crone, that in fact, when I'm rested, well
dressed, and well made up, I look fine. The self-loathing I feel is
neither physically nor intellectually substantial. What I hate is not
me but a disease.

I am not a disease.   23

And a disease is not—at least not singlehandedly—going   24
to determine who I am, though at first it seemed to be going to.

Adjusting to a chronic incurable illness, I have moved through a process similar to that outlined by Elizabeth Kübler-Ross in *On Death and Dying*. The major difference—and it is far more significant than most people recognize—is that I can't be sure of the outcome, as the terminally ill cancer patient can. Research studies indicate that, with proper medical care, I may achieve a "normal" life span. And in our society, with its vision of death as the ultimate evil, worse even than decrepitude, the response to such news is, "Oh well, at least you're not going to *die*." Are there worse things than dying? I think that there may be.

25   I think of two women I know, both with MS, both enough older than I to have served as models. One took to her bed several years ago and has been there ever since. Although she can sit in a high-backed wheelchair, because she is incontinent she refuses to go out at all, even though incontinence pants, which are readily available at any pharmacy, could protect her from embarrassment. Instead, she stays at home and insists that her husband, a small quiet man, a retired civil servant, stay there with her except for a quick weekly foray to the supermarket. The other woman, whose illness was diagnosed when she was eighteen, a nursing student engaged to a young doctor, finished her training, married her doctor, accompanied him to Germany when he was in the service, bore three sons and a daughter, now grown and gone. When she can, she travels with her husband; she plays bridge, embroiders, swims regularly; she works, like me, as a symptomatic-patient instructor of medical students in neurology. Guess which woman I hope to be.

26   At the beginning, I thought about having MS almost incessantly. And because of the unpredictable course of the disease, my thoughts were always terrified. Each night I'd get into bed wondering whether I'd get out again the next morning, whether I'd be able to see, to speak, to hold a pen between my fingers. Knowing that the day might come when I'd be physically incapable of killing myself, I thought perhaps I ought to do so right away, while I still had the strength. Gradually I came to understand that the Nancy who might one day lie inert under a bedsheet, arms and legs paralyzed, unable to feed or bathe herself, unable to reach out for a gun, a bottle of pills, was not the Nancy I was at

present, and that I could not presume to make decisions for that future Nancy, who might well not want in the least to die. Now the only provision I've made for the future Nancy is that when the time comes—and it is likely to come in the form of pneumonia, friend to the weak and the old—I am not to be treated with machines and medications. If she is unable to communicate by then, I hope she will be satisfied with these terms.

Thinking all the time about having MS grew tiresome and in- 27 trusive, especially in the large and tragic mode in which I was accustomed to considering my plight. Months and even years went by without catastrophe (at least without one related to MS), and really I was awfully busy, what with George and children and snakes and students and poems, and I hadn't the time, let alone the inclination, to devote myself to being a disease. Too, the richer my life became, the funnier it seemed, as though there were some connection between largesse and laughter, and so my tragic stance began to waver until, even with the aid of a brace and cane, I couldn't hold it for very long at a time.

After several years I was satisfied with my adjustment. I had 28 suffered my grief and fury and terror, I thought, but now I was at ease with my lot. Then one summer day I set out with George and the children across the desert for a vacation in California. Part way to Yuma I became aware that my right leg felt funny. "I think I've had an exacerbation," I told George. "What shall we do?" he asked. "I think we'd better get the hell to California," I said, "because I don't know whether I'll ever make it again." So we went on to San Diego and then to Orange, and up the Pacific Coast Highway to Santa Cruz, across to Yosemite, down to Sequoia and Joshua Tree, and so back over the desert to home. It was a fine two-week trip, filled with friends and fair weather, and I wouldn't have missed it for the world, though I did in fact make it back to California two years later. Nor would there have been any point in missing it, since in MS, once the symptoms have appeared, the neurological damage has been done, and there's no way to predict or prevent that damage.

The incident spoiled my self-satisfaction, however. It renewed 29 my grief and fury and terror, and I learned that one never finishes adjusting to MS. I don't know now why I thought one would. One does not, after all, finish adjusting to life, and MS is simply a fact of my life—not my favorite fact, of course—but as ordinary as my nose and my tropical fish and my yellow Mazda station wagon. It may at any time get worse, but no amount of worry or anticipation can prepare me for a new loss. My life is a lesson in losses. I learn one at a time.

30   And I had best be patient in the learning, since I'll have to do it like it or not. As any rock fan knows, you can't always get what you want. Particularly when you have MS. You can't, for example, get cured. In recent years researchers and the organizations that fund research have started to pay MS some attention even though it isn't fatal; perhaps they have begun to see that life is something other than a quantitative phenomenon, that one may be very much alive for a very long time in a life that isn't worth living. The researchers have made some progress toward understanding the mechanism of the disease: It may well be an autoimmune reaction triggered by a slow-acting virus. But they are nowhere near its prevention, control, or cure. And most of us want to be cured. Some, unable to accept incurability, grasp at one treatment after another, no matter how bizarre: megavitamin therapy, gluten-free diet, injections of cobra venom, hypothermal suits, lymphocytopharesis, hyberbaric chambers. Many treatments are probably harmless enough, but none are curative.

31   The absence of a cure often makes MS patients bitter toward their doctors. Doctors are, after all, the priests of modern society, the new shamans, whose business is to heal, and many an MS patient roves from one to another, searching for the "good" doctor who will make him well. Doctors too think of themselves as healers, and for this reason many have trouble dealing with MS patients, whose disease in its intransigence defeats their aims and mocks their skills. Too few doctors, it is true, treat their patients as whole human beings, but the reverse is also true. I have always tried to be gentle with my doctors, who often have more at stake in terms of ego than I do. I may be frustrated, maddened, depressed by the incurability of my disease, but I am not diminished by it, and they are. When I push myself up from my seat in the waiting room and stumble toward them, I incarnate the limitation of their powers. The least I can do is refuse to press on their tenderest spots.

This gentleness is part of the reason that I'm not sorry to be a   32
cripple. I didn't have it before. Perhaps I'd have developed it anyway—how could I know such a thing?—and I wish I had more of
it, but I'm glad of what I have. It has opened and enriched my life
enormously, this sense that my frailty and need must be mirrored
in others, that in searching for and shaping a stable core in a life
wrenched by change and loss, change and loss, I must recognize
the same process, under individual conditions, in the lives around
me. I do not deprecate such knowledge, however I've come by it.

All the same, if a cure were found, would I take it? In a   33
minute. I may be a cripple, but I'm only occasionally a loony and
never a saint. Anyway, in my brand of theology God doesn't give
bonus points for a limp. I'd take a cure; I just don't need one. A
friend who also has MS startled me once by asking, "Do you ever
say to yourself, 'Why me, Lord?'" "No, Michael, I don't," I told
him, "because whenever I try, the only response I can think of is
'Why not?'" If I could make a cosmic deal, whom would I put in
my place? What in my life would I give up in exchange for sound
limbs and a thrilling rush of energy? No one. Nothing. I might as
well do the job myself. Now that I'm getting the hang of it.

1986

The Death of the Moth

Virginia Woolf

Moths that fly by day are not properly to be called moths; they   1
do not excite that pleasant sense of dark autumn nights and ivy-
blossom which the commonest yellow-underwing asleep in the
shadow of the curtain never fails to rouse in us. They are hybrid
creatures, neither gay like butterflies nor sombre like their own
species. Nevertheless the present specimen, with his narrow hay-
coloured wings, fringed with a tassel of the same colour, seemed
to be content with life. It was a pleasant morning, mid-September,
mild, benignant, yet with a keener breath than that of the summer

months. The plough was already scoring the field opposite the window, and where the share had been, the earth was pressed flat and gleamed with moisture. Such vigour came rolling in from the fields and the down beyond that it was difficult to keep the eyes strictly turned upon the book. The rooks too were keeping one of their annual festivities; soaring round the tree tops until it looked as if a vast net with thousands of black knots in it had been cast up into the air; which, after a few moments sank slowly down upon the trees until every twig seemed to have a knot at the end of it. Then, suddenly, the net would be thrown into the air again in a wider circle this time, with the utmost clamour and vociferation, as though to be thrown into the air and settle down upon the tree tops were a tremendously exciting experience.

2   The same energy which inspired the rooks, the ploughmen, the horses, and even, it seemed, the lean bare-backed downs, sent the moth fluttering from side to side of his square of the window-pane. One could not help watching him. One was, indeed, conscious of a queer feeling of pity for him. The possibilities of pleasure seemed that morning so enormous and so various that to have only a moth's part in life, and a day moth's at that, appeared a hard fate, and his zest in enjoying his meagre opportunities to the full, pathetic. He flew vigorously to one corner of his compartment, and, after waiting there a second, flew across to the other. What remained for him but to fly to a third corner and then to a fourth? That was all he could do, in spite of the size of the downs, the width of the sky, the far-off smoke of houses, and the romantic voice, now and then, of a steamer out at sea. What he could do he did. Watching him, it seemed as if a fibre, very thin but pure, of the enormous energy of the world had been thrust into his frail and diminutive body. As often as he crossed the pane, I could fancy that a thread of vital light became visible. He was little or nothing but life.

3   Yet, because he was so small, and so simple a form of the energy that was rolling in at the open window and driving its way through so many narrow and intricate corridors in my own brain and in those of other human beings, there was something marvelous as well as pathetic about him. It was as if someone had taken a tiny bead of pure life and decking it as lightly as possible

with down and feathers, had set it dancing and zigzagging to show us the true nature of life. Thus displayed one could not get over the strangeness of it. One is apt to forget all about life, seeing it humped and bossed and garnished and cumbered so that it has to move with the greatest circumspection and dignity. Again, the thought of all that life might have been had he been born in any other shape caused one to view his simple activities with a kind of pity.

After a time, tired by his dancing apparently, he settled on the 4 window ledge in the sun, and, the queer spectacle being at an end, I forgot about him. Then, looking up, my eye was caught by him. He was trying to resume his dancing, but seemed either so stiff or so awkward that he could only flutter to the bottom of the window-pane; and when he tried to fly across it he failed. Being intent on other matters I watched these futile attempts for a time without thinking, unconsciously waiting for him to resume his flight, as one waits for a machine, that has stopped momentarily, to start again without considering the reason of its failure. After perhaps a seventh attempt he slipped from the wooden ledge and fell, fluttering his wings, on to his back on the window sill. The helplessness of his attitude roused me. It flashed upon me that he was in difficulties; he could no longer raise himself; his legs struggled vainly. But, as I stretched out a pencil, meaning to help him to right himself, it came over me that the failure and awkwardness were the approach of death. I laid the pencil down again.

The legs agitated themselves once more. I looked as if for the 5 enemy against which he struggled. I looked out of doors. What had happened there? Presumably it was midday, and work in the fields had stopped. Stillness and quiet had replaced the previous animation. The birds had taken themselves off to feed in the brooks. The horses stood still. Yet the power was there all the same, massed outside, indifferent, impersonal, not attending to anything in particular. Somehow it was opposed to the little hay-coloured moth. It was useless to try to do anything. One could only watch the extraordinary efforts made by those tiny legs against an oncoming doom which could, had it chosen, have submerged an entire city, not merely a city, but masses of human beings; nothing, I knew, had any chance against death. Nevertheless after a pause of exhaustion the legs fluttered again. It was superb this last protest, and so frantic that he succeeded at last in righting himself. One's sympathies, of course, were all on the side of life. Also, when there was nobody to care or to know, this gigantic effort on the part of an insignificant little moth, against a power of such magnitude, to retain what no one else valued or desired to keep, moved one strangely. Again, somehow, one saw life, a pure bead. I lifted the pencil again, useless though I knew it to be. But even as I did so, the unmistakable tokens of death showed themselves. The body relaxed, and instantly grew stiff. The struggle was over. The insignificant little creature now knew death. As I looked at the dead moth, this minute wayside triumph of so great a force over so mean an antagonist filled me with wonder. Just as life had been strange a few minutes before, so death was now as strange. The moth having righted himself now lay most decently and uncomplainingly composed. O yes, he seemed to say, death is stronger than I am.

1942

8

Nature, Science, and Technology

To fully understand the origins and impact of science and technology, we need as well to understand the way science develops, the values implicit in science, and the potential effects science has on the way we lead our lives. While it is common to praise science for our progress—and the accomplishments of medicine, travel, and convenience are just a few areas where scientific and technological advancement has transformed our world—it is less common to acknowledge the social forces behind scientific theory and application. Stephen Jay Gould in "Darwin's Middle Road" does just that in his examination of how Darwin applied the ideas of the social critics and philosophers of the day and ultimately the economic notion of nineteenth-century capitalism to his articulation of evolution as "the survival of the fittest." While Darwin would apply social theory to science, Lewis Thomas applies scientific thought to a theory of society where individuals do not exist as independent entities but are "interlocked." Thomas equates, then, the biology of earth to the ecosystem of a single cell. This metaphor of interdependence is employed by Edward O. Wilson in "Is Humanity Suicidal?"—and it supports a theory of the environment that has long-range social consequences. Unlike Thomas, Wilson sees the earth's "ecosystem" as fragile and recounts the diminishment of our natural resources as a headlong journey into human extinction. The world that Wilson describes is forcefully foretold in Chief Seattle's "Letter to President Pierce." Though the authenticity of the letter has sometimes been questioned, supposedly written on the occasion of Chief Seattle's reluctant agreement to sell his tribal lands to the American government, the sentiments are thought to accurately represent where Chief Seattle believes the philosophy of domination will lead humanity in its relation to nature and society. In "The Clan of One-Breasted Women," Terry Tempest Williams brings this warning home with her heartrending account of the cancer fallout that occurred when the United States developed its program of nuclear testing in Nevada in the fifties. The science fiction writer Ursula K. LeGuin examines as well what science can give and the price it exacts in her allegory of the utopian society of Omelas. Jeremy Rifkin critiques the underbelly of genetic engineering—and the possibility we will ask it to lead us to the perfect human and the perfect world. Charles Krauthammer describes where cloning can lead medically in a Frankenstein version of organ harvesting. However, Howard Rheingold, in "The Virtual Community," reminds us of what technology can offer when he discusses the e-mail communities that helped him as a parent, and how such new technology as these virtual communities can improve life. The selections by LeGuin, Rifkin, and Rheingold in particular reveal how intimate is the connection in our imagination between science and social structure. Science and society interact sometimes directly, as they do on opposite extremes for Terry Tempest Williams and Howard Rheingold, and sometimes indirectly as they did for Darwin, but these selections reveal that science is not an objective pursuit that stands above the fray. Science interacts with society not only in how its accomplishments affect us but also in how the scientific imagination articulates what it knows about our world. Great discoveries have sometimes destructive consequences. As with all things human, however, perhaps science can generate solutions to its own folly.

Darwin's Middle Road

Stephen Jay Gould

1 "We began to sail up the narrow strait lamenting," narrates Odysseus. "For on the one hand lay Scylla, with twelve feet all dangling down; and six necks exceeding long, and on each a hideous head, and therein three rows of teeth set thick and close, full of black death. And on the other mighty Charybdis sucked down the salt sea water. As often as she belched it forth, like a cauldron on a great fire she would seethe up through all her troubled deeps." Odysseus managed to swerve around Charybdis, but Scylla grabbed six of his finest men and devoured them in his sight—"the most pitiful thing mine eyes have seen of all my travail in searching out the paths of the sea."

2 False lures and dangers often come in pairs in our legends and metaphors—consider the frying pan and the fire, or the devil and the deep blue sea. Prescriptions for avoidance either emphasize a dogged steadiness—the straight and narrow of Christian evangelists—or an averaging between unpleasant alternatives—the golden mean of Aristotle. The idea of steering a course between undesirable extremes emerges as a central prescription for a sensible life.

3 The nature of scientific creativity is both a perennial topic of discussion and a prime candidate for seeking a golden mean. The two extreme positions have not been directly competing for allegiance of the unwary. They have, rather, replaced each other sequentially, with one now in the ascendency, the other eclipsed.

4 The first—inductivism—held that great scientists are primarily great observers and patient accumulators of information. For new and significant theory, the inductivists claims, can only arise from a firm foundation of facts. In this architectural view, each fact is a brick in a structure built without blueprints. Any talk or thought about theory (the completed building) is fatuous and premature before the bricks are set. Inductivism once commanded great prestige within science, and even represented an "official" position of sorts, for it touted, however falsely, the utter honesty,

complete objectivity, and almost automatic nature of scientific progress towards final and incontrovertible truth.

Yet, as its critics so rightly claimed, inductivism also depicted science as a heartless, almost inhuman discipline offering no legitimate place to quirkiness, intuition, and all the other subjective attributes adhering to our vernacular notion of genius. Great scientists, the critics claimed, are distinguished more by their powers of hunch and synthesis, than their skill in experiment or observation. The criticisms of inductivism are certainly valid and I welcome its dethroning during the past thirty years as a necessary prelude to better understanding. Yet, in attacking it so strongly, some critics have tried to substitute an alternative equally extreme and unproductive in its emphasis on the essential subjectivity of creative thought. In this "eureka" view, creativity is an ineffable something, accessible only to persons of genius. It arises like a bolt of lightning, unanticipated, unpredictable and unanalyzable—but the bolts strike only a few special people. We ordinary mortals must stand in awe and thanks. (The name refers, of course, to the legendary story of Archimedes running naked through the streets of Syracuse shouting eureka [I have discovered it] when water displaced by his bathing body washed the scales abruptly from his eyes and suggested a method for measuring volumes.)

I am equally disenchanted by both these opposing extremes. Inductivism reduces genius to dull, rote operations; eurekaism grants it an inaccessible status more in the domain of intrinsic mystery than in a realm where we might understand and learn from it. Might we not marry the good features of each view, and abandon both the elitism of eurekaism and the pedestrian qualities of inductivism? May we not acknowledge the personal and subjective character of creativity, but still comprehend it as a mode of thinking that emphasizes or exaggerates capacities sufficiently common to all of us that we may at least understand if not hope to imitate?

In the hagiography of science, a few men hold such high positions that all arguments must apply to them if they are to have any validity. Charles Darwin, as the principal saint of evolutionary biology, has therefore been presented both as an inductivist and as a primary example of eurekaism. I will attempt to show that these interpretations are equally inadequate, and that recent scholarship on Darwin's own odyssey towards the theory of natural selection supports an intermediate position.

8   So great was the prestige of inductivism in his own day, that Darwin himself fell under its sway and, as an old man, falsely depicted his youthful accomplishments in its light. In an autobiography, written as a lesson in morality for his children and not intended for publication, he penned some famous lines that misled historians for nearly a hundred years. Describing his path to the theory of natural selection, he claimed: "I worked on true Baconian principles, and without any theory collected facts on a wholesale scale."

9   The inductivist interpretation focuses on Darwin's five years aboard the *Beagle* and explains his transition from a student for the ministry to the nemesis of preachers as the result of his keen powers of observation applied to the whole world. Thus, the traditional story goes, Darwin's eyes opened wider and wider as he saw, in sequence, the bones of giant South American fossil mammals, the turtles and finches of the Galapagos, and the marsupial fauna of Australia. The truth of evolution and its mechanism of natural selection crept up gradually upon him as he sifted facts in a sieve of utter objectivity.

10   The inadequacies of this tale are best illustrated by the falsity of its conventional premier example—the so-called Darwin's finches of the Galapagos. We now know that although these birds share a recent and common ancestry on the South American mainland, they have radiated into an impressive array of species on the outlying Galapagos. Few terrestrial species manage to cross the wide oceanic barrier between South America and the Galapagos. But the fortunate migrants often find a sparsely inhabited world devoid of the competitors that limit their opportunities on the crowded mainland. Hence, the finches evolved into roles normally occupied by other birds and developed their famous set of adaptations for feeding—seed crushing, insect eating, even grasping and manipulating a cactus needle to dislodge insects from plants. Isolation—both of the islands from the mainland and among the islands themselves—provided an opportunity for separation, independent adaptation, and speciation.

According to the traditional view, Darwin discovered these 11
finches, correctly inferred their history, and wrote the famous
lines in his notebook: "If there is the slightest foundation for these
remarks the zoology of Archipelagoes will be worth examining;
for such facts would undermine the stability of Species." But, as
with so many heroic tales from Washington's cherry tree to the
piety of Crusaders, hope rather than truth motivates the common
reading. Darwin found the finches to be sure. But he didn't recognize them as variants of a common stock. In fact, he didn't even
record the island of discovery for many of them—some of his labels just read "Galapagos Islands." So much for his immediate
recognition of the role of isolation in the formation of new species.
He reconstructed the evolutionary tale only after his return to
London, when a British Museum ornithologist correctly identified
all the birds as finches.

The famous quotation from his notebook refers to Galapagos 12
tortoises and to the claim of native inhabitants that they can "at
once pronounce from which Island any Tortoise may have been
brought" from subtle differences in size and shape of body and
scales. This is a statement of different, and much reduced, order
from the traditional tale of finches. For the finches are true and
separate species—a living example of evolution. The subtle differences among tortoises represent minor geographic variation
within a species. It is a jump in reasoning, albeit a valid one as we
now know, to argue that such small differences can be amplified
to produce a new species. All creationists, after all, acknowledged
geographic variation (consider human races), but argued that it
could not proceed beyond the rigid limits of a created archetype.

I don't wish to downplay the pivotal influence of the *Beagle* 13
voyage on Darwin's career. It gave him space, freedom and endless
time to think in his favored mode of independent self-stimulation.
(His ambivalence towards university life, and his middling performance there by conventional standards, reflected his unhappi-
ness with a curriculum of received wisdom.) He writes from South
America in 1834: "I have not one clear idea about cleavage, stratifi-
cation, lines of upheaval. I have no books, which tell me much and
what they do I cannot apply to what I see. In consequence I draw
my own conclusions, and most gloriously ridiculous ones they

are." The rocks and plants and animals that he saw did provoke him to the crucial attitude of doubt—midwife of all creativity. Sydney, Australia—1836. Darwin wonders why a rational God would create so many marsupials on Australia since nothing about its climate or geography suggests any superiority for pouches: "I had been lying on a sunny bank and was reflecting on the strange character of the animals of this country as compared to the rest of the World. An unbeliever in everything beyond his own reason might exclaim, 'Surely two distinct Creators must have been at work.'"

14   Nonetheless, Darwin returned to London without an evolutionary theory. He suspected the truth of evolution, but had no mechanism to explain it. Natural selection did not arise from any direct reading of the *Beagle's* facts, but from two subsequent years of thought and struggle as reflected in a series of remarkable notebooks that have been unearthed and published during the past twenty years. In these notebooks, we see Darwin testing and abandoning a number of theories and pursuing a multitude of false leads—so much for his later claim about recording facts with an empty mind. He read philosophers, poets, and economists, always searching for meaning and insight—so much for the notion that natural selection arose inductively from the *Beagle's* facts. Later, he labelled one notebook as "full of metaphysics on morals."

15   Yet if this tortuous path belies the Scylla of inductivism, it has engendered an equally simplistic myth—the Charybdis of eurekaism. In his maddeningly misleading autobiography, Darwin does record a eureka and suggests that natural selection struck him as a sudden, serendipitous flash after more than a year of groping frustration:

> In October 1838, that is, fifteen months after I had begun my systematic inquiry, I happened to read for amusement Malthus on Population, and being well prepared to appreciate the struggle for existence which everywhere goes on from long-continued observation of the habits of animals and plants, it at once struck me that under these circumstances favorable variations would tend to be preserved, and unfavorable ones to be destroyed. The result of this would be the formation of new species. Here, then, I had at last got a theory by which to work.

Yet, again, the notebooks belie Darwin's later recollections— 16
in this case by their utter failure to record, at the time it happened,
any special exultation over his Malthusian insight. He inscribes it
as a fairly short and sober entry without a single exclamation
point, though he habitually used two or three in moments of excitement. He did not drop everything and reinterpret a confusing
world in its light. On the very next day, he wrote an even longer
passage on the sexual curiosity of primates.

The theory of natural selection arose neither as a workman- 17
like induction from nature's facts, nor as a mysterious bolt from
Darwin's subconscious, triggered by an accidental reading of
Malthus. It emerged instead as the result of a conscious and productive search, proceeding in a ramifying but ordered manner,
and utilizing both the facts of natural history and an astonishingly
broad range of insights from disparate disciplines far from his
own. Darwin trod the middle path between inductivism and eurekaism. His genius is neither pedestrian nor inaccessible.

Darwinian scholarship has exploded since the centennial of 18
the *Origin* in 1959. The publication of Darwin's notebooks and the
attention devoted by several scholars to the two crucial years between the *Beagle's* docking and the demoted Malthusian insight
has clinched the argument for a "middle path" theory of Darwin's
creativity. Two particularly important works focus on the broadest and narrowest scales. Howard E. Gruber's masterful intellectual and psychological biography of this phase in Darwin's life,
Darwin on Man, traces all the false leads and turning points in
Darwin's search. Gruber shows that Darwin was continually proposing, testing, and abandoning hypotheses, and that he never
simply collected facts in a blind way. He began with a fanciful theory involving the idea that new species arise with a prefixed life
span, and worked his way gradually, if fitfully, towards an idea of
extinction by competition in a world of struggle. He recorded no
exultation upon reading Malthus, because the jigsaw puzzle was
only missing a piece or two at the time.

Silvan S. Schweber has reconstructed, in detail as minute as 19
the record will allow, Darwin's activities during the few weeks before Malthus (The Origin of the *Origin* Revisited, *Journal of the History of Biology*, 1977). He argues that the final pieces arose not from

new facts in natural history, but from Darwin's intellectual wan-
derings in distant fields. In particular, he read a long review of social scientist and philosopher August Comte's most famous work,
the *Cours de philosophie positive.* He was particularly struck by
Comte's insistence that a proper theory be predictive and at least
potentially quantitative. He then turned to Dugald Stewart's *On
the Life and Writing of Adam Smith,* and imbibed the basic belief of
the Scottish economists that theories of overall social structure
must begin by analyzing the unconstrained actions of individuals.
(Natural selection is, above all, a theory about the struggle of individual organisms for success in reproduction.) Then, searching
for quantification, he read a lengthy analysis of work by the most
famous statistician of his time—the Belgian Adolphe Quetelet. In
the review of Quetelet, he found, among other things, a forceful
statement of Malthus's quantitative claim—that population
would grow geometrically and food supplies only arithmetically,
thus guaranteeing an intense struggle for existence. In fact, Darwin had read the Malthusian statement several times before; but
only now was he prepared to appreciate its significance. Thus, he
did not turn to Malthus by accident, and he already knew what it
contained. His "amusement," we must assume, consisted only in
a desire to read in its original formulation the familiar statement
that had so impressed him in Quetelet's secondary account.

20   In reading Schweber's detailed account of the moments preceding Darwin's formulation of natural selection, I was particularly struck by the absence of deciding influence from his own
field of biology. The immediate precipitators were a social scientist, an economist, and a statistician. If genius has any common
denominator, I would propose breadth of interest and the ability
to construct fruitful analogies between fields.

21   In fact, I believe that the theory of natural selection should
be viewed as an extended analogy—whether conscious or unconscious on Darwin's part I do not know—to the laissez faire
economics of Adam Smith. The essence of Smith's argument is
a paradox of sorts: if you want an ordered economy providing
maximal benefits to all, then let individuals compete and struggle for their own advantages. The result, after appropriate sorting and elimination of the inefficient, will be a stable and

harmonious polity. Apparent order arises naturally from the struggle among individuals, not from predestined principles or higher control. Dugald Stewart epitomized Smith's system in the book Darwin read:

> The most effective plan for advancing a people . . . is by allowing every man, as long as he observes the rules of justice, to pursue his own interest in his own way, and to bring both his industry and his capital into the freest competition with those of his fellow citizens. Every system of policy which endeavors . . . to draw towards a particular species of industry a greater share of the capital of the society than would naturally go to it . . . is, in reality, a subversive of the great purpose which it means to promote.

As Schweber states: "The Scottish analysis of society contends [22] that the combined effect of individual actions results in the institutions upon which society is based, and that such a society is a stable and evolving one and functions without a designing and directing mind."

We know that Darwin's uniqueness does not reside in his [23] support for the idea of evolution—scores of scientists had preceded him in this. His special contribution rests upon his documentation and upon the novel character of his theory about how evolution operates. Previous evolutionists had proposed unworkable schemes based on internal perfecting tendencies and inherent directions. Darwin advocated a natural and testable theory based on immediate interaction among individuals (his opponents considered it heartlessly mechanistic). The theory of natural selection is a creative transfer to biology of Adam Smith's basic argument for a rational economy: the balance and order of nature does not arise from a higher, external (divine) control, or from the existence of laws operating directly upon the whole, but from struggle among individuals for their own benefits (in modern terms, for the transmission of their genes to future generations through differential success in reproduction).

Many people are distressed to hear such an argument. Does [24] it not compromise the integrity of science if some of its primary conclusions originate by analogy from contemporary politics and culture rather than from data of the discipline itself? In a famous letter to Engels, Karl Marx identified the similarities between natural selection and the English social scene:

> It is remarkable how Darwin recognizes among beasts and plants his English society with its division of labor, competition, opening up of new markets, 'invention,' and the Malthusian 'struggle for existence.' It is Hobbes' *bellum omnium contra omnes* (the war of all against all).

25 Yet Marx was a great admirer of Darwin—and in this apparent paradox lies resolution. For reasons involving all the themes I have emphasized here—that inductivism is inadequate, that creativity demands breadth, and that analogy is a profound source of insight—great thinkers cannot be divorced from their social background. But the source of an idea is one thing; its truth or fruitfulness is another. The psychology and utility of discovery are very different subjects indeed. Darwin may have cribbed the idea of natural selection from economics, but it may still be right. As the German socialist Karl Kautsky wrote in 1902: "The fact that an idea emanates from a particular class, or accords with their interests, of course proves nothing as to its truth or falsity." In this case, it is ironic that Adam Smith's system of laissez faire does not work in his own domain of economics, for it leads to oligopoly and revolution, rather than to order and harmony. Struggle among individuals does, however, seem to be the law of nature.

26   Many people use such arguments about social context to ascribe great insights primarily to the indefinable phenomenon of good luck. Thus, Darwin was lucky to be born rich, lucky to be on the *Beagle*, lucky to live amidst the ideas of his age, lucky to trip over Parson Malthus—essentially little more than a man in the right place at the right time. Yet, when we read of his personal struggle to understand, the breadth of his concerns and study, and the directedness of his search for a mechanism of evolution, we understand why Pasteur made his famous quip that fortune favors the prepared mind.

1980

The Lives of a Cell

Lewis Thomas

We are told that the trouble with Modern Man is that he has been trying to detach himself from nature. He sits in the topmost tiers of polymer, glass, and steel, dangling his pulsing legs, surveying at a distance the writhing life of the planet. In this scenario, Man comes on as a stupendous lethal force, and the earth is pictured as something delicate, like rising bubbles at the surface of a country pond, or flights of fragile birds. 1

But it is illusion to think that there is anything fragile about the life of the earth; surely this is the toughest membrane imaginable in the universe, opaque to probability, impermeable to death. We are the delicate part, transient and vulnerable as cilia. Nor is it a new thing for man to invent an existence that he imagines to be above the rest of life; this has been his most consistent intellectual exertion down the millennia. As illusion, it has never worked out to his satisfaction in the past, any more than it does today. Man is embedded in nature. 2

The biologic science of recent years has been making this a more urgent fact of life. The new, hard problem will be to cope with the dawning, intensifying realization of just how interlocked we are. The old, clung-to notions most of us have held about our special lordship are being deeply undermined. 3

Item. A good case can be made for our nonexistence as entities. We are not made up, as we had always supposed, of successively enriched packets of our own parts. We are shared, rented, occupied. At the interior of our cells, driving them, providing the oxidative energy that sends us out for the improvement of each shining day, are the mitochondria, and in a strict sense they are not ours. They turn out to be little separate creatures, the colonial posterity of migrant prokaryocytes, probably primitive bacteria that swam into ancestral precursors of our eukaryotic cells and stayed here. Ever since, they have maintained themselves and their ways, replicating in their own fashion, privately, with their own DNA and RNA quite different from ours. They are as much 4 symbionts as the rhizobial bacteria in the roots of beans. Without them, we would not move a muscle, drum a finger, think a thought.

5   Mitochondria are stable and responsible lodgers, and I choose to trust them. But what of the other little animals, similarly established in my cells, sorting and balancing me, clustering me together? My centrioles, basal bodies, and probably a good many other more obscure tiny beings at work inside my cells, each with its own special genome, are as foreign, and as essential, as aphids in anthills. My cells are no longer the pure line entities I was raised with; they are ecosystems more complex than Jamaica Bay.

6   I like to think that they work in my interest, that each breath they draw for me, but perhaps it is they who walk through the local park in the early morning, sensing my senses, listening to my music, thinking my thoughts.

7   I am consoled, somewhat, by the thought that the green plants are in the same fix. They could not be plants, or green, without their chloroplasts, which run the photosynthetic enterprise and generate oxygen for the rest of us. As it turns out, chloroplasts are also separate creatures with their own genomes, speaking their own language.

8   We carry stores of DNA in our nuclei that may have come in, at one time or another, from the fusion of ancestral cells and the linking of ancestral organisms in symbiosis. Our genomes are catalogues of instructions from all kinds of sources in nature, filed for all kinds of contingencies. As for me, I am grateful for differentiation and speciation, but I cannot feel as separate an entity as I did a few years ago, before I was told these things; nor, I should think, can anyone else.

9   *Item.* The uniformity of the earth's life, more astonishing than its diversity, is accountable by the high probability that we derived, originally, from some single cell, fertilized in a bolt of lightning as the earth cooled. It is from the progeny of this parent cell that we take our looks; we still share genes around, and the resemblance of the enzymes of grasses to those of whales is a family resemblance.

10   The viruses, instead of being single-minded agents of disease and death, now begin to look more like mobile genes. Evolution is still an infinitely long and tedious biologic game, with only the

winners staying at the table, but the rules are beginning to look more flexible. We live in a dancing matrix of viruses; they dart, rather like bees, from organism to organism, from plant to insect to mammal to me and back again, and into the sea, tugging along pieces of this genome, strings of genes from that, transplanting grafts of DNA, passing around heredity as though at a great party. They may be a mechanism for keeping new, mutant kinds of DNA in the widest circulation among us. If this is true, the odd virus disease, on which we must focus so much of our attention in medicine, may be looked on as an accident, something dropped.

Item. I have been trying to think of the earth as a kind of or- 11 ganism, but it is no go. I cannot think of it this way. It is too big, too complex, with too many working parts lacking visible connections. The other night, driving through a hilly, wooded part of southern New England, I wondered about this. If not like an organism, what is it like, what is it *most* like? Then, satisfactorily for that moment, it came to me: it is *most* like a single cell.

1974

Is Humanity Suicidal?
If Homo Sapiens Goes the Way
of the Dinosaur, We Have Only
Ourselves to Blame.

Edward O. Wilson

Imagine that on an icy moon of Jupiter—say, Ganymede—the 1 space station of an alien civilization is concealed. For millions of years its scientists have closely watched the earth. Because their law prevents settlement on a living planet, they have tracked the surface by means of satellites equipped with sophisticated sensors, mapping the spread of large assemblages of organisms, from forests, grasslands and tundras to coral reefs and the vast planktonic meadows of the sea. They have recorded millennial cycles in the climate, interrupted by the advance and retreat of glaciers and scattershot volcanic eruptions.

2   The watchers have been waiting for what might be called the Moment. When it comes, occupying only a few centuries and thus a mere tick in geological time, the forests shrink back to less than half their original cover. Atmospheric carbon dioxide rises to the highest level in 100,000 years. The ozone layer of the stratosphere thins, and holes open at the poles. Plumes of nitrous oxide and other toxins rise from fires in South America and Africa, settle in the upper troposphere and drift eastward across the oceans. At night the land surface brightens with millions of pinpoints of light, which coalesce into blazing swaths across Europe, Japan and eastern North America. A semicircle of fire spreads from gas flares around the Persian Gulf.

3   It was all but inevitable, the watchers might tell us if we met them, that from the great diversity of large animals, one species or another would eventually gain intelligent control of Earth. That role has fallen to Homo sapiens, a primate risen in Africa from a lineage that split away from the chimpanzee line five to eight million years ago. Unlike any creature that lived before, we have become a geophysical force, swiftly changing the atmosphere and climate as well as the composition of the world's fauna and flora. Now in the midst of a population explosion, the human species has doubled to 5.5 billion during the past 50 years. It is scheduled to double again in the next 50 years. No other single species in evolutionary history has even remotely approached the sheer mass in protoplasm generated by humanity.

4   Darwin's dice have rolled badly for Earth. It was a misfortune for the living world in particular, many scientists believe, that a carnivorous primate and not some more benign form of animal made the breakthrough. Our species retains hereditary traits that add greatly to our destructive impact. We are tribal and aggressively territorial, intent on private space beyond minimal requirements and oriented by selfish sexual and reproductive drives. Cooperation beyond the family and tribal levels comes hard.

Worse, our liking for meat causes us to use the sun's energy at   5
low efficiency. It is a general rule of ecology that (very roughly)
only about 10 percent of the sun's energy captured by photosyn-
thesis to produce plant tissue is converted into energy in the tissue of herbivores, the animals that eat the plants. Of that amount,
10 percent reaches the tissue of the carnivores feeding on the herbivores. Similarly, only 10 percent is transferred to carnivores that
eat carnivores. And so on for another step or two. In a wetlands
chain that runs from marsh grass to grasshopper to warbler to
hawk, the energy captured during green production shrinks a
thousandfold.

In other words, it takes a great deal of grass to support a   6
hawk. Human beings, like hawks, are top carnivores, at the end of
the food chain whenever they eat meat, two or more links removed from the plants; if chicken, for example, two links, and if
tuna, four links. Even with most societies confined today to a
mostly vegetarian diet, humanity is gobbling up a large part of
the rest of the living world. We appropriate between 20 and 40
percent of the sun's energy that would otherwise be fixed into the
tissue of natural vegetation, principally by our consumption of
crops and timber, construction of buildings and roadways and the
creation of wastelands. In the relentless search for more food, we
have reduced animal life in lakes, rivers and now, increasingly, the
open ocean. And everywhere we pollute the air and water, lower
water tables and extinguish species.

The human species is, in a word, an environmental abnormal-   7
ity. It is possible that intelligence in the wrong kind of species was
foreordained to be a fatal combination for the biosphere. Perhaps
a law of evolution is that intelligence usually extinguishes itself.

This admittedly dour scenario is based on what can be termed   8
the juggernaut theory of human nature, which holds that people
are programmed by their genetic heritage to be so selfish that a
sense of global responsibility will come too late. Individuals place
themselves first, family second, tribe third and the rest of the
world a distant fourth. Their genes also predispose them to plan
ahead for one or two generations at most. They fret over the petty
problems and conflicts of their daily lives and respond swiftly

and often ferociously to slight challenges to their status and tribal security. But oddly, as psychologists have discovered, people also tend to underestimate both the likelihood and impact of such natural disasters as major earthquakes and great storms.

9   The reason for this myopic fog, evolutionary biologists contend, is that it was actually advantageous during all but the last few millennia of the two million years of existence of the genus Homo. The brain evolved into its present form during this long stretch of evolutionary time, during which people existed in small, preliterate hunter–gatherer bands. Life was precarious and short. A premium was placed on close attention to the near future and early reproduction, and little else. Disasters of a magnitude that occur only once every few centuries were forgotten or transmuted into myth. So today the mind still works comfortably backward and forward for only a few years, spanning a period not exceeding one or two generations. Those in past ages whose genes inclined them to short-term thinking lived longer and had more children than those who did not. Prophets never enjoyed a Darwinian edge.

10   The rules have recently changed, however. Global crises are rising within the life span of the generation now coming of age, a foreshortening that may explain why young people express more concern about the environment than do their elders. The time scale has contracted because of the exponential growth in both the human population and technologies impacting the environment. Exponential growth is basically the same as the increase of wealth by compound interest. The larger the population, the faster the growth; the faster the growth, the sooner the population becomes still larger. In Nigeria, to cite one of our more fecund nations, the population is expected to double from its 1988 level to 216 million by the year 2010. If the same rate of growth were to continue to 2110, its population would exceed that of the entire present population of the world.

11   With people everywhere seeking a better quality of life, the search for resources is expanding even faster than the population. The demand is being met by an increase in scientific knowledge, which doubles every 10 to 15 years. It is accelerated further by a parallel rise in environment-devouring technology. Because Earth

is finite in many resources that determine the quality of life—including arable soil, nutrients, fresh water and space for natural ecosystems—doubling of consumption at constant time intervals can bring disaster with shocking suddenness. Even when a non-renewable resource has been only half used, it is still only one interval away from the end. Ecologists like to make this point with the French riddle of the lily pond. At first there is only one lily pad in the pond, but the next day it doubles, and thereafter each of its descendants doubles. The pond completely fills with lily pads in 30 days. When is the pond exactly half full? Answer: on the 29th day.

Yet, mathematical exercises aside, who can safely measure the human capacity to overcome the perceived limits of Earth? The question of central interest is this: Are we racing to the brink of an abyss, or are we just gathering speed for a takeoff to a wonderful future? The crystal ball is clouded; the human condition baffles all the more because it is both unprecedented and bizarre, almost beyond understanding.

In the midst of uncertainty, opinions on the human prospect have tended to fall loosely into two schools. The first, exemptionalism, holds that since humankind is transcendent in intelligence and spirit, so must our species have been released from the iron laws of ecology that bind all other species. No matter how serious the problem, civilized human beings, by ingenuity, force of will and—who knows—divine dispensation, will find a solution.

Population growth? Good for the economy, claim some of the exemptionalists, and in any case a basic human right, so let it run. Land shortages? Try fusion energy to power the desalting of sea water, then reclaim the world's deserts. (The process might be assisted by towing icebergs to coastal pipelines.) Species going extinct? Not to worry. That is nature's way. Think of humankind as only the latest in a long line of exterminating agents in geological time. In any case, because our species has pulled free of old-style, mindless Nature, we have begun a different order of life. Evolution should now be allowed to proceed along this new trajectory. Finally, resources? The planet has more than enough resources to last indefinitely, if human genius is allowed to address each new problem in turn, without alarmist and unreasonable restrictions imposed on economic development. So hold the course, and touch the brakes lightly.

15   The opposing idea of reality is environmentalism, which sees humanity as a biological species tightly dependent on the natural world. As formidable as our intellect may be and as fierce our spirit, the argument goes, those qualities are not enough to free us from the constraints of the natural environment in which our human ancestors evolved. We cannot draw confidence from successful solutions to the smaller problems of the past. Many of Earth's vital resources are about to be exhausted, its atmospheric chemistry is deteriorating and human populations have already grown dangerously large. Natural ecosystems, the wellsprings of a healthful environment, are being irreversibly degraded.

16   At the heart of the environmentalist world view is the conviction that human physical and spiritual health depends on sustaining the planet in a relatively unaltered state. Earth is our home in the full, genetic sense, where humanity and its ancestors existed for all the millions of years of their evolution. Natural ecosystems—forests, coral reefs, marine blue waters—maintain the world exactly as we would wish it to be maintained. When we debase the global environment and extinguish the variety of life, we are dismantling a support system that is too complex to understand, let alone replace, in the foreseeable future. Space scientists theorize the existence of a virtually unlimited array of other planetary environments, almost all of which are uncongenial to human life. Our own Mother Earth, lately called Gaia, is a specialized conglomerate of organisms and the physical environment they create on a day-to-day basis, which can be destabilized and turned lethal by careless activity. We run the risk, conclude the environmentalists, of beaching ourselves upon alien shores like a great confused pod of pilot whales.

17   If I have not done so enough already by tone of voice, I will now place myself solidly in the environmentalist school, but not so radical as to wish a turning back of the clock, not given to driving spikes into Douglas firs to prevent logging and distinctly uneasy with such hybrid movements as ecofeminism, which holds that Mother Earth is a nurturing home for all life and should be

revered and loved as in premodern (paleolithic and archaic) societies and that ecosystematic abuse is rooted in androcentric—that is to say, male-dominated—concepts, values and institutions.

Still, however soaked in androcentric culture, I am radical 18 enough to take seriously the question heard with increasing frequency: Is humanity suicidal? Is the drive to environmental conquest and self-propagation embedded so deeply in our genes as to be unstoppable?

My short answer—opinion if you wish—is that humanity is 19 not suicidal, at least not in the sense just stated. We are smart enough and have time enough to avoid an environmental catastrophe of civilization-threatening dimensions. But the technical problems are sufficiently formidable to require a redirection of much of science and technology, and the ethical issues are so basic as to force a reconsideration of our self-image as a species.

There are reasons for optimism, reasons to believe that we 20 have entered what might someday be generously called the Century of the Environment. The United Nations Conference on Environment and Development, held in Rio de Janeiro in June 1992, attracted more than 120 heads of government, the largest number ever assembled, and helped move environmental issues closer to the political center stage; on Nov. 18, 1992, more than 1,500 senior scientists from 59 countries issued a "Warning to Humanity," stating that overpopulation and environmental deterioration put the very future of life at risk. The greening of religion has become a global trend, with theologians and religious leaders addressing environmental problems as a moral issue. In May 1992, leaders of most of the major American denominations met with scientists as guests of members of the United States Senate to formulate a "Joint Appeal by Religion and Science for the Environment." Conservation of biodiversity is increasingly seen by both national governments and major landowners as important to their country's future. Indonesia, home to a large part of the native Asian plant and animal species, has begun to shift to land-management practices that conserve and sustainably develop the remaining rain forests. Costa Rica has created a National Institute of Biodiversity. A pan-African institute for biodiversity research and management has been founded, with headquarters in Zimbabwe.

21   Finally, there are favorable demographic signs. The rate of population increase is declining on all continents, although it is still well above zero almost everywhere and remains especially high in sub-Saharan Africa. Despite entrenched traditions and religious beliefs, the desire to use contraceptives in family planning is spreading. Demographers estimate that if the demand were fully met, this action alone would reduce the eventual stabilized population by more than two billion.

22   In summary, the will is there. Yet the awful truth remains that a large part of humanity will suffer no matter what is done. The number of people living in absolute poverty has risen during the past 20 years to nearly one billion and is expected to increase another 100 million by the end of the decade. Whatever progress has been made in the developing countries, and that includes an overall improvement in the average standard of living, is threatened by a continuance of rapid population growth and the deterioration of forests and arable soil.

23   Our hopes must be chastened further still, and this is in my opinion the central issue, by a key and seldom-recognized distinction between the nonliving and living environments. Science and the political process can be adapted to manage the nonliving, physical environment. The human hand is now upon the physical homeostat. The ozone layer can be mostly restored to the upper atmosphere by elimination of CFC's, with these substances peaking at six times the present level and then subsiding during the next half century. Also, with procedures that will prove far more difficult and initially expensive, carbon dioxide and other greenhouse gases can be pulled back to concentrations that slow global warming.

24   The human hand, however, is not upon the biological homeostat. There is no way in sight to micromanage the natural ecosystems and the millions of species they contain. That feat might be accomplished by generations to come, but then it will be too late for the ecosystems—and perhaps for us. Despite the seemingly bottomless nature of creation, humankind has been chipping away at its diversity, and Earth is destined to become an impoverished planet within a century if present trends continue. Mass extinctions are being reported with increasing frequency in every part of the world. They include half the freshwater fishes of

peninsular Malaysia, 10 birds native to Cebu in the Philippines, half the 41 tree snails of Oahu, 44 of the 68 shallow-water mussels of the Tennessee River shoals, as many as 90 plant species growing on the Centinela Ridge in Ecuador, and in the United States as a whole, about 200 plant species, with another 680 species and races now classified as in danger of extinction. The main cause is the destruction of natural habitats, especially tropical forests. Close behind, especially on the Hawaiian archipelago and other islands, is the introduction of rats, pigs, beard grass, lantana and other exotic organisms that outbreed and extirpate native species.

The few thousand biologists worldwide who specialize in diversity are aware that they can witness and report no more than a very small percentage of the extinctions actually occurring. The reason is that they have facilities to keep track of only a tiny fraction of the millions of species and a sliver of the planet's surface on a yearly basis. They have devised a rule of thumb to characterize the situation: that whenever careful studies are made of habitats before and after disturbance, extinctions almost always come to light. The corollary: the great majority of extinctions are never observed. Vast numbers of species are apparently vanishing before they can be discovered and named. 25

There is a way, nonetheless, to estimate the rate of loss indirectly. Independent studies around the world and in fresh and marine waters have revealed a robust connection between the size of a habitat and the amount of biodiversity it contains. Even a small loss in area reduces the number of species. The relation is such that when the area of the habitat is cut to a tenth of its original cover, the number of species eventually drops by roughly one-half. Tropical rain forests, thought to harbor a majority of Earth's species (the reason conservationists get so exercised about rain forests), are being reduced by nearly that magnitude. At the present time they occupy about the same area as that of the 48 conterminous United States, representing a little less than half their original, prehistoric cover; and they are shrinking each year by about 2 percent, an amount equal to the state of Florida. If the typical value (that is, 90 percent area loss causes 50 percent eventual extinction) is applied, the projected loss of species due to rain forest destruction worldwide is half a percent across the board of all kinds of plants, animals and microorganisms. 26

27   When area reduction and all the other extinction agents are considered together, it is reasonable to project a reduction by 20 percent or more of the rain forest species by the year 2020, climbing to 50 percent or more by midcentury, if nothing is done to change current practice. Comparable erosion is likely in other environments now under assault, including many coral reefs and Mediterranean-type heathlands of Western Australia, South Africa and California.

28   The ongoing loss will not be replaced by evolution in any period of time that has meaning for humanity. Extinction is now proceeding thousands of times faster than the production of new species. The average life span of a species and its descendants in past geological eras varied according to group (like mollusks or echinoderms or flowering plants) from about 1 to 10 million years. During the past 500 million years, there have been five great extinction spasms comparable to the one now being inaugurated by human expansion. The latest, evidently caused by the strike of an asteroid, ended the Age of Reptiles 66 million years ago. In each case it took more than 10 million years for evolution to completely replenish the biodiversity lost. And that was in an otherwise undisturbed natural environment. Humanity is now destroying most of the habitats where evolution can occur.

29   The surviving biosphere remains the great unknown of Earth in many respects. On the practical side, it is hard even to imagine what other species have to offer in the way of new pharmaceuticals, crops, fibers, petroleum substitutes and other products. We have only a poor grasp of the ecosystem services by which other organisms cleanse the water, turn soil into a fertile living cover and manufacture the very air we breathe. We sense but do not fully understand what the highly diverse natural world means to our esthetic pleasure and mental well-being.

30   Scientists are unprepared to manage a declining biosphere. To illustrate, consider the following mission they might be given. The last remnant of a rain forest is about to be cut over. Environmentalists are stymied. The contracts have been signed, and local landowners and politicians are intransigent. In a final desperate move, a team of biologists is scrambled in an attempt to preserve the biodiversity by extraordinary means. Their assignment is the following: collect samples of all the species of organisms quickly,

before the cutting starts; maintain the species in zoos, gardens and laboratory cultures or else deep-freeze samples of the tissues in liquid nitrogen, and finally, establish the procedure by which the entire community can be reassembled on empty ground at a later date, when social and economic conditions have improved.

The biologists cannot accomplish this task, not if thousands of 31 them came with a billion-dollar budget. They cannot even imagine how to do it. In the forest patch live legions of species: perhaps 300 birds, 500 butterflies, 200 ants, 50,000 beetles, 1,000 trees, 5,000 fungi, tens of thousands of bacteria and so on down a long roster of major groups. Each species occupies a precise niche, demanding a certain place, an exact microclimate, particular nutrients and temperature and humidity cycles with specified timing to trigger phases of the life cycle. Many, perhaps most, of the species are locked in symbioses with other species; they cannot survive and reproduce unless arrayed with their partners in the correct idiosyncratic configurations.

Even if the biologists pulled off the taxonomic equivalent of 32 the Manhattan Project, sorting and preserving cultures of all the species, they could not then put the community back together again. It would be like unscrambling an egg with a pair of spoons. The biology of the microorganisms needed to reanimate the soil would be mostly unknown. The pollinators of most of the flowers and the correct timing of their appearance could only be guessed. The "assembly rules," the sequence in which species must be allowed to colonize in order to coexist indefinitely, would remain in the realm of theory.

In its neglect of the rest of life, exemptionalism fails defini- 33 tively. To move ahead as though scientific and entrepreneurial genius will solve each crisis that arises implies that the declining biosphere can be similarly manipulated. But the world is too complicated to be turned into a garden. There is no biological homeostat that can be worked by humanity; to believe otherwise is to risk reducing a large part of Earth to a wasteland.

The environmentalist vision, prudential and less exuberant 34 than exemptionalism, is closer to reality. It sees humanity entering a bottleneck unique in history, constricted by population and economic pressures. In order to pass through to the other side, within perhaps 50 to 100 years, more science and entrepreneurship will have to be devoted to stabilizing the global environment. That can be accomplished, according to expert consensus, only by halting population growth and devising a wiser use of resources than has been accomplished to date. And wise use for the living world in particular means preserving the surviving ecosystems, micromanaging them only enough to save the biodiversity they contain, until such time as they can be understood and employed in the fullest sense for human benefit.

1997

Letter to President Pierce
Chief Seattle

1 We know that the white man does not understand our ways. One portion of the land is the same to him as the next, for he is a stranger who comes in the night and takes from the land whatever he needs. The earth is not his brother, but his enemy, and when he has conquered it, he moves on. He leaves his fathers' graves, and his children's birthright is forgotten. The sight of your cities pains the eyes of the red man. But perhaps it is because the red man is a savage and does not understand.

2   There is no quiet place in the white man's cities. No place to hear the leaves of spring or the rustle of insect's wings. But perhaps because I am a savage and do not understand, the clatter only seems to insult the ears. The Indian prefers the soft sound of the wind darting over the face of the pond, the smell of the wind itself cleansed by a mid-day rain, or scented with the piñon pine. The air is precious to the red man. For all things share the same breath—the beasts, the trees, the man. Like a man dying for many days, he is numb to the stench.

3   What is man without the beasts? If all the beasts were gone, men would die from great loneliness of spirit, for whatever happens to the beasts also happens to man. All things are connected. Whatever befalls the earth befalls the sons of the earth.

It matters little where we pass the rest of our days; they are 4
not many. A few more hours, a few more winters, and none of the
children of the great tribes that once lived on this earth, or that
roamed in small bands in the woods, will be left to mourn the
graves of a people once as powerful and hopeful as yours.

The whites, too, shall pass—perhaps sooner than other tribes. 5
Continue to contaminate your bed, and you will one night suffo-
cate in your own waste. When the buffalo are all slaughtered, the
wild horses all tamed, the secret corners of the forest heavy with
the scent of many men, and the view of the ripe hills blotted by
talking wires, where is the thicket? Gone. Where is the eagle?
Gone. And what is it to say goodby to the swift and the hunt, the
end of living and the beginning of survival? We might understand
if we knew what it was that the white man dreams, what he describes to his children on the long winter nights, what visions he
burns into their minds, so they will wish for tomorrow. But we are
savages. The white man's dreams are hidden from us.

1855

The Clan of the One-Breasted Women

Terry Tempest Williams

EPILOGUE

I belong to a Clan of One-Breasted Women. My mother, my 1
grandmothers, and six aunts have all had mastectomies. Seven are
dead. The two who survive have just completed rounds of
chemotherapy and radiation.

I've had my own problems: two biopsies for breast cancer 2
and a small tumor between my ribs diagnosed as a "borderline
malignancy."

This is my family history.   3

4   Most statistics tell us breast cancer is genetic, hereditary, with rising percentages attached to fatty diets, childlessness, or becoming pregnant after thirty. What they don't say is living in Utah may be the greatest hazard of all.

5   We are a Mormon family with roots in Utah since 1847. The "word of wisdom" in my family aligned us with good foods—no coffee, no tea, tobacco, or alcohol. For the most part, our women were finished having their babies by the time they were thirty. And only one faced breast cancer prior to 1960. Traditionally, as a group of people, Mormons have a low rate of cancer.

6   Is our family a cultural anomaly? The truth is, we didn't think about it. Those who did, usually the men, simply said, "bad genes." The women's attitude was stoic. Cancer was part of life. On February 16, 1971, the eve of my mother's surgery, I accidentally picked up the telephone and overheard her ask my grandmother what she could expect.

7   "Diane, it is one of the most spiritual experiences you will ever encounter."

8   I quietly put down the receiver.

9   Two days later, my father took my brothers and me to the hospital to visit her. She met us in the lobby in a wheelchair. No bandages were visible. I'll never forget her radiance, the way she held herself in a purple velvet robe, and how she gathered us around her.

10   "Children, I am fine. I want you to know I felt the arms of God around me."

11   We believed her. My father cried. Our mother, his wife, was thirty-eight years old.

12   A little over a year after Mother's death, Dad and I were having dinner together. He had just returned from St. George, where the Tempest Company was completing the gas lines that would service southern Utah. He spoke of his love for the country, the sandstoned landscape, bare-boned and beautiful. He had just finished hiking the Kolob trail in Zion National Park. We got caught up in reminiscing, recalling with fondness our walk up Angel's Landing on his fiftieth birthday and the years our family had vacationed there.

Over dessert, I shared a recurring dream of mine. I told my fa- 13
ther that for years, as long as I could remember, I saw this flash of
light in the night in the desert—that this image had so permeated
my being that I could not venture south without seeing it again,
on the horizon, illuminating buttes and mesas.

"You did see it," he said.   14

"Saw what?"   15

"The bomb. The cloud. We were driving home from River- 16
side, California. You were sitting on Diane's lap. She was pregnant. In fact, I remember the day, September 7, 1957. We had just
gotten out of the Service. We were driving north, past Las Vegas.
It was an hour or so before dawn, when this explosion went off.
We not only heard it, but felt it. I thought the oil tanker in front of
us had blown up. We pulled over and suddenly, rising from the
desert floor, we saw it, clearly, this golden-stemmed cloud, the
mushroom. The sky seemed to vibrate with an eerie pink glow.
Within a few minutes, a light ash was raining on the car."

I stared at my father.   17

"I thought you knew that," he said. "It was a common occur- 18
rence in the fifties."

It was at this moment that I realized the deceit I had been liv- 19
ing under. Children growing up in the American Southwest,
drinking contaminated milk from contaminated cows, even from
the contaminated breasts of their mothers, my mother—members,
years later, of the Clan of One-Breasted Women.

It is a well-known story in the Desert West, "The Day We 20
Bombed Utah," or more accurately, the years we bombed Utah:
above ground atomic testing in Nevada took place from January
27, 1951, through July 11, 1962. Not only were the winds blowing
north covering "low-use segments of the population" with fallout
and leaving sheep dead in their tracks, but the climate was right.
The United States of the 1950s was red, white, and blue. The Korean War was raging. McCarthyism was rampant. Ike was it, and
the cold war was hot. If you were against nuclear testing, you
were for a communist regime.

Much has been written about this "American nuclear tragedy." 21
Public health was secondary to national security. The Atomic

Energy Commissioner, Thomas Murray, said, "Gentlemen, we must not let anything interfere with this series of tests, nothing."

22   Again and again, the American public was told by its government, in spite of burns, blisters, and nausea, "It has been found that the tests may be conducted with adequate assurance of safety under conditions prevailing at the bombing reservations." Assuaging public fears was simply a matter of public relations. "Your best action," an Atomic Energy Commission booklet read, "is not to be worried about fallout." A news release typical of the times stated, "We find no basis for concluding that harm to any individual has resulted from radioactive fallout."

23   On August 30, 1979, during Jimmy Carter's presidency, a suit was filed, *Irene Allen v. The United States of America.* Mrs. Allen's case was the first on an alphabetical list of twenty-four test cases, representative of nearly twelve hundred plaintiffs seeking compensation from the United States government for cancers caused by nuclear testing in Nevada.

24   Irene Allen lived in Hurricane, Utah. She was the mother of five children and had been widowed twice. Her first husband, with their two oldest boys, had watched the tests from the roof of the local high school. He died of leukemia in 1956. Her second husband dies of pancreatic cancer in 1978.

25   In a town meeting conducted by Utah Senator Orrin Hatch, shortly before the suit was filed, Mrs. Allen said, "I am not blaming the government, I want you to know that, Senator Hatch. But I thought if my testimony could help in any way so this wouldn't happen again to any of the generations coming up after us . . . I am happy to be here this day to bear testimony of this."

26   God-fearing people. This is just one story in an anthology of thousands.

27   On May 10, 1984, Judge Bruce S. Jenkins handed down his opinion. Ten of the plaintiffs were awarded damages. It was the first time a federal court had determined that nuclear tests had been the cause of cancers. For the remaining fourteen test cases, the proof of causation was not sufficient. In spite of the split decision, it was considered a landmark ruling. It was not to remain so for long.

In April 1987, the Tenth Circuit Court of Appeals overturned 28
Judge Jenkins's ruling on the ground that the United States was
protected from suit by the legal doctrine of sovereign immunity, a
centuries-old idea from England in the days of absolute monarchs.

In January 1988, the Supreme Court refused to review the Ap- 29
peals Court decision. To our court system it does not matter
whether the United States government was irresponsible,
whether it lied to its citizens, or even that citizens died from the
fallout of nuclear testing. What matters is that our government is
immune: "The King can do no wrong."

In Mormon culture, authority is respected, obedience is 30
revered, and independent thinking is not. I was taught as a young
girl not to "make waves" or "rock the boat."

"Just let it go," Mother would say. "You know how you feel, 31
that's what counts."

For many years, I have done just that—listened, observed, 32
and quietly formed my own opinions, in a culture that rarely asks
questions because it has all the answers. But one by one, I have
watched the women in my family die common, heroic deaths. We
sat in waiting rooms hoping for good news, but always receiving
the bad. I cared for them, bathed their scarred bodies, and kept
their secrets. I watched beautiful women become bald as Cytoxan,
cisplatin, and Adriamycin were injected into their veins. I held
their foreheads as they vomited green-black bile, and I shot them
with morphine when the pain became inhuman. In the end, I witnessed their last peaceful breaths, becoming a midwife to the rebirth of their souls.

The price of obedience has become too high. 33

The fear and inability to question authority that ultimately 34
killed rural communities in Utah during atmospheric testing of
atomic weapons is the same fear I saw in my mother's body.
Sheep. Dead sheep. The evidence is buried.

I cannot prove that my mother, Diane Dixon Tempest, or my 35
grandmothers, Lettie Romney Dixon and Kathryn Blackett Tempest, along with my aunts developed cancer from nuclear fallout
in Utah. But I can't prove they didn't.

My father's memory was correct. The September blast we 36
drove through in 1957 was part of Operation Plumbbob, one of

the most intensive series of bomb tests to be initiated. The flash of light in the night in the desert, which I had always thought was a dream, developed into a family nightmare. It took fourteen years, from 1957 to 1971, for cancer to manifest in my mother—the same time, Howard L. Andrews, an authority in radioactive fallout at the National Institutes of Health, says radiation cancer requires to become evident. The more I learn about what it means to be a "downwinder," the more questions I drown in.

37   What I do know, however, is that as a Mormon woman of the fifth generation of Latter-day Saints, I must question everything, even if it means losing my faith, even it if means becoming a member of a border tribe among my own people. Tolerating blind obedience in the name of patriotism or religion ultimately takes our lives.

38   When the Atomic Energy Commission described the country north of the Nevada Test Site as "virtually uninhabited desert terrain," my family and the birds at Great Salt Lake were some of the "virtual uninhabitants."

39   One night, I dreamed women from all over the world circled a blazing fire in the desert. They spoke of change, how they hold the moon in their bellies and wax and wane with its phases. They mocked the presumption of even-tempered beings and made promises that they would never fear the witch inside themselves. The women danced wildly as sparks broke away from the flames and entered the night sky as stars.

40   And they sang a song given to them by Shoshone grandmothers:

Ah ne nah, nah	Consider the rabbits
nin nah nah—	How gently they walk on the earth—
ah ne nah, nah	Consider the rabbits
nin nah nah—	How gently they walk on the earth—
Nyaga mutzi	We remember them
oh ne nay—	We can walk gently also—
Nyaga mutzi	We remember them
oh ne nay—	We can walk gently also—

The women danced and drummed and sang for weeks, preparing themselves for what was to come. They would reclaim the desert for the sake of their children, for the sake of the land.

A few miles downwind from the fire circle, bombs were being 41 tested. Rabbits felt the tremors. Their soft leather pads on paws and feet recognized the shaking sands, while the roots of mesquite and sage were smoldering. Rocks were hot from the inside out and dust devils hummed unnaturally. And each time there was another nuclear test, ravens watched the desert heave. Stretch marks appeared. The land was losing its muscle.

The women couldn't bear it any longer. They were mothers. 42 They had suffered labor pains but always under the promise of birth. The red hot pains beneath the desert promised death only, as each bomb became a stillborn. A contract had been made and broken between human beings and the land. A new contract was being drawn by the women, who understood the fate of the earth as their own.

Under the cover of darkness, ten women slipped under a 43 barbed-wire fence and entered the contaminated country. They were trespassing. They walked toward the town of Mercury, in moonlight, taking their cues from coyote, kit fox, antelope squirrel, and quail. They moved quietly and deliberately through the maze of Joshua trees. When a hint of daylight appeared they rested, drinking tea and sharing their rations of food. The women closed their eyes. The time had come to protest with the heart, that to deny one's genealogy with the earth was to commit treason against one's soul.

At dawn, the women draped themselves in mylar, wrapping 44 long streamers of silver plastic around their arms to blow in the breeze. They wore clear masks, that became the faces of humanity. And when they arrived at the edge of Mercury, they carried all the butterflies of a summer day in their wombs. They paused to allow their courage to settle.

The town that forbids pregnant women and children to enter 45 because of radiation risks was asleep. The women moved through the streets as winged messengers, twirling around each other in slow motion, peeking inside homes and watching the easy sleep of men and women. They were astonished by such stillness and periodically would utter a shrill note or low cry just to verify life.

46   The residents finally awoke to these strange apparitions. Some simply stared. Others called authorities, and in time, the women were apprehended by wary soldiers dressed in desert fatigues. They were taken to a white, square building on the other edge of Mercury. When asked who they were and why they were there, the women replied, "We are mothers and we have come to reclaim the desert for our children."

47   The soldiers arrested them. As the ten women were blindfolded and handcuffed, they began singing.

> *You can't forbid us everything*
> *You can't forbid us to think—*
> *You can't forbid our tears to flow*
> *And you can't stop the songs that we sing.*

The women continued to sing louder and louder, until they heard the voices of their sisters moving across the mesa:

> *Ah ne nah, nah*
> *nin nah nah—*
> *Ah ne nah, nah*
> *nin nah nah—*
> *Nyaga mutzi*
> *oh ne nay—*
> *Nyaga mutzi*
> *oh ne nay—*

"Call for reinforcements," one soldier said.

48   "We have," interrupted one woman, "we have—and you have no idea of our numbers."

49   I crossed the line at the Nevada Test Site and was arrested with nine other Utahns for trespassing on military lands. They are still conducting nuclear tests in the desert. Ours was an act of civil disobedience. But as I walked toward the town of Mercury, it was more than a gesture of peace. It was a gesture on behalf of the Clan of One-Breasted Women.

50   As one officer cinched the handcuffs around my wrists, another frisked my body. She found a pen and a pad of paper tucked inside my left boot.

51   "And these?" she asked sternly.

"Weapons," I replied.   52

Our eyes met. I smiled. She pulled the leg of my trousers back   53
over my boot.

"Step forward, please," she said as she took my arm.   54

We were booked under an afternoon sun and bused to Tonopah,   55
Nevada. It was a two-hour ride. This was familiar country. The
Joshua trees standing their ground had been named by my ancestors, who believed they looked like prophets pointing west to the
Promised Land. These were the same trees that bloomed each
spring, flowers appearing like white flames in the Mojave. And I
recalled a full moon in May, when Mother and I had walked
among them, flushing out mourning doves and owls.

The bus stopped short of town. We were released.   56

The officials thought it was a cruel joke to leave us stranded in 57
the desert with no way to get home. What they didn't realize was
that we were home, soul-centered and strong, women who recognized the sweet smell of sage as fuel for our spirits.

1991
_____

Those Who Walk Away from Omelas

Ursula K. LeGuin

With a clamor of bells that set the swallows soaring, the Festival of   1
Summer came to the city. Omelas, bright-towered by the sea. The
rigging of the boats in harbor sparkled with flags. In the streets
between houses with red roofs and painted walls, between old
moss-grown gardens and under avenues of trees, past great parks
and public buildings, processions moved. Some were decorous:
old people in long stiff robes of mauve and gray, grave master
workmen, quiet, merry women carrying their babies and chatting
as they walked. In other streets the music beat faster, a shimmering of gong and tambourine, and the people went dancing, the

procession was a dance. Children dodged in and out, their high calls rising like the swallows' crossing flights over the music and the singing. All the processions wound toward the north side of the city, where on the great water-meadow called the Green Fields boys and girls, naked in the bright air, with mud-stained feet and ankles and long, lithe arms, exercised their restive horses before the race. The horses wore no gear at all but a halter without bit. Their manes were braided with streamers of silver, gold, and green. They flared their nostrils and pranced and boasted to one another; they were vastly excited, the horse being the only animal who has adopted our ceremonies as his own. Far off to the north and west the mountains stood up half encircling Omelas on her bay. The air of morning was so clear that the snow still crowning the Eighteen Peaks burned with white-gold fire across the miles of sunlit air, under the dark blue of the sky. There was just enough wind to make the banners that marked the racecourse snap and flutter now and then. In the silence of the broad green meadows one could hear the music winding through the city streets, farther and nearer and ever approaching, a cheerful faint sweetness of the air that from time to time trembled and gathered together and broke out into the great joyous clanging of the bells.

2   Joyous! How is one to tell about joy? How describe the citizens of Omelas?

3   They were not simple folk, you see, though they were happy. But we do not say the words of cheer much any more. All smiles have become archaic. Given a description such as this one tends to make certain assumptions. Given a description such as this one tends to look next for the King, mounted on a splendid stallion and surrounded by his noble knights or perhaps in a golden litter borne by great-muscled slaves. But there was no king. They did not use swords, or keep slaves. They were not barbarians. I do not know the rules and laws of their society, but I suspect that they were singularly few. As they did without monarchy and slavery, so they also got on without the stock exchange, the advertisement, the secret police, and the bomb. Yet I repeat that theses were not simple folk, not dulcet shepherds, noble savages, bland utopians. They were not less complex than us. The trouble is that we have a bad habit, encouraged by pedants and sophisticates, of considering

happiness as something rather stupid. Only pain is intellectual, only evil interesting. This is the treason of the artist: a refusal to admit the banality of evil and the terrible boredom of pain. If you can't lick 'em, join 'em. If it hurts, repeat it. But to praise despair is to condemn delight, to embrace violence is to lose hold of everything else. We have almost lost hold; we can no longer describe a happy man, nor make any celebration of joy. How can I tell you about the people of Omelas? They were not naïve and happy children—though their children were, in fact, happy. They were mature, intelligent, passionate adults whose lives were not wretched. O miracle! but I wish I could describe it better. I wish I could convince you. Omelas sounds in my words like a city in a fairy tale, long ago and far away, once upon a time. Perhaps it would be best if you imagined it as your own fancy bids, assuming it will rise to the occasion, for certainly I cannot suit you all. For instance, how about technology? I think that there would be no cars or helicopters in and above the streets; this follows from the fact that the people of Omelas are happy people. Happiness is based on a just discrimination of what is necessary, what is neither necessary nor destructive, and what is destructive. In the middle category, however—that of the unnecessary but undestructive, that of comfort, luxury, exuberance, etc.—they could perfectly well have central heating, subway trains, washing machines, and all kinds of marvelous devices not yet invented here, floating light-sources, fuelless power, a cure for the common cold. Or they could have none of that: it doesn't matter. As you like it. I incline to think that people from towns up and down the coast have been coming in to Omelas during the last days before the Festival on very fast little trains and double-decked trams and that the train station of Omelas is actually the handsomest building in town, though plainer than the magnificent Farmers' Market. But even granted trains, I fear that Omelas so far strikes some of you as goody-goody. Smiles, bells, parades, horses, bleh. If so, please add an orgy. If an orgy would help, don't hesitate. Let us not, however, have temples from which issue beautiful nude priests and priestesses already half in ecstasy and ready to copulate with any man or woman, lover or stranger, who desires union with the deep godhead of the blood, although that was my first idea. But really it would be better not to have any temples in Omelas—at least, not manned temples. Religion yes, clergy no. Surely the beautiful nudes can just wander about, offering themselves like divine soufflés to the hunger of the needy and the rapture of the flesh. Let them join the processions. Let tambourines be struck above the copulations, and the glory of desire be proclaimed upon the gongs, and (a not unimportant point) let the offspring of these delightful rituals be beloved and looked after by all. One thing I know there is none of in Omelas is guilt. But what else should there be? I thought at first there were no drugs, but that is puritanical. For those who like it, the faint insistent sweetness of *drooz* may perfume the ways of the city, *drooz* which first brings a great lightness and brilliance to the mind and limbs, and then after some hours a dreamy languor, and wonderful visions at last of the very arcana and inmost secrets of the Universe, as well as exciting the pleasure of sex beyond all belief; and it is not habit-forming. For more modest tastes I think there ought to be beer. What else, what else belongs in the joyous city? The sense of victory, surely, the celebration of courage. But as we did without clergy, let us do without soldiers. The joy built upon successful slaughter is not the right kind of joy; it will not do; it is fearful and it is trivial. A boundless and generous contentment, a magnanimous triumph felt not against some outer enemy but in communion with the finest and fairest in the souls of all men everywhere and the splendor of the world's summer: this is what swells the hearts of the people of Omelas, and the victory they celebrate is that of life. I really don't think many of them need to take *drooz*.

4   Most of the processions have reached the Green Fields by now. A marvelous smell of cooking goes forth from the red and blue tents of the provisioners. The faces of small children are amiably sticky; in the benign gray beard of a man a couple of crumbs of rich pastry are entangled. The youths and girls have mounted their horses and are beginning to group around the starting line of the course. An old woman, small, fat, and laughing, is passing out flowers from a basket, and tall young men wear her flowers in their shining hair. A child of nine or ten sits at the edge of the crowd, alone, playing on a wooden flute. Please pause to listen, and they smile, but they do not speak to him, for he never ceases

playing and never sees them, his dark eyes wholly rapt in the sweet, thin magic of the tune.

He finishes, and slowly lowers his hands holding the wooden flute. 5

As if that little private silence were the signal, all at once a 6 trumpet sounds from the pavillion near the starting line: imperious, melancholy, piercing. The horses rear on their slender legs, and some of them neigh in answer. Sober-faced, the young riders stroke the horses' necks and soothe them, whispering, "Quiet, quiet, there my beauty, my hope. . . . " They begin to form in rank along the starting line. The crowds along the racecourse are like a field of grass and flowers in the wind. The Festival of Summer has begun.

Do you believe? Do you accept the festival, the city, the joy? 7 No? Then let me describe one more thing.

In a basement under one of the beautiful public buildings of 8 Omelas, or perhaps in the cellar of one of its spacious private homes, there is a room. It has one locked door, and no window. A little light seeps in dustily between cracks in the boards, second-hand from a cobwebbed window somewhere across the cellar. In one corner of the little room a couple of mops, with stiff, clotted, foul-smelling heads, stand near a rusty bucket. The floor is dirt, a little damp to the touch, as cellar dirt usually is. The room is about three paces long and two wide: a mere broom closet or disused tool room. In the room a child is sitting. It could be a boy or a girl. It looks about six, but actually is nearly ten. It is feeble-minded. Perhaps it was born defective, or perhaps it has become imbecile through fear, malnutrition, and neglect. It picks its nose and occa-sionally fumbles vaguely with its toes or genitals, as it sits hunched in the corner farthest from the bucket and the two mops. It is afraid of the mops. It finds them horrible. It shuts its eyes, but it knows the mops are still standing there; and the door is locked; and nobody will come. The door is always locked; and nobody ever comes, except that sometimes—the child has no understand-ing of time or interval—sometimes the door rattles terribly and opens, and a person, or several people, are there. One of them may come in and kick the child to make it stand up. The others never come close, but peer in at it with frightened, disgusted eyes. The food bowl and the water jug are hastily filled, the door is

locked, the eyes disappear. The people at the door never say anything, but the child, who has not always lived in the tool room,
and can remember sunlight and its mother's voice, sometimes
speaks. "I will be good," it says. "Please let me out, I will be
good!" They never answer. The child used to scream for help at
night, and cry a good deal, but now it only makes a kind of whining, "eh-haa, eh-haa," and it speaks less and less often. It is so thin
there are no calves to its legs; its belly protrudes; it lives on a half-
bowl of corn meal and grease a day. It is naked. Its buttocks and
thighs are a mass of festered sores, as it sits in its own excrement
continually.

9   They all know it is there, all the people of Omelas. Some of
them have come to see it, others are content merely to know it is
there. They all know that it has to be there. Some of them understand why, and some do not, but they all understand that their
happiness, the beauty of their city, the tenderness of their friendships, the health of their children, the wisdom of their scholars,
the skill of their makers, even the abundance of their harvest and
the kindly weathers of their skies, depend wholly on this child's
abominable misery.

10   This is usually explained to children when they are between
eight and twelve, whenever they seem capable of understanding;
and most of those who come to see the child are young people,
though often enough an adult comes, or comes back, to see the
child. No matter how well the matter has been explained to them,
these young spectators are always shocked and sickened at the
sight. They feel disgust, which they had thought themselves superior to. They feel anger, outrage, impotence, despite all the explanations. They would like to do something for the child. But
there is nothing they can do. If the child were brought up into the
sunlight out of that vile place, if it were cleaned and fed and comforted, that would be a good thing, indeed; but if it were done, in
that day and hour all the prosperity and beauty and delight of
Omelas would wither and be destroyed. Those are the terms. To
exchange all the goodness and grace of every life in Omelas for
that single, small improvement: to throw away the happiness of
thousands for the chance of the happiness of one: that would be to
let guilt within the walls indeed.

The terms are strict and absolute; there may not even be a 11 kind word spoken to the child.

Often the young people go home in tears, or in a tearless rage, 12 when they have seen the child and faced this terrible paradox. They may brood over it for weeks or years. But as time goes on they begin to realize that even if the child could be released, it would not get much good of its freedom: a little vague pleasure of warmth and food, no doubt, but little more. It is too degraded and imbecile to know any real joy. It has been afraid too long ever to be free of fear. Its habits are too uncouth for it to respond to humane treatment. Indeed, after so long it would probably be wretched without walls about it to protect it, and darkness for its eyes, and its own excrement to sit in. Their tears at the bitter injustice dry when they begin to perceive the terrible justice of reality and to ac- cept it. Yet it is their tears and anger, the trying of their generosity and the acceptance of their helplessness, which are perhaps the true source of the splendor of their lives. Theirs is no vapid, irre- sponsible happiness. They know that they, like the child, are not free. They know compassion. It is the existence of the child, and their knowledge of its existence, that makes possible the nobility of their architecture, the poignancy of their music, the profundity of their science. It is because of the child that they are so gentle with children. They know that if the wretched one were not there snivelling in the dark, the other one, the flute-player, could make no joyful music as the young riders line up in their beauty for the race in the sunlight of the first morning of summer.

Now do you believe in them? Are they not more credible? But 13 there is one more thing to tell, and this is quite incredible.

At times one of the adolescent girls or boys who go to see the 14 child does not go home to weep or rage, does not, in fact, go home at all. Sometimes also a man or woman much older falls silent for a day or two, and then leaves home. These people go out into the street, and walk down the street alone. They keep walking, and walk straight out of the city of Omelas, through the beautiful gates. They keep walking across the farmlands of Omelas. Each one goes alone, youth or girl, man or woman. Night falls; the traveler must pass down village streets, between the houses with yellow-lit windows, and on out into the darkness of the fields. Each alone, they go west or north, toward the mountains. They go on. They leave Omelas, they walk ahead into the darkness, and they do not come back. The place they go toward is a place even less imaginable to most of us than the city of happiness. I cannot describe it at all. It is possible that it does not exist. But they seem to know where they are going, the ones who walk away from Omelas.

1973

The Ultimate Therapy: Commercial Eugenics on the Eve of the Biotech Century

Jeremy Rifkin

1 While the twentieth century was shaped largely by the spectacular breakthroughs in the fields of physics and chemistry, the twenty-first century will belong to the biological sciences. Scientists around the world are quickly deciphering the genetic code of life, unlocking the mystery of millions of years of biological evolution on Earth. Global life science companies, in turn, are beginning to exploit the new advances in biology in a myriad of ways, laying the economic framework for the coming Biotech Century.

2   Genes are the raw resource of the new economic epoch and are already being used in a variety of business fields—including agriculture, animal husbandry, energy, bioremediation, building and packaging materials, pharmaceuticals, and food and drink—to fashion a bio-industrial world. Nowhere is the new genetic commerce likely to have a bigger impact, however, than in human medicine. For the first time in history, scientific tools are becoming available to manipulate the genetic instructions in human cells. Human gene screening and therapy raise the very real possibility that we might be able to engineer the genetic blueprints of our own species and begin to redirect the future course of our biological evolution on Earth. The new gene splicing techniques will

make it potentially possible to transform individuals and future generations into "works of art," continually updating and editing their DNA codes to enhance physical and mental health. Breakthroughs in genetic technology are bringing us to the edge of a new eugenics era with untold consequences for present and future generations and for civilization itself.

In less than seven years, the global life science companies will 3 hold patents on most of the 100,000 genes that make up the human race as well as patents on the cell lines, tissues, and organs of our species, giving them unprecedented power to dictate the terms by which we and future generations will live our lives. The concentration of power in the global pharmaceutical industry has already reached staggering proportions. The world's ten major pharmaceutical companies currently control 47 percent of the $197 billion pharmaceutical market. The implications of a new market-drive eugenics are enormous and far reaching. Indeed, commercial eugenics could become the defining social dynamic of the new century.

FRIENDLY EUGENICS

Over the next ten years, molecular biologists say they will locate 4 specific genes associated with several thousand genetic diseases. In the past, a parent's genetic history provided some clues to genetic inheritance, but there was still no way to know for sure whether specific genetic traits would be passed on. In the future, the guesswork will be increasingly eliminated, posing a moral dilemma for prospective parents. Parents will have at their disposal an increasingly accurate readout of their individual genetic make-ups, and will be able to predict the statistical probability of a specific genetic disorder being passed on to their children as a result of their biological union.

To avoid the emotional anguish of such decisions, some 5 young people are likely to opt for prevention and avoid marrying someone of the wrong "genotype" for fear of passing along serious genetic diseases to their offspring. Already, part of the Orthodox Jewish community in the United States has established a nationwide program to screen all young Jewish men and women for Tay-Sachs disease. Every young Jew is encouraged to take the test. The results are made available in an easily accessible database to allow young eligible men and women to choose their dating partners with genotype in mind.

6   Some ethicists argue that such programs will become far more commonplace, placing a "genetic stigma" on young people. There's ample precedent for concern. Researchers report that when sickle cell anemia was screened for in Greece, nearly 23 percent of the population was found to have the trait. Fearing stigmatization, many of the carriers concealed their test results, believing that public exposure would seriously jeopardize their marriage prospects.

7   When researchers at the Johns Hopkins Medical Center recently discovered a genetic alteration in one out of every six Jews of Eastern European ancestry that doubles their risk of getting colon cancer, many in the Jewish community began to express their concern that the Jewish population might be singled out and made the object of discrimination. The news of the "Jewish" cancer gene came on top of other discoveries linking breast and ovarian cancer, cystic fibrosis, Tay-Sachs, Gauchers, and Canavan's disease to Jewish blood lines. Of course, scientists point out that other groups are likely to have just as many genetic links to specific diseases, but that the Jewish population has received the most attention to date because "they constitute a well defined, easily identifiable and closely related community—exactly the kind that allows geneticists to start identifying disease-causing genes." Still, the explanations of the researchers were not enough to calm an anxious Jewish community who began to vent their feelings publicly. Amy Rutkin, the director of American affairs for Hadassah, the nation's largest Jewish membership organization, reported that in the aftermath of the colon cancer discovery, the organization has been "receiving phone calls indicating a certain amount of fear and confusion." Rutkin said that "people are asking, is too much research focused on the Jewish community and are we at risk of stigmatization?"

8   Health professionals worry about genetic stigmatization and especially the prospect of selecting potential mates based on

genotyping, but argue that it is still less onerous than selective abortion or sentencing a newborn to premature death or a life of chronic or debilitating illness. Not surprising, there is increasing talk of government mandated genetic testing of couples seeking marriage licenses. Even without a government requirement, it's likely that a growing number of potential marriage partners will want their future partner screened before committing themselves to a life-long relationship.

While genetic screening is already here, human genetic 9 engineering—gene therapy—is just around the corner. Genetic manipulation is of two kinds. In somatic therapy, intervention takes place only within non-sex (somatic) cells and the genetic changes do not transfer into the offspring. In germ line therapy, genetic changes are made in the sperm, egg or embryonic cells, and are passed along to future generations. Somatic gene surgery has been carried out in limited human clinical trials for more than seven years. Germ line experiments have been successfully carried out on mammals for more than a decade and researchers expect the first human trials to be conducted within the next several years.

Despite years of favorable media reports on various somatic 10 gene therapy experiments and the high expectations voiced by the medical establishment and the biotech industry, the results have, thus far, been so disappointing that the NIH itself was recently forced to acknowledge the fact and issue a sober warning to scientists conducting the experiments to stop making promises that cannot be kept. In an extensive survey of all 106 clinical trials of experimental gene therapies conducted over the past five years involving more than 597 patients, a panel of experts convened by the NIH reported that "clinical efficacy has not been definitively demonstrated at this time in any gene therapy protocol, despite anecdotal claims of successful therapy." Even Dr. Leroy B. Walters, a philosophy professor at Georgetown University and the chairperson of the NIH oversight committee that reviewed and approved all of the clinical trials, remarked in a moment of candor that he and the committee had not seen "any solid results yet" after years of experiments. Still, many of the staunchest supporters of the new gene therapies remain convinced that the techniques will bear fruit as methodologies and procedures are honed and new knowledge of the workings of the genes becomes more available to researchers and clinicians.

11   Far more controversial is the prospect of conducting human germ line therapy. Debate over genetic manipulation of human eggs, sperm, and embryonic cells has raged for more than fifteen years. In 1983, a cross-section of the nation's religious leaders and prominent scientists announced their opposition to such experiments, on eugenics grounds, and urged a worldwide ban. (The coalition was put together by The Foundation on Economic Trends.)

12   Programming genetic changes into the human germ line to direct the evolutionary development of future generations is the most radical human experiment ever contemplated and raises unprecedented moral, social, and environmental risks for the whole of humanity. Even so, a growing number of molecular biologists, medical practitioners, and pharmaceutical companies are anxious to take the gamble, convinced that controlling our evolutionary destiny is humankind's next great social frontier. Their arguments are couched in terms of personal health, individual choice, and collective responsibility for future generations.

13   Writing in *The Journal of Medicine and Philosophy*, Dr. Burke Zimmerman makes several points in defense of germ line cell therapy over somatic cell therapy. To begin with, he argues that the increasing use of somatic therapy is only likely to increase the number of survivors with defective genes in their germ lines—genes that will continue to accumulate and further "pollute" the genetic pool of the species, passing an increasing number of genetic problems onto succeeding generations. Secondly, although somatic therapy may be able to treat many disorders in which treatment lies in replacing populations of cells, it might never prove effective in addressing diseases involving solid tissues, organs, and functions dependent on structure—for example the brain—and therefore, germ line therapy is likely the only remedy, short of abortion, against such disorders.

14   Zimmerman and other proponents of germ line therapy argue for a broadening of the ethical mandate of the healing professions to include responsibility for the health of those not yet conceived. The interests of the patient, they say, should be extended to include the interests of "the entire genetic legacy that may result

from intervention in the germ line." Moreover, parents ought not to be denied their right as parents to make choices on how best to protect the health of their unborn children during pregnancy. To deny them the opportunity to take corrective action in the sex cells or at the early embryonic stage would be a serious breach of medical responsibility. Proponents of germ line therapy ask why millions of individuals need to be subjected to painful, intrusive, and potentially risky somatic therapy when the gene or genes responsible for their diseases could be more easily eliminated from the germ line, at less expense, and with less discomfort.

Finally, the health costs to society need to be factored into the   15 equation, say the advocates of germ line therapy. Although the costs of genetic intervention into the germ line to cure diseases are likely to remain high in the early years, the cost is likely to drop dramatically in the future as the methods and techniques become more refined. The lifetime cost of caring for generations of patients suffering from Parkinson's disease or severe Down's syndrome is likely to be far greater than simple prevention in the form of genetic intervention at the germ line level.

GENETIC RESPONSIBILITY

In the coming decades, scientists will learn more about how genes   16 function. They will become increasingly adept at turning genes "on" and "off." They will become more sophisticated in the techniques of recombining genes and altering genetic codes. At every step of the way, conscious decisions will have to be made as to which kinds of permanent changes in the biological codes of life are worth pursuing and which are not. A society and civilization steeped in "engineering" the gene pool of the planet cannot possibly hope to escape the kind of ongoing eugenics decisions that go hand in hand with each new advance in biotechnology. There will be enormous social pressure to conform with the underlying logic of genetic engineering, especially when it comes to its human applications.

Parents in the biotech century will be increasingly forced to   17 decide whether to take their chances with the traditional genetic lottery and use their own unaltered egg and sperm, knowing their children may inherit some "undesirable" traits, or undergo corrective gene changes on their sperm, egg, embryo, or fetus, or substitute egg or sperm from a donor through *in vitro* fertilization and surrogacy arrangements. If they choose to go with the traditional approach and let genetic fate determine their child's biological destiny, they could find themselves culpable if something goes dreadfully wrong in the developing fetus, something they could have avoided had they availed themselves of corrective genetic intervention at the sex cell or embryo stage.

18   In the Biotech Century, a parent's failure to correct genetic defects *in utero* might well be regarded as a heinous crime. Society may conclude that every parent has a responsibility to provide as safe and secure an environment as humanly possible for their unborn child. Not to do so might be considered a breach of parental duty for which the parents could be held morally, if not legally, liable. Mothers have already been held liable for having given birth to crack cocaine addicted babies and babies with fetal alcohol syndrome. Prosecutors have argued that mothers passing on these painful addictions to their unborn children are culpable under existing child abuse statutes, and ought to be held liable for the effect of their lifestyle on their babies.

19   Proponents of human genetic engineering argue that it would be cruel and irresponsible not to use this powerful new technology to eliminate serious "genetic disorders." The problem with this argument, says *The New York Times* in an editorial entitled, "Whether to Make Perfect Humans," is that "there is no discernible line to be drawn between making inheritable repair of genetic defects and improving the species." The *Times* rightly points out that once scientists are able to repair genetic defects, "it will become much harder to argue against additional genes that confer desired qualities, like better health, looks or brains."

20   If diabetes, sickle cell anemia, and cancer are to be prevented by altering the genetic makeup of individuals, why not proceed to other less serious "defects": myopia, color blindness, dyslexia, obesity, short stature? Indeed, what is to preclude a society from deciding that a certain skin color is a disorder? In the end, why would we ever say no to any alteration of the genetic code that

might enhance the well-being of our offspring? It would be difficult to imagine parents rejecting genetic modifications that promised to improve, in some way, the opportunities for their progeny.

It is likely that as new screening technologies become more   21
universally available, and genetic surgery at the embryonic and
fetal stage becomes more widely acceptable, the issue of parental
responsibility will be hotly debated, both in the courts and in the
legislatures. The very fact that parents will increasingly be able to
intervene to ensure the health of their child before birth, is likely
to raise the concomitant issue of the responsibilities and obligations to their unborn children. Why shouldn't parents be held responsible for taking proper care of their unborn child? For that
matter, why shouldn't parents be held liable for neglecting their
child's welfare in the womb in cases where they failed to or refused to screen for and correct genetic defects that could prove
harmful to their offspring?

With Americans already spending billions of dollars on cos-   22
metic surgery to improve their looks and psychotropic drugs to
alter their mood and behavior, the use of genetic therapies to enhance their unborn children also seems a likely prospect. According to a 1992 Harris poll, 43 percent of Americans "would approve
using gene therapy to improve babies' physical characteristics."
Many advocates of germ line intervention are already arguing for
enhancement therapy. They contend that the current debate over
corrective measures to address serious illnesses is too limited and
urge a more expansive discussion to include the advantage of enhancement therapy as well. As to the oft heard criticism that genetic enhancement will favor children of the rich at the expense of
children of the poor—as the rich will be the only ones capable of
paying for genetic enhancement of their offspring—proponents
argue that the children of well-off parents have always enjoyed
the advantages that wealth and inheritance can confer. Is it such a
leap, they ask rhetorically, to want to pass along genetic gifts to
their children along with material riches? Advocates ask us to
consider the positive side of germ line enhancement, even if it
gives an advantage to the children of those who can afford the
technology. "What about . . . increasing the number of talented
people. Wouldn't society be better off in the long run?" asks Dr.
Burke Zimmerman.

23   Perhaps not. Despite the growing enthusiasm among molecular biologists for engineering fundamental changes in the genetic code of human sex cells, it should be emphasized that treating genetic disorders by eliminating recessive traits at the germ line level is far different from treating genetic disorders by way of somatic gene surgery after birth. In the former instance, the genetic deletions can result, in the long run, in a dangerous narrowing of the human gene pool upon which future generations rely for making evolutionary adaptations to changing environments.

24   We learned, long ago, that recessive traits and mutations are essential players in the evolutionary schema. They are not mistakes, but rather variations, some of which become opportunities. Eliminating so-called "bad" genes risks depleting the genetic pool and limiting future evolutionary options. Recessive gene traits are far too complex and mercurial to condemn as simple errors in the code. We are, in fact, just beginning to learn of the many subtle and varied roles recessive gene traits play, some of which have been critically important in ensuring the survival of different ethnic and racial groups. For example, the sickle cell recessive trait protects against malaria. The cystic fibrosis recessive gene may play a role in protecting against cholera. To think of recessive traits and single gene disorders, then, as merely errors in the code, in need of reprogramming, is to lose sight of how things really work in the biological kingdom.

25   Somatic gene surgery, on the other hand, if it proves to be a safe, therapeutic way to treat serious diseases that can not be effectively treated by more conventional approaches, including preventive measures, would appear to have potential value.

26   Many biotech libertarians, however, disdain such distinctions. *The Economist* suggested, in a recent editorial, that society should move beyond old fashioned hand-wringing moralism on the subject and openly embrace the new commercial eugenics opportunities that will soon become available in the marketplace. The editors asked,

> What of genes that might make a good body better, rather than make a bad one good? Should people be able to retrofit themselves with extra neurotransmitters, to enhance various mental powers? Or to change the color of their skin? Or to help them run faster, or lift heavier weights?

The Economist editorial board made clear that its own biases   27
lay firmly with the marketplace. To them, the new commercial eugenics is about ensuring greater consumer freedom so that individuals can make of themselves and their heirs whatever they
choose. The editorial concluded with a ringing endorsement of
the new eugenics:

> The proper goal is to allow people as much choice as possible
> about what they do. To this end, making genes instruments of
> such freedom, rather than limits upon it, is a great step forward.

Dr. Robert Sinsheimer, a long-standing leader and driving   28
force in the field of molecular biology, laid out his eugenics vision
of the new man and woman of the biotech century:

> The old dreams of the cultural perfection of man were always
> sharply constrained by his inherited imperfections and limita-
> tions. . . . To foster his better traits and to curb his worse by cul-
> tural means alone has always been, while clearly not impossible,
> in many instances most difficult. . . . We now glimpse another
> route—the chance to ease the internal strains and heal the inter-
> nal flaws directly, to carry on and consciously perfect far beyond
> our present vision this remarkable product of two billion years of
> evolution. . . . The old eugenics would have required a continual
> selection for breeding of the fit, and a culling of the unfit. . . . The
> horizons of the new eugenics are in principle boundless—for we
> should have the potential to create new genes and new qualities
> yet undreamed. . . . Indeed, this concept marks a turning point in
> the whole evolution of life. For the first time in all time, a living
> creature understands its origin and can undertake to design its
> future. Even in the ancient myths man was constrained by
> essence. He could not rise above his nature to chart his destiny.
> Today we can envision that chance—and its dark companion of
> awesome choice and responsibility.

PERFECTING THE CODE

While the notion of consumer choice would appear benign, the   29
very idea of eliminating so-called genetic defects raises the troubling question of what is meant by the term "defective." Ethicist
Daniel Callahan of the Hastings Center penetrates to the core of the

problem when he observes that "behind the human horror at genetic defectiveness lurks . . . an image of the perfect human being. The very language of 'defect,' 'abnormality,' 'disease,' and 'risk' presupposes such an image, a kind of prototype of perfection."

30   The all consuming preoccupation with "defects" or "errors" among medical researchers and molecular biologists puts them very much at odds with most evolutionary biologists. When evolutionary biologists talk of "mutations," they have in mind the idea of "different 'readings' or 'versions'" of a relatively stable archetype. James Watson and Francis Crick's discovery of the DNA double helix in the 1950s, however, brought with it a new set of metaphors and a new language for describing biological processes which changed the way molecular biologists perceive genetic mutations. The primary building block of life was described as a code, a set of instructions, a program, to be unraveled and read. The early molecular biologists, many of whom had been trained first as physicists, were enamored with what they regarded as the universal explanatory power of the information sciences. Norbert Weiner's cybernetic model and modern communications and information theory provided a compelling new linguistic paradigm for redefining how we talk about both physical and biological phenomena. It is within the context of this new language that molecular biologists first began to talk of genetic variation as "errors" in the code rather than "mutations." The shift from the notion of genetic mutations in nature to genetic errors in codes represents a sea change in the way biologists approach their discipline, with profound repercussions for how we structure both our relationship to the natural world and our own human nature in the coming Biotech Century.

31   The very idea of engineering the human species—by making changes at the germ line level—is not too dissimilar from the idea of engineering a piece of machinery. An engineer is constantly in search of new ways to improve the performance of a machine. As soon as one set of defects is eliminated, the engineer immediately turns his attention to the next set of defects, always with the idea in mind of creating a more efficient machine. The notion of setting arbitrary limits to how much "improvement" is acceptable is alien to the entire engineering conception.

The new language of the information sciences has trans- 32
formed many molecular biologists from scientists to engineers, although they are, no doubt, little aware of the metamorphosis.
When molecular biologists speak of mutations and genetic diseases as errors in the code, the implicit, if not explicit, assumption
is that they should never have existed in the first place, that they
are "bugs," or mistakes that need to be deprogrammed or corrected. The molecular biologist, in turn, becomes the computing
engineer, the writer of codes, continually eliminating errors and
reprogramming instructions to upgrade both the program and the
performance. This is a dubious and dangerous role when we stop
to consider that every human being brings with him or her a number of lethal recessive genes. Do we then come to see ourselves as
miswired from the get-go, riddled with errors in our code? If that
be the case, against what ideal norm of perfection are we to be
measured? If every human being is made up of varying degrees of
error, then we search in vain for the norm, the ideal. What makes
the new language of molecular biology so subtly chilling is that it
risks creating a new archetype, a flawless, errorless, perfect being
to which to aspire—a new man and woman, like us, but without
the warts and wrinkles, vulnerabilities and frailties, that have defined our essence from the very beginning of our existence.

No wonder so many in the disability rights community are 33
becoming increasingly frightened of the new biology. They wonder, if in the new world coming, people like themselves will be
seen as errors in the code, mistakes to be eliminated, lives to be
prevented from coming into being. Then again, how tolerant are
the rest of us likely to be when we come to see everyone around
us as defective, as mistakes and errors in the code?

Already, genetic information is being used by schools, em- 34
ployers, insurance companies and governments to determine educational tracks, employment prospects, insurance premiums,
and security clearances, giving rise to a new and virulent form of
discrimination based on one's genetic profile. Even more chilling,
some genetic engineers envision a future with a small segment of
the human population engineered to "perfection" while others remain as flawed reminders of an outmoded evolutionary design.
Molecular biologist Lee Silver of Princeton University writes

about a not-too-distant future made up of two distinct biological classes which he refers to as the Gen Rich and Naturals. The Gen Rich, which account for 10 percent of the population, have been enhanced with synthetic genes and have become the rulers of society. They include Gen Rich businessmen, musicians, artists, intellectuals, and athletes, each enhanced with specific synthetic genes to allow them to succeed in their respective fields in ways not even conceivable among those born of nature's lottery.

35   At the center of this new genetic aristocracy are the Gen Rich scientists who are enhanced with special genetic traits that greatly increase their mental abilities, giving them the power to dictate the terms of future evolutionary advances on Earth. Silver says that:

> With the passage of time, the genetic distance between Naturals and the Gen Rich has become greater and greater, and now there is little movement up from the Natural to the Gen Rich class. . . . All aspects of the economy, the media, the entertainment industry and the knowledge industry are controlled by members of the Gen Rich class. . . . In contrast, Naturals work as low-paid service providers or as laborers. . . . Gen Rich and Natural children grow up and live in segregated social worlds where there is little chance for contact between them . . . [eventually] the Gen Rich class and the Natural class will become the Gen Rich humans and the Natural humans—entirely separate species with no ability to cross breed and with as much romantic interest in each other as a current human would have for a chimpanzee.

36   Silver acknowledges that the increasing polarization of society into a Gen Rich and Natural class might be unfair, but he is quick to add that wealthy parents have always been able to provide all sorts of advantages for their children. "Anyone who accepts the right of affluent parents to provide their children with an expensive private school education cannot use unfairness as a reason for rejecting the use of reprogenetic technologies," argues Silver. Like many of his colleagues, Silver is a strong advocate of the new genetic technologies. "In a society that values human freedom above all else," writes Silver, "it is hard to find any legitimate basis for restricting the use of reprogenetics."

37   If Silver's predictions about where the new technologies are heading are correct, we face the very real possibility of journeying

into a Huxlian world populated by Alphas, Betas, Gammas, and Deltas. In the new scenario, however, it's the global marketplace and consumer desire, not an oppressive government, that will likely be the ultimate arbiter of the new biology. In the final analysis, commercial eugenics, controlled by global life science companies and mediated by consumer sovereignty, might prove every bit as dangerous to the future prospects of our species as the shrill cries on behalf of purifying the best blood of the Aryan race more than half a century ago in Hitler's infamous Third Reich.

The question, then, is whether or not humanity should begin [38] the process of engineering future generations of human beings by technological design in the laboratory. What are the potential consequences of embarking on a course whose final goal is the "perfection" of the human species?

Today, the ultimate exercise of power is within grasp: the ability to control, at the most fundamental level, the future lives of [39] unborn generations by engineering their biological life process in advance, making them a partial hostage of their own architecturally designed blueprints. I use the word "partial" because, like many others, I believe that environment is a major contributing factor in determining one's life course. It is also true, however, that one's genetic makeup plays a role in helping to shape one's destiny. Genetic engineering, then, represents the power of authorship, albeit limited authorship. Being able to engineer even minor changes in the physical and behavioral characteristics of future generations represents a new era in human history. Never before has such power over human life even been a possibility.

Human genetic engineering raises the very real spectre of a [40] distopian future where the haves and have-nots are increasingly divided and separated by genetic endowment, genetic discrimination is widely practiced, and traditional notions of democracy and equality give way to the creation of a genetocracy based on one's "genetic qualifications." The driving force of this new bioindustrial world are giant life science companies whose control over genetic resources and the new transformative biotechnologies give them the clout to act as commercial agents for a new eugenics era.

COMPETING BIOTECH VISIONS

41 Many in the life sciences field would have us believe that the new gene splicing technologies are irrepressible and irreversible and that any attempt to oppose their introduction is both futile and retrogressive. They never stop to even consider the possibility that the new genetic science might be used in a wholly different manner than is currently being proposed. The fact is, the corporate agenda is only one of two potential paths into the Biotech Century. It is possible that the growing number of anti-eugenic activists around the world might be able to ignite a global debate around alternative uses of the new science—approaches that are less invasive, more sustainable and humane and that conserve and protect the genetic rights of future generations.

42   While the global life science companies favor the introduction and widespread use of gene therapy—genetic engineering—to cure diseases, and enhance the physical, emotional and mental well-being of individuals, a growing number of holistically minded geneticists and health practitioners are beginning to use the new data being generated by the human genome project in a very different way. They are exploring the relationship between genetic mutations and environmental triggers with the hope of fashioning a more sophisticated, scientifically based understanding and approach to preventive health. More than 70 percent of all deaths in the United States and other industrialized countries are attributable to what physicians refer to as "diseases of affluence." Heart attacks, strokes, breast, colon and prostate cancer, and diabetes are among the most common diseases of affluence. While each individual has varying genetic susceptibilities to these diseases, environmental factors, including diet and lifestyle, are major contributing elements that can trigger genetic mutations. Heavy cigarette smoking, high levels of alcohol consumption, diets rich in animal fats, the use of pesticides and other poisonous chemicals, contaminated water and food, polluted air and sedentary living habits with little or no exercise, have been shown, in study after study, to cause genetic mutations and lead to the onset of many of these high profile diseases.

The mapping and sequencing of the human genome is pro- 43
viding researchers with vital new information on recessive gene
traits and genetic predispositions for a range of illnesses. Still,
little research has been done, to date, on how genetic predispositions interact with toxic materials in the environment, the metab-
olizing of different foods, and lifestyle to affect genetic mutations
and phenotypical expression. The new holistic approach to human medicine views the individual genome as part of an embedded organismic structure continually interacting with and being
affected by the environment in which it unfolds. The effort is
geared toward using increasingly sophisticated genetic and environmental information to prevent genetic mutations from occurring. (It needs to be emphasized, however, that a number of
genetic diseases appear to be unpreventable and immune to environmental mediation.)

Some would argue that, in the case of medicine and any num- 44
ber of other fields, there is no reason why both approaches to applied science can't live side by side, each complementing and
augmenting the other. In reality, the commercial market favors
the more reductionist approach for the obvious reason that for
now, at least, that's where the money is to be made. While there
is certainly a growing market for preventive health practices,
programs, and products, far more money is invested in "illness"
based medicine. That could change, but it would require a
paradigm shift in the way we think about science and its applications, with awareness of and support for a science founded in
systems thinking and sensitive to the twin notions of diversity
and interdependence.

While it might seem highly improbable, even inconceivable, 45
to most of the principal players in this new technology revolution
that genetic engineering, with all of its potential promise, might
ultimately be rejected, we need remind ourselves that just a generation ago, it would have been just as inconceivable to imagine
the partial abandonment of nuclear energy which had for years
been so enthusiastically embraced as the ultimate salvation for a
society whose appetite for energy appeared nearly insatiable. It is

also possible that society will accept some and reject other uses of genetic engineering in the coming biotech century. For example, one could make a solid case for genetic screening—with the appropriate safeguards in place—to better predict the onslaught of disabling diseases, especially those that can be prevented with early treatment. The new gene-splicing technologies also open the door to a new generation of lifesaving pharmaceutical products. On the other hand, the use of gene therapy to make corrective changes in the human germ line, affecting the options of future generations, is far more problematic. Society may well say yes to some of the genetic engineering options and no to others. After all, nuclear technology has been harnessed effectively for uses other than creating energy and making bombs.

46   Even rejection of some genetic engineering technologies then, does not mean that the wealth of genomic and environmental information being collected couldn't be used in other ways. While the twenty-first century will be the Age of Biology, the technological application of the knowledge we gain can take a variety of forms. To believe that genetic engineering is the only way to apply our new knowledge of biology and the life sciences is limiting and keeps us from entertaining other options which might prove even more effective in addressing the needs and fulfilling the dreams of current and future generations.

47   The biotech revolution will affect every aspect of our lives. The way we eat; the way we date and marry; the way we have our babies; the way our children are raised and educated; the way we work; the way we engage in politics; the way we express our faith; the way we perceive the world around us and our place in it—all of our individual and shared realities will be deeply touched by the new technologies of the Biotech Century. Surely, these very "personal" technologies deserve to be widely discussed and debated by the public at large before they become a ubiquitous part of our daily lives.

1998

Of Headless Mice and Men

Charles Krauthammer

Last year Dolly the cloned sheep was received with wonder, tit- 1
ters and some vague apprehension. Last week the announcement
by a Chicago physicist that he is assembling a team to produce the
first human clone occasioned yet another wave of Brave New
World anxiety. But the scariest news of all—and largely overlooked—comes from two obscure labs, at the University of Texas
and at the University of Bath. During the past four years, one
group created headless mice; the other, headless tadpoles.

For sheer Frankenstein wattage, the purposeful creation of 2
these animal monsters has no equal. Take the mice. Researchers
found the gene that tells the embryo to produce the head. They
deleted it. They did this in a thousand mice embryos, four of
which were born. I use the term loosely. Having no way to
breathe, the mice died instantly.

Why then create them? The Texas researchers want to learn 3
how genes determine embryo development. But you don't have
to be a genius to see the true utility of manufacturing headless
creatures: for their organs—fully formed, perfectly useful, ripe for
plundering.

Why should you be panicked? Because humans are next. "It 4
would almost certainly be possible to produce human bodies
without a forebrain," Princeton biologist Lee Silver told the London Sunday Times. "These human bodies without any semblance
of consciousness would not be considered persons, and thus it
would be perfectly legal to keep them 'alive' as a future source of
organs."

"Alive." Never have a pair of quotation marks loomed so 5
ominously. Take the mouse–frog technology, apply it to humans,
combine it with cloning, and you are become a god: with a single
cell taken from, say, your finger, you produce a headless replica of

yourself, a mutant twin, arguably lifeless, that becomes your own personal, precisely tissue-matched organ farm.

6   There are, of course, technical hurdles along the way. Suppressing the equivalent "head" gene in man. Incubating tiny infant organs to grow into larger ones that adults could use. And creating artificial wombs (as per Aldous Huxley), given that it might be difficult to recruit sane women to carry headless fetuses to their birth/death.

7   It won't be long, however, before these technical barriers are breached. The ethical barriers are already cracking. Lewis Wolpert, professor of biology at University College, London, finds producing headless humans "personally distasteful" but, given the shortage of organs, does not think distaste is sufficient reason not to go ahead with something that would save lives. And Professor Silver not only sees "nothing wrong, philosophically or rationally," with producing headless humans for organ harvesting; he wants to convince a skeptical public that it is perfectly O.K.

8   When prominent scientists are prepared to acquiesce in—or indeed encourage—the deliberate creation of deformed and dying quasihuman life, you know we are facing a bioethical abyss. Human beings are ends, not means. There is no grosser corruption of biotechnology than creating a human mutant and disemboweling it at our pleasure for spare parts.

9   The prospect of headless human clones should put the whole debate about "normal" cloning in a new light. Normal cloning is less a treatment for infertility than a treatment for vanity. It is a way to produce an exact genetic replica of yourself that will walk the earth years after you're gone.

10   But there is a problem with a clone. It is not really you. It is but a twin, a perfect John Doe Jr., but still a junior. With its own independent consciousness, it is, alas, just a facsimile of you.

11   The headless clone solves the facsimile problem. It is a gateway to the ultimate vanity: immortality. If you create a real clone, you cannot transfer your consciousness into it to truly live on. But if you create a headless clone of just your body, you have created

a ready source of replacement parts to keep you—your consciousness—going indefinitely.

Which is why one form of cloning will inevitably lead to the 12
other. Cloning is the technology of narcissism, and nothing satisfies
narcissism like immortality. Headlessness will be cloning's crowning achievement.

The time to put a stop to this is now. Dolly moved President 13
Clinton to create a commission that recommended a temporary
ban on human cloning. But with physicist Richard Seed threatening to clone humans, and with headless animals already here, we
are past the time for toothless commissions and meaningless bans.

Clinton banned federal funding of human-cloning research, 14
of which there is none anyway. He then proposed a five-year ban
on cloning. This is not enough. Congress should ban human
cloning now. Totally. And regarding one particular form, it should
be draconian: the deliberate creation of headless humans must be
made a crime, indeed a capital crime. If we flinch in the face of
this high-tech barbarity, we'll deserve to live in the hell it heralds.

1998

The Virtual Community

Howard Rheingold

In the summer of 1986, my then-two-year-old daughter picked up 1
a tick. There was this blood-bloated *thing* sucking on our baby's
scalp, and we weren't quite sure how to go about getting it off.
My wife, Judy, called the pediatrician. It was eleven o'clock in the
evening. I logged onto the WELL. I got my answer online within
minutes from a fellow with the improbable but genuine name of
Flash Gordon, M.D. I had removed the tick by the time Judy got
the callback from the pediatrician's office.

What amazed me wasn't just the speed with which we ob- 2
tained precisely the information we needed to know, right when
we needed to know it. It was also the immense inner sense of se-

curity that comes with discovering that real people—most of them parents, some of them nurses, doctors, and midwives—are available, around the clock, if you need them. There is a magic protective circle around the atmosphere of this particular conference. We're talking about our sons and daughters in this forum, not about our computers or our opinions about philosophy, and many of us feel that this tacit understanding sanctifies the virtual space.

3   The atmosphere of the Parenting conference—the attitudes people exhibit to each other in the tone of what they say in public—is part of what continues to attract me. People who never have much to contribute in political debate, technical argument, or intellectual gamesmanship turn out to have a lot to say about raising children. People you knew as fierce, even nasty, intellectual opponents in other contexts give you emotional support on a deeper level, parent to parent, within the boundaries of Parenting, a small but warmly human corner of cyberspace.

4   Here is a short list of examples from the hundreds of separate topics available for discussion in the Parenting conference. Each of these entries is the name of a conversation that includes scores or hundreds of individual contributions spread over a period of days or years, like a long, topical cocktail party you can rewind back to the beginning to find out who said what before you got there.

> *Great Expectations: You're Pregnant: Now What? Part III*
>
> *What's Bad About Children's TV?*
>
> *Movies: The Good, the Bad, and the Ugly*
>
> *Initiations and Rites of Passage*
>
> *Brand New Well Baby!!*
>
> *How Does Being a Parent Change Your Life?*
>
> *Tall Teenage Tales (cont.)*
>
> *Guilt*
>
> *MOTHERS*
>
> *Vasectomy—Did It Hurt?*
>
> *Introductions! Who Are We?*

Fathers (Continued)

Books for Kids, Section Two

Gay and Lesbian Teenagers

Children and Spirituality

Great Parks for Kids

Quality Toys

Parenting in an Often-Violent World

Children's Radio Programming

New WELL Baby

Home Schooling

Newly Separated/Divorced Fathers

Another Well Baby—Carson Arrives in Seattle!

Single Parenting

Uncle Philcat's Back Fence: Gossip Here!

Embarrassing Moments

Kids and Death

All the Poop on Diapers

Pediatric Problems—Little Sicknesses and Sick Little Ones

Talking with Kids About the Prospect of War

Dealing with Incest and Abuse

Other People's Children

When They're Crying

Pets for Kids

People who talk about a shared interest, albeit a deep one 5
such as being a parent, don't often disclose enough about themselves as whole individuals online to inspire real trust in others. In
the case of the subcommunity of the Parenting conference, a few
dozen of us, scattered across the country, few of whom rarely if
ever saw the others face-to-face, had a few years of minor crises to
knit us together and prepare us for serious business when it came

our way. Another several dozen read the conference regularly but contribute only when they have something important to add. Hundreds more every week read the conference without comment, except when something extraordinary happens. . . .

6   Many people are alarmed by the very idea of a virtual community, fearing that is another step in the wrong direction, substituting more technological ersatz for yet another natural resource or human freedom. These critics often voice their sadness at what people have been reduced to doing in a civilization that worships technology, decrying the circumstances that lead some people into such pathetically disconnected lives that they prefer to find their companions on the other side of a computer screen. There is a seed of truth in this fear, for virtual communities require more than words on a screen at some point if they intend to be other than ersatz.

7   Some people—many people—don't do well in spontaneous spoken interaction, but turn out to have valuable contributions to make in a conversation in which they have time to think about what to say. These people, who might constitute a significant proportion of the population, can find written communication more authentic than the face-to-face kind. Who is to say that this preference for one mode of communication—informal written text—is somehow less authentically human than audible speech? Those who critique CMC because some people use it obsessively hit an important target, but miss a great deal more when they don't take into consideration people who use the medium for genuine human interaction. Those who find virtual communities cold places point at the limits of the technology, its most dangerous pitfalls, and we need to pay attention to those boundaries. But these critiques don't tell us how Philcat and Lhary and the Allisons and my own family could have found the community of support and information we found in the WELL when we needed it. And those of us who do find communion in cyberspace might do well to pay attention to the way the medium we love can be abused. . . .

8   Because we cannot see one another in cyberspace, gender, age, national origin, and physical appearance are not apparent unless a person wants to make such characteristics public. People whose physical handicaps make it difficult to form new

friendships find that virtual communities treat them as they always wanted to be treated—as thinkers and transmitters of ideas
and feeling beings, not carnal vessels with a certain appearance
and way of walking and talking (or not walking and not talking).

One of the few things that enthusiastic members of virtual 9
communities in Japan, England, France, and the United States all
agree on is that expanding their circle of friends is one of the most
important advantages of computer conferencing. CMC is a way to
meet people, whether or not you feel the need to affiliate with
them on a community level. It's a way of both making contact
with and maintaining a distance from others. The way you meet
people in cyberspace puts a different spin on affiliation: in traditional kinds of communities, we are accustomed to meeting people, then getting to know them; in virtual communities, you can
get to know people and then choose to meet them. Affiliation also
can be far more ephemeral in cyberspace because you can get to
know people you might never meet on the physical plane.

How does anybody find friends? In the traditional commu- 10
nity, we search through our pool of neighbors and professional
colleagues, of acquaintances and acquaintances of acquaintances,
in order to find people who share our values and interests. We
then exchange information about one another, disclose and discuss our mutual interests, and sometimes we become friends. In a
virtual community we can go directly to the place where our favorite subjects are being discussed, then get acquainted with people who share our passions or who use words in a way we find
attractive. In this sense, the topic is the address: you can't simply
pick up a phone and ask to be connected with someone who
wants to talk about Islamic art or California wine, or someone
with a three-year-old daughter or a forty-year-old Hudson; you
can, however, join a computer conference on any of those topics,
then open a public or private correspondence with the previously
unknown people you find there. Your chances of making friends
are magnified by orders of magnitude over the old methods of
finding a peer group.

You can be fooled about people in cyberspace, behind the 11
cloak of words. But that can be said about telephones or face-to-
face communication as well; computer-mediated communications

provide new ways to fool people, and the most obvious identity swindles will die out only when enough people learn to use the medium critically. In some ways, the medium will, by its nature, be forever biased toward certain kinds of obfuscation. It will also be a place that people often end up revealing themselves far more intimately than they would be inclined to do without the intermediation of screens and pseudonyms. . . .

12   Three different kinds of social criticisms of technology are relevant to claims of CMC as a means of enhancing democracy. One school of criticism emerges from the longer-term history of communications media, and focuses on the way electronic communications media already have preempted public discussions by turning more and more of the content of the media into advertisements for various commodities—a process these critics call commodification. Even the political process, according to this school of critics, has been turned into a commodity. The formal name for this criticism is "the commodification of the public sphere." The public sphere is what these social critics claim we used to have as citizens of a democracy, but have lost to the tide of commodization. The public sphere is also the focus of the hopes of online activists, who see CMC as a way of revitalizing the open and widespread discussions among citizens that feed the roots of democratic societies.

13   The second school of criticism focuses on the fact that high-bandwidth interactive networks could be used in conjunction with other technologies as a means of surveillance, control, and disinformation as well as a conduit for useful information. This direct assault on personal liberty is compounded by a more diffuse erosion of old social values due to the capabilities of new technologies; the most problematic example is the way traditional notions of privacy are challenged on several fronts by the ease of collecting and disseminating detailed information about individuals via cyberspace technologies. When people use the convenience of electronic communication or transaction, we leave invisible digital trails; now that technologies for tracking those trails are maturing, there is cause to worry. The spreading use of computer matching to piece together the digital trails we all leave in cyberspace is one indication of privacy problems to come.

Along with all the person-to-person communications ex- 14
changed on the world's telecommunications networks are vast
flows of other kinds of personal information—credit information,
transaction processing, health information. Most people take it for
granted that no one can search through all the electronic transactions that move through the world's networks in order to pin
down an individual for marketing—or political—motives. Remember the "knowbots" that would act as personal servants,
swimming in the info-tides, fishing for information to suit your
interests? What if people could turn loose knowbots to collect all
the information digitally linked to *you*? What if the Net and cheap,
powerful computers give that power not only to governments
and large corporations but to everyone?

Every time we travel or shop or communicate, citizens of the 15
credit-card society contribute to streams of information that travel
between point of purchase, remote credit bureaus, municipal
and federal information systems, crime information databases,
central transaction databases. And all these other forms of cyberspace interaction take place via the same packet-switched, high-
bandwidth network technology—those packets can contain
transactions as well as video clips and text files. When these
streams of information begin to connect together, the unscrupulous or would-be tyrants can use the Net to catch citizens in a
more ominous kind of net.

The same channels of communication that enable citizens 16
around the world to communicate with one another also allow
government and private interests to gather information about
them. This school of criticism is known as Panoptic in reference to
the perfect prison proposed in the eighteenth century by Jeremy
Bentham—a theoretical model that happens to fit the real capabilities of today's technologies.

Another category of critical claim deserves mention, despite 17
the rather bizarre and incredible imagery used by its most well
known spokesmen—the hyper-realist school. These critics believe
that information technologies have already changed what used to
pass for reality into a slicked-up electronic simulation. Twenty
years before the United States elected a Hollywood actor as president, the first hyper-realists pointed out how politics had become

a movie, a spectacle that raised the old Roman tactic of bread and circuses to the level of mass hypnotism. We live in a hyper-reality that was carefully constructed to mimic the real world and extract money from the pockets of consumers: the forests around the Matterhorn might be dying, but the Disneyland version continues to rake in the dollars. The television programs, movie stars, and theme parks work together to create global industry devoted to maintaining a web of illusion that grows more lifelike as more people buy into it and as technologies grow more powerful.

18   Many other social scientists have intellectual suspicions of the hyper-realist critiques, because so many are abstract and theoretical, based on little or no direct knowledge of technology itself. Nevertheless, this perspective does capture something about the way the effects of communications technologies have changed our modes of thought. One good reason for paying attention to the claims of the hyper-realists is that the society they predicted decades ago bears a disturbingly closer resemblance to real life than do the forecasts of the rosier-visioned technological utopians. While McLuhan's image of the global village has taken on a certain irony in light of what has happened since his predictions of the 1960s, "the society of the spectacle"—another prediction from the 1960s, based on the advent of electronic media—offered a far less rosy and, as events have proved, more realistic portrayal of the way information technologies have changed social customs. . . .

19   What should those of us who believe in the democratizing potential of virtual communities do about the technological critics? I believe we should invite them to the table and help them see the flaws in our dreams, the bugs in our designs. I believe we should study what the historians and social scientists have to say about the illusions and power shifts that accompanied the diffusion of previous technologies. CMC and technology in general have real limits; it's best to continue to listen to those who understand the limits, even as we continue to explore the technologies' positive capabilities. Failing to fall under the spell of the "rhetoric of the technological sublime," actively questioning and examining social assumptions about the effects of new technologies, reminding ourselves that electronic communication has powerful illusory capabilities, are all good steps to take to prevent disasters.

If electronic democracy is to succeed, however, in the face of   20
all the obstacles, activists must do more than avoid mistakes.
Those who would use computer networks as political tools must
go forward and actively apply their theories to more and different
kinds of communities. If there is a last good hope, a bulwark
against the hyper-reality of Baudrillard or Forster, it will come
from a new way of looking at technology. Instead of falling under
the spell of a sales pitch, or rejecting new technologies as instruments of illusion, we need to look closely at new technologies and
ask how they can help build stronger, more humane communities—and ask how they might be obstacles to that goal. The late
1990s may eventually be seen in retrospect as a narrow window of
historical opportunity, when people either acted or failed to act effectively to regain control over communications technologies.
Armed with knowledge, guided by a clear, human-centered vision, governed by a commitment to civil discourse, we the citizens
hold the key levers at a pivotal time. What happens next is largely
up to us.

1993

Acknowledgments

Angelou, Maya. "Graduation" from *I Know Why the Caged Bird Sings* by Maya Angelou. Copyright ©1969 and renewed 1997 by Maya Angelou. Used by permission of Random House, Inc.

Anzaldúa, Gloria. "How to Tame a Wild Tongue" from *Borderlands/La Frontera: The New Mestiza*. Copyright ©1987, 1999 by Gloria Anzaldúa. Reprinted by permission of Aunt Lute Books.

Arendt, Hannah. "Deportations from Western Europe" from *Eichmann in Jerusalem* by Hannah Arendt. Copyright © 1963, 1964 by Hannah Arendt. Used by permission of Viking Penguin, a division of Penguin Putnam Inc.

Atwood, Margaret. "The Female Body" from *Good Bones and Simple Murders* by Margaret Atwood. Copyright © 1983, 1992, 1994 by O.W. Toad Ltd. A Nan A Talese Book. Used by permission of Doubleday, a division of Random House, Inc.

Baker, Russell. "Work in Corporate America." Copyright © 1971 The New York Times Company. Reprinted by permission.

Baldwin, James. From *Notes of a Native Son* by James Baldwin. Copyright © 1955, renewed 1983 by James Baldwin. Reprinted by permission of Beacon Press, Boston.

Barry, Dave. "Red, White, and Beer" from *Dave Barry's Greatest Hits* by Dave Barry. Copyright © 1988 by Dave Barry. Used by permission of Crown Publishers, a division of Random House, Inc.

Bennett, William J. "America at Risk: Can We Survive Without Moral Values." Reprinted from USA Today magazine by Society for the Advancement of Education Inc. November 1994.

Bettelheim, Bruno. "Cinderella: A Story of Sibling Rivalry and Oedipal Conflicts" from *The Uses of Enchantment* by Bruno

Tannen, Deborah. "I'm Sorry, I'm Not Apologizing" from *You Just Don't Understand* by Deborah Tannen. Copyright © 1990 by Deborah Tannen. Reprinted by permission of HarperCollins Publishers, Inc.

Terkel, Studs. "Who Built the Pyramids: Mike Lefevre." Copyright © 1972 by Studs Turkel. Reprinted by permission of Donadio & Olson, Inc.

Thomas, Lewis. "The Lives of a Cell" from *The Lives of a Cell* by Lewis Thomas. Copyright © 1971 by The Massachusetts Medical Society. Used by permission of Viking Penguin, a division of Penguin Putnam Inc.

Tisdale, Sallie. "We Do Abortions Here." Copyright © 1990 by Harper's Magazine. All rights reserved. Reproduced from the October 1990 issue by special permission.

Twitchell, James B. "But First, a Word from Our Sponsor." Permission granted by the author.

Walker, Alice. "Beauty: When the Other Dancer Is the Self" from *In Search of Our Mothers' Gardens: Womanist Prose.* Copyright © 1974 by Alice Walker. Reprinted by permission of Harcourt, Inc.

West, Cornel. "On Black Fathering" from *Faith of Our Fathers* by Andre C. Willis. Copyright © 1996 by Cornel West. Used by permission of Dutton, a division of Penguin Putnam Inc.

White, E.B. "The Meaning of Democracy." By permission of the E.B. White Estate.

Whitehead, Barbara Dafoe. "The Making of a Divorce Culture" from *The Divorce Culture* by Barbara Dafoe Whitehead. Copyright © 1996 by Barbara Dafoe Whitehead. Used by permission of Alfred A. Knopf, a division of Random House, Inc.

Williams, Patricia. "Gilded Lilies and Liberal Guilt." Reprinted by permission of the publisher from *The Alchemy of Race and Rights: Diary of a Law Professor* by Patricia Williams, pp. 17–19, Cambridge, Mass.: Harvard University Press. Copyright © 1991 by the President and Fellows of Harvard College.

Williams, Terry Tempest. "The Clan of the One-Breasted Women" from *Refuge: An Unnatural History of Family and*

Index of Authors and Titles

Index

619